Perritt's

Mutual
Fund
Almanac

Perritt's
Mutual Fund Almanac

Gerald Perritt

Macmillan Spectrum

an imprint of Macmillan • USA

MACMILLAN

A Simon & Schuster Macmillan Company
1633 Broadway
New York, New York 10019-6785

Copyright © 1997 by Gerald Perritt

MACMILLAN is a registered trademark of Macmillan, Inc.

Perritt, Gerald
Perritt's Mutual Fund Almanac/Gerald Perritt

ISBN: 0-02-861492-5

A catalogue record is available from the Library of Congress.

Design by Rachael McBrearty—Madhouse Productions

Manufactured in the United States of America

10 9 8 7 6 5 4 3 2 1

Publisher's Note: Every care has been taken in the preparation of the text to ensure its clarity and accuracy. Readers are cautioned, however, that this book is sold with the understanding that the Publisher is not engaged in rendering legal, accounting, or other professional service. Readers with specific financial problems are urged to seek the professional advice of an accountant or lawyer.

TABLE OF CONTENTS...

Section I: Getting Started in Mutual Funds

Section II: Mutual Fund Financial Statistics

Section III: The 300 Best Mutual Funds in America

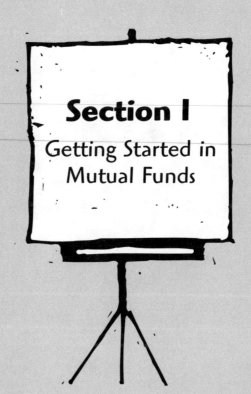

Section I
Getting Started in Mutual Funds

CHAPTER

ONE

A Bit of Mutual Fund History

The origins of the modern-day mutual fund can be traced back to nineteenth-century Europe. Although they gained considerable popularity in England a century and a half ago, mutual funds did not reach America's shores until 1924, when Massachusetts Investors Trust, the first open-end mutual fund, was organized. Today, there are more than six thousand mutual funds, pursuing nearly every imaginable investment objective.

Growth in the mutual fund industry was hampered first by the stock market crash of 1929 and the Great Depression that followed and then by the outbreak of World War II. By the late 1940s, fewer than one hundred mutual funds existed, with combined assets totaling less than $2 billion.

During the first half-century of their existence, mutual funds were restricted to investing in common stocks and corporate bonds. Beginning in the 1970s, however, mutual funds began to broaden their scope. The first money market mutual fund, the Reserve Fund, was organized in November 1971. Tax-exempt money market funds made their initial appearance in 1979. Municipal bond funds made their debut in 1977, after the passage of legislation that permitted funds to pass through tax-exempt income to shareholders. Long-term U.S. government bond funds came on the scene the same year. International bond funds made their debut in 1986. The industry's newest addition, ARM funds, which invest in adjustable rate home mortgages, appeared on the scene in 1990. In 1992, mutual funds began to invest in stocks traded on exchanges located in developing countries. Although investors tend to take the widespread availability of funds of all kinds for granted, the industry is still in its infancy. As the industry matures, expect to see a continuation of changes in the way mutual funds conduct business.

Figures 1, 2, and 3 illustrate the dramatic growth of the mutual fund industry. At the end of 1970, there were 361 stock, bond, and income funds, with combined total assets of $47.6 billion in 10.7 million shareholder accounts. During the next twenty-five years, the popularity of mutual funds with all types of investors skyrocketed. Ownership of mutual funds soared from 6 percent of U.S. households in 1980 to more than 30 percent in 1995. At year-end 1995, investors could choose from 5,761 stock, bond, and money market mutual funds, with more than 400 funds being created that year. That number would grow beyond 6,000 in 1996. Today, there are twice as many mutual funds as there are stocks traded on the New York Stock Exchange.

Total industry assets also expanded dramatically during the last twenty-five years, topping $135 billion in 1980, passing the $1 trillion mark in 1990, and surpassing $2 trillion in 1993. By 1995, total mutual fund assets topped those of all other financial intermediaries except commercial banks. (See figure 5.) Although in-

Figure 1

NUMBER OF MUTUAL FUNDS

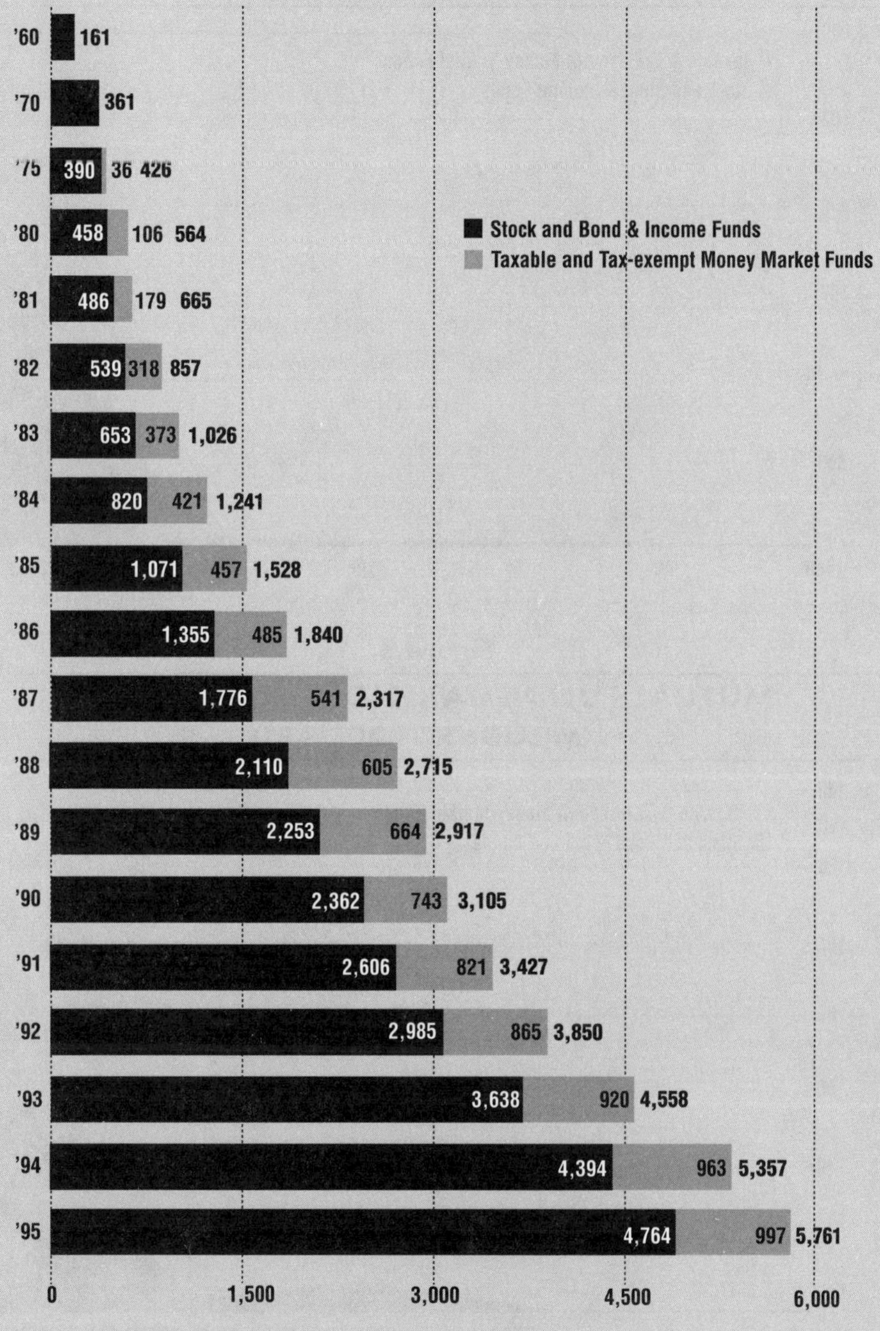

Year	Stock and Bond & Income Funds	Taxable and Tax-exempt Money Market Funds	Total
'60	161		
'70	361		
'75	390	36	426
'80	458	106	564
'81	486	179	665
'82	539	318	857
'83	653	373	1,026
'84	820	421	1,241
'85	1,071	457	1,528
'86	1,355	485	1,840
'87	1,776	541	2,317
'88	2,110	605	2,715
'89	2,253	664	2,917
'90	2,362	743	3,105
'91	2,606	821	3,427
'92	2,985	865	3,850
'93	3,638	920	4,558
'94	4,394	963	5,357
'95	4,764	997	5,761

Source: *1996 Mutual Fund Fact Book*, Investment Company Institute

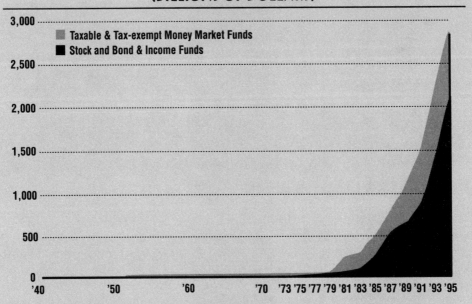

Figure 2

ASSETS OF MUTUAL FUNDS
(BILLIONS OF DOLLARS)

Taxable & Tax-exempt Money Market Funds

Stock and Bond & Income Funds

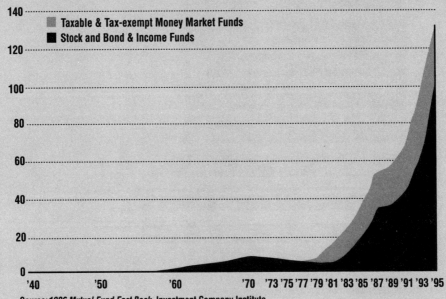

Figure 3

MUTUAL FUND SHAREHOLDER ACCOUNTS
(MILLIONS OF DOLLARS)

Taxable & Tax-exempt Money Market Funds

Stock and Bond & Income Funds

Source: *1996 Mutual Fund Fact Book*, Investment Company Institute

Figure 4

NUMBER OF MUTUAL FUNDS
CLASSIFIED BY INVESTMENT OBJECTIVE

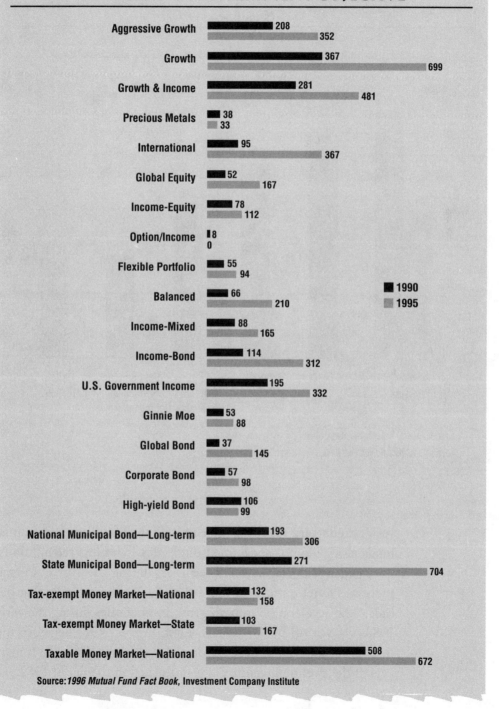

	1990	1995
Aggressive Growth	208	352
Growth	367	699
Growth & Income	281	481
Precious Metals	38	33
International	95	367
Global Equity	52	167
Income-Equity	78	112
Option/Income	8	0
Flexible Portfolio	55	94
Balanced	66	210
Income-Mixed	88	165
Income-Bond	114	312
U.S. Government Income	195	332
Ginnie Moe	53	88
Global Bond	37	145
Corporate Bond	57	98
High-yield Bond	106	99
National Municipal Bond—Long-term	193	306
State Municipal Bond—Long-term	271	704
Tax-exempt Money Market—National	132	158
Tax-exempt Money Market—State	103	167
Taxable Money Market—National	508	672

Source:*1996 Mutual Fund Fact Book*, Investment Company Institute

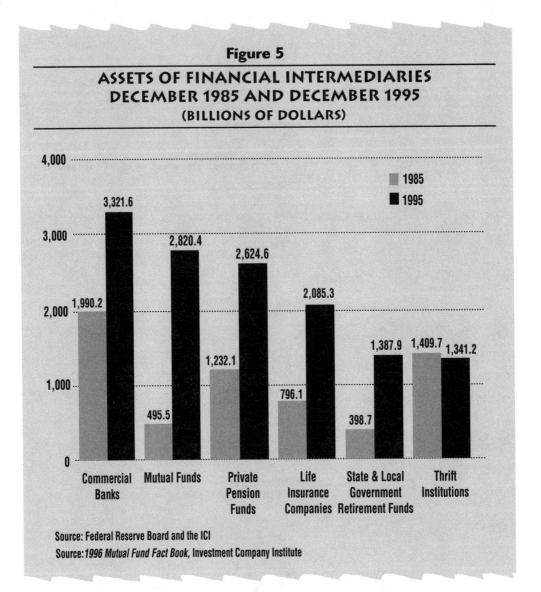

Figure 5

ASSETS OF FINANCIAL INTERMEDIARIES
DECEMBER 1985 AND DECEMBER 1995
(BILLIONS OF DOLLARS)

Source: Federal Reserve Board and the ICI

Source: *1996 Mutual Fund Fact Book,* Investment Company Institute

vestors today are regularly pouring billions of dollars into mutual funds every month, net mutual fund sales (sales less redemptions) were negative during seven of ten years during the 1970s. In fact, there was a net outflow of more than $5.7 billion during that decade. The acceleration in both gross and net sales during the early 1980s was set off by two events. First, interest rates began to top out during mid-1982. Second, one of the most forceful bull markets of the twentieth century was unleashed in the fall of 1982.

Figure 6

A MUTUAL FUND TIME CAPSULE

1924   The first mutual fund in America is launched in Boston.

1940   Mutual fund industry regulated by the federal government with the passage of the Investment Company Act of 1940.

1945   Mutual fund assets top $1 billion for the first time ever.

1951   Mutual fund shareholder accounts top one million.

1953   International equity funds make their initial appearance when Scudder launches the International Fund.

1956   First precious metals fund organized by Van Eck Advisors.

1971   The first money market mutual fund, the Reserve Fund, appears on the scene.

1976   Change in tax laws leads to the formation of the first municipal bond funds.

1979   Tax-exempt money market funds introduced.

1986   First international bond fund, T. Rowe Price International Bond Fund, makes its debut.

1990   Mutual fund assets top $1 trillion.

1996   Mutual fund assets top $3 trillion spread across more than seven thousand funds.

Investors, who were enticed by the high yields offered by money market funds during the late 1970s and early 1980s, began to liquidate their money market fund holdings in early 1983 when interest rates began to drop. Mutual fund families initiated marketing campaigns aimed at their money market fund investors, which enticed large numbers of investors to shift their money fund assets to the families' equity and bond funds. From this modest beginning, the rush was on. In 1984, sales of equity, bond, and income funds fell a scant $4 billion short of total mutual fund sales during the entire decade of the 1970s! And in 1993, investors purchased more than $500 billion of mutual fund shares. During the three years 1991 through 1993, mutual fund companies received more cash than they received during their previous sixty-seven-year history.

Recent Trends in the Mutual Fund Industry

During the past two decades, the mutual fund industry has undergone significant change. In addition to the number and diversity of mutual funds expanding at an astonishing rate, the way funds conduct business also has changed dramatically. The trends described below are more than a historical curiosity. These changes have impacted shareholder returns and require that investors scrutinize a fund's characteristics more carefully before making an investment selection. Awareness of the evolving trends in the mutual fund industry could mean the difference between investment success and failure.

One of the most important changes in the mutual fund industry in recent years concerns the cost of fund investing. During the decade of the 1960s, the vast majority of mutual funds levied a front-end sales charge, or front-end load. The loads, representing commissions primarily paid to stockbrokers, routinely totaled as much as 9.3 percent of the amount of money actually invested in the fund. By the 1970s, only about 30 percent of all mutual fund assets were held by no-load funds sold by sponsors directly to shareholders without a commission.

During the late 1970s and early 1980s, however, sales of no-load funds exploded, and by 1985 the majority of fund assets were controlled by no-load funds. But that trend began to reverse itself with the creation of 12b-1 funds in the mid-1980s, which levy annual distribution fees on fund shareholders. A number of existing no-load funds added 12b-1 fees, and some front-end load funds dropped their front-end charges and combined 12b-1 fees with back-end loads instead. A number of fund families, led by Fidelity, added "low" front-end loads to funds that were previously no-load. In addition, brokerage firms, which had previously acted as distributors of mutual funds for other sponsors, launched their own fund families, nearly all of which were sold with a sales charge of some sort attached. As a result, less than one-third of the more than six thousand funds now available can call themselves 100 percent no-load.

These days, selecting among funds sold by brokerage firms is a little like wading through alphabet soup. These firms have developed a hub-and-spoke approach to marketing their funds. The hub is the investment portfolio, while the spokes emanating from that hub offer a variety of alternative sales fee payment plans. Class A shares are sold with a front-end load. Class B shares are sold with ongoing 12b-1 charges and back-end loads. Some firms have added class C, D, and E shares. (Remember, however, that regardless of the class of shares, all represent the same underlying portfolio of assets. Because of that, I have included only class A shares in fund descriptions in this book.)

In addition to sales fees, management fees also have been on the rise during the past decade. Twenty years ago, the typical management fee amounted to 0.5 percent of fund assets. However, during the 1980s an upward drift in management fees began. These days, most newly organized funds charge an annual adviser fee that ranges from 0.75 percent to 1.00 percent of fund assets. Although fund assets have swelled during recent years, the average equity fund expense ratio is still a relatively high 1.34 percent. And, of course, higher operating expenses result in lower returns to fund shareholders.

With a flood of money pouring into mutual funds in recent years, many modest-sized funds, which sported better-than-average track records, saw their assets swell into the hundreds of millions and even billions of dollars. Although this was a boon to advisers, shareholders were often shortchanged as fund managers found that they could not produce similar investment results because of the loss of investment flexibility that accompanied the fund's rapid growth. While one can find a few exceptions to the contrary, large funds, on average, tend to underperform smaller funds with similar investment objectives and investment strategies. As a result, beginning in the mid-1980s, a number of popular funds began to close their doors to new investors.

Interestingly, mutual fund portfolio turnover ratios also have been on the rise in recent years. My guess is that competition is the culprit. Most mutual fund investors base their fund selections on recent investment performance. Thus, portfolio managers are forced to attempt to produce short-term returns that exceed those of the market. In attempting to do so, these managers jump from one "hot" stock to another. Unfortunately for investors, over the long run, rapid portfolio turnover takes its toll on investment results. Several studies indicate that, over long periods of time, funds with high portfolio turnover ratios underperform similar funds with low portfolio turnover ratios by a significant amount.

Amendments to the Investment Company Act, effected July 1, 1993, have expanded the reporting requirements for most mutual funds. Mutual funds, other than money market funds and index funds, must now disclose the name and title of the person or persons employed by the fund's adviser who are primarily responsible for the day-to-day management of the fund's portfolio. In addition, all funds must include in their prospectuses or annual shareholders' reports a discussion of the factors, strategies, and techniques that materially affected the fund's performance. Finally, funds now are required to provide a line graph comparing the initial account value and subsequent account values at the ends of the most recent ten fiscal years, assuming a $10,000 initial investment made in both the fund and an "appropriate" broad-based securities market index. These changes are a continuation of an ongoing trend by fund regulators to require funds to provide substantive communications to both prospective and current fund shareholders.

A Look Ahead

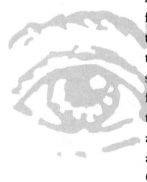

Given the dramatic events of the past decade, what's in store for the mutual fund industry in the future? First, I believe that the mutual fund industry's explosive growth will moderate considerably over the next several years. Although a number of new funds will come to the market in the years ahead, growth will be moderated by consolidation in the industry. A number of fund families are already feeling the pinch of increased competition. As a result, merger activity in the industry has been on the rise in recent years. And merger activity has not been confined to small firms. In 1992, Franklin Funds acquired the Templeton fund family, and in early 1995, the Benham Group announced a merger with Twentieth Century Investors. In October 1996, Franklin Funds acquired Mutual Shares, and late that year the AIM Funds were in merger talks with INVESCO.

The rapid growth in mutual fund assets has not gone unnoticed by the banking industry. In an effort to recapture lost assets, large commercial banks have either bought existing fund families or created their own group of mutual funds. During the last year, a handful of these banks have created dozens of new funds that are being actively marketed to the banks' customers. And a couple of banks have dropped front-end load fees and are now selling no-load fund shares. I look for this trend to continue into the twenty-first century.

I also expect to see a continuation of the trend toward higher-cost funds. Industry sales will be dominated by funds marketed by direct sales forces compensated by expanded sales fees. In addition, administration costs will continue to rise. That, in turn, will cause fund expense ratios to continue to expand.

It is important to note that the Investment Company Act of 1940 has been amended significantly only once (in 1970). Those amendments were aimed at curbing the wild abandon of portfolio managers (dubbed gunslingers by the financial press) during the 1960s and at easing the burden of huge sales commissions levied on the initial share purchases of contractual plans. In light of the technological and innovative changes in financial markets since the act was last amended, I expect significant change during the late 1990s. Recently, the Securities and Exchange Commission (SEC) has suggested several changes to the act that would improve the current level of investor protection, facilitate competition and capital formation by removing barriers, and encourage innovation in the industry.

I believe the discovery of mutual funds by large numbers of investors is one of the big stories of the 1980s and 1990s. Although investors tend to focus their attention on investment returns when evaluating portfolio management results, the reduction of investment risk is the single largest benefit provided by mutual funds. Investors, who otherwise might have held highly concentrated portfolios, saw the wisdom of diversification during the turbulent months of late 1987. Although the stock market crash took its toll on the value of mutual fund portfolios, most of the mutual fund investors who rode out the storm now find that their investment wealth is much greater than it was before October 1987. And long-term-oriented mutual fund investors will continue to prosper in the years ahead.

CHAPTER

TWO

The Very Least You Should Know about Mutual Funds: Before You Invest

There's a lot to learn about mutual funds and mutual fund investing. I've been around the industry for more than a quarter-century, and I'm still learning. The mutual fund industry is in a constant state of flux. New types of funds appear each year, SEC rule changes alter the way funds operate, portfolio managers hop from one fund to another, hundreds of new funds are created every year, and fund families are becoming more innovative in serving shareholder needs.

Although it's wise to know the rules of the road before you slip behind the wheel of an automobile, you don't have to know how to rebuild a carburetor to become a good driver. The same holds true for mutual fund investing. There are a few things you should know about mutual fund investing before you ante up your hard-earned cash. However, you don't need to know how to create and operate a mutual fund to become a successful mutual fund investor. In fact, the faster you begin investing in mutual funds the greater are the odds that you will achieve your financial goals. My advice is to learn the basics, invest in a couple of mutual funds, and learn more as you go. Here's the least you should know before you make your first investment.

The fund. A mutual fund is a financial intermediary that gives individuals the opportunity to pool their capital and invest in a portfolio of securities. Mutual funds are corporations (called investment companies) that have been chartered by a state and whose sole business and reason for existing is to invest in a portfolio of assets. The fund's shareholders are the owners of the corporation. They are responsible for electing the fund's board of directors, who carry out the business affairs of the fund. The fund's shareholders must also approve changes in the fund's objective, the hiring of its investment adviser, and the adviser's compensation, and they must approve the appointment of its auditor.

Investment companies (funds) that engage in interstate commerce are regulated by the Investment Company Act of 1940, which is administered by the SEC. The act requires funds to register with the SEC and to provide "full" disclosure to prospective shareholders in a prospectus, which must be presented before a solicitation is made. Among other things, the act also requires that

(1) adviser contracts be approved by shareholders and the fund's outside directors;

(2) the fund redeem shares offered by shareholders within seven calendar days at the per share net asset value;

(3) shareholders be sent complete financial reports at least semi-annually;

(4) the fund's cash and securities be kept by a bank or a broker who is a member of a national securities exchange.

To qualify as a registered diversified management company under the act of 1940, a fund must have at least 75 percent of its assets invested such that

(1) not more than 5 percent are invested in any one security; and

(2) not more than 10 percent of the voting securities of any corporation are held by the fund. In addition, a mutual fund must register and abide by the laws and regulations of each state in which its shares are sold.

As a shareholder in the fund, you assume a pro rata share of the fund's operating expenses, including the advisory fee, registration fees, expenses for annual meetings, custodial bank and transfer agent fees, interest and taxes, brokerage commissions, expenses related to the fund's purchases and sales of securities, and outside directors' fees and travel expenses. These fees are generally deducted from the dividend and interest income of the fund and accrue daily.

These operating expenses, expressed as a percentage of fund assets, are limited by state statute. No investment advisory fees may be collected by advisers of funds whose expenses exceed the statutory maximum (generally set at 2.5 percent of fund assets).

The fund's investment adviser makes the decisions as to which securities the fund will buy and sell and how much will be invested in each. For its services, the investment adviser receives a fee that generally ranges from 0.75 to 1.00 percent of the fund's average annual assets. Generally, the management fee is set on a declining scale relative to fund size, and in a few instances the contract may include an incentive clause that allows the fee to be adjusted upward or downward according to how the fund performs relative to some stock market average or index.

The fund's adviser is responsible for the day-to-day operation of the fund and in most instances is responsible for and pays the cost of office space and equipment, personnel, compliance with federal and state adviser regulations, and the preparation and distribution of sales material and advertising. The adviser or management company profits to the extent that its management fees exceed its cost of doing business.

The Investment Company Act of 1940 requires that all mutual funds establish a custodial relationship with a bank to protect share-

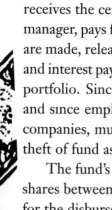

holder assets. The custodial bank holds all of the assets of the fund (cash and securities) in trust for fund shareholders. The custodian receives the certificates for new acquisitions made by the portfolio manager, pays for securities purchased, delivers securities when sales are made, releases cash to pay fund expenses, and accepts dividends and interest payments from the issuers of securities held in the fund's portfolio. Since these assets are held separately from bank assets and since employees who handle money are bonded by insurance companies, mutual fund shareholders are highly protected against theft of fund assets.

The fund's transfer agent facilitates the transfer of mutual fund shares between the fund and its shareholders. It is also responsible for the disbursement of dividends to shareholders and the maintenance of shareholder records.

Net asset value. Purchases and sales of fund shares by investors are made directly with the fund. When you buy fund shares, you remit your payment to the fund, which then issues new shares. When you redeem your shares, you sell them to the fund and they are canceled when they are received. (Rather than receive certificates for shares they buy, most investors elect to have their shares held by the fund's transfer agent, who debits and credits their accounts when new shares are purchased or shares are redeemed by the fund). Because a mutual fund is constantly issuing new shares or canceling shares when they are redeemed, it is known as an open-end investment company.

At the end of each business day, the fund must determine the total value of its portfolio, deduct any liabilities, and divide the result by the number of fund shares outstanding. What results is the fund's per share net asset value (NAV). The NAV is reported to the National Association of Securities dealers each evening and appears the next day in the financial press. If you invest in a no-load mutual fund, its NAV is synonymous with its share price. (Load funds add a sales fee to the NAV to determine the offering price.)

Note that when you purchase fund shares during a regular business day, the fund's NAV is not known until the close of business that day. (This is known as forward pricing.) As a result, purchases and redemptions must be made in dollar terms rather than in shares.

The dollar amount of the purchase or redemption is divided by the fund's NAV at the close of business that day to determine the exact number of shares (including fractions) bought or sold.

For mutual fund shares sold with a front-end load (sales commission), share price is determined by the following formula: NAV/ (1 - % commission). For example, suppose that a fund's NAV at day's end is $10 and the fund is sold with a 5 percent front-end sales commission. The purchase price (called the offering price or offer) is $10/(1 - 0.05), or $10/0.95, which becomes $10.53. In other words, you must pay $1,053 to acquire one hundred shares of the fund, which are valued at $1,000. The difference, $53, is paid to the fund's sales organization and is shared by the broker or financial planner who recommended that you purchase the fund's shares.

Open-end and closed-end funds. A fund that continually issues new shares and redeems outstanding shares is called an open-end fund. A fund with a fixed number of shares outstanding is called a closed-end fund. If you want to purchase closed-end fund shares, you must buy them from an existing shareholder rather than from the fund directly. Similarly, if you sell shares of a closed-end fund, you must find a willing buyer. Because transactions are conducted between investors rather than between investors and the fund, closed-end fund shares are listed on stock exchanges or traded in the over-the-counter market. Although closed-end funds must also determine and report their NAVs, actual share prices are determined by supply and demand. When demand is high relative to supply, closed-end fund shares trade share prices that are above NAV. When supply predominates, the shares usually trade at a discount to NAV. In addition, since transactions are conducted in the secondary market, you must also pay a brokerage commission when buying or selling shares of closed-end funds. Although about two hundred closed-end funds are listed for trading on the New York Stock Exchange, open-end funds, by a wide margin, are the most popular with individual investors.

Load and no-load funds. Open-end funds are sold either with or without a sales commission. When you invest in a no-load fund, every dollar you invest finds its way into fund shares since purchases are made at the NAV. On the other hand, most funds sold by brokers or financial planners are sold with a sales commission attached. You may pay the commission when you initially purchase fund shares (front-end load funds), a commission may be levied when you redeem your shares (back-end load funds), or you may be assessed an ongoing sales fee, called a 12b-1 fee after the SEC rule that permits funds to levy this type of sales fee.

Historically, front-end load funds have been the most widely sold by stock brokers. The up-front charge can be as much as 9 percent of the amount of money actually invested in fund shares. However, as the popularity of no-load funds grew with investors, load funds were forced to become more competitive, and front-end loads now range between 3 and 6 percent of the amount invested. For large investments, load funds will reduce the sales commission. However, to get a reduction in fees you must generally invest hundreds of thousands of dollars in the fund, and as much as $1 million before the load is waived completely.

The important point to remember about load funds is that you are paying someone a commission when you invest in a load fund. These are dollars that find their way into a salesperson's pocket and not into fund shares. As a result, your investment returns are reduced by the amount of the commissions you pay. Think of the commissions as payments for investment advice. If the advice you are getting is not worth the fees you are paying, avoid load funds and invest in no-loads instead.

A growing number of funds have adopted a hub-and-spoke form of organization. These funds are easily recognized because they are designated with capital letters such as A, B, C, or D. These are funds that are sold with different sales fee options.

Here's how it works. A sponsor establishes a single fund (the hub), and the distributor peddles the fund's shares with a variety of sales fee options (the spokes). Class A shares are sold with a front-end sales load only (ranging from 3 percent to 6 percent of the amount you invest). Class B shares possess a back-end load and usually an annual 12b-1 sales fee (back-end loads usually start at 5 or 6 percent and are reduced by one percentage point for each year that you remain invested in the fund). Class C shares are sold with a "level load" (an annual sales fee that ranges from 0.25 percent to 1 percent). Class D shares are usually sold without any sales charges to institutional investors that ante up very large initial investments (usually $250,000 or more).

Which letter of the alphabet is more beneficial? This is a difficult question to answer because it is "fully loaded." The assumption behind it is that one of the share classes is better than another. The truth is that shares sold with some kind of sales charge reduce the fund's returns to its shareholders. It's kind of like being asked how you would like to be executed.

There is really no best choice. If you are pitched a fund with a letter of the alphabet attached, you are being asked how you would like to be stiffed. My advice is to simply say no thanks, and invest instead in a no-load fund that promises to deliver a greater portion of the return that its hard-working portfolio manager actually earns.

Expense ratio. As stated earlier, as a fund shareholder you are responsible for a share of the operating expenses of the fund, including the advisory fee. These expenses are totaled and expressed as a percentage of the fund's total assets (called the fund's expense ratio). Expense ratios average about 1.4 percent for equity funds and about 0.8 percent for bond funds, although they vary considerably for individual funds.

It is important to check a fund's expense ratio before you make an investment because it indicates how much gross returns earned by the fund will be reduced by annual operating expenses. For example, if a fund's portfolio manager earns 12 percent a year before the deduction of 2 percent in annual expenses, you the shareholder will earn a net return of 10 percent. And, over a long period of time, the payment of excessive fund expenses could cost you a bundle. For example, invest $10,000 in a fund that earns 11 percent a year for ten years after deducting 1 percent annually and your portfolio grows to $28,394. Invest in a higher-cost fund that deducts 2 percent annually and returns only 10 percent a year and your initial $10,000 investment will grow to $25,937. That's a difference of $2,457 favoring the lower-cost fund.

Portfolio diversification. The biggest benefit a mutual fund has to offer is the reduction in risk that occurs when a portfolio contains a large number of securities. Own a single stock and you may prosper along with the company that issued it. On the other hand, if the company stumbles and declares bankruptcy, you may lose every cent you invested in its stock. Invest in a mutual fund that has invested in dozens of stocks and you avoid the risk of losing your entire investment because of the failure of one company.

When you invest in a diversified equity mutual fund you experience only one-third the volatility that is experienced by an individual who has bought the shares of one or two companies. Volatility is reduced because the negative impact on portfolio value caused by the declining share prices of companies that are performing poorly are offset by the positive impact of increases in the share prices of companies that are performing well. More importantly, over the long run your mutual fund investment will provide returns that rival those provided by nondiversified investors. In other words, there is very much to be gained and very little to be lost by maintaining a diversified portfolio. In fact, if you invest in a diversified equity fund that possesses a modest expense ratio, you are virtually guaranteed to make money if you hold that fund's shares for a period of ten years or more.

Prospectus. When a mutual fund applies for registration with the SEC, it must submit a registration statement, which outlines the fund's intended objective and its operating policies. This document is distilled and submitted to all prospective investors in the form of the fund's prospectus. These booklets explain the rules of the road. A prospectus tells you what the fund will and won't do with your money. Although it is an important document that should be read thoroughly before you invest in any mutual fund, be prepared for a very boring experience. Most prospectuses are written by lawyers: need I say any more. Here's a guide to the more important sections of a fund's prospectus.

Investment objectives and policies. Here the fund spells out its investment objectives and the strategies that it will use to meet its goals. Some funds tell you little more than that they intend to emphasize capital appreciation, income, or a combination of both. Others are quite specific about what they intend to do with your money. My advice is to invest in only those funds that are specific about their investment goals, philosophies, and portfolio management strategies.

Fund expenses. Fund expenses are expressed as a percentage of the fund's NAV and are displayed prominently near the beginning of the prospectus. Included are sales charges, operating expenses, and advisory fees. In addition, the fund's prospectus must illustrate the total dollar cost you might pay if you invest in the fund for one, three, or five years. Make no investment in any mutual fund until you know what it will cost to make that investment.

Risk factors. This section of the prospectus outlines the risks you are assuming when you make an investment in the fund. Sometimes reading this section can be a scary experience. However, remember that investment return is always coupled with investment risk. The greater the anticipated rewards, the greater the risks you must assume. However, be sure that you know what the risks are before you sink every last dime you have in a fund's shares. If you are not willing to accept the risks offered by the fund under consideration, pass on that fund and look for another that might be much more tame.

Portfolio manager. This is the person minding the store. You will find a description of the portfolio manager's experience in either the fund's prospectus or its annual report. Although it may not be important that a portfolio manager graduated from Harvard rather than the University of Kansas, it may be important to know how long that manager has been at the helm. This is especially true if you are hanging your fund selection decision on the historical return. You want to know whether the person who captured that return is still at the wheel.

Annual and semiannual shareholder reports. This document makes for much more interesting reading than a fund's prospectus. It should also be obtained prior to making an investment in any fund. In it you will find a lengthy discussion of the fund's historical performance by its portfolio manager. Also, the fund is required to list its historical returns and to compare them with a suitable benchmark, such as the Standard & Poor's 500 Index (a commonly used proxy for the stock market). You will also find a list of the fund's investments. Check out this list. Are these the kinds of investments you would make if you were managing your own money? If not, look for another fund that invests in the stocks and bonds you want to own.

How to buy and sell fund shares. Investing in a mutual fund is about the easiest task you will ever perform. Call the fund and obtain a prospectus and purchase application. Read the prospectus, complete the purchase application (which is similar to that required when opening a bank account), and send the fund a check. Ninety-two percent of all funds require that initial investments in the fund exceed some predetermined amount. Sixty percent of the funds around today require a minimum initial investment of $1,000 or less. When you initially invest in a fund, make sure that you get all the services you want: wire transfer, check writing, telephone exchange, automatic investment or regular cash withdrawal, and so on.

When you open an account, the fund will ask how you want to register your fund shares. There are several options. The most common include individual ownership (shares are registered in your name, and upon your death they are placed in your estate and disposed of according to the terms of your will); joint tenancy with right of survivorship (registration creates joint-share ownership, both you and your joint tenant must sign when redeeming shares, and shares revert to the sole survivor when one tenant dies); and joint tenancy (registration is similar to right of survivorship except that if one tenant dies, the shares are placed into the estate of the deceased for disposition according to the will). In addition, fund shares may also be registered with a sole owner as custodian, guardian, or trustee under court order.

Exchanging and redeeming shares is generally as easy as making a purchase. First, if you have telephone exchange privileges, you merely have to call the fund and request the sale of a certain number of shares or their exchange into another fund in the family. Second, you may write directly to the fund's transfer agent and request that shares be sold and the proceeds sent to you. If you are closing an account with a fund family (that is, redeeming all the shares you own), you will be required to send a request in writing. To avoid a delay in the redemption process, make sure that the signature(s) on the redemption request are guaranteed by a bank or a brokerage firm.

Proceeds of share redemptions will be sent as soon as possible. Once the transfer agent receives your request, it takes either one or two days to effect the sale of fund shares. The transfer agent will cut a check for the amount due to you within seven days of the sale. Allowing another four to six days for mail delivery, you can expect to receive a check for the shares you sold within twelve to fifteen days after mailing your redemption request. If you need to receive proceeds sooner, request the transfer agent to wire transfer the proceeds to your bank account.

Check the fund's prospectus for any special conditions that might apply to a switch or sale of fund shares. Some funds charge a redemption fee if shares are redeemed before a specified period of time has elapsed. For example, some funds charge a fee equal to 1 percent of the value of the shares redeemed if the request is made within sixty days of a purchase. Many funds levy a flat dollar charge on telephone exchanges that exceed some threshold number during a year. Also, most funds require that an initial purchase be "on the books" for at least thirty days before allowing a telephone switch to another fund in the family.

All funds offer an automatic investment option. This is a great way to save and invest. When you send your purchase application, you indicate that you want to invest a specific amount of money each and every month. You include a blank check (marked "void") with your purchase application and check the box labeled "Automatic Investment Plan." The fund will do the rest. Every month the amount you specified will be deducted from your bank checking account and invested in additional fund shares. There is no charge for this service. In addition, most funds reduce the amount of their initial investment requirement for investors who elect to invest under the automatic investment option.

THREE

Identifying the Beast:
What Kind of Funds Are Out There?

The number of mutual funds has increased at an incredible rate in recent years; as a result, investors now have opportunities never before available. Because of the great diversity of funds, you can now apply portfolio management strategies once reserved for well-heeled institutional investors. Today, you can most likely find a mutual fund that invests in the categories of assets you desire, applies the investment strategy you prefer, and possesses the return potential and risk level that lie within your return preference and risk tolerance zones. That's a statement I couldn't truthfully make a couple of decades ago.

The accompanying table illustrates the risk and return characteristics for general categories of funds that pursue a wide variety of investment objectives. As can be seen, the more aggressive a fund, the greater has been its historical total returns and the further its share price tumbles during a bear market. I have included the returns of the Standard & Poor's 500 Index as a benchmark for comparison.

Aggressive growth funds. These funds have as their primary objective the pursuit of maximum capital gains. They invest aggressively in the common stocks of rapidly growing, often speculative, companies and tend to stay fully invested at all times. Some aggressive growth funds employ financial leverage (use stock margin) and invest in call options to enhance returns to shareholders. A large number of funds in this category follow an earnings momentum investment strategy (they invest in companies with rapidly expanding earnings and dump these stocks when earnings growth slows) that tends to lead to a high rate of portfolio turnover.

TABLE 1.
FUND CATEGORY FINANCIAL CHARACTERISTICS

Investment Objective	Dividend Yield	Returns 3-Year	Returns 5-Year	Returns 10-Year	Up Market	Down Market
Aggressive Growth	0.3%	14.8%	16.0%	14.4%	242%	-24%
Growth	1.0	14.3	14.2	13.3	170	-17
Growth & Income	2.3	12.1	12.9	11.8	139	-12
Balanced	2.8	9.7	11.0	10.7	111	- 7
International Stock	0.8	9.2	10.2	10.1	57	-10
Precious Metals	1.2	8.5	9.7	5.6	61	-16
Taxable Bond	6.3	4.6	7.3	8.0	69	2
Municipal Bond	4.7	3.7	6.8	7.0	54	2
S&P 500 Index	2.2	17.3	15.2	14.9	167	-15

Up market Nov. 1990 through Sept. 1996; Down market June 1990 through Oct. 1990

Source: CDA/Wiesenberger Mutual Fund Directory

Aggressive growth funds possess relatively low current yields and many don't earn any dividend income at all. In addition, aggressive growth funds tend to concentrate their investments in a few industries that have historically been rapidly expanding such as technology and health care. A large number of funds in this category invest in smaller companies (mid-cap, small-cap, and micro-cap firms) that possess higher levels of risk than those that accompany investment in large blue-chip companies. Most sector funds (that is, funds that concentrate their investments in a single industry) fall into this category. Needless to say, the share prices of aggressive growth funds tend to be highly volatile, performing very well during bull markets and getting trounced during severe market corrections or lengthy bear markets. On average, these funds possess about 15 percent more volatility than the stock market as a whole, and some are 30 percent to 40 percent more volatile. Thus, investment in aggressive growth funds is not for the faint of heart.

Generally, aggressive growth funds are not appropriate for conservative investors unless they form a small portion of a highly diversified mutual fund portfolio. However, these funds are suitable for long-term investors who can assume above average risks and are not bothered by short-term stock market fluctuations. Because of their additional risks, aggressive growth funds possess the highest return potential of all fund groups. Over a ten-year period you can expect to earn an average of about two percentage points more than the overall stock market. In other words, if you are seeking returns that could average well above 12 percent, look no further than the group of aggressive growth equity mutual funds.

Growth funds. As with aggressive growth funds, the primary objective of funds in this group is growth of capital. However, these funds generally do not engage in many of the speculative activities aggressive growth funds employ. Growth funds tend to be more stable than aggressive growth funds since they tend to invest in large, well-established growth companies that pay some cash dividends. You are likely to recognize the names of many of the companies in a growth fund portfolio. In addition, growth funds are likely to diversify their portfolios across a broader range of industries than do aggressive growth funds. Furthermore, a large number of growth funds will build cash positions when it is believed that the stock market is overvalued. Finally, the portfolio managers of growth funds tend to hold their investments a bit longer than those who manage aggressive growth funds.

In general, the performance of growth funds during bull markets tends to be better than that of the S&P 500 Index and nearly matches the performance of the index during bear markets. The overall result is that, over the longer term, the well-managed growth fund can be expected to return between 10 and 12 percent compounded annually, which historically has been about 6 to 7 percent per year more than the rate of inflation.

Growth funds are suitable for nearly every type of investor. Aggressive investors can combine them with their more volatile aggressive funds to moderate portfolio risk. Conservative investors, by combining growth funds with their more conservative cousins, can boost long-term returns. Even income investors may wish to include a 20 percent to 30 percent allocation to growth funds to produce sufficient capital appreciation to offset the negative impact of inflation on the value of their fixed-income portfolios.

Growth and income funds. Growth and income funds seek a combination of dividend income and capital appreciation. Sometimes these funds are referred to as total return funds. Generally, funds in this category invest in common stocks of seasoned, well-established, cash dividend–paying companies. Some funds invest a portion of their assets in convertible bonds in an effort to boost the income portion of the fund's total return. Portfolio managers attempt to provide shareholders with long-term growth while avoiding excessive fluctuations in net asset value. In many instances, their portfolios are packed with utility, bank, and energy stocks. In addition, a number of funds that follow a so-called value stock selection strategy fall into this category because "out of favor" stocks tend to possess generous dividend yields.

Growth and income funds tend to possess less volatility than the overall stock market for several reasons. First, they invest in companies that have a higher degree of earnings predictability. During alternating periods of economic boom and economic recession, the earnings of utility stocks, for example, tend to vary by much less than those of high-growth industrial firms. Second, their portfolios tend to be packed with high-yielding stocks whose continual dividend payments partially offset the erosion in share price during a bear market. Finally, their dividend-paying stocks give portfolio managers an opportunity to invest in value-priced stocks during the throws of a severe bear market.

Because of their relative share price stability and their potential to provide current income, most growth and income funds are suitable for conservative investors. Because their share prices are somewhat sensitive to interest rate changes, they may also be sought after by aggressive investors who are betting that interest rates will decline. Investors who prefer current income may also benefit from ownership of growth and income funds. They provide some income and their potential to produce growth of capital provides an inflation offset.

Balanced funds. These funds seek a balance between current income and capital appreciation by investing in both common stocks and bonds. Portfolios usually consist of 50 to 60 percent high-yielding common stocks and 40 to 50 percent bonds and preferred stocks. Generally, these funds provide about 50 percent more income than stocks contained in the Standard & Poor's 500 Index and are about half as volatile. However, because of their generous allocation to bonds, their portfolios are highly interest rate sensitive and have been known to take a nosedive during a lengthy bear market accompanied by sharply rising interest rates.

Balanced funds are suitable for conservative growth–oriented and income-oriented investors. Their share price stability makes them appealing to investors with relatively short investment horizons. Because of their commitment to bonds, these funds are not suitable for more aggressive investors.

International funds. The first international fund, Scudder International, was introduced in 1953. Since then, international funds have been one of the fastest growing categories of funds, and for good reason. Stock markets located outside of the United States account for nearly two-thirds of the market value of all publicly traded stocks. International funds can be divided into six subcategories:

(1) Global funds invest in both U.S. and foreign stocks.

(2) Diversified international funds invest exclusively in the stocks of companies domiciled outside the United States.

(3) Regional funds invest in specific geographic areas such as Europe, Latin America, or the Pacific Rim.

(4) Emerging-markets funds invest in newly created stock markets in developing countries.

(5) Country-specific funds limit their investments to companies domiciled in a single country.

(6) Specialty funds concentrate their portfolios in specific industries such as global telecommunications, or in market sectors such as small firm stocks.

Investment risks in these international funds tend to parallel their degree of diversification, with the most diversified (global funds) possessing the least risk and the most concentrated (single-country funds) possessing the greatest amount of price volatility. International funds tend to be riskier than domestic funds. International investors are subject to political, foreign exchange, and in some cases, liquidity risks, in addition to the risks inherent in all stocks.

Although international equity funds often contain more risk than those that invest solely in U.S. stocks, the returns of foreign stock markets do not move in lockstep with returns in the U.S. stock market. As a result, a portfolio containing both international and domestic equity funds has less volatility than a portfolio containing one category of funds. In addition, many foreign economies have a much greater growth potential than that in the United States. Thus, investors who combine foreign funds with domestic equity funds experience lower volatility and a higher return potential than investors who hold more concentrated portfolios of funds. When taken as part of a complete investment program, international equity funds are suitable investments for both conservative and aggressive growth-oriented investors.

Precious metals funds. These are funds that, for the most part, invest in gold and silver mining stocks, although some funds actually invest a small portion of their assets in gold and silver bullion. These are the most volatile funds existent. Because of the high fixed costs associated with gold and silver mining operations, small changes in the price of bullion can create large changes in earnings. As a result, a 1 percentage point increase or decrease in the price of gold bullion can cause a 3 to 4 percentage point change in the price of a precious metals fund.

The forces that tend to drive the price of gold higher (for example, inflation, fear, social unrest, currency crises, and so on) tend to drive the prices of most financial assets lower. As a result, a small investment in a precious metals fund, when coupled with investments in stock or bond funds, can reduce portfolio volatility by a significant amount. Thus, precious metals funds make excellent investment hedges. Although investment in a precious metals fund is considered a highly speculative investment, these funds are suitable for both conservative and aggressive investors when used to offset portfolio volatility.

Taxable bond funds. Taxable bond funds can be divided into four subcategories:

(1) Corporate bond funds invest in investment-grade debt securities issued by U.S. corporations.

(2) High-yield bond funds (formerly called junk bond funds) invest in low-rated debt issued by less creditworthy corporations.

(3) Government bond funds invest in U.S. government bonds issued by the Treasury and by government agencies such as the Federal Farm Credit Agency or Government National Mortgage Association (GNMA).

(4) International bond funds invest in the debt obligations of foreign governments and foreign corporations.

Bond fund risk can vary considerably depending on the creditworthiness of bond issuers, interest rate volatility, and the average maturity or duration of the fund's bond portfolio. Generally, high-yield bond funds possess the greatest risk, while government bond funds with relatively short average maturities possess the least.

Although bond funds are highly desired by conservative investors, they are far from safe bets. Bond prices move in the opposite direction of interest rates, and when interest rates spike bond prices can plummet. Interest rate risk is greatest for bonds with longer maturities and lower coupon interest rates. Zero-coupon bonds with long average maturities are the riskiest of all.

Municipal bond funds. As their name implies, these funds invest in bonds issued by city, county, and state governments. In addition, some funds invest in industrial-development bonds, which are tax-exempt bonds issued by corporations and guaranteed by municipalities. The tax exemption on municipal securities is passed through to municipal bond investors. Interest income earned from these funds is not subject to federal income taxes or to income taxes in the states in which the bonds were issued. However, capital gains on both municipal bonds and municipal bond funds are subject to both federal and state taxation.

Since municipal bonds enjoy a tax advantage over those issued by corporations and by the federal government, they offer lower yields. To obtain the tax equivalent yield of a tax-exempt bond divide the municipal bond yield by one minus your marginal income tax rate. If the yield on a fully taxable issue is below this rate, the municipal bond has a net income advantage over the taxable issue.

Like other bond fund prices, municipal bond fund prices move in the opposite direction of interest rates. Generally, the longer the average maturity, the greater is the fund's exposure to interest rate risk. In addition, municipal bond fund investors are subject to default risk. Portfolios containing bonds of lower-rated municipalities and industrial-development bonds contain the greatest degree of default risk. Some funds eliminate default risk by investing only in insured bonds. However, these funds tend to possess slightly lower yields than funds that invest in noninsured bonds.

Some municipal bond funds concentrate their investments in municipal bonds originating within a single state. Shareholders of these funds who reside in the state where the bonds are issued enjoy the advantage of avoiding both federal and state taxes on interest income. However, since the portfolios are concentrated in the issuers inside a single state, share prices tend to be more volatile than diversified municipal bond funds.

CHAPTER

FOUR

Proof of the Pudding Is in the Eating: How to Select Good Funds

With more than six thousand funds to choose from, you might think the task of culling out good funds is insurmountable. Actually, there are so many good funds around these days that if you threw a dozen darts at the *Wall Street Journal*'s list of daily fund quotations, chances are you'd come up with a handful of great funds.

Picking a good mutual fund is much easier than picking a good stock because most funds are so well diversified that their returns tend to track the markets in which they invest. In other words, if the stock market rises, the odds are extremely high that any diversified equity fund that you own will also be trending higher. Here's what I mean. Last October (1996) I asked my computer to list all of the equity mutual funds that had been around for at least fifteen years. My computer found 326 of them. I then obtained the average annual returns for these 326

funds and ranked them from best to worst. Here's what I found.

Of the 326 equity funds that were around the previous fifteen years, the best performing fund, Fidelity Select Health Care, returned an average of 21.9 percent per year. Only three funds posted losses over that period, and two of those three funds were precious metals funds. The return for the fund located in the middle of the list (median fund return) was 14.0 percent, posted by the Vanguard Wellesley Income Fund. In other words, 50 percent of all equity funds in existence during that fifteen-year period returned at least 14 percent per year. (Invest $10,000 and earn 14 percent a year for fifteen years and that investment grows to $71,379.) Furthermore, 266 of the funds in that list (81.6 percent of them) returned at least 12 percent per year.

During the fifteen-year period covered by this study of mutual fund returns, the Standard & Poor's 500 Index (a commonly used indicator of stock market returns) returned an average of 15.8 percent per year. This, however, is an unmanaged index, and its returns have not been adjusted for management fees or transaction costs. Assuming that these expenses would have clipped about 1.5 percent a year from the return, the cost-adjusted return of the U.S. stock market over that fifteen-year period would have amounted to about 14.5 percent. In other words, nearly one half of the equity funds in existence during that period would have posted returns as good as or better than those available in the stock market as a whole.

Had you invested in three or four equity funds that you randomly selected in September 1981 and held them until September 1996, the odds are extremely high that you would have earned an average of more than 12 percent per year. In other words, selecting a well-performing equity mutual fund is not a difficult task at all.

So, is random selection the best way to invest in mutual funds? The answer is a resounding no. There are some very good reasons that some funds underperform for long periods of time. By eliminating these funds from consideration, you improve the odds that your portfolio will deliver all the return you expect. For example, I took the 326 funds identified in the study described above and eliminated all funds with an expense ratio above 1.3 percent. The result was a list of 251 funds. Fidelity Select Health Care still held the top rung of the performance ladder. The bottom rung was occupied by Putnam Global Resources, with a 6.5 percent average annual return. In other words, all losing funds were eliminated when cost was used as a fund selection criteria. Furthermore, the median performer, WPG Growth & Income, returned 14.3 percent, which was a bit better than random selection. Finally, 224 of the 251 (89.2 percent) funds returned an average of at least 12 percent. In other words, if you had selected three or four funds randomly from this new list, the odds that your average annual return would have fallen short of 12 percent were about 100 to 1.

The point being made is that it is relatively easy to invest in well-performing mutual funds because there are so many around. However, remember that when you invest in a mutual fund you are picking an investment style and hiring a professional portfolio manager to deliver the returns that are consistent with the style you have chosen. Thus, you should avoid hiring and firing portfolio managers at will. Take some time investigating potential fund investments, but once you have decided upon the best funds for you, plan to be invested in those funds long term.

In addition, being invested in the top-performing funds is not as important as most investors believe. In fact, about 90 percent of what you will eventually earn on your mutual fund investments will be determined by the categories of assets (equities, bonds, money market funds, and so on) included in your portfolio and the percentage of your assets you allocate to each category. These are known as asset allocation decisions. The balance of what you earn, only 10 percent, will be determined by the quality of funds you select to represent each asset category. Thus, you should spend the bulk of your investment decision time making asset allocation decisions, and only a minimal amount of time making individual fund selections. Besides, I have done most of the work for you. The three hundred funds described in section III are the best funds around. Stick to the funds on this list, diversify properly, and vow to be a long-term investor, and you can't go wrong.

The best way to select funds with solid performance potential is to begin with a list of funds and weed out the potential underachievers. I call this approach winning by not losing. Here's how to weed out funds that could be harmful to your financial health.

Invest in Low-Cost Funds

Most mutual funds don't return what they should because investment expenses siphon off too much of the return that rightfully belongs to you. Unless you rely exclusively on your stockbroker or financial planner to make your mutual fund decisions (and are willing to compensate those people for the services they provide by paying sales commissions on the funds you buy and sell), don't invest in any mutual fund that has either a front-end or back-end sales load. The 3 to 6 percent you pay to invest in a load fund goes directly into some salesperson's pocket and not into the fund you have selected. Investing in funds with hefty sales charges is one of the best ways I know to insure that you earn suboptimal returns.

Remember also, as a mutual fund investor you assume a pro rata share of the fund's operating expenses, including its management fee. These costs are expressed as a percentage of the fund's net assets, called the expense ratio. A fund that earns 12 percent a year and possesses a 2 percent expense ratio will provide a 10 percent net return to its shareholders. A fund with a similar gross return but a 1 percent expense ratio will return 11 percent annually to its shareholders. By limiting your mutual fund search to only those funds with relatively low expense ratios, you boost the odds that you will end up in a better performing fund. As points of reference, here are the average expense ratios by fund category: diversified equity funds, 1.4 percent; international funds, 1.7 percent; and bond funds, 0.8 percent.

Finally, remember that the more a fund's portfolio manager trades, the greater will be the fund's transaction costs and the lower will be its returns. A fund's portfolio turnover ratio (listed in both its annual report and prospectus) is an index of its manager's inclination to trade. The average turnover ratio for equity funds is about 80 percent. That means 80 percent of the stocks the fund holds today won't be there a year from now. If you divide 100 percent by the turnover percentage, you obtain an estimate of the average holding period of the securities in the fund's portfolio. For example, divide 100 percent by 80 percent, and you get a 1.25 year average holding period. A fund with a portfolio turnover ratio of 50 percent holds its investments for an average of 2 years. As a rule of thumb, you can multiply the portfolio turnover rate by 1 percent to obtain an estimate of its annual trading costs. For example, a fund with a 200 percent portfolio turnover ratio experiences approximately 2 percent a year in trading costs (2 multiplied by 1 percent), which correspondingly reduces net returns by 2 percentage points a year.

Before you fill my computer with E-mail, I admit that some load funds that possess high expense ratios and high portfolio turnover ratios appear at the top of the return performance charts from time to time. However, when the performance of these funds is measured over long time periods, such as ten or fifteen years, their good performance fades drastically. It's like trying to overpower gravity. You might be able to jump very high, but gravity will eventually pull you back to earth. That's also true for high-cost funds. They may perform well for a year or two, but their high costs eventually pull their returns back to earth.

Boost Returns by Investing in Higher-Risk Funds

The only hard-and-fast rule in the investment world is that investment return is tied to investment risk. If you are seeking funds with higher return potential, you have to look at funds with higher levels of risk. However, there's a world of difference between being a risk taker and being foolhardy. A risk taker measures increments of risk against increments of return. Furthermore, successful risk takers don't take unnecessary risks. Unnecessary risks are never rewarded on Wall Street. These are risks that can be eliminated by diversifying. For example, you might make a lot of money by sinking every dime you have into one stock that you believe will provide instant riches. However, if the company that issued that stock crashes and burns, your investment capital will go up in flames too. On the other hand, if you invest in the stocks of one hundred high-risk companies, chances are that a few of those stocks will payoff handsomely. Although you may have some big losers, the big winners will more than offset those losses.

Top risk ratings go to aggressive growth, international equity, and sector funds. Within these groups, mid-cap and small-cap funds, emerging markets funds, and technology and biotechnology sector funds are the riskiest of all. Growth funds that invest in blue-chip stocks get the next rung of the risk ladder. On the bottom rung you'll find growth and income, balanced, and convertible bond funds. If statistics are your bag, check out a fund's beta or its standard deviation of return to assess its risk. The greater the beta or standard deviation, the greater is the fund's risk. (If you don't know what I'm talking about, read chapter 12 in this section of the book, entitled "Investment Risk: There Are No Free Lunches, but Don't Pay Too Much.")

Portfolio Managers Can Make a Difference

The key word here is "can." Some do and some don't. Those who do usually have a long tenure in managing a fund. Thus, one tip-off to a good manager is one who has been guiding the fund for a long time. On the other hand, the mutual fund industry has become very competitive, and successful portfolio managers are frequently pirated by competing funds. Thus, if you place a lot of weight on a fund's portfolio manager when making fund selections, you have to know who's where. In addition, a newly appointed portfolio manager may have been groomed by his or her predecessor, and these understudies are frequently capable of extending the fund's successful performance record. In addition, some funds rely on a team approach to security selection or use a computer model to generate a list of potential investments. The Twentieth Century Group of funds is an excellent example. In these instances, the importance of the fund's portfolio manager is lessened. Finally, some funds (sector funds or index funds, for example) employ highly restrictive asset selection strategies. As a result, the role of the portfolio manager is much less important than the performance of the industry or index that the fund tracks.

If you are new to mutual fund investing, but want to entrust your money to only those portfolio managers who have demonstrated that they are capable of delivering meaningful investment returns, here is my short list of fund superstars. You can't go wrong if your favorite fund has one of these people at the helm: Elizabeth Bramwell, James Craig, David Dreman, James Gipson, Ken Heebner, James Oberweis, Michael Price, Charles Royce, Robert Sanborn, Garett Van Wagoner, Ralph Wanger, Donald Yacktman.

Performance History: The Proof Is in the Eating

Some mutual fund investors head right for the performance tables when looking to add another fund to their portfolio. To me, this is one of the worst places to begin your fund search. Remember, you can't buy yesterday's performance, you can only buy tomorrow's potential. A fund that has performed exceptionally well during a short period of time such as a month, a quarter, or even a year, may have done so by accident. Its portfolio manager may have invested in a couple of stocks that blew the roof off the market and pulled the fund's return with them. And the chances that a portfolio manager can duplicate the feat the next month, quarter, or year are probably remote.

Remember also that a fund's return will be pushed and pulled by the segment of the market in which its manager invests. For example, when technology stocks are hot, funds that have a significant allocation in this sector will automatically perform well. On the other hand, if small-cap stocks are in the midst of one of their lengthy underperformance cycles, all small-cap funds will perform poorly. Thus, when assessing return potential based on historical returns, you must go behind the numbers to learn why and how those returns were earned.

This is not to say a fund's performance history is not important; it is. However, you must compare a fund's return to that of its peers if you want to assess a fund's true potential to perform well in the future. Don't just compare a fund with others in a broad class (that is, growth funds, aggressive growth funds, and so on) either. Funds possess varying styles within these broad classes. Among the aggressive growth fund category, for example, you will find groups of funds that differ significantly as to how shareholder assets are invested (for example, small-cap, mid-cap, earnings momentum, high growth, and so on). Meaningful comparisons can be made only if peer groups are sufficiently narrow to allow you to determine which fund has the best investment team.

When you make return comparisons among properly identified fund peer groups, check out returns over both short- and long-term periods (one, three, and five years). Weed out those funds that tend to reside continually in the bottom one-half of the period return ranks. What you are looking for is a fund that meets all the other criteria and has demonstrated a better-than-average record of delivering the goods.

If the Shoe Doesn't Fit, Don't Wear It

I don't care how good a fund might be, if it doesn't contribute to my investment objectives or conform to my risk tolerance level, I won't invest in it, and neither should you. If you are a return chaser, chances are that your portfolio is packed with all kinds of inappropriate funds. Some may be too risky, some may duplicate the efforts of others, some may deliver only capital gains when you need income (or the other way around), and some may possess highly concentrated portfolios that do not give you the benefits of diversification.

Before you invest in any fund, check your current portfolio first. Make sure that you are not duplicating what you already have. If the fund under consideration duplicates the characteristics of one you already own, either pass on that fund or dump the one you already own. Check to see how the new fund will fit with what you already own. Look at the fund's level of risk. Will adding this fund to your portfolio increase total risk to the point that a market setback will damage your financial well-being? If so, pass on that fund. Finally, stop to consider if the fund under consideration fits with your investment objectives. If the shoe doesn't fit, don't ruin your (financial) health by trying to wear it.

CHAPTER

FIVE

The Costs of Investing: If It's Not Worth the Price, Don't Pay It

When investing in mutual funds, or any asset for that matter, consider the costs of obtaining, maintaining, and eventually liquidating the investment. Transaction and portfolio-maintenance costs reduce investment returns and thus should be considered and weighed against potential returns when making any investment. For mutual funds, the prospectus contains the needed data to make cost evaluations.

Mutual fund costs fall into three categories: sales commissions, management fees, and general operating expenses. Until recently, some digging was necessary to uncover all of these various fees and expenses. However, mutual funds are now required to list all costs prominently in a table located within the first few pages of the prospectus. A typical fund expense table is illustrated in figure 7.

You probably wouldn't buy an automobile, a television, or even a pair of shoes without first knowing the price. Most likely, you shop around and pride yourself on obtaining the best price for many of the things you buy. You should take the same approach when buying mutual fund shares. Here are the costs you might face when shopping for a suitable mutual fund.

The Costs of Mutual Fund Investing

Sales charges. Mutual funds come in two varieties—those with sales charges and those without. Front-end load funds take sales fees right off the top. For example, if you invest $1,000 in an 8.5 percent front-end load fund, you pay $85 in commission, and the balance, $915, is invested in fund shares. These days, very few funds charge the maximum front-end load allowable (8.5 percent). Most front-end load funds add sales charges that range from 3 percent to 6 percent.

Some funds forgo a front-end sales charge and take their fees off the back end instead. These are so-called contingent deferred sales charge funds, since the back-end commission is continually reduced the longer you retain your shares. For example, many back-end load funds levy a 5 percent fee if shares are redeemed within one year of purchase, and they reduce the fee by 1 percentage point for each additional year the fund shares are held. The back-end load disappears if the investment is held five or more years.

Other mutual funds levy an ongoing sales charge rather than either front- or back-end loads. These charges, called 12b-1 charges, typically average about 0.5 percent but can range from 0.1 percent to 1.0 percent of the value of your investment. These so-called distribution fees are levied every day you hold the fund's shares.

Finally, some funds combine 12b-1 charges with back-end loads. (In fact, most back-end load funds come with 12b-1 charges attached.) Note that the longer you hold the shares of such funds, the lower the contingent deferred sales charges but the greater the total 12b-1 fees. In other words, invest in one of these funds and what you gain on the one hand you lose on the other.

Figure 7
FUND EXPENSES

The following information is provided in order to assist you in understanding the various costs and expenses that a shareholder of the Fund will bear directly or indirectly. There are certain charges associated with retirement accounts and with certain services offered by the Fund. See "SHAREHOLDER PLANS." Purchases and redemptions may also be made through broker-dealers or others who may charge a commission or other transaction fee for their services. The Annual Fund Operating Expenses are actual expenses incurred during the fiscal year ended October 31, 1995. The Adviser will waive its management fee (0.7%) to the extent that the Fund's total operating expenses exceed 2.5% of the average net assets. See "MANAGEMENT OF THE FUND." The example below is based on the Annual Fund Operating Expenses set forth in the accompanying table.

Shareholder Transaction Expenses

Maximum Sales Load Imposed on Purchases or Reinvested Dividends . . . . . None

Deferred Sales Load . . . . None

Redemption Fee . . . . None

Exchange Fee . . . . None

Annual Fund Operating Expenses

Management Fee 0.70%

12b-1 Fees . . . . None

Other Expenses. 1.37%

Total Fund Operating Expenses. 2.07%

Example:	1 Year	3 Years	5 Years	10 Years
You would pay the following expenses on a $1,000 investment, assuming (1) 5% annual return (2) redemption at the end of each time period:	$21	$64	$109	$235

The example should not be considered a representative of past or future expenses and actual expenses may be greater or less than these shown.

Management and administrative fees. While some investors pay a sales charge when they invest in mutual funds and some do not (those who invest in no-load funds), all mutual fund investors must pay the annual fund management and administrative fees. Management fees are paid to the fund's investment adviser and generally range from 0.5 percent to 1.0 percent of the fund's average assets. Typically, the management fee percentage is reduced as the total assets of the fund increase.

In addition to paying management fees, fund shareholders must foot the bill for such administrative items as shareholder record keeping, auditing, legal services, shareholder reports, the annual meeting, custodial fees, and so on. Management and administrative fees for a typical equity fund range from about 0.2 percent to 2.5 percent and average about 1.4 percent of the fund's total assets.

Figure 8
ESTIMATING FUND EXPENSES: AN EXAMPLE

	Fund A	Fund B	Fund C	Fund D
Sales Charges				
Front-end load	0.00%	8.50%	3.00%	0.00%
Back-end load	3.00	0.00	0.00	0.00
12b-1 fee	1.50	0.00	0.00	0.00
Operating Expenses				
Management Fee	2.25	3.00	2.25	2.10
Admin. Expense	0.90	1.20	0.60	0.90
Estimated Transaction Costs				
Trading Costs	0.75	1.50	3.00	0.60
Total Costs	8.40	14.20	8.85	3.60
Average Annual Expenses	2.80%	4.73%	2.95%	1.20%

NOTE: Annual operating expenses have been multiplied by three to account for a three-year holding period. Transaction costs were estimated by multiplying the portfolio turnover ratio by 1 percent (average cost of a round-trip trade), and multiplying the result by three to account for an intended three-year holding period.

Transaction costs. Finally, mutual fund investors also assume the transaction costs that occur when a portfolio manager adds or deletes securities from the fund's portfolio. Transaction costs include both brokerage commissions and the dealer's bid-ask spread, and vary directly with the level of asset turnover. Transaction costs will differ depending on the number of shares bought or sold and the liquidity in the market where the security is traded. On average, a mutual fund pays from 0.5 percent to 1 percent when making a trade (that is, a cost of about 1 to 2 percent on a round-trip trade). A fund's transaction charges are the most difficult to assess. While funds report the amount of brokerage expenses, such expenses are only a small portion of transaction costs. The bid-ask spread paid to the market maker is the largest component. As this figure is not reported, it must be estimated. Since brokerage commissions and the dealer's bid-ask spread combined average about 1 to 2 percent on a round-trip trade, you can estimate total transaction costs by multiplying the fund's turnover ratio by 1 or 2 percent. For example, a fund with a 50 percent portfolio turnover ratio will experience annual trading costs somewhere in the 0.5 to 1 percent range.

Assessing the Total Cost of Fund Investing

Before you begin to analyze the cost of mutual fund investing, you must estimate the length of time you intend to hold the fund's shares, since some costs are levied only once while others are tacked on every year. Here's how to compare the cost of investing in funds with different fee structures.

Suppose that you plan to invest in a fund and hold it for three years. You have narrowed the alternatives to four funds, and you've decided to invest in the fund with the lowest cost.

Fund A has a deferred contingent sales charge that begins at 5 percent but will be trimmed to 3 percent if the shares are held for three years. In addition, the fund levies an annual 12b-1 fee of 0.5 percent. The management annual fee is 0.75 percent, and annual operating expenses amount to an additional 0.3 percent. The fund's portfolio turnover ratio is 25 percent.

Fund B sports an 8.5 percent front-end load but no 12b-1 or back-end sales fees. Management fees are 1.0 percent per year, and administrative fees add another 0.4 percent annually. The fund's portfolio turnover ratio is 50 percent. Fund C is sold with a 3.0 percent front-end load. The annual management fee is 0.75 percent, and administrative fees average 0.2 percent per year. Portfolio turnover has averaged 100 percent per year. Fund D is a true no-load fund and has no sales charges of any kind. The annual management fee is 0.7 percent, and annual administrative expenses are 0.3 percent. Portfolio turnover is low, averaging 20 percent.

Figure 8 illustrates the total and average annual costs for each fund, assuming a three-year holding period. Although the following analysis does not take the time value of money into consideration, it is sufficiently accurate to make a valid cost comparison.

Note that 12b-1 fees, management fees, and administrative expenses have been multiplied by three—the intended holding period. Note also that total and average annual costs can vary substantially. Finally, note that for some funds, the average annual cost can erode return by a significant amount. For example, the management of Fund B must overcome a hefty burden of 4.73 percent per year, or 3.53 percent more than Fund D to produce a similar return for its shareholders.

While some funds are better managed than others and thus provide greater investment returns to their shareholders, over an investment lifetime, it is frequently the cost of investing that makes the difference between investment success and investment failure. Know what it will cost to invest in a mutual fund and opt to invest in suitable low-cost funds. I can't think of a better way to improve your long-run investment returns.

CHAPTER

SIX

Mutual Fund Portfolios for Each and Every One of Us

Will Rogers once said, "It's easy to make money in the stock market. You buy some stocks, and when they go up, you sell them and make a profit." When asked what happens when they don't go up, he responded: "That's easy, you don't buy 'em."

Several years ago, Groucho Marx was touring the floor of the New York Stock Exchange when a trader asked him where he invested his money. "In Treasury bills," Groucho responded. "They don't pay very much, do they," the trader shot back. "They do if you've got enough of them," Groucho replied.

Unfortunately for us, investing is not as easy as Will Rogers made it out to be, nor do many of us have so much money that we can opt for the safety and low yields of Treasury bills, as did Groucho. This is especially true for individuals contemplating retirement. On the one hand, retirees need the safety that short-term government securities provide. On the other hand, the yield of these securities is generally so low that a 100 percent Treasury bill portfolio rarely provides the needed income to support a life of comfort in retirement. Furthermore, retirees must continually fight an uphill battle against inflation. While short-term government securities provide protection against the loss of your money, fixed-income securities subject their investors to loss of purchasing power due to the continual increase in consumer prices.

Highly risk-averse investors face the proverbial Gordian knot. Safety of principal requires investment in securities that don't pay enough, and the pursuit of additional return means taking on more risk. You can't untie the knot. If you desire a high rate of return you must assume large risks. If you prefer safety, you must settle for small returns. When investing, there are no free lunches. You pay for the returns you get by taking on more risk.

The table below illustrates the returns that have been available to investors during the last fifty-six years. As can be seen, long-run

TABLE 2.
INVESTMENT RETURNS: 1940–1995

Investment Category	Average Annual Return	Inflation-Adjusted Return	Risk
Growth Stocks	16.0%	11.6%	High
Blue-Chip Stocks	11.9	7.5	Moderate
Long-Term Gov't Bonds	5.2	0.8	Low
Treasury Bills	4.3	-0.1	Lowest

Source: *Stocks, Bonds, Bills, and Inflation Yearbook 1996.* Ibbotson Associates.

investment returns decline along with investment risk. In fact, when considered on an after-inflation basis, the lowest-risk investment (Treasury bills) provides no real return at all. On the other hand, an aggressive-growth common stock portfolio has returned an average of 11 percent more than the rate of inflation annually during the last half-century.

To insure preservation of capital (that is, that your investment returns and investment capital will not lose ground against the pressure of increasing consumer prices), investors must allocate some portion of their capital to common stocks. And, of course, the greater the allocation, the greater is the exposure to a decline in portfolio value due to the onset of a bear stock market.

As an investor, your first task is to solve the problem of risk and return trade-off. This means determining the mix of investments that will provide income, preservation of capital, and an inflation hedge, while keeping investment risk within your comfort zone. If you don't require the use of your investment capital for very long periods of time, you can ignore the day-to-day or year-to-year fluctuations in the stock market and allocate most of your capital to common stocks. If you have a shorter investment horizon, you need to find a balance between bonds, Treasury bills, and common stocks. Finally, if you have a very short investment horizon, you must seek a high degree of safety of principal while providing some inflation offset. In other words, you must first address the asset allocation decision before setting off on the task of finding the "best" investments.

Table 3 illustrates the risk of investing in different asset categories as it relates to your investment horizon. Take blue-chip stocks for example. Their best annual return occurred in 1954 when shareholders earned 52.6 percent. Their worst annual return occurred in 1974 when stocks returned a total of -26.5 percent. Thus, investors with very short-term horizons (such as one year) are exposed to the danger of a significant loss if they invest in blue-chip stocks.

On the other hand, investors with longer investment horizons find that time mitigates the risk of investing in common stocks. For example, the blue-chip stock investor's worst five-year return was recorded between 1970 and 1974. During that period, a diversified portfolio of blue-chip common stocks would have declined by an

average of 2.4 percent per year, or by a total of 11.5 percent during the five-year period. Note that while still a loser, the investor with a five-year planning horizon is exposed to less risk than the investor with a one-year horizon. Note also that there has been no ten-year period between 1940 and 1991 in which a blue-chip stock investor would have lost money. The worst ten-year performance for blue-chip stocks occurred between 1965 and 1974. During that period, common stocks returned an average of 1.2 percent annually. Finally, note that the worst performance for blue-chip stocks during any twenty-year period during the last half-century was an annual gain of 6.5 percent. This worst-case scenario for blue-chip stocks was better than the worst-case scenario for any other investment (other than aggressive growth stocks). Since blue-chip stocks performed better than bonds or Treasury bills during twenty-year periods (even when at their worst), long-term investors should opt for portfolios that contain nearly a 100 percent investment in common stocks.

Interestingly, when allocating assets between "safe" and risky investments, most Americans assume a very conservative posture. According to the Federal Reserve Board, which keeps such statistics, Americans invest 48 cents out of every savings dollar in so-called fixed-income assets (bank and thrift CDs, savings accounts, money market funds, and bonds). Of this 48 cents, 30 cents finds its way into interest-bearing accounts at banks and thrifts and 18 cents is invested in bonds.

Only 23 cents out of every savings dollar is invested directly in common stocks or equity mutual funds. With this kind of savings and investment mix, America's savers can expect to earn slightly more than 7 percent on their invested capital over the long run. Given that the rate of inflation during the last half-century has averaged about 4 percent, this asset mix won't cut the mustard for most savers.

Many investors fail to realize that the investment allocation strategy that appears the safest can ultimately become the riskiest. Consider the plight of a retiree who opts for the safety provided by Treasury securities. Suppose this individual invests the proceeds of a $200,000 retirement rollover in ten-year maturity government bonds with a 7 percent annual interest rate. This investor can look

TABLE 3.
INVESTMENT RISK AND INVESTMENT
HOLDING PERIOD: 1940–1995

	Best		Worst	
Annual Returns				
Growth Stocks	88.4%	1943	-30.9%	1973
Blue-Chip Stocks	52.6	1954	-26.5	1974
Long-Term Gov't Bonds	40.4	1982	-9.2	1967
Treasury Bills	14.7	1981	0.0	1940
Five-Year Periods (Annualized Returns)				
Growth Stocks	45.9%	1941–1945	-12.3%	1969–1973
Blue-Chip Stocks	23.8	1950–1954	-2.4	1970–1974
Long-Term Gov't Bonds	21.5	1982–1986	-2.1	1965–1969
Treasury Bills	11.1	1979–1983	0.2	1940–1944
Ten-Year Periods (Annualized Returns)				
Growth Stocks	30.4%	1975–1984	3.2%	1965–1974
Blue-Chip Stocks	20.1	1949–1958	1.2	1965–1974
Long-Term Gov't Bonds	21.6	1982–1991	-0.1	1950–1959
Treasury Bills	9.2	1978–1987	0.4	1940–1949
Twenty-Year Periods (Annualized Returns)				
Growth Stocks	21.1%	1942–1961	8.2%	1955–1974
Blue-Chip Stocks	16.9	1942–1961	6.5	1959–1978
Long-Term Gov't Bonds	9.0	1972–1991	0.7	1950–1969
Treasury Bills	7.7	1972–1991	1.1	1940–1959

forward to receiving $14,000 in interest payments during each of the next ten years and the return of his capital when the bond matures.

Suppose, however, that consumer prices increase at the rate of 4 percent annually during this ten-year period. The purchasing power of next year's interest payment shrinks to $13,462. The following year's interest payment will purchase only $12,944 worth of goods and services.

The final year's interest payment will support only two-thirds the consumption of the first year's interest payment. That is, the last $14,000 payment will buy only $9,459 worth of goods and services. In other words, the fixed-income investing retiree will have to tighten his belt every year. Making matters worse, after ten years, the value of the initial $200,000 investment (in purchasing power terms) will have shrunk to $135,100! Where is the safety in that strategy?

When constructing the following model portfolios, I attempted to balance risk and return for investors with varying planning horizons. Long-term-oriented investor portfolios are heavily tilted toward common stocks. In fact, I recommended some allocation be made to common stocks by all investors. Of course, the percentage allocation to equities declines as one's planning horizon becomes shorter. Also, I have recommended a highly diverse mixture of investments for most investors. These investments include not just domestic stocks, bonds, and money market funds; in some circumstances, I have recommended investment in international stocks and bonds as well.

Although the explosion in the number of mutual funds available to investors in recent years has made investing in funds more confusing, the proliferation in the types of investment portfolios available to individuals has provided an opportunity for additional risk reduction. For example, by investing across a wide spectrum of asset categories, investors can offset declines in the value of some investments by increases in the value of others. Given that the typical equity fund has only one-third the risk of a single stock and that the highly diversified portfolio of mutual funds has only one-half the risk of the typical equity fund, the mutual fund industry has provided individual investors with risk-reduction opportunities heretofore only available to large institutional investors.

Lifetime Portfolio Management

History indicates that over the long run aggressive growth equity funds produce the highest total returns. However, these funds are highly volatile, and they produce very little current income. Thus, they may not be well suited for all investors. However, for younger investors who are setting aside dollars for their retirement, aggressive growth mutual funds are ideal investment vehicles since investors with long planning horizons can tolerate a high degree of short-term price volatility.

When investing for retirement that will take place several years in the future, your investment view should be long term. Thus, week-to-week, month-to-month, or even year-to-year variations in portfolio value can be ignored. In fact, individuals who invest equal amounts of money on a regular basis should welcome a high degree of portfolio volatility because their periodic investments will buy a larger number of mutual fund shares when share prices decline. Furthermore, since current dividend and interest income are subject to taxation when distributed, wealth-accumulating investors' needs are better served by mutual funds that pay little or no current income. Thus, the full measure of return is left to compound over future years.

Additionally, bond funds provide the highest current income. Moreover, bond funds generally hold a large number of different issues, and thus they protect investors from the default risk that they would face by holding a handful of bonds. Since retired investors generally expect their investment portfolios to provide income, bond funds are highly touted to retirees by brokers and financial planners. If investing life were that simple, wealth-accumulating investors could merely invest in a few aggressive growth mutual funds and then exchange those funds for bond funds when they retire. However, life is anything but simple. And, sad to say, neither is lifetime portfolio management.

Accumulating Wealth for Retirement

Investors with more than a five-year planning horizon should adopt a highly aggressive investment posture. The goal should be to maximize investment return rather than minimize investment risk. Of course, risk management is important. Wealth-accumulating investors should avoid taking unnecessary risks by holding diversified portfolios and making regular cash contributions to their retirement programs.

While all stocks fall during a bear market, a highly diversified portfolio of common stocks will eventually head for higher ground. And that statement cannot be made about a portfolio containing one or two stocks. Thus, by investing in a handful of growth and aggressive growth mutual funds, investors ensure against having temporary losses turn into permanent ones. Furthermore, by investing equal dollar amounts at regular intervals, wealth-accumulating investors benefit from dollar cost averaging. When stock prices are inordinately low, these investors accumulate more fund shares than when stock prices are inflated. Thus, when stock prices ultimately head higher, these investors magnify their investment returns. Finally, since retirement contributions will not be needed until sometime in the distant future, there is little need to hold cash reserves such as money market funds or bank CDs.

Keeping these points in mind, here is a simplified model portfolio for wealth-accumulating investors.

Aggressive Growth Funds	35%
Growth Funds	35
International Equity Funds	30

Some diversification across types of capital appreciation funds is recommended because return relationships can be unstable during the short run. For example, during the past ten years, growth funds, on average, have provided greater returns than aggressive growth funds. On the other hand, aggressive growth funds have provided higher returns over the last fifteen to twenty years. International equity funds are recommended because of their relatively low correlation to returns with funds that invest solely in domestic stocks. By combining international equities with domestic equities, you can reduce portfolio risk without sacrificing investment return. Furthermore, during periods marked by a weak dollar, these funds can produce handsome returns. For example, during the last decade, international equity funds returned an average of 17 percent compounded annually, or about 2.5 percent per year more than any other group of equity funds. Over the long run, this aggressive portfolio will provide an average annual return of between 11 and 14 percent.

A Nearing-Retirement Strategy

It is no secret that investors who are retired need a balance between portfolio return and risk. First, since retirees are usually not contributing to their investment portfolios, losses cannot be tempered by dollar cost averaging. Instead of adding cash to their portfolios, most retirees are making regular withdrawals. Second, since retirees depend on income from their investments to support current consumption, predictable income streams are preferred over those that vary from year to year. Finally, because of periodic withdrawals, retirees run the risk of having to sell more equity fund shares when prices are depressed to meet their required monthly cash flow. The result is exactly opposite that of dollar cost averaging. That is, they sell funds at a loss during market declines, and they gain less on market rebounds since they were required to effect inordinately large security sales when prices were depressed.

Investors who contemplate making an abrupt shift from growth funds to income funds upon retirement also suffer from temporary stock market declines that might occur shortly before the shift in assets occurs. For example, an aggressive growth portfolio is subject to a decline of 50 percent or more during steep bear stock markets. If such a bear market were to occur shortly before retirement, income could be permanently decreased by more than one-half. Thus, years of careful planning could be undone in a few short months.

To avoid this possibility, I recommend that investors with less than five years until retirement gradually reduce the risk of their portfolios. This can be accomplished by shifting from aggressive growth funds to growth and income funds and bond funds. Here is one recommendation:

Growth Funds	20%
Growth and Income Funds	20
International Equity Funds	15
Domestic Bond Funds	15
International Bond Funds	15
Money Market Funds	15

Note that more than one-half of this portfolio is invested in equity funds. Thus, the portfolio has the potential to provide capital growth as well as income. The 45 percent allocation to bond funds and money market funds provides stability as well as current income. As a result, this portfolio could be expected to decline by one-third less than an aggressive portfolio during a steep bear market. However, over a five-year market cycle, this portfolio can be expected to return about 9 to 10 percent annually. Thus, a 40 percent reduction in investment risk is accompanied by only a 20 percent reduction in long-term total return.

A Modest-Risk Retirement Portfolio

As a new retiree, you must remember that your investment portfolio will be required to support you for twenty years or more. In other words, if you have recently retired you must still invest for the long term. That means that you must continue to seek growth of investment capital to offset the impact of inflation. For example, if consumer prices were to rise at an average of 3 percent annually, the prices of goods and services would be 80 percent higher twenty years from now. Thus, even a modest amount of inflation can be devastating to a retiree.

Consider the case of a retired investor who purchased "safe" government bonds with twenty-year maturities twenty years ago. If this individual had invested $200,000 in these bonds in 1972, the portfolio (then yielding about 7.5 percent) would have provided an annual income of $15,000. Twenty years later, this portfolio would still be providing $15,000 in annual income. However, because of escalating consumer prices, it would have taken an annual income of $50,000 to maintain the same standard of living as when the initial investment was made. Or to put it another way, the purchasing power of a $15,000 initial income stream would have fallen to $4,500 by the time the twenty-year bond matured. And the purchasing power of the initial $200,000 bond investment would have fallen to $60,000!

To protect investment income and portfolio value from the detrimental effects of inflation, an investment portfolio must be structured to provide some growth in income and capital over the long term. This, of course, requires investment in common stock mutual funds. Here is a model portfolio that provides both growth and a high level of current income:

Growth Funds	10%
Growth and Income Funds	10
International Equity Funds	10
Domestic Bond Funds	30
International Bond Funds	20
Money Market Funds	20

Note that this portfolio contains a 30 percent allocation to equity funds. These funds, in addition to providing some current income, can be expected to grow by an average of about 7 percent annually and thus provide an overall portfolio growth rate of approximately 2 percent per year (about half the rate of inflation during the last fifty years). Furthermore, during periods when stock prices are advancing at a greater-than-average pace, the portfolio can be rebalanced by selling some equity shares and diverting the proceeds to bond and money market funds. By taking profits when stock prices are inordinately high, an investor obtains the potential to increase the portfolio's average growth rate. Furthermore, this portfolio can be expected to provide a greater current income than is generally obtainable from bank certificates of deposit, Treasury bills, or money market mutual funds. Finally, because of the large allocation to fixed-income investments, the portfolio possesses less than one-third the risk contained in the stock market.

A Highly Conservative Retirement Portfolio

It may come as a bit of a surprise to some investors that my recommended portfolio for very conservative retirees is not much different from the portfolio recommended for younger retirees. In fact, my recommended allocations are exactly the same: 30 percent to equity funds, 50 percent to bond funds, and 20 percent to money market funds. The only difference is that I recommend the 10-percent growth fund allocation be shifted to growth and income funds (bringing the total allocation to this fund category to 20 percent). This shift will both decrease portfolio variability (risk) and increase current income. Generally, growth and income funds have betas less than 0.60 (about half the variability of the stock market) and provide about two hundred basis points less yield than Treasury bills. (A basis point is equal to 0.01 percent). This reduces the downside risk to less than one-fourth that of the stock market, while providing a growth potential of more than 1.5 percent annually.

Here is the recommended portfolio:	
Growth and Income Funds	20%
International Equity Funds	10
Domestic Bond Funds	30
International Bond Funds	20
Money Market Funds	20

Although I have attempted to provide a bare-bones outline of portfolio strategies for broad groups of investors with varying income and capital appreciation needs, one can see that maintaining a lifetime investment plan can be somewhat complex. However, the proliferation of mutual funds has simplified the implementation aspect of lifetime financial planning. Individual investors can obtain a wide degree of diversification by investing in mutual funds that specialize in particular categories of financial assets. Thus, investment risk can be controlled to a much greater extent today than was possible only a decade ago. In addition, since the selection of individual stocks and bonds is left to each mutual fund's investment adviser, investors can concentrate their decision making on asset allocation rather than on individual asset selection.

Weatherproof Your Portfolio with an All-Weather Portfolio

Although most investors know that the best time to buy stocks is after they have taken a nasty tumble, many fear that the stock market will continue to trend downward and are reluctant to make a purchase when stock prices are continually falling. On the other hand, a large number of investors are lured to the stock market after prices have risen substantially. They then bail out at the first sign that prices are heading lower. These investors practice the "buy low, sell high" strategy in reverse. Other savers seem to find an excuse for not investing in the stock market. Both of these groups of individuals are doomed to investment failure.

This behavior is understandable. Investors, like most other decision makers, tend to fear the unknown. Like all rational decision makers, they are risk averse. That is, given the choice between two investments with equal potential returns, they will select the one that has the least risk. However, few investors know how to quantify the risks they face when investing. They know that stocks are risky, Treasury bills (and money market fund investments) are safe, and bonds possess a level of risk that's somewhere in between. As a result of such confusion, many investors take a simple approach to the asset allocation decision. Highly risk-averse investors tend to keep the bulk of their capital in bank CDs, Treasury bills, and money market funds. Those who place a premium on interest income opt for bonds or bond funds, while those who seek growth invest primarily in domestic equities. I call this approach asset allocation by default.

Interestingly, most mutual fund investors begin the investment decision process by attempting to find the "best" mutual funds. These investors place a premium on past performance and spend hours scrutinizing lists of historic fund returns. Some invest in last quarter's or last year's best performers. Others look for funds that have performed well during three-, five-, or even ten-year periods. Unfortunately, these investors place the cart in front of the horse. As a result, they generally never get anywhere. Many of these investors spend their investment lifetimes jumping from one fund to another without giving consideration to whether or not these funds are appropriate for their needs or lie within their risk tolerance zones. As a result, these investors not only end up with inappropriate portfolios, but also generally earn far less than they should given the effort they have expended or the risks they have taken.

Why Asset Allocation Reduces Portfolio Volatility

Different types of assets perform differently in different economic environments. In other words, economic events that cause the prices of some assets to fall cause the prices of others to rise. Take bond prices and gold prices for example. Accelerating rates of inflation can be devastating to bond prices. If investors believe that consumer prices will rise by 5 percent next year, they might demand a 10 percent yield on their bond investments. If inflation expectations rise to 8 percent, these investors might demand that bonds pay them 13 percent. And when interest rates go up, bond prices go down. On the other hand, the price of gold bullion tends to rise and fall with the rate of inflation (or the expectation of inflation). The greater the expected rate of inflation, the higher the price of gold will rise. Thus, a portfolio that contains both gold and bonds will be less variable than one that contains bonds only, because the losses on one of the investments tend to be offset by gains in the other. The result: The price volatility of a portfolio of these two assets tends to be less than the price volatility of either of them considered independently. In this instance, the whole is less than the sum of the parts, and therefore is more desirable. And this is true whenever the returns of two or more assets do not move in lockstep with one another.

The beauty of a portfolio that is diversified across a wide spectrum of assets such as stocks, bonds, international assets, gold, and money market funds is that the returns of each asset category do not move in harmony with the others. Thus, by allocating some capital to each category, overall portfolio volatility (that is, portfolio risk) is reduced.

But what about investment return? Lower investment risk is usually associated with lower return potential. However, in the case of a portfolio diversified across a wide spectrum of assets, the reduction in investment risk far exceeds the slight reduction in return potential. The result is a portfolio that contains less risk per unit of return (or to put it another way, the portfolio contains more return per unit of risk).

All-Weather Investing

If you can't beat the market, why not own it? That's exactly what I propose with my "All-Weather Portfolio." However, my definition of "the market" is different than that offered by most investment advisers. The market, to capital asset pricing theorists, consists of all assets held in proportions equal to their market values relative to the total value of all assets. Of course, it is impossible to hold a portfolio that contains an allocation to all of the world's assets. (How do you go about investing in farmland in Bosnia?) However, I have identified seven major categories of assets that together act as a suitable proxy for the world-market portfolio. These asset categories include blue-chip stocks, small-cap stocks, international stocks, international bonds, domestic bonds, gold, and money market funds. Although most of these categories of assets contain a relatively high degree of volatility (risk), the fact that their returns do not move in lockstep produces a portfolio that has less than one-half the risk of the stock market in general but produces a similar long-run rate of return.

The accompanying table illustrates the rates of return produced by an All-Weather Portfolio during the last two decades. The All-Weather Portfolio consists of equal percentage investments made to each of the seven asset categories listed above. The portfolios were rebalanced at the end of each year. Note that the portfolio returned significantly more than a Treasury bill portfolio and about the same as the broadly based Standard & Poor's 500 Index of blue-chip stocks. Although the All-Weather Portfolio's average annual return was slightly above that provided by the stock market, note the reduced return volatility. The All-Weather Portfolio suffered losses during 1981, 1990, and 1994, with the largest annual loss amounting to only 4.3 percent.

It would have been very difficult to assemble an All-Weather

Portfolio a decade ago unless you were extremely wealthy. That's because it would have taken a considerable amount of money to assemble a diversified portfolio of assets representing each of the seven categories. However, today mutual funds can be found to represent each asset category. By investing in mutual funds, you assure that you obtain proper diversification with each asset category by investing as little as $1,000. Furthermore, you have left the selection of individual assets to professional investors. Your asset allocation tasks are limited to making the proper allocations to the various asset categories and the rebalancing of the portfolio on a periodic basis. What could be more simple?

Active or Passive Asset Allocation?

There are two views on this question. The passive view holds that, since the goal of an All-Weather Portfolio is risk reduction, declines in the value of one segment of the portfolio will largely offset gains in another. If investors knew which asset class was going to produce the greatest returns during the year, they should allocate all of their capital to that asset class. However, by actively managing the portfolio in that manner, investors increase risk due to forecasting errors, which the All-Weather Portfolio was designed to limit in the first place.

A second view holds that some degree of active management can be beneficial as long as reallocations among asset classes are modest and are not made with a high degree of frequency. Thus, when it appears that one segment of the portfolio contains assets that are highly overvalued, the proportion of capital committed to that segment should be reduced. By making reallocations in this manner, investors may increase long-run returns without engaging in forecasting the short-run direction of asset prices since relative values rather than trends are used as the basis for reallocating capital. This is the approach I recommend.

Table 5 illustrates the allocation boundaries for each asset class. When the returns in an asset category are on a strong upward trend, expand your allocation toward the upper allocation limit. When you believe that an asset category is overvalued and due for a correction, limit your investment to the bottom of the recommended per-

TABLE 4.
ALL-WEATHER PORTFOLIO RETURNS

Year	All-Weather Portfolio	S&P 500 Index	Treasury Bills
1973	2.8%	-14.7%	6.9%
1974	1.3	-26.5	8.0
1975	21.9	37.2	5.8
1976	14.0	23.8	5.1
1977	11.9	-7.2	5.1
1978	17.3	6.6	7.2
1979	20.4	18.4	10.4
1980	28.6	32.4	11.2
1981	-2.0	-4.9	14.7
1982	17.8	21.4	10.5
1983	12.1	22.5	8.8
1984	2.2	6.3	9.8
1985	26.5	32.2	7.7
1986	23.3	18.5	6.2
1987	8.7	5.2	5.5
1988	8.6	16.8	6.3
1989	11.9	31.5	8.5
1990	-4.3	-3.2	7.8
1991	16.8	30.5	5.6
1992	4.4	7.7	3.5
1993	15.7	10.0	3.0
1994	-0.7	1.3	3.9
1995	18.9	37.4	5.6
Annualized Return	12.8%	11.8%	7.2%
Standard Deviation	9.2	17.3	2.7

centage allocation. Note that this strategy requires that you be invested in each asset category, no matter how unappealing its return prospects may be.

Note that you can change the character of the All-Weather Portfolio without changing the percentage allocations. For example, suppose that you have opted for an equal allocation strategy and allocate one-seventh of your assets to each category. However, suppose that you believe that interest rates will soon be headed upward. Rather than change the percentage allocation to bond funds, you could switch your investment from a bond fund with a long-term average maturity to one with a relatively short maturity. As a result, the portfolio has become somewhat insulated against the effects of rising interest rates and tumbling bond prices. Similarly, you could switch your common stock investments from a growth to a growth and income fund (that possesses a much lower beta) if you believe the stock market is due for a tumble. This form of strategic asset allocation allows room for acting on forecasts without subjecting the portfolio to the extreme risk that usually results by taking an all-or-nothing approach.

Even if you assume a passive strategy and opt to make equal allocations to each asset class, you must rebalance the portfolio pe-

TABLE 5.
ASSET ALLOCATION PARAMETERS

Asset Category	Allocation Range
Small-Cap Equity Funds	10%–20%
Large-Cap Equity Funds	10–20
International Equity Funds	10–20
U.S. Bond Funds	10–30
International Bond Funds	5–15
Gold Funds	5–15
Money Market Funds	5–25

riodically. Rebalancing is necessitated by the fact that allocation percentages will change as asset prices change. However, the good news is that by rebalancing back to the initial allocations you must sell some shares of the funds that have increased in price and buy shares in those whose prices are temporarily depressed. In other words, periodic rebalancing forces you to follow a buy low, sell high strategy. And only good can result.

The question of when to rebalance is subjective. Rebalance frequently enough to take advantage of financial market fluctuations. However, frequent rebalancing causes you to constantly make minor adjustments in your portfolio and negates some of the benefits of all-weather investing, namely reduced costs and expenditure of effort.

I suggest that you rebalance whenever the percentage invested in any category rises or falls by 3 percentage points. For example, if you allocate 20 percent of your assets to blue-chip stock funds and that percentage rises to 23 percent because of rising stock prices, rebalance back to the initial percentage. In addition, I recommend that you rebalance at least once each year. My suggestion is to rebalance at least every January. I have selected the month of January since most mutual funds make their annual capital distributions in December. Thus, you avoid the problem of buying someone else's capital gains.

Individual Fund Selection

When selecting individual funds for each investment category, look for three characteristics. First, remember that investment costs reduce investment returns. Since you are making both fund selection and asset allocation decisions, invest in no-load funds only. In addition, seek funds with low expense and portfolio turnover ratios. A high portfolio turnover ratio is indicative of a fund that is incurring high transaction costs when it trades the stocks or bonds in its portfolio.

Second, make sure that the funds adequately represent the appropriate category of assets. A small-cap equity fund should invest in small firm stocks, and so on. Index funds provide ideal matches with category returns. (In addition, most index funds have low expense and portfolio turnover ratios.)

Finally, select funds that tend to stay fully invested at all times. Remember that you are making the allocations among asset classes. If you allocate 20 percent of your portfolio to money market funds, you obtain redundant results if one of your equity funds has allocated 20 percent of its assets to cash also.

Protecting your hard-earned assets requires widespread portfolio diversification. The All-Weather Portfolio provides that protection while maintaining the potential to earn double-digit long-run returns. Over a period of five years or more, this portfolio should average a return in excess of 10 percent annually while experiencing less than one-half the downside risk of the stock market. In fact, I have yet to uncover an economic scenario that would cause the value of the All-Weather Portfolio to decline by more than 15 percent on a temporary basis. And that's a lot of protection given the high volatility in today's financial markets.

The All-Weather Portfolio is similar to a growth and income portfolio. In fact, about 40 percent of the long-run return is due to interest and dividend income with 60 percent reserved for capital appreciation. Although some of the components carry a high degree of risk (small-cap stock funds and gold funds for example), when they are combined into a single portfolio, overall risk is reduced significantly.

All investors should find room in their financial plans for an All-Weather Portfolio. Income-oriented investors, for example, could combine an income portfolio with an All-Weather Portfolio. The all-weather portion would insure long-term growth of capital and thus hedge the income portfolio from the ravages of inflation. On the other hand, the All-Weather Portfolio provides a degree of stability for growth-oriented investors who combine it with an aggressive equity fund portfolio. It is an excellent portfolio for retirees who desire above-average returns while maintaining a high degree of capital preservation. The All-Weather Portfolio is neither fad nor fiction. It is the best way to provide decent returns while maintaining asset protection for a lifetime.

It Pays to Keep Your Balance

Where should aggressive growth investors put their money these days? If you ponder the question of whether to invest in the stock market long enough, you probably will find good reason to avoid equities no matter what's going on in the financial markets. Frequently, investors are so fearful of the stock market that they tend to be underinvested in equity funds at all times. However, history indicates that the best approach to equity investing is to spread capital across three categories of equities (large-cap, small-cap, and international equity funds) and periodically rebalance that portfolio. That's because the relationship among the returns of blue-chip stocks, small-cap stocks, and international equities is less than perfectly correlated. In other words, when one asset category is performing poorly, another category tends to be performing much better. Aggressive equity investors who diversify across categories of equity mutual funds can lower the risk of their portfolios without sacrificing a significant amount of return. As a result, the risk per unit of return of a balanced portfolio of equity funds is reduced to a minimum.

To illustrate what happens to a balanced portfolio of equity funds, I tracked the returns of blue chips, small-caps, and foreign stocks during the past two decades. (See table 6.) I then computed the average return and standard deviations of return (risk index) for each of the three categories and for a portfolio consisting of equal dollar investments in each of the three categories (assuming the portfolio was rebalanced to an equal allocation at the end of each year). Here's what I found.

If you are a conservative growth-oriented investor and wish to minimize total risk, the portfolio of choice is U.S. blue-chip stocks. However, this portfolio, as you might expect, also delivered the lowest average annual return (13 percent). If your goal is to obtain the highest average annual rate of return (17.7 percent in this case), U.S. small-cap stocks are your cup of tea. Of course, this portfolio is also the riskiest. If your goal is to obtain the greatest return while taking the least amount of risk, the equally balanced portfolio delivers the goods. Note that its average return is 2.4 percentage points greater than that of a blue-chip equity portfolio, yet its standard deviation is only 0.8 percentage points greater. As a result, the balanced portfolio's risk per unit of return falls to 1.19.

Although many investors seek to invest where they believe they can earn the greatest short-run returns, prudent investors know that by keeping their balance they can keep their portfolios' returns from falling off a cliff because of a forecasting error (that is, being in the wrong place at precisely the wrong time). In the case of equity fund investing, the appropriate strategy is to allocate capital across blue-chip, small-cap, and international equity funds.

There Are No Guarantees: Hedging for Safety

If you want the most from your investment capital, there is no place like the stock market. However, pour all of your money into the stock of a promising company that suffers an unexpected catastrophe and your entire nest egg could disappear overnight. Of course, you can reduce this extreme level of risk by investing in a diversified equity mutual fund. However, even diversified funds can suffer during bear markets. For example, during the 1973–1974 bear stock market, the S&P 500 Index declined by nearly 50 percent, and so did nearly every equity mutual fund around back then. When you invest in the stock market there are no guarantees. If you need the return of your investment capital within a short period of time, say five or ten years, you may decide to avoid the stock market and put your cash to work in a safe CD or money market mutual fund.

These alternatives may not be as "safe" as they first appear. The returns from certificates of deposit or money market funds are low, and most of what you earn is eroded by rising consumer prices. As my mother used to tell me, "you can't have your cake and eat it too." Similarly, when investing, you can't have both safety and meaningful investment returns. However, you can hedge your bets. Here's how.

Invest a portion of your capital in a zero-coupon Treasury bond that, at maturity, will return an amount equal to the value of your initial investment capital. Invest the balance in the stock market.

TABLE 6.
A BALANCED APPROACH TO
GROWTH-STOCK INVESTING

Year	Blue-Chip Stocks	Small-Cap Stocks	International Stocks	Equal Allocation
1972	19.0%	4.4%	40.9%	21.4%
1973	-14.7	-30.9	-14.4	-19.9
1974	-26.5	-19.9	-24.0	-23.5
1975	37.2	52.8	37.5	42.5
1976	23.8	57.4	6.0	29.1
1977	-7.2	25.4	15.6	11.3
1978	6.6	23.5	34.3	21.5
1979	18.4	43.5	12.9	24.9
1980	32.4	39.9	25.1	32.5
1981	-4.9	13.9	-2.1	2.3
1982	21.4	28.8	-0.6	16.3
1983	22.5	39.7	25.1	29.1
1984	6.3	-6.7	5.1	1.6
1985	32.2	24.7	47.2	34.7
1986	18.5	6.9	55.5	26.9
1987	5.2	-9.3	5.0	0.3
1988	16.8	22.9	17.3	19.0
1989	31.5	10.0	23.9	21.8
1990	-3.2	-21.6	-12.0	-12.3
1991	30.5	44.6	11.1	28.7
1992	7.7	23.3	-14.0	15.6
1993	10.0	21.0	1.0	10.7
1994	1.3	3.1	6.2	3.5
Average Return	12.4%	17.2%	13.5%	14.7%
Standard Deviation	16.7	24.4	21.0	17.7
Risk/return	1.35	1.41	1.55	1.19

For example, if you have $100,000 to invest today and want to guarantee the return of at least that amount in ten years, you could invest $50,000 in a zero-coupon Treasury bond that matures in 2006 (currently selling at 50 percent of face value) and $50,000 in a portfolio of equity mutual funds. Although it is impossible to tell what will happen to the value of your equity fund investments ten years from now, the value of your zero-coupon bond, at maturity, will be $100,000—the total value of your original investment capital.

If, at the end of ten years, your equity fund returns match those experienced during the worst ten-year period since 1940 (a total ten-year return of 12.7 percent), the value of your $50,000 equity fund investment will have grown to $56,300, and the value of your total portfolio at the end of ten years will amount to $156,300. Your annualized annual return will have averaged 4.6 percent. In other words, under the worst of conditions, your portfolio would have returned more than the rate of inflation.

I do not recommend this strategy for everyone because it results in a hefty allocation to bonds and a skimpy allocation to stocks. However, if you are one of those investors who is so frightened by the prospect of losing money in the stock market that you avoid investing any of your capital in equity mutual funds, this strategy will enable you to invest a portion of your capital in the stock market without exposing yourself to the prospect of investment losses.

Some financial planners recommend that you subtract your age from one hundred to obtain the percentage you should allocate to equity funds. Implementation of this strategy would require a thirty-year-old investor to put 70 percent of his or her assets in the stock market, and a sixty-year old to decrease that allocation to 40 percent. Although this strategy recognizes the safety needed by people who are nearing retirement age, it is overly simplified. It fails to consider the level of interest rates and the level of stock prices, and, most of all, it allocates too small a portion to equities for most investors.

The zero-coupon bond strategy corrects all of these shortfalls. To see why, consider the properties of zero-coupon bonds. First, the current price is lower the longer the time to the zero-coupon bond's maturity. Thus, younger investors who apply this strategy, who presumably will not need to use their investment capital as soon as older investors, are required to invest a lesser percentage of their capital to bonds and a greater percentage in the stock market. Second, when interest rates are high (and presumably headed lower in the future), this hedging strategy requires a smaller investment in zero-coupon bonds and a greater investment in the stock market. When interest rates are low and have room to move only higher, the zero-coupon strategy reduces the required allocation to the stock market. Since stock prices tend to head in the opposite direction of interest rates, this strategy allows investors to load up on equity funds when rates are high and to reduce the equity commitment when interest rates are exceptionally low.

Because this strategy guarantees the eventual return of all your capital, it tends to work best when the equity allocation is made to aggressive growth funds. Remember, when you invest a portion of your capital in a zero-coupon bond, you are reducing investment risk. However, you are also reducing investment return potential. Because of the risk hedge, you can afford to take greater risks with the equity portion of your portfolio. In addition, these higher risk funds will provide higher returns over the long run. As a result, you can offset some of the reduction in return caused by investing in a bond fund by balancing that investment with a potentially high-return equity fund.

What if you are currently retired, need income from your investment portfolio, and need to avoid extreme risks? My hedging strategy can be employed with a couple of modifications. First, determine your life expectancy (consult the life expectancy tables in IRS Publication 939), and divide the number of years by two. This is the number you should apply to the current date to determine the applicable zero-coupon bond maturity date. For example, if you are retired, are withdrawing capital from your portfolio, and have a life expectancy of twenty-two years, the applicable zero-coupon bond is one that matures in eleven years. Before you obtain the price of this bond and invest that percentage in a zero-coupon bond, you must make one other adjustment. Take the amount you desire to withdraw from your portfolio each year, and multiply that amount by two. Invest this amount in a money market fund, allocate the appropriate percentage of the remainder of your portfolio to a zero-coupon bond, and invest the balance in an equity fund.

The adjustment for money market fund investments is made to relieve the impact of having to sell some of your equity fund shares to meet your living requirements in the middle of a severe bear stock market. Instead of selling equity fund shares at depressed prices, you can withdraw cash from your money market fund, which has a stable price. I have chosen a two-year period because bear markets tend to last an average of about one year. An additional year cash cushion has been added to allow the value of your equity investments time to rebound before you begin selling equity fund shares once again.

Admittedly, this strategy becomes a bit more complicated when you are constantly adding new capital to your investment portfolio. However, it provides an economically justifiable and relatively simple answer to the most basic of investment questions: How should I divide my capital between stocks, bonds, and money market funds? Furthermore, it requires that everyone, no matter how old, allocate a portion of their capital to the stock market. Finally, the hedging strategy allows investors to assume equity risks they might not otherwise assume, and as a result boost their overall long-term investment returns as well.

If you prefer to invest in a zero-coupon bond fund rather than directly in Treasury securities, check out the Benham/Twentieth Century Group (800-321-8321). Benham offers six "Target" bond portfolios. These funds invest in zero-coupon Treasury securities that will mature in the target year (currently 2000, 2005, 2010, 2015, 2020, and 2025). The fund portfolios are liquidated in the target year when per share net asset value reaches 100 percent. The share prices of these Target Maturity Funds indicate the percentage of capital you need to allocate to the fund. For example, if the Target 2010 Portfolio's share price is $48, you should allocate 48 percent of your capital to that fund (assuming that you have an investment horizon of approximately fifteen years) and 52 percent of your capital to equity mutual funds.

The benefits of using Benham Target Maturity portfolios are that you can invest smaller amounts of money ($1,000 minimum initial investment requirement) and you avoid brokerage costs that could be onerous for small purchases of Treasury securities. The downside is that you must assume a portion of the fund's operating expenses.

CHAPTER

SEVEN

Playing the Market by the Numbers

The only sure bet you'll find on Wall Street is that there are no sure bets. When you invest, you part with cash in the hopes of obtaining more cash in the future. Since no one can predict the future with perfect certainty, all investments possess an element of risk. In fact, investment return is nothing more than a reward for assuming investment risk. If you want greater rewards, you must assume greater investment risks.

Most investors place the bulk of their investment decision-making emphasis on the search for assets that will produce the best returns. However, this is only one dimension of the investment decision process. The other, of course, is the assessment of investment risk. Although most investors believe that they can produce the best returns by searching for the best-performing mutual funds, the truth is that the best way to enhance long-run returns is to manage investment risks. Risk management

73

entails first determining the level of risk you can tolerate and then establishing an investment plan that minimizes risk for a given level of return.

The application of a few simple rules can reduce investment risk substantially, usually without a sacrifice of investment return. These rules include maintaining a diversified portfolio, easing into and out of the market rather than making giant leaps in either direction, and periodically rebalancing your portfolio back to predetermined targets to maintain an overall level of portfolio risk that lies within your risk tolerance zone. Here are a couple of techniques that can aid in controlling portfolio risk. The first, dollar cost averaging (DCA) reduces risk because it eliminates market timing decisions that tend to cost investors plenty. The second, formula investing, is a systematic portfolio rebalancing strategy that insures that portfolio risk stays well within your predetermined risk tolerance zone.

Dollar Cost Averaging

Dollar cost averaging entails making periodic payments of a fixed amount of money over a lengthy period to purchase individual securities or mutual funds. DCA works best in retirement savings plans: It forces you to make a disciplined, long-term commitment to an investment that grows tax-deferred until you take distributions at retirement. When you buy in a disciplined manner, you buy more shares at a lower price when prices are falling. On the upside, you also accumulate shares at lower prices if the market keeps rising. Over the long term, your periodic purchases will result in an average cost that will be lower than the average market price.

DCA is a safe way for the average person to invest because it eliminates market timing decisions. Most investors tend to buy at market peaks when mutual funds or stocks are near the points at which the market usually plunges. Or, in a falling market, investors typically buy, hold, and pray and eventually panic and sell at the worst possible times, as the market bottoms just before rebounding.

Dollar cost averaging eliminates the guesswork. You always will be fully invested to catch the turns in the market. This hypothetical example shows how it works.

In a declining market, if you made a series of $400 investments, your breakdown might look like this:

Investment	Share Price	Shares Bought
$400	$16	25
400	10	40
400	8	50
400	8	50
400	5	80
$2,000	$47	245

As you can see, the price of the shares dropped from $16 to $5. Your average share cost was $8.16, or $2,000 divided by 245. Your average share price was $9.40, or $47 divided by 5. When the market moves up, your DCA program might look like this:

Investment	Share Price	Shares Bought
$400	$5	80
400	8	50
400	10	40
400	10	40
400	16	25
$2,000	$49	235

Your average share cost was $8.51, or $2,000 divided by 235. The average share price was $9.80, or $49 divided by 5.

Dollar cost averaging is one of the safest ways to play the stock market, but the method does have its pitfalls. You can't absolutely guarantee that the average cost will be lower than the market value when you redeem. You also must be careful not to invest too large a sum at once, otherwise your losses could mount up quickly.

Bull markets historically last longer than bear markets, so in many cases investors may not be able to buy enough low-cost shares during down cycles to make DCA as profitable as investing a lump sum in a bull market. For investors to accumulate enough money in a dollar cost averaging program to earn substantial profits usually takes from five to ten years. Over the short term, the performance of dollar cost averaging will lag behind other investing methods. And, although aggressive stock funds or gold funds are the best vehicles for DCA because they are volatile and DCA capitalizes on their price fluctuation, the danger always exists that the fund will not rebound sufficiently.

You must be patient to succeed at dollar cost averaging. You may experience years during which the market is flat and you are accumulating shares at about the same price. These are the times that DCA performs poorly because the difference between share price and average cost will be relatively small. You also may experience a period when the financial markets move like a seesaw. A jerky market means few time periods when you can buy shares at a price low enough for regular buying to pay off.

DCA is not a perfect way to invest, but in a well-thought-out, diversified investment plan, it is a safe way to invest for long-term horizons of ten years or more. Furthermore, it lends itself well to mutual fund investing. First, you can establish an automatic investment plan with nearly any mutual fund worth owning. As little as $50 a month can be deducted directly from your checking account and invested directly in the shares of your fund of choice. Second, since you can purchase fractional shares of mutual funds, the full amount of your selected periodic investment amount can be fully invested in fund shares. Finally, because most equity mutual funds are widely diversified, there is virtual assurance that over a long period of time, say ten years, the average price of fund shares will be higher than their average cost. In fact, I can't think of a better way to accumulate capital than to invest regularly in a diversified portfolio of equity mutual funds.

Formula Investing

Formula investing strategies enable you to take profits when prices are high, to buy more shares when prices decline, and to reduce portfolio risk. Using predetermined sell points to rebalance your portfolio works well when you allocate capital among several categories of assets such as stocks, bonds, and money market funds.

Investors who bought and held stocks or bonds over the last ten years, despite some scary corrections, realized sizable capital gains. You would have quadrupled your money in the stock market and more than doubled it in the bond market. The October 1987 stock market crash, however, still is imbedded in people's minds. That experience, coupled with today's uncertain economic environment and historically high stock valuations, dictates considering more than just a buy-and-hold investment scheme.

Of course, who knew ten years ago that we would experience one of the greatest bull markets in history? How many investors have the intestinal fortitude to hold on to sizable lump-sum investments as they lose money? The Twentieth Century Fund, a successful aggressive growth fund, has returned an average of 16.4 percent annually during the last fifteen years. However, the value of this fund declined 29 percent between December 1983 and May 1984, 33 percent in October 1987, and 18 percent between July and October 1990.

Constant-dollar and constant-ratio investment strategies are variations on dollar cost averaging that help control risk and eliminate market-timing sell decisions. Formula investing is based on the simple idea that you take predetermined levels of profits in your aggressive investments and salt away the money in conservative investments such as money market mutual funds or bond funds. This switching enables you to avoid market timing decisions. When your aggressive investments decline to a specified level, you switch money from your conservative portfolio into your aggressive portfolio. When your aggressive investments increase in value, you sell a portion and park the profits in a safe place. Thus, you take profits when stock prices rise and dollar cost average when stock prices decline.

The constant-dollar value plan is one tactic that employs the principles of dollar cost averaging and risk aversion to build wealth. Under this plan, the dollar value of your aggressive investments will remain constant after passing through a predetermined time period. Money then would be channeled into a bond fund or from the bond fund into a stock fund to maintain the constant-dollar investment strategy. Bond or money market funds are appropriate counterbalances because they have low correlations to equities. As a result, during recessionary periods when stocks perform poorly, gains in bonds will offset losses in the equity markets as interest rates decline. For investors who do not want the volatility associated with bond funds, money funds may be the safest parking place.

Here is how the constant-dollar strategy would work using an aggressive growth stock and a bond or money fund: You decide to keep a constant-dollar amount of $10,000 in your aggressive portfolio and are willing to accept a 20 percent gain or loss in that portfolio every six months. After six months, if the value of your stock fund has grown to $12,000, you would take out $2,000 and move it into your bond or money fund. Conversely, if the value of your stock fund has dropped to $8,000 after six months, you would switch $2,000 out of bonds and into stocks to maintain the constant dollar value of $10,000. You use the bond fund or money fund as a parking place.

The accompanying table shows how the trades are made. You invested $10,000 in both a stock and bond fund and are willing to take out $2,000 in profits, or 20 percent, when the value of your stock fund grows to $12,000 after six months. You are also willing to take $2,000 or more out of your bond fund when the value of your stock fund declines to $8,000 or less. Your trades might look like this: In the second half of 1992 you earned $2,700 in your stock fund. You rebalance your stock fund back to $10,000 and put the profits in your bond fund. In the second half of 1993, however, the market value of your stock fund declined $3,000, so you took money out of your bond fund and rebalanced the equity side to $10,000. Over the next eighteen months, the value of the stock fund fluctuates within your trading limits, and by the middle of 1995 the fund is worth $11,800. But by year-end 1995, the fund has grown to $13,900, and the total value is $33,000.

The trick with the constant-dollar plan is to match your risk tolerance with the appropriate evaluation period. If you take profits too quickly, you could end up with too many trades and miss major market moves on the upside. In addition, if the investments are not part of a retirement savings plan, you end up paying taxes prematurely on your realized gains. It is best to check your aggressive portfolio semiannually to maintain a constant dollar amount in eq-

STOCK AND BOND FUND TRADES

Date	Stock Fund	Bond Fund	Total Value
6/92	$10,000	$10,000	$20,000
7/92 to 12/92	12,700	12,480	25,180
Rebalance	10,000	15,180	25,180
1/93 to 6/93	11,000	16,610	27,610
7/93 to 12/93	8,000	16,859	24,859
Rebalance	10,000	14,859	24,859
1/94 to 6/94	9,150	13,859	23,009
1/95 to 6/95	11,800	17,683	29,483
7/95 to 12/95	13,900	19,100	33,000
Rebalance	10,000	23,000	33,000

uities. A 15 to 20 percent gain or loss is an appropriate benchmark. At these levels, you are banking profits and buying when minor market corrections turn into bear markets.

The past ten years present a difficult time period in which to evaluate the performance of formula investing. Few down periods occurred during which an investor would have used a 15 to 20 percent switching signal to move from bonds to stocks. As a result, a buy-and-hold strategy would have produced better returns than the use of constant-dollar rebalancing strategy. However, stock and bond market volatility is currently on the upswing. And indications are that the next ten years in the financial markets will not be similar to those experienced during the past ten years. If so, the formula plan approach should provide optimal profits and will limit portfolio risk.

Formula investing is not a get-rich-quick scheme. It must be used over several business cycles. The constant-dollar tactic earns most in a market with a steep drop, in which you average down, followed by a resurgent bull market. You also must choose the right type of aggressive stock fund to make formula investing work. Look for no-load aggressive equity funds that show strong rebounds from their lows. Total return funds or mutual funds that adjust their cash, stock, and bond mixes, may be inappropriate. Aggressive funds that remain fully invested in the stock market allow you to maximize your returns and place profits into cash or bonds. Always look at the investment strategy of an equity fund before you invest this way.

The constant-ratio investment plan is another way to buy more shares when prices decline. By maintaining a constant ratio of stocks to bonds or cash over a period of time, you are rebalancing your portfolio by taking profits on the upside and dollar cost averaging on the downside when the investment declines.

If you keep one-third of your investment in a growth stock fund and two-thirds in a money or bond fund, that combination would translate into a ratio of 50 percent—one-third divided by two-thirds equals 0.50. Every six months you would check the ratio of stocks to bonds or cash and bring it back to 50 percent, if necessary. You would rebalance in a way similar to the method depicted in the table above.

If you started with $20,000 ($6,600 in a growth fund and $13,400 in a money market fund that earned 3.5 percent semiannually) and the growth fund lost 5.6 percent over six months, the new value of your portfolio would be $6,244 in stocks and $13,869 in cash, a total of $20,113. The ratio of stocks to bonds has dropped to 45 percent, so you must readjust it. You shift your money to position $7,626 (or one-third of the total value) into stocks and the remaining two-thirds, or $13,947, into cash. The constant-ratio methodology combines the best of both worlds: You have a predetermined sell point and you dollar cost average as prices fall.

Money market funds provide an essentially risk-free return. Thus, keeping two-thirds of your investable money in such a fund is a conservative, safety-oriented move. If you can tolerate the additional volatility of placing this portion of your money into bonds, the constant-ratio strategy will enable you to earn profits in both stocks and bonds and cost average in both when prices slump.

The important point about rebalancing is the process: spreading your risks and realizing your profits without trying to guess the best time to buy or sell. The 20 percent rebalancing tactic works well to reduce risk. This percentage breakdown may not be ideal for everyone, however. A couple approaching retirement should take less risk than a young professional couple with a relatively high level of income. Younger people can afford to seek growth and take more risk because they can buy and hold for a longer time. In addition, their incomes may increase substantially over time. The preretirement couple may want some growth, but they also need safety. They would be aghast to see the value of their portfolio drop 20 percent a few years before they retire.

This is why it is important to match investment risk with financial needs and risk tolerance. When you look at your risk level and income and growth requirements, you can set a better investment mix. Examine the following two factors:

(1) How closely do investments move in tandem with each other? You want a mix where the investments will move in opposite directions part of the time.

(2) You want to combine investments to obtain the best return with the least amount of price volatility. Ideally, you will lower your risk and still receive the return you need to build your wealth. If you could choose between an investment offering an annual return of 16 percent with a downside price fluctuation of 24 percent, or an investment mix providing a 12-percent return with a 12-percent downside margin, which would you choose? The answer depends on how much you want to risk. Hint: Before choosing the former alternative, think honestly about how you would feel if you lost nearly $24,000 on each $100,000 you invested in a single year.

There are no sure things in the investment world. Thus, the best an investor can do is tilt the odds of investment success in their favor. Application of dollar cost averaging or formula planning strategies don't just reduce the extreme risks that face many investors, they tilt the odds of winning the investment game solidly in your favor.

CHAPTER

EIGHT

Ten Ways to Improve Your Mutual Fund Profits Today

During the last half-century, common stocks have returned an average of 12 percent per year, or about 9 percent annually more than the rate of inflation. Earn a 9 percent real rate of return and the purchasing power of your investment portfolio doubles every eight years.

Although 12 percent may not seem like a huge return, you could have easily built a fortune during the last fifty years if you had earned an average of 12 percent annually on your investment portfolio. For example, a $10,000 investment made in 1947 would be worth $2,890,000 at the end of 1996 if investment wealth expanded by 12 percent annually. However, very few investors have been able to build multimillion-dollar fortunes by investing in the stock market. That's because investors unknowingly nip away at the returns available to them each and every year. Give away one-quarter percent here and one-half percent there, and, over a long period of time, investment wealth suffers tremendously. If you don't believe me, check out the following examples.

Suppose you invest $2,000 annually in an IRA and earn an average of 12 percent per year. After twenty-five years, your retirement account will grow to $298,660. Give away just one percent a year, reducing your annual return from 12 percent to 11 percent, and the value of your IRA grows to $257,510. That's a total cost of $41,150. Invest $15,000 a year in a 401(k) or SEP retirement plan and earn an average of 12 percent a year. At the end of fifteen years, your retirement account will grow to $2,240,000. Earn just 8 percent a year, and the value of your retirement account shrinks to $1,184,000. That's a total cost of $1,055,000.

How many people knowingly would flush a million dollars down the drain? I venture to guess not one. However, hundreds of thousands of investors (perhaps even millions) are doing just that. They pay too much to invest in mutual funds, they assume large risks that don't pay off, they allocate their retirement assets improperly, and so on. As a result, their long-term returns suffer, and so does their investment wealth. Here are ten ways to improve your mutual fund returns. Each of these tips can add thousands of dollars to your investment nest egg. All are easy to employ. If you are not applying one or two of these strategies, you could be giving away the opportunity to gain financial freedom. Here's how you can begin to increase your mutual fund profits today.

Vow to never again invest one penny of your hard-earned investment capital in ANY mutual fund that levies either a front-end or back-end sales charge. Before investing in any mutual fund, obtain the fund's latest prospectus and immediately turn to the section entitled "Expenses and Performance." All mutual funds are required by law to outline the costs of investing. Included in a fund's expense table are the following items: maximum sales load, deferred sales load, redemption fee, exchange fee, management fee, 12b-1 fee, and other expenses. Avoid investing in any fund that levies a sales load or a deferred sales load. Also, avoid any fund with an annual 12b-1 fee in excess of 0.25 percent.

How does this strategy boost investment profits? Here's an example. Suppose that you invest in a fund recommended by your broker that levies a "modest" 4-percent front-end sales load. The broker pockets $400 of every $10,000 you remit and invests the balance, $9,600, in the fund. If this fund returns 12 percent annually over a twenty-year period, the value of your investment will grow from $9,600 to $92,604, a tidy profit. However, if you had invested in a no-load fund that also provided a 12-percent average annual return, your investment of $10,000 would have grown to $96,463, a difference of $3,895! In other words, the initial payment of a $400 sales fee eventually cost you nearly ten times that amount. Multiply the losses in this example by several $10,000 investments made over an investment lifetime, and you will have thrown away tens, if not hundreds, of thousands of dollars in mutual fund profits.

Surprisingly, a large number of investors opt to invest in load funds sold by financial planners and stockbrokers. These people are throwing away their hard-earned money. Of the $1.4 trillion invested in equity and bond funds, $879 billion has been poured into funds that are sold with front-end loads, deferred sales charges, or 12b-1 fees that exceed 0.25 percent. That represents sixty-four cents of every dollar currently invested in long-term mutual funds.

Make your asset allocation decision first. Then go about the process of identifying the individual funds you want to own. Most mutual fund investors put the cart before the horse and let the tail wag the dog. Worn out cliches, perhaps, but descriptive of the decision process of a large number of mutual fund investors.

Millions of mutual fund investors believe that the way to earn superior returns is to invest in the best-performing funds. In the end, these investors' returns fail to live up to their expectations because the investors spend a lot of time trying to find the best funds and completely ignore the most important decisions of all, those involving asset allocation.

Asset allocation decisions involve determining the categories of assets you want in your portfolio (that is, stocks, bonds, money funds, and so on) and the percentage of assets you wish to allocate to each category. Since studies have shown that nearly 90 percent of the returns you ultimately earn are determined by asset allocation decisions (versus asset selection and market timing decisions), this is where you should concentrate the bulk of your investment decision-making time. Here's why. Suppose that the stock market returns 10 percent during the year. Suppose further that you owned a couple of exceptional mutual funds that provided a 15 percent return that year. However, suppose that you allocated only 30 percent of your capital to these funds and 70 percent to a money market fund that returned 5 percent. Even though you had the good fortune (or foresight) to invest in superior-performing funds, your overall portfolio return is just 8 percent, 2 percentage points below that of the market. Another investor could have bought an index fund that replicated the stock market's return, placed 70 percent of his or her assets in that fund and the balance in a money market fund, and earned 8.5 percent that year.

Ignoring the asset allocation decision can also erode investment returns because you may end up allocating more to a particular investment category than you intended. For example, suppose that a 20 percent decline in the value of your portfolio would cause undue stress or financial hardship. Thus, you decide to allocate only one-half of your capital to equity mutual funds and one-half to money market funds. Because of this allocation, it would take a stock market decline in excess of 40 percent to produce an overall portfolio loss amounting to 20 percent. Suppose, however, that stock prices, and the value of your equity fund investments, advance by 40 percent. Because of the escalation in the value of your equity fund investments, your portfolio would now contain a 58 percent allocation to the stock market and a 42 percent allocation to money market funds. Given this allocation, a severe bear market that drives stock prices downward by 40 percent would result in a 23 percent decline in the value of your entire portfolio, a decline beyond your tolerance zone. If this decline causes you to bail out of your equity investments, you will miss the opportunity to recoup some of your losses when stock prices eventually rebound. In other words, ignoring the asset allocation decision caused you to make a decision that you would not have made otherwise. And, that decision caused losses that you could have sidestepped had you remained in the stock market.

Forget trying to time the market and do something productive instead. Most market timers seek to avoid losses during a stock market decline by being on the investment sidelines when other investors are suffering losses. Timers are fond of pointing out how much your wealth suffers during declining market, and how much **you** would have saved if you would have bailed out of stocks before the stock market took a plunge. However, what market timers don't tell you is that of the two types of mistakes you can make (being in the market when it is falling and being out of the market when it is rising) the most costly is being out the market when stock prices advance. And missing market moves to the upside can be extremely costly. Here are a couple of examples.

Suppose that you invested $100,000 in the stock market in early 1976 and maintained a fully invested position until the end of 1995. That portfolio would have attained a value of $1,526,480. Had you bailed out of the stock market during 1988, after the October 1987 stock market crash erased nearly 30 percent of your portfolio's value, and remained out the entire year (advice many investment advisers were giving their clients back then), the value of your portfolio at year-end 1995 would have amounted to $1,386,640, a cost of $139,840.

If you had invested $100,000 in the stock market in early 1976 and decided to sit on the sidelines during 1995 (when stock prices advanced by nearly 38 percent), you would have missed a $374,000 portfolio gain. In early 1995, nearly 60 percent of all investment newsletter writers were urging their subscribers to abandon the stock market because they feared another disaster. However, the real disasters were reserved for those investors who decided to take their advice.

What market timers forget is that stock market declines are only temporary. Losses experienced during a bear market are recouped during the stock market's ultimate rebound. However, if you miss a market move to the upside, you lose these returns *forever*, and your portfolio is doomed to underperform. Furthermore, although the stock market spends more time going up than going down, major market moves occur very quickly. For example, a recent University of Michigan study that covered the stock market's performance between 1963 and 1993 showed that 95 percent of the gains over that period came in just 1.2 percent of the trading days. If an investor had missed those particular ninety days out of the entire seventy-five hundred trading days that were examined, his or her total return would have amounted to only one-half that provided by money market funds over that thirty-year period. In other words, a few timing mistakes can cost you plenty.

Consider allocating more of your capital to equity funds. One common thread seems to run through the financial magazines that I read these days: "Investors have too much money in the stock market." I argue, instead, that many investors are underinvested in equity mutual funds. Here's why.

Of the more than $3 trillion invested in mutual funds these days, approximately one-third resides in money market funds, one-third has been invested in bond funds, and one-third has been placed in equity mutual funds. During the last half-century, the stock market has returned an average of 12 percent per year; long-term bonds have returned approximately 6 percent per year; and money market instruments have returned about 4 percent annually. An equal allocation to each of these three investment categories would have produced a 7.3 percent average annual return. On the other hand, a 65 percent allocation to equities and a 35 percent allocation to money market funds over that period would have produced a 9.2 percent average annual return. That's nearly 2 percentage points more per year.

Of course, this strategy would have also increased investment risk. However, not by as much as you might initially imagine. Suppose that the stock market declines by 30 percent when interest rates are rising, which in turn causes bond prices to tumble by 15 percent. A portfolio that contains a one-third allocation to stocks, bonds, and money market funds would decline by 15 percent during this severe bear market. A portfolio that contains a 65-percent allocation to stocks and a 35-percent allocation to money market funds would have declined by 18 percent. A $100,000 portfolio that declines in value by 15 percent produces a $15,000 loss while a decline of 18 percent produces a loss of $18,000, a difference of only $3,000. Remember also, this loss is only temporary while the long-term gain that results from a heftier allocation to equity funds is permanent. For example, $100,000 equally allocated to stocks, bonds, and Treasury bills will be worth $202,300 after ten years. On the other hand, the value of a portfolio containing 65 percent equities and 35 percent money market funds would be worth $241,100, a gain of $38,000. In other words, you have traded a temporary 3-percent decline for a permanent 38-percent increase in portfolio value. The moral of this tale should be clear. For long-term-oriented investors "more (equity funds) is better." Increasing your target allocation to equity mutual funds is one of the best ways I know to increase your long-term investment profits and improve your well-being.

If you are an income-seeking investor, avoid GNMA funds and opt for funds that invest in Treasury securities or corporate bonds instead. GNMAs are pools of mortgages whose interest payments and principal repayments are guaranteed by the U.S. government. Holders of GNMAs receive both interest income and a return of principal each month because home buyers' monthly payments include principal and interest. GNMAs are bonds and their prices are affected by interest rates. Thus, rising interest rates can cause short-term losses even though payments are guaranteed by the U.S. government.

As with all bonds, when interest rates rise, the prices of GNMA bonds fall. Their prices also rise when interest rates fall. However, GNMA bonds don't rise as much as comparable risk bonds when interest rates fall because many home buyers choose to refinance their mortgages when interest rates decline. When this happens, GNMA holders receive the principal amount of the note and are left to fend for themselves in a lower interest rate environment. As a result, government and corporate bonds tend to produce greater long-term returns than GNMAs. If current income is what you seek, invest in government and corporate bond funds and avoid GNMA funds.

Recently, I obtained the fifteen-year returns for the five GNMA funds that had been around that long. Their annual returns ranged from 11.3 percent to 10.2 percent and averaged 10.6 percent. During the same period, both Treasury and long-term corporate bonds returned 13.5 percent a year. In other words, you would have given away 2.9 percent in return annually over this fifteen-year period by investing in GNMA funds. Even a portfolio consisting of 70 percent long-term Treasury bonds and 30 percent Treasury bills (a very conservative portfolio) would have returned an average of 11.6 percent per year. Thus, the typical GNMA investor gives away profits that amount to as much as $21,500 for every $10,000 invested over a fifteen-year period.

Check the expense ratio of your prospective mutual fund investments and switch to a comparable fund with a lower expense ratio. When you invest in a mutual fund, you assume a share of the expenses incurred to operate that fund. For the typical equity fund, these annual expenses range from 0.25 percent to as much as 4 percent. Since these fees are levied each and every year, high-cost funds can trim investment returns by a significant amount over a long period of time. For example, the Vanguard Index 500 Fund (an unmanaged fund that seeks to replicate the returns of the Standard & Poor's 500 Index by investing in all 500 stocks contained in the index) resides among the top 25 percent of the 248 general equity funds when ranked by their fifteen-year returns. Although this is an unmanaged fund, its return topped that of 75 percent of the funds in existence mainly because its expense ratio (0.25 percent) was far less than that of any other fund. In other words, many actively managed funds fail to deliver sufficient returns to offset their higher annual operating costs.

Give away one-half of one percent return annually by investing in high-cost funds and, over an investment lifetime, your wealth can suffer greatly. For example, a $10,000 investment made in a fund with an annual expense ratio of 1.0 percent that delivers an 11 percent average annual return for forty years will grow to $650,000. Invest instead in a fund with an annual expense ratio of 1.5 percent that delivers a 10.5 percent net return and the value of that investment shrinks by $107,400.

Don't sell your equity fund shares during stock market declines—buy more. It's probably an understatement to say that most bear markets scare investors. They sit, day after day, watching the value of their portfolios decline. Eventually, many investors become so upset that they dump their equity funds, often at or near the market's bottom.

Wise investors, on the other hand, take advantage of these temporary dips in stock prices to accumulate more equity fund shares. These investors know that prices will eventually stop falling and begin to rise. Buying equity funds during bear markets reduces your average cost and, when the stock market eventually rebounds, allows you to move back into the black much faster than those who failed to average down. Here's an extreme example.

Had you invested $10,000 in an equity portfolio mirroring the return of the Standard & Poor's Composite Index in August 1929, before the October 1929 stock market crash and the ensuing Great Depression, the value of that investment would have hit bottom in May 1932 at $1,664. Had you continued to hold that portfolio, it would have taken until January 1946, a total of fifteen years and five months, before the value of your initial investment would have returned to $10,000. However, if you added an additional $1,000 to that portfolio each time the stock market declined by 20 percent, you would have made eight additions to your portfolio by the time the market hit bottom in May 1932, a total investment of $18,000. By December 31, 1935, that $18,000 portfolio would have attained a value of $20,528. You would have more than recouped all of your losses in six years and four months. By January 1945, when other investors were just beginning to break even, the value of your portfolio would have been $34,295, almost twice that of your initial investment.

Invest in equity funds the same way you shop for other things in life. When prices are marked down and bargains appear, make the purchase. The biggest successes in the stock market are reserved for those investors who swim upstream and add to their portfolios when other investors are dumping their stocks and are willing to accept bargain-basement prices.

Don't select a mutual fund merely because it was one of last year's best performers. Remember, you want to select the best-performing funds before the year begins, not after it ends. Many mutual fund investors use last year's mutual fund performance ranks as their primary method of fund selection. This is understandable since last year's performance is the most publicized mutual fund statistic. The successes of last year's best-performing portfolio managers are lauded in the financial press, and herds of investors are attracted to the funds piloted by these mutual fund stars. The problem, however, is that these stars tend not to shine too long.

The danger in investing in a fund that "beat the market" by an extreme amount in any single year is that usually the fund's portfolio manager assumed some large risks that happen to pay off. Over the long run, things tend to even out, and large gains are balanced by eventual large losses. Thus, investors who climb aboard these speeding trains are usually just in time to experience the great train wreck as investment risk comes home to roost.

I'm not saying that you shouldn't pay attention to historical returns. Funds that have performed better than their peers during periods of one to three years tend to continue their better-than-average performance. However, in extreme cases, the mathematical law known as "gravitation toward the mean" tends to hold true. That is, those funds that produce extremely attractive returns during one period tend to underperform during subsequent periods.

If you are seeking high returns but want to dodge extreme investment risk, diversify your portfolio. During the last fifteen years, the stock market has returned an average of 15 percent per year. That's much more than the 11 percent average annual return it has provided during the last century. The abnormally high stock market return in recent years has raised the expectations of nearly all investors. Many investors are upset if their equity funds don't return 20 percent or more annually. I suspect that many investing newcomers have yet to learn that investment return is welded to investment risk. Investors who seek greater return potential must assume greater risk. These investors are usually the first to bail out and lock in investment losses when the stock market takes a nasty tumble. Although we haven't seen a bear market since 1980, they tend to occur with a great deal of frequency. They sneak up on investors after the market has headed skyward for a lengthy period of time and after many investors have forgotten about investment risk.

The best way to obtain better-than-average long-term investment returns is to diversify widely. Losses that occur in one investment category are usually offset by gains in other categories. A portfolio that contains allocations to aggressive growth funds, growth funds, precious metals funds, international equity funds, bond funds (both domestic and international), and money market funds generally contains about one-half the risk of the stock market. In other words, the value of this portfolio will fall by less than one-half that of the stock market during a long bear market. However, over the long run, this portfolio tends to provide an average annual rate of return that equals that of the stock market. In fact, my research fails to uncover any period when the value of this portfolio would have declined by more than 15 percent, and that includes the great bear market that accompanied the Great Depression in the 1930s.

Long-term investors usually fare best. However, to win the game in the long run you must survive in the short run. And the best way to survive in the short run is to reduce your portfolio's volatility by diversifying widely.

The surest way to increase your investment profits is to investigate before you invest. Before investing in any mutual fund, get a copy of the fund's prospectus, its latest annual or semi-annual report, and a statement of additional information. Then do three things. First, study the statement of investment objectives. Are the objectives a good match with those that are best for your portfolio? If not, pass on this fund and look for another. Don't be tempted to undermine your own objectives because a particular fund has an attractive track record. Second, examine the list of stocks shown in the annual report. Are these the types of stocks you would buy? If not, look for another fund. Third, compare the fund's year-by-year historical returns to those of the S&P 500 Index. Take special note of large swings in the fund's return. The greater the ups and downs, the greater is the fund's risk. Chances are, future returns will continue to gyrate wildly. Be aware that the fund's management has chosen that course.

These three steps are meant to familiarize you with the potential severity of the fund's roller-coaster ride before you buy a ticket. If you think you can stand the ride, the fund is probably an acceptable investment. If not, look for a fund with a level of risk that's more tolerable.

Avoid the investment mistakes made by millions of mutual fund investors and improve your well-being. Mutual fund profits are waiting for you at nearly every turn. However, to capture the full measure of the return being offered, you must dodge the potholes that dot the road to investment success.

CHAPTER

NINE

When to Hold 'Em and When to Fold 'Em

Over the years, I have heard numerous investors bemoan the fact that mutual fund shares are "easy to buy but difficult to sell." This statement is, in part, understandable. When you are ready to invest, you have already set the time—you want to invest now. You also know what type of fund you want to own (municipal bond fund, small-cap growth fund, and so on). It is relatively easy to weed out undesirable funds (that is, those with onerous cost structures, those that fail to perform as well as their peers, and so on). And you most likely are filled with optimism—you want to buy.

Most of the mutual fund advice I have come across focuses on the mutual fund selection decision and ignores a discussion of when to sell. I understand why. When you invest in a mutual fund you are actually hiring an investment adviser, and you wouldn't want to change your investment adviser every month. In short, mutual funds are to buy and not to sell. Find a few good funds whose risk and return characteristics meet your current investment objectives and your risk tolerance requirements, and stick with those funds for the long term. More often than not, you will earn a better return than investors who hire and fire their portfolio managers at will.

I've never liked market timing strategies. Miss one major market updraft and you could relegate your portfolio return to mediocrity during your entire lifetime. Trade too frequently and your long-run returns are eroded by the premature payment of income taxes. Jump from one fund to another and you end up spending an inordinate amount of time analyzing mutual fund investments and less time on the more important things in life.

Mutual funds are not meant to be actively traded, so resist the urge to jump from one fund to another frequently. Frequent fund switchers usually cause themselves more harm than good. In fact, a growing number of mutual fund families are not only cautioning their funds' investors against frequent switching, but also beginning to tell frequent traders that they are not welcome because they are disruptive and saddle longer-term shareholders with higher costs.

However, there are times when it is appropriate to jump ship. Some funds perform better during certain stages of the economic cycle than do others. At times, the financial markets may become significantly overvalued, and it may be appropriate to sell some fund shares to reduce your risk exposure. Finally, some funds change their business practices, which creates good reasons to sell.

When deciding whether or not to sell, you should ask yourself why you invested in the fund in the first place. If that reason no longer applies, bail out. For example, suppose you invest in a government bond fund because it yields 10 percent, and you believe that interest rates are about to fall. Suppose further that, as you expected, the fund's yield declines to 6 percent, and you capture the lion's share of the fund's appreciation potential. Because rates have little room to fall further, the reason you bought the fund no longer is valid, and you should sell. Similarly, suppose you invest in an aggressive growth fund because you believe that the economy and corporate profits will expand at above-average rates. Instead, the economy begins to weaken and corporate profit growth fails to materialize. Because the primary reasons you bought the fund did not materialize, you should sell.

A Few More Reasons to Sell

A fund manager who produced better-than-average returns relative to funds with similar objectives and investment strategies relinquishes the helm. You may not wish to bail out immediately because it will take the new portfolio manager a while to restructure the fund's portfolio. However, if you invested in the fund because of the portfolio manager's ability to deliver exceptional returns, consider selling when that manager departs. For example, Selected American Shares' return has suffered since the departure of superstar portfolio manager Donald Yacktman, and Fidelity Magellan has never been the same since the departure of Peter Lynch.

A fund that has performed reasonably well changes its investment style. This frequently happens to reasonably successful small- and mid-cap funds that attract a flood of new capital and are forced to invest in the stocks of larger companies. In other words, successes and growth in popularity with investors cause the fund to depart from the investment strategy it knows best. Chances are, the fund will lose its performance edge.

A fund closes its doors to new investors. Closing a fund to new shareholders can eliminate one of the reasons for the fund's success (the opportunity to invest fresh cash in positions already held or to capitalize on new investment ideas). Some investors believe they are in a select group when they own shares of a fund that will no longer admit newcomers. However, I have found that once a fund closes its doors, its returns tend to suffer. If you insist on sticking around, you will have joined a select group of investors, those who earn inferior returns. When a fund closes its doors, I recommend that you seek out a similar fund (similar investment objective, similar investment style, similar size, and so on) that has been providing better-than-average returns and switch your investment into that fund.

A fund's return falls below average relative to its peers over a twelve-month period. Recent research indicates that a fund with a better-than-average performance record over a twelve-month period has better than a fifty-fifty chance of continued success, while one with a poor track record (relative to its peers) has a better-than-average chance of continuing its lackluster performance. Upgrade your investment to a similar fund whose twelve-month performance ranks in the top third among its peers. Remember, you don't need to own the top-performing fund to obtain handsome returns, you need only own one that performs better than average. In fact, there are a number of reasons to avoid top performers. To obtain extreme returns, portfolio managers usually have to assume extreme risks that just happen to pay off in a prior period. In addition, top-performing funds create potential tax liabilities for new shareholders who weren't around when those gains were being earned.

An actively managed equity fund grows inordinately large. Large funds have more difficulty outperforming smaller funds for a variety of reasons. First, the purchase and sale of huge blocks of stock often distorts share prices. The block trader bids up price when buying and depresses price when selling. Second, you generally can't beat the market if you own it, and gigantic funds must spread their capital over so many stocks that they end up with a portfolio whose returns correlate strongly with the S&P 500 Index. Even the mighty Fidelity Magellan Fund succumbed to the weight of its $56 billion in assets. For funds that invest in small-cap stocks, the size threshold is about $400 million. For other equity funds, sell those whose assets swell beyond two or three billion dollars.

A period of declining interest rates sends an intermediate-term or long-term bond fund's yield below the annual rate of inflation plus 3 percent. In this instance, the fund's interest rate risk does not justify its long-run return potential. Rarely do long-term bond yields fall far below this threshold during periods marked by low or modest rates of inflation. Remember, bond prices fall when interest rates rise, and the probability that the next move in interest rates will be to the upside increases substantially when bond yields fall below the rate of inflation plus 3 percent.

You wish to rebalance your overall portfolio. No matter how well your funds are performing, this is an excellent reason to sell some of its shares. For example, suppose you decide to maintain a 50 percent allocation to both equity funds and money market funds. Rising stock prices cause the equity portion to increase to 70 percent. Your portfolio now contains significantly more risk than you can probably tolerate given your initial target allocations. You should sell some equity fund shares and rebalance the portfolio to its target allocations. Similarly, if stock prices fall and your equity fund allocation shrinks as a result, you should sell some money fund shares and reinvest in equity fund shares. If you practice periodic rebalancing, you ensure that you will buy equities when prices are low and that you sell when prices head skyward.

You change your investment objectives. This should not happen too often. However, review your personal financial circumstances at least once each year, and decide whether to stay the course or change the proportion of capital you allocate to various categories of assets. If you become worried about continued employment, if you are approaching retirement, if you require cash to make a major expenditure, such as the purchase of a home, you should place needed assets in low-risk investments. On the other hand, an inheritance, a job promotion, or an increase in salary give you the opportunity to increase the growth potential of your portfolio through the assumption of a higher degree of risk.

The share price of your fund falls below its two-hundred-day or thirty-nine week moving average. This is one of the market timing techniques that has some statistical validity. Recent academic research indicates that following this sell signal can marginally improve long-run investment returns. However, don't become too enamored of this sell signal. If you are spending most of your free time charting the progress of your mutual fund investments, you are probably missing out on more important things in life. Remember, the goal of investing is not to make all of the money you can, but to provide the resources that can be used to increase the quality of your life and the lives of your loved ones. In other words, wealth is not an end in itself, instead it is the means to other ends.

You wish to spend some of your investment profits on the good things in life. I have met too many people who believe that spending any of their investment capital is a cardinal sin. Frequently, these individuals suffer undue hardships because the income from their investments falls short of their preferred lifestyles, and they avoid relying on their capital to make up the difference. Remember, the stock market over the long run has returned an average of nearly 12 percent annually. Thus, equity investors can withdraw up to 12 percent of their portfolios each year without ever depleting their nest eggs. In fact, with the differential tax rate of capital gains versus other income, you may be money ahead if you withdraw 6 percent of your capital from your equity fund's portfolio each year **rather than investing** in a "safe" bond fund with a 6 percent yield.

Mutual funds are much different from individual securities. First, the diversification most mutual funds provide reduces investment risk significantly. Second, professional managers direct mutual fund portfolios. Third, funds generally stick with their mandated investment objectives and preferred investment styles. Thus, you have fewer reasons to sell a mutual fund than a specific stock or bond. However, there are times when you should sell. Do not become complacent about your mutual fund investments. Your investment portfolio should reflect the ongoing changes in your life, current conditions in the financial markets, the state of the economy, and the characteristics of individual funds.

CHAPTER

TEN

Navigating the Mutual Fund Tax Maze: Don't Give Uncle Sam More Than He Deserves

Subchapter M of the Internal Revenue Code allows mutual funds to escape one of life's biggest burdens, paying income taxes. Instead, funds can heap that burden on shareholders, provided that the funds diversify properly, receive less than 30 percent of their income from the sales of securities held less than three months, and distribute at least 90 percent of their taxable income to shareholders annually. Nearly all funds follow these rules and pass along their income tax obligations to their shareholders.

If you own fund shares outside such tax-deferred vehicles as IRAs, SEPs, or 401(k) retirement accounts, you are required to share any good fortune with your Uncle Sam. Welcome to the mutual fund tax maze. Navigation in this domain can be costly to your financial well-being, if you don't have a well-marked map. Here, I explain the special tax status of mutual funds, describe the types of mutual fund income that are subject to federal taxation, outline various methods that can be used to determine the cost basis of shares you have sold, present strategies that you can employ to reduce your federal tax liability, and answer some of the most frequently asked questions concerning mutual fund taxation.

Income from Mutual Funds

Mutual funds earn income by investing in portfolio securities and by obtaining income in the form of cash dividends and interest paid to the fund by security issuers. The fund can also earn capital gains income resulting from price changes of its assets. Capital gains or losses may be either realized by the fund (if it has disposed of securities during the tax year) or unrealized (if the securities continue to be held by the fund at the end of the tax year). Increases or decreases in fund income, whether realized or not, are instantaneously transmitted to fund shareholders through increases or decreases in the value of total assets and thus in the fund's per share net asset value.

When you sell your mutual fund shares, realized gains or losses may result. You may also obtain income from distributions made by the fund. These distributions usually consist of interest and dividend income and realized capital gains. On the ex-distribution date (the date the distribution is made), the per share net asset value of the fund will fall by the amount of the distribution. Thus, the income received from the distribution is offset exactly by the decrease in the value of the fund shares held. For example, if a fund's per share net asset value is $10 and the fund distributes $2 per share, its per share net asset value will decline from $10 to $8. At year-end, your fund will send you a statement (Form 1099-DIV) that reports the sources of income that it has distributed to you during the calendar year. Since income distributed to shareholders is realized by them and is taxed accordingly, the fund must indicate the source of the components of all distributions paid during the year.

Investment income. This is the income earned by the fund from cash dividends and the interest payments it receives. It also includes investment income and short-term capital gains realized by the fund. Annual income from these sources is reduced by fund operating expenses and adviser fees. The difference, called net investment income, is distributed to fund shareholders. This income is considered to be ordinary income and is thus taxed at the taxpayers marginal rate.

Capital gains income. In trading securities, the fund may realize capital gains and losses. The gains and losses are netted, and the excess realized capital gains are paid to shareholders. If the combination of realized capital gains and losses results in a net loss, the fund is allowed to carry the loss forward and use the loss to offset net realized capital gains in future periods.

Since mutual fund cash distributions result in an immediate decline in per share net asset value equal to the amount of the distribution, individuals who purchase mutual fund shares immediately before the ex-distribution date effectively have a portion of their investment capital returned to them. The distribution is considered a taxable event, and even though the distribution equals the decrease in net asset value, investors are left worse off by the amount of the tax they must pay on the distribution. Therefore, under normal circumstances, taxpaying investors should wait to make their fund purchases immediately after the ex-distribution date. Contact a fund's sales representative to obtain the date on which a distribution will be made.

Buying Gains and Losses

Whenever you invest in a mutual fund, you may be buying either a tax liability or benefit. For example, a fund may have substantial capital gains on some of the investments it currently holds in its portfolio. These are gains on investments that may have been made months or even years ago but have yet to be realized. If the fund were to liquidate these investments shortly after you invested in the fund, the gains become realized gains and you become liable for the taxes due even though you may have held the fund's shares only a day or two. To determine the extent of the potential tax liabilities (or the benefits of buying a loss carry-forward) consult the fund's latest annual or semiannual report, which lists the total value of net unrealized gains or losses. Divide this amount by the number of shares outstanding to determine the approximate unrealized gain or loss per share. If this amount represents a substantial percentage of the fund's current share price, you may wish to consider investing in another fund with similar investment objectives that possesses a lower potential tax liability.

The Tax Advantage of Losses

Since mutual funds can carry forward net realized capital losses, it is possible for new investors to "buy" the tax advantage of losses suffered by others. First, I must point out the fact that, whenever possible, mutual fund managers try not to distribute capital gains to shareholders; yet they cannot risk endangering the fund's conduit status. They recognize the fact that gains in per share net asset value (rather than distributed capital gains) are more desired by shareholders since unrealized capital appreciation goes untaxed, while capital gains distributions are taxed in the year they were distributed. Thus, as year-end approaches, a portfolio manager may attempt to reduce the amount of the year-end capital gains distribution by realizing some losses to offset gains realized early in the year.

A fund with a net unrealized loss position can provide a distinct advantage over a fund with a net unrealized gain position. So does a fund that is "carrying forward" realized losses. The following example illustrates the potential benefit of prior period losses to new shareholders. Suppose two mutual funds currently own exactly the same assets. Both are no-load funds with per share net asset values equal to $10. One fund purchased its portfolio of securities at about one-half of today's market value and thus the fund has a large net unrealized capital gain position. The other fund acquired the securities in its portfolio recently, after liquidating securities that had declined in value over the preceding year and thus has net realized losses to carry forward.

Even though the portfolios of both funds are identical, the fund with a loss carry-forward is more desirable than the fund with substantial unrealized gains. To see why, consider what would happen if the securities held by both funds rise in price. If the fund carrying forward losses sells some of its holdings, it can utilize the losses being carried forward to offset any realized gains. On the other hand, if the fund with unrealized gains sells some of its securities, it must distribute the realized gains and its shareholders are required to pay taxes on the income they receive.

Identifying Gains and Losses

To determine the gain or loss on an exchange or redemption of mutual fund shares, you need to know their cost basis. Generally, the cost basis is the price you paid to acquire the shares and includes the commission or front-end sales load. If you sell shares of a fund that you have acquired all at one time, your taxable gain (or loss) is the difference between your purchase and sale prices. However, if the shares were acquired at different times, you need to know the cost basis of the particular shares you sold in order to determine your gain or loss.

There are several methods that you can use to identify which shares were sold. The specific identification method allows you to select exactly which shares you wish to sell and can be advantageous if you want to designate shares that will produce a particular gain or loss. In addition, you may elect to average the cost basis of all of your shares under either a single-category or double-category method. Finally, a first-in-first-out method will be assumed by the IRS if you do not specifically identify the shares or make an average cost election for the shares being sold.

It is important that you maintain adequate records of all share purchases, including shares purchased through reinvestment of distributions. Your fund will send you an annual summary report of all purchase and sale activity in your fund shortly after year-end. In addition, you will receive a confirmation statement each time you purchase or sell fund shares. These documents should be preserved so that you can determine the cost basis of shares that are subsequently sold. Although some funds have begun to provide their shareholders with historical records of their fund transactions, not all funds do so. Thus, if you haven't kept a personal record, it may be virtually impossible to determine or substantiate investment gains or losses.

Identifiable cost method. When using the identifiable cost method of accounting for share costs, the IRS places the burden of proof on the taxpayer. That is, you must be able to trace the sale to a specific block of shares. The easiest method for doing that is to request, periodically, that your fund send you stock certificates that represent your holdings. When a sale is made, record the certificate number(s) and the date of acquisition along with the original cost and proceeds received. If you leave your shares on deposit with the fund (as most fund investors do), keep a record of each purchase made. When a sale is made, write to the fund and instruct it to sell a specific block of shares acquired on a specific date. Request that the fund verify the sale in writing.

Average cost method. You may elect to average the cost of shares acquired at different times and prices. (You may use either the single-category or the double-category averaging method.) The election applies to mutual fund shares held by an agent, usually a bank. Although you'll still need records to substantiate your cost basis, averaging avoids the difficult task of identifying the exact shares being sold when those shares were acquired at different times and at different prices. Some funds will even ease the record-keeping burden by providing a statement showing the average cost basis under the single category for shares redeemed. If you use the single- or double-averaging method, attach a note to your tax return specifying the chosen method. Once you have elected one of these methods, you must continue to apply the same method for all sales or exchanges of shares in the same fund. However, you may use any of the available cost basis methods for other funds, even if they are members of the same fund family.

If you use single-category averaging, you determine the average cost per share by dividing your total cost for all shares in the account by the number of shares you own. This average becomes the cost of the shares you are selling. To determine whether your gain is long term or short term, the IRS assumes that you sold shares in the order you acquired them (that is, the shares purchased first are the shares deemed to be sold).

If you elect double-category averaging, you must separate your shares into long term (shares held more than one year) and short term (shares held one year or less). You determine the average cost per share in each category by dividing the total basis for all shares in that category by the number of shares in that category. You should indicate to the agent handling share transactions the category from which you are selling. If you don't, the long-term shares are deemed to have been sold first. If the number of shares sold exceeds the number held long term, the difference is treated as being held short term.

First-in-first-out (FIFO) method. If you do not specifically identify the cost of the shares sold or do not elect to average the cost basis, the IRS requires you to determine the gain or loss as if shares were sold in the order that you acquired them. In other words, the first shares purchased are assumed to be the first shares sold. Because shares held over a long period of time will most likely have appreciated in value, shares acquired in the most distant past will probably be those with the lowest cost basis and will result in the greatest tax liability when they are sold. Thus, use of methods other than FIFO will most likely result in lower tax payments.

Don't Rely on Your Memory

Over the years I have met a number of mutual fund investors who have paid taxes on their income, not once but twice. This usually occurs because these investors did not keep adequate records and relied instead on their memories to determine their cost basis. For example, suppose that you invested $2,000 in a fund five years ago. Suppose that you sell the fund's shares and receive $5,000. The fact that you remembered investing $2,000 in that fund and receiving $5,000 when you sold might lead you to conclude that you must report a $3,000 capital gain on your income tax return. However, suppose that the fund made distributions during this period totaling $3,000, and you elected the option of reinvesting distributions in additional fund shares during the previous five-year period. Since these distributions were subject to taxation in prior years, the sale creates no tax liability at all.

Avoid Getting Blindsided

Most mutual funds distribute their net realized capital gains in late December. And a fund that makes a substantial distribution can blindside an unwary taxpaying investor who invests in the fund shortly before the distribution. Thus, you want to avoid making such an ill-advised investment. However, the rub is that you won't know the size of a fund's capital gains distribution until it is paid. Your fund will usually not tell what the distribution will be since most don't know until a final tally is made shortly before the distribution date.

So what can you do? Look for a few telltale signs before making an investment near the end of the year. (In fact, before you invest in any fund, ask the sales representative when the next income or capital distribution is expected to be paid.) First, if the fund has a high portfolio turnover ratio and a decent return, most likely that fund will be forced to pay a hefty distribution in December. On the other hand, new funds with low portfolio turnover ratios can usually avoid paying large capital distributions. That is usually true for funds that are signing up a horde of new investors. That's because the total dollar value of realized gains are being distributed across a growing number of shares, and thus the pro rata share of the realized gains is diminished. In addition, funds that have had poor recent performance usually have plenty of losses to balance future gains. For example, most gold funds returned more than 80 percent during 1993, but losses that piled up during the previous five years, when the price of gold slumped badly, enabled most precious metals funds to avoid large capital distributions that year.

Check a fund's latest annual or semiannual report, which lists unrealized gains and losses, and postpone your intended investment in any fund with a high potential tax liability until after the distribution date. Remember, those gains were earned by someone else. If a fund surprises you with a hefty capital gains distribution before year-end, dump that fund immediately. Your realized loss (caused by the fall in share price equal to the amount of the capital gains distribution) will offset the realized capital gains you received. Reinvest the proceeds in another fund with a similar investment objective and investment style. Remember, it is not always what you earn that's the key to investment success; sometimes it's what you get to keep that really matters.

Tax-Loss Fund Switching

Mutual funds are ideal vehicles to use in a tax-loss switching strategy. In tax-loss switching you sell a security that has declined in price then immediately purchase another security with similar characteristics. The sale allows you to realize a loss, which can be used to offset gains realized earlier in the year and thereby reduce your income tax liability. Because you have reinvested in another security with similar return potential, you are not sacrificing potential gains that might be missed if you merely sold your losing positions.

The beauty of this strategy using mutual funds is that it is easy to locate another fund with similar characteristics. Generally, this requires investment in a similar category of funds (that is, small-caps, growth and income, technology sector, and so on). You should obtain the financial reports of your intended investment before you make the tax-loss sale so that you can examine its investment strategy and the securities in its portfolio to ensure that you have an adequate match. In the case of bond funds, look for suitable switches that invest in the same categories of bonds (for example, governments, corporates, junk bonds, and so on) and possess a similar average maturity or duration. If you invest in a wide range of fund categories, chances are that you can reduce your annual federal income tax payments on a frequent basis, since the returns of various categories of assets tend not to move in lockstep. In fact, some categories of funds (gold funds and bond funds) tend to provide returns that move in opposite directions. Thus, losses in one area can be used to offset realized gains in another. Remember also, if you do not currently have realized gains, $3,000 of losses in any one year can be used to offset income from other sources.

Invest in Tax-Managed Funds

A growing number of fund families have become aware of investors' desire to limit tax payments on investment gains. As a result, these families have introduced what is now called the tax-managed fund. A tax-managed fund limits its distributions to shareholders in a number of ways. For example, an equity fund might invest in nondividend-paying common stocks to eliminate any distribution that would result from passing along cash dividends to fund shareholders. That fund might also avoid realizing gains on its investments by holding them rather than engaging in active trading practices. In addition, the fund might realize a capital gain only when it has adequate losses that it can use to offset that gain and thus avoid making a distribution to shareholders.

Tax-managed funds that are designed to provide both growth of capital and current income usually invest in a combination of nondividend-paying common stocks (the growth portion) and tax-exempt municipal bonds (the income portion). These funds also tend to hold their investments for long periods of time to reduce the likelihood of having to distribute a realized capital gain. If you are intrigued by the tax-managed fund concept, contact the Vanguard Group of Funds, which offers several alternatives (800-662-7447).

I hate to pay taxes. Moreover, I detest trying to decipher the Internal Revenue Code to determine what taxes I actually owe. One wag suggested that the IRS Form 1040 be simplified to contain one line to indicate what you earned during the year. That line was followed by the instruction: "Send it in." Don't blindly pay taxes you can avoid. Take the time to plan your mutual fund purchases and sales, keep adequate records, and invest in tax-efficient funds. Remember, the money you save is your own.

Figure 9

FORM 1099-DIV

Shortly after the end of the year, your mutual fund's sponsor will send you Form 1099-DIV, which contains the information necessary to complete your federal income tax return. This form may include several types of dividends or other distributions that your fund may have made during the year. This tax information is submitted to the IRS by your fund sponsor, and you may be subject to a penalty or other sanction if this income is taxable and it is not reported on your federal tax return.

Ordinary dividends. In box 1b, your fund will report your share of earnings from interest from cash equivalents (such as Treasury bills and commercial paper), interest from bonds, and cash dividends from corporate stocks. Also reported here are short-term capital distributions representing your share of the fund's short-term profits (net of short-term losses). The amount reported as ordinary income is net of your share of the fund's operating expenses.

Capital gains distributions. The fund's distributions from long-term capital gains are reported in box 1c. These distributions represent your share of the fund's realized long-term profits on sales of portfolio securities (net of any realized losses). You must report these gains on your tax return as long-term capital gains regardless of how long you have held your mutual fund shares.

Nontaxable distributions. On rare occasions, your mutual fund may report (in box 1d) some income as a nontaxable distribution. This distribution is called a return of capital, and, while not taxable as income, it reduces the cost basis of your fund shares.

Total distributions. The total from boxes 1b, 1c, and 1d are reported in box 1a. Note that the total in this box may include both taxable and nontaxable distributions.

Foreign income distributions. In box 3, your fund will report your share of the taxes paid to a foreign government. Box 4 contains the name of the foreign country to which the taxes have been paid. Distributions from income are taxable, but you may be able to claim either a foreign tax credit (on Form 1116) or a deduction on Schedule A for the amount of foreign taxes paid. Generally, your fund will give you instructions for claiming the foreign tax credit or deduction.

Frequently Asked Tax Questions

Q. *Do I have to pay taxes on distributions that are automatically reinvested in my account?*

A. Yes. It doesn't matter to the IRS whether you take them in cash or reinvest them. Of course, income from municipal bond funds is usually exempt from federal taxation, and income and net capital gains distributed to IRA and other retirement accounts are tax-sheltered until withdrawn.

Q. *If I switch shares from one fund to another in the same fund family, is this a taxable event?*

A. Yes, unless the switch occurred in a tax-sheltered retirement plan or money market fund. An exchange of assets from one fund to another is the same as a sale and purchase for tax purposes.

Q. *What are short-term and long-term capital gains?*

A. If you sell shares of a fund that were held longer than twelve months, the resulting gain or loss is classified as long term, while shares held twelve months or less usually create a short-term gain or loss. The exception to this rule occurs when you realize a capital loss on shares held less than six months and you received a long-term capital gains distribution from the fund during those six months. In this case, only the portion of your loss that exceeds the amount of the distribution can be reported as short term. The portion that is equal to or less than the distribution is considered long term.

Q. *Are short-term and long-term gains taxed at different rates?*

A. Long-term gains realized on your sale of fund shares, as well as those distributed by a mutual fund, are taxed at a maximum rate of 28 percent. Short-term gains are taxed at ordinary income rates and are included with ordinary income on your 1099-DIV.

Q. *Does the "wash sale" rule apply to mutual fund shares?*

A. Yes. If you sell shares at a loss, you can't claim the loss if you purchased additional shares in the same fund within thirty days before or after the sale.

Q. *Can nondeductible contributions be commingled with deductible contributions on my IRA?*

A. Yes, you can make both deductible and nondeductible contributions to the same account. However, it is your responsibility to report nondeductible amounts on Form 8606 and attach it to Form 1040. You report deductible contributions directly on Form 1040.

TABLE 7.
SCHEDULE OF IRA DEDUCTIBILITY

Filing Status	Adjusted Gross Income	Allowable Deduction
Single	$25,000 or less	Full amount
	$25,001–34,999	Partial deduction
	$35,000 or more	No deduction
Married, filing jointly	$40,000 or less	Full amount
	$40,001–$49,999	Partial deduction
	$50,000 or more	No deduction
Married, filing separately	Up to $10,000	Partial deduction
	$10,000 and above	No deduction

CHAPTER

ELEVEN

Investment Return: Realistic Expectations and Castles in the Air

When I was young, I was fond of fairy tales. I liked to read about genies, magic lamps, and wonderful castles in the air. At times I even imagined climbing bean stalks, slaying giants, and spiriting away the riches I would find hidden in castles in the clouds. Those indeed were the wonder years.

It's been decades since I have imagined instant riches. Over the years, I have learned that you get only what you pay for. There is no easy path to great wealth. Although it is possible to amass a fortune, that outcome is usually reserved for those who know that building wealth requires hard work, sacrifice, and prudent risk taking—or is it?

During the last fifteen years, the stock market has rewarded investors handsomely. Since the beginning of this great bull market in late 1982, the Standard & Poor's

500 Index has returned an average of more than 15 percent per year. More than a handful of fortunate investors have earned an average of 20 percent or more on their mutual fund portfolios during that period. Invest $25,000, earn an average of 20 percent per year, and after twenty years that initial investment will grow to more than $958,000. Invest $10,000 every year, earn 20 percent, and you will have piled up more than $2.2 million after twenty years and an astounding $88 million after forty years!

Before you set off to make a fortune in the financial markets, stop for a reality check. If you believe you can earn 20 percent or more from your mutual fund investments year after year, you are chasing castles in the air. Of the 457 mutual funds that have been around during the last fifteen years, only two, CGM Capital Development and Fidelity Select Health Care, have produced average annual returns in excess of 20 percent. Furthermore, the stock market has produced exceptional returns during the last fifteen years. To obtain a true picture of what returns the financial markets are capable of delivering, you must take a longer view of history.

The following table lists the average annualized returns for various classes of assets that have prevailed during the last half-century. Chances are they are much more modest than you might have expected, ranging from about 14 percent for small company growth stocks to slightly less than 5 percent for short-term Treasury bills. Furthermore, these are the returns of various market indices. They are unmanaged portfolios and do not reflect the costs of investing or the payment of income taxes. In other words, if you expect to earn 15 percent or more from your mutual fund investments, you are expecting far too much.

If I have shattered your dreams of castles in the air, I apologize. However, before you become so discouraged that you abandon your investment plan, remember the power of compound returns. Invest over a long period of time, earn modest returns, plow back as much of what you earn as you can, and you will build a very comfortable

TABLE 8.
A HALF-CENTURY'S INVESTMENT RETURNS

Small Company Growth Stocks	13.8%
Blue-Chip Stocks	11.9
Long-Term Corporate Bonds	5.8
Long-Term Government Bonds	5.3
Intermediate-Term Government Bonds	5.9
Treasury Bills	4.8
Inflation	4.4

Source: *Stocks, Bonds, Bills and Inflation Yearbook,* Ibbotson Associates

nest egg. For example, invest $2,000 each year in an Individual Retirement Account for thirty years, earn 10 percent a year, and that retirement account will reach a value of approximately $362,000. Stretch your annual average return to 12 percent, and the account's value will top $540,000.

The historical return data also illustrate the danger of being too conservative. For example, invest $2,000 each year for thirty years in an IRA packed with bond and money market mutual funds and your average annual rate of return can skid to as low as 5 percent. If so, your retirement nest egg will attain a value of only $140,000. Furthermore, much of what you earn will most likely be eroded by rising consumer prices. Note that the annual rate of inflation during the last half-century has averaged 4.4 percent. In other words, over that period Treasury bills returned an average of only 0.4 percent per year more than the rate of inflation (called the "real" rate of return), and government and corporate bonds have provided little more in the way of real return.

Although mutual funds will not allow you to obtain that castle in the air, they will provide a very comfortable nest here on earth. Depending on where you invest and the amount of risk you assume, you can earn from 5 to 14 percent annually on your mutual fund investments. Invest as much as you can for as long as you can and your wealth will grow to a tidy sum.

TABLE 9.
SAVE AND INVEST $100 A MONTH AND HERE'S WHAT YOU'LL HAVE

Years	Annual Percentage Return				
	5%	8%	10%	12%	15%
5	$6,829	7,397	7,808	8,247	8,968
10	15,592	18,417	20,655	23,334	27,866
15	26,840	34,835	41,792	50,458	67,686
20	41,275	59,295	76,570	99,915	151,595
25	59,799	95,737	133,798	189,764	328,407
30	83,573	150,030	227,933	352,991	700,982

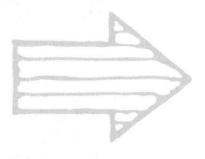

CHAPTER

TWELVE

Investment Risk: There Are No Free Lunches, but Don't Pay Too Much

Bring up your favorite mutual fund at a dinner party and the first question you are usually asked is, "What has it returned?" Rarely will someone ask you about the fund's risk. Will Rogers once quipped, "When I invest, I am not so much concerned about the return on my money as I am about the return of my money." And everyone knows that "a fool and his money are soon parted." When you invest, you give up your money today in the hopes of obtaining more money in the future. Given that the future is uncertain, by definition, investing involves the assumption of a degree of risk. The amount of risk is influenced by two factors: (1) the risk of the individual securities you hold and (2) how those securities have been assembled in a portfolio.

Figure 10 illustrates the hierarchy of risk in the mutual fund industry. At the bottom of the risk pyramid are money market funds. These funds invest in Treasury bills, large denomination certificates of deposit, commercial paper (short-term loans to America's highest quality corporations), bankers acceptances (which are created in the course of international trade), and repurchase agreements (government securities that someone has guaranteed to repurchase near term at a stated price). At the top of the pyramid are the most volatile funds around, sector and precious metals funds.

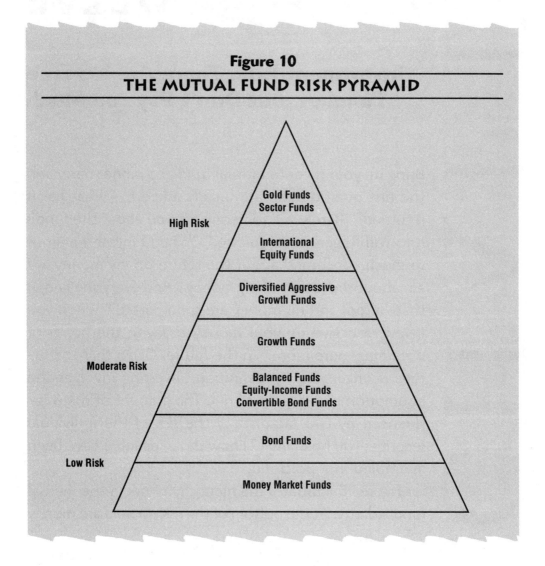

Figure 10

THE MUTUAL FUND RISK PYRAMID

Risk is a necessary evil. You must take the bad when you are seeking the good. For example, during the last fifty years, Treasury bills, the safest investment you can make, returned an average of 4.8 percent a year. During that period, the Consumer Price Index (CPI) increased at a 4.4 percent annual rate, leaving Treasury bill investors with a 0.4 percent annual expansion in real wealth. Long-term government bond investors improved on that return a bit, earning an average of 5.3 percent per year before inflation and 0.9 percent after deducting the annual rate of expansion in the CPI. On the other hand, common stocks, as measured by the return of the Standard & Poor's 500 Index, have returned an average of 11.9 percent a year during the last half-century. That's a whopping 7.5 percent a year more than the rate of inflation. In other words, if you dodge investment risk you will most likely dodge any meaningful investment return as well.

Although the assumption of risk is necessary when pursuing meaningful investment returns, there is a world of difference between taking necessary risks and being foolhardy. All investors, whether their portfolios are packed with risky common stocks or low-risk Treasury bills, are exposed to inflation risk. This is the risk that your capital will shrink in value because the prices of goods and services are rising. Even a low rate of inflation can erode wealth by a significant amount over a long period of time. For example, suppose that you invest $10,000 in a Treasury bond that yields 7 percent annually. Every year you receive interest payments totaling $700. If you spend that income, you will have a portfolio valued at $20,000 when the bond matures twenty years later. However, if consumer prices rise by an average of 3 percent per year during that period, the purchasing power of your portfolio declines from $20,000 to $11,074. Invest in government bonds and you add interest rate risk to inflation risk. When interest rates rise, the price of bonds declines. For example, if you purchase a $1,000 Treasury bond that yields 7 percent (pays $70 a year) and interest rates rise to 10 percent, a newly issued Treasury bond will pay $100 interest each year. Thus, the price of a bond that yields 7 percent will fall to the point at which the total return of the two bonds is equated. The extent of the decline in a bond's price is a function of its stated interest payment and the time until the bond matures. Generally, the higher the stated interest rate and the shorter the time until maturity, the less will be the decline in bond price as a response to rising interest rates. Thus, most risky of all are zero-coupon bonds with long maturities. Table 10 illustrates the percentage decline in bond prices that results from a 1-percent rise in interest rates. As can be seen, even small changes in interest rates can cause some bond prices to decline by a significant amount.

Invest in corporate or municipal bonds and you add credit risk to inflation and interest rate risk. Credit risk is the possibility that the bond issuer will not make timely interest payments or repayment of principal. Of course, investors demand to be paid for taking the additional risk. Thus, corporations with lower credit quality possess higher yields than those with better credit quality. Bonds with the highest ratings are referred to as "investment grade." Bonds with low ratings are referred to as "junk (or high yield) bonds."

Invest in the stock market and you add business and market risk. Stock prices rise and fall with a corporation's economic fortunes. When a corporation's revenues are growing, its profit margins are expanding, and its earnings are on the rise, its stock price can be expected to rise as well, and vice versa. Additionally, common stock investors are exposed to the oscillations of the stock market. When the market goes up, so do the prices of most stocks. However, when

TABLE 10.
CHANGE IN BOND PRICES AS A RESULT OF A
1 PERCENTAGE POINT RISE IN INTEREST RATES

	Bond Yield				
Average Maturity	**6%**	**7%**	**8%**	**9%**	**10%**
2 Years	-1.9	-1.8	-1.7	-1.6	-1.5
10 Years	-7.0	-6.7	-6.4	-6.2	-5.8
25 Years	-11.7	-10.7	-9.8	-9.2	-8.0

the stock market takes a nosedive, the stock prices of good companies are taken down with the bad.

Although investing in stocks can be a risky business, diversification comes to the rescue. The typical diversified equity mutual fund possesses only one-third the risk of a portfolio containing one or two stocks. Because some companies are performing well when others are doing poorly, business risk can be completely eliminated if you diversify properly. What remains is market or beta risk. Simply stated, beta measures portfolio risk in relation to the riskiness of the market as a whole. The market is assumed to have a beta of 1.0. A diversified portfolio with a beta of 1.2 has 20 percent more risk than the stock market, that is, it is about 20 percent more volatile. For diversified portfolios the relationship between beta risk and portfolio return is as follows:

Portfolio Return = Risk-Free Return + Beta (Market Return - Risk-Free Return)

Portfolio Return = 0.06 + 0.5 (.12-.06) = 0.09, or 9%

Figure 11 illustrates the trade-off between investment risk and investment return, known as the capital market line. The upward-sloping line represents the combinations of risk and return found in well-diversified portfolios. The risk-free rate of return (RF) is the yield on short-term Treasury bills. The market return (RM) is the expected return of the Standard & Poor's 500 Index. Also located on the capital market line are the expected returns from two portfolios, one with a beta of 0.5 and one with a beta of 1.5. The annual returns of these two portfolios were estimated assuming that Treasury bills will yield 6 percent and the S&P 500 Index will return a total of 12 percent.

Although beta cannot predict the direction the stock market will take, it anticipates the responsiveness of a portfolio's value extremely well, given changes in the stock market as a whole. For example, if

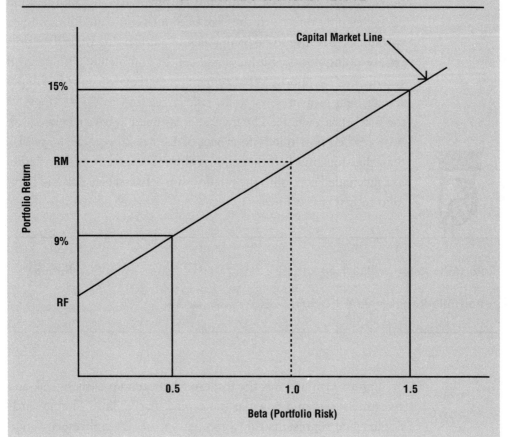

Figure 11

PORTFOLIO RISK AND RETURN
THE CAPITAL MARKET LINE

the stock market declined by 50 percent over a prolonged period, a portfolio whose beta is 1.2 could be expected to decline in value by 60 percent. Of course, if stock prices were to rise by 50 percent, the value of this portfolio would climb by 60 percent.

Figure 12 illustrates the changes in quarterly returns for three funds: Oberweis Emerging Growth (beta 1.6), the Vanguard Index 500 Portfolio (beta 1.0), and Lindner Dividend (beta 0.6). As you can see, the quarterly returns of Oberweis Emerging Growth, with its higher-than-average beta, are much more volatile than the returns of the other two funds. The Lindner Dividend Fund, with its lower-than-average beta, has been the least volatile of the three funds.

It is important to note that beta does not distinguish a good fund from a bad one. It indicates only the extent to which a fund's shares will rise and fall, given changes in the overall stock market. However, because investment return is linked to investment risk, high beta funds tend to provide greater long-term returns than low beta funds. Whether you invest in a high or low beta fund depends on your personal preference.

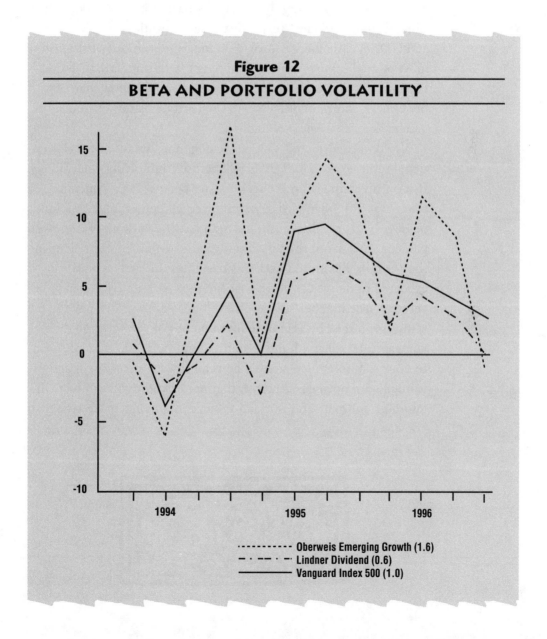

Figure 12

BETA AND PORTFOLIO VOLATILITY

·········· Oberweis Emerging Growth (1.6)
— · — — · — Lindner Dividend (0.6)
———— Vanguard Index 500 (1.0)

Remember, however, that beta provides a reliable risk index only for those funds that are well-diversified. Mutual funds that maintain concentrated portfolios, such as gold funds and industry sector funds, may be much riskier than indicated by their betas. That's because the lion's share of these funds' risk is asset specific. Since the volatility of these funds is relatively unrelated to stock market volatility, most investors use the standard deviation of return to measure the risk of highly concentrated mutual fund portfolios. Mutual fund statistical services such as Morningstar, Value Line, and CDA/Wiesenberger provide standard deviations of return for most mutual funds. Although a discussion of standard deviation is beyond the scope of this presentation, you should know that, as with beta, the greater a mutual fund's standard deviation of return, the greater is its share price volatility.

If you are attracted to a particular fund because of its exceptional return, take a look at its risk before committing your money. If it's a diversified fund, check out its beta; if it's a concentrated fund, look at its standard deviation. Remember, average-risk funds possess betas of about 1.0 and standard deviations of about 20 percent. Check out the fund's return after adjusting for risk, using the formula illustrated earlier. Over the long run, a fund can be expected to deliver a return that lines up with its risk. There are very few free lunches served on Wall Street. You must pay for the returns you seek by assuming investment risk. Determine the risk you can tolerate and build a mutual fund portfolio that conforms to your risk tolerance zone. The road toward investment success is filled with potholes. Smooth that road as best you can by maintaining a mutual fund portfolio that contains no more risk than you can tolerate.

CHAPTER

THIRTEEN

Bear Market Strategies

Investors of all kinds have been on a buying binge, and stock prices have rocketed skyward since late 1990. In mid-October 1990, the Dow Jones Industrial Average was hovering around the 2,365 level. In early October 1996, the Dow broke through the 6,000 mark—an astounding gain of more than 3,600 points. That represented an average annual return of more than 18 percent, making that bull market the longest and strongest in history. During that six-year period, the stock market didn't experience correction of 15 percent or more. Never before in history has that happened. The last severe bear market occurred in late 1987, and you have to go back to the mid-1970s to locate a prolonged bear stock market. Back then, there were less than four hundred mutual funds available to individual investors. In short, there are plenty of mutual fund investors who have never experienced a painful bear stock market.

If you began investing in mutual funds sometime during the last two decades, you haven't seen what can happen to your investment nest egg during a prolonged bear market. And I suspect that a large number of novice investors will panic and bail out of their stock and bond mutual funds should a prolonged bear market develop this year or next. Many of these investors, while licking their wounds, will probably vow never to stray very far from investing in "safe" bank certificates of deposit ever again. If you are wringing your hands or losing sleep worrying about your mutual fund investments, you are probably headed for big trouble during the next severe bear market.

Despite the stock market's recent resilience, a longer view of history tells us that stock market corrections occur suddenly, swiftly, and with a high degree of regularity. For example, I tracked the Standard & Poor's 500 Index since January 1941 and recorded every stock market decline of 5 percent or more that occurred during the 660-month period ending December 1995. Here's what I found.

During the last fifty-five years, there were forty-five periods when the stock market slumped by 5 percent or more, eighteen periods with declines of 10 percent or more, twelve market drops exceeding 15 percent, and four periods during which stock prices fell by more than 25 percent. In aggregate, these market backslides covered 182 months. In other words, since early 1941, the stock market has spent more than 25 percent of the time in retreat. The percentage decline in the stock market during these forty-five periods averaged 12.5 percent, with an average duration of about four months.

These statistics indicate that steep market corrections are often swift. By the time you realize you are in the midst of a significant stock market decline, the worst is usually behind you. In other words, by the time your emotions tell you it's time to unload your equity mutual funds, it's probably too late to do any good, and most likely just at the point in time when a sale will do the most damage to your long-run investment returns.

If your emotions are not going to protect you during a stock market slump, how can you protect yourself? Although I am sure that a number of self-proclaimed stock market gurus are going to be advertising that they correctly predicted the next major stock market decline, the plain truth is that over the long run, stock market timing does not produce the results being claimed and can cause a lot of damage as well.

Stock market timers are quick to boast about their success in calling stock market turns. And some of their claims are true. However, market timers are usually mute about the times when their signals called market moves that came up croppers. And it's these timing mistakes that harm investors most, especially during those periods when market timers mistakenly get their clients out of the stock market when it is going up.

For example, during the last fifty years, the Standard & Poor's 500 Index has returned 12.3 percent compounded annually. Had you been able to dodge the market's five worst years during that period, your compound annual rate of return would have increased 150 basis points to 13.8 percent. On the other hand, if you mistakenly sat on the sidelines during the stock market's five best years during that fifty-year period, your compound annual return would have declined by 370 basis points to 8.6 percent. In other words, there is more to lose by being out of the stock market when it is going up than there is to gain by being out of the market when it is going down. In fact, after more than fifty years of scientific scrutiny by the academic community, there has yet to be uncovered a stock market timing rule that increases investment returns over those of a comparable-risk, buy-and-hold strategy. Furthermore, adviser sentiment has proved to be an excellent contrary indicator. When a large percentage of investment advisers believe that the stock market is on the verge of a significant decline, history indicates that the stock market is usually poised for a major rise. If stock market timing provides little protection, what else can you do? The best answer is to construct a portfolio of mutual funds that contains a level of risk that lies well within your risk tolerance zone. Long-term investors invariably are among the stock market's most successful investors. These people weather the market's foul moods and rack up profits when stock prices are rising. However, to win in the long run, you must be able to navigate the short run. By that I mean that you must stick around to capture the stock market's full move to

TABLE 11.
SIGNIFICANT STOCK MARKET DECLINES 1941-1995

Period	Percent Decline	Number of Months
Aug. 1941–April 1942	26.3%	9 months
July 1943–Nov. 1943	10.8	5
June 1946–May 1947	24.7	12
July 1948–June 1949	15.5	12
Jan. 1953–Aug. 1953	12.2	8
Aug. 1956–Feb. 1957	12.4	7
Aug. 1957–Dec. 1957	16.5	5
Jan. 1960–Oct. 1960	10.6	10
Jan. 1962–June 1962	23.5	6
Feb. 1966–Sept. 1966	17.6	8
Dec. 1968–June 1970	32.9	19
Jan. 1973–Sept. 1974	46.2	21
July 1975–Sept. 1975	11.9	3
Jan. 1977–Feb. 1978	19.0	14
Feb. 1980–March 1980	10.6	2
Dec. 1980–July 1982	23.8	20
Sept. 1987–Nov. 1987	30.2	3
June 1990–Oct. 1990	15.8	5

the upside. And, like market down drafts, moves to the upside are usually robust and swift.

The stock market's biggest losers are usually those individuals who take more risks than they should and eventually bail out of a declining market after mounting losses cause their emotions to override their sense of rationality. They are the people who are never around when the stock market begins its upward trek once again.

To dodge this grievous error, you must allocate your capital between cash and equities in such a manner that you will not be overtaken by your emotions during a stock market decline. By assuming a level of risk you can tolerate, you can sit tight during a stock market decline and insure that you remain a long-term investor.

Suppose, for example, that a stock market decline of 15 percent or more would cause you to bail out of your equity mutual fund investments prematurely. If you allocate 50 percent of your capital to money market mutual funds and 50 percent to well-managed equity funds that tend to stay fully invested in the stock market at all times, a 30 percent plunge in stock prices would result in a 15 percent decline in the total value of your portfolio. Thus, in all but the most severe bear markets, you insure that your portfolio will not decline by more than 15 percent. Since the decline is within your risk tolerance zone, you will not be overcome by the urge to save what you have left and flee the stock market at exactly the wrong time. Because the percentage of your portfolio allocated to cash increases during a stock market decline, you have the opportunity to rebalance your portfolio (that is, increase your equity fund investments) at the optimum time, when stock prices are bargain priced.

If you are in the stage of your investment life when you are adding to your portfolio every year, stock market declines should make you happy rather than sad. During a stock market slump, you can invest in the shares of quality equity mutual funds that have temporarily been put on sale. It's like finding that automobile you wanted marked down by 20 percent or more. Rather than being less attractive, that automobile becomes more attractive at the lower price. Learn to shop for stocks and bonds the same way that you shop for other things in life; you bargain hard, and when you find quality merchandise at a reasonable price, you make the purchase.

If you fear that the day after you make an investment in an equity mutual fund the stock market will take a sudden dip, here are the results of an experiment that should lift your spirits. I assumed a hypothetical $5,000 investment in the stock market (the Standard & Poor's 500 Index) each year for twenty years beginning in 1976. At the end of that period, I had invested a total of $100,000 in the stock market. Furthermore, I assumed that each year's investment was made at the stock market high for the year. This is the ultimate version of the worried investor's nightmare. Every single annual investment in the market, soon after it was made, declined in value. Even so, after twenty years of investing this way, my hypothetical portfolio had attained a value of $512,000, representing a 13.8 percent compound annual return. My point is to illustrate that patient investors who can regularly add to their investment portfolios should do so no matter what their feelings about the stock market may be.

Of course, if you want to earn the highest return on your capital, find the one single investment that you believe will perform best and sink every dollar you can get hold of into it. That, of course, is also one of the surest ways to financial ruin. Prudent investors know the value of spreading their capital among several different types of investments. By doing so, these investors forgo high return potential for the safety that diversification provides. Interestingly, these investors tend to fare the best of all. That's because the most important variable in the compound return equation is time. Diversified investors ensure that they will stay in the investment arena the longest and thus allow their capital to compound year after year.

Finally, you must give yourself a chance to win. A money market mutual fund, a Treasury bill, and a bank certificate of deposit are by far the safest investments you can make. However, after the payment of taxes and the erosion of purchasing power caused by creeping inflation, these safe investments are guaranteed losers. To earn meaningful returns (that is, net returns in excess of the rate of inflation), you must assume some degree of investment risk. That is the one hard fact of life in the investment world. Thus, you must allocate some portion of your capital to assets that contain some risk. How much, of course, depends on your risk tolerance level.

The table above illustrates the range of annual returns obtainable from stocks, bonds, and money market funds. Use these returns to guide your asset allocation decisions. Construct a hypothetical portfolio and obtain an estimate of the return that portfolio will provide by computing its weighted average annual return. For example, a portfolio that contains an equal allocation to equity, bond, and money market mutual funds will provide a return somewhere in the 6 percent to 8 percent range, or an average of about 7 percent over the long run. A portfolio equally distributed between money market funds and equity mutual funds will return an aver-

TABLE 12.
MUTUAL FUND CATEGORIES AND
ANNUAL RETURN POTENTIAL

Investment Category	Average Annual Returns
Equity Funds	10% to 14%
Bond Funds	5% to 7%
Money Market Funds	3% to 5%

age of about 8 percent per year, or about 4.5 percentage points annually more than the historical rate of inflation. The goal of this exercise is to establish target portfolio allocations that will provide both meaningful returns and the protection you need during a prolonged bear stock market.

Although most investors fear severe stock market declines, several groups of investors actually benefit when the stock market heads to lower ground. These groups include

(1) Investors who were reluctant to invest in the stock market during the past couple of years. These people would finally get the opportunity to put their cash to work as valuations retreat to more reasonable levels.

(2) Investors who regularly invest new capital in the stock market (that is, dollar cost averagers). Remember, dollar cost averaging works because investors buy more shares when stock prices are low and fewer shares when stock prices are high. When stock prices continually move to higher ground, dollar cost averaging loses its power as each purchase is made at a higher price.

(3) Investors who allocate their capital among stocks, bonds, and money market funds and periodically rebalance that portfolio back to its target percentage allocations. Rebalancing enhances returns because investors sell equity fund shares and purchase money market shares after stock prices have risen and sell money market fund shares and buy equity fund shares after stock prices have declined. In other words, periodic rebalancing forces investors to sell high and buy low.

(4) Investors who are about to retire and receive a lump-sum pension payment that must be rolled over into an IRA. A prolonged stock market decline will allow these investors to gradually deploy their cash into the stock market while prices are decreasing. When the bull market resumes, these investors will reap handsome rewards.

Although some investors will be hurt by a steep stock market decline, most investors should welcome market volatility during their capital accumulating years. Remember, the only time you want the stock market to be at an all-time high is the day you cash out.

The rules of successful investing are few: diversify, invest for the long term, and minimize the cost of investing. Furthermore, you must realize that the stock market spends a lot of time in retreat. Use these frequent stock market slumps to add to your equity portfolio and avoid the urge to dump your equity funds when their prices are declining. Follow these few simple rules and prosper.

CHAPTER

FOURTEEN

One-Stop Shopping in Mutual Fund Supermarkets

As I have described it, investing in mutual funds is not difficult. You find a fund you like, call the fund and request a prospectus and purchase application, fill out the application, and send it with your check to the fund's transfer agent. The fund's custodian bank holds your shares and sends you periodic statements detailing the progress of your investment. Although you can switch your investment in one fund to another in the same fund family by making a phone call, you must repeat the whole process when you want to exchange an investment in one fund for another offered by a different family. In other words, you must request in writing that shares of the former fund be redeemed, wait for the fund to send you a check, deposit the check in your bank account, then send a personal check to the transfer agent of the fund you wish to buy. If you repeat these activities for a dozen or more funds, the process can take time; and, in this instance, time is money. You end up swimming in account statements every month, and your money spends a lot of time in the U.S. postal system, not in your favorite funds.

A growing number of brokerage firms now offer an alternative to the mass of paperwork that accompanies investing with several different fund families. As Charles Schwab's Tom Taggart puts it simply: "Not all top-rated funds are in the same fund family." Although a number of "full service" brokerage firms, including American Express, Merrill Lynch, and Smith Barney, have recently begun to offer mutual fund trading to their customers, the big three, Charles Schwab, Jack White & Company, and Fidelity Investments, dominate the mutual fund supermarket industry. Schwab's Mutual Fund Marketplace, Fidelity Investments' FundsNetwork, and Jack White & Company's Mutual Fund Network each offers you the opportunity to invest in hundreds of funds drawn from scores of fund families in a convenient one-stop shopping environment. For a small commission, these discount brokers will buy and sell fund shares for you. The brokerage firm keeps the shares, and you receive a consolidated statement of your mutual fund investments every month. Furthermore, these discount brokers have been rapidly expanding the number of funds that you can buy without paying a brokerage commission. The fund families that participate in these "no transaction fee" programs rebate a portion of their management fees to the brokerage firms that sell their shares. Thus, you enjoy the convenience of being able to switch among mutual fund families cost-free with a single telephone call. You eliminate investment downtime, and you pay relatively low fees (or no additional fees) to conduct business. Although the services offered by the big three discounters are similar, there are subtle differences in the way they operate. Depending on the amount of capital you invest, the amount of trading you do, and your general investment style, one of the firms may better suit your needs than the others.

Charles Schwab's Mutual Fund Marketplace (800-266-5623) offers more than eight hundred mutual funds from which to choose.

Schwab's OneSource program includes about six hundred funds from dozens of fund families, which are available to investors on a no-transaction-fee basis. Funds pay Schwab 0.20 percent of the value of the assets resting at Schwab annually. Schwab maintains the shareholder accounts, fields investors' telephone calls, sends fund prospectuses, assembles statements, and so on. The participating fund family gains hassle-free assets through the OneSource program and does not necessarily mind handing over a small portion of its income. Investors find the program ultraconvenient because they need remember only one telephone number, Schwab's, and they receive one statement that details their investment activity. The advantage ends when you purchase a no-load fund through Schwab that does not participate in the OneSource program (for example the Vanguard and T. Row Price funds). Since you pay Schwab a transaction fee to acquire the shares of these funds, it is cheaper to purchase the fund directly from the sponsor. The OneSource division of Schwab's Mutual Fund Marketplace has become so popular among no-load investors that assets have swelled beyond $80 billion since it began operations a few years ago.

Fidelity Investments' FundsNetwork program (800-544-9697) is set up like Schwab's Mutual Fund Marketplace and flaunts the same major advantage: the ability to purchase several no-load mutual funds from among different families without paying transaction fees. Fidelity profits the same way Schwab does from its relationship with no-load groups, and you experience a similar degree of convenience (one statement, one telephone call, and so on). Although Fidelity offers significantly more funds to choose from overall (more than 1,700), only about 250 non-Fidelity funds are sold without a transaction fee. Additionally, if you purchase a no-load fund not offered through Fidelity's no-transaction-fee program, you pay a slightly higher commission at Fidelity than at Schwab.

You will find one advantage to Fidelity's FundsNetwork that you will not have at another discount broker—the availability of Fidelity funds on a no-transaction-fee basis. The Fidelity funds have quite a following, and fans of this group may choose not only from among several no-load groups, but also from Fidelity's family of well-managed funds.

Although other discount brokers probably would love to get their hands on Fidelity's high-quality no-load funds for their no-transaction-fee programs, the chances of Fidelity allowing this are slim. If you plan to invest primarily in Fidelity's funds, this program should be right for you.

Jack White and Company (800-233-3411) has packed its supermarket shelves with far more mutual funds than either Schwab or Fidelity. In addition, its no-transaction-fee Mutual Fund Network offers more costless choices (840) than the other two discounters. And its transaction fee for the purchase or sale of nonparticipating no-load funds is less than Schwab's. However, each purchase or sale transaction has a $5,000 minimum. Neither Schwab nor Fidelity imposes minimum dollar amounts on transactions. Jack White saddles transactions of less than $5,000 with a $27 fee.

If you plan to trade in large chunks, though, consider Jack White. This broker provides the same conveniences as the others and offers more funds and lower fees. Additionally, Jack White sets no limit on the number of short-term transactions, while both Schwab and Fidelity limit investors to five short-term trades each year.

CHAPTER

FIFTEEN

Don't Just Take My Advice: Mutual Fund Advisory Newsletters

Until a few years ago, the *Wall Street Journal* wouldn't accept advertising from financial advisory newsletters. The *Journal's* reasoning was that financial newsletter writers were a bunch of lunatic self-promoters. The *Journal's* editors probably arrived at that conclusion because some financial newsletter writers are lunatic self-promoters. These are the people who flood your mailbox with promises of instant riches. Their goal is to make not you, but themselves, rich, by selling worthless and, in some instances, irresponsible investment advice.

"If you had followed my surefire strategy last year, you would have multiplied your wealth by five or six times.... This little-known stock market secret will make you 1,250% or more each and every year.... Earn 25 percent to 30 percent year after year with little risk by following my stock market advice.... My stock of the week selections are up an amazing 2,400% in just six months.... My number one stock pick, now priced at $5, is set for a run that could push its price well beyond $200 during the next twelve months."

We have all seen those ads. Some of you probably believed some of the claims and signed up as subscribers. After following the newsletter's advice for a year, you probably figured out that there is no surefire way to instant riches in the financial markets. In fact, numerous studies indicate that security prices reflect new information so fast that neither newsletter writers nor Wall Street analysts can outguess their short-term direction. According to these "efficient market" studies, you should cancel your newsletter subscriptions, fire your investment adviser, and buy and hold a diversified portfolio.

Although security markets are more efficient than most investors believe, there is still a need for responsible security analysts and investment newsletter writers. Efficient market theorists recognize that there is a strong relationship between investment risk and investment return. Investors can change the return potential of their portfolios by changing portfolio risk, increasing it to provide a higher return potential, and lowering it to produce more staid returns. Given that investors have different risk tolerance levels, there is a need for investment information and advice that allows investors to tailor a portfolio to their individual needs. Thus, security analysis and investment advice provide investors with an economic benefit, even though the financial markets are highly efficient. Mark Hulbert, editor of the Hulbert Financial Digest, has followed the recommendations of newsletter writers and tracked their performance for nearly two decades. He has found that while it is extremely hard to beat the market, it can be done. Furthermore, investment ideas don't occur in a vacuum. An investor must either search for investment ideas himself or rely on his broker to provide recommendations. However, very few individual investors possess the time or economic resources to go it alone. And relying on one's stockbroker exclusively for investment recommendations creates the possibility of a conflict of interest. A stockbroker is paid not to give investment advice but to generate commissions for the firm. The more your broker gets you to trade, the greater the firm's and his income. On the other hand, once you ante up a few dollars to subscribe to an investment newsletter, the financial relationship between adviser and client disappears. The newsletter writer's income is now tied to subscription renewals, and the adviser/newsletter writer can generate a better renewal rate by giving useful advice.

There are now more than six thousand mutual funds on the market, and hundreds of new funds are being created each year. It has become nearly impossible for individual investors to keep abreast of the mutual fund marketplace. Enter the mutual fund advisory newsletter. Many of these newsletters present lists of recommended funds, model investment portfolios tailored to varying risk levels, information on the funds they have recommended such as portfolio management changes, changes in performance trends, and so on, as well as descriptions of newly created funds. For $50 to $100 a year, a mutual fund investor can get timely and useful information on a wide spectrum of funds.

Fifteen years ago, there were fewer than a half-dozen newsletters focusing on mutual fund investing. Today, I have counted more than four dozen that offer mutual fund information and advice. These newsletters differ widely in philosophy as well as scope. Some confine their editorial content to market analysis and individual fund recommendations. Others include model portfolios. The newsletter(s) suitable for you depends on your specific needs and your personal investment style. If you are a buy-and-hold investor, for example, there is little reason to subscribe to a newsletter packed with short-term market timing advice. If you want investment portfolio guidance as well as new investment ideas, look for a newsletter that offers a model portfolio that fits your comfort zone.

Before you subscribe to any mutual fund advisory newsletter, determine the type of advice you want. Ask the publisher to send you a back issue so that you can review the letter's content. Because of escalating costs, many newsletter publishers have ceased the practice of sending free issues to prospective subscribers. In these instances, I recommend that you obtain a short-term trial subscription and check out the advice given in a couple of issues before following the editor's recommendations. If you want to compare the performance of one newsletter's recommendations against the recommendations of other newsletters, consider subscribing to the *Hulbert Financial Digest*, which offers a five-issue trial subscription for $37.50 (703-683-5905).

The quality of advice offered by mutual fund newsletters varies all over the lot. Some are filled with harebrained schemes that have no chance of providing meaningful returns. Others require that you follow advice dispensed daily on an investment hotline. And, sad to say, a few are written by lunatic self-promoters. Here are a few newsletters that have stood the test of time. In my opinion, these are among the best mutual fund advisory newsletters currently available.

Fidelity Insight. This is one of a growing number of newsletters that focus exclusively on Fidelity funds. The newsletter is not affiliated with Fidelity; however, its editor, Eric Kobren, worked in Fidelity's marketing department for a number of years before creating this newsletter.

It is the first newsletter to focus exclusively on Fidelity funds. Kobren offers not only up-to-date Fidelity fund news but also four model portfolios, ranging from conservative (Income and Preservation Portfolio) to highly aggressive (Speculative Portfolio). The letter's model portfolios are usually well-balanced and, according to the *Hulbert Financial Digest*, have delivered market-beating risk-adjusted returns. If you invest in Fidelity funds and are looking for guidance, this is the advisory letter for you.

Fund Exchange. Although I remain skeptical about the benefits of market timing, I enjoy reading Paul Merriman's newsletter, which is packed with financial planning and investment advice. Interestingly, unlike most market timers, Merriman tends to position his portfolios very conservatively. As a result, they rarely reach the top of the performance charts. However, they are rarely at the bottom either. Subscribers can choose from five model portfolios with varying risk characteristics. Included with an annual subscription is access to a 24-hour "Switch Alert" hotline, a recorded message alerting subscribers to buy-and-sell signals for his equity, bond, and gold portfolios.

Mutual Fund Forecaster. Founded by Norman Fosback and Glen King Parker in 1985, this is the most widely read mutual fund advisory, with more than 150,000 subscribers. Editor Fosback has produced some of the best mutual fund research reports that I have seen. Every month the letter presents both "Buy" and "Best Buy" recommendations as well as a "Trader's Portfolio." Six model portfolios, including a Fidelity Family Portfolio, guide subscribers. In addition, each issue contains profit projections and risk ratings for hundreds of no-load and low-load funds.

The Mutual Fund Letter. Published and edited by the author of this book, this is by far my favorite mutual fund advisory letter. (Why not?) If you would like to make up your own mind, I'll send you the latest issue free of charge (800-326-6941). The newsletter has been published since February 1984, and each issue contains no-load fund buy-hold-sell advice, four model portfolios, market outlook, fund family focus, and a host of articles outlining investment strategies and tactics. Because the letter focuses on long-run returns, you won't find a telephone hotline or alert fax reports.

No-Load Fund Investor. Edited by Sheldon Jacobs, this monthly newsletter has a lot to like. Model portfolios, top-rated funds by investment category, and historical returns for the best no-load funds in the industry are but a few of the letter's features. Best of all, Sheldon's fund recommendations have tended to be right on the mark. You might not get rich following one of his newsletter's model portfolios, but the advice given is sensible and has enabled thousands of his followers to earn returns consistent with the risks they have taken. His annual statistical manual, the *No-Load Fund Investor*, is packed with no-load fund data and information.

No-Load Fund *X*. Burt Berry has spent more than two decades giving investors solid mutual fund advice. His proprietary model ranks funds in four classes: most speculative, speculative, growth, and total return. Ranks are determined by averaging the latest twelve-, six-, three-, and one-month fund returns and adding bonus points for consistency. Model portfolios consist of the top six funds in each category. In addition to tipping off subscribers to the hottest funds, each issue contains historical return data for hundreds of no-load funds.

Popular Mutual Fund Advisory Newsletters

All Star Funds

(Formerly *The Sector Ace*)
Editor: Ronald E. Rowland
P.O. Box 203427
Austin, TX 78720
Tel: 800-299-4223
Published monthly since 1991
Annual subscription: $249
Includes hotline updates
Fax service: $75 additional

Asset Allocator

Editor: Ted Kunzog
2408 Chestnut Street
Joliet, IL 60435
Tel: 800-850-1522
Published monthly since 1990
Annual subscription: $139
Three-issue trial: $10

Bob Brinker's Marketimer

Editor: Robert J. Brinker
P.O. Box 229
Irvington, NY 10533
Tel: 800-700-1030
Published monthly since 1986
Annual subscription: $185
Home page: http://www.adpad.com/brinker

The Chartist Mutual Fund Timer

Editor: Dan Sullivan
P.O. Box 758
Seal Beach, CA 90740
Tel: 310-596-2385
Published monthly since 1988
Annual subscription: $100; two years: $180
Six-month trial: $55

Closed End Country Fund Report

Editor: James R. Libera
725 Fifteenth Street
Suite 501
Washington, DC 20005
Published monthly since 1990
Annual subscription: $190; two years: $295

Closed End Fund Digest

Editor: Patrick Winton
1224 Coast Village Circle
Suite 11
Santa Barbara, CA 93108
Tel: 805-565-5651
Published monthly since 1987
Annual subscription: $199; two years: $249
Three-month trial: $49

Donoghue's Wealthletter

Editor: William E. Donoghue
Donoghue Group, Inc.
Money Market Square East
P.O. Box 309
Milford, MA 01757
Tel: 800-982-2455
Published twice monthly since 1996
Annual subscription: $298
Free sample of latest issue on
request

Equity Fund Outlook

Editor: Thurman L. Smith
P.O. Box 76
Boston, MA 02117
Tel: 617-397-6844
Published monthly by Equity Fund
Research since 1988
Annual subscription: $115; two
years: $205
Six-month trial: $69

Fabian's Domestic Investment Resource

Editor: Doug Fabian
P.O. Box 2538
Huntington Beach, CA 92647
Tel: 800-950-8765
Published monthly since 1977
Annual subscription: $119
Fax/Weekly hotline: $99 annually

Fidelity Insight

Editor: Eric M. Kobren
Mutual Fund Investors Association
20 William Street
P.O. Box 9135

Wellesley Hills, MA 02181-9135
Tel: 800-444-6342
Published monthly since 1985
Annual subscription: $177

Fidelity Monitor

Editor: Jack Bowers
P.O. Box 1294
Rocklin, CA 95677-7294
Published monthly since 1986
Annual subscription: $96, including
toll-free hotline service
Five-month trial: $48

Foreign Markets Advisory

Editor: David G. Muller, Jr.
P.O. Box 75
Fairfax Station, VA 22039
Published monthly since 1992
Annual subscription: $225
Fax or E-mail service: $25 addi-
tional
E-mail address:
dgmuller@interramp.com

Fund Exchange

Editor: Paul A. Merriman
1200 Westlake Avenue North
Suite 700
Seattle, WA 98109-3530
Published monthly since 1983
Annual subscription: $125, including
fax alerts
Free subscription on E-mail
Home page: http://
www.paulmerriman.com
E-mail address:
clientservices@paulmerriman.com

Fund Kinetics

Editor: Byron B. McCann
Venture Catalyst, Inc.
2841 23rd Avenue West
Seattle, WA 98199
Published weekly since 1987
Annual subscription: $175
Six-week trial: $49
Weekly fax service: $75 additional
Home page: http://
www.luckydog.com/fundkinetics
E-mail address: fundkinetx@aol.com

Fundline

Editor: David H. Menashe
P.O. Box 663
Woodland Hills, CA 91365
Tel: 818-346-5637
Published monthly since 1968
Annual subscription: $127
Includes weekly hotline
Four-month trial: $47

FundsNet Insight

Editor: Eric M. Kobren
Mutual Fund Investors Association
20 William Street
P.O. Box 9131
Wellesley Hills, MA 02181-9131
Tel: 800-444-6342
Published monthly since 1994
Annual subscription: $17

Graphic Fund Forecaster

Editor: Fred W. Hohn
6 Pioneer Circle
Andover, MA 01810-3413
Tel: 800-532-2322
Published monthly since 1984

Annual subscription: $129
Four-month trial: $30
E-mail address: tysfred@gnn.com

Growth Fund Guide

Editors: Walter J. Rouleau and William
H. Rouleau
Growth Fund Research Building
P.O. Box 6600
Rapid City, SD 57709-9968
Tel: 800-621-8322
Published monthly since 1968
Annual subscription: $99; two years:
$179
Includes hotline service
Six-month trial: $59

Growth Stocks Report

Editor: Jay Saxena
Vital Information
107 Edinburgh South, Suite 207
Cary, NC 27511
Tel: 800-237-8400
Published monthly since January 1995
Annual subscription: $199
Three-month trial: $59
Includes free weekly fax and E-mail
updates
Home page: http://www.vital-info.com
E-mail: info@vital-info.com

Income Fund Outlook

Editor: Norman G. Fosback
Institute for Econometric Research
2200 S.W. 10th Street
Deerfield Beach, FL 33442
Tel: 800-442-9000
Published monthly since 1981

Annual subscription: $49; two years: $88
Includes weekly hotline reports via telephone, fax, or E-mail
E-mail address: letters@mag.com

InvestTech Mutual Fund Advisor

Editor: James B. Stack
2472 Birch Glen
Whitefish, MT 59937-3349
Tel: 800-955-8500
Published every three weeks since 1986
Annual subscription: $175
Seven-month trial: $99
Web site in the planning stages

Louis Rukeyser's Mutual Funds

Editor: Brian Smith
Financial Services Associates
1101 King Street, Suite 400
Alexandria, VA 22314
Tel: 800-892-9702
Published monthly since 1992
Annual subscription: $48 (introductory rate); two years: $96

Moneyletter

(Formerly: *Donoghue's Moneyletter*)
Editor: Walter Frank
Agora Financial Publishing
1217 St. Paul Street
Baltimore, MD 21202
Tel: 800-433-1528
Published bimonthly since 1979

Morningstar Mutual Funds

Editor: Amy C. Arnott
Morningstar, Inc.
225 West Wacker Drive

Chicago, IL 60606
Tel: 800-876-5005
Published biweekly since 1987
Annual subscription: $425
Three-month trial: $55
One-page fax reports on individual funds: $5
Also eighteen other publications; call for catalog

Mutual Fund Advisor

Editor: Donald H. Rowe
The Wall Street Digest
One Sarasota Tower, Suite 602
Sarasota, FL 34236
Tel: 800-966-7693
Published monthly since 1989
Annual subscription: $150
Available via fax, $49 additional every three months

Mutual Fund Forecaster

Editor: Norman G. Fosback
Institute for Econometric Research
2200 S.W. Tenth Street
Deerfield Beach, FL 33442
Tel: 800-442-9000
Published monthly since 1985
Annual subscription: $49; two years: $88

Mutual Fund Investing

Editor: Jay Schabacker
Phillips Publishing
7811 Montrose Road
Potomac, MD 20854
Tel: 800-777-5005
Published monthly since 1985
Annual subscription: $199
Includes telephone hotline

The Mutual Fund Letter

Editor: Dr. Gerald W. Perritt
12514 Starkey Road
Largo, FL 33773
Tel: 800-326-6941
Published monthly since 1984
Annual subscription: $99
Six-month trial: $59
Home page: http://
www.mutletter.com/
E-mail address: mutletter@aol.com

The Mutual Fund Strategist

Editors: Charlie Hooper and Holly
Hooper
P.O. Box 446
Burlington, VT 05402
Published monthly since 1982
Annual subscription: $149
Three-month trial: $52
Fax hotline: add $69 per year

Mutual Fund Technical Trader

Editor: Stephen Parker
Investment Concepts, Inc.
P.O. Box 4560
Burlington, VT 05406-4560
Tel: 802-864-3128
Published monthly since 1989
Annual subscription: $139; two
years: $250
Home page: http://
www.selectfunds.com

National Trendlines

Editor: Douglas A. Jimerson
National Investment Advisors, Inc.
14001 Berryville Road

North Potomac, MD 20874
Tel: 800-521-1585
Published monthly since January 1986
Annual subscription: $75
Six-month trial: $39

No-Load Fund Analyst

Editor: Ken Gregory
L/G Research, Inc.
4 Orinda Way, Suite 230-D
Orinda, CA 94563
Tel: 800-776-9555
Fax: 510-254-0335
Published monthly since 1987
Annual subscription: $225
Three-month trial: $55

No-Load Fund Investor

Editor: Sheldon Jacobs
P.O. Box 318
Irvington, NY 10533
Tel: 800-252-2042
Published monthly since 1980
Annual subscription: $129
Add $30 for *Handbook for No-Load
Fund Investors*

No-Load Fund Selections and Timing

Editor: Stephen L. McKee
100 N. Central Expressway
Suite 1112
Richardson, TX 75080-5328
Tel: 800-800-6563
Published monthly since 1985
Annual subscription: $180
Three-month trial: $25
Includes telephone hotline

No-Load Fund *X*

Editors: Burton Barry and Janet Brown
235 Montgomery Street
Suite 662
San Francisco, CA 94104
Tel: 800-763-8639
Published monthly since 1976
Annual subscription: $125
Mid month report: $49 additional
Monthly two-page fax service:
add $36

No-Load Portfolios

Editors: W. J. Corney and Pat Goodall
8635 Sahara, Suite 420
The Lakes, NY 89117
Fax: 702-255-1682
Annual subscription: $89

Prudence & Performance

Editor: Dr. Arnold Langsen
The Langsen Group, Inc.
22112 NE 23rd Street
Redmond, WA 98053
Published monthly since 1991
Annual subscription: $125

CHAPTER

SIXTEEN

Planning Your Financial Future: Save Your Money, Watch It Grow, Spend It

A famous economist once proclaimed, "in the long run, we are all dead." Perhaps it's notions such as this that cause many of us to ignore our financial future. Interestingly, the younger we are the less we tend to our future well-being. That's unfortunate, because the young have "the force" with them. The force is the power of compound return. And it stems from time. The longer an investment is left to compound its value (its returns are reinvested to earn additional returns), the more powerful is the force.

A friend of mine commented recently that her grandmother was about to celebrate her one-hundredth birthday. She also commented that her grandmother had an investment portfolio worth about $3 million. Although a portfolio that size is impressive, I got to thinking about how easy it must have been for my friend's grandmother to amass that fortune. If that woman had invested a mere $400 at age twenty-one in an equity portfolio that returned an average of 12 percent a year, that investment would now be worth $3.09 million! No wonder when asked what was man's most powerful invention, Albert Einstein was reported to have responded, "compound interest."

Here are a few more examples of the power of compound return. Invest $22,000 in a tax-deferred account at age twenty-five and you can withdraw $22,000 beginning at age fifty every year for as long as you live. Invest $2,000 in an IRA each year for the next twenty-five years, earn 12 percent, and you can withdraw $35,840 every year forever and never touch the principal. Invest $2,000 in a tax-deferred account for your newborn child and earn an average of 12 percent a year. When your son or daughter turns sixty-five, that investment will be valued at $3.16 million. Even though a 3 percent average annual rate of inflation will reduce the value of the portfolio to $463,000 stated in today's dollars, that's still more money than most of today's sixty-five-year-olds have been able to salt away during their lifetimes.

The message in these examples should be clear. Invest as much as you can, as often as you can, as early as you can, and your financial future will be bright. Think of invested money as rabbits. Breed a pair of rabbits and continue to breed their offspring. After about eight years you and your family can eat rabbit stew every day of the year and you will never run out of rabbits. That's because, left unchecked, rabbit populations grow geometrically. The same is true of investment wealth. If left untouched for many years, it too will grow by geometric proportions.

Table 13 illustrates the future value of $1 invested today for various time periods and rates of return. To find the future worth of an investment made today, merely multiply the amount of that investment by the number given at the intersection of the relevant row and column. For example, suppose that you invest $5,000 in a tax-exempt municipal bond fund that yields an average of 6 percent a year. Suppose further that you reinvest all distributions and allow the investment to grow for twenty-five years. The intersection of the column headed by 6 percent and the row marked twenty-five years contains the number 4.292. Multiply this number by your initial investment ($5,000) and you obtain the value of your investment twenty-five years from today, $21,460. If your mutual fund investment had returned 14 percent per year for twenty-five years, it would be worth 26.461 multiplied by $5,000, or $132,305. Make up a few examples, use table 13 to compute the future value of your investment, and you will see just how easy it is to build an investment fortune.

Once you get the hang of using table 13, graduate to table 14. In Chicago, it is said that some politicians get elected term after term because their constituents vote early and vote often. If you want to obtain your financial goals, you must adopt the political strategy employed in Chicago: Invest early and invest often. Here's how it works.

Suppose that at age twenty-one you begin investing $2,000 at the beginning of each year in a tax-deferred individual retirement account (IRA). If your portfolio of equity mutual funds earns an average of 10 percent a year during the forty years that you make annual contributions, your IRA will have grown in value to $973,700. To determine the value of the IRA, I employed the data in table 14. I located the number at the intersection of the column headed by 10 percent and the row labeled forty years. I then multiplied that number (486.85) by the annual IRA contribution ($2,000) to obtain the account's future value $973,700. Make up a few examples and give table 14 a try. Now you will really see how easy it is to reach your financial goals.

Let's now use tables 13 and 14 in combination to solve some common financial problems. For example, suppose that you want to save and invest regularly to provide sufficient financial resources to send your son or daughter to college. Suppose that your child is now age five and will begin college in thirteen years. Suppose that it now costs $10,000 a year ($40,000 for four years) to attend a state university. Furthermore, suppose that college costs increase at the

TABLE 13.
FUTURE VALUE OF $1

Years	Return Rate									
	5%	6%	7%	8%	9%	10%	12%	14%	15%	16%
1	1.050	1.060	1.070	1.080	1.090	1.100	1.120	1.140	1.150	1.160
2	1.103	1.124	1.145	1.166	1.188	1.210	1.254	1.300	1.323	1.346
3	1.158	1.191	1.225	1.260	1.295	1.331	1.405	1.482	1.521	1.561
4	1.216	1.263	1.311	1.360	1.412	1.464	1.574	1.689	1.749	1.811
5	1.276	1.338	1.403	1.469	1.539	1.611	1.762	1.925	2.011	2.100
6	1.340	1.419	1.501	1.587	1.677	1.772	1.974	2.195	2.313	2.436
7	1.407	1.504	1.606	1.714	1.828	1.949	2.211	2.502	2.660	2.826
8	1.478	1.594	1.718	1.851	1.992	2.144	2.476	2.853	3.059	3.278
9	1.551	1.690	1.839	1.999	2.172	2.358	2.773	3.252	3.518	3.803
10	1.629	1.791	1.967	2.159	2.367	2.594	3.106	3.707	4.046	4.411
11	1.710	1.898	2.105	2.332	2.580	2.853	3.479	4.226	4.652	5.117
12	1.796	2.012	2.252	2.518	2.813	3.138	3.896	4.818	5.350	5.936
13	1.886	2.133	2.410	2.720	3.066	3.452	4.364	5.492	6.153	6.886
14	1.980	2.261	2.579	2.937	3.342	3.798	4.887	6.261	7.076	7.988
15	2.079	2.397	2.759	3.172	3.643	4.177	5.474	7.138	8.137	9.266
16	2.183	2.540	2.952	3.426	3.970	4.595	6.130	8.137	9.358	10.748
17	2.292	2.693	3.159	3.700	4.328	5.055	6.866	9.277	10.761	12.467
18	2.407	2.854	3.380	3.996	4.717	5.560	7.690	10.575	12.375	14.462
19	2.527	3.026	3.617	4.316	5.141	6.116	8.613	12.055	14.231	16.776
20	2.653	3.207	3.870	4.661	5.604	6.728	9.646	13.743	16.366	19.460
21	2.786	3.400	4.141	5.034	6.109	7.400	10.803	15.667	18.821	22.574
22	2.925	3.604	4.430	5.437	6.659	8.140	12.100	17.861	21.644	26.186
23	3.072	3.820	4.741	5.872	7.258	8.954	13.552	20.361	24.891	30.376
24	3.225	4.049	5.072	6.341	7.911	9.850	15.178	23.212	28.625	35.236
25	3.386	4.292	5.427	6.849	8.623	10.834	17.000	26.461	32.918	40.874
26	3.556	4.549	5.807	7.396	9.399	11.918	19.040	30.166	37.856	47.414
27	3.734	4.822	6.214	7.988	10.245	13.110	21.324	34.389	43.535	55.000
28	3.920	5.112	6.649	8.627	11.167	14.421	23.883	39.204	50.065	63.800
29	4.116	5.418	7.114	9.317	12.172	15.863	26.749	44.693	57.575	74.008
30	4.321	5.744	7.612	10.062	13.267	17.449	59.959	50.950	66.211	85.849
40	7.040	10.285	14.974	21.724	31.409	45.259	93.050	188.880	378.720	278.200

TABLE 14.
VALUE OF $1 INVESTED AT THE BEGINNING OF EACH YEAR

Years	Return Rate									
	5%	6%	7%	8%	9%	10%	12%	14%	15%	16%
1	1.050	1.060	1.070	1.080	1.090	1.100	1.120	1.140	1.150	1.160
2	2.153	2.184	2.215	2.246	2.278	2.310	2.374	2.440	2.473	2.506
3	3.310	3.375	3.440	3.506	3.573	3.641	3.779	3.921	3.993	4.067
4	4.526	4.637	4.751	4.867	4.985	5.105	5.323	5.610	5.742	5.877
5	5.802	5.975	6.153	6.336	6.523	6.716	7.115	7.536	7.754	7.978
6	7.142	7.384	7.654	7.923	8.200	8.487	9.089	9.730	10.066	10.413
7	8.549	8.896	9.259	9.636	10.028	10.435	11.299	12.232	12.726	13.240
8	10.026	10.491	10.978	11.487	12.021	12.579	13.775	15.085	15.785	16.518
9	11.577	12.180	12.816	13.486	14.192	14.937	16.548	18.337	19.303	20.321
10	13.206	13.971	14.783	15.645	16.560	17.531	19.654	22.044	23.349	24.732
11	14.917	15.869	16.888	17.977	19.140	20.384	23.133	26.270	28.001	29.850
12	16.713	17.882	19.140	20.495	21.953	23.522	27.029	31.088	33.351	35.786
13	18.598	20.015	21.550	23.214	25.019	26.975	31.392	36.581	39.504	42.672
14	20.578	22.276	24.129	26.152	28.360	30.772	36.279	42.842	46.580	50.659
15	22.657	24.672	26.888	29.324	32.003	34.949	41.753	49.980	54.717	59.925
16	24.840	27.212	29.840	32.750	35.973	39.544	47.883	58.117	64.075	70.673
17	27.132	29.905	32.999	36.450	41.301	44.599	54.749	67.394	74.836	83.140
18	29.539	32.760	36.379	40.446	45.018	50.159	62.439	77.969	87.211	97.603
19	32.066	35.785	39.995	44.762	50.160	56.275	71.052	90.024	101.440	114.370
20	34.719	38.992	44.865	49.422	55.760	63.002	80.698	103.760	117.810	133.840
21	37.505	42.392	49.005	54.456	61.873	70.402	91.502	119.430	136.630	156.410
22	40.430	45.995	52.436	59.893	68.531	78.543	103.600	137.290	158.270	182.600
23	43.502	49.815	57.176	65.764	75.789	87.497	117.150	157.650	183.160	212.970
24	46.727	53.864	62.249	72.105	83.700	97.347	132.330	180.870	211.790	248.210
25	50.113	58.156	67.676	78.954	92.323	108.180	149.330	207.330	244.710	289.080
26	53.669	52.705	73.483	86.350	101.720	120.090	168.370	237.480	282.560	336.500
27	57.402	67.528	79.697	94.338	111.960	133.200	189.690	271.880	326.100	391.500
28	61.322	72.639	86.346	102.960	123.130	147.630	213.580	311.090	376.160	455.300
29	65.438	78.058	93.460	112.280	135.300	163.490	240.330	357.780	434.740	529.310
30	69.76	83.80	101.07	122.34	148.56	180.93	270.29	408.73	500.95	615.16
40	126.83	164.05	213.60	279.77	368.29	486.85	859.14	1530	2045	2738

rate of 5 percent a year during the next thirteen years. How much do you need to save each year to provide for your child's education?

First determine how much money you will need in thirteen years. Since college costs are expected to expand by an average of 5 percent a year, you can obtain an estimate of the amount required for a four-year education by expanding today's requirement ($40,000) by 5 percent compounded for thirteen years. That's right, you can determine this amount with the aid of table 13. Locate the number at the intersection of the column headed by 5 percent and the row labeled thirteen years. Multiply that number (1.886) by today's college cost ($40,000) and you get $75,440. To determine how much you must set aside each year to obtain this amount, use table 14. Determine your target rate of return (say 12 percent). Locate the number at the intersection of this rate of return and thirteen years (31.392). In other words, if you invest $1 each year for thirteen years, you will have a portfolio worth $31.39. To determine how much you need to set aside each year to obtain $75,440, divide it by 31.39. The answer is $2,403, or about $200 a month. Note that if you had begun the college education savings and investment program the day your child was born, your annual savings requirement would have declined to $1,208, or about $100 per month. (To find the answer of this revised plan divide the number located at the intersection of the column headed by 12 percent and the row labeled eighteen years, 62.439, into the estimated cost of a four-year college education, $75,440). See what I mean about investing early and often. Had you begun your investment program in this example five years earlier, your monthly savings requirement would have declined by one-half. As the old song goes, "What a difference a day makes."

Here's another example. Suppose that you are planning for your retirement and determine that you will need a pretax annual income of $60,000 stated in the value of today's dollars. You are planning to retire in thirty years and believe that you can earn 10 percent a year on your investment portfolio. How much will you be required to save each year in a tax-deferred investment program to obtain this goal?

First determine your annual income requirements stated in the value of future dollars. For example, if the rate of inflation averages

3 percent a year during the next thirty years, your annual income requirement grows to $145,620. (Use table 13 to determine the future value of $1 after thirty years, growing at the rate of 3 percent a year, and multiply this number by the required $60,000). If you can earn 10 percent a year on your investment portfolio, you will need a portfolio worth $1.46 million in thirty years. To obtain this number, I divided the annual income requirement by 0.10 (the estimated rate of return). To determine the annual savings needed to build a portfolio this size, use table 14. The intersection of the column headed 10 percent and the row labeled thirty years contains the number 181.94. Divide it into the required portfolio value ($1.46 million), and you get an annual savings requirement of $8,004, or $667 a month.

Make up a few examples using your required time frames and estimated investment returns. Chances are that you are going to get some pretty scary numbers. It may seem that you will never be able to save as much as is required. In fact, I'll bet that some of you will look at the requirements and become depressed. The astronomical savings requirements that some of you might obtain from the arithmetic may even cause you to abandon all hope of ever being able to reach your financial goals. However, don't overlook other financial resources. Remember, if your son or daughter goes to college, financial aid will most likely be available. This will offset some of the savings requirements. Your child may also have to work a few hours a week while in college to defray some of the costs. In other words, don't give up. Instead, begin saving whatever you can today. Squeeze out a few dollars from your current monthly expenditures and set those aside, too. Finally, consider increasing the return potential of your investment portfolio. If a 10 percent return will not do the trick, increase your allocation to aggressive growth mutual funds and boost the return potential by another percentage or two.

If it appears that you are headed for the financial poorhouse when you retire because of your inability to save the required amount each month, you too may be worrying needlessly. Don't forget the contribution to your retirement needs made by Social Security or by a company pension plan. Also, chances are that your living requirements when you retire will not be as high as you assume. Remember, you probably have spent a lifetime acquiring things that you will not need to purchase when you retire. In addition, inflation may not be as large a problem as it initially appears. If you own your own home, for example, expansion in rent or real estate prices, a large component of the Consumer Price Index, will not negatively impact your future living requirements. In fact, if you view your home as a financial asset, inflation will probably increase the value of this asset as you get older. This asset could be used to supply a portion of annual income requirements. The sale of your home and replacement with a smaller dwelling could free up plenty of cash. Perhaps the use of a reverse mortgage (the bank pays you monthly to acquire your home over a long period of time) could make up the annual income shortfall. In other words, don't become discouraged. However, if this section has awakened you to the need to set aside investment dollars regularly, I have succeeded in my goal.

Figure 13 contains a simplified retirement planning worksheet that can be used to estimate the amount of annual savings required to build a retirement portfolio that can be used to supplement retirement income from other sources. Although it is labeled a "Retirement Savings Worksheet," it can be used to estimate savings requirements for other purposes, such as a child's education, the purchase of a vacation home, and so on.

The amounts illustrated in the example are stated in current rather than future dollars. To account for inflation, I have used an after-inflation adjusted return on line 7 to make the adjustments needed. First, estimate the annual income you would need if you retired today (adjusted for outlays that may not be required when you plan to retire). Next, subtract an estimate of annual income that you will receive from other sources when you retire. The difference (line 3) is the income you require from your retirement portfolio. To estimate the size of the portfolio required to produce this income, divide the annual income requirement by the rate of return (expressed as a decimal) you believe that you will be able to earn on your investment portfolio while in retirement. (Note, because of risk considerations, this rate may be less than the rate you plan to earn while accumulating retirement assets.) In this example,

Figure 13

RETIREMENT SAVINGS WORKSHEET

	Example	Your Worksheet
(1) Pretax annual income desired	$80,000	_____
(2) Social Security and pension income	$30,000	_____
(3) Investment income required: Subtract line (2) from line (1)	$50,000	_____
(4) Estimate of retirement portfolio return	8% (0.08)	_____
(5) Investment portfolio required: Divide line (3) by line (4)	$625,000	_____
(6) Number of years until retirement	20	_____
(7) Target annual investment return	10%	_____
(8) Factor obtained from table 14	63.00	_____
(9) Annual savings requirement: Divide line (5) by line (8)	$9,920	_____

I assumed that a conservative portfolio containing equity and bond funds would produce an 8 percent (0.08) return. Dividing $50,000 by 0.80 yields a portfolio value of $625,000.

To determine the annual savings required to produce a portfolio valued at $625,000, determine the number of years until planned retirement (line 6) and the rate of return you plan to earn while accumulating retirement assets. Adjust this target rate for the expected rate of inflation and place on line 7. In this example, I assumed an annual return of 13 percent and reduced this annual rate by 3 percentage points (the expected rate of inflation during the asset accumulation period). Thus, the adjusted annual return (expressed as a real rate of return) becomes 10 percent. Using twenty years and a real rate of 10 percent, locate the appropriate factor using table 14. Divide this factor into the value of the required portfolio to obtain your annual savings requirements, $9,920 in this example.

Although this is a simplified approach to savings planning, remember that the future is highly uncertain. Any financial plan requires making certain assumptions about the future. Since the inputs are only estimates, little is gained by applying sophisticated computerized models to establish a plan that, on the surface, appears to be precise. Although this worksheet is not sophisticated, it contains all the relevant inputs to a sound financial plan—an estimate of what you think you will need when you retire, the value of a portfolio that will meet this requirement, and a schedule of savings that will allow you to reach your goal. If nothing else, this exercise should get you thinking about establishing a savings plan. Remember, however, that savings plans are a lot like dieting. A good plan is not enough. You must have the resolve to carry out that plan to achieve the desired results.

CHAPTER

SEVENTEEN

Investing toward the Twenty-First Century: A Few Surprises in the Offing

I have long recommended investing for the longer term. To some, this means looking a year or two ahead; to me the long run extends at least five to seven years into the future. This belief is based on the fact that financial market cycles can, and do, last for several years. For example, small-cap stocks have both outperformed and underperformed large-cap stocks for periods that have lasted five to ten years. In addition, trends in the relative performance of low Price-Earnings multiple value stocks versus high Price-Earnings multiple earnings momentum stocks have persisted for periods that can stretch for five or more years. Finally, some economic trends can last for a decade or more. For example, the U.S. economy experienced hyperinflation at the consumer level for a period extending from the mid-1960s to the early 1980s. During that period, the Standard & Poor's 500 Index returned a paltry 6.8 percent annually (including the reinvestment of cash dividends)—about 5 percentage points below its long-term historical average return. Investors holding long-term Treasury securities fared even worse. Between the beginning of 1965 and the end of 1981, long-term government bonds returned 2.5 percent a year. And that return was more than erased by a 6.7 percent annual rate of expansion in consumer prices. On the other hand, the returns of "real" assets such as real estate and precious metals soared. To prosper in the financial markets, you must make long-term return projections and chart the course of your asset allocation strategy accordingly. Of course, you must continually tune your allocations to unfolding events and be willing to make changes in your portfolio if your long-run forecasts prove wide of the mark. Like a careful driver, you must have one eye on the road ahead and the other on the horizon. Both views are required if you wish to dodge the potholes in the road while making meaningful progress toward your eventual destination.

In the pages that follow, I present my outlook for the financial markets during the next decade, including specific return forecasts for several asset categories. I freely admit that I do not possess a magic crystal ball. However, by focusing on historical financial asset returns, current trends, and significant economic variables that could affect the financial markets, I believe I can provide guidelines that will increase your odds of achieving investment success.

Forecasting long-term investment returns is not as difficult as it might appear. That's because distortions in short-run returns caused by system "noise" tend to be reduced over time; random events ultimately cancel out one another over long periods. Thus, the negative impact on returns caused by unexpected unfavorable events are offset by the positive forces exerted by unexpected positive events. The result is similar to that obtained by portfolio diversification, where random disturbances may positively affect some assets and negatively affect others. The negatives are canceled out by the positives, and overall volatility is reduced because many assets are held in a single portfolio. As a result, the returns from diversified portfolios are more predictable than the returns from a single asset. Similarly, the predictability of asset-category returns increases as the length of time over which the predictions are being made increases.

TABLE 15.
INVESTMENT RETURNS
(COMPOUND ANNUAL RATES)

Asset Category	1940–1995	1982–1995
Small-Cap Stocks	16.0%	14.2%
Blue-Chip Stocks	11.9	16.4
Long-Term Gov't Bonds	5.2	14.4
Treasury Bills	4.3	6.6
Inflation	4.4	3.6

The U.S. Stock Market: 1997–2005

If you invest in the U.S. stock market, what return will you get over the long run? To find an answer to this all-important question, I turned to data supplied by lbbotson Associates, a Chicago-based investment consulting firm. This firm has assembled investment returns for various categories of assets from 1926 to the current date. Large capitalization stock returns are those generated by a hypothetical portfolio of stocks contained in the Standard & Poor's 500 Index. Between the beginning of 1926 and the end of 1995, the S&P 500 has provided a 10.5 percent average compound annual rate of return. However, this period includes the 1929 stock market crash and the era of the Great Depression. Between October 1929 and February 1933, the value of the S&P 500 tumbled an astounding 81 percent. Thus, one might argue that the historical return during this period understates the actual return potential of a diversified portfolio of blue-chip stocks. When measured over the period 1940 through 1995, the average annual compounded return of the S&P 500 increases to 11.9 percent. Thus, I suspect that the true performance potential of a blue-chip equity portfolio, when viewed over a long period of time, lies somewhere between the two figures (10 percent to 12 percent per year).

Common stock investors garner returns from two sources: capital appreciation and cash dividends. During the last fifty years, per share earnings of the S&P 500 have grown by an average of 7 percent per year; as might be expected, so have share prices. Dividend payments have supplied about 4 percent of the annual portfolio return. Combine these two numbers and you get an 11 percent portfolio return potential. Although this number corresponds to the historical returns generated by the S&P 500 during this century, it too has been constructed from historical data and therefore might also be somewhat skewed.

Here is a third approach to forecasting long-term equity returns. Since the growth in corporate earnings, when taken in aggregate, should parallel the growth in the U.S. economy over long periods of time, one can add the growth in annual real gross domestic product (GDP) to the anticipated rate of inflation to obtain an estimate of nominal economic and corporate earnings growth. For example, during the late 1940s and 1950s, government economic policymakers set 5 percent annually as a target real rate of expansion in the U.S. economy. Add to that a 2 to 3 percent expansion in industrial and consumer prices, and you get a nominal growth rate of between 7 and 8 percent. Add a 4 percent dividend yield to this rate of capital expansion, and you get a potential return on common stocks of between 11 and 12 percent.

Although the three methods yielded nearly identical forecasts of blue-chip stock returns (ranging from 10 to 12 percent annually), the economic outlook for the remainder of the decade indicates that blue-chip stock portfolios may underperform their historical average return for a period extending several years into the future.

Suppose, for example, the U.S. economy expands at a 2.5 percent real annual rate for the remainder of the decade. Suppose further that consumer prices expand at near their current rate—3 percent per year. The sum of these two numbers indicates that the U.S. economy will expand at a 5.5 percent nominal annual rate. Add the dividend yield of the S&P 500 Index (currently about 2 percent) to this total, and you obtain a total annual return potential of 7 to 8 percent. That's a far cry from the 11 percent annual return potential suggested by historical data.

To muddy the waters even more, consider the fact that since the beginning of 1982 the S&P 500 Index has returned more than 16 percent annually. Given that a large number of people made their first-ever investment during the current bull market, I suspect that, if asked, many investors would guess that a diversified portfolio of blue-chip stocks should return 15 percent or more annually, not the 11 percent indicated by history or the 7 to 8 percent suggested by economic analysis. I also suspect that many of today's growth fund investors are going to be very disappointed by the returns offered by the stock market during the next dozen years.

For a host of reasons, whenever equities return substantially more or substantially less than their long-term annual average, the performance streak usually takes a 180-degree turn. For example, between the beginning of 1926 and the end of 1941, the S&P 500 returned an average of 3.0 percent per year. During the subsequent sixteen years (1942 through 1957), this hypothetical portfolio returned an average of 16.2 percent per year. A similar change in fortune occurred for index returns during the ten years 1969 through 1978 (a 3.2 percent average annual return) and the subsequent ten years, 1979 through 1988 (a 16.3 percent average annual return).

A pattern of return reversals can also be found after prolonged periods of stock market overperformance. During the fourteen years from 1943 through 1956, the S&P 500 returned an average of 18.1 percent per year. During the next fourteen years (1957 through 1970), this portfolio's average annual return declined to 8.6 percent. Similarly, during the thirteen-year stretch from 1949 through 1961, the S&P 500 returned an average of 18.3 percent per year. During the next thirteen years, its average annual return skidded to 3.0 percent.

That takes me to the stock market's present run of exceptional luck. Equity investors will eventually have to pay for the exceptional returns the stock market has delivered during the last fourteen years. Payment will be collected by a stock market that ultimately provides returns that are far below average for a period that could stretch for more than a decade. The stock market will fail to deliver not only the 15-plus percent annual returns that many investors have come to expect, but also the 11 percent annual returns suggested by history.

Although no one can say for certain when a period of subpar performance will begin, I suspect that it will begin soon. First, the current run of exceptional performance has lasted more than fourteen years. Rarely has the stock market been able to deliver exceptional returns for a longer period. Second, extended periods of overperformance begin when stocks are selling at below average price-earnings multiples. On the other hand, streaks of underperformance usually begin when price-earnings multiples are near their historic highs, as is the case today. The stock market's current average price-earnings multiple of about seventeen times trailing earnings is around two and one-half points above its long-term average. Third, Federal Reserve Board Chairman Alan Greenspan, in testimony before the House Banking Committee, has suggested that the U.S. economy could grow at a modest nominal annual rate well into the next century. According to the head of the nation's central bank, a real (after inflation) GDP growth rate of between 2.5 percent and 3.0 percent and an annual rate of inflation of between 1 and 2 percent is desirable. If you add these averages together, you obtain a target nominal economic growth rate of 4.3 percent. Add the current S&P 500 dividend yield (2.0 percent) to this rate of growth, and you get a stock market with an annual return potential of slightly more than 6 percent.

Looking ahead to the turn of the century, I believe that a large number of equity investors are going to be disappointed by the performance of their equity portfolios. My analysis indicates that blue- chip stock portfolios will return somewhere between 6 and 9 percent per year during the next dozen years.

Don't Settle for Below-Average Yields

During the last fifteen years, you could have invested in nearly any growth or aggressive growth mutual fund and earned double-digit returns. Falling interest rates and two lengthy economic expansions virtually guaranteed that a diversified portfolio of common stocks would produce handsome returns. However, interest rates are near their thirty-year lows, price-earnings multiples are somewhat rich, and the U.S. economy is nearing capacity. Thus, to earn above-average (or even average) stock market returns, investors will have to become more selective when making their equity fund selections. Funds that specialize in low price-earnings ratio stocks are going to fare better than the S&P 500 Index. Small-cap funds are also appealing. Finally, some industries will fare much better than others during the next decade or so. Included in this group are telecommunications, computer technology (software—not hardware), health care, and energy. When investing in any of these sectors, make your initial purchases after a significant stock market correction, and add to your holdings on future market declines.

The Appeal of Small-Cap Funds

I have demonstrated that a large-cap equity portfolio should produce an average annual return of about 12 percent over lengthy periods of time. Small-firm stocks, because of their greater growth potential, should return even more. While large-firm stocks are capable of growing at a 7 percent annual rate, small-firm stocks can grow at average rates of 10 to 15 percent. Because of the need to reinvest earnings to expand capacity, small-cap stocks pay out a much smaller portion of current earnings in cash dividends than do large-caps. It's not surprising that, on average, small-cap stocks provide about 1 percent annually in dividend yield. Thus, on a total return basis, small-caps should return about 16 percent per year over a long period of time. And, in fact, they have done just that. From the beginning of 1940 through the end of 1995, a portfolio of the entire universe of small-cap stocks returned 16.0 percent compounded annually. This compares to an 11.9 percent average annual return for large-caps during the same period.

Like large-cap stocks, small-caps can overperform and underperform their long-term average for lengthy periods. For example, between the beginning of 1975 and the end of 1983, small-caps returned an average of 33.3 percent per year. But between the beginning of 1984 and the end of 1990, the average annual small-cap return was a disappointing 2.6 percent.

Because small-cap stocks have failed to keep pace with the price appreciation of large-caps in recent years, small-caps are priced more reasonably than large-caps. I believe that the best performance years are still ahead for small-cap stocks. Although I doubt that the average return in this sector will be as high as it was between 1975 and 1984, I believe that during the remainder of this decade small-cap returns should easily double those of large-caps.

Fixed-Income Returns

Although blue-chip stock investors have fared best during the bull market that dates back to 1982, fixed-income investors were treated almost as kindly. Falling interest rates boosted bond prices, and generous yields that were carried over from the inflation years of the 1970s provided fixed-income investors with the best returns in history. Between 1982 and 1995 long-term Treasury securities returned an average of 14.4 percent compounded annually. That's an incredible 8.9 percentage points per year more than their average annual return during the last half-century.

The yield on long-term bonds peaked in early 1981 at 14.2 percent. Since then, yields have drifted lower. The current 7 percent yield has not been seen since 1972. Although bond yields are as low as they have been in more than two decades, they could go even lower. If so, that would boost returns as bond prices rise. How low can long-term interest rates go? The answer depends on the rate of inflation. Although long-term bond yields fluctuate widely, over the long run their yields average about three hundred basis points more than the rate of inflation. That is, they tend to provide a real yield of approximately 3 percent. If the advance in consumer prices averages about 3 percent during the next decade, look for long-term government bond yields to decline to around 6 percent. Should the rate of increase in consumer prices slow to 2 percent, government bond yields could fall to 5 percent.

Ideally, the Federal Reserve would like to eliminate inflation entirely. At a zero rate of inflation, bond yields could fall as low as 3 percent. However, I believe this to be an unrealistic expectation. The chance of bond yields falling to the 3-percent level in our lifetime is remote.

The key to a favorable outlook for inflation and interest rates lies with the Congress and the president. A balanced budget would reduce the demand for goods and services (from the government), reduce the expansion in public debt, and provide the private sector with increased borrowing capacity.

Although both political parties want to bring the federal government budget into balance, they can't agree on a suitable time frame. Furthermore, a balanced budget will require deep cuts in transfer payments such as welfare, Social Security, and Medicare. Balancing the budget in the short term is a difficult, if not impossible, task. Even if the government can eliminate the deficit in seven or eight years, the mountain of federal debt would increase in the meantime. Thus, I believe that the rate of expansion in consumer prices will not be held below a 2-percent annual rate and that the yield on long-term Treasury securities will not fall below 5 percent. And there is always the chance that unforeseen events could reverse the downward course in interest rates. In fact, the probability that interest rates will be higher than they currently are ten years from now is much greater than the probability that rates will be lower.

Even if bond yields dip another one hundred basis points later in this decade, bond returns will not approach those experienced during the last dozen years. Since the annual expense ratios of income funds can clip from fifty to one hundred basis points from the yield of their bond portfolios, income fund investors should fare poorly during the next decade. On average, bond funds will return between 5 and 7 percent annually. And given the erosion in principal that results from an unexpected rise in interest rates, I believe that current yields do not compensate investors for the risks they are being asked to assume.

If you must invest in bond funds, look for funds with short durations or limited average maturities. Risks are dramatically reduced for portfolios with average maturities of five years or less. And given the relatively high returns being offered by taxable money market funds, I believe that these vehicles offer the most favorable risk/return trade-off.

Foreign Stocks Could Provide Pleasant Surprises

Take some time to list the economic, financial, political, and social problems around the world, and you probably would never send one cent of your investment capital beyond the U.S. border. The world is a big place. Look long enough and you will always find significant problems. The flip side, however, is that you will find profit opportunities as well.

Foreign markets have become too large and too important to ignore. Currently, stocks traded in the United States make up less than one-third of the aggregate equity capitalization of the world's publicly traded companies. And the share of market for publicly traded common stocks outside U.S. borders will continue to expand as more economies adopt a capitalist system in an effort to boost productivity, wealth, and social well-being. If you are seeking above-average growth opportunities, you must direct capital to those economies that are expanding rapidly.

Developed economies such as the United States, Japan, and western Europe are projected to grow at a real rate of about 3 percent during the next decade. On the other hand, real annual growth in developing economies is expected to top 5 percent. In other words, the growth potential for equities in developing countries is about twice that of U.S. equities.

Although the reward potential in foreign stock markets is high, so are the risks. Currency and political risk can be added to the risks faced by investors in the stocks of companies domiciled in the United States. Because the returns of foreign stocks are less than perfectly correlated with the returns from U.S. stocks, a portfolio containing cross-border equity investments actually possesses less risk than a portfolio consisting exclusively of domestic stocks.

Conservative, growth-oriented investors should consider investing in diversified international equity funds. More venturesome investors should include an emerging-markets fund in their portfolios. However, a long-term orientation is required. The recent Mexican financial debacle underscores the short-term risk in investing in emerging-markets stocks. It also underscores the need to diversify rather than commit investments to a single country.

I expect diversified emerging-markets investments to produce average annual returns in excess of 20 percent during the next decade. My optimism stems from a combination of the relatively poor performance of foreign stocks in recent years and the growing interest of sophisticated investors in emerging markets.

The best time to invest in any asset category is not after prices have risen rapidly, but after they have taken a nasty tumble. In Europe, stocks have underperformed since the collapse of the Berlin Wall in 1989. In the late 1980s, euphoria over a united Europe and pent-up demand by Eastern bloc nations drove European stocks well beyond reasonable values.

Japanese stocks continue to be mired in a six-year bear market, and a looming banking crisis threatens to send prices even lower. Finally, the devaluation of the Mexican peso cut Mexican stock prices by nearly half. Some South American markets took their cue from Mexico and tumbled shortly thereafter. As a result, foreign stocks are much more reasonably priced now than they were a few years ago.

Although foreign stocks have languished in recent years, a flood of new money is being invested outside U.S. borders. For example, foreign equity investment has risen nearly tenfold—to a yearly average of almost $100 billion in the early 1990s from about $10 billion a year in the early 1980s. Even so, large corporate pension funds are underinvested in foreign stocks. Today, U.S. corporate pension funds have only about 8 percent of their $2 trillion in assets invested in foreign markets, with about 20 percent of that amount in emerging markets. By the turn of the century, a number of experts predict, these pension funds will have about 15 to 20 percent of their assets invested internationally. And 20 percent of this amount is expected to be allocated to emerging markets. That would provide a $200 billion capital injection into developing markets. In addition, emerging-markets funds have only about 1 percent of worldwide fund assets under management today, but this is expected to rise to above 3 percent by the turn of the century, for a total of more than $250 billion.

The important point is that emerging markets are very small. An additional $10 billion or $20 billion added to any particular market would cause stock prices to soar. And that was exactly what happened in 1993 and during most of 1994. To profit handsomely from international investments, you must be on board before the stampede begins, and I believe the time is now.

Precious Metals

I have never been a gold bug, and considering what has happened to the price of gold during the last fifteen years, I'm glad I wasn't. Beginning at a price of about $200 an ounce, when it became legal for Americans to speculate in the gold market in 1972, the price of gold soared to near $800 an ounce in early 1980 when the Hunt brothers were attempting to corner the silver market and the fear of systemic inflation was spreading across the country. Gold collapsed shortly thereafter, and the price has wandered between $300 and $400 an ounce since then.

Although economic and financial fears (or the lack of them) drive the price of gold in the short run, over the long run, the price of gold is closely tied to the rate of inflation. In the 1930s, gold speculation in the United States was banned, and the price of gold was pegged at $35 an ounce. During the next sixty years, consumer prices expanded at about a 4 percent average annual rate. Inflate the price of an ounce of gold at this rate for six decades and you obtain a price of $390 an ounce, which is very close to the current world market price.

With the annual rate of inflation in the United States below 3 percent, the prospects for rapid appreciation in the price of gold are slim. However, I believe that gold prices will rise by more than the rate of inflation in the United States during the next decade. First, inflation in developing nations is more severe than in the United States. Thus, there is a greater need for an inflation hedge abroad than here at home. In addition, the rate of wealth expansion in many countries is far greater than in the United States. Thus you can expect the demand for gold to expand as a result of rapid economic growth in such developing regions as Asia and Latin America.

Some well-known gold bugs expect an ounce of gold to trade above $800 before the turn of the century, but I believe this is pure fantasy. However, if the price of gold rises above $400 an ounce, a substantial resistance area will have been broken, and the price of gold could rise another $100 an ounce during a very short time. Since the expansion in gold-mining stock prices tends to rise by 2 to 3 times the percentage increase in the price of gold bullion, a gold fund investment could produce returns of 50 percent to 75 percent shortly after this important resistance level is broken.

The most important characteristic of precious metals is that their returns tend to be negatively correlated with those of stocks and bonds. Thus, a small allocation to a diversified gold fund can significantly reduce portfolio volatility. This is especially important to fixed-income investors, since the inflation pressures that drive bond prices downward also drive gold prices upward.

My advice to long-term-oriented investors, given the benign inflation outlook in the United States, is to avoid gold funds. Investors who need to hedge their bond or stock portfolios should allocate no more than 3 percent to 5 percent of assets to gold funds.

Forecast Highlights

U.S. economy. During the 1950s and 1960s, the real rate of domestic economic growth averaged about 3.5 percent per year. In fact, the Commission on Money and Credit in the early 1950s established a 4 percent real annual economic growth rate as a viable target. During the last twenty-five years, the secular rate of economic growth in the United States has steadily declined. At present, the Fed has targeted a 2.5 percent annual expansion in real GDP as an optimal rate of economic expansion. Probabilities favor a continuation of real GDP expansion at a 2.5 percent average annual rate through the year 2000.

The number-one priority on the Federal Reserve's list of concerns is inflation. During the past few years, the Consumer Price Index has expanded at below 3 percent annually. And economists estimate that the official rate of inflation is overstated by as much as one hundred basis points. In short, the Fed has largely achieved its goal of eliminating inflation at the consumer level. Will the benign inflation-rate environment continue? Absent external shocks, I believe that inflation will remain in check during the remainder of the decade.

Bond market. To obtain an estimate of long-term government bond yields, add three hundred basis points to the expected rate of inflation. Should the annual rate of inflation hover around 2 percent, look for government bond yields to dip to 5 percent during this decade. Short-term Treasury bills usually mirror the rate of inflation. Thus, my optimistic inflation forecast indicates that short-term bond yields could fall into the 3 to 4 percent range.

Add about two hundred basis points to the long-term Treasury bond yield to obtain the yield on high-grade corporate bonds (that is, 7.0 to 7.5 percent). Trim the corporate bond yield by about one-third to get an estimate of long-term municipal bond yields (that is, about 5 percent).

Although a one-hundred-basis-point dip in interest rates is expected in the long-term bond market, this is a very optimistic forecast that could easily be derailed by unforeseen events. Keep the maturities of your bond portfolios on the short side, and invest in only low-cost bond funds.

U.S. stock market. I have argued that returns on blue-chip stocks will be muted during the remainder of the decade, because of modest current dividend yields and a lower rate of corporate earnings expansion. However, small-cap stock investors should prosper in an economy marked by a stable dollar, low inflation, and the absence of an overly restrictive monetary policy.

Foreign stocks. Although I expect international markets to provide double-digit annual returns, the best returns during the remainder of this decade will come from emerging markets. Volatility in these markets will be high, but investors oriented toward the long term should earn average returns that could top 20 percent annually well into the twenty-first century.

Precious metals. The price of gold in the short run is driven by social unrest, political instability, and/or hyperinflation. My optimistic inflation forecast along with the trends toward more friendly relations with Russia, China, and Korea indicate that gold bullion will continue to be a subpar investment performer. However, in the long run, the price of gold bullion should rise due to expanding demand, especially in so-called developing nations.

Special situations. Long-term-oriented investors should continue to benefit from trends that have been ongoing in certain industries for more than a decade. In the United States, these industries include computer software, technology, telecommunications, health care, and energy.

CHAPTER EIGHTEEN

Knowledge Is Power: Some Other Good Investment Books to Read

The last time I stopped by my neighborhood Barnes & Noble bookstore, I noticed more than three dozen books that focused specifically on mutual fund investing. Some of these books were written by financial reporters, others by editors of mutual fund advisory newsletters, and (surprisingly) quite a few by people who have no professional financial background whatsoever. These three dozen–plus books were sprinkled among more than two hundred titles crammed into a relatively small investment section of the store's business bookshelf.

Thank goodness prime retail space doesn't come cheap, otherwise browsers might be subject to miles of how-to investment books. The proliferation of investment books is understandable. The stock and bond markets, as of this writing, are in the midst of one of the strongest bull markets of all times. In August 1982, the Dow Jones Industrial Average dipped as low as 776. By October 1996, it had risen beyond 6,000, a gain of more than 5,000 points! During that period, average-risk common stock portfolios returned an average of more than 15 percent per year. A $140,000 investment in an average-performing equity mutual fund made in late 1982 would have been worth more than $1 million by the fall of 1996. In other words, there are plenty of investors out there who think they are much smarter than they really are. No doubt, many of today's investment book authors have confused brains with a bull market.

Decades ago, the surgeon general required tobacco companies to put warning labels on their products—"Warning: Cigarette smoking may be dangerous to your health." It's too bad the secretary of the Treasury didn't require that a warning be placed on the vast majority of investment books—"Warning: The contents of this product may be dangerous to your financial well-being." If I had a "get rich quick" scheme, I wouldn't give away my secret, and most likely no one else would either. Books titled *How I Turned Pocket Change into $1 Million* and *Wealth Without Work* should be banned from booksellers' investment shelves and relegated to the current fiction shelves instead.

Make no mistake about it, most of us who write investment books do so because we seek the fame or have a product to promote, or we do it simply for the money. However, every once in a while someone writes a book that needs to be written. These authors are straight shooters who have plenty to say and convey much to be heeded. These books contain lessons learned by years of experience, easy-to-read explanations of sophisticated research studies, or descriptions of periods of financial upheaval that, because of the cyclical nature of the financial markets, are destined to be heaped upon us when we least expect them.

Here's a list of my favorite investment books. Some have come to market recently, others were written more than a decade ago, and one was first published in 1841. They all have one thing in common, however—they all contain stuff worth knowing.

Bogle on Mutual Funds
John C. Bogle
Dell Publishing (1994)
Paperback: 320 pages, $13.95

Mr. Bogle is the founder and chairman of the Vanguard Group of mutual funds, the second largest mutual fund family in the world and the largest offering no-load-only funds to investors. The premise of this book is that investment outcomes are a combination of potential returns, underlying risks, and prevailing costs. The value in this book lies not so much in what Mr. Bogle tells you to do, but in his advice about what you shouldn't do. Don't believe any "free lunch" offers, don't forget about investment risk when you are promised large investment rewards, avoid the excessive costs of investing, and avoid the urges to jump in and out of the market and from fund to fund. Although he continually relates his fondness for Vanguard mutual funds, there is much here that can be applied to investing in well-managed funds offered by other fund families.

Extraordinary Popular Delusions and the Madness of Crowds
Joseph de la Vega
John Wiley and Sons (1966)
Paperback: 214 pages, $19.95

If you want to understand the stock market's frequently erratic behavior, spend a few hours with this book. Although the tales related between the covers occurred three centuries ago, when you are through reading the book you will see how the Dow Jones Industrial Average could plunge more than five hundred points in a single day and how Japanese stocks could lose 90 percent of their value over a half-decade. Although stock markets tend to be rational arenas, at times fear and greed send the prices of their merchandise zigging and zagging far from a true course. If you want an insight to the future, study the past. Although the merchandise may differ and the buyers and sellers described in this book may be centuries removed from today's technology-dependent trading pits, there are many lessons to be learned. If you are in awe of the five-thousand-point rise the Dow Jones Industrial Average has experienced during the last decade-and-a-half and are currently fully invested to capture the next ten-thousand-point rise, you too may have become subject to one of the stock market's biggest motivators. If you haven't bought a stock since the crash of 1987, you most likely have succumbed to its other driving force.

Funding Your Future
Jonathan Clements
Warner Books (1993)
Paperback: 224 pages

Written by an award-winning columnist from the *Wall Street Journal*, this book is packed with tips on how to successfully manage your mutual fund portfolio. Unlike a number of how-to books that are filled with some guru's flaky ideas about making money in mutual funds, this book dispenses advice based on years of solid academic and professional research. Whether you are young or old, conservative or aggressive, a novice mutual fund investor or an old hand, Jonathan Clements tells you how to build and manage a mutual fund portfolio to meet your goals and objectives. His advice is right on the mark, and it is delivered in jargon-free language that is informative, interesting, and even entertaining. Implement the strategies given in this book and you will no doubt become more wealthy from the experience.

The Complete Idiot's Guide to Making Money with Mutual Funds
Alan Lavine and Gail Liberman
Alpha Books (1995)
Paperback: 297 pages, $16.95

This husband-and-wife team relies on their wealth of experience in the financial arena. He has been a long-time financial columnist with the *Boston Herald* and she has spent a couple of decades as a financial journalist and editor of the *Bank Rate Monitor*. Like other "Idiot's Guides," the book is packed with sidebars that alone are worth its price. In between sidebars, however, you will find a wealth of information about mutual funds and the mutual fund industry. Although I prefer the term novice over idiot, this book is mandatory reading for anyone who is planning to open a mutual fund shareholder account. The authors explain in plain language the types of funds available, their potential returns and risks, and the rudiments of portfolio management.

Investment Policy: Winning the Losers Game
Charles D. Ellis
Irwin Professional Publishing (second edition, 1993)
Hardcover: 94 pages, $35.00

This book illustrates that good things often come in small packages. At thirty-seven cents per page, this is one of the most expensive investment books you will find. However, it will most likely save you tens of thousands of dollars over an investment lifetime. Although few believe it, investing is a loser's game. To win, you must lose less than everyone else, and the way to do that is to establish a correct investment policy, locate investments that are consistent with that policy, and employ low-cost strategies that will make you more successful than others. This short book, written by an investment professional and former editor of *The Financial Analysts Journal*, is a consumers guide to investment management designed to meet the needs of the many individual investors who entrust their family savings to mutual funds, trust companies, and investment advisers. It does not teach you how to invest, but how to become a successful investor.

Mutual Funds Made Easy
Gerald W. Perritt
Dearborn Financial Publishing (1995)
Paperback: 201 pages, $9.95

Written by the author of this book, *Mutual Funds Made Easy* presents a guided tour through the maze of mutual fund investing. Although written for the novice investor, the book contains plenty of tips for seasoned investors as well. Revealed are tried-and-true investment strategies that will get your investment program rolling on a high-return course. Learn how to reduce the costs and avoid the mistakes that can cost you even more; how to build a weather-resistant group of funds that stands up to any market conditions; how to pay for your children's education, contribute to your own IRA and fund your goals, and obtain the tools to identify what types of funds you need to include in your portfolio; and how many funds to own and when to sell. This book gives you all the tools to make your investment decisions with confidence.

The New Money Masters
John Train
HarperBusiness (1989)
Paperback: 385 pages, $14.00

Sixteen years ago, John Train dazzled readers with his national bestseller *The Money Masters*, which described the winning investment strategies of nine great investors (Grahm, Buffett, Templeton, T. Rowe Price, among others). This book was must reading (and still is) for anyone with control over an investment portfolio. This sequel focuses on today's successful investors, most of whom either have managed or currently do manage billions of dollars of mutual fund assets. The reader gets insights to the techniques that have propelled eight more "money masters" to the top of the heap. Included are such superstars as Soros, Lynch, Rogers, Neff, and Wanger. When you are finished with this book, pick up a copy of *The Money Masters*. No matter how good an investor you believe you are, the insights in these two books will make you better.

A Random Walk down Wall Street
Burton G. Malkiel
W.W. Norton and Company (1996)
Paperback: 528 pages, $15.95

If you haven't read this book, you are probably not getting nearly enough out of your investment experience. It has been mandatory reading for every financial analyst I have ever hired. This former securities analyst, member of the President's Council of Economic Advisors, and dean of the Yale School of Organization and Management takes the reader through more than two decades of academic research concerning the securities markets. In a most humorous fashion, he debunks nearly every myth surrounding Wall Street and security trading. He discusses specific rules and investment opportunities for investors at every level. This is not a "get rich quick" book. It is, however, a book that will most assuredly keep you from getting your pocket picked by slick salespeople and stock market operators.

Terry Savage's New Money Strategies for the 90s
Terry Savage
HarperBusiness (1994)
Paperback: 560 pages, $14.00

This is a no-nonsense guide to financial security. If you ever opened a savings account, obtained a loan, bought a mutual fund, invested in stocks and bonds, or shopped for insurance, this book is meant for you. A registered investment adviser, columnist for the *Chicago Sun Times*, and veteran CBS financial reporter, Ms. Savage explores all facets of the investment world. The premise is that people don't invest, they consume investment products. What are the best deals? What should you avoid? How should you allocate your money among competing financial products? These are the broad topics covered in this A-to-Z consumers guide. The book makes an excellent gift for young adults who are beginning their wealth-building years and is a fact-filled reference guide for the rest of us.

Section II

Mutual Fund
Financial Statistics

Mutual Fund Financial Statistics

This section contains a wealth of financial statistics for various categories of mutual funds. Some of the funds in the tables are also described in detail in Section III, "The 300 Best Mutual Funds in America." The purpose of this section is to acquaint investors with the various types of funds currently available and to allow investors to compare the operations of like-kind funds.

A number of funds contained in these tables are capable of producing handsome returns even though they are not included on my "Best 300 Funds" list. For example, the index funds listed in table 21 possess a number of favorable attributes: They have low turnover ratios and low expense ratios, and they are highly diversified. Because these funds are "unmanaged" and seek to replicate some financial market index, they were excluded from my list of the 300 best. Similarly, income-oriented investors should give consideration to the bond funds listed in table 33. These are the lowest-cost bond funds you will find anywhere. Because costs are low, these funds have produced some of the best long-term returns in their respective category. I have also included a list of top-rated funds that are currently not selling shares to new investors. If you are not currently a shareholder in any of these funds, you cannot buy their shares. However, all are top-notch funds, and you may wish to consider making an investment in these funds if they open their doors and begin to sell shares to the public once again.

If you currently hold the shares of any of the funds on these lists, you may wish to compare the costs and returns of your fund with others that possess similar investment objectives. If your current fund comes up short on the comparisons, you may wish to upgrade your investment to another fund with more favorable prospects.

CHAPTER

NINETEEN

America's 50 Largest Taxable Money Market Funds

Money market mutual funds invest in debt securities with very short maturities. Some money market funds confine their portfolios to Treasury securities. Others invest in private debt securities, which include commercial paper (short-term corporate unsecured IOUs), bank certificates of deposit, bankers' acceptances (which arise from international trade transactions), and other short-term debt.

Securities and Exchange Commission (SEC) regulations restrict both types of securities that money market funds can invest in and the composition of their portfolios. Like other mutual funds, a money market fund cannot invest more than 5 percent of its assets in a single company or more than 25 percent in a single industry. In addition, SEC regulations prohibit a money market fund from investing in commercial paper below the two top grates, securities rated A1 and A2 by Standard & Poor's or P1 and P2 by Moody's. Also, money market funds are prohibited from investing in debt with a maturity of more than one year or from holding a dollar-weighted average portfolio maturity of more than ninety days. In mid-1994, the SEC toughened its rules regarding derivative investments by requiring that money market funds avoid investment in floating-rate securities if their prices can drop below their par values.

Money market funds are the least risky of all mutual funds. Those that invest in Treasury bills are nearly free of risk altogether. Some of these funds, however, introduce an element of risk by investing some of their capital in repurchase agreements. While money fund investors have never lost one dime of their assets, money funds that invest in private debt subject their shareholders to default risk. In fact, a handful of money market funds suffered losses when some companies defaulted on their commercial paper a few years ago. However, the funds' advisers assumed these losses, and money fund shareholders were left whole.

The popularity of money market funds among savers is understandable. These funds generally pay a higher rate of interest than bank savings accounts, they provide shareholders with free checking accounts, and they extend wire transfer privileges.

Money market fund share prices are fixed at $1. Interest income earned is credited to shareholder accounts daily and reinvested in additional fund shares. While share price is fixed, interest rates fluctuate daily. Money funds report their current yields two ways, an annualized seven-day average yield and an annualized seven-day compound yield. At a particular point in time, yields among money funds will vary. The differences arise because of differences in portfolio composition, average maturities, and fund expenses.

TABLE 16.
THE 50 LARGEST TAXABLE MONEY MARKET FUNDS

Fund	Total Assets ($Bil)	Telephone
Alex Brown Cash Reserves Prime	2.4	1-800-767-3524
Alliance Capital Reserves	5.3	1-800-221-5672
Alliance Government Reserves	3.4	1-800-221-5672
Alliance MMF Prime	2.7	1-800-221-5672
Benchmark Diversified Assets	3.1	1-800-595-9111
Capital Preservation Fund	3.0	1-800-472-3389
Cash Equivalent Fund/MM Portfolio	2.8	1-800-621-1048
Cash Mgmt Trust of America	3.3	1-800-621-1048
Centennial Money Market Trust	7.7	1-800-525-7048
Daily Cash Accumulation Fund	3.6	1-800-525-7048
Daily Passport Cash Trust	4.3	1-800-752-2347
Dean Witter Active Assets	7.9	1-800-869-3863
Dean Witter Liquid Assets	11.6	1-800-869-3863
Dreyfus Cash Mgt. Plus "A"	6.4	1-800-782-6620
Dreyfus Cash Mgt. "A"	2.9	1-800-782-6620
Dreyfus Government Cash Mgt. "A"	4.4	1-800-782-6620
Dreyfus Liquid Assets	4.7	1-800-782-6620
Dreyfus Treasury Prime Cash Mgt. "A"	3.2	1-800-782-6620
Dreyfus World-Wide Dollar	2.0	1-800-782-6620
Evergreen US Treasury MMP "A"	2.6	1-800-326-3241
Federated Trust US Treasury	2.5	1-800-245-0242
Fidelity Cash Reserves	20.6	1-800-752-2347
Fidelity Daily MF	2.6	1-800-752-2347
Fidelity MMT Retirement	5.5	1-800-752-2347
Fidelity MMT Retirement Government	2.6	1-800-752-2347

continues

Fund	Total Assets ($Bil)	Telephone
Fidelity Spartan MMF	8.9	1-800-752-2347
Great Hall Prime MMF	2.7	1-800-333-0813
IDS Cash Mgt Fund	2.9	1-800-328-8300
Kemper MMF	4.3	1-800-621-1048
Lehman Brothers Prime	2.1	1-800-451-2010
Merrill Lynch CMA Money Fund	37.7	1-800-225-1576
Merrill Lynch Ready Assets	7.3	1-800-225-1576
Merrill Lynch Retirement Reserve	9.4	1-800-225-1576
Nations Prime Fund Trust A	2.4	1-800-321-7854
Pain Webber Cash Fund	5.1	1-800-647-1568
Pain Webber RMA MM Port	7.8	1-800-647-1568
Paine Webber Retirement MF	3.6	1-800-647-1568
Prudential Money Market Assets	7.5	1-800-225-1852
Prudential Command MF	5.7	1-800-225-1852
Putnam Money Market A	2.1	1-800-225-1581
Schwab Money Market Fund	16.9	1-800-266-5623
Schwab Value Advantage	9.7	1-800-266-5623
Seven Seas Series MMF "A"	3.9	1-800-227-4193
Smith Barney Cash Portfolio A	26.0	1-800-221-8806
Smith Barney Government Portfolio A	4.3	1-800-221-8806
Stagecoach MMF	3.9	1-800-338-2550
T. Rowe Price Prime Reserve	4.3	1-800-225-5132
Vanguard MMR Federal Portfolio	3.0	1-800-635-1511
Vanguard MMR Prime	21.6	1-800-635-1511
Vanguard MMR Treasury Portfolio	2.9	1-800-635-1511

CHAPTER

TWENTY

The 25 Largest Tax-Free Money Market Funds

Like taxable money market funds, tax-exempt money market funds have a share price fixed at $1, pay interest daily, and reinvest the interest in additional fund shares. However, there the similarity with taxable money market funds ends. Tax-exempt funds do not participate in the "money market," but invest in a combination of short-term municipal securities and put bonds, the latter of which are long-term municipal bonds. Put-bond holders have the option to sell (put) these bonds to other investors at a stated price within a short period of time. Because of the popularity of tax-exempt money market funds, the demand for short-term municipal securities far outstripped supply. Generally, municipalities raise capital by issuing long-term bonds to finance fixed assets such as schools, water delivery systems, and sewage treatment plants. Thus, the overwhelming proportion of municipal debt consists of long-term bonds rather than short-term notes. The put bond (a derivative security) was created to accommodate the demand for short-term paper by tax-exempt money market funds.

Interest earned on tax-exempt money market funds is exempt from federal taxes and from state taxes on interest earned by shareholders residing in the same state as the bond issuers. Because of the tax-exempt feature of these funds, their yields are less than those offered by taxable money funds. To convert the yield offered by tax-exempts to a fully taxable yield, divide the yield on the tax-exempt security by one minus your marginal tax rate. For example, if a tax-exempt money fund's yield is 4 percent and your marginal tax rate is 28 percent, divide 4 percent by 0.72 to obtain a taxable equivalent yield, 5.56 percent. Compare this adjusted rate to the current yield on taxable money funds. If the money fund yield is greater than this adjusted rate, you will be money ahead by investing in the taxable fund rather than the tax-exempt fund.

TABLE 17.
THE 25 LARGEST TAX-EXEMPT MONEY FUNDS

Fund	Total Assets ($Bil)	Telephone
Alliance Muni Trust General	1.2	1-800-221-5672
CMA California Municipal MF	1.5	1-800-225-1576
CMA New York Municipal MF	1.1	1-800-225-1576
CMA Tax-Exempt MF	7.8	1-800-225-1576
Calvert Tax-Free Reserves 0 Shares	1.6	1-800-368-2745
Centennial Tax-Exempt Trust	1.5	1-800-525-7048
Dean Witter Active Assets Tax-Free	1.6	1-800-869-3863
Dreyfus Tax-Exempt Cash Mgt. A	1.4	1-800-782-6620
Fidelity Municipal MMF	3.7	1-800-752-2347
Fidelity Spartan California Muni MMF	1.4	1-800-752-2347
Fidelity Spartan Municipal MF	2.5	1-800-752-2347
Nations Tax-Exempt Fund A	1.0	1-800-321-7854
Northern Municipal MMF	1.2	1-800-595-9111
Pain Webber RMA Tax-Free	2.0	1-800-647-1568
Prudential Command Tax-Free Fund	1.2	1-800-225-1852
Schwab California Tax-Exempt Sweep Shares	1.7	1-800-266-5623
Schwab Tax-Exempt Sweep	3.7	1-800-266-5623
Smith Barney Muni Fund CA	1.3	1-800-221-8806
Smith Barney Municipal	5.3	1-800-221-8806
Stagecoach CA Tax-Free MMF	1.2	1-800-338-2550
Strong Municipal MMF	1.7	1-800-368-3863
USAA Tax-Exempt MMF	1.5	1-800-382-8722
Vanguard CA Tax-Free MMP	1.4	1-800-635-1511
Vanguard Muni Bond	4.8	1-800-635-1511
Vanguard PA Tax-Free	1.3	1-800-635-1511

CHAPTER TWENTY-ONE

The Largest Equity Funds You Can Find

The long bull stock market has created a love affair between investors and equity mutual funds. From a modest $161 million in 1986, total equity fund assets topped $1.3 trillion in 1996. By year-end 1995, equity funds made up 45 percent of industry assets, double the figure recorded ten years earlier. The flood of money into equity funds has caused a large number of popular funds to grow to gigantic proportions. There are now more than 270 equity funds whose assets have swollen beyond $1 billion. The largest of them all, the once-mighty Fidelity Magellan Fund, has more than $50 billion in investment assets. That's a lot of money. It's enough to buy 1.7 million Cadillac automobiles or all the football franchises in the National Football League (and still have $42 billion left over to spend acquiring all the other professional sports franchises in America). Or, to view it from another perspective, its assets are more than six times the gross national product of Liechtenstein.

If you invest in giant equity funds, you obtain a well-diversified portfolio because the managers of these funds are forced to spread the funds' money around. A mutual fund is prohibited from owning more than 10 percent of the shares of stock of any one company. For example, it can invest only $10 million in the common stock of a $100 million equity cap firm. To invest $1 billion in companies of this size, the fund would have to invest in at least one hundred different companies. Thus, you obtain a considerable degree of safety when you invest in a multibillion dollar equity mutual fund. Furthermore, since fund operating expenses are shared by so many investors, the expense ratios of giant funds tend to be lower than those of funds that have a "mere" hundred million or so to invest.

On the other hand, there are a number of downsides to investing in multibillion dollar funds. First, you can't beat the market if you own it, and large funds are forced to invest in so many companies that their portfolios' characteristics tend to mirror those of the stock market as a whole. (At one point, for example, Fidelity Magellan held the common stocks of more than fourteen hundred different companies.) If you want to own the market, the simplest way is to buy an index fund. Second, large funds are forced to invest in only large companies that can accommodate a large volume of trading. They must pass on investments in smaller, more rapidly growing companies that have the potential of providing greater long-run returns. Finally, giant funds don't have the flexibility of smaller funds. It takes longer to build meaningful positions in favored companies and a lot of time to liquidate those positions. It's like an elephant attempting to squash a bothersome mouse. The elephant knows it can easily trample the mouse, but it has to catch the little creature first.

The accompanying table lists the twenty-five largest domestic equity funds in the industry. To make the list, a fund has to possess at least $9 billion in total assets. In aggregate, these twenty-five funds have $402 billion in total assets, representing approximately 31 percent of the $1.3 trillion invested in all equity funds.

TABLE 18. THE WORLD'S LARGEST EQUITY FUNDS

Fund	Total Assets ($Bil)	Year Began	Sales Charges %	Expense Ratio %	Turnover Ratio %
Fidelity Magellan	54	1963	3.00%	0.95%	155%
Investment Company of America	28	1934	5.75%	0.60%	7%
Vanguard Index 500	24	1976	NL	0.20%	6%
Washington Mutual Investors	22	1952	5.75%	0.66%	23%
Fidelity Contrafund	20	1967	3.00%	0.90%	199%
Fidelity Growth & Income	20	1985	NL	0.75%	41%
20th Century Ultra Investors	17	1981	NL	1.00%	87%
Fidelity Puritan	17	1947	NL	0.74%	139%
Income Fund of America	15	1973	5.75%	0.65%	26%
Vanguard Windsor	15	1958	NL	0.45%	38%
Euro Pacific Growth	14	1984	5.75%	0.95%	22%
Janus Fund	14	1970	NL	0.87%	118%
Fidelity Equity Income II	14	1990	NL	0.74%	47%
Vanguard Wellington	14	1929	NL	0.33%	24%
Vanguard Windsor II	13	1985	NL	0.40%	30%
Fidelity Equity-Income	12	1966	NL	0.68%	40%
Dean Witter Dividend Growth	11	1981	5.00%	1.31%	10%
Fidelity Asset Manager	11	1988	NL	0.98%	114%
New Perspective	11	1973	5.75%	0.83%	22%
Putnam Fund for Growth & Income	10	1957	5.75%	0.89%	58%
AIM Constellation A	10	1976	5.50%	1.16%	45%
Growth Fund of America	9	1973	5.75%	0.75%	27%
Templeton Foreign I	9	1982	5.75%	1.15%	22%
Fidelity Growth Company	9	1983	3.00%	0.94%	77%
Fidelity Blue Chip Growth	9	1987	3.00%	0.98%	206%

Average Annual Returns			Minimum Investment		Portfolio Manager	Since	Telephone
1 Year %	3 Year %	5 Year %	Initial $	Subsequent $			
3.0%	11.9%	15.1%	2,500	250	Bob Stansky	1996	1-800-544-0202
17.1%	14.4%	13.2%	250	50	Team Mgt.	NA	1-800-421-0180
20.2%	17.3%	15.1%	3,000	100	George Sauter	1987	1-800-662-7447
20.2%	16.4%	15.5%	250	50	Team Mgt.	NA	1-800-421-0180
14.2%	15.0%	18.3%	2,500	250	Will Danoff	1990	1-800-544-0202
20.8%	16.5%	16.8%	2,500	250	Steven Kaye	1993	1-800-544-0202
11.1%	13.1%	17.0%	2,500	50	Team Mgt.	NA	1-800-345-2021
13.3%	11.5%	14.5%	2,500	250	Bettina Doulton	1996	1-800-544-0202
14.0%	11.2%	12.8%	1,000	50	Team Mgt.	NA	1-800-421-0180
13.3%	14.1%	16.0%	Closed	NA	Charles Freeman	1996	1-800-662-7447
13.0%	12.1%	13.0%	250	50	Thierry Vandeventer	1984	1-800-421-0180
20.0%	15.0%	14.3%	2,500	100	James Craig, III	1986	1-800-525-3713
15.9%	14.2%	16.8%	2,500	250	Brian Posner	1992	1-800-544-0202
15.4%	13.7%	13.4%	3,000	100	Ernst H. von Metzsch	1995	1-800-662-7447
20.6%	16.1%	16.0%	3,000	100	Multi Manager	NA	1-800-662-7447
18.2%	15.1%	16.6%	2,500	250	Stephen Petersen	1993	1-800-544-0202
18.9%	14.1%	13.6%	1,000	100	Paul Vance	1981	1-800-869-6397
10.4%	8.0%	11.0%	2,500	250	Dick Habermann	1996	1-800-544-0202
10.6%	13.9%	13.6%	250	50	Mark Denning	1993	1-800-421-0180
19.5%	16.1%	15.1%	500	50	Anthony Kreisel	1993	1-800-225-1581
10.4%	17.6%	19.9%	500	50	Bob Kippes	1993	1-800-959-4246
6.4%	12.3%	13.3%	1,000	50	Team Mgt.	NA	1-800-421-0180
10.1%	11.1%	11.4%	100	25	Mark Holowesko	1987	1-800-342-5236
13.8%	16.4%	16.1%	2,500	250	Larry Greenberg	1996	1-800-544-0202
8.8%	16.0%	18.4%	2,500	250	John McDowell	1996	1-800-544-0202

CHAPTER

TWENTY-TWO

Granddaddy Funds

Excluding money market funds, more than four thousand mutual funds have appeared on the scene during the past dozen years. The number of funds has expanded geometrically, as has their variety. In addition to diversified growth, growth and income, and aggressive growth funds, you can now invest in international equity funds (global, regional, or country specific); international bond funds; convertible bond funds; industry-sector funds (domestic and global); emerging-markets funds; mid-cap, small-cap, and micro-cap funds; leveraged funds; domestic bond funds of all types; asset allocation funds; and so on. Think of an investment strategy and chances are that you will be able to locate a handful of funds that implement it.

If you discovered mutual funds only recently, you may be surprised to find that mutual funds have been around for a long time. In fact, you can invest in more than sixty funds whose histories stretch back more than fifty years. A dozen funds that were initiated before the stock market crash of October 1929 still are in operation. The first mutual fund in America, the Massachusetts Investors Trust, established in 1924, is still around today. (Mutual funds existed in nineteenth-century England, and money invested in English and Scottish investment companies, called trusts, helped finance the post–Civil War economy in America.)

Most of these graybeards offer staid investment strategies. A large number are balanced funds (that is, those that invest in a fixed ratio of stocks and bonds), a few are bond funds, and the rest invest in dividend-paying common stocks (that is, equity-income funds) or seek growth of capital by pursuing "plain vanilla" asset selection strategies. Most of these funds are sold with a sales charge of some kind. That's because that was the way funds were sold a half-century ago.

The accompanying table lists the oldest funds in America. Over the years, many of these funds have changed their names, a handful have changed their investment advisory relationships, and a few have changed their investment objectives and asset selection strategies. However, all have one thing in common: They all have celebrated their fifty-eighth birthday.

TABLE 19. GRANDDADDY FUNDS

Fund	Investment Objectives	Year Began	Total Assets ($Mil)	Sales Charges %	Expense Ratio %
Alliance Balanced Shares	Growth & Income	1932	109	4.25%	1.32%
Alliance Fund	Growth	1938	927	4.25%	1.08%
Alliance Growth & Income	Growth & Income	1932	529	4.25%	1.05%
American Balanced	Balanced	1932	3,529	5.75%	0.67%
Investment Company of America	Growth & Income	1934	28,127	5.75%	0.60%
Century Shares Trust	Sector	1928	244	NL	0.94%
Colonial Fund	Growth & Income	1904	1,174	5.75%	1.16%
Delaware Fund	Balanced	1938	484	4.75%	0.97%
Dodge & Cox Balanced	Balanced	1931	2,729	NL	0.57%
Eaton Vance Traditional Investors	Balanced	1922	238	4.75%	0.95%
Federated Stock & Bond	Capital Appreciation	1934	137	5.50%	1.21%
Fidelity Fund	Growth & Income	1930	3,943	NL	0.64%
Founders Blue Chip	Growth & Income	1938	484	NL	1.22%
Franklin Equity	Capital Appreciation	1933	367	4.50%	0.95%
Fundamental Investors (American Funds)	Growth & Income	1932	5,969	5.75%	0.70%
Invesco Growth	Growth	1935	572	NL	1.06%
Massachusetts Investors Growth	Growth	1932	1,231	5.75%	0.73%
Massachusetts Investors Trust	Growth & Income	1924	2,330	5.75%	0.78%
Nationwide	Capital Appreciation	1933	900	4.50%	0.63%
Nicholas Income	Income	1929	29	NL	0.58%
Pioneer Fund	Growth & Income	1928	2,651	5.75%	1.09%
George Putnam Fund of Boston	Growth & Income	1937	1,494	5.75%	0.91%
Putnam Investors	Growth	1925	1,155	5.75%	0.99%
Safeco Equity	Growth & Income	1932	685	NL	0.84%
Scudder Growth & Income	Growth & Income	1928	3,548	NL	0.79%
Scudder Income	Income	1928	571	NL	0.99%
Selected American Shares	Growth & Income	1933	1,064	NL	1.09%
Seligman Common Stock	Growth & Income	1930	636	4.75%	1.10%
Sentinel Common Stock	Growth & Income	1934	1,168	5.00%	1.10%
Vanguard Wellington	Balanced	1929	14,152	NL	0.33%

Average Annual Returns			Minimum Investment		Portfolio Manager	Since	Telephone
1 Year %	3 Year %	5 Year %	Initial $	Subsequent $			
8.2%	7.8%	8.8%	250	50	Kevin O'Brien	1996	1-800-881-5672
8.2%	12.0%	14.9%	250	50	Alfred Harrison	1989	1-800-221-5672
20.3%	14.2%	13.1%	252	50	Paul Rissman	1994	1-800-881-5672
13.4%	11.6%	12.2%	500	50	George Miller	1965	1-800-421-0180
17.1%	14.4%	13.2%	250	50	Jon Lovelace	1958	1-800-421-0180
11.1%	7.4%	14.2%	500	25	Allen Fulkerson	1976	1-800-321-1928
12.3%	11.9%	13.1%	1,000	50	Daniel Rie	1993	1-800-248-2828
13.7%	10.5%	11.5%	1,000	100	George Burwell	1992	1-800-523-4640
12.1%	12.5%	13.5%	2,500	100	Team Mgt.	1931	1-800-621-3979
13.7%	11.1%	11.6%	1,000	50	Thomas Faust, Jr.	1993	1-800-225-6265
11.9%	9.8%	10.0%	500	50	Christopher Wiles	1996	1-800-341-7400
20.0%	16.6%	15.3%	2,500	250	Beth Terrana	1993	1-800-544-8888
21.0%	15.9%	13.7%	1,000	100	Brian Kelly	1996	1-800-525-2440
16.9%	16.5%	12.1%	100	25	Conrad Herrmann	1993	1-800-632-2301
17.6%	16.0%	16.2%	250	50	James Drasdo	1984	1-800-421-0180
23.3%	13.0%	13.3%	1,000	50	Douglas Pratt	1995	1-800-525-8085
18.4%	13.2%	14.0%	1,000	50	Christian Felipe	1995	1-800-225-2606
26.7%	17.9%	15.7%	1,000	50	Parke/Laupheimer	1992	1-800-225-2606
21.6%	16.5%	12.4%	250	25	Charles Bath	1985	1-800-848-0920
17.7%	10.3%	13.8%	500	100	Albert Nicholas	1967	1-414-272-6133
14.8%	12.9%	13.5%	50	50	John Carey	1987	1-800-225-6292
15.4%	12.8%	12.4%	500	50	Bousa/Taubes/Thompson	94/93/95	1-800-225-1581
21.0%	15.7%	15.4%	500	50	Cother/Weiss/Santos	95/96/94	1-800-225-1581
18.0%	18.7%	18.9%	1,000	100	Richard Meagley	1995	1-800-624-5711
20.1%	15.8%	15.8%	1,000	100	Tobert Hoffman	1991	1-800-225-2470
5.1%	4.5%	7.6%	1,000	100	William Hutchinson	1987	1-800-225-2470
19.5%	14.9%	13.9%	1,000	100	Shelby Davis	1993	1-800-243-1575
13.6%	12.9%	13.2%	1,000	100	Charles Smith	1992	1-800-221-2450
19.9%	14.4%	13.4%	1,000	50	Keniston Merrill	1982	1-800-282-3863
15.4%	13.7%	13.4%	3,000	100	Ernst Von Metzsch	1995	1-800-662-7447

CHAPTER

TWENTY-THREE

Old Hands

The mutual fund industry has become highly competitive in recent years. Fund families not only compete against one another for investor dollars, but also often launch vigorous campaigns to lure top-performing portfolio managers away from the competition. As a result, fewer than 10 percent of the funds around these days can make the claim that their portfolio manager has been at the helm for a decade or more.

Does it really matter whether or not a portfolio manager has significant tenure with the fund? It certainly does if your fund selection criteria includes historical performance. You want to be sure that the captain of the ship today is the same one who successfully guided its entry into port. In addition, the long-term success of some funds is the result of the eccentricity of their portfolio managers. In many instances, these managers have either invented a better mousetrap, or they have improved upon the mundane. Highly successful portfolio managers such as Ken Heebner, Peter Lynch, Albert Nicholas, Michael Price, John Templeton, and Ralph Wanger quickly come to mind.

On the other hand, the role of the portfolio manager in generating returns is much less important at other funds. Index fund returns, for example, are dependent on the performance of the underlying index and how much those returns are reduced by fund expenses rather than on the expertise of the funds' portfolio managers. To a lesser extent, so are the returns of most industry-sector funds, whose returns tend to be dominated by conditions in a specific industry rather than on a portfolio manager's ability to locate standout investments. Furthermore, a large number of funds are run by a team of managers. Still others, such as those offered by Twentieth Century, are highly dependent on sophisticated computer models that screen potential investments according to a predetermined set of criteria. Thus, when evaluating the potential success of a particular fund, you have to know the nature of the beast before you put an inordinate amount of weight on its jockey.

The accompanying list of funds consists of those whose portfolio managers have been guiding the fund for more than fifteen years. Some of these funds have recently added co-portfolio managers (as they no doubt should). In those instances, I have listed the portfolio manager with the most tenure. Collectively, the portfolio managers listed here have been at the helm for a total of 732 years.

TABLE 20. OLD HANDS

Fund	Total Assets ($Mil)	Year Began	Sales Charges %	Expense Ratio %	Turnover Ratio %
American Growth	105	1958	5.75%	1.75%	173%
Analytic Optioned Equity	49	1978	NL	1.38%	32%
Armstrong Associates	14	1971	NL	1.80%	12%
Bridges Investment	27	1962	NL	0.89%	7%
Century Shares Trust	244	1928	NL	0.94%	5%
CGM Capital Development	603	1961	NL	0.85%	270%
CGM Mutual	1,149	1929	NL	0.91%	291%
Copley Fund	75	1978	NL	1.03%	5%
Dean Witter Tax Exempt	1,220	1980	4.00%	0.48%	21%
Dreyfus Muni Bond	3,734	1976	NL	0.70%	52%
Enterprise Growth	151	1968	4.75%	1.60%	45%
General Securities	38	1951	NL	1.50%	24%
Guardian Park Avenue	1,159	1972	4.50%	0.81%	78%
IDS High-Yield Tax Exempt	5,989	1979	5.00%	0.72%	14%
Mairs and Power Growth	104	1958	NL	0.99%	4%
Mathers	191	1965	NL	0.98%	58%
Merrill Lynch Basic Value A	3,588	1977	5.25%	0.59%	12%
Mutual Shares	5,921	1949	NL	0.69%	79%
New England Growth	1,204	1992	5.75%	1.61%	15%
Nuveen Municipal Bond	2,795	1986	4.50%	0.83%	17%
Pax World	496	1971	NL	0.97%	29%
Pennsylvania Mutual	538	1962	NL	0.98%	10%
Salomon Bros. Opportunity	145	1979	NL	1.18%	8%
Sentry	94	1970	NL	0.86%	27%
Smith Barney Appreciation	2,002	1970	5.00%	1.02%	57%
SoGen International	3,307	1970	3.75%	1.25%	10%
T. Rowe Price New Era	1,297	1969	NL	0.79%	23%
United Accumulative	1,221	1940	5.75%	0.80%	229%
United Income	4,376	1940	5.75%	0.84%	18%
Valley Forge	12	1971	NL	1.30%	16%
Van Kampen Amercian Corp Bond	162	1971	4.75%	1.13%	25%
WPG Tudor	192	1969	NL	1.30%	80%

| Average Annual Returns | | | Minimum Investment | | Portfolio Manager | Since | Telephone |
1 Year %	3 Year %	5 Year %	Initial $	Subsequent $			
6.4%	10.2%	14.0%	0	0	Robert Brody	1958	1-800-525-2406
14.2%	11.5%	9.8%	5,000	0	Chuck Dobson	1978	1-800-374-2633
5.4%	10.2%	11.8%	250	0	C.K. Lawson	1968	1-214-720-9101
17.2%	13.9%	11.6%	800	200	Edson Bridges II	1963	1-402-397-4700
11.1%	7.4%	14.2%	500	25	Allan W. Fulkerson	1976	1-800-321-1928
25.0%	11.5%	16.9%	Closed	50	G. Kenneth Heeber	1976	1-800-345-4048
11.0%	7.2%	11.5%	2,500	50	G. Kenneth Heeber	1981	1-800-345-4048
6.7%	3.2%	9.5%	1,000	100	Irving Levine	1978	1-508-674-8459
6.3%	4.3%	7.1%	1,000	100	James Willison	1980	1-800-869-6397
5.4%	3.2%	6.6%	2,500	100	Richard Mognihan	1976	1-800-645-6561
33.0%	23.6%	18.5%	1,000	50	Ron Cahakaris	1980	1-800-432-4320
12.6%	15.4%	12.4%	1,500	100	Jack Robinson	1951	1-800-577-9217
16.6%	14.1%	18.4%	1,000	100	Charles Albers	1972	1-800-343-0817
5.5%	4.2%	6.7%	2,000	100	Kurt Larson	1989	1-800-272-4445
21.5%	24.3%	19.8%	2,500	100	George Mairs III	1980	1-800-304-7404
-1.1%	1.6%	1.7%	1,000	200	Henry G. Van Der Eb, Jr.	1975	1-800-962-3863
15.3%	14.4%	15.5%	1,000	50	Paul Hoffman	1977	1-609-282-2800
13.6%	16.0%	17.5%	5,000	100	Michael Price	1975	1-800-553-3014
8.3%	12.1%	10.7%	Closed	50	Kenneth Heeber	1976	1-800-225-5478
6.9%	5.3%	6.9%	1,000	100	Thomas Spalding	1978	1-800-621-7227
16.4%	12.8%	7.7%	250	50	Anthony Brown	1971	1-800-767-1729
5.8%	8.6%	10.9%	2,000	50	Charles Royce	1973	1-800-221-4268
10.7%	13.9%	14.9%	1,000	100	Irving Brilliant	1979	1-800-725-6666
13.5%	12.4%	10.5%	500	50	Keith Ringberg	1977	1-800-533-7827
17.0%	14.0%	12.3%	1,000	50	Hersh Cohen	1979	1-212-723-9218
12.1%	11.4%	13.0%	1,000	100	Jean-Marie Eveillard	1979	1-800-628-0252
20.3%	15.6%	11.8%	2,500	100	George A. Roche	1979	1-800-638-5660
11.0%	13.4%	13.3%	500	0	Antonio Intagliata	1979	1-913-236-2000
15.2%	14.9%	14.8%	500	0	Russ Thompson	1979	1-913-236-2000
4.7%	7.1%	9.0%	1,000	100	Bernard Klawans	1971	1-800-548-1942
3.5%	4.4%	7.8%	500	25	David Troth	1979	1-800-421-5666
26.2%	16.1%	15.0%	100	50	Melville Straus	1973	1-800-223-3332

CHAPTER

TWENTY-FOUR

Index Funds

Indexing, once considered a mere hedging device, has come into its own in recent years. Increasingly, investors are turning away from actively managed portfolios for the assurance of market returns offered by passively managed index funds. Index funds seek to parallel the returns of some market index by maintaining a portfolio that replicates the composition of the underlying index. For example, mutual funds that replicate the Standard & Poor's 500 Index invest in the five hundred stocks contained in the index and allocate a percentage of portfolio assets to each stock based on the ratio of the market value of each company to the aggregate market value of all stocks in the index.

The number of index mutual funds has grown rapidly since 1974, when the first index fund made its debut. (However, a large number of these newly created index funds offer their shares to institutional investors only.)

Whereas the original index funds tracked the S&P 500 Index, the universe of index funds has since expanded to encompass an array of market segments, including the Dow Jones Industrial Average, Wilshire 4500, and the Russell 2000, to name but a few. The largest concentration of index funds is offered by the Vanguard Group of no-load funds.

Why has indexing gained such popularity? The answer has its roots in both theory and practice. The concept of indexing was first pioneered in the mid-1970s as a logical response to the Efficient Market Hypothesis (EMH), which proposed that the stock and bond markets work with such efficiency that beating the broad market averages is virtually impossible. If you can't beat the market, then buy it, say proponents of EMH.

Even for those who question the validity of EMH, the case for indexing is difficult to refute. Over long periods of time, the broad stock market averages have outperformed the majority of actively managed portfolios. For example, the Vanguard Index 500 portfolio's return tops that of 75 percent of the actively managed equity funds that have been around that long. As the task of beating the market becomes increasingly difficult, if not impossible, for active portfolio managers, more and more investors find themselves attracted to the benefits of indexing.

Although it may sound un-American to settle for the average, the benefits of indexing are indisputable. First, an index portfolio offers highly predictable results in line with its benchmark in every year. For example, if small-cap stocks return 40 percent during a particular year, a small-cap index fund will ensure that most of that return heads for your pocket. Although you may be giving up superior performance by investing in an index fund, you are virtually guaranteed that your portfolio will not significantly underperform the market averages. In other words, index fund investors win the investment game by not losing. Moreover, an index strategy involves substantially lower costs than active portfolio management. Low portfolio turnover keeps transaction costs minimal, while low trading and minimal research needs often allow fund sponsors to waive all or a portion of the management fee. In fact, the reason that index funds tend to perform better than their actively managed counterparts is that they fork over more of their gross investment returns to shareholders.

Of course, passive investment strategies also have some drawbacks. For starters, the market doesn't always rise. Index funds stay 100 percent invested at all times, whereas actively managed portfolios often hold at least some cash. Thus, while index funds give shareholders the full measure of the market's return on the upside, they also ensure that their shareholders will suffer all of the pain inflicted by plummeting stock market prices.

The degree to which an index fund succeeds in minimizing transaction and operating costs is critical. All else being equal, the lower a fund's costs, the better its chances of meeting its objective. If you opt for the index route, limit your selections to no-load funds with relatively low expense and portfolio turnover ratios.

TABLE 21. INDEX FUNDS

Fund	Index Replicated	Total Assets ($Mil)	Year Began	Expense Ratio %
ASM Fund	Dow Jones Average	19	1990	2.50%
Benham Global Natural Resource Index	DJWSI	51	1994	0.76%
California Investment S&P 500 Index	S&P 500	43	1992	0.20%
California Investment S&P Mid-Cap Index	S&P Midcap 400	34	1992	0.40%
Dreyfus Mid-Cap Index	S&P Midcap 400	157	1991	0.85%
Dreyfus S&P 500 Index	S&P 500	500	1990	0.55%
Fidelity Market Index	S&P 500	1,113	1990	0.45%
Galaxy II Large Company Index	S&P 500	264	1990	0.40%
Galaxy II Small Company Index	Small Co. Index	304	1990	0.40%
Galaxy II Utility Index	Utility Index	55	1993	0.40%
One Group Equity Index	S&P 500	322	1991	0.56%
Portico Equity Index	S&P 500	33	1989	0.72%
Rushmore American Gas Index	American Gas Assoc.	206	1989	0.85%
Schwab 1000 Index	Schwab 1000 Index	1,534	1991	0.49%
Schwab International Index	Schwab Int'l Index	242	1993	0.69%
Schwab Small Cap Index	Schwab Small Cap Index	200	1993	0.59%
Seven Seas S&P 500 Index	S&P 500	684	1992	0.19%
T. Rowe Price Equity Index	S&P 500	668	1982	0.84%
Vanguard Index Extended Market	Wilshire 4500	1,746	1987	0.25%
Vanguard Index Growth	S&P/BARRA Growth Index	511	1992	0.20%
Vanguard Index Small Cap	Russell 2000	1,450	1992	0.25%
Vanguard Index Total Stock Market	Wilshire 5000	2,865	1992	0.25%
Vanguard Index Value	S&P/BARRA Value Index	765	1992	0.20%
Victory Stock Index	S&P 500	244	1993	0.56%

| Turnover Ratio % | Average Annual Returns | | | Minimum Investment | | Telephone |
	1 Year %	3 Year %	5 Year %	Initial $	Subsequent $	
340.0%	21.2%	15.9%	13.4%	1,000	100	1-800-445-2763
39.0%	12.9%	NA	NA	2,500	250	1-800-345-2021
4.0%	20.2%	17.1%	NA	5,000	250	1-800-225-8778
12.0%	13.8%	13.0%	NA	5,000	250	1-800-225-8778
20.0%	13.3%	12.8%	14.8%	2,500	100	1-800-645-6561
4.0%	19.6%	16.7%	14.7%	2,500	100	1-800-645-6561
5.0%	20.0%	17.1%	14.8%	2,500	250	1-800-544-8888
5.0%	20.0%	17.0%	14.7%	2,500	100	1-800-628-0414
14.0%	16.2%	13.4%	14.9%	2,500	100	1-800-628-0414
12.0%	2.0%	3.8%	NA	2,500	100	1-800-628-0414
2.7%	19.9%	16.9%	14.6%	1,000	100	1-800-480-4111
4.6%	19.6%	16.8%	14.6%	100	100	1-800-228-1024
10.0%	20.6%	6.9%	11.3%	2,500	0	1-800-343-3355
2.0%	19.1%	16.2%	14.9%	1,000	100	1-800-266-5623
0.0%	9.8%	8.8%	NA	1,000	100	1-800-266-5623
24.0%	13.8%	NA	NA	1,000	100	1-800-266-5623
38.0%	20.0%	17.1%	NA	1,000	0	1-800-647-7327
26.0%	20.0%	17.1%	14.7%	2,500	100	1-800-638-5660
15.0%	16.1%	14.8%	15.9%	3,000	100	1-800-662-7447
24.0%	21.9%	19.6%	NA	3,000	100	1-800-662-7447
28.0%	14.6%	13.9%	16.3%	3,000	100	1-800-662-7447
3.0%	18.2%	16.0%	NA	3,000	100	1-800-662-7447
27.0%	18.4%	15.0%	NA	3,000	100	1-800-662-7447
11.9%	19.7%	NA	NA	500	25	1-800-539-3863

CHAPTER

TWENTY-FIVE

Up-and-Coming Funds

I have always believed that the proof of the pudding is in the eating. When searching for funds with exceptional performance potential, I generally limit my selections to funds that have been in business for a while. That's because I've been around the investment business for more than a quarter-century and have learned to approach exaggerated claims of an individual fund's ability to provide generous investment returns with a sensible degree of skepticism. To those who claim to have built a better mousetrap I say, "Show me the dead rodents."

Similarly, I like to view a mutual fund's performance before I ante up my client's or my money. I want to know what type of stocks a portfolio manager has bought and is likely to buy, how frequently the manager turns over the portfolio, and what the fund's expenses will be. Although a newly created fund's prospectus is required to outline its investment objectives and portfolio management strategies, these required statements tend to be too broad to tell me specifically what the fund's manager will do with my money. Thus, I tend to consider only those funds that have been around for a while before I make a monetary commitment.

As is usually the case, there are exceptions to this rule of thumb. The most notable is the one I make because I know the portfolio manager and have monitored his or her performance while at the helm of another fund. For example, Garret Van Wagoner's performance while at the helm of the Govett Small Cap Fund is legendary. When he left that fund to start his own mutual fund family, you knew what you were going to get—an aggressively managed smaller-cap portfolio that followed an earnings momentum strategy. That, of course, is what attracted large numbers of investors, who poured more than a billion dollars into the Van Wagoner Funds during the course of a few months.

The funds in the accompanying list are start-up funds that did not make my "300 Best" list because of their recency. However, they are all diamonds in the rough. These funds are either managed by individuals who have built a successful track record while managing a fund with similar investment objectives or are sponsored by fund families that possess sufficient analytical resources and portfolio management talent to give the fund a high probability of achieving investment success. Among them you will find funds managed by such superstars as Ron Baron, Louis Navillier, Bill Nasgovitz, Jim Oberweis, Chuck Royce, Eric Ryback, and Garret Van Wagoner. All funds on this list have posted enviable returns during their few months in existence, and there is little doubt that a number of them will appear on my best funds list in the not-too-distant future.

TABLE 22. UP AND COMING FUNDS

Fund	Investment Objective	Total Assets ($Mil)	Sales Charges %
Baron Growth & Income	Growth & Income	172	NL
Berger Small Company Growth	Small Cap	816	NL
Bridgeway Aggressive Growth	Capital Appreciation	1	NL
Bridgeway Ultra Small Cap	Micro Cap	4	NL
Dreyfus Large Company Value	Growth	24	NL
Dreyfus Small Company Value	Small Cap	10	NL
Heartland Small Cap Contrarian	Small Cap	222	NL
Janus Olympus	Capital Appreciation	379	NL
Linder/Ryback Small Cap	Micro Cap	10	NL
Montgomery Small Cap Opportunities	Small Cap	136	NL
Navellier Aggressive Growth	Capital Appreciation	80	NL
Oakmark Small Cap	Small Cap	121	NL
Oberweis Micro Cap	Micro Cap	45	NL
PBHG Select Equity	Capital Appreciation	434	NL
Robertson Stephens Growth & Income	Growth & Income	301	NL
Royce Low Price Stock	Micro Cap	14	NL
Royce Total Return	Growth & Income	4	NL
Stein Roe Special Venture	Small Cap	120	NL
Stein Roe Young Investors	Growth	115	NL
Strong Small Cap	Small Cap	78	NL
T. Rowe Price Health Sciences	Sector	162	NL
20th Century Value	Growth & Income	1,088	NL
USAA Growth Strategy	Growth	84	NL
Van Wagoner Emerging Growth	Small Cap	783	NL
Van Wagoner Micro Cap	Micro Cap	140	NL
Van Wagner Mid Cap	Mid Cap	93	NL

Return 1 Year %	Minimum Investment		Portfolio Manager	Telephone
	Initial $	Subsequent $		
25.8%	2,000	0	Ronald Baron	1-800-992-2766
31.3%	500	50	William Keithler	1-800-333-1001
38.0%	2,000	500	John Montgomery	1-800-661-3550
29.7%	2,000	500	John Montgomery	1-800-661-3550
31.3%	2,500	100	Timothy Ghriskey	1-800-645-6561
30.1%	2,500	100	Team Mgt.	1-800-645-6561
20.8%	1,000	100	William Nasqovitz	1-800-432-7856
NA	2,500	100	Scott Schoelzel	1-800-525-8983
20.4%	3,000	100	Ryback/Wang	1-314-727-5305
NA	1,000	100	Castro/Boich	1-800-572-3863
NA	2,000	100	Allen Alpers	1-800-887-8671
NA	1,000	100	Steve Reid	1-800-625-6275
NA	1,000	100	James Oberweis	1-800-323-6166
45.2%	2,500	0	Pilgrim/Baxter	1-800-809-8008
24.0%	5,000	100	John Wallace	1-800-766-3863
13.6%	2,000	50	Charles Royce	1-800-221-4268
19.4%	2,000	50	Scott Colbert	1-800-221-4268
31.8%	2,500	50	Dunn/Peterson	1-800-338-2550
35.5%	2,500	50	Gustafson/Brady/McQue	1-800-338-2550
NA	1,000	50	Mary Lisanti	1-800-368-1030
NA	2,500	100	Joesph Klein III	1-800-638-5660
22.6%	2,500	50	Zuger/Davidson	1-800-345-2021
25.4%	1,000	50	David Parsons	1-800-531-8448
NA	1,000	50	Garrett Van Wagoner	1-800-228-2121
NA	1,000	50	Garrett Van Wagoner	1-800-228-2121
NA	1,000	50	Garrett Van Wagoner	1-800-228-2121

CHAPTER

TWENTY-SIX

The Most Efficient Equity Funds Around

The easiest and surest way to improve your investment returns is to reduce the costs of investing. For example, during the last six decades the Standard & Poor's 500 Index has returned 10.8 percent per year. This is the long-run average return you can expect to earn from a well-diversified, average-risk portfolio of blue-chip stocks before deducting the costs of acquiring and maintaining that portfolio. If, for example, annual portfolio maintenance costs average 2.8 percent, your average net annual return from this portfolio declines to just 8.0 percent. If you could trim your annual expenses to 1.3 percent, your net returns increase to 9.5 percent. Although this may not seem like much, when compounded over many years, small additions to net returns mean a lot. Check out these examples.

Contribute $2,000 to an IRA every year for twenty years. Invest in a diversified portfolio of blue-chip stocks. If you earn 10.8

percent compounded annually, your portfolio would be worth $140,160. Earn only 8 percent per year and the value of the portfolio declines to $98,884. That's an earnings shortfall of more than $40,000, or a 30-percent decline in your wealth. Earn 9.5 percent compounded annually and your portfolio will be worth $118,760, an improvement of $18,882 for every $2,000 in annual investments. Little by little, the gains mount.

When you invest in a mutual fund, there are three ways the fund's gross investment return can be shaved before it gets into your pocket. First, some funds levy sales charges that reduce returns. These charges may take the form of a front-end load, a back-end load (called a contingent deferred sales charge), or an annual 12b-1 "distribution fee." Pay any of these fees and you reduce your investment return and your ultimate net worth. Second, gross investment returns are reduced by the fund's transaction costs. These are the payments to brokers and market makers to buy and sell securities. The more the fund's portfolio manager trades, the greater is the reduction in gross returns. For example, if a round-trip trade (security purchase and subsequent sale) results in a 1-percent transaction charge, and the fund turns over its portfolio once each year (a portfolio turnover rate of 100 percent), its gross return declines by 1 percentage point. If the fund's portfolio turnover ratio balloons to 200 percent, gross returns get trimmed by 2 percentage points. In other words, the higher a fund's portfolio turnover ratio, the more return its portfolio manager is giving away and the less you get to keep. Finally, annual fund operating expenses clip gross investment returns by the amount of the annual fee (that is, expense ratio). Invest in funds that levy sales charges, turn over their portfolios frequently, and possess high annual operating expense ratios, and you may be giving away tens, if not hundreds, of thousands of dollars over an investment lifetime.

The following table lists some of the most efficient funds around. All are sold without sales charges of any kind, have low portfolio turnover ratios, and possess annual expense ratios of less than 1 percent. (Index funds, usually the most efficient funds of all, have been excluded from this list since they are listed elsewhere in this book.) How do your funds stack up against those on this list? If you find you're paying too much, consider making a change, and put more than change into your pocket.

TABLE 23.   HIGHLY EFFICIENT EQUITY FUNDS

Fund	Investment Objective	Total Assets ($Mil)	Year Began	Expense Ratio %	Turnover Ratio %
Acorn Fund	Growth	2,813	1970	0.57%	26%
Babson Growth	Growth	281	1960	0.85%	17%
Babson Value	Growth & Income	514	1984	0.98%	6%
Compass Value Equity	Growth & Income	23	1992	1.22%	12%
Consulting Group Large Cap Value	Growth	1,507	1991	0.83%	21%
Dodge & Cox Balanced	Balanced	2,729	1931	0.57%	20%
Dodge & Cox Stock	Growth	1,750	1964	0.60%	13%
Dreyfus Appreciation	Growth	605	1984	0.92%	5%
Elfon Trusts	Growth	1,386	1935	0.13%	15%
First Omaha Equity	Growth	236	1992	0.99%	27%
Homestead Value	Growth & Income	190	1990	0.84%	10%
Lindner Dividend	Balanced	2,293	1976	0.61%	30%
Lindner Growth	Growth & Income	1,447	1973	0.54%	25%
Mairs & Power Growth	Growth	104	1958	0.99%	4%
Monitor Income Equity Trust	Growth & Income	161	1989	0.82%	17%
Neuberger & Berman Guardian	Growth & Income	5,000	1950	0.84%	26%
Nicholas Fund	Growth	3,789	1969	0.74%	26%
Nicholas II	Growth	769	1983	0.66%	20%
Parnassus Income Balanced	Balanced	30	1992	0.72%	15%
Pennsylvania Mutual	Growth	538	1962	0.98%	10%
Preferred Value	Growth & Income	267	1992	0.89%	29%
RSI Core Equity	Growth & Income	8	1991	1.00%	25%
Scudder Growth & Income	Growth & Income	3,548	1970	0.79%	27%
Sentry Fund	Growth	94	1970	0.80%	27%
T. Rowe Price Balanced	Balanced	788	1939	0.95%	13%
T. Rowe Price Equity Income	Growth & Income	6,332	1985	0.85%	22%
T. Rowe Price Growth & Income	Growth & Income	2,058	1982	0.84%	26%
T. Rowe Price New Era	Sector	1,297	1969	0.79%	23%
Vanguard Wellington	Balanced	14,152	1929	0.33%	24%

| Average Annual Returns | | | Minimum Investment | | Portfolio Manager | Since | Telephone |
1 Year %	3 Year %	5 Year %	Initial $	Subsequent $			
16.6%	10.4%	18.6%	1,000	100	Wagner/McQuaid	70/95	1–800–922–6769
17.7%	14.9%	13.6%	500	50	Kirk/Gribbell	85/95	1–800–422–2766
17.2%	17.9%	17.8%	1,000	100	Nick Whitridge	1984	1–800–422–2766
20.5%	16.0%	NA	500	100	Gaskins/Capaldi	94/95	1–888–426–6727
15.8%	12.7%	NA	100	0	Team Mgt.	NA	1–212–816–8725
12.1%	12.5%	13.5%	2,500	100	Team Mgt.	NA	1–800–621–3979
16.5%	16.8%	16.4%	2,500	100	Team Mgt.	NA	1–800–621–3979
24.9%	20.9%	14.8%	2,500	100	Fayez Sarofim & Co.	1990	1–800–645–6561
22.4%	18.0%	15.5%	100	25	David Carlson	1988	1–800–242–0134
26.3%	14.2%	12.9%	500	50	Team Mgt.	NA	1–800–662–4203
16.9%	16.8%	16.0%	1,000	0	Stuart Teach	1990	1–800–258–3030
10.2%	8.4%	13.0%	2,000	100	Eric Ernest Ryback	1982	1–314–727–5305
17.3%	12.7%	13.8%	2,000	100	Lange/Ryback	77/82	1–314–727–5305
21.5%	24.3%	19.8%	2,500	100	George Mairs III	1980	1–800–304–7404
17.9%	12.9%	11.6%	1,000	500	James Buskirk	1989	1–800–253–0412
7.2%	14.3%	16.2%	1,000	100	Marx/Simons/Risen	81/88/96	1–800–877–9700
22.3%	15.2%	14.2%	500	100	Albert Nicholas	1969	1–414–272–6133
21.3%	16.1%	13.6%	1,000	100	David Nicholas	1993	1–414–272–6133
11.2%	8.5%	NA	2,000	50	Jerome Dodson	1992	1–800–999–3505
5.8%	8.6%	10.9%	2,000	50	Charles Royce	1973	1–800–221–4268
21.3%	17.3%	NA	1,000	50	Jim Coughlin	1992	1–800–662–4769
22.2%	20.1%	18.5%	2,500	250	Jim Coughlin	1991	1–800–772–3615
20.1%	15.8%	15.8%	1,000	100	Team Mgt.	NA	1–800–225–2470
13.5%	12.4%	10.5%	500	50	Keith Ringberg	1977	1–800–533–7827
13.4%	11.0%	12.0%	2,500	100	Richard Whitney	1991	1–800–638–5660
20.5%	17.2%	16.3%	2,500	100	Brian Rogers	1985	1–800–638–5660
4.2%	5.2%	6.6%	2,500	100	Stephen Boesel	1987	1–800–638–5660
20.3%	15.6%	11.8%	2,500	100	George Roche	1979	1–800–638–5660
15.4%	13.7%	13.4%	3,000	100	Ernst von Metzsch	1995	1–800–662–7447

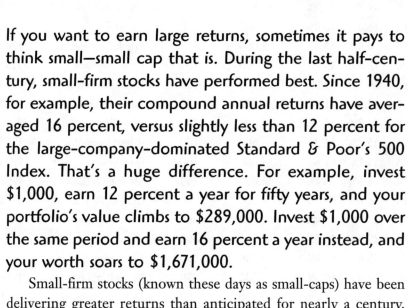

CHAPTER TWENTY-SEVEN

Small-Cap Funds

If you want to earn large returns, sometimes it pays to think small—small cap that is. During the last half-century, small-firm stocks have performed best. Since 1940, for example, their compound annual returns have averaged 16 percent, versus slightly less than 12 percent for the large-company-dominated Standard & Poor's 500 Index. That's a huge difference. For example, invest $1,000, earn 12 percent a year for fifty years, and your portfolio's value climbs to $289,000. Invest $1,000 over the same period and earn 16 percent a year instead, and your worth soars to $1,671,000.

Small-firm stocks (known these days as small-caps) have been delivering greater returns than anticipated for nearly a century. These extra returns have become known in academic circles as "the small-firm effect." According to efficient market theory, investment returns are linked to investment risk and nothing else. If you want to earn a greater return in an efficient market, you must take on additional investment risk. However, this has not been true for small-firm stocks. Although the stocks of small firms are riskier than those of large, blue-chip companies, they have consistently been providing larger returns than can be explained by their increased risk. In other words, Wall Street has been serving up a free lunch to small-cap investors for a long time. If you want to fill your plate with one of the few free lunches the stock market has to offer, consider investing a portion of your capital in a well-managed small-cap fund.

These days, more than two hundred mutual funds include the phrases "small firm" or "emerging growth" in their statements of investment objectives. However, if you check out the stocks that many funds have bought, you'll no doubt find a number of companies with equity market values (share price multiplied by the number of shares of stock outstanding) beyond $1 billion. By any stretch of the imagination, these companies don't qualify as being small. So, if you're after the extra returns that small-cap portfolios provide, you must weed out the pretenders and focus your attention on true small-cap funds. These are funds that have the majority of their assets invested in companies with equity market values of less than $350 million.

When selecting a small-cap fund, look for those with relatively low portfolio turnover ratios. Small firms must be given time to grow, and investors who exhibit patience are those that reap the extra returns that small-growth companies provide. In addition, look for funds with modest levels of total assets. Funds with plenty of money to invest are forced to include the stocks of larger companies in their portfolios. Finally, look for funds that have performed better than the average small-cap fund. Remember, proof of the pudding is in the eating.

The funds listed in the accompanying table qualify as small-cap funds (by my definition). All have the majority of their assets invested in companies with equity market values of less than $350 million. Excluded from the list are small-cap index funds. Index funds have all the attributes I like in a small-cap fund and should be considered by aggressive-growth-oriented investors. If an index fund is your cup of tea, check out those listed in Chapter 24, "Index Funds."

TABLE 24. SMALL-CAP FUNDS

Fund	Total Assets ($Mil)	Year Began	Sales Charges %	Expense Ratio %
Cappielo Rushmore Emerging Growth	45	1992	NL	1.50%
Excelsior Early Life Cycle	92	1992	4.50%	0.90%
Fidelity Low Priced Stock	4,625	1982	3.00%	1.05%
First American Regional Equity	26	1992	4.50%	1.15%
Founders Discovery	272	1989	NL	1.63%
GIT Special Growth	16	1983	NL	1.41%
Galaxy Small Cap Value	33	1992	3.75%	1.04%
Hotchkis & Wiley Small Cap	16	1985	NL	0.10%
Kemper-Dreman Small Cap A	70	1992	5.75%	1.83%
Manning & Napier Small Cap	100	1992	NL	1.07%
Oberweis Emerging Growth	207	1987	NL	1.52%
Omni Investment	32	1984	NL	1.64%
Pacific Advisors Small Cap	6	1993	5.75%	2.49%
Pathfinder	5	1987	NL	1.50%
PBHG Emerging Growth	1,204	1993	NL	1.47%
Pennsylvania Mutual	538	1973	NL	0.98%
Perkins Opportunity	139	1993	4.75%	1.97%
Perritt Capital Growth	8	1988	NL	1.92%
Royce Micro Cap	135	1991	NL	1.94%
Royce Value	148	1982	NL	1.76%
Schooner	6	1993	NL	1.50%
Shadow Stock	39	1987	NL	1.13%
Skyline Special Equities	167	1987	NL	1.51%
Stratton Small Cap Yield	20	1993	NL	1.46%

Average Annual Return			Minimum Investment		Portfolio Manager	Since	Telephone
1 Year %	3 Year %	5 Year %	Initial $	Subsequent $			
-3.6%	11.0%	NA	2,500	0	Frank A. Cappiello	1992	1-800-622-1386
-2.4%	10.9%	NA	500	50	Timothy W. Evnin	1992	1-800-446-1012
12.7%	16.0%	19.2%	2,500	2,500	Joel Tillinghast	1989	1-800-544-8888
11.0%	18.7%	NA	1,000	100	Regional Value Team	NA	1-800637-2548
20.1%	13.6%	16.1%	1,000	100	David G. Kern	1995	1-800-525-2440
8.0%	8.7%	8.6%	2,500	50	Tennes/Burgess	95/96	1-800-336-3063
20.8%	16.6%	NA	0	0	Peter Larson	1992	1-800-628-0414
10.7%	10.4%	13.4%	5,000	0	Hitchman/Miles	94/95	1-800-346-7301
22.0%	21.6%	NA	1,000	100	Michael Berry	1995	1-800-621-1048
-1.1%	12.1%	NA	2,000	100	Team Mgt.	NA	1-800-446-3863
22.9%	18.2%	18.7%	1,000	100	James Oberweis	1987	1-800-323-6166
16.3%	16.7%	17.2%	3,000	1,000	Perkins/Wolf	1984	1-800-323-6166
25.2%	16.4%	NA	0	0	Team Mgt.	NA	1-800-223-9790
20.2%	16.2%	9.1%	0	25	Edwin R. Bernstein	1989	1-800-444-4778
32.6%	33.4%	NA	2,500	0	Christine M. Baxter	1993	1-800-433-0051
5.8%	8.6%	10.9%	2,000	50	Charles Royce	1973	1-800-221-2468
5.1%	30.1%	NA	2,500	100	Richard & Daniel Perkins	1993	1-800-366-8361
12.7%	12.2%	11.0%	1,000	250	Gerald W. Perritt	1988	1-800-338-4268
7.4%	11.4%	NA	2,000	50	Charles Royce	1991	1-800-221-4268
7.4%	8.8%	10.9%	2,000	50	Charles Royce	1982	1-800-221-4268
5.4%	8.1%	NA	5,000	1,000	Gipson/Grey	93/94	1-800-420-7556
10.9%	10.0%	13.0%	2,500	100	Scliemann/Whitridge	1987	1-800-422-2766
20.0%	13.0%	20.3%	1,000	100	William M. Dutton	1987	1-800-458-5222
11.6%	9.0%	NA	500	100	James W. Stratton	1993	1-800-634-5726

CHAPTER

TWENTY-EIGHT

Buy-and-Hold Funds

One of the best ways to improve your investment returns is to reduce the costs of investing. The costs of mutual fund investing include sales charges, operating expenses, and transaction costs. Sales charges can be avoided by investing in only no-load funds. Operating expenses can be reduced by investing in funds with low annual expense ratios. Portfolio transaction costs can be lessened by investing in funds with low portfolio turnover ratios. While most mutual fund investors are cognizant of sales charges and operating expenses, very few consider the negative impact on investment returns that can be caused by high portfolio turnover. A fund's turnover ratio is determined by taking the lesser of annual security purchases or sales and dividing that figure by average annual assets.

The average annual turnover ratio for diversified equity funds is approximately 80-percent. During the course

222

of a year, funds with an 80-percent turnover ratio replace 80 percent of their investments with new investments. An estimate of a fund's average annual security
holding period can be obtained by dividing 100 percent
by the fund's portfolio turnover ratio. For example, a
fund with an 80 percent turnover ratio holds its investments an average of one and one-quarter years, or fifteen months. A fund with a 200 percent turnover ratio,
keeps its investments an average of six months.

Think of a fund's turnover ratio as an index of its trading costs.
For example, if transaction costs average about 2 percent on a round-
trip trade (security purchase and subsequent sale), a fund with a 200
percent turnover ratio experiences 4 percent annually in transaction costs. In other words, this fund's portfolio manager has to earn
a 20 percent return before trading costs to produce a portfolio return of 16 percent.

Over the long term, funds with exceptionally low portfolio turnover ratios tend to produce better-than-average returns for their
shareholders because they do not give away a large portion of the
returns their portfolio managers earn. The accompanying table lists
some of the most patient funds around, based on their exceptionally low portfolio turnover ratios. These funds hold their investments an average of approximately ten years. Although most of the
funds on this list are conservatively managed, nearly all have produced handsome returns during the last five years.

TABLE 25. BUY-AND-HOLD FUNDS

Fund	Investment Objective	Total Assets ($Mil)	Sales Charges %	Expense Ratio %	Turnover Ratio %
Babson Enterprise II	Growth	46	NL	1.45%	15%
Babson Value	Growth & Income	514	NL	0.98%	6%
Copley Fund	Growth	75	NL	1.03%	5%
Davis New York Venture	Growth	2,189	4.75%	0.90%	15%
Dean Witter Dividend Growth	Growth & Income	10,519	NL	1.31%	6%
Dodge & Cox Stock	Growth	1,750	NL	0.60%	13%
Domini Social Equity	Growth	81	NL	0.98%	5%
Dreyfus Appreciation	Growth	605	NL	0.92%	5%
FAM Value	Growth	267	NL	1.25%	10%
Fortis Capital	Growth	305	4.75%	1.24%	14%
Franklin Growth	Growth	960	4.50%	0.90%	1%
Franklin Rising Dividends	Growth & Income	267	4.50%	1.43%	15%
Galaxy Equity Growth	Growth	148	3.75%	1.48%	14%
Mairs & Power Growth	Growth	104	NL	0.99%	4%
Oppenheimer Value Stock	Growth	144	5.75%	1.28%	12%
Pennsylvania Mutual	Growth	538	NL	0.98%	10%
Princor Growth	Growth	216	4.75%	1.16%	13%
Royce Value	Growth	148	NL	1.76%	14%
Salomon Brothers Opportunity	Growth	145	NL	1.18%	8%
Stagecoach Corporate Stock	Growth	365	NL	0.96%	6%
Third Avenue Value	Aggressive Growth	503	NL	1.33%	15%
Value Line Special Situations	Aggressive Growth	20	NL	1.06%	10%
Wayne Hummer Growth	Growth	103	NL	1.06%	3%

Average Annual Returns			Minimum Investment		Portfolio Manager	Since	Telephone
1 Year %	3 Year %	5 Year %	Initial $	Subsequent $			
23.6%	12.4%	14.4%	1,000	100	Schliemann/James	91/91	1-800-422-2766
17.2%	17.9%	17.8%	1,000	100	Nick Whitridge	1984	1-800-422-2766
6.7%	3.2%	9.5%	1,000	100	Irving Levine	1978	1-508-674-8459
15.4%	14.7%	18.2%	1,000	50	S. Davis/C. Davis	69/96	1-800-279-0279
18.9%	14.1%	13.6%	1,000	100	Paul Vance	1981	1-800-869-3863
16.5%	16.8%	16.4%	2,500	100	Team Mgt.	NA	1-800-621-3979
19.3%	15.8%	14.5%	1,000	0	Amy Domini	1991	1-800-762-6814
24.9%	20.9%	14.8%	2,500	100	Fayez Sarofim & Co	1990	1-800-645-6561
6.4%	10.0%	12.0%	2,000	50	Putnam/Van Buren	87/87	1-800-932-3271
11.4%	13.1%	12.5%	500	50	Stephen Poling	1983	1-800-800-2638
19.7%	19.1%	13.6%	100	25	Palmieri/Herrmann	65/91	1-800-342-5236
17.8%	11.1%	9.1%	100	25	Lippman/Baughman /McGee	87/87 /88	1-800-342-5236
18.3%	15.9%	12.9%	2,500	100	Edward Klieziewicz	1990	1-800-628-0414
21.5%	24.3%	19.8%	2,500	100	George Mairs III	1980	1-800-304-7404
17.7%	15.0%	13.6%	1,000	25	James McAllen	1996	1-800-525-7048
5.8%	8.6%	10.9%	2,000	50	Charles Royce	1973	1-800-221-4268
14.0%	16.8%	15.4%	300	50	Hamilton/Craven	87/93	1-800-247-4123
7.4%	8.8%	10.9%	2,000	50	Charles Royce	1982	1-800-221-4268
10.7%	13.9%	14.9%	1,000	100	Irving Brilliant	1979	1-800-725-6666
19.1%	16.2%	14.0%	1,000	100	Hom/Seto	84/91	1-800-222-8222
12.4%	13.1%	16.4%	1,000	1,000	Martin Whitman	1990	1-800-443-1021
1.3%	11.2%	9.4%	1,000	100	Team Mgt.	NA	1-800-223-0818
13.2%	10.7%	9.9%	1,000	500	Thomas Rowland	1996	1-800-621-4477

TWENTY-NINE

High-Volatility Funds

Investment return does not come free of charge. You always pay for it by taking risks. Generally, the most potentially rewarding investments contain the greatest risks. Investment risk is defined as return volatility. The more volatile are returns, the greater is investment risk. Equity investors face two types of risk: company-specific risk and market risk. Company-specific risk results from the business the firm is in, how it finances its operations, competitive forces, and chance. Market risk is the volatility of return that results from changing conditions in the financial markets. When the stock market falls, for example, the share prices of good companies are taken down with the bad. Similarly, during a stampeding bull market, even the share prices of mediocre companies rise along with the market.

The beauty of investing in an equity mutual fund is that the lion's share of company-specific risk is eliminated by diversification. Adverse events that cause the prices of some stocks to fall are offset by positive events that cause the share prices of others to rise. The result is muted volatility. However, mutual funds that invest in rapidly growing companies that command high price-earnings multiples tend to be much more volatile than those that invest in slower-growing companies whose year-to-year per share earnings are much more predictable. Of course, portfolios packed with highly volatile growth-company stocks return much more over the long run than do funds that contain a lower level of market risk.

The diversified equity funds that appear here are some of the most volatile around. (Absent from the list are industry-sector and precious metals funds.) As one might suspect, they have produced exceptional returns during the last five years. These funds are not suitable for conservative investors or investors with short-term investment horizons. However, long-term-oriented, aggressive-growth investors should find a number of these funds appealing. To make the list, a fund had to return more than 40 percent during 1995 and suffer a double-digit percentage loss during the three-month stock market correction ending July 31, 1996.

TABLE 26. HIGHLY VOLATILE FUNDS

Fund	Total Assets ($Mil)	Year Began	Sales Charges %	Expense Ratio %	Turnover Ratio %
Alger Mid Cap Growth	105	1993	5.00%	2.39%	121%
Alger Small Cap	558	1986	5.00%	2.11%	97%
Bull & Bear Special Equities	53	1986	NL	2.43%	154%
Columbia Special	1,609	1985	NL	0.98%	183%
Dean Witter Developing Growth	754	1983	5.00%	1.77%	114%
Dreyfus Special Growth	67	1982	NL	1.15%	69%
Founders Discovery	272	1990	NL	1.63%	118%
Govett Smaller Companies	416	1993	4.95%	1.95%	280%
Hancock Special Equities	957	1986	5.00%	1.50%	82%
Invesco Emerging Growth	298	1991	NL	1.49%	228%
Ivy Emerging Growth	64	1993	5.75%	1.95%	86%
Kemper Small Cap A	633	1969	5.75%	1.14%	102%
Navellier Aggressive Small Cap	246	1994	3.00%	1.75%	170%
Neuberger Berman Manhattan	584	1979	NL	0.98%	44%
Oberweis Emerging Growth	207	1987	NL	1.52%	79%
PBHG Emerging Growth	1,204	1993	NL	1.47%	97%
Perkins Opportunity	139	1993	4.75%	1.97%	92%
Phoenix Aggressive Growth	240	1981	4.75%	1.29%	331%
Putnam OTC Emerging Growth	1,695	1982	5.75%	1.14%	116%
Scudder Development	1,039	1971	NL	1.32%	42%
Stein Roe Capital Opportunities	1,316	1969	NL	1.25%	60%
Strong Discovery	582	1988	NL	1.40%	516%
20th Century Gift Trust	841	1983	NL	1.00%	105%
20th Century Vista	2,258	1983	NL	0.98%	89%
USAA Aggressive Growth	671	1981	NL	0.86%	86%
United New Concepts	548	1983	5.75%	1.25%	125%
Warburg Pincus Emerging Growth	968	1988	NL	1.26%	126%
Wasatch Mid Cap	163	1992	NL	1.75%	175%

Average Annual Returns			Minimum Investment		Portfolio Manager	Since	Telephone
1 Year %	3 Year %	5 Year %	Initial $	Subsequent $			
5.9%	20.9%	NA	0	0	Alger/Khoo/Tartaro	1993	1-800-992-3863
1.3%	16.0%	15.6%	0	0	Alger/Khoo/Tartaro	1993	1-800-992-3863
2.8%	6.6%	14.7%	1,000	100	Brett Sneed	1988	1-800-847-4200
14.3%	15.1%	17.7%	2,000	100	Chad Fleischman	1995	1-800-547-1707
17.5%	16.3%	18.1%	1,000	100	Jayne Stevlingson	1994	1-800-869-6397
6.4%	0.6%	11.5%	2,500	100	Michael Schonberg	1996	1-800-645-6561
20.1%	13.6%	16.1%	1,000	100	David Kern	1995	1-800-525-2440
10.7%	34.0%	NA	500	25	Jeffrey Bernstein	1995	1-800-821-0803
22.7%	19.7%	25.5%	1,000	0	Michael DiCarlo	1988	1-800-225-5291
31.1%	15.5%	NA	1,000	50	Schroer/Rasplicka	92/94	1-800-525-8085
25.8%	22.3%	NA	1,000	100	James Broodfoot	1993	1-800-456-5111
16.3%	13.4%	15.9%	1,000	100	Gary Langbaum	1995	1-800-621-1048
23.1%	NA	NA	2,000	500	Louis Navellier	1994	1-800-887-8671
0.3%	9.5%	13.0%	1,000	100	Mark Goldstein	1992	1-800-877-9700
22.9%	18.2%	18.7%	1,000	100	James Oberweis	1987	1-800-323-6166
32.6%	33.4%	NA	2,500	0	Pilgrim/Baxter	1993	1-800-433-0051
5.1%	30.1%	NA	2,500	100	Richard & Daniel Perkins	1993	1-800-366-8361
25.3%	19.3%	15.7%	500	25	Van Harissis	1996	1-800-243-1574
26.6%	24.2%	25.0%	500	50	James Callinan	1994	1-800-225-1581
17.5%	17.3%	15.2%	1,000	100	McKay/Chin	88/93	1-800-225-5163
49.6%	28.1%	24.5%	2,500	100	Gloria Santella	1991	1-800-338-2550
0.3%	11.0%	12.0%	1,000	50	Strong/Paquelet	88/96	1-800-368-3863
10.9%	23.4%	27.8%	500	50	Stowers III/Puff/Fogle	83/83/90	1-800-345-2021
13.5%	18.9%	17.5%	2,500	50	Stowers III/Fogle	83/90	1-800-345-2021
33.2%	25.4%	17.0%	1,000	50	Cabell/Efron	1995	1-800-531-8181
8.5%	17.3%	17.3%	500	100	Mark Seferovich	1989	1-913-236-1303
14.1%	15.9%	19.7%	2,500	100	Dater/Lurito	88/90	1-800-927-2874
-2.5%	20.0%	NA	2,000	100	Stewart/Barker	92/92	1-800-551-1700

CHAPTER

THIRTY

Asset Allocation Funds

"Asset allocation" has become a modern-day finance buzzword used to describe portfolios that contain more than two different classes of assets (for example, stocks, bonds, Treasury bills, and so on). Even some market timers who switch their investments back and forth between stocks and cash refer to themselves as asset allocators. To me, however, a true asset allocation fund is one that spreads its investments among several asset classes whose returns do not move in perfect harmony. Thus, the objective of the true asset allocator is to reduce portfolio variability (risk).

Asset allocation funds differ widely on the selection of asset classes to be included in their portfolios. However, most include several assets from the following classes: U.S. stocks, foreign stocks, precious metals, real estate stocks, domestic bonds, foreign bonds, foreign currencies, and money market instruments. Some asset allocation funds, such as the T. Rowe Price Spectrum Funds, invest in other mutual funds. When managing asset allocation funds, some portfolio managers apply a passive reallocation strategy, such as rebalancing the portfolio back to its initial allocation once each quarter. Others attempt to forecast returns in the various categories in which they invest. They then reallocate the fund's assets, giving more weight to those asset classes that are expected to produce the best returns. Thus, when investing in an asset allocation fund, it is very important to know which classes of assets the fund will invest in as well as whether management follows a passive or active reallocation strategy.

In theory, asset allocation funds should provide meaningful returns with reduced portfolio volatility. Unfortunately, asset allocation funds are relatively new additions to the investment world (the grandfather of asset allocation funds, the Permanent Portfolio Fund, commenced operations during 1982). Thus, there is insufficient data to tell how investment fact measures up to investment theory. However, if 1987 in any way represents asset allocation fund performance during a chaotic investment climate, these funds are all that they claim to be. By year-end 1987, the four asset allocation funds in existence at that time managed to beat the market. The group's best performer returned more than 16 percent during 1987. During 1987's turbulent fourth quarter, when the S&P 500 Index tumbled nearly 27 percent, asset allocation funds declined an average of only 10 percent, about one-third the decline of the typical equity mutual fund during that period.

During recent years, asset allocation funds have been underperformers when compared to the returns provided by the S&P 500 Index. However, that does not imply that asset allocation funds have been consistent underachievers. It is unfair to compare the returns of asset allocation funds with those of popular stock market indexes. Since most asset allocation funds invest in bonds, cash equivalents, and other assets such as gold and precious metals, they tend to possess far less risk than the typical equity fund. In fact, the median beta (market-risk exposure) of the funds described here is about two-thirds that of the typical equity mutual fund. Thus, when judged on a risk-adjusted return basis, they obtain relatively high marks. Asset allocation funds are ideally suited for conservative, growth-oriented investors, because they possess relatively low risk, provide a modest current yield, and are capable of producing double-digit annual returns over longer periods of time. Should the financial markets experience turbulence during the latter half of the 1990s, these funds could reside among the industry's best performers.

TABLE 27. ASSET ALLOCATION FUNDS

Fund	Total Assets ($Mil)	Year Began	Sales Charges %	Expense Ratio %	Turnover Ratio %
Crabbe Huson Asset Allocation	145	1989	NL	1.48%	226%
Dean Witter Strategist	1,303	1988	5.00%	1.63%	179%
Dreyfus Asset Allocation Total Return	62	1993	NL	1.25%	370%
Fidelity Asset Manager	10,790	1989	NL	0.97%	137%
Flex-Funds Muirfield	127	1988	NL	1.26%	NA
Fortis Advantage Asset Allocation	141	1988	4.75%	1.57%	94%
Galaxy Asset Allocation	106	1991	3.75%	1.54%	41%
Guardian Asset Allocation	79	1993	4.50%	1.25%	219%
Montgomery Asset Allocation	128	1994	NL	1.30%	96%
Oppenheimer Disciplined Allocation	259	1985	5.75%	1.17%	55%
Overland Express Asset Allocation	54	1988	4.50%	1.30%	47%
Permanent Portfolio	77	1982	NL	1.42%	10%
Preferred Asset Allocation	96	1992	NL	1.11%	18%
Prudential Allocation Strategy	105	1990	5.00%	1.33%	180%
Seafirst Asset Allocation	159	1988	NL	0.95%	NA
Stagecoach Asset Allocation	1,103	1986	4.50%	0.84%	15%
Strong Asset Allocation	269	1981	NL	1.17%	326%
USAA Cornerstone	1,045	1984	NL	1.13%	33%
Value Line Asset Allocation	63	1986	NL	1.39%	244%
Vanguard Asset Allocation	2,181	1988	NL	0.49%	34%

Average Annual Returns			Minimum Investment		Portfolio Manager	Since	Telephone
1 Year %	3 Year %	5 Year %	Initial $	Subsequent $			
6.6%	9.0%	11.3%	2,000	500	Team Mgt.	NA	1-800-541-9732
15.2%	11.2%	10.9%	1,000	100	Mark Bavoso	1988	1-800-869-3863
7.4%	10.5%	NA	2,500	100	Timothy Ghriskey	1996	1-800-645-6561
10.4%	8.0%	11.0%	2,500	250	Richard Habermann	1996	1-800-544-8888
2.5%	9.8%	10.8%	2,500	100	Robert Meeder	1988	1-800-325-3539
9.1%	10.0%	11.1%	500	50	Poling/Hudson/Hayek	88/95/95	1-800-800-2638
14.9%	11.6%	NA	2,500	50	Don Jones	1996	1-800-628-0414
10.8%	9.3%	NA	1,000	100	Frank Jones	1993	1-800-343-0817
18.1%	NA	NA	1,000	100	Stevens/Honour/Pratt	94/94/94	1-800-572-3863
13.7%	11.7%	12.1%	1,000	25	Richard Rubenstein	1991	1-800-525-7048
16.1%	14.4%	13.8%	1,000	100	Janet Campagna	1996	1-800-552-9612
-0.8%	3.8%	5.9%	1,000	100	Terry Coxon	1982	1-800-531-5142
13.8%	12.3%	NA	1,000	50	Hazuka/Peters	92/92	1-800-995-4769
8.1%	8.3%	9.7%	1,000	100	Smith/Goldberg	95/95	1-800-225-1852
13.0%	11.8%	11.0%	500	0	Pyle/Vielhaber	94/94	1-800-852-9730
10.5%	10.0%	11.7%	1,000	100	Derringer/Sakamoto	88/91	1-800-222-8222
9.4%	8.7%	10.0%	250	50	Bradley Tank	1993	1-800-368-1030
14.3%	10.0%	12.3%	3,000	50	Harry Miller	1990	1-800-383-8722
29.3%	20.3%	NA	1,000	100	Team Mgt.	NA	1-800-223-0818
15.3%	13.2%	13.4%	3,000	100	Thomas Hazuka	1988	1-800-662-7447

CHAPTER

THIRTY-ONE

Precious Metals Funds

The following table contains financial statistics for funds that invest in precious metals. Some of the funds invest in gold bullion and the shares of gold-mining companies only; others include investments in silver and platinum. A few funds restrict their investments to specific geographic areas such as South Africa or North America.

On average, the share prices of precious metals funds tend to be more volatile than the underlying prices of gold or silver bullion. That is because most funds invest heavily in mining stocks, whose earnings and share prices possess high volatility as a result of doing business in a high-fixed-cost industry. As a result of a high degree of operating leverage, small percentage changes in the price of gold can lead to large percentage changes in mining profits.

One basic force drives the price of gold: fear (or the lack of it). Political instability, the prospect of higher inflation, and a falling value of the U.S. dollar tend to drive the price of gold higher. Thus, the returns from investing in a precious metals fund tend to fluctuate in an opposite direction from the returns of most financial assets. As a result, investment in gold tends to lower portfolio variability (that is, investment risk) when combined with other investments such as stocks and bonds. However, to the extent that many precious metals funds invest in gold mining shares of companies doing business outside of the United States, there are also elements of political and foreign exchange risk inherent in these investments.

Given the depressed conditions that have existed in the gold and silver bullion markets in recent years, it is not surprising that precious metals funds as a group have been among the industry's poorest performers during the past fifteen years.

Although precious metals funds sport relatively low average betas, their share prices are extremely volatile. The low beta results from a very low correlation with returns from equities. On average, these funds pay very little current income, the exception being funds specializing in South African gold-mining shares.

TABLE 28. PRECIOUS METALS FUNDS

Fund	Total Assets ($Mil)	Year Began	Sales Charges %	Expense Ratio %	Turnover Ratio %
Benham Global Fund	515	1988	NL	0.64%	35%
Blanchard Precious Metals	107	1989	NL	2.29%	176%
Dean Witter Prec. Metals & Minerals	65	1990	5.00%	2.29%	23%
Fidelity Select American Gold	416	1985	3.00%	1.39%	56%
Fidelity Select Prec. Metals & Minerals	309	1981	3.00%	1.52%	53%
Franklin Gold	369	1969	4.50%	0.95%	6%
IDS Precious Metals	103	1981	5.00%	1.65%	50%
Invesco Strategic Gold	244	1984	NL	1.42%	72%
Keystone Precious Metals	183	1974	4.00%	2.28%	39%
Lexington Gold Fund	136	1975	NL	1.70%	40%
Lexington Strategic Investments	58	1974	5.75%	1.70%	115%
Lexington Strategic Silver	74	1984	5.75%	1.82%	44%
Midas Fund	176	1986	NL	2.26%	47%
Oppenheimer Gold	162	1983	5.75%	1.36%	358%
Pioneer Gold	36	1990	5.75%	1.75%	60%
Rydex Precious Metals	37	1993	NL	1.38%	1765%
Scudder Gold	175	1988	NL	1.65%	42%
Smith Barney Natural Resources	47	1986	5.00%	1.99%	40%
So-Gen Gold	60	1993	3.75%	1.41%	22%
United Services Gold Shares	152	1974	NL	1.42%	33%
United Services World Gold	251	1985	NL	1.55%	28%
USAA Gold	140	1984	NL	1.28%	35%
Van Eck Resources Gold	153	1986	5.75%	1.81%	6%
Van Eck Int'l Investors Gold	506	1955	5.75%	1.42%	4%
Vanguard Specialized Gold & Prec. Metals	582	1984	NL	0.60%	5%

Average Annual Returns			Minimum Investment		Portfolio Manager	Since	Telephone
1 Year %	3 Year %	5 Year %	Initial $	Subsequent $			
-3.2%	5.1%	9.7%	2,500	250	Bill Martin	1992	1-800-345-2021
19.3%	11.0%	13.3%	3,000	200	Peter Cavelti	1988	1-800-922-7771
7.3%	6.8%	4.0%	1,000	100	Konrad Krill	1994	1-800-869-3863
27.4%	14.7%	17.4%	2,500	250	Larry Rakers	1995	1-800-522-7297
8.3%	12.5%	13.3%	2,500	250	Lawrence Rakers	1996	1-800-522-7297
-1.2%	6.5%	6.6%	100	25	Wiskemann/Killea	72/94	1-800-342-5236
5.2%	28.5%	22.4%	2,000	100	Richard Warden	1991	1-800-328-8300
44.9%	16.4%	15.6%	1,000	50	Dan Leonard	1989	1-800-525-8085
2.7%	7.3%	10.9%	1,000	0	John Madden	1995	1-800-343-2898
11.7%	10.7%	9.4%	1,000	50	Robert Radsch	1994	1-800-526-0056
-6.6%	9.7%	6.1%	1,000	50	Robert Radsch	1994	1-800-526-0056
3.2%	11.7%	7.8%	1,000	50	Robert Radsch	1994	1-800-526-0056
22.3%	22.1%	23.5%	500	50	Kjeld Thygesen	1992	1-800-400-6432
1.8%	8.4%	8.3%	1,000	25	Diane Sobin	1995	1-800-525-7048
0.6%	5.8%	8.7%	1,000	50	David Tripple	1990	1-800-225-6292
-6.1%	NA	NA	15,000	0	Mike Byrum	1993	1-800-820-0888
40.5%	20.7%	16.4%	1,000	100	Donald/Wallace	88/88	1-800-225-2470
20.3%	11.2%	11.5%	1,000	50	Ailsing O'Duffy	1991	1-212-723-9147
-0.7%	6.7%	NA	1,000	0	Jean-Marie Eveillard	1993	1-800-628-0252
-25.7%	-6.9%	-8.9%	1,000	50	Victor Flores	1992	1-800-873-8637
28.7%	16.1%	18.9%	1,000	50	Victor Flores	1990	1-800-873-8637
1.2%	5.0%	7.9%	1,000	50	Mark Johnson	1994	1-800-382-8722
-0.3%	3.1%	9.9%	1,000	100	Lucille Palermo	1992	1-800-826-2333
-8.5%	4.1%	6.2%	1,000	100	Lucille Palermo	1996	1-800-826-2333
1.0%	7.2%	8.2%	3,000	100	David Hutchins	1987	1-800-662-7447

CHAPTER

THIRTY-TWO

Regional International Funds

The biggest benefit provided by mutual fund investing is the risk reduction that results from a well-diversified portfolio. Mutual funds that possess highly concentrated portfolios subject their shareholders to risks that are not present in diversified funds. Thus, I have never been a fan of investing in highly concentrated funds. However, as with most rules, there are some exceptions. Regional international funds invest in the securities of companies domiciled either in a single country or in a geographic area. The downside to investing in regional funds is the extra risk they possess. The upside is that some regional funds concentrate their investments in some of the fastest-growing economies in the world. Thus, these funds possess exceptional return potential and should be considered by long-term aggressive growth investors.

These funds tend to produce their best returns when the value of the U.S. dollar is either stable or in a slight decline. That's because nondollar-denominated assets get a return boost due to favorable currency translation. Although the potential rewards of investing in the world's great growth economies, such as Latin America, the Pacific Rim, and China are high, so are the risks. In fact, tumbling stock prices in Latin America and Japan in late 1994 and early 1995 nearly wiped out all returns earned by their shareholders during the last three years. However, the significant decline in stock prices in so-called developing economies has produced some of the most reasonably priced stocks around these days.

If regional international funds strike your fancy, remember that their extreme volatility requires that you invest for the long term. If you can't hold your investments in these funds for at least three to five years, you have no business investing in them. In addition, because of the extreme risks, allocate no more than 10 percent of your total portfolio to funds on this list.

TABLE 29. LOW COST REGIONAL INTERNATIONAL EQUITY FUNDS

Fund	Total Assets ($Mil)	Year Began	Sales Charges %	Expense Ratio %	Turnover Ratio %
Fidelity Europe	666	1986	3.00%	1.26%	52%
Fidelity Europe Capital Appreciation	165	1993	3.00%	1.32%	163%
Fidelity Hong Kong & China	84	1995	3.00%	2.00%	96%
Fidelity Japan	328	1992	3.00%	1.09%	104%
Fidelity Japan Small Company	122	1995	3.00%	1.38%	51%
Fidelity Latin America	665	1993	3.00%	1.37%	76%
Fidelity Pacific Basin	629	1986	3.00%	1.23%	133%
Fidelity Southeast Asia	825	1993	3.00%	1.14%	94%
Guiness Flight China	165	1994	NL	1.98%	18%
Invesco European	255	1986	NL	1.48%	96%
Invesco European Small Company	116	1995	NL	1.68%	141%
Invesco Latin American Growth	36	1995	NL	2.00%	29%
Invesco Pacific Basin	157	1984	NL	1.66%	56%
Japan Fund	511	1962	NL	1.14%	80%
Nomura Pacific Basin	33	1985	NL	1.78%	45%
Scudder Greater Europe Growth	92	1994	NL	1.50%	37%
Scudder Latin America	623	1992	NL	2.11%	40%
Scudder Pacific Opportunity	352	1992	NL	1.74%	64%
Strong Asia Pacific	84	1993	NL	2.00%	104%
T. Rowe Price European Stock	623	1990	NL	1.20%	17%
T. Rowe Price Japan	214	1992	NL	1.38%	62%
T. Rowe Price Latin America	196	1993	NL	1.82%	19%
T. Rowe Price New Asia	2,369	1991	NL	1.10%	47%
Vanguard International Equity European	1,281	1990	NL	0.35%	2%
Vanguard International Equity Pacific	990	1990	NL	0.35%	1%

Average Annual Returns			Minimum Investment		Portfolio Manager	Since	Telephone
1 Year %	3 Year %	5 Year %	Initial $	Subsequent $			
16.4%	16.7%	12.7%	2,500	250	Sally Walden	1992	1-800-544-8888
13.6%	NA	NA	2,500	250	Kevin McCarey	1993	1-800-544-8888
NA	NA	NA	2,500	250	Joseph Tse	1995	1-800-544-8888
1.0%	-1.2%	NA	2,500	250	Shigeki Makino	1994	1-800-544-8888
NA	NA	NA	2,500	250	Simon Fraser	1995	1-800-544-8888
23.1%	2.2%	NA	2,500	250	Patti Satterthwaite	1993	1-800-544-8888
-0.5%	3.1%	7.2%	2,500	250	Shigeki Makino	1996	1-800-544-8888
10.7%	11.7%	NA	2,500	250	Allan Liu	1993	1-800-544-8888
22.2%	NA	NA	5,000	250	Lynda Johnstone	1994	1-800-915-6565
18.5%	14.3%	9.8%	1,000	50	Stephen Chamberlain	1990	1-800-525-8085
25.7%	NA	NA	1,000	50	Crossley/Griffiths	1991	1-800-525-8085
18.7%	NA	NA	1,000	50	Jarvis/Lyon	1996	1-800-525-8085
5.3%	6.2%	6.2%	1,000	50	Steven Chamberlin	1987	1-800-525-8085
-2.2%	-6.3%	-1.4%	1,000	100	Seung Kwak	1994	1-800-535-2726
6.3%	3.5%	5.7%	1,000	0	Iwao Komatsu	1994	1-800-833-0018
22.8%	NA	NA	1,000	100	Franklin/Bratt/Gregory	1994	1-800-225-2470
19.5%	8.3%	NA	1,000	100	Games/Kenney/Rogers	1992	1-800-225-2470
2.4%	5.5%	NA	1,000	100	Allan/Brat/Cornell	1992	1-800-225-2470
4.5%	NA	NA	1,000	250	Anthony Cragg	1993	1-800-368-1030
19.4%	17.0%	12.4%	2,500	100	Martin Wade	1990	1-800-638-5660
-0.9%	-2.1%	NA	2,500	100	Martin Wade	1991	1-800-638-5660
18.5%	NA	NA	2,500	100	Martin Wade	1993	1-800-638-5660
6.9%	6.4%	13.0%	2,500	100	Martin Wade	1990	1-800-638-5660
14.4%	14.7%	12.1%	3,000	100	George Sauter	1990	1-800-662-7447
3.8%	2.6%	5.1%	3,000	100	George Sauter	1990	1-800-662-7447

THIRTY-THREE

Emerging-Markets Funds

Emerging-markets investing has great appeal because economically disadvantaged countries have the potential to sustain much higher growth rates than developed countries. In the United States, for example, a 2 or 3 percent annual real expansion in gross domestic product is considered healthy. In emerging economies, growth targets are twice this rate, and China has been growing at close to a 10 percent annual real rate for nearly a decade. And as growth stock investors know, the best returns are usually reserved for rapidly growing companies. Long-term, emerging-market investments should return an average of 15 to 18 percent annually. Thus, growth-oriented investors should consider making a long-term commitment to rapid-growth, emerging markets.

Given that most of the world's population lives in economic hardship, developing economies can grow at rapid rates for a long period of time before economic expansion slows to rates experienced by developed societies. Of the world's 5.5 billion people, 59 percent reside in Asia, 12 percent in Africa, 8 percent in Latin America, and 6 percent in the former Soviet Union. Although poor in terms of per capita gross domestic product, developing countries, because of their sheer size, are dominant economic forces. For example, five of the world's twelve largest economies are those of developing countries. China, India, Russia, Brazil, and Mexico all have gross domestic products larger than Canada's. And China is the world's third-largest economy, behind the United States and Japan.

After gaining an average of nearly 80 percent in 1993, emerging-market funds fell on hard times in 1994, with most funds posting double-digit losses. This experience tells you that investment risk in these markets is extremely high. Emerging-markets investment is not for everybody. Anyone with a low tolerance for risk should steer clear of these markets. Furthermore, emerging stock markets are highly unpredictable. For example, nearly everyone was caught off guard when the Mexican peso collapsed and the Mexican stock market plunged. Thus, emerging-markets investors must take a very long-term view when looking to rack up potential profits. If you can't stick with your emerging-markets funds for at least five years, you have no business investing in them.

Volatility in emerging markets is so high because the markets are so small. In India, for example, the total market capitalization of all stocks traded there is a minuscule $80 billion. As a result, mood swings by well-heeled investors can have a pronounced effect on share prices. Finally, even venturesome investors should limit their allocations to emerging-markets funds. At present, emerging markets represent less than 10 percent of the world equity market capitalization. Thus, I suggest that portfolio allocations also be limited to 10 percent of portfolio assets.

TABLE 30. EMERGING-MARKETS FUNDS

Fund	Total Assets ($Mil)	Year Began	Sales Charges %	Expense Ratio %	Turnover Ratio %
Biltmore Emerging Markets	107	1994	4.50%	2.15%	17%
Consulting Group Emerging Markets	96	1994	NL	1.75%	89%
Fidelity Emerging Markets	1,459	1990	3.00%	1.34%	80%
Glenmede Emerging Markets	94	1994	NL	1.81%	50%
Govett Emerging Markets A	85	1992	4.95%	2.50%	14%
GT Global Emerging Markets	266	1992	4.75%	2.14%	52%
Lexington Worldwide Emerging Market	331	1969	NL	1.88%	93%
Merrill Lynch Developing Capital Market	343	1992	5.25%	1.62%	71%
Montgomery Emerging Markets	931	1992	NL	1.80%	92%
Pioneer Emerging Markets	43	1994	5.75%	2.25%	247%
Robertson Stephens Developing Countries	58	1994	NL	1.83%	124%
Seven Seas Emerging Markets	117	1994	NL	1.25%	20%
T. Rowe Price Emerging Markets Stock	61	1995	NL	1.75%	29%
Templeton Developing Markets I	2,982	1991	5.75%	2.10%	10%
USAA Emerging Markets	52	1994	NL	2.50%	35%
Vanguard Int'l Equity Emerging Market	514	1994	NL	0.60%	3%
Warburg Pincus Emerging Markets	234	1994	NL	1.00%	69%

| Average Annual Returns | | | Minimum Investment | | Portfolio Manager | Since | Telephone |
1 Year %	3 Year %	5 Year %	Initial $	Subsequent $			
7.8%	NA	NA	250	50	Scott Sadler	1995	1-800-994-4414
8.7%	NA	NA	100	0	Rachael Maunder	1994	1-212-816-8725
10.2%	7.6%	11.9%	2,500	250	Richard Hazlewood	1993	1-800-544-8888
-2.8%	NA	NA	25,000	1,000	Douglas Polunim	1994	1-800-442-8299
4.9%	4.9%	NA	500	25	Rachael Maunder	1992	1-800-821-0803
1.7%	5.6%	NA	500	100	Jonathan Chew	1993	1-800-824-1580
6.9%	5.6%	9.4%	1,000	50	Richard Saler	1992	1-800-526-0056
9.6%	8.3%	11.3%	1,000	50	Grace Pineda	1989	1-800-637-3863
7.5%	6.5%	NA	1,000	100	Team Mgt.	NA	1-800-572-3863
16.3%	NA	NA	1,000	50	Mark Madden	1994	1-800-225-6292
6.6%	NA	NA	5,000	100	Michael Hoffman	1994	1-800-766-3863
7.5%	NA	NA	1,000	0	Robert Furdak	1994	1-800-647-7327
7.9%	NA	NA	2,500	100	Wade/Bruce	1995	1-800-225-5132
12.0%	8.6%	NA	100	25	Mark Mobius	1991	1-800-342-5236
10.4%	NA	NA	3,000	50	Travis Selmier II	1994	1-800-531-8181
12.9%	NA	NA	3,000	100	George Sauter	1994	1-800-662-2739
7.9%	NA	NA	2,500	100	King/Nicholas	89/89	1-800-927-2874

CHAPTER THIRTY-FOUR

Top-Rated Funds Closed to New Investors

Investors have poured more than $1.2 trillion into mutual funds during the last ten years. Although more than two thousand new funds were created during that period, a lot of money was channeled into funds that had exhibited "hot" performance numbers. Some funds received so much money that their boards of directors believed that further cash inflows could compromise the fund's investment strategy. As a result, a growing number of funds quit selling shares to new investors.

The "cash-flow effect" has been most pronounced for funds that invest in the small-cap sector of the market. Since small-cap stocks are highly illiquid, the purchase and sale of large blocks of small-caps requires that portfolio managers pay a premium over the current offer price to buy, and accept a discount below the bid price when they sell. The alternative to large block trading is to spread capital among hundreds of stocks or move up the target a notch and invest in mid-cap rather than small-cap stocks. Rather than fish in larger ponds, several small-cap funds cut off the flood of money by closing their doors to new investors.

However, there is a strong relationship between equity fund performance and cash flow. Equity funds with larger amounts of new cash tend to outperform similar equity funds that are not experiencing an influx of cash. This is especially true of funds that invest in small-cap stocks. Funds receiving a flood of new cash to invest can increase their positions in their favorite stocks, thereby buoying their price. In addition, a continual stream of cash allows portfolio managers an opportunity to add new, promising investments to their portfolios without being forced to sell their stellar performers. When a hot fund closes its doors to new investors, it also turns off the money flow. As a result, the fund loses some of the flexibility it once had, and the fund's relative performance tends to suffer.

What should you do when a fund closes its doors to new money? First, there is generally no reason to sell your shares immediately. As long as the fund continues to perform well, and as long as its management style fits your needs, you should continue to hold the fund's shares. If either of these two conditions changes, sell.

What about making additional investments in a closed fund? The answer is, it depends. Some funds close their doors before they become too large to effectively carry out their mandated investment objectives. Thus, making additional investments in these funds should not be bothersome. On the other hand, some funds close their doors only after they have been flooded with so much money that their portfolio managers' investment strategies become compromised. In these instances, there is little reason to remain a shareholder. Although you will be unable to get back into these funds once you liquidate your investments, so what? Your objective in selling is to find more promising investments elsewhere.

TABLE 31. TOP-RATED FUNDS CLOSED TO NEW INVESTORS

Fund	Total Assets ($Mil)	Year Began	Average Annual Returns		
			1 Year %	3 Year %	5 Year %
Babson Enterprise	225	1983	14.3%	11.7%	15.5%
CGM Capital Development	603	1960	25.0%	11.5%	16.9%
Fidelity Congress Street	86	1960	23.6%	20.9%	14.8%
Fidelity Exchange	250	1976	21.3%	18.6%	14.9%
Fidelity New Millennium	1,153	1992	25.6%	22.3%	NA
Franklin Balance Sheet	621	1990	12.9%	13.8%	18.5%
Harbor International	3,963	1987	15.9%	15.7%	14.4%
Heartland Value	2	1984	12.9%	15.8%	22.6%
IAI Emerging Growth	735	1991	30.8%	22.9%	24.7%
Janus Venture	1,906	1984	8.4%	15.0%	13.9%
Longleaf Partners	2,161	1987	14.9%	18.9%	19.8%
Montgomery Micro-Cap	306	1994	16.9%	NA	NA
Montgomery Small-Cap	275	1990	25.0%	14.1%	17.8%
Sequoia	2,329	1970	22.9%	18.1%	17.5%
Strong Common Stock	1,150	1989	15.7%	15.1%	18.3%
T. Rowe Price New Horizons	4,099	1960	24.9%	24.5%	22.2%
T. Rowe Price Small Cap Value	1,249	1988	18.7%	15.9%	18.7%
Vanguard Prime Cap	3,827	1984	10.0%	20.1%	18.2%
Vanguard Windsor	14,615	1958	13.1%	14.1%	16.0%
Wasatch Aggressive Equity	299	1986	-1.1%	12.6%	12.5%

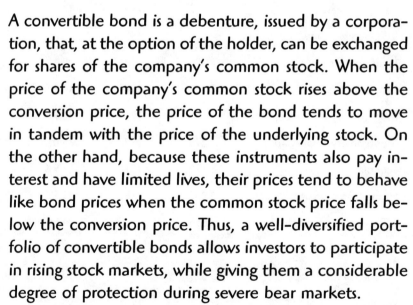

THIRTY-FIVE

Convertible Bond Funds

A convertible bond is a debenture, issued by a corporation, that, at the option of the holder, can be exchanged for shares of the company's common stock. When the price of the company's common stock rises above the conversion price, the price of the bond tends to move in tandem with the price of the underlying stock. On the other hand, because these instruments also pay interest and have limited lives, their prices tend to behave like bond prices when the common stock price falls below the conversion price. Thus, a well-diversified portfolio of convertible bonds allows investors to participate in rising stock markets, while giving them a considerable degree of protection during severe bear markets.

Although investment in convertible bonds at first glance appears to be the ideal investment strategy for risk-averse, growth-oriented investors, a convertible bond strategy does not come without its pitfalls. The convertible bond market tends to be a rather thinly traded market. Thus, bid and ask prices can widen substantially when a large block of bonds is purchased or sold. In addition, the price of convertible bonds can sink when a bear stock market results from rising interest rates. First, the bonds lose value because their underlying stocks are losing value. Second, the value of the instrument as a bond also decreases along with other bonds in a rising-interest-rate environment.

Convertible bond funds differ significantly from each other with respect to the degree to which they stress convertibles' fixed-income and equity characteristics. In varying degrees, most convertible bond funds blend the pursuit of growth and income. But some funds go to extremes, greatly prioritizing one over the other. A convertible bond fund's risks are directly related to the degree to which it stresses growth over income.

You can gain much insight into a convertible bond fund's objectives by looking at its yield. Generally, the higher a fund's yield, the more it stresses income and price stability at the expense of potential capital gains. At the opposite end of the spectrum are bolder vehicles that aggressively pursue growth. These types of funds tend to invest heavily in securities of emerging-growth companies and stress high-growth industries such as technology, health care, and pollution control. The majority of convertible bond funds, however, fall somewhere in between these two extremes.

Convertible bond funds tend to possess far less volatility than the typical growth-stock fund (average beta of about 0.60). In addition, while the yields of convertible bond funds are less than those of comparable-risk debentures, the returns are greater than those for most common stocks. As a result, convertible bond funds make excellent additions to the portfolios of conservative investors who seek a balance between growth of capital and current income.

TABLE 32. CONVERTIBLE BOND FUNDS

Fund	Total Assets ($Mil)	Year Began	Sales Charges %	Expense Ratio %	Turnover Ratio %
Calamos Convertible	27	1985	4.75%	1.50%	65%
Davis Convertible Securities	64	1992	4.75%	1.18%	54%
Dean Witter Convertible Securities	216	1985	5.00%	1.96%	138%
Franklin Convertible Securities	117	1987	4.50%	1.03%	109%
Gabelli Global Convertible Securities	16	1994	NL	2.41%	152%
Lexington Convertible Securities	10	1988	NL	2.52%	11%
Mainstay Convertible	43	1986	5.50%	1.47%	243%
Northern Income Equity	60	1994	NL	1.00%	67%
Oppenheimer Bond for Growth	38	1986	5.75%	1.08%	58%
Pacific Horizon Capital Income	253	1987	4.50%	1.23%	57%
Phoenix Convertible	213	1970	4.75%	1.18%	79%
Putnam Convertible Income Growth	854	1982	5.75%	1.16%	48%
Smith Barney Convertible	36	1992	5.00%	1.40%	48%
Value Line Convertible	70	1982	NL	1.08%	129%
Vanguard Convertible Securities	160	1986	NL	0.75%	46%

Average Annual Returns			Minimum Investment		Portfolio Manager	Since	Telephone
1 Year %	3 Year %	5 Year %	Initial $	Subsequent $			
13.0%	10.1%	12.7%	500	50	John & Nick Calamos	85/88	1-800-823-7386
16.0%	9.9%	NA	1,000	25	Andrew Davis	1994	1-800-279-0279
14.7%	11.0%	12.3%	1,000	100	Michael Knox	1994	1-800-869-6397
14.0%	11.9%	14.9%	100	25	Edward Jamieson	1987	1-800-342-5236
7.0%	NA	NA	1,000	0	Hartswell Woodson III	1993	1-800-422-3554
12.8%	10.1%	11.3%	1,000	50	Richard B. Russell	1988	1-800-526-0056
11.3%	11.3%	16.1%	500	50	Laplaige/Feinberg	91/92	1-800-522-4202
18.3%	NA	NA	2,500	50	Theordore Southworth	1995	1-800-595-9111
7.4%	NA	NA	1,000	25	Mike Rosen	1986	1-800-525-7048
17.7%	11.6%	15.9%	500	50	Ed Cassens	1994	1-800-346-2087
10.1%	7.6%	9.7%	500	25	John Hamlin	1992	1-800-243-1574
16.0%	12.0%	15.2%	500	50	Mullin/Pohl	1992	1-800-225-1581
10.1%	7.8%	NA	1,000	50	Robert Swab	1995	1-800-221-8806
20.2%	10.4%	13.4%	1,000	250	Team Mgt.	NA	1-800-223-0818
15.4%	9.3%	12.7%	3,000	100	Rohit Desai	1986	1-800-662-7447

CHAPTER THIRTY-SIX

Low-Cost Bond Funds

At the onset of the decade of the 1980s, fewer than 120 bond funds of all types existed. By 1996, that number had swelled to more than 2,200. During that fifteen-year period of frenetic growth, several categories of specialized bond funds were created, including Ginnie Mae funds, government income funds, international bond funds, and municipal bond funds that concentrate their investments in the issues of a single state. In addition, a growing number of funds "target" their maturities by investing in zero-coupon bonds with a specific target maturity. More recently, investors have been offered the opportunity to invest in renegotiable-rate home mortgages, which dominate the portfolios of so-called Adjustable Rate Mortgage (ARM) funds. Thus, today's income-oriented investor can find bond funds that assume a wide spectrum of risks in the pursuit of current income.

U.S. government bond funds invest in a variety of government securities. These include U.S. Treasury bonds, federally guaranteed mortgage-backed securities, and issues of government agencies such as the Federal Home Loan Bank, Federal Farm Credit, Student Loan Marketing, and Tennessee Valley Authority. These bonds pay interest that is taxable at the federal level but free of state and local taxes. U.S. government bond fund shareholders receive a pass-through of the exemption from state and local taxes on interest income earned.

GNMA (Government National Mortgage Association, or Ginnie Mae) funds invest in government-backed mortgage securities. To qualify for this category, a fund must always have 65 percent of its portfolio invested in mortgage-backed securities. ARM funds, for the most part, are short-term GNMA funds.

Corporate bond funds seek a high level of income by concentrating their portfolios in high-rated corporate bonds (called investment-grade bonds) and, to a lesser extent, in U.S. Treasury bonds or bonds issued by government agencies.

High-yield bond funds invest in lower-quality or unrated corporate bonds, known as junk bonds. These days, a growing number of junk bond funds also invest in bonds with investment-grade ratings.

While individuals have the option of investing directly in government securities, bond funds provide several advantages. First, bond funds make investment in government securities possible for investors with limited resources. Instead of buying bonds in large denominations, income investors can purchase a diversified portfolio by initially investing $2,500 or less in an appropriate government bond fund. Second, by investing in a bond fund, individuals obtain needed risk reduction since they own a pro rata share of a highly diversified portfolio rather than a small handful of issues. Third, bond investors are burdened with significant transaction costs when they trade small lots of bonds. In some instances, transaction costs can amount to an entire year's interest income. Finally, bond fund investors obtain a high degree of liquidity. Since the fund must purchase shares tendered at the end of a business day, investors with changing investment needs can easily adjust their bond fund holdings.

Tax-exempt, or municipal, bonds are debt obligations of local and state governments. The interest on these bonds is exempt from federal taxes and from state and local taxes in the states where the bonds are issued. Even though these bonds are called tax-exempt, municipal bond investors generally must pay state and local taxes on interest income earned on bonds issued outside the investor's state of residence. In addition, capital gains income earned on municipal bond investments is not exempt from federal taxation.

Municipal bonds are classified as general obligation bonds (interest and principal repayments are met by the taxing power of municipalities and states) and revenue bonds (ability to pay principal and interest is a function of the income earned by facilities such as toll roads, hospitals, and so on). Single-state municipal bond funds are similar to other municipal bond funds except that their portfolios contain the issues of only one state. Residents of that state receive a so-called triple tax advantage, since interest income is exempt from federal, state, and local taxation.

The Tax Reform Act of 1976 allowed mutual funds to pass through tax-free interest income to shareholders. (Prior to that time, only unit investment trusts were granted the tax-free pass-through.) The Kemper Municipal Bond Fund, the nation's first "minifund," was born in April of that year. Since then, more than one thousand tax-exempt bond funds have come to market. Some invest in only high-quality issues, while others seek a higher current yield by investing in bonds of marginal credit quality (generally revenue bonds). Other municipal bond funds invest in only insured issues. In addition, investors can find municipal bond funds whose managers target their average maturities to specific periods, such as short-term, intermediate-term, and long-term. With the expansion of tax rates levied by states and cities, municipal bonds issued outside an investor's state of residence have lost some of their tax-advantage appeal. As a result, a number of fund companies greatly expanded their offerings of single-state municipal bond funds. This has been one of the fastest-growing areas in the bond fund category in recent years.

Like taxable bond funds, municipal bond funds offer shareholders several advantages. First, they offer a high degree of liquidity. Most municipal bonds are traded infrequently; however, municipal bond fund shareholders can purchase or sell bond fund shares daily.

Second, because of the relatively low level of trading activity, municipal bonds possess very large bid-ask spreads. Thus, when purchasing and selling municipal bonds directly, investors trading in lots of less than $100,000 face trading costs that can easily erode an entire year's interest income. Finally, bond fund investors can obtain a high degree of portfolio diversification with the investment of a modest amount of money.

TABLE 33. LOW-COST BOND FUNDS

Fund	Total Assets ($Mil)	Expense Ratio %	Average Annual Returns			Minimum Investment $	Telephone
			1 Year %	3 Year %	5 Year %		
Corporate Investment Grade Bonds							
Dodge & Cox Income	390	0.54%	4.7%	5.4%	8.3%	2,500	1-800-621-3979
Hotchkis & Wiley Low Duration	189	0.58%	7.3%	7.8%	NA	5,000	1-800-346-7301
One Group Income Bond	520	0.58%	4.4%	4.1%	6.6%	1,000	1-800-338-4345
One Group Intermediate Bond	231	0.51%	4.9%	4.4%	NA	1,000	1-800-338-4345
One Group Limited Volatility Bond	605	0.50%	5.1%	4.6%	6.2%	1,000	1-800-338-4345
T. Rowe Price Spectrum Income	1,195	0.00%	8.2%	7.4%	9.2%	2,500	1-800-225-5132
Vanguard Bond Index Intermediate Term	470	0.20%	4.3%	NA	NA	3,000	1-800-635-1511
Vanguard Bond Index Short Term	283	0.20%	5.3%	NA	NA	3,000	1-800-635-1511
Vanguard Bond Index Total Market	3,336	0.20%	4.9%	4.9%	7.3%	3,000	1-800-635-1511
Vanguard Fixed Income Interm. Term Corporate	490	0.28%	4.5%	NA	NA	3,000	1-800-635-1511
Vanguard Fixed Income Long Term Corporate Bond	3,315	0.31%	3.4%	4.9%	9.3%	3,000	1-800-635-1511
Vanguard Fixed Income Short Term Corporate Bond	3,990	0.27%	5.7%	5.2%	6.6%	3,000	1-800-635-1511
Corporate High-Yield Bond							
Nicholas Income	168	0.58%	11.5%	8.6%	10.1%	500	1-414-272-6133
Vanguard Fixed Income High Yield Corporate	3,117	0.34%	9.5%	8.5%	11.9%	3,000	1-800-635-1511
U.S. Government Bonds							
Benham Treasury Note	300	0.51%	4.8%	4.0%	6.3%	1,000	1-800-472-3389
Dreyfus 100% US Treasury Long Term	134	0.87%	3.3%	2.9%	8.1%	2,500	1-800-782-6620

Fund	Total Assets ($Mil)	Expense Ratio %	Average Annual Returns			Minimum Investment $	Telephone
			1 Year %	3 Year %	5 Year %		
Schwab Short/Intermediate Government Bond	138	0.49%	4.8%	3.3%	NA	1,000	1-800-266-5623
Vanguard Fixed Income Interm. Term US Govt.	1,216	0.28%	4.0%	4.3%	NA	3,000	1-800-635-1511
Vanguard Fixed Income Long Term US Treasury	893	0.27%	2.0%	4.0%	8.8%	3,000	1-800-635-1511
Vanguard Fixed Income Short Term Federal	1,334	0.27%	5.5%	4.7%	6.2%	3,000	1-800-635-1511
Vanguard Fixed Income Short Term US Treasury	935	0.27%	5.1%	4.7%	NA	3,000	1-800-635-1511
GNMA Bonds							
Benham GNMA Income	1,099	0.58%	5.0%	5.4%	6.9%	1,000	1-800-472-3389
USAA GNMA	303	0.13%	4.0%	5.6%	6.9%	3,000	1-800-382-8722
Vanguard Fixed Income GNMA	7,031	0.29%	5.7%	6.0%	7.1%	3,000	1-800-635-1511
Municipal Bonds							
Columbia Municipal Bond	371	0.56%	4.8%	3.7%	6.3%	1,000	1-800-547-1707
Fidelity Limited Term Municipal	910	0.56%	4.9%	4.2%	6.9%	2,500	1-800-544-8888
Fidelity Municipal Income	1,820	0.59%	6.5%	3.7%	6.8%	2,500	1-800-544-8888
One Group Intermediate Tax Free	217	0.78%	5.2%	3.8%	6.0%	1,000	1-800-338-4345
One Group Muni Income	240	0.80%	5.3%	4.3%	NA	1,000	1-800-338-4345
SAFECO Municipal Bond	479	0.14%	7.2%	4.2%	7.4%	1,000	1-800-624-5711
Scudder Limited Term Tax-Free	122	0.50%	4.3%	NA	NA	1,000	1-800-225-2470
Strong High Yield Muni Bond	227	0.70%	5.4%	NA	NA	2,500	1-800-368-3863
T. Rowe Price Tax Free Income	1,340	0.57%	6.2%	4.2%	7.5%	2,500	1-800-225-5132
T. Rowe Price Tax Free Short/Intermediate	435	0.57%	4.0%	3.9%	5.1%	2,500	1-800-225-5132
USAA Tax Exempt Intermediate Term	1,654	0.37%	5.4%	4.6%	7.0%	3,000	1-800-382-8722

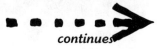

continues

Fund	Total Assets ($Mil)	Expense Ratio %	Average Annual Returns			Minimum Investment $	Telephone
			1 Year %	3 Year %	5 Year %		
USAA Tax Exempt Long Term	1,848	0.28%	6.9%	4.0%	7.1%	3,000	1-800-382-8722
USAA Tax Exempt Short Term	762	0.40%	4.5%	4.2%	5.0%	3,000	1-800-382-8722
Vanguard Muni High Yield	1,964	0.21%	6.7%	5.0%	8.0%	3,000	1-800-635-1511
Vanguard Muni Insured Long Term	1,946	0.21%	6.8%	4.7%	7.9%	3,000	1-800-635-1511
Vanguard Muni Intermediate Term	5,853	0.21%	4.8%	4.7%	7.2%	3,000	1-800-635-1511
Vanguard Muni Limited Term	1,738	0.21%	4.1%	3.9%	5.3%	3,000	1-800-635-1511
Vanguard Muni Long Term	1,100	0.21%	7.3%	4.9%	8.0%	3,000	1-800-635-1511
Vanguard Muni Short Term	1,411	0.21%	3.9%	3.7%	4.2%	3,000	1-800-635-1511
Single State Municipal Bonds							
Benham CA Muni High Yield	139	0.51%	9.0%	5.4%	7.7%	1,000	1-800-472-3389
Benham CA Tax Free Insured	190	0.50%	7.1%	4.3%	7.5%	1,000	1-800-472-3389
Benham CA Tax Free Intermediate Term	439	0.48%	4.8%	4.1%	6.3%	1,000	1-800-472-3389
Benham CA Tax Free Limited Term	100	0.51%	4.1%	3.7%	NA	1,000	1-800-472-3389
Benham CA Tax Free Long Term	285	0.49%	7.4%	4.4%	7.4%	1,000	1-800-472-3389
Fidelity CA Insured Muni	210	0.60%	6.5%	3.1%	6.9%	2,500	1-800-544-8888
Fidelity CA Municipal Income	476	0.58%	6.8%	3.9%	7.0%	2,500	1-800-544-8888
Fidelity MA Municipal Income	1,102	0.58%	5.9%	4.4%	7.2%	2,500	1-800-544-8888
Fidelity MI Municipal Income	458	0.59%	5.5%	3.1%	6.9%	2,500	1-800-544-8888
Fidelity MN Municipal Income	299	0.60%	5.1%	3.8%	6.3%	2,500	1-800-544-8888
Fidelity NY Insured Municipal Income	318	0.61%	5.4%	3.7%	6.9%	2,500	1-800-544-8888
Fidelity NY Municipal Income	409	0.60%	6.2%	4.1%	7.2%	2,500	1-800-544-8888
Fidelity OH Municipal Income	382	0.60%	5.5%	4.3%	7.2%	2,500	1-800-544-8888
Schwab CA Long Term Tax Free Bond	102	0.49%	7.3%	4.0%	NA	1,000	1-800-266-5623

Fund	Total Assets ($Mil)	Expense Ratio %	Average Annual Returns			Minimum Investment $	Telephone
			1 Year %	3 Year %	5 Year %		
Scudder MA Tax Free	316	0.75%	6.2%	4.5%	8.1%	1,000	1-800-266-5623
T. Rowe Price MD Tax Free	799	0.54%	6.1%	4.2%	7.2%	2,500	1-800-225-5132
USAA CA Bond	413	0.42%	8.3%	4.6%	7.3%	3,000	1-800-382-8722
USAA VA Bond	269	0.34%	7.0%	4.6%	7.3%	3,000	1-800-382-8722
Vanguard CA Tax Free Insured Intermediate	271	0.21%	5.7%	NA	NA	3,000	1-800-635-1511
Vanguard CA Tax Free Insured Limited Term	992	0.20%	7.5%	4.8%	7.7%	3,000	1-800-635-1511
Vanguard FL Insured Tax Free	462	0.21%	6.9%	4.9%	NA	3,000	1-800-635-1511
Vanguard NJ Tax Free Insured Long Term	803	0.21%	5.7%	4.3%	7.5%	3,000	1-800-635-1511
Vanguard NY Insured Tax Free	890	0.22%	6.1%	4.5%	7.6%	3,000	1-800-635-1511
Vanguard OH Tax Free Insured Long Term	204	0.21%	6.1%	4.4%	7.5%	3,000	1-800-635-1511
Vanguard PA Tax Free Insured Long Term	1,580	0.20%	6.4%	4.6%	7.7%	3,000	1-800-635-1511

Section III

The 300 Best
Mutual Funds
in America

The 300 Best Mutual Funds in America

The following pages contain descriptions of the three hundred best mutual funds that money can buy. If you are bewildered by the growing number of funds and don't know where to begin your search for those that suit your needs, confine your search to the equity funds described here. In my opinion, these are the best funds around. Of course, the operative phrase is "in my opinion." Everyone is entitled to his own opinion. However, I know plenty of opinionated people who possess wacky ideas. To these people, I usually say: "You are entitled to your own opinion, but you're wrong."

Given that this list of funds is based on my opinion, am I also wrong? I may be. Bring two dozen mutual fund experts together and you are sure to get a couple of dozen lists of the best funds in America. Although these rosters would include a number of common listings, I'll bet that the total number of distinct funds would total nearly one thousand. Personal biases and varying criteria would account for the differences in list composition. Besides, there are plenty of great mutual funds around these days.

The plain truth is that there are no hard rules that allow one to distinguish between funds that will perform well and those that will deliver mediocre performance. So, why not just screen the universe of funds for those that have performed best in the past? There are two problems with this approach. First, the question of performance over what time horizon arises. Should you use one year, three years, five years, or an even longer time period? Second, there is no guarantee that a fund that has provided an exceptional return over some previous time period will do so in the future. In fact, the Securities and Exchange Commission requires all funds that advertise their historical returns to include the phrase "past returns are no guarantee of future results" in their advertisements. (Most relegate this phrase to the smallest size type they can find and bury it at the bottom of their ad copy.)

So, why not pin a list of all available funds to your wall and heave darts? The strategy is not very scientific (not to mention that you are going to have a lot of holes to repair). However, if you throw enough darts and hold the shares selected by your well-focused aim over the long term, you will probably outperform nearly half of the thirty-eight million people who invest in mutual funds. Although this approach has some appeal, there is a better way to select funds.

Although no one knows precisely which funds will perform best in the future, a large number of funds that appear on best-performance lists possess a number of common traits. Over time, the best-performing funds tend to be relatively low-cost ones: those that are run by portfolio managers who have been managing the fund's portfolio for a relatively long time and who tend to show a degree of patience with their investment selections, those with a well-delineated investment philosophy and a sound investment strategy, and those that have stood the test of time.

In selecting funds for my list of the best equity funds in America, I sought these characteristics. I did not require every fund to possess all of the aforementioned traits; however, all possess one or more of the items that tend to lead to exceptional performance. I began my search by screening the more than thirty-seven hundred equity funds using five variables. I looked for funds with at least $30 million in total assets and at least a three-year life, that were currently selling shares to the general public, that had an annual expense ratio of 2 percent or less, and that required a minimum initial investment of $5,000 or less.

The application of these general screens reduced the universe to approximately fourteen hundred funds. I then divided the funds into seven groups according to their general investment objectives: aggressive growth, growth, growth and income, industry sector, international, and precious metals. Grouping was necessary to insure that a sufficient number of funds in each group would make the final list. This ensures that all investors will be able to invest in a portfolio of the best funds that also suit their individual needs and investment objectives. Finally, I examined the funds in each category and discarded those that did not contain the requisite characteristics. I repeated the process of elimination several times until the final list contained the three hundred funds described on the following pages.

What You Will Find Here

The three hundred funds described on the following pages represent about 8 percent of the equity funds in existence. They are funds that have a three-year operating history, with relatively low minimum initial investment requirements, and that are currently selling shares to individual investors. Included are seventy aggressive growth funds, seventy growth funds, seventy growth and income funds (including both balanced and equity-income funds), fifty international funds (including both global and foreign funds), thirty industry-sector funds, and ten precious metals funds.

Included are both no-load and load funds. Although I personally prefer to invest exclusively in no-load funds, there are a large number of well-managed funds that possess modest annual distribution fees or modest front-end loads. Some of these load funds waive the sales fee if they are purchased in company-sponsored 401(k) or SEP retirement accounts. Others are sold without sales charges to financial advisers who manage the assets of individual investors. Others waive the load for bulk purchases of $100,000 or more. The aim of this presentation is to serve the needs of all types of investors.

The three hundred funds have been drawn from ninety-three different families. Ten fund families are heavily represented. These include (with number of funds in parentheses): Dreyfus (six), Fidelity (thirty-seven), Founders (seven), Janus (six), INVESCO (fourteen), Scudder (ten), Strong (six), T. Rowe Price (nineteen), USAA (seven), and Vanguard (twelve). These ten families supply approximately 40 percent of the funds that make the "best" list. This does not mean that these families have a corner on the best funds. For example, you would expect to find a large representation by Fidelity, which has a family of more than one hundred funds. Relatively few fund families offer industry-sector funds (that is, Fidelity, INVESCO, and Vanguard), which ballooned the number of funds in these fund families. In addition, some fund families (such as Benham and Franklin) offer predominately bond rather than equity funds. Finally, my strong bias toward no-load funds has no doubt led to an increased presence of funds from a number of these families, that offer no-load funds only.

What You Won't Find Here

I have made every attempt to provide a list of funds that are usable by individual investors. Thus, a number of well-managed funds were excluded from consideration. These include funds and fund families that sell their shares to institutional investors only (such as Dimensional Fund Advisors, Federated, and so on); funds that have discontinued selling shares to new investors (for example, Babson Enterprise, Strong Common Stock, and Vanguard Windsor); well-managed funds with large initial investment requirements (for example, Brandywine, which has a $25,000 initial investment requirement); relatively new funds or fund families that have a limited operating history (for example, Van Wagoner Funds); and passively managed index funds (a list of these funds appears in section II). In the case of funds selling various classes of shares (A, B, C, and so on), I have opted to include the front-end loaded A shares.

How to Use this List

I have tried to include enough information about each of the funds listed here so that you can reduce the number of funds that suit your needs to a manageable few. The next step is to contact the funds that have peaked your interest and obtain the latest prospectuses and shareholder financial reports. Read these documents carefully before making your final selections.

The data contained in these fund descriptions have been obtained from the mutual funds themselves. Although reasonable care has been exercised, data and compilations cannot be guaranteed. As with any almanac, the descriptions are limited to the latest data available prior to publication. During the course of the year it is reasonable to expect changes in fund operations and financial statistics. Some funds may close their doors, while funds that were previously closed to new investors may resume selling their shares to new investors. Mergers between funds or fund families might cause some funds to cease to exist. Changes in operating policies might change minimum investment requirements or fund expenses. Finally, changing conditions in the financial markets can cause historical returns to fluctuate widely.

This almanac is unique in several respects. First, to get this year's edition on your booksellers' shelves early in 1997, I used September 30, 1996, as the terminal date when computing one-year, three-year, five-year, and since-inception average annual returns. Second, I have included two descriptive sections not normally included in other mutual fund annuals, "Suitability" and "Portfolio Implications." Although it is the responsibility of readers to determine the specific funds that are suitable to their needs and objectives, I have attempted to provide some assistance. The "Portfolio Implications" section describes how a fund might be best combined with other funds. The goal is to assist investors in assembling a portfolio of mutual funds that offers an optimal combination of portfolio return and portfolio risk. Finally, I have included, whenever possible, a fund's home page on the World Wide Web. In addition to a presentation of the latest financial statistics, these home pages frequently allow investors to download prospectuses and purchase applications. In short, I have attempted to make the almanac as user-friendly as possible. I welcome reader comments and suggestions that will improve future editions. Please address your correspondence to: Gerald Perritt, Investment Information Services, Inc., 12514 Starkey Road, Largo, Florida 33773, or to my E-mail address, MutLetter@aol.com.

CHAPTER

THIRTY-SEVEN

Aggressive Growth Funds

Aggressive growth funds have as their primary investment objective the pursuit of maximum capital gains. They invest aggressively in speculative stocks and tend to stay fully invested at all times. Some funds use financial leverage (stock market margin) in an attempt to enhance returns, others invest in mid-cap and small-cap firms, while still others attempt to purchase common stocks of the fastest-growing companies regardless of whether they are large or small. Some funds in this category invest in highly concentrated portfolios consisting of a handful of stocks drawn from two or three industries.

Needless to say, the share prices of aggressive growth funds are quite volatile, performing very well in bull markets and faring very poorly in bear markets. A number of funds in this group possess betas of 1.20 or more. Thus, investment in these funds is not for the faint of heart. Generally, aggressive growth funds are suitable for long-term investors (with investment horizons of five years or more) who can assume above-average risks and are not bothered by short-term stock market fluctuations. However, over the long run, because of the risks assumed, these funds tend to provide the greatest investment returns.

Since their portfolios are packed with the stocks of growth companies that retain most of their earnings, aggressive growth funds possess scant current yields. In fact, a vast majority of the funds described on the following pages provide no current income at all. In addition, these funds tend to possess very high portfolio turnover ratios.

After underperforming the S&P 500 Index between 1986 and 1990, aggressive growth fund returns exploded to the upside. Rising interest rates during nearly all of 1994 put a lid on stock market returns and caused double-digit percentage losses among some aggressive growth funds. However, aggressive growth funds have resumed their skyward trek during the last two years.

Among the better performers in recent years were funds that reside in relatively small fund families such as Govett, Robertson Stephens, and Oberweis. In addition, the top performers were heavily invested in technology stocks and mid- and small-cap issues.

Not too surprisingly, most of the funds with better-than-average performance during the last five- and ten-year periods are high-risk, high-beta funds. Although these funds are well managed and should continue to produce market-topping returns over the long run, the onset of a major bear stock market could send the share prices of these funds reeling. Thus, investors attracted to aggressive growth funds with outstanding short-run returns should consider their personal risk tolerance level before making an initial investment in any of them.

ACORN FUND

Wanger Asset Management
227 West Monroe Street
Suite 3000
Chicago, IL 60606
800-922-6769

Inception: *1970*
Total Assets: *$2.8 Billion*
Ticker Symbol: *ACRNX*
Home Page: *None*

Objective and Strategy: This well-managed fund seeks to capitalize on the above-average returns supplied by smaller companies. Focus is placed on above-average growth, niche companies with market values generally below $800 million that sell at modest multiples to book value and per share earnings. Because of a large influx of new money, the fund closed its doors to new shareholders in 1990. It began selling shares again last year. Traditionally, the fund has focused on tiny, growth companies. However, its large asset base has forced management to focus on mid-cap stocks. In addition, Mr. Wanger has turned to markets overseas in the search for reasonably valued stocks. Thus, this growth vehicle possesses more diversification than might first meet the eye.

Portfolio Manager: Ralph Wanger since the fund's inception in 1970. He is now assisted by Charles P. McQuaid and Terence M. Hogan, who have worked with him for eighteen and ten years, respectively.

Suitability: This fund is suitable for all growth-oriented investors. However, because Mr. Wanger takes a long-term view when adding new investments, the best results are obtained by investors who also are long-term oriented.

Annualized Returns
1-Year 16.6%
3-Year 10.4%
5-Year 18.6%

Portfolio Implications: The fund's portfolio may duplicate other small- and mid-cap fund holdings. In addition, its large allocation to foreign stocks provides some overlap for highly diversified investors.

Risk: This fund contains more volatility than indicated by its modest 0.82 beta. First, it invests in smaller companies, and its overseas investments expose investors to a degree of currency and political risk. The fund's share price tumbled more than 24 percent during the 1990 bear market.

Costs: This is one of the lowest-cost, actively managed funds around. The fund is sold with a no-load format, possesses a very low 0.57-percent annual expense ratio, and its 29-percent portfolio turnover ratio is well below average for aggressive growth funds.

Distributions: Income distributions are paid in June and December, and capital gains distributions occur in late December.

How to Buy and Sell: Minimum initial investment $1,000; IRA $200; subsequent investments $100. Telephone exchange with other Acorn funds and several other money market funds.

AIM CONSTELLATION

AIM Distributors
11 Greenway Plaza
Suite 1919
Houston, TX 77046
800-347-4246

Inception: 1976
Total Assets: $10.5 Billion
Ticker Symbol: CSTGX
Home Page: http://
www.aimfunds.com

Objective and Strategy: This fund seeks capital appreciation by investing in common stocks of small to mid-sized companies. There is a tendency for this fund to turn its portfolio over rather quickly because management focuses on earnings momentum stocks. Depending on the stock market environment, the fund will hold traditional high-growth industries such as health care and technology or more sedate sectors such as retail or industry cyclicals. Like most momentum players, the fund sells a stock following any slowdown in earnings growth. As one might expect, performance is exceptional during bull markets. However, the fund has also performed rather well during market downturns too. The fund's hefty front-end load cuts into its exceptional portfolio performance statistics.

Annualized Returns
1-Year 10.4%
3-Year 17.6%
5-Year 19.9%

Portfolio Manager: Team managed by Robert M. Kippes (1993), Kenneth A. Zschappel (1996), Charles D. Scavone (1996), and David P. Barnark (1996).

Suitability: This well-managed fund is designed for people aggressively seeking capital growth. Its hefty front-end load requires a long-term investment orientation.

Portfolio Implications: This fund's portfolio will provide some duplication with small- and mid-cap funds. The fund performs best during the lengthy overperformance legs of the so-called small-cap performance cycle.

Risk: As you might expect, this fund reaches for hefty returns and investors pay the price by assuming extreme volatility. The fund's beta is a hefty 1.27, and its share price plunged by slightly more than 29 percent during the 1990 bear market.

Costs: Purchasers pay a hefty 5.5-percent front-end load. However, once you pay the entrance fee, operating expenses tend to be below average. Last year its expense ratio averaged 1.16 percent, and its 45-percent portfolio turnover ratio is below average for the group.

Distributions: Both income and capital gains distributions are paid in mid-December.

How to Buy and Sell: Minimum initial investment $500; IRA $250; subsequent investments $25. Telephone exchange with other AIM funds. Shares also available at Charles Schwab.

ALGER GROWTH

Fred Alger Management Company
75 Maiden Lane
New York, NY 10038
800-992-3863

Inception: 1986
Total Assets: $247 Million
Ticker Symbol: AFGPX
Home Page: http://
www.networth.galt.com

Objective and Strategy: This fund seeks long-term growth of capital by investing in companies that demonstrate high historical and potential earnings growth. Generally, these stocks command above-market price-earnings ratios. Management invests in companies with market capitalizations of $1 billion or greater. David Alger, portfolio manager, prefers to invest in companies that are still in the development state or in older companies that appear to be entering a new stage of growth. This approach has led him to invest heavily in technology stocks during the last couple of years. Should a company disappoint, it is quickly swept out of the portfolio. Given the thirst for growth and an earnings momentum strategy, this fund is one of the most aggressive of its fund group.

Annualized Returns
1-Year 3.5%
3-Year 16.0%
5-Year 16.4%

Portfolio Manager: David D. Alger since the fund's inception in 1986. Seilai Khoo and Ronald Tartaro also co-manage the fund and have been with the adviser since 1989 and 1990, respectively.

Suitability: This fund is suitable for only the most aggressive growth-oriented investors. If you can't tolerate a sharp plunge in share price that at times can cut your investment in half, stay away from this vehicle. Given the hefty deferred sales charge, this is not a fund to trade.

Portfolio Implications: Because of the aggressive nature of this fund, investors should limit their allocations to no more than 15 percent of portfolio assets. Because of its technology bent, its portfolio will closely track the various technology sector indices.

Risk: This is one of the highest-risk aggressive growth funds you will find. Its beta is a whopping 1.29, and its heavy technology concentration adds to its short-term volatility. Its share price tumbled more than 16 percent during the 1990 bear market.

Costs: Shares are sold with a contingent deferred sales charge that begins at 5.0 percent and is reduced by 100 basis points each year the shares are held. In addition, shareholders are assessed a hefty 0.75-percent ongoing 12b-1 distribution fee. The 2.09-percent annual expense ratio is above average as is its 118-percent portfolio turnover ratio.

Distributions: Both income and capital gains distributions are paid in December.

How to Buy and Sell: No minimum initial or subsequent investment requirement. Telephone exchange with other Alger funds. Shares may also be obtained by institutional clients of Charles Schwab and at Fidelity Brokerage. Beware of the fund's large exit fee.

ALGER MIDCAP GROWTH

Fred Alger Management Company
75 Maiden Lane
New York, NY 10038
800-992-3863

Inception: 1993
Total Assets: $105 Million
Ticker Symbol: AMCGX
Home Page: http://
www.networth.galt.com

Objective and Strategy: If you are after whopping return potential, and extreme share price volatility doesn't frighten you, this is the fund for you. The fund seeks long-term capital appreciation by investing in mid-sized companies that offer promising growth potential. The fund may also invest in small-cap companies, such as those held in the Alger Small-Cap Fund, and some large-cap companies held in the Alger Growth portfolio, keeping the overall portfolio's market cap weighting within the range of the companies included in the S&P Mid-Cap 400 Index. Historically, its portfolio has been somewhat compact, containing about sixty stocks, about 80 percent of which do not pay cash dividends. David Alger has not been shy about paying up for the exceptional growth stocks he prefers.

Portfolio Manager: David D. Alger since the fund's inception in 1993. Seilai Khoo and Ronald Tartaro also comanage the fund and have been with the adviser at other Alger funds since 1989 and 1990, respectively.

Suitability: If you like the thrill of jumping out of airplanes, you'll love this fund. It is only suitable for the most aggressive growth-seeking investors. Its exit fee dictates a long-term view.

Annualized Returns
1-Year 5.9%
3-Year 20.9%
5-Year NA

Portfolio Implications: This fund gives you a cross section of all the Alger funds. Thus, ownership of this fund will be somewhat duplicated by the company's other offerings. The fund has a heavy technology exposure. It works best when combined with more sedate growth funds.

Risk: You won't find too many more funds with volatility in excess of this one. Its beta is a whopping 1.32. This relatively young fund has yet to experience a severe bear stock market, but you can expect a plunge in share price when one eventually occurs.

Costs: Shares are sold with a contingent deferred sales charge that begins at 5.0 percent and is reduced by 100 basis points each year the shares are held. In addition, shares are assessed a hefty 0.75-percent ongoing 12b-1 distribution fee. The 2.39-percent annual expense ratio is well above average as is its 120-percent portfolio turnover ratio.

Distributions: Income and capital gains distributions are paid annually, usually in December.

How to Buy and Sell: Hefty exit fee. No minimum initial or subsequent investment requirements. Telephone exchange with other Alger funds. Shares available to institutional investors at Charles Schwab.

ALLIANCE QUASAR CLASS A

Alliance Funds Distributors
500 Plaza Drive, 3rd Floor
Secaucus, NJ 07094
800-221-5672

Inception: 1969
Total Assets: $221 Million
Ticker Symbol: QUASX
Home Page: http://
www.alliancecapital.com

Objective and Strategy: Although billed as a small-cap growth fund, this fund's portfolio has been packed with medium- to large-cap growth company stocks from the computer technology and telecommunications industries, which were poor performers a few years ago. Since then, however, the fund's sector bets have paid off handsomely. Today, its portfolio is chock-full of smaller companies involved in the exploration of new products, new markets, and new technologies. Thus, heavy emphasis is placed on telecommunications, computers, health care, and retail. At times, the fund's portfolio will contain unlisted and foreign securities. This is one of the better growth vehicles around. Our only concern is that it has had three different lead portfolio managers during the last six years.

Portfolio Manager: Alden M. Stewart since 1994, Randall E. Haase since 1994, and Timothy Rice since 1993. Previously Stewart and Haase were associated with Equitable Capital and Rice with Alliance.

Suitability: The fund's shares are suitable for aggressive, long-term, growth-oriented investors. Conservative investors should limit their investment in this fund to no more than 10 percent of portfolio assets.

Annualized Returns

1-Year 42.4%
3-Year 21.3%
5-Year 16.6%

Portfolio Implications: Large-cap growth investors gain a degree of diversification benefit from investing in this smaller-cap fund. The fund works best when added to a portfolio containing growth and international equity funds.

Risk: This is another highly volatile, high beta (1.22) aggressive growth fund. During the 1990 bear market, this fund's share price plunged nearly 31 percent.

Costs: The fund is one of the more costly aggressive growth vehicles. Investors pay a 4.25-percent front-end load and a 0.30-percent annual 12b-1 fee. Its 1.83-percent expense ratio is above average as is its 160-percent portfolio turnover ratio.

Distributions: Income and capital gains distributions are paid annually, usually in early December.

How to Buy and Sell: Investors pay a front-end sales fee. Minimum initial investment $250; IRA $250; subsequent investments $50. Telephone exchange with other Alliance funds. Class B and C shares also available. Shares also available at Fidelity Brokerage.

BABSON ENTERPRISE II

Jones & Babson
2440 Pershing Road
Kansas City, MO 64108-2518
800-422-2766

Inception: 1991
Total Assets: $46 Million
Ticker Symbol: BAETX
Home Page: http://
www.jbfunds.com

Objective and Strategy: This is the most recent addition to the Babson family of no-load funds. It began selling shares at about the time Babson Enterprise closed its doors to new investors. Although its portfolio contains some small-cap stocks, its emphasis is on the mid-cap sector of the market and it is not meant to be a clone of Enterprise. In fact, in recent years, this fund has performed much better than its older namesake. That shouldn't be too surprising, given investors' interest in this market sector. Management uses a strict value discipline and thus is not as heavily invested in high-tech companies as are many of its peers. Before a company's stock finds its way into this portfolio it must demonstrate its growth potential and be reasonably priced relative to sales, earnings, and book value.

Annualized Returns
1-Year 23.6%
3-Year 12.4%
5-Year 14.4%

Portfolio Manager: Peter C. Schliemann and Lance F. James have been comanagers since the fund's inception in 1991. Schliemann is also portfolio manager of the Babson Enterprise and Babson Shadow Stock funds.

Suitability: This growth vehicle is suitable for both aggressive and conservative growth-oriented investors. Its lower-than-average portfolio turnover ratio suggests shares are suitable for patient investors only.

Portfolio Implications: This is one growth fund that can be added to any equity fund portfolio. Its emphasis on mid-cap value stocks provides little duplication with other mid-cap growth funds.

Risk: This is one of the lowest-risk mid-cap funds around. Its beta is a below-average 0.77. Although it has yet to experience a giant bear market, it should fare better than its peers when one eventually comes stalking.

Costs: The fund is sold with a no-load format. Like most Babson offerings, its operating costs are modest. Its 1.45-annual expense ratio is below average for a small fund, and its 15-percent portfolio turnover ratio is among the lowest in the group.

Distributions: Income and capital gains distributions are paid in late December.

How to Buy and Sell: Minimum initial investment $1,000; IRA $250; subsequent investments $100. Telephone switch with other Babson funds. Shares are also available at both Charles Schwab and Fidelity Brokerage with no transaction fees.

BARON ASSET FUND

The Baron Funds
767 Fifth Avenue
24th Floor
New York, NY 10153
800-992-2766

Inception: 1987
Total Assets: $1.1 Billion
Ticker Symbol: BARAX
Home Page: None

Objective and Strategy: The ambitious goal of this aggressively managed small-cap growth fund is to "double shareholder's net worth every three to five years." With a 20-plus percent annual return during the last five years, the fund has exceeded its goal. In general, management follows a "sunrise industry" theme when selecting stocks. These are the stocks of companies in which our children are likely to be employed. The stocks benefit from various demographic trends including growth of the Hispanic population, an aging population, government privatizations, and growth in the temporary help and human resource outsourcing businesses. The portfolio is packed with high-growth, high price-earnings ratio stocks. Stocks are sold quickly if growth falls below expectations.

Portfolio Manager: Ron Baron since the fund's inception in 1987. He is president of Baron Capital, has more than twenty-one years experience as a portfolio manager, and has built an enviable reputation as a growth stock investor.

Suitability: The fund is suitable for long-term, growth-oriented investors. It is an ideal vehicle to use in funding a child's education or for younger employees seeking to grow their retirement assets.

Annualized Returns
1-Year 21.3%
3-Year 20.1%
5-Year 21.0%

Portfolio Implications: The fund is best used in conjunction with small-cap value funds or any growth-seeking large-cap fund. Its portfolio might provide some duplication with small- and mid-cap aggressive growth funds.

Risk: Although its beta is a modest 1.06, there is more risk here than first meets the eye. Simply stated, you can't earn 21-percent annual returns without investing in above-average risk stocks. Its share price plunged more than 33 percent during the 1990 bear market.

Costs: This is a modest-cost aggressive growth vehicle. It is sold with no front-end or back-end loads. Although shareholders pay an ongoing 0.25-percent 12b-1 fee, its annual expense ratio is an average 1.44 percent. Portfolio turnover is also a below-average 35 percent.

Distributions: Income and capital gains are distributed in late December.

How to Buy and Sell: Minimum initial investment $2,000; no minimum subsequent investment requirement. Shares also available at Jack White and Company and through both Charles Schwab and Fidelity Brokerage with no transaction fees.

COLUMBIA SPECIAL

Columbia Financial Center, Inc.
1301 South West Fifth Avenue
P. O. Box 1350
Portland, OR 97207-1350
800-547-1707

Inception: 1985
Total Assets: $1.6 Billion
Ticker Symbol: CLSPX
Home Page: None

Objective and Strategy: Capital appreciation is this fund's primary objective. The fund intends to invest in companies that are more aggressive than the market, so the fund carries an above-average beta. Started in 1985, the fund has obtained an enviable performance record. It owes its success to management's skillful implementation of a sector rotation strategy. Trading rapidly, it shifts assets among relatively few aggressive growth industries that it believes will perform well in the near future. A small-cap fund in its early years, the fund's ballooning assets has sent management into the mid- and large-cap sectors of the market in search of growth. Its demonstrated skill at picking stocks and sectors and its generally good timing suggest that the fund will continue to provide excellent long-term results.

Annualized Returns
1-Year 14.3%
3-Year 15.1%
5-Year 17.7%

Portfolio Manager: Chad L. Fleischman since 1995. He joined the Columbia organization in 1980 and assisted in the management of Special from 1989 to June 1994.

Suitability: This is an aggressively managed fund and thus is suitable for aggressive investors only. Because of extreme short-term volatility, the fund is best suited for accounts that have a long-term termination date.

Portfolio Implications: This fund is best combined with small- and large-cap growth funds. Its portfolio will provide some duplication with mid-cap equity funds.

Risk: Although its beta is a slightly above-market 1.06, there is plenty of short-term share price volatility here. For example, the fund's share price dropped by more than 33 percent during the 1990 bear market.

Costs: Turnover ratio aside, this is a low-cost aggressive growth vehicle. It is sold with a no-load format; its annual expense ratio is a below-average 0.98 percent. Portfolio turnover is a hefty 183 percent.

Distributions: Both income and capital gains distributions are paid in late December.

How to Buy and Sell: Minimum initial investment $2,000; IRA $1,000; subsequent investments $100. Telephone exchange with other Columbia funds. Shares are also available without transaction fees from Charles Schwab.

CRABBE HUSON SPECIAL

Crabbe Huson Funds
P.O. Box 8413
Boston, MA 02266-8413
800-638-3148

Inception: 1987
Total Assets: $684 Million
Ticker Symbol: CHSPX
Home Page: http://
www.contrarian.com

Objective and Strategy: Don't be misled by the recent poor performance of this fund. It is extremely well managed. However, like all Crabbe Huson funds, its managers are contrary investors. They view stocks increasing in price as candidates for sale and stocks declining in price as potential acquisitions. As a result, their investment results generally do not mirror those of the market. In addition, this fund has the ability to short sell selected stocks that management believes are significantly overvalued. During a roaring bull market, this fund can be expected to underperform. However, because of its very conservative posture, it performs exceptionally well during a flat or down market. Over the long run this approach has produced market-topping returns. You want to own this fund during a bear market.

Portfolio Manager: James E. Crabbe and Richard S. Huson since the fund's inception in 1987. Both are controlling shareholders of the fund's adviser and have served in various management positions with the adviser since 1980.

Suitability: Although a growth vehicle, this fund's shares are suitable for both aggressive and conservative investors. However, this is not a fund to trade. You want to own its shares for three years or more.

Portfolio Implications: This is an excellent fund to combine with high-risk funds because of its ability to short sell individual stocks. Its inclusion will reduce portfolio volatility significantly while allowing for above-average growth potential.

Risk: This fund's contrarian stance and ability to short sell stocks has resulted in a very low 0.68 beta for an aggressive growth fund. The fund's share price declined by nearly 17 percent during the 1990 bear market.

Costs: This is a modest-cost aggressive growth fund. It is sold without a front-end or back-end sales fee. However, shareholders are assessed an on-going 0.25-percent 12b-1 fee. Its 1.40-percent annual expense ratio is slightly below average. However, portfolio turnover is a high 123 percent.

Distributions: Both income and capital gains distributions are paid in December.

How to Buy and Sell: Minimum initial investment $2,000 (regular and IRA accounts); subsequent investments $500. Shares are also available through Charles Schwab with no transaction fees.

Annualized Returns

1-Year	-3.8%
3-Year	11.2%
5-Year	15.3%

DAVIS NEW YORK VENTURE

Davis Selected Advisors, L.P.
124 East Marcy Street
Santa Fe, NM 87504
800-279-2279

Inception: 1969
Total Assets: $2.2 Billion
Ticker Symbol: NYZTX
Home Page: None

Objective and Strategy: This fund invests in companies that offer superior opportunities for long-term growth. Management follows a consistent philosophy of investing in large, fundamentally sound growth companies that appear to be undervalued and can be held for the long term. It emphasizes large, established companies that are well managed and fast growing. Many of its current holdings are household names such as American Express, Wells Fargo, Coca-Cola, Intel, General Motors, etc. Historically, the fund has maintained a very low portfolio turnover ratio. Some of its stocks remain in its portfolio for a decade. This approach has served shareholders well with average annual returns exceeding 18 percent for more than two decades.

Portfolio Manager: Shelby M. C. Davis since inception in 1969. Assisted by Christopher C. Davis, who has been with the adviser since 1989.

Suitability: This fund is suitable for all heritage portfolios. Growth-oriented investors who want to own a fund's shares for decades are best served by this vehicle.

Annualized Returns

1-Year 15.4%
3-Year 14.7%
5-Year 18.2%

Portfolio Implications: If you own this fund, you don't need any other large-cap growth fund. Combine investment in the fund with small-cap growth and international equity funds for best results.

Risk: With an emphasis on established companies, it's no surprise to find a near-market beta of 1.06. Its share price declined 15 percent during the severe 1990 bear market.

Costs: It's a shame that this fund is sold with a 4.75-percent front-end load. Otherwise it would be an ideal investment for all growth investors. Portfolio turnover is extremely low at 15 percent, and its 0.90-percent expense ratio is well below average for the group.

Distributions: Income and capital gains distributions are paid in late December.

How to Buy and Sell: Minimum initial investment $1,000; IRA $250; subsequent investments $25. Don't forget the 4.75-percent front-end load.

DELAWARE TREND CLASS A

Delaware Distributors, L.P.
1818 Market Street
Philadelphia, PA 19103
800-523-4640

Inception: 1968
Total Assets: $498 Million
Ticker Symbol: DEITX
Home Page: None

Objective and Strategy: This small-cap fund invests in rapidly growing businesses that can adapt to and profit from trends within the U.S. economy and society. Generally, the fund invests in relatively young companies that are in the early phases of their life cycles, a period that generally offers the greatest capital appreciation potential. Stock selection decisions are based on a time horizon of at least two years. Management focuses on companies that have the capital and talent to capitalize on changes in the marketplace, financially sound companies with conservative accounting practices, and companies with a strong competitive advantage. It should be no surprise that this selection model has led management to make hefty investments in the health care and technology sectors. Although this is a high-risk fund, its potential rewards are also high.

Portfolio Manager: Edward N. Antoian since 1984. Prior to joining the Delaware group in 1984, he was with E. F. Hutton. He holds an M.B.A. from the University of Pennsylvania, Wharton School.

Suitability: The fund is suitable for aggressive long-term investors only. It should be

appealing to young investors who are investing for future retirement.

Portfolio Implications: Small-cap and technology-oriented funds will probably duplicate many of the investments in this fund. It performs exceptionally well during a bull market, but it can get whacked during sharp market declines.

Risk: The fund's beta is a higher-than-average 1.13. Because of its concentration in small-cap stocks, liquidity risk is also high. The fund's share price declined a whopping 37 percent during the 1990 bear market.

Costs: The fund's class A shares are sold with a 4.75-percent front-end load and an ongoing 0.24-percent 12b-1 fee. However, its 1.36-percent annual expense ratio is below average, as is its 64-percent portfolio turnover ratio.

Distributions: Income and capital gains distributions are paid in late July.

How to Buy and Sell: Minimum initial investment $1,000; IRA $250; subsequent investments $100. Telephone exchange with other Delaware funds. Class B (back-end loaded) and C shares also available.

Annualized Returns
1-Year 17.0%
3-Year 13.5%
5-Year 19.8%

DREYFUS NEW LEADERS

Dreyfus Service
200 Park Avenue
7th Floor
New York, NY 10166
800-782-6620

Inception: 1985
Total Assets: $737 Million
Ticker Symbol: DNLDX
Home Page: http://www.dreyfus.com

Objective and Strategy: As the name implies, this fund invests primarily in mid-sized, emerging growth companies with innovative products, services, and/or processes. Management mitigates the volatility usually associated with investing in smaller companies by adjusting the fund's asset mix in response to market conditions and by stressing diversification. (At last count the portfolio contained 120 issues.) The main criteria for choosing a stock are how a company gets its cash and how it plans to use it. This, coupled with the fund's willingness to raise cash in the face of market and economic uncertainty, has enabled it to produce above-average returns since its inception. The fund is one of Dreyfus's best growth stock offerings.

Portfolio Manager: Thomas A. Frank since 1985 when he joined Dreyfus. Frank holds an M.B.A. from Columbia University and has previous portfolio management experience with Neuberger and Berman and Chase Investors Management Corp.

Suitability: Investment in this fund is suitable for all growth-oriented investors. However, conservative investors should limit investment in the fund to no more than 10 percent of portfolio assets.

Annualized Returns

1-Year 16.0%
3-Year 13.5%
5-Year 15.5%

Portfolio Implications: This fund will duplicate the performance of most small- and mid-cap aggressive growth funds. The fund is best used when coupled with large-cap growth funds.

Risk: The fund is one of the tamest aggressive growth funds, with a below-market beta of 0.92. However, share price can decline significantly during a severe bear market as witnessed by its 20-percent decline during the 1990 bear market.

Costs: This is a modest-cost aggressive growth fund. It is sold with a no-load format (it eliminated its 12b-1 fee in 1995); its annual expense ratio is a below-average 1.21 percent. However, its 109-percent portfolio turnover ratio is slightly above average for the group.

Distributions: Both income and capital gains distributions are paid in mid-December.

How to Buy and Sell: Minimum initial investment $2,500; IRA $1,000; subsequent investments $100. Telephone exchange with other Dreyfus funds. One-percent redemption fee for shares held less than six months. Shares also available without transaction fees at Charles Schwab.

ECLIPSE EQUITY

P.O. Box 2196
Peach Tree City, GA 30269
800-872-2710

Inception: 1987
Total Assets: $162 Million
Ticker Symbol: EEQEX
Home Page: http://
www.eclipsefund.com

Objective and Strategy: The fund is one of four portfolios in the Eclipse Asset Trust. It seeks a high total return from equity investments, primarily from investing in stocks with an average market capitalization that is below the average market capitalization in the Standard & Poor's 500 Index. When selecting individual issues, management gives approximately equal weight to estimated relative intrinsic value, expected future earnings growth, and current and expected dividend income. Thus, although characterized as an aggressive growth fund, the fund at times will exhibit characteristics of total return, value and growth, and equity-income funds. Although conservatively managed, it has delivered above-average long-term returns.

Portfolio Manager: Wesley G. McCain, chairman and director of Toweley Capital Management (the adviser) since its founding in 1971, is primarily responsible for the day-to-day management of the fund's portfolio.

Suitability: This is an aggressive growth fund that is suitable for both aggressive and conservative investors. Its emphasis on total return produces some dividend income.

Portfolio Implications: Because of its desire for total return and investment in smaller

Annualized Returns

1-Year 20.5%
3-Year 11.5%
5-Year 14.5%

companies, this fund can be combined with nearly any other equity fund.

Risk: This is one of the lowest-risk aggressive growth funds around. Its beta is a very modest 0.78. However, the illiquidity that accompanies investing in smaller companies can result in a sharp decline in share price during severe bear markets as witnessed by its near 23-percent decline during the 1990 bear market.

Costs: This is a very modest-cost aggressive growth fund. It is sold with a no-load format. Its 1.14-percent annual expense ratio is well below average for the group, as is its 74-percent portfolio turnover ratio. In short, you get to keep most of what this fund's portfolio delivers.

Distributions: Both income and capital gains distributions are paid in early January.

How to Buy and Sell: Minimum initial investment $1,000; IRA $1,000; no subsequent minimum investment requirement. Telephone exchange with the other three funds in the trust. Shares also available at Jack White and Company with no transaction fees.

FASCIANO FUND

Fasciano Company
190 South LaSalle Street
Suite 2800
Chicago, IL 60603
800-848-6050

Inception: 1988
Total Assets: $29 Million
Ticker Symbol: FASCX
Home Page: http://
www.networth.galt.com

Objective and Strategy: If you are looking for a place to park some of your cash, this is one fund to consider. Since he began managing this fund, Mr. Fasciano has been literally "pounding the pavement" in search of reasonably priced small- and mid-cap growth stocks. Although his namesake fund's returns pale next to those of high-flying momentum players who have poured their money into "hot" IPOs and Internet-related technology stocks, he has been able to deliver solid returns by maintaining investments in more mundane companies. For example, the fund's largest holding, International Speedway, has been in the fund's portfolio since 1988. Fasciano has also been reaping rewards from an investment in Central Parking, owner and manager of parking lots. His off-beat ideas have one thing in common, they deliver exceptional returns.

Annualized Returns
1-Year 23.8%
3-Year 17.8%
5-Year 14.3%

Portfolio Manager: Michael F. Fasciano since the fund's inception in 1988. The son-in-law of fabled growth stock investor Albert O. Nicholas, Mr. Fasciano has been in the securities industry since 1978.

Suitability: This fund is best suited for patient growth investors. Whether you are aggressive or conservative, you will want to

buy and hold an investment in this relatively small fund.

Portfolio Implications: This value-based smaller company fund works extremely well when combined with more aggressive growth vehicles. You will find very little portfolio duplication with your other aggressive growth funds.

Risk: The fund's 0.63 beta is extremely low for an aggressive growth fund. The illiquidity of some of its holdings will produce some short-term share price volatility. However, that should not be bothersome for long-term investors. Its share price declined 15 percent during the 1990 bear market.

Costs: This is a very modest-cost fund, given its small size. It is sold with a no-load format; its 1.70-percent annual expense ratio is slightly above average, but its 38-percent portfolio turnover ratio is well below average.

Distributions: Both income and capital gains distributions are paid in late December.

How to Buy and Sell: Minimum initial investment $1,000; IRA $1,000; subsequent investments $100. This is the only fund in the Fasciano family.

FIDELITY CAPITAL APPRECIATION

Fidelity Distributors
82 Devonshire Street
Mail Zone L7B
Boston, MA 02109
800-752-2347

Inception: 1986
Total Assets: $1.6 Billion
Ticker Symbol: FDCAX
Home Page: http://www.fidelity.com

Objective and Strategy: In seeking growth of capital, management looks for companies in industries that have been depressed and are about to improve. The fund favors companies involved in prospective acquisition, spin-offs, consolidations, and liquidations. Management generally uses a value-oriented strategy of buying the stocks of companies that are undervalued in relation to their potential for growth in earnings and book value. These kinds of stocks are generally overlooked and undervalued by researchers. The fund holds a mixture of large, established and mid-cap companies. Its largest sectors include technology, retail, and leisure. Although there is a danger in investing in out-of-favor companies that may not return to favor soon, the strategy has proved fruitful in certain years.

Portfolio Manager: Thomas Sweeney since the fund's inception in 1986. Previously, he managed Select Paper and Forest Products. Sweeney joined Fidelity in 1985.

Suitability: Investment in this fund is suitable for both aggressive and conservative investors. However, conservative investors should limit their allocations to this fund to no more than 10 percent of portfolio assets.

Annualized Returns

1-Year 3.5%
3-Year 12.3%
5-Year 14.0%

Portfolio Implications: This value-oriented fund performs best during weak markets. It should be combined with more aggressive vehicles for best results. It works well when combined with small-cap growth funds.

Risk: The fund's value bent has produced a below-market 0.80 beta. However, share price volatility can be high at times as witnessed by its 22-percent decline during the 1990 bear market.

Costs: Like many Fidelity funds, investors pay a 3-percent front-end load. However, there is no ongoing 12b-1 fee. Its 1.03 annual expense ratio is well below the group average. However, its 250-percent portfolio turnover ratio is extremely high.

Distributions: Both income and capital gains distributions are paid in late December.

How to Buy and Sell: Minimum initial investment $2,500; IRA $500; subsequent investments $250. Telephone exchange with other Fidelity funds (credit for loads previously paid). Shares are also available through Fidelity Brokerage without transaction fees.

FIDELITY EMERGING GROWTH

Fidelity Distributors
82 Devonshire Street
Mail Zone L7B
Boston, MA 02109
800-752-2347

Inception: 1990
Total Assets: $2.0 Billion
Ticker Symbol: FDEGX
Home Page: http://www.fidelity.com

Objective and Strategy: This relatively young fund invests in growth wherever management can find it. However, to be a candidate for the portfolio, a company's revenue must historically grow at 20 percent per year. This criterion leads to many firms that have just been jump-started for one reason or another. They are either very young companies or they are recovering from adverse conditions. Also, the criterion has led to investments in developing economies overseas, where high growth is the norm. Not surprisingly, the fund typically carries an unusually high average price-earnings ratio, for the fund is forced to pay up for exceptionally high-growth stocks. During the last year, from one-third to nearly one-half of its assets were invested in technology stocks.

Annualized Returns
1-Year 4.4%
3-Year 16.3%
5-Year 17.1%

Portfolio Manager: Lawrence Greenberg since October 1993. He also manages VIP Growth and has managed Select Environmental Services and Select Medical Delivery since joining Fidelity in 1986.

Suitability: This fund is suitable for only the most aggressive growth-oriented investors. A long-term orientation should be maintained.

Portfolio Implications: Because of this fund's high-risk investments, investors should limit allocations to this fund to no more than 15 percent of portfolio assets. Overall portfolio volatility can be reduced by combining investment in this fund with small-cap value funds and international equity funds.

Risk: Depending on market conditions, this fund can be either a big winner or a big loser. It sports an above-average 1.13 beta. This relatively new fund has yet to experience a severe bear market.

Costs: Investors pay a 3-percent front-end sales fee but no ongoing 12b-1 fee. The fund's 1.11-percent annual expense ratio is below average, but its 139-percent portfolio turnover ratio is relatively high.

Distributions: Income and capital gains distributions are paid in either late December or early January.

How to Buy and Sell: Minimum initial investment $2,500; IRA $500; subsequent investments $250. Telephone exchange with other Fidelity funds (credit given for sales load paid). Shares are also available at Fidelity Brokerage without transaction fees.

FIDELITY LOW PRICED STOCK

Fidelity Distributors
82 Devonshire Street
Mail Zone L7B
Boston, MA 02109
800-752-2347

Inception: 1989
Total Assets: $4.6 Billion
Ticker Symbol: FLPSX
Home Page: http://www.fidelity.com

Objective and Strategy: This fund aggressively seeks capital appreciation by investing in a portfolio of low-priced stocks. During its first few years in existence, the fund defined "low price" as any stock priced under $15 per share. However, as the assets of the fund ballooned, management was forced to invest in larger, more liquid stocks. Thus, it now invests in stocks trading below $25 per share at time of purchase or those that have a price per share that places the stock in the bottom 40 percent of the stocks included in the Wilshire 500 Index. Even so, the fund has been forced to spread its assets among the stocks of more than five hundred different companies, and this number should grow as assets continue to swell. The good news is that the wide-spread diversification will reduce risk substantially.

Annualized Returns
1-Year 12.7%
3-Year 16.0%
5-Year 19.2%

Portfolio Manager: Joel Tillinghast since the fund's inception. M. M., Northwestern University, Kellogg School of Management, 1983.

Suitability: The fund is suitable for aggressive, long-term-oriented investors. If you are young and saving for retirement or maintaining an education savings plan for your young children, this fund is an ideal investment alternative.

Portfolio Implications: Although a low-priced stock does not imply a small-cap investment, most of the stocks in this portfolio are small-caps. With hundreds of stocks, the fund has nearly attained index status.

Risk: Although this fund invests in high-risk stocks, its emphasis on low price has led it to invest in many value stocks. Thus, its beta is a low 0.67, and its share price declined by only 13 percent during the severe 1990 bear market.

Costs: Investors pay a 3-percent front-end load but no ongoing 12b-1 fee. Its annual expense ratio is a very low 1.05 percent of assets, and its 80-percent portfolio turnover ratio is right at the group average. On balance this is a low-cost fund for long-term, small-cap investors.

Distributions: Income and capital gains distributions are paid in either September or December.

How to Buy and Sell: Minimum initial investment $2,500; IRA $500; subsequent investments $250. A 1.5-percent redemption fee is imposed on shares held less than ninety days. Telephone exchange with other Fidelity funds (credit given for sales load paid).

FIDELITY OTC PORTFOLIO

Fidelity Distributors
82 Devonshire Street
Mail Zone L7B
Boston, MA 02109
800–544–8888

Inception: 1984
Total Assets: $3.2 Billion
Ticker Symbol: FOCPX
Home Page: http://www.fidelity.com

Objective and Strategy: As the name suggests, the fund seeks capital growth by investing in stocks traded in the over-the-counter market. These are often the stocks of smaller, less well-known companies, which may have limited marketability. However, its largest investments have recently been in large companies such as Intel, Microsoft, Dell Computer, etc. The fund has an excellent long-term performance record, a 19.6-percent average annual return since inception in 1984. However, its best returns were posted in its early years when it was managed by Morris Smith, who left the fund to manage the giant Magellan Fund. Since then, the fund has had three different portfolio managers. However, if you are looking to participate in over-the-counter (now called NASDAQ) stocks, this fund is an excellent vehicle.

Annualized Returns

1-Year 13.9%
3-Year 16.0%
5-Year 15.6%

Portfolio Manager: Charles Magnum since June 1996. While at Fidelity he has managed Convertible Securities, Select Health Care, and Select Medical Delivery. He received his M.B.A. from the University of Chicago in 1990.

Suitability: The fund is suitable only for aggressive growth-oriented investors who can assume above-average risks.

Portfolio Implications: This fund is an excellent fit with funds that index stocks traded on organized stock exchanges or with small-cap growth or value funds.

Risk: The fund's beta is a modest 0.87 percent. However, the long bull market has masked some of the risk present. Its share price declined by slightly more than 16 percent during the severe 1990 bear market.

Costs: Investors pay a 3-percent front-end load but no ongoing 12b-1 fee. The fund's expense ratio is a very low 0.83 percent of assets but its 133-percent portfolio turnover ratio is well above-average.

Distributions: Income and capital gains distributions are paid in September and December.

How to Buy and Sell: Minimum initial investment $2,500; IRA $500; subsequent investments $250. Telephone exchange with other Fidelity funds (credit is given for sales load paid). Shares also available through Fidelity Brokerage without transaction fees.

FIRST AMERICAN REGIONAL EQUITY

SEI Financial Management
  Corporation
680 East Swedesford Road
Wayne, PA 19087
800-637-2548

Inception: 1992
Total Assets: $26 Million
Ticker Symbol: FAREX
Home Page: None

Objective and Strategy: This bank-sponsored fund seeks capital appreciation by investing at least 65 percent of its assets in smaller companies headquartered in Minnesota, North and South Dakota, Montana, Wisconsin, Michigan, Iowa, Nebraska, Colorado, and Illinois. Small-sized companies are deemed those with market capitalizations of less than $1 billion. These companies often have established a market niche or have developed unique products or technologies that are expected to produce superior growth in revenues and earnings. The fund benefits from a unique multiple management style approach. This tiny fund has maintained a rather compact portfolio ranging from three to four dozen different companies. However, management tends to be longer-term investors, rather than frequent traders.

Portfolio Manager: Albin S. Dubiak, Roland P. Witcomb, and Jeff A. Johnson since the fund's inception in 1992. Each manages at least two other First American investment funds.

Suitability: This fund is appropriate for investors with long-term time horizons who can tolerate an above-average degree of price fluctuation.

Annualized Returns
1-Year 11.0%
3-Year 18.7%
5-Year NA

Portfolio Implications: This fund makes an ideal higher growth component of a diversified mutual fund portfolio. Given its emphasis on small companies and regional orientation, there is little overlap with other growth funds.

Risk: The fund's beta is a below-market 0.95. Although this relatively young fund has yet to experience a severe bear market, its investments are somewhat illiquid and share price would most likely take a larger-than-average dip during a prolonged bear market.

Costs: Class A shares are sold with a 4.50-percent front-end load and an ongoing 0.24-percent 12b-1 fee. However, its 1.15-percent expense ratio is exceptionally low for a small fund, and its 42-percent portfolio turnover ratio is far below average for its category.

Distributions: Income is distributed quarterly and capital gains are distributed annually in December.

How to Buy and Sell: Minimum initial investment $1,000; IRA $250; subsequent investments $100. Telephone exchange with other First American funds. Class B shares (back-end loaded) are also available.

FOUNDERS DISCOVERY

Founders Asset Management
2930 East Third Avenue
Denver, CO 80206
800–525–2440

Inception: 1989
Total Assets: $272 Million
Ticker Symbol: FDISX
Home Page: http://
www.networth.galt.com/founders

Objective and Strategy: Wondering who the leading companies of tomorrow are? Look no further than the Discovery Fund. This aggressively managed fund seeks capital appreciation by investing in the common stocks of small, rapidly growing U.S. companies with market capitalizations between $10 million and $500 million. Typically, these stocks are traded over-the-counter. Kern's bottom-up approach to stock selection has generated an investment portfolio of eighty to ninety small companies with strong managements, competitive market positions, and innovative products. Discovery has ranked in the top 20 percent of its peer group for performance during the last one-, three-, and five-year periods. However, you pay for these extra returns by assuming extreme short-term volatility.

Portfolio Manager: David G. Kern joined Founders in 1995 and became sole portfolio manager of the fund in the third quarter of that year. Previously, he served as assistant portfolio manager with the Delaware Management Company.

Suitability: This fund is suitable for only the most aggressive, growth-seeking investors.

Portfolio Implications: This fund will boost portfolio returns when combined with

Annualized Returns

1-Year 20.1%
3-Year 13.6%
5-Year 16.1%

more sedate growth funds. If your portfolio is packed with large-cap growth funds, a 10- to 15-percent allocation to this fund can add one to two percentage points to your long-run annual average return.

Risk: You'll not find a more volatile domestic equity fund around. The portfolio tends to be packed with technology stocks that sell at high price-earnings multiples. Its 1.33 beta is extremely high. However, the fund suffered a modest 13-percent decline during the severe 1990 bear market.

Costs: The fund is sold without a front-end or back-end load, but with a 0.25-percent ongoing 12b-1 fee instead. However, its 1.63-percent annual expense ratio is about average for the group. It sports a greater-than-average 118-percent portfolio turnover ratio.

Distributions: Income distributions are paid quarterly and capital gains are distributed annually in December.

How to Buy and Sell: Minimum initial investment $1,000; IRA $500; subsequent investments $50. Telephone switch with other Founders funds. Shares also available at Charles Schwab and Fidelity Brokerage with no transaction fees.

FOUNDERS FRONTIER

Founders Asset Management
2930 East Third Avenue
Denver, CO 80206
800-525-2440

Inception: 1987
Total Assets: $369 Million
Ticker Symbol: FOUNX
Home Page: http://
www.networth.galt.com/founders

Objective and Strategy: This fund invests primarily in small and medium-sized companies with market capitalizations ranging from $150 million to $600 million. The fund may invest in large companies or foreign stocks if management believes market conditions warrant such action. A few years ago, the fund generally invested in companies with equity market values below $300 million, but that role has been filled by the company's Discovery fund. Although returns have been trimmed a bit since the company began pursuing larger companies, its volatility has declined as well. The fund has historically traded rapidly, adjusting its tactics to market conditions. This fund is destined to outperform in a market that favors growth over value stocks. However, it can be expected to underperform during market downturns.

Annualized Returns

1-Year 18.6%
3-Year 15.3%
5-Year 15.6%

Portfolio Manager: Michael K. Haines since 1990. He has been comanager of Founders Special since 1996 and co-portfolio manager of Founders Discovery from 1989 to July 1995. He has been with Founders for nine years.

Suitability: This fund is suited for aggressive and modestly aggressive investors. It pays very little in the way of current income. Thus, it is suited for longer-term investors.

Portfolio Implications: This is a mid-cap fund that provides little overlap with small-cap or large-cap funds. Its emphasis on growth and an earnings momentum strategy complement growth portfolios packed with funds that follow a value philosophy.

Risk: This is a volatile fund. Its beta is 1.13 and it experienced a 20-percent decline in its share price during the 1990 bear market.

Costs: This is a very reasonable-cost aggressive growth vehicle. It is sold without a front-end or back-end load, but with a 0.25-percent ongoing 12b-1 fee instead. Even so, its 1.57-percent expense ratio is about average for the group. Its portfolio turnover ratio is slightly above average at 92 percent.

Distributions: Income distributions are paid quarterly and capital gains are distributed annually in December.

How to Buy and Sell: Minimum initial investment $1,000; IRA $500; subsequent investments $50. Telephone exchange with other Founders funds ($100 minimum). Shares can also be obtained through Charles Schwab and Fidelity Brokerage without transaction fees.

FOUNDERS SPECIAL

Founders Asset Management
2930 East Third Avenue
Denver, CO 80206
800-525-2440

Inception: 1961
Total Assets: $376 Million
Ticker Symbol: FRSPX
Home Page: http://
networth.galt.com/founders

Objective and Strategy: Above-average long-term capital appreciation is the goal of this fund, which it attempts to achieve via investments in domestic and foreign companies. Prior to mid-1992, the fund invested exclusively in high-growth, smaller company issues and has since then made a transition to the mid- and slower-growth large-cap markets. When making stock selections, management seeks companies with depressed earnings that have turnaround potential. Although it is now more heavily invested in larger-cap stocks, it continues to favor investment in high-growth industries such as health care, computers, telecommunications, and recreation. In addition, the fund uses aggressive techniques such as leveraging and rapid trading in an attempt to enhance returns.

Annualized Returns

1-Year 8.3%
3-Year 12.2%
5-Year 14.2%

Portfolio Manager: Michael K. Haines and Edward F. Keely since 1996. Mr. Haines is also the lead portfolio manager of Frontier, and Mr. Keely is lead manager of Founders Growth Fund.

Suitability: Like other Founders growth funds, this fund is suitable for aggressive growth-oriented investors only.

Portfolio Implications: Combine this fund with Founders Discovery and Frontier and you cover just about the waterfront in terms of company size. Add a couple of value funds (both small- and large-cap) and you will have assembled a diversified, high growth-potential portfolio.

Risk: If you are seeking better-than-market returns, you have to assume above-market risks, and this fund delivers on both counts. Its 1.27 beta is extremely high, and the fund's share price declined by nearly 17 percent during the 1990 bear stock market.

Costs: The fund is sold without a front-end or back-end load, but with a 0.25-percent annual 12b-1 fee instead. However, this is a low-cost aggressive growth fund. Its 1.35-percent annual expense ratio is below average. However, it is a vigorous trader, sporting a hefty 263-percent portfolio turnover ratio.

Distributions: Income distributions are paid quarterly and capital gains are distributed annually in December.

How to Buy and Sell: Minimum initial investment $1,000; IRA $500; subsequent investments $50. Telephone exchange with other Founders funds. Shares may also be obtained through Charles Schwab and Fidelity Brokerage with no transaction fees.

FRANKLIN CALIFORNIA GROWTH

Franklin Advisors, Inc.
777 Mariners Island Boulevard
San Mateo, CA 94404
800-632-2301

Inception: 1991
Total Assets: $98 Million
Ticker Symbol: FKCGX
Home Page: None

Objective and Strategy: California is known as the "golden state," a place where entrepreneurs come to pursue their dreams. It is home to some of the nation's most dynamic universities and industries, as well as companies that have become global leaders and household names. Formerly known as the Franklin California 250 Growth Fund, the fund changed its investment strategy and name in July 1993. The goal of this fund is to "mine" California gold by investing in growth companies headquartered or conducting the majority of their operations in California. These are companies that may have market capitalizations up to $2.5 billion at the time of purchase. When one thinks of California-based companies, "silicone valley" quickly comes to mind; however, only one-third of the fund's portfolio is concentrated in the "high tech" sector.

Annualized Returns

1-Year 23.3%
3-Year 29.5%
5-Year NA

Portfolio Manager: The portfolio is team managed by Conrad B. Herrmann, Frank Fallaciously, Nick Moore, and Kea Yamamoto.

Suitability: The fund is suitable for aggressive growth investors who seek to capitalize on California's great growth companies. Given its regional concentration of investments, it is suitable for only a small portion of a growth-oriented portfolio.

Portfolio Implications: As the California economy goes, so go the fortunes of this fund. It should be combined with other growth or aggressive growth funds that invest a significant portion of their assets in companies outside the state.

Risk: There is plenty more risk here than first meets the eye. Its beta is a below-market 0.85. However, since changing its objective, it has experienced a stock market that has only gone one way: up. Its emphasis on higher price-earnings multiple, growth companies introduces a significant degree of risk.

Costs: Like most Franklin funds, this one is sold with a 4.50-percent front-end load. Shareholders also experience a 0.13-percent annual 12b-1 fee. On the other hand, operating costs are low. Its 1.27-percent expense ratio is below average, as is its 79-percent portfolio turnover ratio.

Distributions: Income distributions are paid in June and December and capital gains are distributed annually in December.

How to Buy and Sell: Minimum initial investment $100; IRA $100; subsequent investments $100. Telephone exchange with other Franklin/Templeton funds.

HEARTLAND SMALL CAP CONTRARIAN

Heartland Advisors
790 North Milwaukee Street
Milwaukee, WI 53202
800-432-7856

Inception: 1995
Total Assets: $222 Million
Ticker Symbol: HRSMX
Home Page: None

Objective and Strategy: Normally, young funds need more seasoning before they appear on my recommended list. However, this fund is just too good to pass up. Its portfolio manager built a solid reputation investing in tiny companies while at the helm of Heartland Value. With that fund now closed to new investors, you must invest in this fund to get Bill's expertise. In fact, you also get many of the same companies that the much larger $1 billion-plus Value Fund holds. You also get something else, downside protection. This fund has the ability to short sell overvalued stocks as well buy reasonably valued small-cap stocks. The result is that you end up on both sides of the market. You make money when stock prices advance, and you offset some of the losses that occur when the market takes a nosedive.

Annualized Returns
1-Year 20.8%
3-Year NA
5-Year NA

Portfolio Manager: William J. Nasgovitz since the fund's inception in 1995. He has been president of Heartland Advisors since 1982 and also manages the highly successful Heartland Value Fund, which is now closed to new investors.

Suitability: This fund is suitable for all growth-oriented investors, whether conservative or not. Given its sometimes short positions, this fund has far less risk than the typical small-cap fund.

Portfolio Implications: If you are looking for a way to protect the value of your portfolio during a market decline, consider adding this fund to your portfolio. Also, consider making an investment in the fund soon. Chances are that investors will flock to its doors in the not-too-distant future, and it too will be forced to discontinue selling shares to new investors.

Risk: Because of its ability to short sell what are believed to be overvalued stocks, this fund has less volatility than the typical aggressive growth vehicle. Although it has yet to experience a severe bear market, chances are that it will weather the storm quite well.

Costs: A great fund and low costs too. It is sold with an ongoing 0.25-percent 12b-1 fee. However, total annual expenses are a low 1.45 percent of assets (and will fall further as assets rise). Its portfolio turnover ratio is a very low 23 percent.

Distributions: It plans to make both income and capital gains distributions in December. Its short sales could result in large income distributions.

How to Buy and Sell: Minimum initial investment $1,000; IRA $500; subsequent investments $100. Shares also available with transaction fees through Charles Schwab, Jack White, and Fidelity Brokerage.

IAI MID CAP GROWTH

IAI Mutual Funds
3700 First Bank Place
P.O. Box 357
Minneapolis, MN 55440-0357
800-945-3863

Inception: 1992
Total Assets: $137 Million
Ticker Symbol: IAMCX
Home Page: http://
www.networth.galt.com/iai

Objective and Strategy: This fund seeks capital appreciation by investing in mid-cap stocks (i.e., those with equity market values between $500 million and $5 billion). These are stocks that are small enough to grow rapidly yet large enough to survive a poor economy. They also are led by more experienced management teams than small-caps, and many remain undiscovered by Wall Street analysts. Individual selections are the stocks of companies that possess a competitive advantage such as a patent or superior technology, are growing revenue and earnings at a 15- to 20-percent annual rate, and possess enough cash flow to fund growth without having to issue a lot of debt. This fund has garnered superior returns ever since it was launched in 1992.

Portfolio Manager: Suzanne Zak since the fund's inception in 1992. She is also comanager of IAI's Growth Fund. Prior to joining IAI, she managed the Seligman Growth Fund. She has a B.B. from Princeton and an M.B.A. from Rutgers.

Suitability: The fund is suitable for both aggressive and somewhat conservative growth-seeking investors. However, conservative investors should limit allocations to no more than 10 percent of portfolio assets.

Annualized Returns
1-Year 17.1%
3-Year 17.3%
5-Year NA

Portfolio Implications: This is a true mid-cap fund. It is ideally positioned to complement investments in both large-cap and small-cap funds. The fund also works well when coupled with international equity funds.

Risk: The fund has a modest 0.95 beta, which indicates a slightly below-market level of risk. However, the fund has yet to experience a severe bear market, which would most likely drive the share price of this fund down by a double-digit percentage.

Costs: Like all of the IAI funds, this fund is sold with a no-load format. In addition, its 1.25-percent annual expense ratio and its 15-percent portfolio turnover ratio are both well below average relative to its peers. In other words, this is a very low-cost aggressive growth fund.

Distributions: Income and capital gains distributions are paid annually in June.

How to Buy and Sell: Minimum initial investment is a hefty $5,000; IRA $2,000; subsequent investments $100. An automatic monthly investment program is available with a $100 monthly minimum. Shares are also available with no transaction fees through Charles Schwab, Fidelity Brokerage, and Jack White and Company.

INVESCO DYNAMICS FUND

Invesco Funds Group
P.O. Box 173706
Denver, CO 80217-3706
800-525-8085

Inception: 1967
Total Assets: $794 Million
Ticker Symbol: FIDYX
Home Page: http://www.invesco.com

Objective and Strategy: This fund has been churning out exceptional returns for many years. By using aggressive investment techniques, this fund seeks to attain its goal of capital appreciation. When choosing stocks for the fund's portfolio, management looks at several factors, including the growth of earnings per share, increasing profit margins, future growth of sales, and current market data on the company. Generally, these are vibrant companies that are just now developing new ideas and establishing a consumer base. The fund's core investments are primarily classic growth stocks in technology, health care, and consumer growth. These high-quality companies include Microsoft, Disney, Oracle, Cisco Systems, and Oxford Health Plans. Interestingly, retail stocks were among the largest holdings during 1996.

Portfolio Manager: Timothy J. Miller since 1993. He joined Invesco in 1992 and in mid-1996 took over the reins of the Invesco Growth Fund. He obtained an M.B.A .from the University of Missouri.

Suitability: Suitable for growth-seeking investors who can withstand considerable short-term volatility and have the patience to grow their capital over a longer period of time.

Annualized Returns

1-Year 21.7%
3-Year 16.4%
5-Year 19.0%

Portfolio Implications: This fund's portfolio is quite similar to many other aggressive growth vehicles. Thus, considerable duplication may result from combining this fund with other diversified aggressive growth funds. It works well, however, with small-cap offerings.

Risk: This fund's rewards have been high, but so has its risk. Its beta of 1.04 is only slightly higher than that of the stock market as a whole. However, its share price sunk nearly 23 percent during the 1990 bear market, indicating there is more risk here than first meets the eye.

Costs: This is a modest-cost aggressive growth vehicle. Its shares are sold without a front-end or back-end load. However, it possesses a 0.25-percent ongoing 12b-1 fee. Its expense ratio is a modest 1.21 percent, but it sports a high (176 percent) portfolio turnover ratio.

Distributions: Both income and capital gains distributions are paid in late October or early November.

How to Buy and Sell: Minimum initial investment $1,000; IRA $250; subsequent investments $250. Telephone switch with other Invesco funds. Shares may also be obtained through Charles Schwab, Fidelity Brokerage, and Jack White and Company without transaction fees.

INVESCO EMERGING GROWTH

Invesco Funds Group
P.O. Box 173706
Denver, CO 80217-3706
800-525-8085

Inception: 1991
Total Assets: $298 Million
Ticker Symbol: FIEGX
Home Page: http://www.invesco.com

Objective and Strategy: This fund (which will change its name to the Small Company Growth Fund in early 1997) aggressively seeks capital growth by investing in the stocks of companies with equity market values below $1 billion while attempting to keep volatility to a minimum. This combination of appreciation with reasonable risk is sought through a fundamental approach that focuses on a company's revenue, strong return on equity, high profit margins, low debt, and attractive products or services that will allow the company to meet or beat expectations on earnings. As might be expected the fund's two largest areas of investment are technology and health care. The fund's philosophy is to remain fully invested over the market cycle. However, its high portfolio turnover ratio is indicative of an earnings momentum strategy.

Annualized Returns
1-Year 31.1%
3-Year 15.5%
5-Year NA

Portfolio Manager: John R. Schroer since 1995. Schroer, who joined Invesco in 1992, also comanages the Health Sciences Portfolio. He obtained a B.S. and M.B.A. from the University of Wisconsin.

Suitability: The fund is suitable for aggressive and modestly aggressive growth-oriented investors. It is a strong addition to your more aggressive investments if you are just starting out, or if you're in your peak earning years.

Portfolio Implications: This fund fills the niche between micro-cap and large-cap investments. Investors should consider combining this fund with an international equity fund to obtain the optimal benefits of diversification.

Risk: As might be expected, the fund's beta is an above-average 1.17. Although this young fund has yet to experience a severe bear market, its concentration of investments in relatively high price-earnings ratio stocks indicates that its share price will decline by more than the market during a downturn.

Costs: This is an average-cost small-cap vehicle. The fund levies a 0.25-percent ongoing 12b-1 fee in lieu of either a front-end or back-end load. Its 1.49-percent expense ratio is right at the group average. However, its portfolio turnover ratio is an exceptionally high 228 percent.

Distributions: Both income and capital gains distributions are paid annually in late December.

How to Buy and Sell: Minimum initial investment $1,000; IRA $250; subsequent investments $50. Telephone exchange with other Invesco funds. Shares may also be obtained through Charles Schwab, Fidelity Brokerage, and Jack White and Company without transaction fees.

IVY EMERGING GROWTH CLASS A

Mackenzie Funds Distribution
P.O. Box 5007
Boca Raton, FL 33431
800-777-6472

Inception: 1993
Total Assets: $64 Million
Ticker Symbol: IVEGX
Home Page: http://
www.ivymackenzie.com

Objective and Strategy: This fund seeks long-term growth of capital through investment in common stocks of small and medium-sized companies that are early in their life cycles and have the potential for rapid growth of sales and earnings. Management emphasizes companies that operate in fertile industry environments including network computing, data communications, software, health care information and services, specialty retailing, and financial and business services. Preference is given to companies that have good visibility in terms of their business model and product life cycle. Normally the fund holds a large number of stocks (about 250 at last count) to minimize the impact of unexpected company-specific events. Since inception in April 1993, the fund has earned an average of more than 30 percent annually.

Portfolio Manager: James W. Broadfoot since the fund's inception in 1993. He also manages Ivy Growth. He joined Ivy in 1990 and earned an M.B.A. from the Wharton School of the University of Pennsylvania. Broadfoot is the author of *Investing in Emerging Growth Stocks.*

Suitability: This fund is recommended for aggressive growth investors only. Because of extreme short-term volatility, investors should adopt a long-term investment horizon.

Annualized Returns
1-Year 25.8%
3-Year 22.3%
5-Year NA

Portfolio Implications: The fund's small- and mid-cap investments make it a good fit with a portfolio dominated by large-cap funds. Because small companies derive most of their revenues from the domestic economy, investors should consider coupling this fund with an international equity fund for best overall results.

Risk: Although this fund has yet to experience a severe bear market, its above-average returns since inception indicate a higher-than-average level of risk as does its extremely high 1.35 beta.

Costs: Sold with a 5.75-percent front-end load and ongoing 0.25-percent 12b-1 charge. Thus, the entrance fee is rather steep. In addition, its 1.95-percent expense ratio is above average for the group. Its 86-percent portfolio turnover ratio is about at the group average. In short, this is an expensive fund, but one that has delivered solid net returns to shareholders.

Distributions: Both income and capital gains distributions are paid annually, usually in late December.

How to Buy and Sell: Minimum initial investment $1,000; IRA $1,000; subsequent investments $25. Telephone exchange with other Ivy and Mackenzie funds. Shares may be obtained with no transaction fees by investment advisers from Charles Schwab.

KAUFMANN FUND

The Kaufmann Fund, Inc.
140 East 45th Street, 43rd Floor
New York, NY 10017
800-261-0555

Inception: 1986
Total Assets: $4.7 Billion
Ticker Symbol: KAUFX
Home Page: http://
www.networth.galt.com/kaufmann

Objective and Strategy: This fund, originally incorporated in 1967, was acquired by current management in 1986. Since then, performance has been nothing short of spectacular. Portfolio managers Utsch and Auriana have applied an aggressive strategy, which frequently involves assuming positions in initial public offerings (IPOs) and gradually adding to those positions over time as their confidence in and understanding of the company's business prospects grows. Aside from hot IPOs, the managers have an appetite for smaller, rapidly growing companies and are usually willing to pay high price-earnings multiples for them. These companies are generally leaders in their markets as a result of proprietary technology or know-how. The fund constantly strives to take advantage of market corrections (by adding to positions) to improve the fund's long-term performance.

Portfolio Manager: Hans P. Utsch and Lawrence Auriana since the fund's resurrection in 1986. They cofounded Edgemont, the fund's investment adviser, in 1984 and have both worked in the securities business since the early 1960s.

Suitability: This fund is suitable for highly aggressive growth-oriented investors only.

Annualized Returns

1-Year 24.3%
3-Year 23.8%
5-Year 23.1%

Portfolio Implications: If you're looking to boost the return of your growth portfolio, consider adding a small allocation to this fund. Its relatively compact portfolio will provide little duplication to your other holdings.

Risk: Large bets on individual companies and a portfolio packed with high price-earnings ratio stocks have resulted in a portfolio marked by extreme short-term volatility that is not fully reflected by the modest 1.13 beta. The fund suffered a 30-percent share price decline during the 1990 bear market.

Costs: Although the fund is sold without a front-end or back-end sales fee, it is an above-average cost fund. Shareholders pay a 0.53-percent ongoing 12b-1 fee and a 1.50-percent annual management fee. Despite its more than $4 billion in total assets, the total expense ratio stands at a hefty 2.17 percent.

Distributions: Both income and capital gains distributions are paid annually in December.

How to Buy and Sell: Minimum initial investment $1,500; IRA $1,500; subsequent investments $1,000. Fund shares may also be obtained through Charles Schwab, Fidelity Brokerage, and Jack White and Company without transaction fees.

LOOMIS SAYLES SMALL CAP

Loomis Sayles & Company, L.P.
One Financial Center
Boston, MA 02111
800-633-3330

Inception: *1991*
Total Assets: *$109 Million*
Ticker Symbol: *LSSLX*
Home Page: *None*

Objective and Strategy: This fund was selected for the aggressive growth section because it invests in small-cap stocks, not because it employs risky, aggressive investment tactics. In fact, to mitigate risk, this fund invests in a unique mixture of both growth and value companies. Thus, this isn't a sink or swim offering whose fate hangs on the current stock market environment. Small-cap growth and small-cap value stocks exhibit some independence, with one group overperforming for extended periods followed by underperformance for several years. By combining both in a single portfolio, investors obtain all of the return promised by the small-cap sector of the market while experiencing far less risk than the typical small-cap fund.

Annualized Returns

1-Year 22.8%
3-Year 13.5%
5-Year 18.2%

Portfolio Manager: Jeffrey C. Petherick, vice president of the trust and of Loomis Sayles, since the fund's inception in 1991. Mary C. Champagne co-portfolio manager since 1995.

Suitability: This is one small-cap fund that is suitable for both aggressive and conservative growth-oriented investors. However, a long-term orientation is required. This fund is well suited for younger investors who are saving for retirement or older investors with a long-term view.

Portfolio Implications: This fund provides a high degree of diversification within the small-cap sector of the market because of its unique combination of growth and value stocks. If you invest in this small-cap fund, there is no need to invest in another. The fund makes an ideal addition to a large-cap fund portfolio.

Risk: This is one of the lowest beta (0.88) small-cap funds around. As a relatively young fund, it has yet to experience a severe bear market. However, given its small-cap orientation, you can expect its share price to decline during down markets because of limited liquidity of its holdings.

Costs: Although the fund has a higher-than-average portfolio turnover ratio (155 percent), it has a very modest cost structure. It is sold with a no-load format and has a below-average 1.25-percent expense ratio.

Distributions: Both income and capital gains distributions are paid annually in mid-September.

How to Buy and Sell: Minimum initial investment $2,500; IRA $250; subsequent investments $50. Telephone switch with other Loomis Sayles funds. Shares may also be obtained through Charles Schwab without transaction fees.

MANAGERS CAPITAL APPRECIATION

The Managers Funds, L.P.
40 Richards Avenue
Norwalk, CT 06854-2325
800-835-3879

Inception: 1984
Total Assets: $97 Million
Ticker Symbol: MGCAX
Home Page: None

Objective and Strategy: This is one of ten funds in the Managers Trust. Managers has a unique structure whereby the trustees select various management companies to manage individual portfolios in the trust. This fund is managed by two different investment advisory firms. Dietche and Field pursues a value style and looks for the presence of a catalyst that will have a positive impact on the stock's price. Hudson Capital seeks securities that have financial or earnings dynamics within an identified secular investment theme. Securities with low valuations are favored along with companies that show potential for change. The firm looks for companies with increasing earnings growth, new products, and new management, as well as companies influenced by structural changes including mergers, spin-offs, and lower raw materials prices.

Annualized Returns
1-Year 11.5%
3-Year 13.8%
5-Year 14.2%

Portfolio Manager: Lincoln P. Field from Dietche and Field since 1984 and Howard W. Shaun from Hudson Capital since 1987.

Suitability: Because of its growth with value bent, this aggressive fund is recommended for both aggressive and conservative growth-oriented investors. It is only one of a handful of aggressive growth funds that has continually paid cash dividends.

Portfolio Implications: The fund's value-oriented posture makes it an excellent candidate to combine with an aggressive growth, earnings momentum fund. Its portfolio is dotted with both mid-cap and large-cap stocks. It includes a smattering of international equities as well.

Risk: This is a modest-risk aggressive growth vehicle with a 1.00 portfolio beta. Its value style tends to limit losses during severe bear markets as witnessed by its modest 15-percent decline during the 1990 bear market.

Costs: This is a modest-cost fund. Its shares are sold with a no-load format. Its 1.3-percent annual expense ratio is below average for the group. However, its 134-percent portfolio turnover ratio is relatively high.

Distributions: Both income and capital gains distributions are paid annually in December.

How to Buy and Sell: Minimum initial investment $2,000; IRA $500; no minimum subsequent investment requirement. Telephone exchange with the other nine funds in the trust. Shares are also available without transaction fees from Charles Schwab and Jack White and Company.

MANAGERS SPECIAL EQUITY

The Managers Funds, L.P.
40 Richards Avenue
Norwalk, CT 06854-2325
800-835-3879

Inception: 1984
Total Assets: $169 Million
Ticker Symbol: MGSEX
Home Page: None

Objective and Strategy: This is one of ten funds in the Managers Trust. Managers administrates the trust and supervises the activities of outside portfolio managers who supervise the day-to-day operations of an individual portfolio within the trust. Special Equity utilizes three management firms: Liberty Investment, Westport Asset Management, and Pilgrim Baxter. Thus, the portfolio is a composite of three investment philosophies. Liberty invests in companies with less than $300 million equity capitalizations that have consistent, predictable growth and those for which a catalyst exists that will cause recognition in value. Westport invests more aggressively in smaller companies that have the potential to increase earnings or return on equity. Pilgrim invests in small-caps with accelerated earnings growth. The combination of three styles has served shareholders well.

Annualized Returns

1-Year 28.6%
3-Year 18.3%
5-Year 18.8%

Portfolio Manager: Tim Ebright of Liberty Investment Management, Andy Knuth of Westport Asset Management, and Gary Pilgrim of Pilgrim, Baxter and Associates.

Suitability: The fund is suitable for both aggressive and modestly aggressive growth-oriented investors. For best results, assume a long-term orientation.

Portfolio Implications: Although the fund focuses on small-cap stocks, you get three different portfolio managers who act independently of one another in a single portfolio. This fund should serve the needs of all investors who want to include small-cap stocks in their growth portfolio. Consider coupling investment in this fund with an international equity fund.

Risk: The combination of three investment styles has produced a modest-risk small-cap fund. Its beta is a below-market 0.98, which is unusual for a small-cap vehicle. However, the fund's share price sank nearly 24 percent during the 1990 bear market.

Costs: This is a modest-cost fund. Its shares are sold with a no-load format, and its annual expense ratio is right at the group average, 1.44 percent. Portfolio turnover, however, is above average at 144 percent.

Distributions: Both income and capital gains distributions are paid annually in December.

How to Buy and Sell: Minimum initial investment $2,000; IRA $500; no minimum subsequent investment requirement. Telephone exchange with the other nine funds in the trust. Shares are also available without transaction fees from Charles Schwab and Jack White and Company.

MONETTA MID CAP EQUITY FUND

Monetta Funds
1776-A South Naperville Road
Suite 207
Wheaton, IL 60187
800-666-3882

Inception: 1993
Total Assets: $18 Million
Ticker Symbol: MMCEX
Home Page: None

Objective and Strategy: This relatively young fund seeks long-term capital appreciation by investing in common stocks believed to have above-average growth potential. An aggressive, earnings momentum style dominates portfolio management at all Monetta funds. Individual funds differ on the basis of the size of companies included in their portfolios. This fund concentrates its holdings among companies with market capitalizations of $1 billion to $5 billion. Under normal market conditions, the fund invests at least 90 percent of its total assets in equity securities. The fund has shunned large investments in technology issues and has opted instead to invest heavily in the consumer, financial, and industrial industries. At the time of this writing, management was considering the addition of stocks in the retail, oil, and telecommunications industries.

Portfolio Manager: John M. Alogna since inception in 1993. He has also managed the Large-Cap and Balanced Funds since their inceptions and the Intermediate-Term Bond Fund and Government Money Market Fund since January 1994.

Annualized Returns

1-Year 12.8%
3-Year 14.8%
5-Year NA

Suitability: This fund is recommended for aggressive and modestly aggressive growth-oriented investors.

Portfolio Implications: This is a true mid-cap fund. You will find little portfolio duplication when combining it with either small-cap or large-cap offerings.

Risk: This relatively young fund has yet to experience a severe bear market. However, its modest beta (0.79) suggests that its shares will fare better than most aggressive growth vehicles during a stock market sell-off.

Costs: Although the fund has a high portfolio turnover ratio (209 percent), its costs are modest. Its shares are sold with a no-load format, and it possesses a below-average 1.25-percent annual expense ratio.

Distributions: Both income and capital gains distributions are paid annually in December

How to Buy and Sell: Minimum initial investment $1,000; IRA $250; subsequent investments $50. Telephone exchange with other Monetta funds. Shares may also be obtained without transaction fees from Jack White and Company.

NEUBERGER & BERMAN GENESIS

Neuberger & Berman
  Management, Inc.
605 Third Avenue, 2nd Floor
New York, NY 10158–0180
800-877-9700

Inception: 1988
Total Assets: $185 Million
Ticker Symbol: NBGNX
Home Page: http://
www.nbfunds.com

Objective and Strategy: Guided by a strict value orientation, this pure small-company fund has been riding the tide of the popularity of small-cap stocks since its inception in 1988. Management's patience has proved fruitful since the fund's inception. Management expects recent strength in small-cap stocks to continue for another couple of years. While its tiny companies are vulnerable to stock market corrections, Neuberger and Berman's excellent track record, its concern for quality, and its value orientation suggest that the fund will continue to prove rewarding to shareholders over time. At present, it invests in companies with market caps below $750 million (median market cap $500 million). Top sector investments include industrial products, electronics, and energy.

Annualized Returns

1-Year 23.2%
3-Year 15.9%
5-Year 15.4%

Portfolio Manager: Judith M. Vale since February 1994. Prior to joining Neuberger and Berman in 1992, she worked as a portfolio manager and analyst for other prominent investment advisers since 1987.

Suitability: This fund is suitable for all growth-oriented investors. It should be especially appealing for the retirement programs of younger investors or for those setting aside money for a young child's education fund.

Portfolio Implications: This small-cap value fund is best used in combination with other small-cap funds that possess a more aggressive style or with large-cap funds.

Risk: Its modest beta (0.72) suggests a below-average risk level. However, because of the limited liquidity of smaller company stocks, the fund's share price will take a hit during a severe down market as witnessed by its near 26-percent decline during the 1990 bear market.

Costs: This is a very low-cost fund. Its shares are sold with a no-load format. Its 1.33-percent annual expense ratio is far below the average for its group, as is its 37-percent portfolio turnover ratio. In short, shareholders get to keep most of what the fund's portfolio manager earns.

Distributions: Both income and capital gains distributions are paid annually in December.

How to Buy and Sell: Minimum initial investment $1,000; IRA $250; subsequent investments $100. Telephone exchange with other Neuberger and Berman funds. Shares may also be obtained through Charles Schwab and Fidelity Brokerage without transaction fees.

NICHOLAS II

The Nicholas Company
700 Water Street
Suite 1010
Milwaukee, WI 53202
800-227-5987

Inception: 1983
Total Assets: $769 Million
Ticker Symbol: NCTWX
Home Page: None

Objective and Strategy: Like all the Nicholas equity funds, this fund seeks long-term capital appreciation by investing in reasonably valued common stocks. The fund differs from Nicholas and Limited Edition in the size of the companies that are included in the portfolio. This is a mid-range fund that invests in small (equity market values less than $500 million) and mid-sized (equity market values between $500 million and $2 billion) companies. Management seeks growth stocks that represent good value (i.e., where the price-earnings ratio is low in relation to earnings growth or where the price is reasonable in relation to book value). Above-average secular earnings growth and strong current earnings momentum are also important factors in stock selection. Once the stocks are purchased, management has exhibited a great deal of patience with its holdings.

Portfolio Manager: David O. Nicholas, son of the company's founder, took over portfolio management responsibilities for this fund from his father, Albert O. Nicholas, in March 1993. He has been with the firm since 1985.

Suitability: This fund is suitable for long-term, aggressive growth investors only. It is

Annualized Returns

1-Year 21.3%
3-Year 16.1%
5-Year 13.6%

best used by younger investors setting aside money for retirement.

Portfolio Implications: As a mid-cap fund, it is best combined with small-cap and large-cap growth vehicles.

Risk: This is Nicholas's mid-risk offering. Its share price can be expected to be slightly more volatile than the stock market as a whole. However, it sports a modest 0.82 beta. Its share price declined by slightly more than 20 percent during the 1990 bear market.

Costs: Like all Nicholas's offerings, this is a very low-cost growth fund. Its shares are sold with a no-load format. Its annual expense ratio is a very low 0.66 percent, as is its 20-percent portfolio turnover ratio.

Distributions: Both income and capital gains distributions are paid annually, usually in December.

How to Buy and Sell: Minimum initial investment $1,000; IRA $1,000; subsequent investments $50. Telephone exchange with other Nicholas funds (minimum $1,000) with payment of $5 fee. Management frowns on frequent switching.

NICHOLAS LIMITED EDITION

Nicholas Limited Edition, Inc.
700 North Water Street
Suite 1010
Milwaukee, WI 53202
800-227-5987

Inception: 1987
Total Assets: $229 Million
Ticker Symbol: NLLEX
Home Page: None

Objective and Strategy: This fund seeks capital growth by investing in small-cap stocks, defined as those with equity market values below $500 million. Once stocks are purchased, management tends to hold on to them for several years. Like all Nicholas funds, it is managed with a value bent. It is different from other Nicholas growth funds in the size of the companies that are included in the portfolio. Management seeks growth stocks that represent good value. These are stocks with low price-earnings or low price-to-book value ratios. Above-average secular earnings growth and strong current earnings momentum are also important factors in stock selection. This fund will close its doors to new investors when the number of shares outstanding reaches ten million. It has closed its doors once before and probably will be forced to do so again during 1997.

Portfolio Manager: David O. Nicholas, son of the company's founder, took over portfolio management responsibilities for this fund from his father, Albert O. Nicholas, in March 1993. He has been with the firm since 1985.

Suitability: This fund is suitable for long-term, aggressive growth investors only. It is best used by younger investors setting aside money for retirement.

Annualized Returns

1-Year 25.5%
3-Year 16.5%
5-Year 15.9%

Portfolio Implications: As a small-cap fund, it is best combined with mid-cap and large-cap growth vehicles. Investors should also consider combining this fund with an international equity fund.

Risk: This is Nicholas's highest-risk offering. Its share price can be expected to be more volatile than the stock market as a whole. However, it sports an unusually low 0.74 beta. Its share price declined by slightly more than 21 percent during the 1990 bear market.

Costs: Like all Nicholas' offerings, this is a very low-cost growth fund. Its shares are sold with a no-load format. Its annual expense ratio is a very low 0.90 percent as is its 35-percent portfolio turnover ratio.

Distributions: Both income and capital gains distributions are paid annually, usually in December.

How to Buy and Sell: Minimum initial investment $2,000; IRA $2,000; subsequent investments $100. Telephone exchange with other Nicholas funds (minimum $1,000) with payment of $5 fee. Four exchanges per account per year are allowed. Fund will close its doors when shares outstanding reach ten million.

OBERWEIS EMERGING GROWTH

The Oberweis Funds
951 Ice Cream Drive, Suite 200
North Aurora, IL 60542
800-323-6166

Inception: 1987
Total Assets: $207 Million
Ticker Symbol: OBEGX
Home Page: None

Objective and Strategy: This highly aggressive smaller company (average market cap of approximately $600 million) fund employs the "Oberweis Octagon" when selecting individual stocks. This is an eight-pronged strategy that includes a minimum of 30-percent revenue and pretax income growth, P-E not more than one-half potential annual growth rate, products that offer substantial future growth, favorable recent earnings and revenue trends, reasonable price-to-sales ratio, conservative accounting practices, and high relative strength in the market, in that the company's stock has outperformed at least 75 percent of other stocks over the previous twelve months. As might be expected, this approach has led to extreme portfolio volatility, but exceptional long-term returns.

**Annualized
Returns**
1-Year 22.9%
3-Year 18.2%
5-Year 18.7%

Portfolio Manager: James D. Oberweis since the fund's inception in 1987. He also manages the Micro-Cap Portfolio and the Mid-Cap Portfolio. He received an M.B.A. from the University of Chicago.

Suitability: This fund is suitable for the most aggressive growth-oriented investors only. It is a highly volatile fund and may not suit the needs of more conservative investors.

Portfolio Implications: Invest a small portion of your portfolio in this fund and forget about it, that is, if you can tolerate extreme volatility and want to boost the long-term returns of your mutual fund portfolio.

Risk: You won't find a riskier domestic equity fund than this one. Share price can move up or down by 50 percent or more in a single year. It sports a high 1.58 beta and its share price plunged nearly 32 percent during the 1990 bear stock market.

Costs: This is a modest-cost aggressive growth vehicle. It is sold without either a front-end or back-end load, but possesses a 0.25-percent annual 12b-1 fee. Its annual expense ratio (1.52) is at the group average as is its 79-percent portfolio turnover ratio.

Distributions: Income and capital gains distributions are paid annually in late November.

How to Buy and Sell: Minimum initial investment $1,000; IRA $1,000; subsequent investments $100. Telephone exchange with other Oberweis funds. Shares may also be obtained without transaction fees from Charles Schwab, Fidelity Brokerage, and Jack White and Company.

OPPENHEIMER DISCOVERY CLASS A

Oppenheimer Funds Distributor
10200 East Girard, Suite A
Denver, CO 80231
800-525-7048

Inception: 1986
Total Assets: $1.1 Billion
Ticker Symbol: OPOCX
Home Page: None

Objective and Strategy: Like many Oppenheimer-managed funds, Discovery interprets its mandate with a wide degree of latitude. Although it primarily invests in small, emerging growth companies, it freely purchases large company stocks that meet its growth and value parameters. Management relies on both top-down and bottom-up approaches to identify macroeconomic industry and market trends and their potential beneficiaries. Although the fund's approach has the potential to backfire, its excellent long-term returns imply that the strategy works well. Although the fund's holdings are diversified across many industry sectors, it has had a lot of success with its investments in technology and health care stocks. The fund has made a heavy bet on software stocks, which management believes will benefit from corporate America's shift to network-computing.

Annualized Returns

1-Year 27.8%
3-Year 14.6%
5-Year 19.3%

Portfolio Manager: Jay W. Tracey III since October 1991. He has managed other Oppenheimer funds during the past five years. Prior to joining Oppenheimer, he worked for Founders and Berger.

Suitability: This fund is suitable for aggressive growth investors only. Its hefty front-end load makes this fund suitable for long-term investors only.

Portfolio Implications: This fund's portfolio looks like a number of other funds that emphasize mid-cap stocks drawn from the computer technology and health care sectors. If you plan to invest in this fund, check your other aggressive growth funds first for potential duplication.

Risk: To the victor go the spoils and to the high risk funds go the best returns. This high return vehicle is accompanied by high risk as witnessed by its above-average 1.22 beta. Interestingly, its share price decline during the 1990 bear market (slightly less than 20 percent) was less than most aggressive growth funds.

Costs: Once you become a shareholder, this is a modest-cost fund. However, you must ante up a hefty 5.75-percent front-end load sales fee to get in the door. In addition, the fund levies a 0.24-annual 12b-1 fee. Its 1.33-percent annual expense ratio is slightly below the group average, but its 106-percent portfolio turnover ratio is slightly above average.

Distributions: Both income and capital gains distributions are paid annually in December.

How to Buy and Sell: Shares are sold by brokers and financial planners. Minimum initial investment $1,000; IRA $250; subsequent investments $25. Telephone switch with other Oppenheimer funds. Shares available at Fidelity Brokerage with small commission charge.

PARKSTONE SMALL CAP CLASS A

BISYS Fund Services
3435 Stelzer Road
Columbus, OH 43219
800-451-8377

Inception: 1988
Total Assets: $187 Million
Ticker Symbol: PKSAX
Home Page: None

Objective and Strategy: This fund invests for long-term capital appreciation in companies that offer a wide range of growth opportunities. Its small company investments are those whose earnings increases have historically resulted in higher share prices, those that are driven by innovation and new ideas, and those that may become the well-established industry leaders of tomorrow. Management defines small-cap as any company with market value of equity below $1 billion. The fund is one of the most volatile in the Parkstone fund family. Although a diversified fund, its strong performance numbers over the years have resulted from investment in a few big winners and large sector bets that paid off.

Portfolio Manager: Roger H. Stamper since the fund's inception in 1988. He also manages the Parkstone Equity Fund, Balanced Fund, and High Income Equity Fund.

Suitability: This is another aggressively managed small-cap vehicle and is suitable for only those aggressive growth investors who can tolerate extreme short-term portfolio volatility.

Portfolio Implications: The best use of this fund is to add a small allocation to a growth-oriented portfolio. It possesses extremely high return potential but is accompanied by high short-term share price volatility.

Risk: You don't earn an average of 26 percent annually over a five-year period without assuming large risks. This fund is no exception. Its beta is an astronomical 1.51, that's 50 percent more risk than the S&P 500 Index. Its share price tumbled 24 percent during the 1990 bear market.

Annualized Returns

1-Year 31.2%
3-Year 25.5%
5-Year 26.0%

Costs: The fund is sold with a 4.50-percent front-end load and a 0.25-percent annual 12b-1 fee. Thus, sales fees tend to be rather high. On the other hand, its annual expense ratio is about average at 1.55 percent, and its portfolio turnover ratio, 50 percent, is below the group average.

Distributions: Income and capital gains distributions are paid annually in mid-December.

How to Buy and Sell: Shares sold by brokers and financial planners. Class B shares also available. Minimum initial investment requirement $1,000; IRA $1,000; subsequent investments $50. Shares also available without transaction fees to investment advisers through Charles Schwab.

PBHG EMERGING GROWTH

The PBHG Funds, Inc.
P.O. Box 419534
Kansas City, MO 64141–6534
800-433-0051

Inception: 1993
Total Assets: $1.2 Billion
Ticker Symbol: PBEGX
Home Page: http://www.pbhg.com

Objective and Strategy: This fund aggressively seeks capital appreciation by investing in the stocks of emerging U.S. companies. Like most PBHG funds it employs an earnings momentum strategy. The strategy is to invest in rapidly growing companies that consistently meet and exceed growth expectations. Management uses proprietary software and research models that incorporate attributes such as positive earnings surprises, upward earnings estimate revisions, and accelerating sales and earnings growth to guide the fundamental research effort. Critical to the fundamental research is an assessment of the company's earnings quality and the sustainability of the company's current growth trends. Stocks are sold when they fail to sustain strong earnings. No more than 40 percent of assets are invested in any one sector and no more than 3 percent in any one security.

Annualized Returns

1-Year 32.6%
3-Year 33.4%
5-Year NA

Portfolio Manager: Christine M. Baxter and Gary L. Pilgrim since the fund's inception. Baxter has been with the company since 1991. Pilgrim also comanages the Emerging Growth, Large-Cap, and Select Equity Funds.

Suitability: This fund is suitable for aggressive growth-oriented investors only. Its extreme share price volatility during the short term precludes investment by more conservative investors.

Portfolio Implications: This fund employs an earnings momentum strategy and dumps stocks if they underperform. A small allocation to this fund, held for the longer term, can boost portfolio returns without substantially increasing risk. Limit investments in this fund to no more than 15 percent of portfolio assets.

Risk: This relatively young fund has yet to experience a severe bear market. However, the use of an earnings momentum strategy, investment in small companies, and a 1.51 beta suggest extreme portfolio volatility.

Costs: This is a modest-cost aggressive growth vehicle. It is sold with a no-load format, possesses an average annual expense ratio (1.47 percent) and a slightly above-average 97-percent portfolio turnover ratio.

Distributions: Both income and capital gains distributions are paid annually in December.

How to Buy and Sell: Minimum initial investment $2,500; IRA $2,000; no subsequent minimum investment requirement. Telephone switch with other PBHG funds. Shares also available through Charles Schwab, Jack White, and Fidelity Brokerage (no transaction fees).

PBHG GROWTH

The PBHG Funds, Inc.
P.O. Box 419534
Kansas City, MO 64141-6534
800-433-0051

Inception: 1985
Total Assets: $5.0 Billion
Ticker Symbol: PBHGX
Home Page: http://www.pbhg.com

Objective and Strategy: The only difference between this fund and PBHG Emerging Growth is the size of the companies in its portfolio. This fund invests in mid-cap firms. It aggressively seeks capital appreciation by utilizing an earnings momentum style. The strategy is to invest in rapidly growing companies that consistently meet and exceed growth expectations. Management uses proprietary software and research models that incorporate attributes such as positive earnings surprises, upward earnings estimate revisions, and accelerating sales and earnings growth to guide the fundamental research effort. Critical to the fundamental research is an assessment of the company's earnings quality and the sustainability of the company's current growth trends. Stocks are sold when they fail to sustain strong earnings. No more than 3 percent of assets are invested in any one security, an attempt to mitigate investment risk.

Portfolio Manager: Gary L. Pilgrim since the fund's inception in 1985. He also co-manages the Emerging Growth, Large-Cap, and Select Equity funds.

Suitability: This fund is suitable for aggressive growth-oriented investors only. Its extreme share price volatility during the short run precludes investment by more conservative investors.

Portfolio Implications: This fund employs an earnings momentum strategy and dumps stocks if they underperform. A small allocation to this fund, held for the longer term, can boost portfolio returns without substantially increasing overall portfolio risk. Highly aggressive investors may wish to allocate up to 20 percent of portfolio assets to this fund.

Risk: This is a high volatility fund as witnessed by its 1.29 portfolio beta. Its share price tumbled more than 31 percent during the 1990 bear market.

Costs: This is a relatively low-cost aggressive growth vehicle. Its shares are sold with an no-load format. Its annual expense ratio (1.45 percent) is slightly below the group average as is its surprisingly low 45-percent portfolio turnover ratio.

Distributions: Both income and capital gains distributions are paid annually in December.

How to Buy and Sell: Minimum initial investment $2,500; IRA $2,000; no subsequent investment requirement. Telephone switch with other PBHG funds. Shares also available through Charles Schwab, Jack White, and Fidelity Brokerage (no transaction fees).

Annualized Returns

1-Year 29.6%
3-Year 24.6%
5-Year 31.9%

PERKINS OPPORTUNITY

730 East Lake Street
Wayzata, MN 55391
800-366-8361

Inception: 1993
Total Assets: $139 Million
Ticker Symbol: POFDX
Home Page: http://
www.firstfund.com

Objective and Strategy: Although it pursues long-term capital appreciation, this fund does not neatly fit into any category. Although the fund tends to emphasize smaller companies, it will invest in any company that presents an opportunity. About half of the stocks in its portfolio are of companies that are located in the upper Midwest (the fund is based in Minneapolis). Its stock selection strategy also cuts across the spectrum of earnings momentum, growth, and value. Management looks for companies that have some positive change taking place that it believes will result in a significant upward movement in its stock. Management admits that it is not looking for a 20-percent return; it wants to own stocks whose prices will multiply several times over. Management also employs technical analysis of chart patterns when determining when to buy and sell individual stock issues.

Annualized Returns
1-Year 5.1%
3-Year 30.1%
5-Year NA

Portfolio Manager: Richard W. Perkins and Daniel S. Perkins since the fund's inception in 1993. They have been in the investment advisory business since 1984.

Suitability: Although this is a well-managed fund, its share price is highly volatile and thus its shares are suitable for aggressive growth-oriented investors only.

Portfolio Implications: This fund's holdings span across small-, mid- and large-cap stocks. Thus, its portfolio may provide some duplication with other aggressive growth vehicles.

Risk: This very high-risk fund sports an unusually high 1.53 beta. Although this relatively young fund has yet to experience a severe bear market, its aggressive investment style indicates that share price will decline by more than the overall market during a sustained market correction.

Costs: Shares are sold by financial planners and brokers with a 4.75-percent front-end load. In addition, shareholders assume a 0.20-percent ongoing 12b-1 fee. Its annual expense ratio (1.97 percent) is above average for the group as is its 93-percent portfolio turnover ratio.

Distributions: Income is distributed semiannually in June and December, and capital gains are distributed annually in December.

How to Buy and Sell: Minimum initial investment $2,500; IRA $2,000; subsequent investments $100. The fund's shares are available to institutional investors (investment advisers) through Charles Schwab without transaction fees.

PERRITT CAPITAL GROWTH

Perritt Capital Management
120 South Riverside Plaza
Suite 1745
Chicago, IL 60609

Inception: 1988
Total Assets: $9 Million
Ticker Symbol: PRCGX
Home Page: http://
www.perrittcap.com

Objective and Strategy: When compiling a list of the best equity funds around, I just couldn't resist including my own fund. This fund invests in the stocks of small companies (market cap under $150 million at time of purchase) that possess greater-than-average earnings growth but sell at below-market price-earnings ratios. When selecting individual stocks from among the more than two thousand small-caps, Perritt seeks those with relatively little debt, price-earnings ratios less than twice the anticipated three- to five-year earnings growth rates, and the shares of companies whose operating managers hold a significant amount of the company's common stock. Stocks are generally held until their equity market caps top $400 million. The fund generally maintains a portfolio consisting of the stocks of fifty to seventy different companies.

Portfolio Manager: Me, since the fund's inception in early 1988. Dr. Perritt, president of Perritt Capital Management, which he founded in 1987, obtained a D.B.A from the University of Kentucky in 1974.

Suitability: This is one of a handful of true small-cap funds sold with a no-load format. It is suitable for both aggressive and modestly aggressive growth-oriented investors. Best results are obtained when investing for longer-term capital appreciation.

Annualized Returns

1-Year 12.7%
3-Year 12.2%
5-Year 11.0%

Portfolio Implications: There is generally little overlap with other small-cap fund portfolios because of the small size of this fund's portfolio holdings. For best overall portfolio performance, combine this fund with funds that concentrate their holdings in large-caps and/or international equities.

Risk: This fund is packed with value stocks. It sports one of the lowest betas (0.80) in its investment category. However, because of the limited liquidity of small-caps, the fund can exhibit high downside volatility during severe bear markets as witnessed by its 21-percent decline during the 1990 bear market.

Costs: This is a modest-cost fund, considering its small size. Its shares are sold with a no-load format, and it possesses a below-average 58-percent portfolio turnover ratio. However, the annual expense ratio, 1.92, is above average, but should decline as assets grow.

Distributions: Both income and capital gains distributions are paid in late November.

How to Buy and Sell: Minimum initial investment $1,000; IRA $250; no minimum subsequent investment requirement. Shares may also be obtained through Jack White and Company and Olde Brokerage without transaction fees and through Charles Schwab with a small fee.

PRINCOR EMERGING GROWTH CLASS A

Princor Financial Services
P.O. Box 10423
Des Moines, IA 50392
800-247-4123

Inception: 1987
Total Assets: $205 Million
Ticker Symbol: PRGWX
Home Page: http://
www.principal.com

Objective and Strategy: This fund seeks long-term capital appreciation by investing a significant portion of its assets in emerging growth companies that have equity market values below $1 billion. However, anything might turn up in this fund's portfolio. Its holdings include seasoned companies and IPOs, large-cap and small-cap stocks, stocks with both low and high price-earnings multiples. In short, management will invest anywhere it believes it can obtain greater than average capital appreciation. Founded during the aftermath of the great 1987 stock crash, management has built an enviable performance record. Since inception the fund has returned an annual average in excess of 28 percent.

Annualized Returns
1-Year 15.2%
3-Year 17.5%
5-Year 17.7%

Portfolio Manager: Mike Hamilton since fund's inception in December 1987. MBA, Bellarmine College. Also manages Princor Growth Fund.

Suitability: The fund is suitable for aggressive and modestly aggressive growth-oriented investors who can hold their investments through long bear markets.

Portfolio Implications: This is a highly diversified mid-cap growth fund. It works well with more conservatively managed large-cap funds and aggressively managed small-cap funds.

Risk: Although the fund's portfolio sports a modest 0.92 beta, its concentration in mid-cap stocks gives its share price a bit more volatility than first meets the eye. During the 1990 bear market, its share price declined by slightly more than 22 percent.

Costs: The fund's shares are primarily sold by financial planners and brokers. Investors must ante up a 4.75-percent front-end sales load and assume an ongoing 0.25-percent 12b-1 fee. Its annual expense ratio (1.47 percent) is about average for the group while its 36-percent portfolio turnover ratio is well below average for aggressive growth funds.

Distributions: Income distributions are paid semiannually in June and December; capital gains are distributed in December.

How to Buy and Sell: Minimum initial investment $1,000; IRA $250; subsequent investments $50. Class B shares (4-percent contingent deferred sales fee and 1-percent 12b-1 fee) are also available.

PUTNAM OTC EMERGING GROWTH "A"

One Post Office Square
Boston, MA 02109
800–225–1581

Inception: 1982
Total Assets: $61 Million
Ticker Symbol: POEGX
Home Page: http://
www.putnaminv.com

Objective and Strategy: This fund seeks capital appreciation by investing in common stocks of small to medium-sized emerging-growth companies traded in the over-the-counter market that management believes have potential for capital appreciation. When choosing investments, management seeks public companies in relatively early states of development with records of profitability and strong financial positions. These companies may have new technologies, unique proprietary products, or profitable market niches. In addition, preference is given to companies that are experiencing strong unit sales growth and in which management has a substantial equity stake. As might be expected, the fund's portfolio historically has been packed with technology stocks.

Portfolio Manager: Steven L. Kirson and Michael J. Mufson since June 1996. Both have worked with this fund since joining Putnam in 1989 and 1993, respectively. Mufson also manages Putnam Vista.

Suitability: This very aggressively managed fund is suitable for highly aggressive investors only.

Portfolio Implications: The fund's investments will provide significant overlap with

Annualized Returns
1-Year 26.0%
3-Year NA
5-Year NA

other aggressive small-cap funds that invest heavily in technology stocks. Consider combining this fund with more value-oriented small-cap and large-cap funds.

Risk: This fund's portfolio, packed with high price-earnings ratio growth stocks, possesses extreme short-term share price volatility as witnessed by its higher-than-average 1.41 beta. The fund's share price tumbled nearly 31 percent during the 1990 bear market.

Costs: The fund's class A shares are sold with a hefty 5.75-percent front-end load. However, operating costs are relatively moderate. Its annual expense ratio is a below-average 1.14 percent, but its portfolio turnover ratio is a higher-than-average 116 percent.

Distributions: Both income and capital gains distributions are paid annually in December.

How to Buy and Sell: Shares are sold by financial planners and brokers. Minimum initial investment $500; IRA $250; subsequent investments $25. Class B shares (higher 12b-1 fee and contingent deferred sales charge) are also available. Shares are also available through Fidelity Brokerage with a small commission charge.

PUTNAM VOYAGER CLASS A

One Post Office Square
Boston, MA 02109
800-225-1581

Inception: *1969*
Total Assets: *$7.8 Billion*
Ticker Symbol: *PVOYX*
Home Page: *http://*
www.putnaminv.com

Objective and Strategy: The fund seeks capital appreciation primarily by investing in common stocks of mid-sized companies. The portfolio typically contains a core of smaller companies that it holds for the long run. The fund also leaves some room in its asset base for short-term opportunities as they arise, such as cyclical issues entering a positive phase of the business cycle, turn-around situations, and special situations. Recently, two-thirds of the fund's portfolio was concentrated in three industry sectors: consumer, technology, and health care. Top individual stock holdings included Computer Associates, America Online, Oxford Health Plan, and Citicorp. The dichotomous strategy has served shareholders well as witnessed by the fund's return, which has averaged more than 19 percent during the last five years.

Annualized Returns
1-Year 23.0%
3-Year 19.4%
5-Year 19.1%

Portfolio Manager: Robert R. Beck, Charles H. Swanberg, and Roland W. Gillis since 1995.

Suitability: Investment in this fund is suitable for both aggressive and modestly aggressive investors. However, investors should limit their investment in the fund to no more than 15 percent of portfolio assets.

Portfolio Implications: This is another plain-vanilla aggressive growth fund whose portfolio will probably duplicate the risk-return characteristics of other successful aggressive growth vehicles. Thus, you need to examine your other fund holdings before investing in this fund.

Risk: This is a highly volatile fund with a beta of 1.21. During the 1990 bear market its share price declined by nearly 21 percent.

Costs: This fund's class A shares are sold with a hefty 5.75-percent front-end load. However, operating costs are reasonable. Its annual expense ratio is well below average at 1.07 percent, and its portfolio turnover ratio (65 percent) is also below average for the group.

Distributions: Both income and capital gains distributions are paid annually in December.

How to Buy and Sell: Shares are sold by financial planners and brokers. Minimum initial investment $500; IRA $250; subsequent investments $25. Class B shares (higher 12b-1 fee and contingent deferred sales charge) are also available. Shares are also available through Fidelity Brokerage with a small commission charge.

ROBERTSON STEPHENS CONTRARIAN

Robertson Stephens & Company
555 California Street
San Francisco, CA 94104
800-766-3863

Inception: 1993
Total Assets: $883 Million
Ticker Symbol: RSCOY
Home Page: http://www.rsim.com

Objective and Strategy: One of the few true contrarian funds around today, it has the ability to short sell individual securities and buy put options on indexes as well as individual securities. While the market has done nothing but post new highs in recent years, you might think this fund would have performed miserably. To the contrary, management has provided shareholders with a better than 20 percent annual average return since the fund's inception in June 1993. The secret to its success is shorting some high-flying technology stocks and owning a basket of commodity-based stocks, such as petroleum companies. Another part of Stephens's approach is staying clear of companies owned by a lot of institutional investors. With the market now trading at all time highs and basis valuation measures near historic highs, this fund has a great deal of appeal.

Portfolio Manager: Paul H. Stephens since the fund's inception in June 1993. As a founder of Robertson Stephens, he has also managed investment portfolios for individuals since 1975. He obtained an M.B.A. from the University of California, Berkeley.

Suitability: The fund is suitable for both aggressive and conservative growth-oriented investors. Over long periods of time, the fund's short positions could trim returns, thus it is ideal for investors with shorter investment horizons.

Annualized Returns
1-Year 23.4%
3-Year 19.8%
5-Year NA

Portfolio Implications: This fund's portfolio is usually both long and short the market. Thus, it has upside potential while maintaining plenty of downside protection. It is an excellent investment vehicle for late stock market cycle investing when valuation multiples tend to be well above average and the odds of a market setback are high. Because its short positions can result in abnormally high income distributions, the fund is best used in a tax-sheltered portfolio.

Risk: Believe it or not, the beta of this relatively young fund is actually *minus* 0.06. In other words, its returns have nearly no relationship to the stock market as a whole. Adding it to any growth-oriented portfolio will actually lower overall volatility.

Costs: This is an above-average cost fund. Although investors do not pay a front-end or back-end sales fee, the fund levies a hefty 0.75-percent ongoing 12b-1 fee that has caused its annual expense ratio to balloon to 2.46 percent. However, its portfolio turnover ratio is a below-average 34 percent.

Distributions: Both income and capital gains are distributed annually in December.

How to Buy and Sell: Minimum initial investment $5,000; IRA $1,000; subsequent investments $100. Shares also available without transaction fees from Charles Schwab, Fidelity, and Jack White.

ROBERTSON STEPHENS EMERGING GROWTH

Robertson Stephens & Company
555 California Street
San Francisco, CA 94104
800-766-3863

Inception: 1987
Total Assets: $193 Million
Ticker Symbol: RSEGX
Home Page: http://www.rsim.com

Objective and Strategy: In recent years this fund has gradually changed its strategy. Once a small-company fund, the fund has attempted to fulfill its objective of capital appreciation by investing its assets in many mid-sized and even large firms. Still, the fund has continued to emphasize a few sectors, which adds aggressiveness to the fund. Primarily stocks are selected from the technology, health care, or environmental sectors. These companies usually have earnings growth of at least 25 percent and a return on equity of 20 percent. In mid-1996 the fund switched portfolio managers in an apparent attempt to return to its roots as a small-cap fund. Its new manager, Jim Callinan, is a well-known authority on smaller stocks. He looks for companies with strong management and a proprietary advantage, such as a patent or low-cost operating position.

Portfolio Manager: James Callinan since June 1996. Prior to joining Robertson Stephens in 1996, he served as portfolio manager of the Putnam OTC Emerging Growth Fund. He has an M.B.A. from Harvard.

Suitability: This is a very aggressive fund and is therefore suitable for only aggressive growth-oriented investors. Its technology bent requires a longer-term investment horizon.

Annualized Returns

1-Year 17.7%
3-Year 17.9%
5-Year 12.9%

Portfolio Implications: This fund's relatively compact portfolio includes many companies favored by other aggressive growth investors. Thus, some duplication with other aggressive growth funds should be expected. Check the portfolios of your current aggressive growth fund holdings before making a significant investment in this fund.

Risk: The fund's 1.33 beta suggests extreme short-term share price volatility. However, the fund's share price declined by about 20 percent during the 1990 bear market, which is a bit less than the declines posted by other aggressive growth funds.

Costs: This is an average-cost aggressive growth fund. Its shares are sold without a front-end or back-end load. However, shareholders assume an ongoing 0.25-percent 12b-1 fee. Its expense ratio is about average at 1.64 percent, but its portfolio turnover ratio is an above-average 280 percent.

Distributions: Both income and capital gains distributions are paid annually in late December.

How to Buy and Sell: Minimum initial investment $5,000; IRA $1,000; subsequent investments $100. Telephone switch with other Robertson Stephens funds. Shares are also available through Charles Schwab, Fidelity Brokerage, and Jack White and Company without transaction fees.

ROBERTSON STEPHENS VALUE & GROWTH

Robertson Stephens & Company
555 California Street
San Francisco, CA 94104
800-766-3863

Inception: 1992
Total Assets: $743 Million
Ticker Symbol: RSVPX
Home Page: http://www.rsim.com

Objective and Strategy: In seeking its objective of capital appreciation, this fund invests in small and medium-sized companies that offer good shareholder value based on growth prospects, earnings momentum, and company assets. Although this fund reserves the right to engage in short sales and options trading in order to hedge its long positions, it is normally quite conservative in this respect. During its first four years of operation, investment results have been just short of spectacular. However, the fund's name is somewhat misleading. The portfolio is relatively compact and contains a significant (40 percent) allocation to higher price-earnings multiples technology stocks. A couple of big winners have propelled returns higher. However, as with any compact strategy, a few big losers could also derail its stellar track record.

Portfolio Manager: Ronald E. Elijah since the fund's inception in April 1992. He is also the portfolio manager of Information Age Fund. He obtained an M.B.A. from Golden Gate University.

Suitability: Despite being called a "value" fund, this fund's shares are suitable for only the most aggressive growth-seeking investors. Consider taming its volatility by combining an investment in this fund with a true value growth fund. Limit investments in this fund to no more than 15 percent of portfolio assets.

Annualized Returns
1-Year -9.3%
3-Year 23.8%
5-Year NA

Portfolio Implications: This is an aggressive growth vehicle, pure and simple. It is also loaded with technology stocks. If your other growth funds already have a significant position in the technology sector, this fund will most likely provide significant duplication.

Risk: Although the fund's 1.15 beta suggests that its share price is only modestly more volatile than that of the market, its compact portfolio indicates otherwise. This relatively young fund has yet to experience a severe bear market, however its share price could tumble during a quick stock market sell-off.

Costs: This is an average price aggressive growth vehicle. Its shares are sold without a front-end or back-end sales load. However, shareholders assume a 0.25-percent annual 12b-1 fee. Its 1.45-percent expense ratio is slightly below average for the aggressive growth group. However, its portfolio turnover ratio is a high 232 percent.

Distributions: The fund has yet to make income or capital gains distributions, but when required to do so, it plans to make these distributions annually.

How to Buy and Sell: Minimum initial investment $5,000; IRA $1,000; subsequent investments $100. Shares also available through Charles Schwab, Fidelity, and Jack White (without fees).

ROYCE MICRO-CAP FUND

The Royce Funds
1414 Avenue of the Americas
New York, NY 10019
800–221–4268

Inception: 1991
Total Assets: $135 Million
Ticker Symbol: RYOTX
Home Page: http://
www.roycefunds.com

Objective and Strategy: Royce Micro-Cap (formerly the Royce OTC Fund) selects its companies on a value basis, and the majority of its investments are traded on NASDAQ. These are typically very small companies that are less well known and are, therefore, more likely to offer value. Specifically, the fund will only consider investing in companies with equity market values below $300 million. To mitigate the inherent risks that accompany investing in this sector of the market, the fund tries to choose companies with strong fundamentals. The fund uses cash flow and a company's use of excess cash flow as its primary gauge of a company's worth. This is one of the few funds that gives investors the opportunity to capture the extra risk-adjusted returns supplied by true small companies. Its value focus is an added benefit.

Annualized Returns

1-Year 7.4%
3-Year 11.4%
5-Year NA

Portfolio Manager: Charles M. Royce since the fund's inception in 1991. He is assisted by Jack E. Fockler, Jr. and W. Whitney George. They also team up to manage the Royce Value, Total Return, and Global Services Fund.

Suitability: This is one of the few small company funds that is a suitable investment for all growth-oriented investors.

Portfolio Implications: There are only a small handful of true small-cap value funds around. Chances are that investment in this fund will not provide duplication with any of your other equity fund investments. It is a fund that works well with any equity fund portfolio, and its value bent can offset risks of your other aggressive growth funds.

Risk: This is the lowest-risk small-cap fund around. Its beta is less than half that of the stock market as a whole (0.47). Although this relatively young fund has yet to experience a severe bear market, its very conservative small-cap investments suggest that it will weather occasional stock market storms well.

Costs: The fund is sold with a no-load format. However, its management fee (1.45 percent) produces a higher-than-average 1.94-percent annual expense ratio. Offsetting these higher operating costs, however, is the fund's very modest 25-percent portfolio turnover ratio.

Distributions: Income and capital gains are distributed annually in December.

How to Buy and Sell: Minimum initial investment $2,000; IRA $500; subsequent investments $50. Telephone exchange with other Royce funds. A 1-percent redemption fee (paid to the fund) is levied on shares held less than one year. Shares may also be obtained through Fidelity Brokerage and Jack White and Company without transaction fees.

ROYCE PREMIER

The Royce Funds
1414 Avenue of the Americas
New York, NY 10019
800-221-4268

Inception: 1991
Total Assets: $285 Million
Ticker Symbol: RYPRX
Home Page: http://
www.roycefunds.com

Objective and Strategy: This fund seeks long-term growth by investing in a limited portfolio of the small-cap sector of the market defined by the fund's adviser as having superior financial characteristics. The portfolio will typically own companies that have market capitalizations between $300 million and $1 billion. The Royce funds have been value investing in small companies for over twenty years. The Royce approach is to understand and value a company's "private worth," the price the company would command if the entire enterprise were sold in a private transaction to a rational buyer. To obtain this estimate of worth requires acquiring an estimate of a company's future cash flow prospects and then discounting the annual cash flow estimates by an investor's required rate of return. By its very nature, it is a conservative valuation model.

Portfolio Manager: Charles M. Royce since the fund's inception in 1991. He is assisted by Jack Fockler, Jr. and W. Whitney George. They team up to manage the Royce Value, Total Return, and Global Services Fund.

Suitability: Like other Royce growth funds, this fund is suitable for all types of growth-oriented investors, whether aggressive or highly conservative.

Annualized Returns
1-Year 9.9%
3-Year 12.6%
5-Year NA

Portfolio Implications: Because of the fund's value selection model, most of its portfolio holdings rarely appear in other small- and mid-cap funds that invest in higher price-earnings ratio stocks. Thus, this fund makes an excellent addition to any growth-seeking portfolio.

Risk: In the mode of all Royce funds, this is one of the lower-risk entrants in the mid-cap fund group. Its beta is a low 0.51, about one-half that of the overall market. Although this relatively young fund has yet to experience a severe stock market correction, chances are that it will weather financial storms well.

Costs: This is a very low-cost mid-cap growth fund. Its 1.25-percent annual expense ratio is well below average as is its 39-percent portfolio turnover ratio.

Distributions: Both income and capital gains distributions are paid annually in December.

How to Buy and Sell: Minimum initial investment $2,000; IRA $500; subsequent investments $50. Telephone exchange with other Royce funds. A 1-percent redemption fee (paid to the fund) is levied for shares held less than one year. Shares may also be obtained through Fidelity Brokerage and Jack White and Company without transaction fees.

SCUDDER DEVELOPMENT

Scudder Investor Services
175 Federal Street
Boston, MA 02110
800-225-2470

Inception: 1971
Total Assets: $1.1 Billion
Ticker Symbol: SCDVX
Home Page: http://
www.scudder.com

Objective and Strategy: This fund seeks long-term capital growth by investing in the securities of relatively small or little-known companies often referred to as emerging growth companies. The fund strives to identify smaller companies operating in emerging growth industries or niches. These companies can provide above-average long-term growth opportunities that can translate into strong long-term performance. To help reduce risk, the fund allocates its assets among many companies and industries. Recent emphasis has been on energy stocks. The fund has reduced its holdings of stocks that are most vulnerable to a rise in interest rates, and it has been paring back on some of its holdings that have grown too large for the fund's capitalization range. The fund has returned an average of about 17 percent a year during the last twenty years.

Portfolio Manager: Roy C. McKay since he joined Scudder in 1988. Peter Chin, who has been with Scudder since 1973, has comanaged the fund since 1993.

Suitability: This volatile fund is suitable for highly aggressive growth-seeking investors only.

Annualized Returns

1-Year 17.5%
3-Year 17.3%
5-Year 15.2%

Portfolio Implications: This mid-cap fund's portfolio is highly diverse. If you invest in this fund, there is little need to add another mid-cap fund to your portfolio. It is best combined with micro-cap and large-cap growth funds.

Risk: This is an extremely volatile fund. Its 1.50 beta is one of the highest in the aggressive growth category. During the 1990 bear market, the fund's share price declined by nearly 24 percent.

Costs: This is a low-cost aggressive growth fund. Its shares are sold with a no-load format. Its annual expense ratio is a below-average 1.32 percent, as is its 42-percent portfolio turnover ratio.

Distributions: Both income and capital gains distributions are paid semiannually, usually in June and December.

How to Buy and Sell: Minimum initial investment $1,000; IRA $500; subsequent investments $50. Telephone exchange with other Scudder funds. Shares may also be obtained without transaction fees from Charles Schwab and Fidelity Brokerage.

SELECTED SPECIAL

Selected Funds
124 East Marcy Street
Santa Fe, NM 87501
800-243-1575

Inception: *1939*
Total Assets: *$62 Million*
Ticker Symbol: *SLSSX*
Home Page: *None*

Objective and Strategy: This fund seeks growth of capital by investing primarily in both mid-cap and large-cap growth stocks. The fund, which was part of the Kemper financial group, became associated with Venture Advisors in late 1993. During the last four years, the fund has had four different portfolio managers including the latest, Elizabeth Bramwell, who left Gabelli to form her own investment firm. The fund is now in capable hands, and it is hoped that Bramwell Capital Management (the fund's subadviser) can bring some management stability to a fund that first began selling its shares to the public in 1939. The fund's portfolio is relatively compact, containing about seventy different stocks. It largest sector bets include financial services, industrial products, and technology.

Annualized Returns
1-Year 9.3%
3-Year 11.8%
5-Year 12.9%

Portfolio Manager: Elizabeth Bramwell since February 1994. Prior to 1994, Ms. Bramwell managed the Gabelli Growth fund since its inception in 1987.

Suitability: This fund is suitable for all growth-oriented investors. Conservative investors should limit their investment in this fund to no more than 15 percent of portfolio assets.

Portfolio Implications: Although concentrating in smaller companies, this is a plain-vanilla aggressive growth fund. Its emphasis on value stocks mitigates risk a bit. If you invest in this fund, plan on being around for the long term.

Risk: This fund's risk level is near the low end of the aggressive growth fund spectrum. Its beta is a modest 0.91. However, like most aggressive growth vehicles, its share price declined by a hefty 21.5 percent during the 1990 bear market.

Costs: This is a very low-cost aggressive growth fund. Its shares are sold without a front-end or back-end sales charge. Even though shareholders assume a 0.25-percent ongoing 12b-1 fee, the fund's annual expense ratio (including this fee) is a very low 1.09 percent. Its portfolio turnover ratio, 27 percent, is also well below average for the aggressive growth fund group.

Distributions: Both income and capital gains are distributed annually, usually in March.

How to Buy and Sell: Minimum initial investment $1,000; IRA $250; subsequent investments $100. The fund's shares may also be obtained through Charles Schwab and Company without transaction fees.

SEVEN SEAS SMALL CAP

The Seven Seas Series Fund
Two International Place, 35th Floor
Boston, MA 02110
617-654-6089

Inception: 1992
Total Assets: $49 Million
Ticker Symbol: SVSCX
Home Page: None

Objective and Strategy: This fund aggressively seeks capital growth by investing in small- and mid-cap stocks, defined as those with equity market values between $100 million and $1.5 billion. Prior to November 22, 1994, the fund was passively managed under the name The Seven Seas Series S&P Midcap Index Fund. Both its name and investment objective were changed on that date. Its mandated objective is to outperform the Russell 2000 (small-cap) Index while maintaining characteristics similar to those of the index. The fund minimizes macroeconomic bets such as movements in interest rates, industry timing, and style rotation bets. The investment approach identifies attractive stocks based on fundamental changes in earnings expectations. The universe of stocks upon which it draws are those contained in the Russell 2000 Index.

Annualized Returns
1-Year 24.6%
3-Year 19.9%
5-Year NA

Portfolio Manager: Jeffrey Adams since December 1994. Mr. Adams has been with State Street Bank and Trust Company (the fund's adviser) since 1990 as portfolio manager and account administrator.

Suitability: The fund is suitable for all growth-oriented investors who wish to include small-cap stocks in their portfolios.

Portfolio Implications: Although the fund is actively managed, its financial characteristics are highly similar to those of the Russell 2000 Index. Small-cap investors may wish to use this fund as their core holding in this sector of the market.

Risk: The fund's beta (0.91) is slightly below that of the market generally. Thus, its volatility is a bit below that of the Russell 2000 Index. Although this relatively young fund has yet to experience a severe bear market, its investments possess limited liquidity and would be expected to participate in a prolonged stock market decline.

Costs: This is a very reasonable-cost small-cap fund. Management has capped the fund's annual expense ratio at 1.00 percent. Its shares are sold without a front-end or back-end load. Its small 12b-1 fee becomes irrelevant because of the fund's limit on its expense ratio.

Distributions: Income distributions are paid quarterly and capital gains are distributed annually, usually in early September.

How to Buy and Sell: Minimum initial investment $1,000; IRA $1,000; no minimum subsequent investment requirement. Shares are also available without transaction fees from Jack White.

SKYLINE SPECIAL EQUITIES

Skyline Funds
311 South Wacker Drive
Suite 4500
Chicago, IL 60606
800-458-5222

Inception: 1987
Total Assets: $167 Million
Ticker Symbol: SKSEX
Home Page: None

Objective and Strategy: This fund seeks capital appreciation by investing primarily in stocks with market capitalizations below $300 million. Management has consistently stressed a value-oriented philosophy and has had strong success with it. Despite what has been an earnings-driven, high-growth bull market for small-cap stocks in recent years, this fund's return ranks high when compared to other much more aggressive small-cap funds. This fund will really shine in a stock picker's market, as it did in 1992 when it returned a whopping 42.4 percent in an otherwise lackluster market environment. The fund attempts to identify companies with above-average revenue and earnings growth but below-average price-earnings ratios. Also special situations are regularly considered. Closed for two years, the fund recently reopened its doors to new investors.

Portfolio Manager: William M. Dutton since the fund's inception in 1987. He obtained a B.A. from Princeton University and a masters degree in accounting from the University of Illinois.

Suitability: This fund is suitable for all growth-oriented investors. Its conservative investment philosophy has resulted in one of the few aggressive growth funds suitable for conservative investors.

Annualized Returns

1-Year 20.0%
3-Year 13.0%
5-Year 20.3%

Portfolio Implications: You usually won't see many of Bill Dutton's picks in other aggressive growth portfolios because of his penchant for value-priced stocks. Thus, the fund works well when combined with nearly every other growth vehicle around.

Risk: Although the fund sports a very low beta (0.80) for an aggressive growth fund, its holdings have limited liquidity and thus are susceptible to a stock market downturn as witnessed by the fund's 27-percent decline during the 1990 bear market.

Costs: This is a very modest-cost aggressive growth fund. Its shares are sold with a no-load format. Its 1.51-percent annual expense ratio is about average for the group, and its 71-percent portfolio turnover ratio is slightly below the group's average.

Distributions: Both income and capital gains distributions are paid annually in mid-December.

How to Buy and Sell: Minimum initial investment $1,000; IRA $1,000; subsequent investments $100. The fund closed its doors to new investors for a few years because it was receiving a flood of new money but has recently reopened. Shares can be obtained from Charles Schwab, Fidelity Brokerage, and Jack White and Company without transaction fees.

SKYLINE SPECIAL EQUITIES II

Skyline Funds
311 South Wacker Drive
Suite 4500
Chicago, IL 60606
800-458-5222

Inception: 1993
Total Assets: $96 Million
Ticker Symbol: SPEQX
Home Page: None

Objective and Strategy: This fund seeks capital appreciation by investing in mid-cap growth stocks. It began operations around the time that Special Equities closed its doors to new investors because a flood of new money was compromising that fund's small-cap investment strategy. It was not meant to be a clone of Special Equities, but rather to focus on stocks with market capitalizations above those held in that fund's portfolio. Its portfolio is also marked by a very conservative investment decision strategy, which emphasizes out-of-favor growth stocks that sell at price-earnings multiples well below those commanded by those favored by earnings momentum-seekers.

Portfolio Manager: Kenneth S. Kailin since the fund's inception in 1993. He also manages portfolios for institutional clients. He obtained an M.B.A. from the University of Chicago.

Suitability: This fund is suitable for all growth-oriented investors. Its conservative investment philosophy has resulted in one of the few aggressive growth funds suitable for conservative investors.

**Annualized
Returns**
1-Year 16.5%
3-Year 13.1%
5-Year NA

Portfolio Implications: You usually won't see many of this fund's selections in other aggressive growth portfolios because of its inherent conservatism. It works well with most other aggressive growth and growth vehicles.

Risk: Although the fund sports a very low beta (0.88) for an aggressive growth fund, its holdings have limited liquidity and thus are susceptible to a stock market down draft. This young fund has yet to experience a severe bear market.

Costs: This is a very modest-cost aggressive growth fund. Its shares are sold with a no-load format. Its 1.52-percent annual expense ratio is about average for the group, and its 71-percent portfolio turnover ratio is slightly below the group average.

Distributions: Both income and capital gains distributions are paid annually in mid-December.

How to Buy and Sell: Minimum initial investment $1,000; IRA $1,000; subsequent investments $100. Shares can be obtained from Charles Schwab, Fidelity Brokerage, and Jack White and Company without transaction fees.

STEIN ROE CAPITAL OPPORTUNITIES

Stein Roe & Farnham
P.O. Box 804058
Chicago, IL 60680
800-338-2550

Inception: 1969
Total Assets: $1.3 Billion
Ticker Symbol: SRFCX
Home Page: http://
www.steinroe.com

Objective and Strategy: The fund seeks long-term capital appreciation by investing in aggressive growth companies, such as securities of smaller emerging companies as well as securities of well-seasoned companies of any size that offer strong earnings growth potential. Management searches for aggressive growth companies that may benefit from new products or services, technological developments, or changes in management. Although the fund invests primarily in common stocks, the managers may invest in all types of equity securities, including preferred stocks and convertible securities. Preference is given to companies with sustainable earnings growth, which are sought early in the growth cycle and are held for the long-term. In fact, the preoccupation with long-term performance is one characteristic that distinguishes this fund from other aggressive growth funds.

Annualized Returns
1-Year 49.6%
3-Year 28.1%
5-Year 24.5%

Portfolio Manager: Gloria J. Santella and Eric S. Maddix since 1991 and 1996, respectively. Santella joined Stein Roe in 1979 and Maddix in 1987. Both received their M.B.A.s from the University of Chicago.

Suitability: This is Stein Roe's most volatile fund. Its shares are suitable for highly aggressive investors who can tolerate share price volatility that is well above that of the market.

Portfolio Implications: If you add this fund to your growth-oriented portfolio, you will most likely not need another aggressive growth fund. Furthermore, you must view the fund's return potential from the perspective of a five-year or greater investment horizon. This find works well in a dollar cost averaging program.

Risk: If you want big returns, you have to take big risks, and this fund is no exception to that rule. Its beta (1.29) is well above that of the market. Its share price tumbled more than 37 percent during the 1990 bear market.

Costs: This is a very efficient aggressive growth fund. Its shares are sold with a no-load format, and its 1.25-percent expense ratio is well below the average for the aggressive growth fund group, as is its 45-percent portfolio turnover ratio.

Distributions: Both income and capital gains distributions are paid annually in December.

How to Buy and Sell: Minimum initial investment $2,500; IRA $500; subsequent investments $100. Telephone switch with other Stein Roe funds. Shares may also be obtained through Charles Schwab, Fidelity Brokerage, and Jack White and Company with no transaction fees.

STRONG DISCOVERY

Strong Funds
P.O. Box 2936
Milwaukee, WI 53201
800-368-3863

Inception: 1987
Total Assets: $582 Million
Ticker Symbol: STDIX
Home Page: http://www.strong-funds.com

Objective and Strategy: This fund seeks capital appreciation by uncovering emerging investment trends and attractive growth opportunities. It attempts to identify companies that are poised for accelerated earnings growth due to innovative products or services, new management, or favorable economic or market cycles. These companies are usually small, unseasoned firms in the early stages of development, but they may also include more mature organizations. Whatever the size, history, or industry of the companies, the adviser believes their potential earnings growth is not yet reflected in the market value and that, over time, the market prices of these securities will move higher. As with any strategy that seeks to invest in undervalued, out-of-favor companies, the fund's return at times will not move in lockstep with the market. Such has been the case recently, as performance has suffered. However, this fund will perform well over a complete market cycle.

Portfolio Manager: Richard S. Strong since the fund's inception in 1987. Strong founded the advisory company in 1974. Charles A. Paquelet joined the fund as comanager in August 1996.

Suitability: The fund is suitable for patient, aggressive growth-oriented investors. It works best when coupled with funds that

Annualized Returns
1-Year 0.3%
3-Year 11.0%
5-Year 12.0%

concentrate their portfolios in the large-cap sector of the market.

Portfolio Implications: This is a heritage fund. You want to buy and hold its shares over a very long time period to benefit from the full measure of the market cycle. It is also an excellent fund to use in dollar cost averaging programs.

Risk: The fund's beta (1.23) is well above that of the market. However, its love for out-of-favor stocks can provide a degree of protection during severe bear markets as witnessed by the fund's 13-percent share price decline during the 1990 bear market.

Costs: The fund's shares are sold with a no-load format, and the fund possesses a slightly below-average annual expense ratio (1.40 percent). However, like a number of equity funds in the Strong family, its portfolio turnover is exceptionally high at 516 percent.

Distributions: Income distributions are paid quarterly and capital gains are distributed annually in December.

How to Buy and Sell: Minimum initial investment $1,000; IRA $250; subsequent investments $50. Telephone exchange with other Strong funds. Shares may also be obtained without transaction fees from Charles Schwab, Fidelity Brokerage, and Jack White and Company.

T. ROWE PRICE OTC SECURITIES

T. Rowe Price Investor Services
100 East Pratt Street
Baltimore, MD 21202
800-225-5132

Inception: *1956*
Total Assets: *$343 Million*
Ticker Symbol: *OTCFX*
Home Page: *http://*
www.troweprice.com

ION III
Aggressive Growth Funds

Objective and Strategy: Formerly part of USF&G, this fund received more than its share of bruises during the 1980s. Since T. Rowe Price became the fund's investment adviser in August 1992, the fund has chalked-up exceptional performance numbers. The fund seeks capital appreciation by investing in securities traded in the U.S. over-the-counter market, primarily stocks of small to medium-sized companies. When selecting individual stocks, management looks for the following characteristics: capable management, attractive business niches, pricing flexibility, sound financial and accounting practices, and a demonstrated ability to grow revenues, earnings, and cash flow consistently. More than fifty years ago, Thomas Rowe Price pioneered the growth stock theory, and he would be proud of this fine growth fund's investment philosophy.

Portfolio Manager: Gregory McCrickard since 1992. He joined T. Rowe Price in 1986 and has been managing investments since 1991. He is assisted by Preston Athey, Lise Buyer, Hugh Evans III, and James Kennedy.

Suitability: All growth-oriented mutual fund investors should own at least one T. Rowe Price growth vehicle, and this fund is an excellent candidate. More conservative investors, however, should limit their invest-

Annualized Returns
1-Year 22.6%
3-Year 18.1%
5-Year 18.0%

ments in this fund to no more than 10 percent of portfolio assets.

Portfolio Implications: Couple this fund with both a well-managed small-cap fund and a fund packed with blue-chip stocks and you will have a complete growth fund portfolio.

Risk: If you want to earn large returns, you have to take large risks. However, this growth vehicle sports a very low 0.78 beta. However, its short-term volatility during market corrections is much higher than this beta indicates. During the 1990 bear market, for example, the fund's share price declined slightly more than 26 percent.

Costs: This is another low-cost growth fund in the T. Rowe Price stable. It is sold with a no-load format, sports a very low 1.11-percent expense ratio and a below-average 58-percent portfolio turnover ratio.

Distributions: Income distributions (which are minimal) and capital gains are paid annually in December.

How to Buy and Sell: Minimum initial investment $2,500; IRA $1,000; subsequent investments $100. Telephone exchange with other T. Rowe Price funds, although the company frowns on frequent switching.

T. ROWE PRICE MID-CAP GROWTH

T. Rowe Price Investment Services
100 East Pratt Street
Baltimore, MD 21202
800-225-5132

Inception: 1992
Total Assets: $655 Million
Ticker Symbol: RPMGX
Home Page: http://
www.troweprice.com

Objective and Strategy: This fund seeks capital appreciation by investing in growth stocks with market capitalizations in the $300 million to $4 billion range. The average market capitalization of the fund is currently $1.7 billion. When selecting individual stocks, portfolio manager Brian Berghuis seeks companies with annual earnings growth rates in excess of 12 percent that are in industries where there is good growth because of a positive backdrop. Generally, these companies exhibit good operating leverage, where there are recurring revenues and where there is a high degree of confidence that the companies will achieve their earnings targets. They are also companies that are market share leaders or those that have a clear competitive advantage. When buying, Berghuis acquires those stocks that are trading at reasonable price-earnings ratios relative to the market as a whole.

Annualized Returns
1-Year 24.9%
3-Year 21.4%
5-Year NA

Portfolio Manager: Brian Berghuis since 1992. He has been managing investments since joining Price in 1985. Assisted by Marc Baylin, James Kennedy, and John Wakeman.

Suitability: This is one aggressive growth fund that is suitable for all growth-oriented investors. However, conservative investors should limit their allocations to this fund to no more than 10 percent of portfolio assets.

Portfolio Implications: This is a true mid-cap fund. It is best combined with growth funds that invest in small-cap and large-cap stocks.

Risk: The fund's beta is a modest 0.93, indicating less risk than the market as a whole. However, the fund is relatively young and has been operating in a market in which mid-cap stocks have continually trended higher. Thus, chances are that its beta is understated.

Costs: Like all T. Rowe Price funds, this is a low-cost offering. Its shares are sold with a no-load format, its annual expense ratio is a modest 1.25 percent and its portfolio turnover ratio is a below-average 58 percent.

Distributions: Both income and capital gains distributions are paid annually in December.

How to Buy and Sell: Minimum initial investment $2,500; IRA $1,000; subsequent investments $100. Telephone exchange with other Price funds, although the company frowns on frequent switching.

TWENTIETH CENTURY GIFTRUST

Twentieth Century Investors
4500 Main Street
P.O. Box 418210
Kansas City, MO 64111
800–345–2021

Inception: 1983
Total Assets: $841 Million
Ticker Symbol: TWGTX
Home Page: http://
www.americancentury.com

Objective and Strategy: This well-managed, capital gains–seeking fund has a unique format. It is an irrevocable trust in which an investor establishes the account as a gift to an individual who will receive Giftrust shares on a specified maturity date. There is a ten-year minimum holding period, perfect for encouraging long-term investing, and an aggressive growth strategy that has been phenomenally successful in the past. The fund is managed according to the Twentieth Century philosophy in which assets are invested in highly successful companies whose earnings and revenues are growing at accelerating rates. Stocks are identified through the use of a proprietary computer screening program and then are scrutinized by a team of managers. It largest investment concentrations include computer software, business services, medical equipment, and biotechnology.

Annualized Returns
1-Year 10.9%
3-Year 23.4%
5-Year 27.8%

Portfolio Manager: The fund's portfolio is team managed under the leadership of James E. Stowers III, company chairman.

Suitability: Giftrust could help provide a child with a financially independent retirement, provide a pint-sized future astro-

physicist with college funds, or establish a sound financial foundation for a beloved friend or relative.

Portfolio Implications: This fund has an extremely high beta, which almost assures that it will handily beat the market over any twenty-year period. It should only be used for investment needs that are in the very distant future.

Risk: This is one of the highest-risk, aggressive growth funds around (beta 1.58). But who cares? Investments in the trust must be held at least ten years, thus negating any concern about short-run share price fluctuations. Its share price declined by 28 percent during the 1990 bear market.

Costs: This is another low-cost Twentieth Century offering. It is sold with a no-load format and its annual expense ratio is limited to 1.00 percent of assets. Its portfolio turnover ratio (105 percent) is slightly above average.

Distributions: Both income and capital gains distributions are paid in December.

How to Buy and Sell: Minimum initial investment $500; subsequent investments $50.

TWENTIETH CENTURY ULTRA

Twentieth Century Investors
4500 Main Street
P.O. Box 418210
Kansas City, MO 64111
800-345-2021

Inception: *1981*
Total Assets: *$18 Billion*
Ticker Symbol: *TWCUX*
Home Page: *http://*
www.americancentury.com

Objective and Strategy: This fund aggressively seeks capital appreciation. It once was Twentieth Century's most aggressive fund and its performance leader. However, the popularity of the fund with investors ballooned portfolio assets, thus channeling its emphasis on small-cap stocks toward mid-cap and large-cap holdings. This trend toward investing in larger companies has both reduced its long-run performance potential and its investment risk. In an attempt to boost returns, the fund establishes positions early in the life cycle of fast-growing companies. (Like all Twentieth Century equity funds, this fund seeks the stocks of companies whose earnings growth rates are expanding.) Predictably, this has led the fund into hefty investments in technology stocks. It has also added a 5-percent allocation to international stocks.

Portfolio Manager: The fund is managed using a team approach under the leadership of James E. Stowers III since the fund's inception in 1981.

Suitability: This fund is suitable for aggressive and modestly aggressive growth-oriented investors. A long-term orientation is required.

Annualized Returns

1-Year 11.1%
3-Year 13.1%
5-Year 17.0%

Portfolio Implications: The fund has had to abandon its investment in true small-cap stocks for those with billion-dollar equity capitalizations. Thus, it is beginning to look a lot like other aggressive growth funds. Its large asset base almost assures duplication of investments with other aggressive growth funds.

Risk: Once a high-risk vehicle, its beta has steadily declined as its asset base has grown. Today, it sports a near-market beta of 1.01. Its share price declined by slightly more than 17 percent during the 1990 bear market.

Costs: Like all Twentieth Century equity offerings, this is a very low-cost fund. Its shares are sold with a no-load format, its annual expense ratio is capped at 1.00 percent, and it sports an average 87-percent portfolio turnover ratio.

Distributions: Both income and capital gains distributions are paid annually in December.

How to Buy and Sell: Minimum initial investment $1,000; IRA $1,000; subsequent investments $50. Telephone exchange with other Twentieth Century/Benham Funds. Shares may also be obtained through Charles Schwab without transaction fees.

USAA AGGRESSIVE GROWTH

USAA Investment Management
  Company
9800 Fredricksburg Road
San Antonio, TX 78288
800-531-8181

Inception: 1981
Total Assets: $671 Million
Ticker Symbol: USAUX
Home Page: None

Objective and Strategy: This no-load, capital appreciation–seeking fund places most of its bets on small emerging growth companies with market capitalizations below $500 million. It has the option of investing up to 10 percent of its assets in foreign firms. Stock selection tends to follow industry selection. However, when choosing stocks, management seeks companies with strong earnings growth, experienced management, and proven product-development capabilities. The fund's roller-coaster performance of the past couple of years is what investors can expect, with significant rewards coming to only those who stick around for the long run. Its recent largest industry concentrations include computer software, health care and medical supplies, and communication equipment manufacturers.

Annualized Returns

1-Year 33.2%
3-Year 25.4%
5-Year 17.0%

Portfolio Manager: John K. Cabell, Jr. and Eric M. Efron since March 1995. Cabell holds an M.A. and B.S. from the University of Alabama. Efron obtained an M.B.A. from New York University.

Suitability: This fund is suitable for aggressive, long-term investors only. It is an excellent vehicle to fund retirement programs by young investors or as a component of a young child's education fund.

Portfolio Implications: This is a middle of the road aggressive growth fund. Its portfolio characteristics will most likely be highly similar to other diversified aggressive growth funds. It is best combined with a large-cap, value-oriented fund.

Risk: This is another big risk, big return fund. Its 1.48 beta indicates a portfolio with significant short-term volatility. In fact, that risk came home to roost during the 1990 bear market, when the fund's share price declined more than 30 percent.

Costs: This is a very modest-cost fund. Its shares are sold with a no-load format. Its 0.86-percent expense ratio is well below the group average. However, its 138-percent portfolio turnover ratio is well above average.

Distributions: Income and capital gains distributions are paid annually in September.

How to Buy and Sell: Minimum initial investment $3,000; IRA $250; subsequent investments $50. Telephone switch with other USAA funds.

UNITED NEW CONCEPTS CLASS A

Waddell & Reed Financial Services
6300 Lamar Avenue
P.O. Box 29217
Shawnee Mission, KS 66201
913-236-2000

Inception: 1983
Total Assets: $548 Million
Ticker Symbol: UNECX
Home Page: http://
www.waddell.com

Objective and Strategy: This fund seeks capital appreciation by investing in the common stocks of new or unseasoned companies that are in the early stages of development or in smaller companies positioned in new and emerging industries where opportunity for rapid growth is above average. The fund has been known to make large bets on particular sectors, which paid off in 1988 with a huge 88-percent annual gain. Since then, however, the fund's return has cooled. Still, its five-year average annual return is in excess of 17 percent, which is quite respectable when compared to its peers. When purchasing individual issues, management looks for companies with aggressive or creative management, technological expertise, new or unique products or services, entry into new or emerging industries, or special situations arising out of governmental priorities and programs.

Annualized Returns
1-Year 8.5%
3-Year 17.3%
5-Year 17.3%

Portfolio Manager: Mark G. Seferovich since March 1989. He joined Waddell and Reed, the fund's adviser, in February 1989.

Suitability: The fund's shares are suitable investments for aggressive and moderately aggressive investors.

Portfolio Implications: This is another aggressive growth vehicle that focuses its attention on smaller companies. Its portfolio characteristics will most likely be highly similar to other funds with a comparable investment objective, thus the potential for portfolio duplication is high.

Risk: Although the fund invests in emerging growth–type companies, its beta is a below-market 0.92. During the 1990 bear market, the fund's share price declined slightly less than 20 percent.

Costs: This fund's entrance fee is relatively high. Investors must pay a 5.75-percent front-end sales fee. However, once aboard, operating expenses are quite modest. Despite its 0.15-percent ongoing 12b-1 fee, its annual expense ratio is a below-average 1.25 percent, as is its 28-percent portfolio turnover ratio.

Distributions: Both income and capital gains distributions are paid annually in mid-December.

How to Buy and Sell: Class A shares are sold by financial planners and stock brokers with a 5.75-percent front-end sales charge. Class Y shares (available to institutional investors only) are also available. Telephone exchange with other United funds.

VALUE LINE LEVERAGED GROWTH

Value Line Securities
220 East 42nd Street
New York, NY 10017
800-223-0818

Inception: 1972
Total Assets: $378 Million
Ticker Symbol: VALLX
Home Page: None

Objective and Strategy: This fund seeks capital appreciation by buying common stocks on margin. The fund employs leverage by borrowing money to purchase additional securities. Thus, the fund is sometimes more than 100 percent invested. The fund stays almost fully invested in common stocks or convertible securities and can write covered call options. The fund posted an outstanding 37-percent return in 1995, the best in the fund's history that spans nearly a quarter century. Recently, its largest investments were concentrated in the financial services, computer and peripherals, computer software, and semiconductor industries. Generally, its growth stock offerings are drawn from the large-cap sector of the market, and many of its holdings are household names. The Value Line rating system provides the backbone for stock selection.

Portfolio Manager: Alan N. Hoffman since April 1993. Hoffman also manages the Value Line Multinational Fund as well as other pension accounts. He has been with Value Line since 1988.

Suitability: This fund is suitable for aggressive and moderately aggressive investors. Because of its use of financial leverage, it is suggested that investors allocate no more than 10 percent of portfolio assets to this fund.

Annualized Returns
1-Year 20.3%
3-Year 15.5%
5-Year 15.3%

Portfolio Implications: This is a blue-chip, aggressive growth vehicle with a leverage kicker. Its portfolio will most likely provide significant duplication with other aggressive growth funds.

Risk: Although the fund may use financial leverage, its risk is about equal to the average for the aggressive growth group of funds (beta 1.18). Its share price declined by a modest 15 percent during the severe 1990 bear market.

Costs: This is a very low-cost aggressive growth fund. Its shares are sold with a no-load format; its annual expense ratio is very low at 0.88 percent, as is its 54-percent portfolio turnover ratio.

Distributions: Both income and capital gains distributions are paid annually in late December.

How to Buy and Sell: Minimum initial investment $1,000; IRA $1,000; subsequent investments $100. Telephone exchange with other Value Line funds. Shares may also be obtained through Charles Schwab, Fidelity Brokerage, and Jack White and Company with no transaction fees.

VANGUARD EXPLORER

Vanguard Group
Vanguard Financial Center
P.O. Box 2600
Valley Forge, PA 19482
800-635-1511

Inception: 1962
Total Assets: $2.2 Billion
Ticker Symbol: VEXPX
Home Page: http://
www.vanguard.com

Objective and Strategy: This fund seeks capital appreciation by investing in companies with small equity market values (those with an average market value between $100 million and $500 million). These companies tend to be unseasoned but are considered to have favorable prospects for growth. The fund may also invest, to a limited degree, in short-term fixed-income securities. In recent years, the fund's management has stressed investment in smaller firms in the technology sector. In late 1990 the assets of the Explorer II Fund were merged into Explorer, and in late 1994 the fund acquired the assets of the Vanguard Technology fund. After many years of poor performance, a steadfast dedication to its small-cap strategy has finally allowed shareholders to reap big rewards, as can be seen by the returns of the past few years.

Annualized Returns
1-Year 15.9%
3-Year 14.6%
5-Year 16.0%

Portfolio Manager: Multimanaged: 53 percent by Kenneth Abrams of Wellington Management since 1994 and 47 percent by John Granahan of Granahan Investment Management since 1985. Granahan previously managed the Explorer fund from 1972 to 1979.

Suitability: The fund is suitable for investors seeking long-term growth, willing to assume above-average risk, desiring an aggressive fund as part of a balanced program, and planning to invest for at least five years.

Portfolio Implications: This is another small-cap, high-tech fund that will provide a degree of overlap with a large number of small-cap, aggressive growth funds. Its portfolio is highly diversified with about three hundred different small-cap firms represented.

Risk: The beta of this fund is a reasonable 0.95. However, there is more risk here than first meets the eye. Small-cap stocks are somewhat illiquid and technology stocks can experience significant price volatility. The fund's share price declined by nearly 25 percent during the 1990 bear market.

Costs: Like all Vanguard equity funds, this fund is one of the lowest-cost aggressive growth funds you will find. Its shares are sold with a no-load format. Its annual expense ratio is a very low 0.68 percent and its 66-percent portfolio turnover ratio is below the group average.

Distributions: Income and capital gains distributions are paid annually in December.

How to Buy and Sell: Minimum initial investment $3,000; IRA $1,000; subsequent investments $100. Telephone switch with other Vanguard funds, but the fund family will not tolerate frequent switching.

WASATCH MID CAP

68 South Main Street
Salt Lake City, UT 84101
800-551-1700

***Inception:** 1992*
***Total Assets:** $163 Million*
***Ticker Symbol:** WAMCX*
***Home Page:** None*

Objective and Strategy: This fund invests in companies with annual sales under $500 million that are growing earnings at least 15 percent per year. Insider ownership should be at least 10 percent, and the company's price-earnings ratio should not exceed its five-year projected earnings growth rate. The fund's stock-picking agenda does not stop there. A company must have an important patent, a business that is difficult to copy, or be a leader among competition. Management mitigates risk by keeping a balanced portfolio of stocks with momentum alongside core companies that represent very low risk relative to their potential rewards. While not a technology fund, the fund has a large percentage of its holdings in technology-related companies in keeping with its nature of investing in high-quality companies capable of rapid earnings growth.

Portfolio Manager: Samuel S. Stewart, Jr., Ph.D. since the fund's inception in 1992. Stewart also manages the Income and Aggressive Equity funds. Assisted by Karey Barker, who has been at Wasatch since 1989.

Suitability: The fund is suitable for aggressive investors with long-term (five years or more) investment horizons.

Annualized Returns
1-Year -2.5%
3-Year 20.0%
5-Year NA

Portfolio Implications: High-tech, rapidly growing companies. If this describes the holdings of your other aggressive growth funds, watch out for portfolio duplication. Couple an investment in this fund with a more staid, value-based fund.

Risk: This is another high-risk, aggressive growth vehicle. It sports a high 1.37 beta. Although this relatively young fund has yet to experience a severe bear market, its high beta suggests that its downside vulnerability is exceptionally high.

Costs: This is a modest-cost aggressive growth fund. Its shares are sold with a no-load format, its 1.75-percent expense ratio is slightly above average. However, the fund exhibits patience, and its 46-percent portfolio turnover ratio is well below average for the aggressive fund group.

Distributions: Both income and capital gains distributions are paid annually in December.

How to Buy and Sell: Minimum initial investment $2,000; IRA $1,000; subsequent investments $100. Telephone exchange with other Wasatch funds. Shares may also be obtained through Charles Schwab, Fidelity Brokerage, and Jack White and Company without transaction fees.

WARBURG PINCUS CAPITAL APPRECIATION

Warburg Pincus Funds
466 Lexington Avenue
New York, NY 10017
800–257–5614

Inception: 1987
Total Assets: $339 Million
Ticker Symbol: CVCAX
Home Page: None

Objective and Strategy: The fund seeks capital appreciation by investing in a broadly diversified portfolio consisting primarily of equity securities of domestic companies. Management attempts to identify sectors of the market and companies within market sectors that it believes will outperform the overall market. It focuses on the stocks of medium-sized companies, which it defines as those with equity market values between $500 million and $4.5 billion. These are companies deemed to have above-average earnings growth prospects or where significant fundamental changes are taking place that augur well for improved earnings. Recently, financial stocks represented a significant portion of the fund's portfolio (20 percent of assets). These stocks will be the beneficiaries of ongoing consolidation in the banking industry and from increasing margins during a declining interest rate environment.

Portfolio Manager: George U. Wyper and Susan L. Black since December 1994. Wyper joined Warburg in August 1994 and Black in 1985.

Suitability: The fund is suitable for growth-oriented investors, whether aggressive or more conservative. However, a longer-term orientation is required.

Annualized Returns

1-Year 24.0%
3-Year 16.3%
5-Year 16.4%

Portfolio Implications: This is another mid-cap vehicle that could possibly duplicate the holdings of other aggressive growth funds in your portfolio. It is best used in combination with funds that invest in large-cap stocks and those that select value-based stocks.

Risk: This is a modest-risk aggressive growth fund. Its beta is a moderate 1.05, and its share price declined by less than 15 percent during the severe 1990 bear market.

Costs: This is a modest-cost equity fund. Its shares are sold with a no-load format. Its annual expense ratio is a below-average 1.12 percent. However, it sports a higher-than-average 146-percent portfolio turnover ratio.

Distributions: Both income and capital gains distributions are paid annually, usually in either November or December.

How to Buy and Sell: Minimum initial investment $2,500; IRA $500; subsequent investments $100. Telephone exchange with other Warburg Pincus funds. Shares may also be obtained through Charles Schwab, Fidelity Brokerage, and Jack White and Company without transaction fees.

WARBURG PINCUS EMERGING GROWTH-COMMON

Warburg Pincus Funds
466 Lexington Avenue
New York, NY 10017
800-257-5614

Inception: *1988*
Total Assets: *$968 Million*
Ticker Symbol: *CVEGX*
Home Page: *None*

Objective and Strategy: If you're looking for a big bang for your buck, you'll get it here. The fund seeks maximum capital appreciation. It is a nondiversified management investment company, meaning that its portfolio, at times, can be relatively compact. The fund invests the bulk of its assets in emerging growth companies, defined as small or medium-sized companies that have passed their start-up phase and show positive earnings and prospects of achieving significant profit and gain in a relatively short period of time. These are companies that stand to benefit from new products or services, technological developments, or changes in management. The portfolio is packed with special situation companies, including reorganizations, recapitalizations, mergers, liquidations, or favorably resolved litigation.

Portfolio Manager: Elizabeth B. Dater since the fund's inception in 1988 and Stephen Lurito since 1990. Dater holds a B.A. from Boston University. Lurito obtained an M.B.A. from the Wharton School of the University of Pennsylvania.

Suitability: Despite its modest beta, this fund is suitable for only those investors with very high risk tolerance levels who can hold their shares for the long run (five years or more).

Annualized Returns

1-Year 14.1%
3-Year 15.9%
5-Year 19.7%

Portfolio Implications: This fund is far from a balanced investment program. However, if you are aggressive and growth-oriented, a small investment in this fund will complement your other aggressive equity fund holdings. Its emphasis on special situations is a big plus.

Risk: The fund's beta (1.12) is about average for the aggressive fund group. Its shares exhibit higher-than-average volatility. Its share price declined by more than 21 percent during the 1990 bear market.

Costs: This is a low-cost aggressive growth vehicle. Its shares are sold with a no-load format, and its annual expense ratio (1.26 percent) is well below the average for the group. It sports an average portfolio turnover ratio of 84 percent.

Distributions: Both income and capital gains are distributed annually in either November or December.

How to Buy and Sell: Minimum initial investment $2,500; IRA $500; subsequent investments $100. Telephone exchange with other Warburg Pincus funds. Shares may also be obtained through Charles Schwab, Fidelity Brokerage, and Jack White and Company without transaction fees.

WPG TUDOR

WPG Mutual Funds
One New York Plaza
New York, NY 10004
800-223-3332

Inception: 1970
Total Assets: $192 Million
Ticker Symbol: TUDRX
Home Page: None

Objective and Strategy: This fund seeks capital appreciation by investing in growth stocks. It may place up to 50 percent of its assets in special situations that offer prospects for appreciation in the short run. Management has shifted the fund's focus from blue-chip to mid-cap and small-cap companies, for it believes the smaller issues are poised for a period of sustained superior performance. To be sure, the fund pays a price for the highest-growth companies that it prefers, for the fund's price-earnings ratio is consistently one of the highest in the aggressive growth group. The fund also tends to place big bets on individual sectors, adding an additional element of risk. However, the largest rewards usually go to the investors willing to assume above-average investment risks, and this fund's shareholders have benefitted from the risks the fund has assumed.

Annualized Returns
1-Year 26.2%
3-Year 16.1%
5-Year 15.0%

Portfolio Manager: Melville Straus since 1973. Straus also assumed portfolio management responsibilities for the WPG Growth Fund in March 1996.

Suitability: This fund is suitable for only very aggressive, growth-oriented investors who can hold their investments for the long term (at least five years).

Portfolio Implications: This very aggressive vehicle should be combined with more sedate growth funds to provide a balanced investment program. Because of the extreme volatility of this fund's shares, investors should not allocate more than 15 percent of portfolio assets to this fund.

Risk: The fund sports a very high beta (1.49). Its portfolio tends to be packed with high price-earnings ratio stocks, and thus share price could suffer during a recession induced a bear market when P-E ratios collapse. The fund's shares declined slightly more than 18 percent during the 1990 bear market.

Costs: This is an average-cost aggressive growth vehicle. Its shares are sold with a no-load format, and its expense ratio is slightly below average (1.30 percent). However, its 123-percent portfolio turnover ratio is above the equity fund average.

Distributions: Both capital gains and income distributions are paid annually in September.

How to Buy and Sell: Minimum initial investment $2,500; IRA $250; subsequent investments $100. Telephone exchange with other WPG funds. Shares may also be obtained through Jack White and Company without transaction fees.

CHAPTER

THIRTY-EIGHT

Growth Funds

As the name implies, growth funds attempt to obtain long-term growth of investment capital as their primary investment objective. The portfolio managers of these funds do not engage in speculative tactics such as using financial leverage (i.e., buying common stocks on margin) or short selling. However, on occasion, some managers will use stock or index options to hedge their portfolio positions.

Growth fund returns are less volatile than those of funds classified as aggressive growth. Their average volatility tends to parallel that of the S&P 500 Index because they usually invest in the common stocks of large, well-established companies. Because most blue-chip companies regularly pay some cash dividends to their shareholders, growth funds tend to provide a modest amount of current income. A growth fund investor is likely to find companies with household names such as AT&T, Ford, IBM, and DuPont in these portfolios. Although a handful of growth funds attempt to boost returns by engaging in market timing tactics, the vast majority of funds in this group tend to stay fully invested over the stock market cycle. As a result, their portfolio turnover ratios are less than those of equity funds in general.

While a small but growing number of growth fund portfolio managers have adopted short-term trading strategies, most hold their investments for long-term capital appreciation. A large percentage of growth fund managers tend to hold their common stock investments for approximately two years, and one can find numerous funds with significantly longer average holding periods.

Many of the funds listed in this section have been operating for decades. Thus, you will find many familiar funds described here. All are actively managed. (Index funds, which generally fall into the growth fund category, are described in Section II.)

Over the long run, you can expect the typical growth fund's return to just about match that of the stock market. Thus, they are suitable for all growth-oriented investors. Conservative investors should combine growth funds with lower volatility growth and income funds. Aggressive investors should limit their allocation to growth funds to a maximum of 50 percent of portfolio assets and tilt the balance of their portfolios toward funds with greater return potential such as aggressive growth, small-cap, and international equity funds.

AIM VALUE CLASS A

AIM Distributors
11 Greenway Plaza, Suite 1919
Houston, TX 77046
800–347–4246

Inception: 1984
Total Assets: $4.4 Billion
Ticker Symbol: AVLFX
Home Page: http://
www.aimfunds.com

Objective and Strategy: This fund's primary objective is long-term growth of capital, with income a secondary objective. Fund management searches out undervalued equity securities that may include out-of-favor cyclicals, stocks with low price-earnings ratios, and companies whose securities are selling at prices that do not reflect the value of their underlying assets. In the hunt for value, portfolio manager Dobberpuhl has gone overseas, and about 20 percent of portfolio assets are invested in foreign stocks. However, the fund has continued with its long-term game plan of buying low-expectation stocks with improved earnings in a high-expectation market. Stocks from sectors such as electric power, medical, tobacco, and financial and consumer credit have begun to play an important role in the portfolio.

Annualized Returns

1-Year 5.3%
3-Year 14.5%
5-Year 17.6%

Portfolio Manager: Joel E. Dobberpuhl since 1992 and Claude Cody IV since joining AIM in 1992. Dobberpuhl joined AIM in 1990. Cody also manages the Balanced and Global Utilities funds.

Suitability: The fund is suitable for growth-oriented investors who can take a long-term view. Although the fund seeks growth, its love of undervalued issues tends to lead it to dividend-paying stocks.

Portfolio Implications: In a search for value anything might turn up in this fund's portfolio. It has held hefty positions in foreign equities and cash equivalents at times. Thus, unlike a number of growth vehicles, this fund's flavor is anything but plain-vanilla.

Risk: The fund prides itself in behaving well in both up and down markets, however that is not always the case. Despite a lower-than-market beta (0.95), its share price tumbled more than 19 percent during the 1990 bear market.

Costs: This is one of the higher cost growth fund offerings. Its Class A shares carry a 5.50-percent front-end load and a 0.25-percent ongoing 12b-1 fee. Its annual expense ratio (1.12 percent) is below average, but it sports a hefty 151-percent portfolio turnover ratio.

Distributions: Both income and capital gains are distributed annually.

How to Buy and Sell: Class B shares (higher 12b-1 fee and back-end load) are also available. Minimum initial investment $500; IRA $250; subsequent investments $50. Telephone exchange with other AIM funds.

ACCESSOR GROWTH

Bennington Capital Management
Pacific First Center
Seattle, WA 98101
800-759-3504

Inception: 1992
Total Assets: $56 Million
Ticker Symbol: AGROX
Home Page: None

Objective and Strategy: This fund seeks capital growth by investing in equity securities with greater than average growth characteristics selected from the five hundred stocks contained in the Standard & Poor's 500 Index. Specifically, management attempts to equal or exceed the total return performance of the S&P/BARRA Growth Index over a market cycle of five years by investing in the stocks of companies that are expected to experience higher than average growth of earnings or growth of stock price. The portfolio is managed by the State Street Bank and Trust Company. Although its portfolio tends to be relatively compact (about eighty companies being represented), assets are spread across about three dozen industry sectors. Its largest allocations are to drugs and pharmaceuticals, food processing, and telecommunications.

Annualized Returns
1-Year 17.0%
3-Year 18.6%
5-Year NA

Portfolio Manager: Douglas T. Holmes of State Street since the fund's inception in 1992. He also manages funds for other fund families.

Suitability: This is a pure growth portfolio and is suitable for modest or highly aggressive growth-seeking investors.

Portfolio Implications: Divide the Standard & Poor's 500 Index stocks into those with high and low growth rates and check out the former category and you will find most of the stocks contained in this fund's portfolio. These are high P-E and price-to-book value stocks.

Risk: Because the fund focuses on higher growth stocks, its share price can be expected to perform better than the market on the upside and worse on the downside. However, its beta is a relatively modest 0.86. This young fund has yet to experience a major bear market.

Costs: This is a modest-cost fund. Its shares are sold with a no-load format. Its 1.13-percent expense ratio is below average for the group, but its portfolio turnover ratio (99 percent) is above average.

Distributions: Small income distributions are paid quarterly and capital gains are distributed in December.

How to Buy and Sell: Minimum initial investment $1,000; IRA $1,000; subsequent investments $1,000. Telephone exchange with other Accessor funds.

ALLIANCE GROWTH CLASS A

Alliance Capital Management
1345 Avenue of the Americas
New York, NY 10105
800-247-4154

Inception: 1990
Total Assets: $432 Million
Ticker Symbol: AGRFX
Home Page: http://
www.alliancecapital.com

Objective and Strategy: This fund seeks long-term growth of capital by investing in equity securities of companies with favorable earnings outlooks and whose long-term growth rates are expected to exceed that of the U.S. economy. The fund style is best described as flexible and opportunistic. Although portfolio manager Tyler Smith emphasizes large- and medium-capitalization growth stocks, he will purchase cyclical or emerging growth companies when market conditions or company fundamentals are attractive. At times you may even see lower-rated bonds or even zero-coupon bonds in the fund's portfolio. Smith seeks stocks that have good earnings potential, capable management, and a strong market niche. The bulk of his investments are concentrated in a few industries, most notably technology, telecommunications, retail, and financial services.

Portfolio Manager: Tyler Smith since the fund's inception in 1990. Smith has been associated with Alliance since 1993 and previously was employed by Equitable Capital Management before its acquisition by Alliance.

Suitability: If you have a long-term investment time frame and are seeking growth of capital through an overall investment portfolio, consider this fund.

Annualized Returns

1-Year 15.7%
3-Year 13.9%
5-Year 18.0%

Portfolio Implications: Three themes tend to dominate Tyler Smith's investment strategy: technology, retail, and financial services. Thus, the fund contains a mixture of stocks with highly diverse financial characteristics (e.g., high and low P-E's, dividend-payers, and earnings-retainers, etc.).

Risk: You need look no further than the fund's five-year returns to realize that there is risk here. The fund's beta is an average 1.05, but its portfolio is packed with high-tech stocks, which introduce an additional element of risk. This young fund has yet to experience a major bear market.

Costs: The fund's Class A shares are sold with a 4.25-percent front-end load and a 0.30-percent ongoing 12b-1 fee. However, its annual expense ratio is about average at 1.35 percent, and its portfolio turnover ratio is a very low 15 percent.

Distributions: Both income and capital gains are distributed annually.

How to Buy and Sell: Minimum initial investment $250; IRA $250; subsequent investments $50. Telephone exchange with other Alliance funds. A 1-percent redemption fee is imposed on redemptions within one year.

AMERICAN CENTURY EQUITY GROWTH

The Benham Group
1665 Charleston Road
Mountain View, CA 94043
800–321–8321

Inception: 1991
Total Assets: $197 Million
Ticker Symbol: BEQGX
Home Page: http://
www.americancentury.com

Objective and Strategy: This fund seeks capital growth by maintaining a portfolio that is fully invested in common stocks at all times. Like the other Benham equity offerings, the fund utilizes a statistical technique known as portfolio optimization (creating a portfolio with the greatest return given a target risk level) to construct a portfolio with the desired parameters. The technique is a cross between indexing and active portfolio management. Stocks are drawn from a universe consisting of the 1,500 largest companies traded in the United States (ranked by market value of equity). The result is a portfolio consisting of the common stocks of approximately 150 companies. That portfolio has a dividend yield approximately equal to that of the Standard & Poor's 500 Index and an average price-earnings ratio that is about 20 percent lower than that of the Index.

Annualized Returns

1-Year 22.2%
3-Year 15.6%
5-Year 15.3%

Portfolio Manager: Steven Colton since May 1991. Colton joined Benham Management in 1987 and has also managed the Benham Utilities Index Fund since its inception in March 1993.

Suitability: The portfolio is suitable for modestly aggressive investors who desire a combination of capital appreciation and current dividend income.

Portfolio Implications: Portfolio optimization insures that, over the long run, the portfolio will produce the highest level of return possible given a specified level of risk. In this instance, the target risk level is approximately equal to that of the S&P 500 Index. The technique increases the odds that the fund's portfolio will top that of its benchmark index (before operating costs).

Risk: The fund's beta is slightly below that of the market (0.88) but can be expected, in the short run, to exhibit share price volatility nearly equal to that of the S&P 500 Index. This relatively young fund has yet to experience a major bear market.

Costs: This is a reasonable-cost fund. Its shares are sold with a no-load format. Its annual expense ratio is a below-average 0.71 percent, but its portfolio turnover ratio is rather high (126 percent).

Distributions: Income is paid in March, June, September, and December. Capital gains are distributed in December.

How to Buy and Sell: Minimum initial investment $1,000; IRA $1,000; subsequent investments $100. Telephone exchange with other Benham/Twentieth Century funds. Shares may also be obtained through Charles Schwab, Jack White, and Fidelity Brokerage with no transaction fees.

BABSON GROWTH

Jones & Babson
2440 Pershing Road, Suite G-15
Kansas City, MO 64108-2518
800-422-2766

Inception: 1959
Total Assets: $281 Million
Ticker Symbol: BABSX
Home Page: http://
www.jbfunds.com

Objective and Strategy: This is Babson's original fund offering and is considered the "flagship" of the company. Since its inception in 1959, it has sought long-term growth by purchasing stocks that have demonstrated an above-average ability to increase their earnings and dividends and have favorable prospects of sustaining growth. The fund avoids large concentrations in sectors or specific stocks, preferring to pursue a more diversified approach to achieving growth. The approach to stock selection is to filter data from over one thousand companies and identify those experiencing accelerating growth in their core business (i.e., growing earnings, revenues, and cash flow). According to the fund's portfolio manager, "evaluation of a company's historic performance is important, but secondary. Instead, judgements are made about future growth."

Portfolio Manager: James B. Gribbell, comanager with David Kirk since 1993, recently took over sole management responsibilities. Gribbell joined Babson in 1991 as a research analyst.

Suitability: This company prides itself on taking a long-term perspective to growth and desires that its shareholders do the

Annualized Returns

1-Year 17.7%
3-Year 14.9%
5-Year 13.6%

same. Suitable for modestly aggressive and aggressive growth seekers.

Portfolio Implications: What you get here is a large-cap growth portfolio. As such, its portfolio holdings are not too much different than those of other well-managed growth funds.

Risk: This is a highly diversified growth stock portfolio. Thus, it should not be too surprising to find that its beta is slightly below that of the market (0.89). However, like growth portfolios generally, its share price can tumble during a severe bear market as witnessed by its 20-percent decline during the 1990 bear market.

Costs: This is a low-cost growth fund. Its shares are sold with a no-load format, its annual expense ratio is a low 0.85 percent, and its portfolio turnover ratio is a very low 17 percent.

Distributions: Income is paid in June and December as are capital gains distributions.

How to Buy and Sell: Minimum initial investment $500; IRA $250; subsequent investments $50. Telephone exchange with other Babson funds. Shares are available through Fidelity Brokerage with no transaction fees.

BABSON VALUE

Jones & Babson
2440 Pershing Road, Suite G–15
Kansas City, MO 64108
800-422-2766

Inception: 1984
Total Assets: $514 Million
Ticker Symbol: BVALX
Home Page: http:// www.jbfunds.com

Objective and Strategy: This fund seeks long-term growth by purchasing stocks that are unpopular and undervalued based on their earnings, assets, and/or dividends. The fund's goal is to invest in stocks that offer above-average potential for growth in principal and income while assuming less than market risk. An important factor in the selection of investments is financial strength. Says its portfolio manager: "My preference always has been to buy something for less than list price. It's just common sense." The portfolio is fully invested at all times in about forty stocks. Stocks are held throughout the cycle from undervalued to fully valued and are sold when their relative price strength begins to subside. The fund's style may be b-o-r-i-n-g but is sure has been profitable for shareholders. This fund is high on my preference list.

Portfolio Manager: Roland (Nick) Whitridge since the fund's inception in 1984. He joined Babson in 1974 and has over thirty years of investment management experience.

Suitability: I can't think of an investor that wouldn't want to own this fund. Conservative investors should limit holdings to 15 percent of portfolio assets.

Annualized Returns

1-Year 17.2%
3-Year 17.9%
5-Year 17.8%

Portfolio Implications: This fund's portfolio turnover ratio has averaged less than 10 percent in recent years. It's not a buy-and-hold portfolio, but close to it. Its portfolio is quite compact, with investments in about forty issues. This is a good fund to combine with small-cap or aggressive growth offerings.

Risk: Despite its modest 0.84 beta, there is risk here. It stems from a fully invested posture. Its share price declined by slightly more than 22 percent during the 1990 bear market.

Costs: This is a very cost-efficient fund. Its shares are sold with a no-load format and its 0.98-percent annual expense ratio is below average. Its 6-percent portfolio turnover ratio is one of the lowest in the growth fund group.

Distributions: Income is paid in March, June, September, and December. Capital gains are distributed in December.

How to Buy and Sell: Minimum initial investment $1,000; IRA $250; subsequent investments $100. Telephone exchange with other Babson funds. Shares may also be obtained through Charles Schwab, Fidelity Brokerage, and Jack White with no transaction fees.

BERGER 100

Berger Associates
P.O. Box 5005
Denver, CO 80217
800-333-1001

Inception: 1974
Total Assets: $2.1 Billion
Ticker Symbol: BEONX
Home Page: http://
www.bergerfunds.com

Objective and Strategy: This fund seeks capital appreciation. Any income produced by the fund's portfolio is incidental to the achievement of capital appreciation. Portfolio manager Rodney Linafelter is always looking for the same thing in the companies that he seeks to own: predictable earnings. Rather than target some particular earnings growth rate, he prefers to own companies that continually beat analysts' earnings estimates. These tend to be stocks that have a good story attached to them such as Intel, which, he says, "not only controls its own destiny but everyone else's as well." He also seeks out broad investment themes. These themes can lead to overweightings in a handful of sectors which recently have included energy services, health care, and retail. At times the fund has produced exceptional returns.

Portfolio Manager: Patrick Adams since 1997. Also manages the Berger 100 Fund.

Suitability: This fund is suitable for aggressive investors only. Its share price at times has been extremely volatile and income distributions have been scant.

Annualized Returns

1-Year 9.4%
3-Year 7.7%
5-Year 13.5%

Portfolio Implications: The portfolio is usually relatively compact, with the stocks of about six dozen companies being represented. Emphasis is on high growth rate companies that can sell at relatively high price-earnings multiples.

Risk: Although the portfolio's beta is a near-market 0.98, its share price can be highly volatile during short-run periods as witnessed by the fund's 20-percent decline during the 1990 bear market.

Costs: This is an average-cost fund. Its shares are sold without either a front-end or back-end load, but sport a 0.25-percent ongoing 12b-1 fee. The annual expense ratio (1.47 percent) is above average as is its 114-percent portfolio turnover ratio.

Distributions: Income (if any) is paid in December, and capital gains are distributed in December.

How to Buy and Sell: Minimum initial investment $2,000 (recently raised from $500); IRA $1,000; subsequent investments $50. Telephone exchange with other Berger funds. Shares may also be obtained without transaction fees from Charles Schwab, Fidelity Brokerage, and Jack White and Company.

CAPPIELLO-RUSHMORE GROWTH

Cappiello–Rushmore Trust
4922 Fairmont Avenue
Bethesda, MD 20814
800-622-1386

Inception: 1992
Total Assets: $32 Million
Ticker Symbol: CRGRX
Home Page: None

Objective and Strategy: Formerly known as the Rushmore Stock Market Index Plus Fund, this fund seeks capital growth by investing in common stocks and convertible securities of larger, established companies that have demonstrated consistent sales and earnings growth. The fund may also invest up to 20 percent of its assets in American Depository receipts (foreign stocks traded in the United States). Although the fund may invest in companies of any size, it has maintained a larger capitalization focus in recent years. Emphasis has been placed on the technology, energy, financial services, health care, and retailing sectors. Its best-performing stocks in recent months were Federated Department Stores, Reynolds & Reynolds, Shared Medical Systems, Student Loan Marketing, and Coca-Cola.

Portfolio Manager: Frank Cappiello since the fund's inception in 1992. Prior experience includes manager of institutional research for a major brokerage firm. He is a graduate of the University of Notre Dame and Harvard University's Graduate School of Business.

Suitability: Make no mistake about it, this is an aggressively managed fund and is suitable for aggressive investors only.

Annualized Returns
1-Year 3.3%
3-Year 15.1%
5-Year NA

Portfolio Implications: What you will get here is a portfolio packed with high-growth companies that are capable of producing exceptional returns during short-run periods. However, large sector bets can also lead to underperformance as well.

Risk: The fund's growth company portfolio possesses a beta of 1.13. Although the fund has yet to experience a bear market, its holdings hint that volatility could be exceptionally high.

Costs: This is an average-cost fund. Its shares are sold with a no-load format, its 1.50-percent annual expense ratio is slightly above average, and its 71-percent portfolio turnover ratio is slightly below average.

Distributions: Net investment income is paid in December as are capital gains.

How to Buy and Sell: Minimum initial investment $2,500; IRA $500; no minimum subsequent investment requirement. Telephone exchange with other Rushmore funds. Shares may also be obtained without transaction fees through Charles Schwab, Fidelity Brokerage, and Jack White and Company.

CLIPPER FUND

9601 Wilshire Boulevard
Beverly Hills, CA 90210
800-776-5033

Inception: 1984
Total Assets: $465 Million
Ticker Symbol: CFIMX
Home Page: None

Objective and Strategy: This fund seeks long-term growth of capital. An avowed value investor and asset allocator, portfolio manager James Gipson will invest in a stock only if he believes it is significantly underpriced relative to its underlying earnings power and/or asset values. The aim is to identify a price that a rational private investor would pay to acquire the entire company. Stocks are purchased if they are priced at 30 percent or more below this target valuation. Because of the rigid value strategy, very few stocks cut the mustard at Clipper. Thus, the portfolio tends to be highly concentrated in a small number of stocks. In addition, should the values not appear, Gipson is not shy about parking assets in Treasury securities. His contrarian tactics may involve some setbacks from time-to-time, but his willingness to stay the course and his doggedness have allowed long-term shareholders to prosper.

Portfolio Manager: James H. Gipson since establishing the fund in 1984. Previously, he was a portfolio manager with Battery March. He is also portfolio manager of the Schooner Fund.

Suitability: If your investment objective contains growth, you'll want to own some shares of this fund. It is ideally suited to be used as the core of a retirement or child's education savings program.

Portfolio Implications: Two characteristics stand out. The portfolio is concentrated in a handful of companies and, at times, the portfolio can hold a significant position in Treasury securities. Generally, when the market is overvalued, you'll find plenty of cash in this fund's portfolio.

Risk: Targeting large returns usually results in a high-risk portfolio. However, that hasn't been the case at Clipper. Its portfolio beta is a modest 1.06, and its share price declined by more than 18 percent during the 1990 bear market.

Costs: This is a cost-efficient fund. Its shares are sold with a no-load format. Its 1.11-percent expense ratio is below average as is its 31-percent portfolio turnover ratio.

Distributions: Both net investment income and capital gains are distributed annually in December.

How to Buy and Sell: Minimum initial investment $5,000; IRA $2,000; subsequent investments $1,000 (IRA $200).

Annualized Returns

1-Year 21.0%

3-Year 19.2%

5-Year 18.1%

COLONIAL GROWTH SHARES CLASS A

Colonial Investment Services
One Financial Center, 10th Floor
Boston, MA 02110
800-248-2828

Inception: *1949*
Total Assets: *$233 Million*
Ticker Symbol: *COLGX*
Home Page: *http://www.lib.com*

Objective and Strategy: A computer-driven strategy that stresses value and earnings momentum has enabled this growth-seeking fund to produce steady, above-average results in a wide variety of markets. The computer searches for companies with low price-earnings multiples and low levels of volatility given their above-average growth prospects. These criteria have yielded primarily small- and mid-cap stocks, with a unique mix of growth and value. Like many funds that pursue pure growth, the fund is heavily invested in the technology, consumer cyclical, financial, and health care sectors. Although the fund focuses on smaller companies, the large-capitalization sector of the market is represented by investments in such companies as Phillip Morris, Safeway, Microsoft, and Loews.

Portfolio Manager: Daniel Rie since 1986. He also manages the Colonial Fund, Colonial Global Equity, and Colonial U.S. Federal Growth.

Suitability: Investment in the fund is suitable for aggressive and modestly aggressive investors. Generally, the fund's investments do not provide a significant amount of dividend income.

Annualized Returns

1-Year 20.7%

3-Year 17.2%

5-Year 15.5%

Portfolio Implications: This fund's portfolio is concentrated in a number of stocks also held in other well-managed growth fund portfolios. Look out for duplication when coupling this fund with other growth vehicles.

Risk: Although the fund sports a slightly above-market beta (1.05), its share price can exhibit extreme volatility during severe market sell-offs as witnessed by its more than 22-percent decline during the 1990 bear market.

Costs: The fund's shares are sold with a hefty 5.75-percent front-end load and 0.22-percent ongoing 12b-1 fee. Its annual expense ratio is a modest 1.12 percent, and its portfolio turnover ratio is slightly above average (92 percent).

Distributions: Income and capital gains are distributed semiannually in June and December.

How to Buy and Sell: Class A shares sold with front-end load. Class B shares also available (higher 12b-1 fee and contingent deferred sales charge). Minimum initial investment $1,000; IRA $1,000; subsequent investments $50. One-percent redemption fee for shares held less than eighteen months.

COLUMBIA GROWTH

Columbia Financial Center, Inc.
1301 South West Fifth Avenue
P.O. Box 1350
Portland, OR 97207–1350
800–547–1707

Inception: 1967
Total Assets: $989 Million
Ticker Symbol: CLMBX
Home Page: None

Objective and Strategy: Columbia Growth succeeds where few others do. Although it seems that the fund's rapid trading and sector rotation tactics would invite whipsaw, this hasn't been the case. Generally moderate results are interspersed with an occasional banner year, giving this fund one of the better risk-adjusted return records of any growth fund. Its success owes to management's skill at interpreting macroeconomic and/or industry trends and identifying reasonably priced, well-run companies that are poised to benefit. That the fund features a mix of stocks of varying sizes bodes well for its continued success. However, during flat markets, earnings momentum strategies tend to perform less than value strategies. However, over the long term you can bet on this fund to shine.

Annualized Returns

1-Year 18.4%
3-Year 15.3%
5-Year 15.8%

Portfolio Manager: Alexander S. Macmillan since 1992. Prior to joining the investment team, he was portfolio manager for Gardner and Preston Moss (1982–1989). He received his M.B.A. from Amos Tuck School at Dartmouth.

Suitability: This growth vehicle is better suited to investors with more aggressive styles. In addition, investors should plan on holding this fund's shares for several years to obtain the best returns.

Portfolio Implications: Sometimes this is a "now you see it, now you don't" portfolio. Companies that disappoint are quickly dumped and new investments acquired whose shares are advancing smartly, usually on the heels of a positive earnings surprise.

Risk: This is one of the more aggressive funds in the growth category. Its beta is 1.09, and its share price tumbled slightly more than 16 percent during the 1990 bear market.

Costs: This fund has reasonable costs. Its shares are sold with a no-load format. Its annual expense ratio is a below-average 0.62 percent, but its portfolio turnover ratio (95 percent) is above average.

Distributions: Both income and capital gains distributions are paid annually in December.

How to Buy and Sell: Minimum initial investment $1,000; IRA $1,000; subsequent investments $100. Telephone exchange with other Columbia funds. Shares may also be obtained without transaction fees through Charles Schwab and Company.

CRABBE HUSON EQUITY

Crabbe Huson Funds
P.O. Box 8413
Boston, MA 02266-8413
800-638-3148

Inception: 1989
Total Assets: $478 Million
Ticker Symbol: CNEYX
Home Page: http://
www.contrarian.com

Objective and Strategy: This fund seeks capital appreciation by investing in common stocks of large companies that are actively traded and widely held. Like most of the offerings of this relatively small but highly successful fund family, management stresses a value approach to asset selection. Portfolio manager James Crabbe tends to march to his own drummer, and shareholders can expect to find the fund's portfolio dotted with beaten-down, out-of-favor companies. This strategy has worked exceptionally well over long time periods. However, Mr. Crabbe's requirement that the fund's investments represent real values has led the fund to underperform recently as the stock market's rapid rise has led to ballooning valuation multiples. However, the contrarian strategy practiced here will add significant value when the stock market returns to a more normal pattern.

Annualized Returns
1-Year 13.3%
3-Year 14.7%
5-Year 16.6%

Portfolio Manager: Management team led by James E. Crabbe since the fund's inception. He founded the fund's adviser in 1980. He is assisted by John Maack, Jr., Marian Kessler, and John Anton.

Suitability: If you like to buy straw hats in the winter, swim against the tide, and are unwilling to pay retail price for anything, this is the fund for you. It is ideally suited for conservative investors who seek growth of capital as well as current income.

Portfolio Implications: The contrarian tactics practiced by management usually result in a portfolio of stocks that are not owned by other growth vehicles. Thus, this portfolio makes a good companion to the more aggressively managed growth funds in your portfolio.

Risk: This fund's shares experience average volatility. Its beta is a modest 0.86, and its share price declined by 18 percent during the 1990 bear market. The real risk is lack of participation during a runaway bull market.

Costs: The fund's shares are sold without either a front-end or a back-end load but sport a modest 0.23-percent ongoing 12b-1 fee. Its annual expense ratio is an average 1.40 percent, and its portfolio turnover ratio (92 percent) is slightly above average.

Distributions: Both income and capital gains distributions are paid in December.

How to Buy and Sell: Minimum initial investment $2,000; IRA $2,000; subsequent investments $500. Telephone exchange with three other Crabbe Huson equity funds. Shares are also available without transaction fees from Charles Schwab and Jack White and Company.

DREYFUS APPRECIATION

Premier Mutual Fund Services
The Pan Am Building
200 Park Avenue, 7th Floor
New York, NY 10166
800-645-6561

Inception: 1984
Total Assets: $605 Million
Ticker Symbol: DGAGX
Home Page: http://www.dreyfus.com

Objective and Strategy: This fund's primary objective is to provide long-term capital growth consistent with the preservation of capital. Late in 1990, this fund, which formerly invested in small- and mid-cap stocks, came under new management. In a prime example of bad timing, the new management began dumping the smaller issues in favor of large-cap, blue-chip stocks. As fortune would have it, small-caps were about to embark on a period of overperformance. However, current management's large-cap, buy-and-hold strategy was sound, and when blue-chip stocks began to dominate a few years later, the fund came into its own and its performance is just short of phenomenal. The fund's portfolio is relatively compact, with about five dozen companies being represented. However, these companies are some of the best managed in the world.

Portfolio Manager: Fayez Sarofim of Fayez Sarofim and Company (the fund's sub-adviser) since 1990.

Suitability: This "heritage fund" is suitable for all growth-oriented investors. By heritage fund, we mean one to buy now and hold for decades. Conservative investors may wish to limit their investments in the fund.

Annualized Returns

1-Year 24.9%

3-Year 20.9%

5-Year 14.8%

Portfolio Implications: This fund is an excellent core holding. Like its portfolio manager, you'll want to hold these shares for years. If you are saving for a child's education or setting aside retirement dollars, consider investing some of those dollars in this fund's shares.

Risk: Despite its rapid growth company orientation, this fund sports a modest 0.96 beta. Furthermore, its share price declined by a somewhat modest 14 percent during the 1990 bear market.

Costs: This is a very cost-efficient fund. Its shares are sold with a no-load format. Its annual expense ratio is a modest 0.92 percent, and its portfolio turnover ratio is an exceptionally low 5 percent.

Distributions: Both net investment income and capital gains distributions are paid annually.

How to Buy and Sell: Minimum initial investment $2,500; IRA $750; subsequent investments $100. Telephone exchange with other Dreyfus funds. Shares may also be obtained without transaction fees through Charles Schwab and Jack White and Company.

DREYFUS CORE VALUE FUND

Premier Mutual Fund Services
The Pan Am Building
200 Park Avenue, 7th Floor
New York, NY 10166
800-782-6620

Inception: 1947
Total Assets: $61 Million
Ticker Symbol: DCVIX
Home Page: http://www.dreyfus.com

Objective and Strategy: This fund has recently gone through a series of name changes. It has been called the Boston Company Capital Appreciation Fund, the Laurel Capital Appreciation Fund and now, Dreyfus Core Value. Growth is the primary investment objective, while income receives secondary consideration. The fund invests primarily in common stocks and convertible securities of large companies selling at low price-earnings multiples and may invest up to 20 percent of its assets in foreign securities. Securities are selected for the fund based on a continuous study of trends in industries and companies, earning power, and growth features. Although the fund's investments tend to be broadly diversified, management emphasizes high-growth industries. Its major industry sectors include financial services, health care, and consumer services.

Annualized Returns
1-Year 17.5%
3-Year 15.8%
5-Year NA

Portfolio Manager: The fund is managed by a committee of portfolio managers of Dreyfus, and no single person is primarily responsible for making recommendations to the committee.

Suitability: The fund is suitable for all growth-seeking investors.

Portfolio Implications: This is a typical growth fund portfolio with the exception of a near 20-percent allocation to foreign stocks. The portfolio is well diversified, and its foreign investments complement its diverse U.S. growth stock holdings.

Risk: This is a modest-risk fund with a beta of 0.98. Although this young fund has yet to experience a major bear market, its foreign stock holdings may limit its losses during a sharp stock market sell-off.

Costs: This fund has reasonable costs. Its shares are sold without either a front-end or a back-end load but sport a 0.25-percent ongoing 12b-1 ratio. Its annual management fee is a below-average 1.15 percent as is its 54-percent portfolio turnover ratio.

Distributions: Income is paid quarterly and capital gains are distributed annually.

How to Buy and Sell: Minimum initial investment $2,500; IRA $750; subsequent investments $100. Telephone exchange with other Dreyfus funds. Shares may also be obtained without transaction fees from Charles Schwab and Jack White and Company.

DREYFUS THIRD CENTURY

Premier Mutual Fund Services
The Pan Am Building
200 Park Avenue, 7th Floor
New York, NY 10166
800-782-6620

Inception: 1972
Total Assets: $465 Million
Ticker Symbol: DRTHX
Home Page: http://www.dreyfus.com

Objective and Strategy: The fund invests in U.S. common stocks and convertible securities of companies that, in the opinion of the fund's management, not only meet traditional investment considerations but simultaneously demonstrate that they conduct their business in a manner which contributes to the quality of life in America in the areas of (1) protection and improvement in the environment, (2) occupation health and safety, (3) consumer protection and product safety, and (4) equal employment opportunity. Potential investment candidates are screened first for suitability using traditional financial analysis. Then Dreyfus staff members initiate direct company contact and a search of publicly available information. If no areas of concern arise with respect to the fund's social responsibility criteria, the companies are declared eligible for purchase. This is one of a handful of "socially responsible" funds that also sports a relatively attractive performance record.

Annualized Returns
1-Year 22.6%
3-Year 14.8%
5-Year 11.9%

Portfolio Manager: Eric W. Steedman since May 1996 and Maceo K. Sloan since 1994. Steedman joined Dreyfus in early 1995 and Sloan has been employed by NCM (the fund's subadviser) since 1986.

Suitability: The fund's shares are suitable for growth-oriented investors generally and specifically for investors who wish to direct their investment capital toward socially responsible corporations.

Portfolio Implications: The fund's special investment considerations limit the availability of investment opportunities (such as the exclusion of tobacco, gambling or military companies) more than is customary with other funds.

Risk: The fund sports an average 1.03 beta, and its share price declined by about the same percentage as the market (15 percent) during the 1990 bear market.

Costs: This is a reasonable-cost fund. Its shares are sold with a no-load format. Its annual expense ratio is a below-average 1.12 percent, but its portfolio turnover ratio (133 percent) is above average.

Distributions: Both income and capital gains distributions are paid annually.

How to Buy and Sell: Minimum initial investment $2,500; IRA $750; subsequent investments $100. Telephone exchange with other Dreyfus funds. Shares may also be obtained without transaction fees through Charles Schwab and Jack White and Company.

ENTERPRISE GROWTH

Enterprise Group of Funds, Inc.
1200 Ashwood Parkway
Atlanta, GA 30338
800-432-4320

Inception: *1968*
Total Assets: *$151 Million*
Ticker Symbol: *ENGRX*
Home Page: *None*

Objective and Strategy: This fund has long pursued a moderate growth strategy that has enabled it to achieve competitive returns in just about every year during the past ten years. Management looks for growing companies at times when special developments or depressions in price may temporarily provide suitable buying opportunities. Limitations on small or large companies are not made, and the fund may invest in foreign securities if it deems such investments appropriate. The equity selection process is often referred to as "growth at a price." It emphasizes the stocks of companies that are expected to experience strong earnings growth and have attractively priced shares. The fund's low-risk profile is also enhanced by a move to cash when management can't find attractively priced stocks or when management is confident that the stock market is near a top and is due for a correction.

Portfolio Manager: Ronald E. Canakaris since 1980. He joined Montag and Caldwell, the subadviser, in 1972 and became president in 1984. He has a B.S. in business administration from the University of Florida.

Suitability: This fund's shares are suitable for all modestly aggressive long-term investors.

Annualized Returns
1-Year 33.0%
3-Year 23.6%
5-Year 18.5%

Portfolio Implications: As you might suspect, the fund's portfolio contains several household names, such as Coca-Cola, Proctor & Gamble, Intel, Microsoft, Walt Disney, and Gillette. Thus, it looks a lot like many blue-chip stock indices.

Risk: This is one of the higher-risk entries in the growth fund category. Its beta is 1.10 and its share price declined by slightly more than 17 percent during the 1990 bear market.

Costs: The fund's class A shares are sold with a 4.75-percent front-end sales charge and a 0.45-percent ongoing 12b-1 fee. Its annual expense ratio (1.60 percent) is slightly above average, but its 45-percent portfolio turnover ratio is below average.

Distributions: Income and capital gains distributions are paid annually.

How to Buy and Sell: Class B shares (higher 12b-1 fee and contingent deferred sales charge) are also available. Minimum initial investment $1,000; IRA $250; subsequent investments $100. Telephone exchange with other Enterprise offerings. Shares are offered through Charles Schwab to institutions only without transaction fees.

Fidelity Distributors
82 Devonshire Street
Mail Zone L7B
Boston, MA 02109
800-752-2347

Inception: 1987
Total Assets: $9.0 Billion
Ticker Symbol: FBGRX
Home Page: http://www.fidelity.com

Objective and Strategy: This fund seeks to provide growth of capital by investing mainly in common stocks of well-known and established companies. This fund's affinity for rapidly growing companies that are experiencing good earnings momentum leads it into expensive, high-expectation stocks. The strategy of a portfolio containing popular growth stocks worked like a charm over the recent past, playing into the hands of an earnings-driven market. Still, hefty price-earnings and price-to-book value ratios make the fund extremely vulnerable to big jolts in the face of any actual or anticipated earnings disappointments. As such, this fund is not for risk-wary investors. Patient, risk-tolerant shareholders can expect to be amply rewarded over the long haul, but they might not get a smooth ride.

Annualized Returns
1-Year 5.5%
3-Year 14.9%
5-Year 17.7%

Portfolio Manager: John McDowell since March 1996. He joined Fidelity in 1986 and has managed the Select Retail and Large Cap Stock Funds. He has an M.B.A. from Harvard.

Suitability: You have to be able to tolerate a bit of risk to invest in this fund. To mitigate risk, you must take a long-term orientation and be willing to add to your shareholdings during periods marked by sharp stock market declines.

Portfolio Implications: This is a growth fund you will want to own during a runaway bull market. However, the fund provides little protection during the early stages of a bear market because of management's affinity for high price-earnings ratio stocks.

Risk: Despite its below-market beta (0.93), this fund's shares can experience a wild roller-coaster ride. Even so, its share price declined by a modest 13.6 percent during the 1990 bear market.

Costs: Like most of Fidelity's equity offerings, this fund is sold with a 3-percent front-end sales charge. Its expense ratio (0.98 percent) is below average, but it rapidly turns over its portfolio (206 percent portfolio turnover rate).

Distributions: Both income and capital gains are distributed in September and December.

How to Buy and Sell: Minimum initial investment $2,500; IRA $250; subsequent investments $250. Telephone exchange with other Fidelity funds with waiver of front-end load. Shares may also be obtained through Fidelity Brokerage without transaction fees.

FIDELITY CONTRAFUND

Fidelity Distributors
82 Devonshire Street
Mail Zone L7B
Boston, MA 02109
800-752-2347

Inception: 1967
Total Assets: $21.3 Billion
Ticker Symbol: FCNTX
Home Page: http://www.fidelity.com

Objective and Strategy: This is a growth fund that seeks to increase shareholder wealth over the long term by investing in equity securities of companies that are undervalued or out of favor. Contrafund has whipped most rivals and the Standard & Poor's 500 Index in recent years. Its success owes to its moderate value orientation and its taste for healthy niche companies and turnaround situations with unrecognized but solid earnings prospects. An adept use of cash, which explains the fund's resistance to severe market downturns, also has boosted performance. The fund is among the very few value players to have performed well in growth-driven markets. The fund's recent success has brought a flood of new cash from investors eager to climb on the fund's bandwagon, which has ballooned total assets beyond $21 billion.

Annualized Returns
1-Year 10.8%
3-Year 13.8%
5-Year 17.6%

Portfolio Manager: William Danoff since 1990. He joined Fidelity in 1986 and managed the Select Retail Fund. He also manages a variable annuity Contrafund product. He has an M.B.A. from the University of Pennsylvania, Wharton School of Business.

Suitability: This fund is suitable for both modestly aggressive and aggressive growth-oriented investors. Take a position in this fund and hang on for years and years. You'll be glad you did.

Portfolio Implications: If there is one downside to this well-managed fund, it is the fund's gigantic size. Although it has continued to provide competitive returns, you only have to look at the experience of Magellan to realize that giant funds are more difficult to manage.

Risk: The fund's strategy of providing growth with value has limited this fund's volatility. Its beta is a below-market 0.94, and its share price declined by a modest 11.8 percent during the 1990 bear market.

Costs: Like most of Fidelity's equity offerings, this fund is sold with a 3-percent front-end sales charge. Its expense ratio (0.90 percent) is below average, but it rapidly turns over its portfolio, which adds to transactions costs (199-percent portfolio turnover ratio).

Distributions: Both income and capital gains are distributed in February and December.

How to Buy and Sell: Minimum initial investment $2,500; IRA $500; subsequent investments $250. Telephone exchange with other Fidelity funds with waiver of front-end load. Shares may also be obtained through Fidelity Brokerage without transaction fees.

FIDELITY FUND

Fidelity Distributors
82 Devonshire Street
Mail Zone L7B
Boston, MA 02109
800-752-2347

Inception: 1930
Total Assets: $4.1 Billion
Ticker Symbol: FFIDX
Home Page: http://www.fidelity.com

Objective and Strategy: This is the oldest fund in the Fidelity stable. Since its inception in 1930, the fund has provided investors with a 10.7-percent annual average return. Although this may not appear to be impressive, a $2,000 investment in the fund at inception would now be worth $1.64 million (assuming reinvestment of distributions). Under the direction of portfolio manager Beth Terrana, the fund seeks capital appreciation with reasonable current income by investing in growth-oriented common stocks. A bottom-up investment strategy is employed (i.e., selecting stocks based solely on their own merits rather than first drawing economic conclusions and making industry sector commitments). This rapidly traded fund offers investors a bit more capital appreciation than most growth and income funds (thus its placement in the growth fund category), but this comes at the expense of the fund's current yield.

Portfolio Manager: Beth Terrana since July 1993. She previously managed Equity-Income, VIP Equity-Income, and Growth and Income. She joined Fidelity in 1983 after obtaining an M.B.A. from Harvard.

Suitability: This fund is suitable for both modestly aggressive and aggressive growth-oriented investors.

Annualized Returns

1-Year 20.0%
3-Year 16.6%
5-Year 15.3%

Portfolio Implications: Although a number of other Fidelity funds have taken center stage in recent years, this old-timer is capable of delivering the goods. Although it sounds silly to call a fund with $4 billion in assets small, that's far less money than has been invested in some of Fidelity's popular funds. Thus, management has a bit more flexibility.

Risk: This is another modest-risk equity growth fund. Its beta is a below-market 0.94 percent, and its share price declined by a modest 13.6 percent during the 1990 bear market.

Costs: This is one of the few equity funds offered by Fidelity with a no-load format. The fund's expense ratio is a low 0.63 percent, although its portfolio turnover ratio is a hefty 150 percent.

Distributions: Income is paid in March, June, September, and December, and capital gains are distributed in August and December.

How to Buy and Sell: Minimum initial investment $2,500; IRA $500; subsequent investments $250. Shares may also be obtained through Fidelity Brokerage without transaction fees.

FIDELITY GROWTH COMPANY

Fidelity Distributors
82 Devonshire Street
Mail Zone L7B
Boston, MA 02109
800-752-2347

Inception: 1983
Total Assets: $8.9 Billion
Ticker Symbol: FDGRX
Home Page: http://www.fidelity.com

Objective and Strategy: This fund, which has returned an average of 17.5 percent since its inception in January 1983, seeks capital appreciation by investing primarily in the common stocks of companies believed to have above-average growth characteristics. Its investments include both smaller companies in new and emerging areas of the economy and larger companies operating in mature industries or declining industries that have been revitalized. The fund's mix of small- and large-capitalization company stocks has allowed it to participate in the market's run-up in recent years while side-stepping the steep bear market in emerging growth stocks that persisted during most of 1990. The fund tends to ride bull markets well. Like most growth-oriented fund's these days, it holds hefty positions in technology, health care, and retail stocks.

Portfolio Manager: Lawrence Greenberg since 1996. He also manages Emerging Growth and previously managed Select Environment and Select Medical Delivery. He joined Fidelity in 1986.

Suitability: The fund is suitable for both modestly aggressive and aggressive investors who prefer growth of capital over current income. It makes an excellent core holding for a retirement program or a child's education savings plan.

Annualized Returns

1-Year 10.4%
3-Year 15.3%
5-Year 15.4%

Portfolio Implications: You get a bit of everything in this portfolio, high P-E and low P-E ratio stocks, small-cap and large-cap stocks, and in-favor and out-of-favor companies. This is a highly diversified equity portfolio and deserves consideration by most investors.

Risk: This is one of the higher-risk entrants in the growth fund category. Its beta is an above-market 1.09, and its share price tumbled more than 19 percent during the 1990 bear market.

Costs: Like most of Fidelity's equity offerings, this fund is sold with a 3-percent front-end sales charge. Its expense ratio (0.94 percent) is below average as is its 77-percent portfolio turnover ratio.

Distributions: Both net investment income and capital gains are distributed in January and December.

How to Buy and Sell: Minimum initial investment $2,500; IRA $500; subsequent investments $250. Telephone exchange with other Fidelity funds with waiver of front-end load. Shares may also be obtained through Fidelity Brokerage without transaction fees.

FIDELITY STOCK SELECTOR

Fidelity Distributors
82 Devonshire Street
Mail Zone L7B
Boston, MA 02109
800-752-2347

Inception: 1990
Total Assets: $1.6 Billion
Ticker Symbol: FDSSX
Home Page: http://www.fidelity.com

Objective and Strategy: This fund seeks growth of capital by investing in a broad range of companies both domestic and international. Management attempts to identify undervalued industries through the use of its computer models. After identifying the most attractive industries, individual stock selection is made based on product line, quality of management, earnings momentum, and historical performance. Although the fund will be more volatile because of its concentration in a handful of industries, no more than 25 percent of its total assets can be allocated to any specific industry. The fund has turned in an impressive performance record since it began offering its shares to investors in September 1990 (a 21.5-percent compound annual return). Nearly two-thirds of its assets are invested in four industry sectors: finance, utilities, technology, and health care.

Portfolio Manager: Bradford Lewis since 1990. He also manages the Small Cap Stock and Disciplined Equity portfolios and previously managed Select Air Transportation, Select Defense and Aerospace, and Select Medical Delivery.

Suitability: Like most Fidelity equity offerings, this aggressively managed growth vehicle is suitable for more aggressive growth-oriented investors.

Portfolio Implications: Investors either sink or swim with the large sector bets made by this fund's management. Since inception, however, shareholders have been riding a rising tide.

Risk: Stock Selector possesses a beta that is slightly above that of the market (1.04). Although this young fund has yet to experience a major bear market, its aggressive posture suggests that its share price will flow with the outgoing tide during a market downturn.

Annualized Returns
1-Year 9.0%
3-Year 14.2%
5-Year 16.8%

Costs: This is one of a handful of Fidelity equity offerings to be sold with a no-load format. Its 0.98-percent annual expense ratio is below average, but its portfolio turnover ratio (298 percent) is quite hefty.

Distributions: Both income and capital gains are distributed in December.

How to Buy and Sell: Minimum initial investment $2,500; IRA $500; subsequent investments $250. Shares may also be obtained through Fidelity Brokerage without transaction fees.

FIDELITY VALUE

Fidelity Distributors
82 Devonshire Street
Mail Zone L7B
Boston, MA 02109
800-752-2347

Inception: *1978*
Total Assets: *$7.0 Billion*
Ticker Symbol: *FDVLX*
Home Page: *http://www.fidelity.com*

Objective and Strategy: Founded as Fidelity Asset Investment Trust in late 1978, the fund has returned a remarkable 15.7 percent annually during its seventeen-year history. The fund invests in the stocks of companies with valuable assets or those thought to be undervalued based on company assets, earnings, or growth potential. Portfolio manager Rich Fentin prefers to invest in cheap stocks that he believes will benefit from some sort of catalyst. The list of investments include many companies that are leaders in their respective industries, such as Wal-Mart and Dayton Hudson (retail), American Express (financial services), and Deluxe (check printing). In recent months Fentin has added to his retail stock holdings with shares of Toys R Us and Office Depot. Although the fund's name implies conservatism, the fund is more of a pure growth vehicle.

Portfolio Manager: Rich Fentin since 1996. He previously managed the Puritan Fund for nine years (1987 through 1996) and has managed the Growth Company and Value funds. He joined Fidelity in 1980 after receiving an M.B.A. from Harvard.

Suitability: This is more of a pure growth fund than a value play. Thus, its shares are more suited for modestly aggressive,

Annualized Returns
1-Year 16.1%
3-Year 16.3%
5-Year 18.0%

growth-oriented investors who can assume market risks.

Portfolio Implications: Although management prefers to invest in growing companies, the fund is packed with nontraditional growth industries such as consumer durables, energy, retail, basic industries, and industrial equipment.

Risk: Although dubbed a value fund, there is a bit more risk here than in other value players. The fund's beta is a below-market 0.84, and its share price tumbled more than 17 percent during the 1990 bear market.

Costs: The fund's shares are sold with a no-load format. Its annual expense ratio (0.97 percent) is below average, but its portfolio turnover ratio is a hefty 193 percent, which increases transaction costs.

Distributions: Both net investment income and realized capital gains are distributed in December.

How to Buy and Sell: Minimum initial investment $2,500; IRA $500; subsequent investments $250. Telephone exchange with other Fidelity funds. Shares may also be obtained through Fidelity Brokerage without transaction fees.

FOUNDERS BLUE CHIP

Founders Asset Management
2930 East Third Avenue
Denver, CO 80206
800-525-2440

Inception: 1938
Total Assets: $484 Million
Ticker Symbol: FRMUX
Home Page: http://
www.networth.galt.com/founders

Objective and Strategy: This fund seeks long-term growth of capital and income by investing in the common stocks of large, well-established, stable, and mature companies with market capitalizations or annual revenues in excess of $1 billion. Most of the securities in the portfolio pay cash dividends. Like most Founders' funds, this fund delivers solid growth of capital using a strategy driven by diligent and extensive research. The fund has chalked-up remarkably consistent performance numbers during its long history. Its shareholders have garnered returns of 13.8 percent, 13.6 percent, and 15.6 percent during the last five, ten, and fifteen years, respectively. The fund is in the capable hands of Brian Kelly, who earned a solid reputation as a portfolio manager with Founders' cross-town rival, Invesco.

Annualized Returns
1-Year 8.0%
3-Year 15.5%
5-Year 13.7%

Portfolio Manager: Brian Kelly since 1996. He assumed the helm of Blue Chip after moving across town from Invesco, where he managed several of that company's funds.

Suitability: This fund is suitable for conservative and modestly aggressive investors who focus on total return (a combination of current income and capital gains).

Portfolio Implications: As its name implies, what you get here is a highly diversified portfolio of blue-chip stocks. This fund is one that you want to buy and hold. It is ideally suited as the core investment in a retirement program or a child's college savings plan.

Risk: This is a modest-risk fund, and reinvestment of periodic cash dividends can reduce risk further. Its portfolio beta is 0.89, and its share price declined by a very modest 9 percent during the 1990 bear market.

Costs: This is a modest-cost equity fund. Its shares are sold without either a front-end or a back-end load, but investors assume an ongoing 0.25-percent 12b-1 fee. Its annual expense ratio is a modest 1.22 percent, but its portfolio turnover ratio is a hefty 235 percent.

Distributions: Income is paid quarterly in March, June, September, and December, and capital gains are distributed in December.

How to Buy and Sell: Minimum initial investment $1,000; IRA $500; subsequent investments $100. Telephone exchange with other Founders funds. Shares may also be obtained without transaction fees through Charles Schwab and Fidelity Brokerage.

FOUNDERS GROWTH

Founders Asset Management
2930 East Third Avenue
Denver, CO 80206
800–525–2440

Inception: 1962
Total Assets: $841 Million
Ticker Symbol: FRGRX
Home Page: http://
www.networth.galt.com/founders

Objective and Strategy: This fund seeks long-term growth of capital by investing in the common stocks of well-established, high-quality growth companies. These companies tend to have strong performance records, solid market positions, and reasonable financial strength. The fund has gained an exceptional track record of strong long-term performance (a 16.7-percent compound annual return during the last fifteen years) by emphasizing a diverse portfolio of companies in the mid- and large-cap universes. It seeks to identify securities that have demonstrated the ability to consistently generate real revenue and earnings growth. This fund's portfolio is slightly more aggressive than that of Founders Blue Chip and contains few dividend-paying stocks. Its largest investments are in the computer and software, leisure and entertainment, retail, and telecommunications industries.

Annualized Returns

1-Year 18.6%
3-Year 16.9%
5-Year 19.3%

Portfolio Manager: Edward Kelly, CFA, joined Founders in 1989 and assumed lead portfolio responsibilities in 1994. He also has served as co-lead manager of Founders Special.

Suitability: This fund's shares are suitable for modestly aggressive and aggressive investors who prefer capital gains over current income.

Portfolio Implications: The fund is heavily invested in the traditional growth industries favored by other well-managed growth funds. You should compare this portfolio's holdings with those of your other growth funds before making an investment to avoid possible duplication.

Risk: High returns are usually accompanied by high risk, and this fund is no exception. Its portfolio beta is a hefty 1.29, although its share price decline during the severe 1990 bear market was in line with that of the market generally (16.4 percent).

Costs: The fund's shares are sold without either a front-end or a back-end sales fee, but shareholders assume a 0.25-percent ongoing 12b-1 fee. Its annual expense ratio is 1.28, about average for the group, but its portfolio turnover ratio is a hefty 130 percent.

Distributions: Income is paid in March, June, September, and December, and capital gains are distributed annually in December.

How to Buy and Sell: Minimum initial investment $1,000; IRA $500; subsequent investments $100. Telephone exchange with other Founders funds. Shares may also be obtained without transaction fees through Charles Schwab and Fidelity Brokerage.

GABELLI ASSET FUND

Gabelli & Company
One Corporate Center
Rye, NY 10580-1434
800-422-3554

Inception: 1986
Total Assets: $1.1 Billion
Ticker Symbol: GABAX
Home Page: http://www.gabelli.com

Objective and Strategy: This fund seeks capital appreciation by investing in common stocks of companies with underlying assets and/or business franchises that it believes are undervalued by the market. Strong franchise telecommunications, motion picture, and cable-television stocks dominate its portfolio. Portfolio manager Mario Gabelli prides himself on being able to ferret out potential takeover candidates and his focus on unexploited asset-based companies proved highly successful in the late 1980s, when the fund's large stakes in numerous deal stocks played into the hands of a take-over-driven market. A slowdown in corporate restructurings during the first half of the 1990s has trimmed the fund's performance numbers a bit. However, this disciplined fund still can be expected to produce excellent results over the long haul.

Portfolio Manager: Mario J. Gabelli since the fund's inception in 1986. Mr. Gabelli is the president of the fund's investment adviser.

Suitability: This fund's shares are suitable for modestly aggressive, patient, growth-seeking investors.

Portfolio Implications: You have to be patient with this fund. Mr. Gabelli is a master at identifying companies that are selling well below their value as private companies. However, to capitalize on Gabelli's investment style, you have to be patient and wait for a suitor to eventually bid up the prices of the fund's core holdings.

Risk: Although a value player, the fund's share price volatility is slightly above that of the market (beta 1.05). However, its share price declined by a modest 11 percent during the 1990 bear market.

Costs: The fund's shares are sold without either a front-end or a back-end load. However, shareholders assume a 0.25-percent ongoing 12b-1 fee which has lifted its annual expense ratio to a slightly above-average 1.44 percent. Its portfolio turnover ratio is also a hefty 140 percent.

Distributions: Both income and capital gains are distributed annually.

How to Buy and Sell: Minimum initial investment $1,000; IRA $1,000; no minimum subsequent investment requirement. Telephone exchange with other Gabelli funds. Shares may also be obtained without transaction fees from Charles Schwab, Fidelity Brokerage, and Jack White and Company.

Annualized Returns	
1-Year	12.4%
3-Year	11.5%
5-Year	14.3%

GABELLI GROWTH FUND

Gabelli & Company
One Corporate Center
Rye, NY 10580
800-422-3554

Inception: 1987
Total Assets: $589 Million
Ticker Symbol: GABGX
Home Page: http://www.gabelli.com

Objective and Strategy: This fund seeks growth of capital. It features a mix of large- and small-firm stocks that it believes represent undervalued earning power. Management stresses companies that show above-average growth in market share, increasing profitability, and good earnings momentum. Most of the fund's major industries, which include retail, entertainment, and telecommunications, underscore its high-growth aspirations. Its largest holdings recently include First Data, General Electric, Home Depot, State Street Boston, and Gillette. Still, a hefty stake in low-multiple, basic industry stocks also reveals a sound value discipline at work. This dual emphasis on growth and value has so far proven highly successful, allowing the fund to whip most of its rivals in a variety of markets since its inception in 1987.

Portfolio Manager: Howard Frank Ward since 1995. Prior to joining Gabelli, Ward was with Scudder, Stevens and Clark, where he served as the portfolio manager of the Growth and Balanced funds.

Suitability: This fund, packed with blue-chip stocks with reasonable valuations, is suitable for both conservative and modestly aggressive investors who seek growth of capital.

Annualized Returns

1-Year 20.0%
3-Year 14.6%
5-Year 13.8%

Portfolio Implications: Like many well-managed growth funds, its portfolio is packed with companies with household names. Thus, there is the potential for portfolio duplication with other well-managed growth vehicles.

Risk: Like most Gabelli equity funds, this fund sports a slightly above-average beta (1.03). However, its value-orientation tends to shore-up its share price during severe bear markets as witnessed by its modest 11-percent share price decline during the 1990 bear market.

Costs: Shares are sold without either a front-end or a back-end sales charge. However, shareholders assume a 0.25-percent ongoing 12b-1 fee. Its 1.44-percent annual expense ratio is slightly above average for the group as is its 140-percent portfolio turnover ratio.

Distributions: Both income and capital gains distributions are paid annually.

How to Buy and Sell: Minimum initial investment $1,000; IRA $1,000; no minimum subsequent investment requirement. Telephone exchange with other Gabelli funds. Shares may also be obtained without transaction fees through Charles Schwab, Fidelity Brokerage, and Jack White and Company.

GABELLI VALUE FUND

Gabelli & Company
One Corporate Center
Rye, NY 10580
800-422-3554

Inception: 1989
Total Assets: $515 Million
Ticker Symbol: GABVX
Home Page: http://www.gabelli.com

Objective and Strategy: This fund, which is organized as a nondiversified fund, seeks capital appreciation by investing in the securities of undervalued companies. Reflecting manager Mario Gabelli's private market value methodology (companies, that in the public market, are selling at a significant discount to the value the adviser believes informed industrialists would be willing to pay to acquire companies with similar characteristics), the fund features a mix of strong franchise telephone, media, and consumer products stocks. Gabelli hopes to profit by the recognition of hidden values by the market or by participating in corporate takeovers. This strategy was out of sync with the market's taste for recession proof earnings during its first two years in existence (when corporate takeovers virtually came to a halt), but when this situation reversed in 1992, this portfolio's significant unrecognized value was realized and the fund has continued to shine ever since.

Portfolio Manager: Mario J. Gabelli since the fund's inception in September 1989. He is chairman and chief investment officer of the fund's adviser.

Suitability: This fund is suitable for growth-oriented investors who have considerable patience. It is a nondiversified fund and is not suitable for highly conservative investors.

Annualized Returns
1-Year 9.1%
3-Year 10.6%
5-Year 16.5%

Portfolio Implications: This is one of the few "takeover" funds around. Its shareholders capitalize during corporate takeovers of the fund's holdings. The fund can invest up to 50 percent of its assets in securities for which a tender or exchange offer has been made.

Risk: The fund sports a market beta. However, its risk arises when it concentrates a significant portion of its assets in a few investments involved in a takeover or reorganization. Its share price tumbled by more than 17 percent during the 1990 bear market.

Costs: This is the highest-cost fund in the Gabelli fund family. Its shares are sold with a 5.50-percent front-end sales charge; its annual expense ratio is an above-average 1.50 percent, although its portfolio turnover ratio (65 percent) is slightly below average.

Distributions: Income and capital gains distributions are paid annually.

How to Buy and Sell: Minimum initial investment $1,000; IRA $250; subsequent investments $100. Shares are sold with a rather hefty front-end sales fee attached.

HARBOR CAPITAL APPRECIATION

Harbor Funds
One Seagate
Toledo, OH 43666
800-422-1050

Inception: *1987*
Total Assets: *$1.5 Billion*
Ticker Symbol: *HACAX*
Home Page: *None*

Objective and Strategy: This fund, which was originally developed for the Owens-Illinois pension fund, seeks capital appreciation by investing in companies with market capitalizations in excess of $1 billion. Managements seeks companies with superior absolute and relative earnings growth. In addition, these companies also demonstrate high sales growth, high unit growth, high or improving returns on assets and equity, and strong balance sheets. After following a conservative, value orientation during its first two years of operation, the fund switched to a more growth-intensive approach in 1990. Although the fund's new aggressive tactics have been in sync with the market's recent earnings orientations, shareholders should expect to see considerably greater share price volatility from this fund than they have experienced in the past. In addition, the fund may become concentrated in specific industries, as witnessed by its recent 40-percent stake in technology stocks.

Portfolio Manager: Spiros "Sig" Segalas since 1990. He has been with Jennison Associates (an independent subsidiary of Prudential Insurance) since 1969. He is also

Annualized Returns

1-Year 12.1%
3-Year 19.0%
5-Year 18.6%

the manager of the Owens-Illinois pension portfolio.

Suitability: This fund is suitable for only more aggressive growth-oriented investors. Patience is also required.

Portfolio Implications: The fund's assets are usually concentrated in the stocks of about sixty companies. At times, its largest holdings have accounted for 4 percent of portfolio assets each, and it has not been shy about making relatively large sector bets.

Risk: This is a high-risk growth fund, as indicated by its high 1.22 beta. Extreme share price volatility is exemplified by its more than 20-percent decline during the 1990 bear market.

Costs: This is a cost-efficient growth fund. Its shares are sold with a no-load format; its annual expense ratio is modest at 0.75 percent, as is its 52-percent portfolio turnover ratio.

Distributions: Income (if any) and capital gains are distributed in October.

How to Buy and Sell: Minimum initial investment $2,000; IRA $500; subsequent investments $100.

IAI REGIONAL

IAI Mutual Funds
3700 First Bank Place
P.O. Box 357
Minneapolis, MN 55440-0357
800-945-3863

Inception: 1980
Total Assets: $589 Million
Ticker Symbol: IARGX
Home Page: http://
networth.galt.com/iai

375

Growth Funds

Objective and Strategy: The fund seeks growth of capital by investing at least 80 percent of its assets in companies located in Minnesota, Wisconsin, Illinois, Iowa, Nebraska, Montana, North Dakota, and South Dakota. More importantly, it owes its top-notch, long-term returns not only to spectacular single-year gains, but also to its ability to produce at least moderately above-average results in most markets. Excellent stock selection, a fairly strict price discipline, and an effective use of cash have made the fund one of the growth category's most consistent performers. The Regional fund owns a collection of stocks in companies which should continue to generate strong growth regardless of the fortunes of the overall U.S. economy. It is an excellent selection for patient investors.

Annualized Returns
1-Year 16.3%
3-Year 12.6%
5-Year 11.9%

Portfolio Manager: Mark C. Hoonsbeen served as comanger since 1995 before becoming lead manager in 1996. He was a portfolio manager with the St. Paul Companies prior to joining IAI in 1994.

Suitability: Although capital appreciation is the fund's primary objective, its shares are suitable for conservative as well as more aggressive investors.

Portfolio Implications: The bulk of its investments are drawn from companies located in the upper Midwest. However, the portfolio is well-diversified across a wide spectrum of industries and thus, its performance is not tied directly to that of the region in which it primarily invests.

Risk: The fund sports a modest 0.96 beta, and its share price declined by less than the overall stock market (13.5 percent) during 1990 severe bear market.

Costs: This is a modest-cost fund. Its shares are sold with a no-load format, and its annual expense ratio is a below-average 1.21 percent. Its portfolio turnover ratio, however, is slightly above average (90 percent).

Distributions: Both income and capital gains are distributed annually.

How to Buy and Sell: Minimum initial investment $5,000; IRA $2,000; subsequent investments $100. Telephone exchange with other IAI funds. Shares may also be obtained without transaction fees through Charles Schwab, Fidelity Brokerage, and Jack White and Company.

IDS NEW DIMENSIONS

IDS Financial Services
IDS Tower 10
Minneapolis, MN 55440
800-437-4332

Inception: 1968
Total Assets: $8.8 Billion
Ticker Symbol: INNDX
Home Page: http://
www.americanexpress.com/advisors

Objective and Strategy: This fund seeks long-term capital appreciation by investing primarily in common stocks of companies that show the potential for significant growth. The fund can also invest a portion of its assets, but not more than 30 percent, in foreign securities. Like most of its IDS siblings, the fund follows a growth-intensive strategy, focusing on relatively expensive, large-capitalization growth stocks with significantly above-average growth in earnings. Theoretically, the fund's growth-intensive approach would involve greater-than-average risk. However, management's effective use of cash has prevented this from being the case for this fund. The fund's investments are concentrated in sectors where economic or technological change is rapidly taking place. Thus, it's no surprise to find that its largest industry allocations have been made to computers and office equipment, electronics, and health care.

Portfolio Manager: Gordon Fines since 1991. He managed the IDS Management Retirement Fund from 1985 to 1991 and currently leads the growth team for American Express Financial. He joined IDS in 1981.

Annualized Returns	
1-Year	24.1%
3-Year	16.5%
5-Year	16.8%

Suitability: The fund's shares are suitable for more aggressive growth-seeking investors.

Portfolio Implications: What you find in this fund's portfolio are traditional high-growth stocks. These are in such highly visible companies as Intel, Pfizer, General Electric, Amgen, and McDonalds, which make up a significant portion of the fund's portfolio.

Risk: This growth-seeking fund possesses above-average risk. Its beta is slightly above that of the market (1.09). However, its share price declined a rather modest 12 percent during the 1990 bear market.

Costs: Class A shares are sold with a hefty 5.00-percent front-end sales load. However, its operating costs are quite modest. Its annual expanse ratio is below-average at 0.93 percent, as is its 54-percent portfolio turnover ratio.

Distributions: Both income and capital gains are distributed annually.

How to Buy and Sell: Class B and Y shares are also available with varying sales charges. Minimum initial investment $2,000; IRA $2,000; subsequent investments $100. Telephone exchange with other IDS funds.

INVESCO GROWTH

Invesco Funds Group
P.O. Box 173706
Denver, CO 80217-3706
800-525-8085

Inception: 1935
Total Assets: $572 Million
Ticker Symbol: FLRFX
Home Page: http://
www.invesco.com

Objective and Strategy: This fund is designed to provide long-term capital appreciation plus quarterly income by investing in nationally listed common stocks. There are two ways a fund can pursue growth of capital. It can run flat-out, taking the market spurts, jumps, and falls in stride, or it can opt for a slower, steadier path. This fund has chosen the latter. Management seeks companies whose annual earnings are growing faster than the market average. It employs a top-down investment strategy, which first identifies those industries expected to do well in the forecasted economy, then selects specific securities from those market segments. Surprisingly, technology stocks are the portfolio's largest representatives, followed by consumer cyclicals and staples and finance. Individual stocks all sport household names.

Portfolio Manager: Comanaged by Timothy J. Miller and Trent May since June 1996. Miller also manages the Invesco Dynamics Fund.

Suitability: If you believe that slow and steady wins the growth race, this is the fund for you. It is suitable for both conservative and modestly aggressive growth-seeking investors.

Annualized Returns

1-Year 23.3%
3-Year 13.0%
5-Year 13.3%

Portfolio Implications: Although the fund espouses a buy-and-hold philosophy, the fund sports a hefty portfolio turnover ratio. Its investments are all established, easily recognized growth companies, and its portfolio may provide duplication with the portfolios of other well-managed growth funds.

Risk: The fund sports a slightly below-market beta (0.97), and its large-cap orientation provides some protection during down markets. Its share price declined by about 18 percent during the 1990 bear market.

Costs: The fund's shares are sold without either a front-end or a back-end sales load. However, shareholders assume an ongoing 0.25-percent 12b-1 fee. The annual expense ratio is a modest 1.06 percent, but portfolio turnover is a hefty 111 percent.

Distributions: Income distributions are paid quarterly, and capital gains are distributed annually in December.

How to Buy and Sell: Minimum initial investment $1,000; IRA $250; subsequent investments $50. Telephone exchange with other Invesco offerings. Shares may also be obtained without transaction fees from Charles Schwab, Fidelity Brokerage, and Jack White and Company.

JANUS FUND

Janus Service Corporation
100 Fillmore Street
Denver, CO 80206-4923
800-525-3713

Inception: 1970
Total Assets: $14.4 Billion
Ticker Symbol: JANSX
Home Page: http://www.janus.com

Objective and Strategy: This well-managed fund seeks growth of capital by investing in a diversified portfolio of larger-sized companies. Janus's superb risk-reward profile is matched by few rivals. Over the long haul, the fund has achieved one of the better total returns of any growth fund, while also showing one of the lower levels of risk. (Since inception in February 1970, Janus's shareholders have been rewarded with an enviable 16.6-percent average annual return.) Its excellent results are attributable to management's skill at adapting to market trends. Regardless of market trends, the fund usually is caught holding very timely, popular stocks. Besides excellent stock selection, this no-load fund also has benefitted from extremely well-timed retreats to cash, which have enabled it to resist sharp bear market declines.

Portfolio Manager: James P. Craig since 1986. He previously managed the Venture and Balanced funds. He obtained an M.A. in finance from the Wharton School of the University of Pennsylvania.

Suitability: All growth-oriented investors, whether aggressive or conservative, should consider an investment in this well-run fund. It is an ideal candidate for the core of

a retirement program or a child's education savings plan.

Portfolio Implications: Given the fund's large size, it must focus on billion-dollar companies. However, the magic of James Craig has put the fund's assets in the right companies year in and year out. Periodic retreats to cash also result in protection during down markets.

Risk: The fund's beta is a modest 0.88. However, its risk-reward ratio is quite low as witnessed by the modest 12.7-percent decline in share price during the 1990 bear market.

Costs: This is a reasonable-cost fund. Its shares are sold with a no-load format. Its 0.87-percent annual expense ratio is well below average for the growth fund category. However, its portfolio turnover ratio (118 percent) is higher than average.

Distributions: Both income and capital gains are paid annually in December.

How to Buy and Sell: Minimum initial investment $2,500; IRA $500; subsequent investments $100. Telephone exchange with other Janus funds. Shares may also be obtained without transaction fees through Charles Schwab and Fidelity Brokerage.

Annualized Returns

1-Year 20.0%
3-Year 15.0%
5-Year 14.3%

JANUS ENTERPRISE

Janus Service Corporation
100 Fillmore Street
Denver, CO 80206-4923
800-525-3713

Inception: 1992
Total Assets: $699 Million
Ticker Symbol: JAENX
Home Page: http://www.janus.com

Objective and Strategy: This fund seeks long-term growth of capital. It is organized as a nondiversified fund and concentrates its assets in a relatively small number of mid-sized companies whose market capitalizations fall within the range of companies in the S&P MidCap 400 Index (equity capitalizations between $11 million and $7.5 billion). Portfolio manager James Goff is a stock picker whose stock-by-stock approach has produced a diverse array of high-growth, well-managed companies. Recently, foreign securities accounted for about 10 percent of portfolio assets. At times, Goff will hedge the portfolio with S&P futures contracts. Reflecting the fund's concentrated portfolio strategy, its portfolio contained fifty different equity issues, with the fund's ten largest holdings accounting for 44 percent of portfolio assets. Portfolio themes include wireless communications, business services and outsourcing, pharmaceuticals, and a diverse assortment of retailers.

Annualized Returns
1-Year 21.9%
3-Year 19.2%
5-Year NA

Portfolio Manager: James P. Goff since the fund's inception in 1992. He joined Janus Capital in 1988 and has served as comanager of the Janus Venture Fund. He has a B.A. from Yale University.

Suitability: This is not a diversified fund. Its portfolio is concentrated in a few stock issues and therefore is not suitable for conservative investors.

Portfolio Implications: As a nondiversified fund, this is as far away from a balanced program as you can get. Its success depends on stock-picking ability and the performance of a handful of stocks in its portfolio. It should be combined with other growth and aggressive growth funds.

Risk: This is an extremely high-risk growth fund, although its portfolio beta is a modest 0.97. This young fund has yet to experience a major bear market, but you can expect its share price to tumble along with the stock market.

Costs: The fund's shares are sold with a no-load format; its annual expense ratio is an average 1.26 percent, but its portfolio turnover ratio is a hefty 194 percent.

Distributions: Both income and capital gains distributions are paid in December.

How to Buy and Sell: Minimum initial investment $2,500; IRA $500; subsequent investments $100. Telephone exchange with other Janus funds. Shares can also be obtained through Charles Schwab and Fidelity Brokerage without transaction fees.

JANUS MERCURY

Janus Service Corporation
100 Fillmore Street
Denver, CO 80206
800-525-3713

Inception: 1993
Total Assets: $2.0 Billion
Ticker Symbol: JAMRX
Home Page: http://www.janus.com

Objective and Strategy: This is another Janus nondiversified offering. It seeks capital growth by investing in a concentrated portfolio of common stocks of companies of any size. Recently, foreign stocks accounted for about 20 percent of portfolio assets. Stocks are selected for their growth characteristics. Portfolio manager Warren Lammert has chosen to emphasize five broad investment themes: technology, telecommunications, pharmaceuticals, financial services, and business services (primarily companies that provide outsourcing services). In keeping with its large bets on a few stocks, the portfolio's ten largest holdings accounted for 35 percent of portfolio assets. The fund has lived up to its name, producing a 25-percent average annual return since its inception in May 1993.

Annualized Returns
1-Year 17.6%
3-Year 24.1%
5-Year NA

Portfolio Manager: Warren B. Lammert since the fund's inception in 1993. He also manages the Venture Fund and managed the Balanced Fund from 1992 to 1993. He joined Janus Capital in 1987.

Suitability: This is a nondiversified fund. Its portfolio is concentrated in a few stock issues and therefore is not suitable for conservative (or even possibly modestly aggressive) investors.

Portfolio Implications: As a nondiversified fund, this is far from a balanced investment program. Its success depends on management's stock-picking ability and the performance of a handful of stocks. Investors should combine this fund with other growth fund offerings.

Risk: This is an extremely high-risk growth fund, although its portfolio beta is a modest 1.01. This young fund has yet to experience a major bear market, but you can expect its share price to tumble along with the stock market.

Costs: The fund's shares are sold with a no-load format; its annual expense ratio is a modest 1.14 percent, but its portfolio turnover ratio is a very high 201 percent.

Distributions: Both income and capital gains distributions are paid in December.

How to Buy and Sell: Minimum initial investment $2,500; IRA $500; subsequent investments $100. Telephone exchange with other Janus funds. Shares can also be obtained through Charles Schwab and Fidelity Brokerage without transaction fees.

KEMPER-DREMAN CONTRARIAN

Kemper Funds
120 South LaSalle Street
Chicago, IL 60603
800-621-1048

Inception: 1988
Total Assets: $35 Million
Ticker Symbol: KDCAX
Home Page: http://
www.kemper.com

Objective and Strategy: This fund provides a combination of capital growth and current income through the implementation of a strategy that seeks to capitalize on the historic performance advantage of low price-earnings multiple stocks. Its portfolio is packed with out-of-favor stocks whose prices have suffered as the result of overreaction by investors to unfavorable news about the companies. Management's strict value strategy also considers other factors, such as financial strength, book-to-market value, five- and ten-year growth rates above 10 percent annually, size of institutional ownership, and year-ahead earnings estimates. In short, management tries to buy companies when no one wants them and sell them when they return to favor.

Portfolio Manager: Christian C. Bertelsen since March 1996. Prior to joining Kemper, he served as portfolio manager of an unaffiliated investment company. He has an M.B.A. from Boston University.

Suitability: This is an excellent growth vehicle for conservative investors. However, patience is required to allow out-of-favor companies to return to favor.

Annualized Returns

1-Year	17.5%
3-Year	16.6%
5-Year	14.2%

Portfolio Implications: The fund's new portfolio manager began taking profits in financial and consumer stocks last March and began reinvesting the proceeds from these sales into stocks in four categories: industrial stocks, inflation hedges, retail, and technology.

Risk: Although a contrarian approach generally leads to a low-risk portfolio, this fund sports a hefty 1.12 beta. In addition, its share price plunged nearly 21 percent during the 1990 bear market.

Costs: Class A shares are sold with a hefty 5.75-percent front-end sales charge. The fund's annual expense ratio is an above-average 1.66 percent. However, its portfolio turnover ratio is a very low 30 percent.

Distributions: Income is paid quarterly and capital gains are distributed annually.

How to Buy and Sell: Minimum initial investment $1,000; IRA $1,000; subsequent investments $100. Class B, C, and I shares (which sport different sales load structures) are also available.

LINDNER GROWTH

Lindner Investments
7711 Carondelet Avenue
Suite 700
St. Louis, MO 63105
888-733-3769

Inception: 1973
Total Assets: $1.5 Billion
Ticker Symbol: LDNRX
Home Page: http://
www.lindnerfunds.com

Objective and Strategy: This fund seeks long-term capital appreciation with current income as a secondary objective. It changed its name from the Lindner Fund in August 1995. Since its inception twenty years ago, the fund has consistently maintained a conservative bent. While conservatism usually is equated with modest returns in the investment world, this fund provided shareholders with an average annual return in excess of 21 percent during the 1980s. The fund's success was not only achieved by generating handsome returns during bull markets, but also by avoiding significant losses during bear markets. Its returns have moderated in recent years because management has refused to jump on the earnings momentum bandwagon. In fact, management has remained skittish about the runaway bull market and has insulated the portfolio from a severe market decline by allocating about 20 percent of assets to foreign stocks, holding a hefty cash balance, and increasing allocations to financial, energy, and mining stocks. The fund possesses one of the lowest risk profiles of any growth fund and provides an excellent bear market hedge.

Portfolio Manager: Eric Ryback since 1984, Lawrence Callahan since 1993, and Robert Lange since 1977. Each also manages at least one other fund in the Lindner/Ryback family.

Annualized Returns

1-Year 17.3%
3-Year 12.7%
5-Year 13.8%

Suitability: This fund is well suited for conservative growth-seeking investors. It possesses a low-risk profile and could perform well during a bear stock market.

Portfolio Implications: This fund will not be a top performer during a runaway bull market. However, by saving ground during bear markets, it can be expected to produce handsome returns long term. This is an excellent fund for use as a hedge in a growth-oriented portfolio.

Risk: The fund has an unusually low risk level, which has boosted its risk-reward ratio. Its beta is a modest 0.82, and its share price declined by a modest 14 percent during the 1990 bear market.

Costs: This is a very cost-efficient fund. Its shares are sold with a no-load format. Its annual expense ratio is a low 0.54 percent, as is its 25-percent portfolio turnover ratio.

Distributions: Both income and capital gains are distributed annually in September.

How to Buy and Sell: Minimum initial investment $2,000; IRA $250; subsequent investments $100. Telephone exchange with other Lindner/Ryback funds. Shares may also be obtained through Jack White and Company without transaction fees.

LOOMIS SAYLES GROWTH

Loomis Sayles & Company, L.P.
One Financial Center
Boston, MA 02111
800-633-3330

Inception: 1991
Total Assets: $50 Million
Ticker Symbol: LSGRX
Home Page: None

Objective and Strategy: This new entry to the Loomis Sayles stable of well-managed growth funds primarily seeks capital growth by investing in high-growth companies, both large and small. Since inception, its returns have kept pace with those of the Standard & Poor's 500 Index, which is no small feat for a fund with a diverse portfolio of growth stocks. Management prefers to invest in companies that are capable of growing at a 20-plus percent annual rate and usually has to pay up for them. Thus, the portfolio's price-earnings ratio tends to be a bit above that of the typical growth fund. Recently, management has placed emphasis on niche retailers (Starbucks and PetSmart), technology (Cascade and Microsoft), and energy (Schlumberger and Enron), and those bets have paid off handsomely.

Portfolio Manager: Jerome A. Castellini, vice president of the trust and of Loomis Sayles, has served as portfolio manager since the fund's inception in 1991.

Suitability: Given this fund's emphasis on growth and its higher-than-average portfolio price-earnings ratio, its shares are suitable for more aggressive growth-seeking investors.

Annualized Returns
1-Year 9.7%
3-Year 10.7%
5-Year 11.2%

Portfolio Implications: This fund is best combined with a growth fund that stresses out-of-favor companies that sell at lower price-earnings ratios. That combination will give you both a growth and value play and lower overall portfolio volatility.

Risk: The fund's beta (1.08) is slightly above average for the growth fund category. This relatively young fund has yet to experience a severe bear market, but given its affinity for higher price-earnings ratio stocks, its shares could suffer during a sharp market sell-off.

Costs: This is a modest-cost fund. Its shares are sold with a no-load format. Its annual expense ratio is a below-average 1.08 percent, as is its 48-percent portfolio turnover ratio.

Distributions: Both income and capital gains are paid annually.

How to Buy and Sell: Minimum initial investment $2,500; IRA $250; subsequent investments $50. Telephone exchange with other Loomis Sayles funds. Shares may also be obtained through Charles Schwab and Jack White and Company without transaction fees.

MFS VALUE FUND CLASS A

MFS Financial Services
500 Boylston Street, 15th Floor
Boston, MA 02116
800-225-2606

Inception: 1983
Total Assets: $352 Million
Ticker Symbol: MVLFX
Home Page: http://www.mfs.com

Objective and Strategy: Formerly MFS Special, this fund's name was changed to MFS Value to more accurately reflect its value discipline. The fund's portfolio tends to span sixty to one hundred different stocks drawn from what management believes are promising undervalued issues, both domestic and foreign. Like many value-oriented investors these days, management has had to turn to markets overseas in search of value. Currently, foreign securities represent about 12 percent of the fund's portfolio. In growth-led markets, this fund can be expected to underperform and with the stock market exhibiting an earnings momentum bent during 1995 and 1996, the fund's returns have lagged the market. However, over a longer-term market cycle the fund can be expected to deliver the goods.

Annualized Returns

1-Year 18.8%
3-Year 18.1%
5-Year 19.4%

Portfolio Manager: John F. Brennan, Jr. since September 1991. He has been a portfolio manager with MFS since 1985.

Suitability: The fund's shares are suitable for both conservative and modestly aggressive growth-seeking investors.

Portfolio Implications: This value investor has recently tilted its portfolio more toward growth stocks. Besides a growing international component, the fund has assumed a hefty investment in entertainment stocks.

Risk: High-return portfolios usually contain higher-than-average risk and this fund's portfolio is no exception. Its beta is slightly above that of the market (1.07), and its share price declined by nearly 18 percent during the 1990 bear market.

Costs: The fund's class A shares are sold with a hefty 5.75-percent front-end load and a 0.25-percent ongoing 12b-1 fee. Its annual expense ratio is an average 1.35 percent, and its portfolio turnover ratio (109 percent) is above the growth fund average.

Distributions: Both income and capital gains distributions are paid annually.

How to Buy and Sell: Class B shares (contingent deferred sales charge) are also available. Minimum initial investment $1,000; IRA $250; subsequent investments $50.

MAIRS & POWER GROWTH FUND

Mairs & Power, Inc.
W-2062 First Bank Building
St. Paul, MN 55101
800-304-7404

Inception: 1958
Total Assets: $104 Million
Ticker Symbol: MPGFX
Home Page: None

Objective and Strategy: This growth-oriented fund invests in both large and small companies that are located or do business in the Midwest. Portfolio manager George Mairs (the third Mairs to direct the fund's portfolio) has produced respectable double-digit annual returns during the last twenty-seven years. He attained this notable performance record by stressing long-term investing while minimizing fund expenses. Over the past ten years, the fund's portfolio turnover ratio has averaged less than 4 percent, giving a true meaning to "long-term" investing. Mairs has always maintained a compact portfolio containing the common stocks of less than three dozen companies. However, the fund's risk profile has been extremely low. Unfortunately, the fund's shares are registered for sale in a limited number of states.

Annualized Returns

1-Year 21.5%
3-Year 24.3%
5-Year 19.8%

Portfolio Manager: George A. Mairs III since the fund's inception in 1958. Mr. Mairs has been an officer and director of Mairs and Power, Inc. since 1961.

Suitability: If you are a true long-term investor and can get your hands on the shares of this well-run fund, do so.

Portfolio Implications: This is a buy-and-hold fund and you must be a buy-and-hold investor to reap its potential rewards. The fund makes an excellent core holding for a retirement program or for a young child's college education plan.

Risk: With its large returns, you'd expect plenty of risk. However, the fund's beta is a very low 0.69. Its share price declined with the overall market during the 1990 bear market (16.3 percent).

Costs: This is a very cost-efficient fund. Its shares are sold with a no-load format. Its annual expense ratio is a below-average 0.99 percent, and its 4-percent portfolio turnover ratio is one of the lowest you'll find among equity funds.

Distributions: Income distributions are paid in June and December, and capital gains are distributed in December.

How to Buy and Sell: The fund's shares are sold in a limited number of states. Minimum initial investment $2,500; IRA $1,000; subsequent investments $100.

MONTGOMERY GROWTH

Montgomery Securities
101 California Street
San Francisco, CA 94111
800-572-3863

Inception: 1993
Total Assets: $1.0 Billion
Ticker Symbol: MNGFX
Home Page: None

Objective and Strategy: This fund seeks capital appreciation by investing in common stocks, usually those of domestic companies that have market capitalizations of $500 million or more. This young fund began operations in a favorable stock market environment in late 1993 and has posted an enviable 26.4-percent average annual return since its inception. Management seeks growth at reasonable value, identifying companies with sound fundamental value and potential for substantial growth. The fund selects its investments based on a combination of quantitative screening techniques and fundamental analysis. The initial stock list is developed by screening the targeted universe on changes in rates of growth and valuation ratios such as price to sales, price to earnings, and price to cash flows. The goal is to identify rapidly growing companies with reasonable valuations and accelerating growth rates or those with low valuations and initial signs of growth. Application of rigorous fundamental analysis of income statements and balance sheets, as well as company visits, narrows the list to those eventually selected for the porfolio.

Portfolio Manager: Roger W. Honour and Andrew Pratt. Honour served as a portfolio manager with Twentieth Century Advisors and Alliance Capital. Pratt joined Montgomery from Hewlett-Packard, where he managed a portfolio of small-cap growth stocks.

Suitability: This fund is suitable for more aggressive growth-seeking investors. It can be used as the core of a long-term retirement program or as part of a child's education savings plan.

Portfolio Implications: What you get here are plenty of mid-cap, rapid-growth companies. However, these companies may be relatively young and their share prices can be highly volatile.

Risk: This is a higher-risk growth fund with an above-market beta. This relatively young fund has yet to experience a severe bear market. However, given its penchant for higher price-earnings multiple stocks, its shares could easily get caught up in a market slide.

Costs: This fund's shares are sold with a no-load format. Its 1.49-percent annual expense ratio is slightly above average, and its portfolio turnover ratio is a hefty 110 percent.

Distributions: Both income and capital gains distributions are paid annually.

How to Buy and Sell: Minimum initial investment $1,000; IRA $1,000; subsequent investments $100. Telephone exchange with other Montgomery funds.

Annualized Returns
1-Year 22.8%
3-Year 26.4%
5-Year NA

NEUBERGER & BERMAN FOCUS

Neuberger & Berman Management, Inc.
605 Third Avenue, 2nd Floor
New York, NY 10158-0180
800-877-9700

Inception: 1955
Total Assets: $1.1 Billion
Ticker Symbol: NBSSX
Home Page: http://www.nbfunds.com

Objective and Strategy: If you like to invest in concentrated portfolios but can't tolerate the risk inherent in sector fund investing, here's an alternative. This fund seeks capital appreciation by investing in common stocks selected from thirteen multi-industry sectors. To maximize potential return, the portfolio makes 90 percent or more of its investments in not more than six sectors it identifies as undervalued. It seeks undervalued, out-of-favor stocks of companies with solid balance sheets, strong managements, and low prices. According to the fund's portfolio manager, "undervalued stocks generally tend to be clustered within a limited number of sectors—not spread evenly over the economy as a whole. In particular, we like to buy the stocks of the strongest companies in these out of favor industries." These days 75 percent of the fund's assets are concentrated in four industries: financial services, technology, heavy industry, and entertainment.

Annualized Returns

1-Year 6.0%
3-Year 15.6%
5-Year 17.3%

Portfolio Manager: Kent C. Simons and Lawrence Marx III since 1988. Comanager Kevin L. Risen joined the team in 1996. The three also manage the Guardian Fund.

Suitability: Given its industry concentration, this fund's shares are suitable for more aggressive growth-oriented investors.

Portfolio Implications: Investing in this fund is somewhat like owning a sector fund: You get the potential for exceptional profits during short-run periods. However, by diversifying across at least six sectors, the fund possesses far less risk than the typical sector fund.

Risk: As you might expect, this fund's portfolio concentration is accompanied by enhanced volatility as witnessed by its 1.17 beta. However, the fund's share price declined by a modest 13.7 percent during the 1990 bear market.

Costs: This is a modest-cost fund. Its shares are sold with a no-load format. Its annual expense ratio is a below-average 0.92 percent, as is its 36-percent portfolio turnover ratio.

Distributions: Both income and capital gains distributions are paid annually.

How to Buy and Sell: Minimum initial investment $1,000; IRA $250; subsequent investments $100. Telephone exchange with other Neuberger and Berman funds. Shares may also be obtained without transaction fees through Charles Schwab and Fidelity Brokerage.

NEUBERGER & BERMAN MANHATTAN

Neuberger & Berman Management, Inc.
605 Third Avenue, 2nd Floor
New York, NY 10158-0180
800-877-9700

Inception: 1979
Total Assets: $584 Million
Ticker Symbol: NMANX
Home Page: http://
www.nbfunds.com

Objective and Strategy: The Manhattan fund keeps on an even keel. The fund, which stresses above-average growth at a reasonable price, has produced consistently moderate returns in almost every year during the past decade. Its success owes to a number of factors, including its preference for quality companies, its price consciousness, and its practice of keeping market-level representation in most major sectors. Management wants to own the stocks of financially sound companies that have a competitive advantage or a product that makes them particularly attractive over the long term. Recently, management has been stressing financial services, communications, technology, and health care issues. Generally, the fund's portfolio is fully invested in growth stocks at all times.

Annualized Returns

1-Year 0.3%
3-Year 9.5%
5-Year 13.0%

Portfolio Manager: Mark Goldstein since 1992 and Susan Switzer since 1995. Prior to joining Neuberger and Berman, Goldstein was an analyst with Merrill Lynch and the College Retirement Equity Fund.

Suitability: Because of its higher-than-average risk level, this fund is suitable for more aggressive growth-seeking investors.

Portfolio Implications: This fund has invested in higher-growth companies that sport higher-than-average valuations, despite management's cost-conscious mentality. The portfolio has about ninety companies and a $2.8 billion median equity capitalization.

Risk: This is an exceptionally high-risk growth fund with a beta of 1.20. Its share price declined by nearly 19 percent during the 1990 bear market.

Costs: Like most Neuberger and Berman offerings, this fund's operating costs are quite reasonable. Its shares are sold with a no-load format, its annual expense ratio is 1.02 percent, and its portfolio turnover ratio is 44 percent.

Distributions: Both income (if any) and capital gains are distributed in December.

How to Buy and Sell: Minimum initial investment $1,000; IRA $250; subsequent investments $100. Telephone exchange with other Neuberger and Berman funds. Shares may also be obtained without transaction fees from Charles Schwab and Fidelity Brokerage.

NEUBERGER & BERMAN PARTNERS

Neuberger & Berman Management, Inc.
605 Third Avenue, 2nd Floor
New York, NY 10158-0180
800-877-9700

Inception: 1975
Total Assets: $2.0 Billion
Ticker Symbol: NPRTX
Home Page: http://
www.nbfunds.com

Objective and Strategy: The Partners fund was designed for the cautious investor. Giving top priority to capital preservation, the fund stresses relatively inexpensive growth stocks. Most of its companies show strong underlying fundamentals but sell at depressed valuations because of negative market sentiment and/or temporary difficulties. Despite the fact that the stock market has been led by high price-earnings multiples growth stocks during the last few years, the fund has performed reasonably well over the long term. It ranks in the top third of all funds in terms of performance during the past ten years, has had only two down years since Neuberger and Berman began running the fund in 1975, and has returned an average of about 18 percent per year since 1975. This fund offers good downside protection without missing strong bull markets.

Portfolio Manager: Michael M. Kassen since 1990 and Robert I. Gendelman since 1994. Both were portfolio managers before joining Neuberger and Berman, Kassen with Fidelity and Gendelman with Harpel Advisors.

Suitability: The fund is suitable for modestly aggressive and aggressive investors who prefer a mix of growth and current income.

Annualized Returns
1-Year 17.5%
3-Year 15.2%
5-Year 16.7%

Portfolio Implications: On a risk-reward basis, this is one of Neuberger and Berman's better funds. If you are the kind of person who is willing to "take the road less traveled" to find bargains, this fund is for you. Not too surprising is the fact that insurance, banking and financial services, and real estate sectors are heavily emphasized.

Risk: This fund sports a higher-than-market beta (1.11), but its share price held up reasonably well during the 1990 bear market, declining by slightly more than 12 percent during that turbulent period.

Costs: The fund sports reasonable operating costs. Its shares are sold with a no-load format. Its annual expense ratio is a below-average 0.87 percent, but its portfolio turnover ratio (96 percent) is slightly above average.

Distributions: Both income and capital gains are distributed annually in December.

How to Buy and Sell: Minimum initial investment $1,000; IRA $250; subsequent investments $100. Telephone exchange with other Neuberger and Berman funds. Shares may also be obtained without transaction fees from Charles Schwab and Fidelity Brokerage.

NICHOLAS FUND

700 Water Street
Milwaukee, WI 53202
414-272-6133

Inception: 1969
Total Assets: $3.8 Billion
Ticker Symbol: WICSX
Home Page: None

Objective and Strategy: This fund successfully achieves its objective of providing long-term capital growth and moderate risk through investments in mid-sized companies. The fund's investment style is best described as "price-conscious growth." Most of the fund's quality companies show above-average earnings growth, high returns on shareholder's equity, low leverage, and strong franchises, but sell at low valuations. The fund has returned an average of slightly more than 13.5 percent since its inception in 1969, or about two hundred basis points a year more than the Standard & Poor's 500 Index, while maintaining a level of volatility (risk) below that of the Index. Its superb performance record illustrates management's ability to discover undervalued mid-sized companies. Albert Nicholas is also a patient investor who holds on to the stocks of these companies for an average of more than four years.

Portfolio Manager: Albert O. Nicholas since the fund's inception in 1969. He is also portfolio manager of the Equity Income and Income funds. He also ran Nicholas II and Limited Edition from each fund's inception until 1993.

Annualized Returns
1-Year 22.3%
3-Year 15.2%
5-Year 14.2%

Suitability: If you want to participate in the mid-cap sector of the market but are afraid of the risks involved, this fund is for you. Its shares are suitable for both conservative and more aggressive growth-seeking investors.

Portfolio Implications: This fund sits squarely between small- and large-cap funds. Its combination with a fund that specializes in either small- or large-cap stocks provides significant diversification benefits.

Risk: This modest-risk, mid-cap fund sports a below-market beta (0.91). However, its share price tumbled more than 20 percent during the 1990 bear market, underscoring the short-term volatility of mid-cap stock prices.

Costs: If you like your funds to come cheap, this one's for you. Its shares are sold with a no-load format. Its annual expense ratio is a low 0.74 percent, as is its 26-percent portfolio turnover ratio.

Distributions: Income and capital gains are paid in May and December.

How to Buy and Sell: Minimum initial investment $500; IRA $500; subsequent investments $100.

OAKMARK FUND

Harris Associates, L.P.
2 North LaSalle Street
Chicago, IL 60602
800-625-6275

Inception: *1991*
Total Assets: *$4.0 Billion*
Ticker Symbol: *OAKMX*
Home Page: *None*

Objective and Strategy: This highly successful fund seeks capital appreciation and, to a small degree, investment income by investing in reasonably priced mid- and large-cap companies. This fund began selling shares during the stock market's revival in August 1991, but that doesn't account for all of its success. During the last five years, the fund has returned an average of 28 percent a year, which places it on the top rungs of the mutual fund performance ladder. Portfolio manager Robert Sanborn will only purchase a company's stock if it is selling at a significant discount to its intrinsic value. He also prefers to invest in companies whose managers have a large ownership stake. Once he sets his sights on a company, he's not shy about taking a position. In fact, his ten largest holdings account for about half of the portfolio's assets. He also gives his stocks time to reach their potential, turning over the portfolio about once every four years.

Portfolio Manager: Robert J. Sanborn since the fund's inception in 1991. Previously, he managed individual portfolios at Harris Associates. He has an M.B.A. from the University of Chicago.

Suitability: This well-managed fund is suitable for both conservative and more aggressive growth-seeking investors. Conservative investors, however, may wish to limit their allocation to this fund to 10 percent of portfolio assets.

Portfolio Implications: This is a relatively compact portfolio, given its large asset base. In addition, assets tend to be concentrated in a handful of stocks, which means that the fund will either sink or swim. But it has performed swimmingly since its inception. Couple this fund with another growth fund or two for maximum diversification benefits.

Risk: Despite its exceptional returns, the fund possesses a below-market beta (0.89). This relatively young fund has yet to experience a major bear market.

Costs: This fund sports reasonable costs. Its shares are sold with a no-load format. Its 1.40-percent annual expense ratio is about average for the group, but its portfolio turnover ratio (18 percent) is one of the lowest around.

Distributions: Income and capital gains are distributed in December.

How to Buy and Sell: Minimum initial investment $2,500; IRA $1,000; subsequent investments $100. Telephone exchange with other Oakmark funds.

Annualized Returns

1-Year 15.5%
3-Year 18.0%
5-Year 28.0%

OPPENHEIMER MAIN STREET INVESTORS GROWTH

*Oppenheimer Fund Management
   Corporation
3410 South Galena Street
Denver, CO 80231
800-525-7048*

*Inception: 1988
Total Assets: $3.2 Billion
Ticker Symbol: OPPSX
Home Page: None*

Objective and Strategy: This unique fund seeks a high total return by investing in a combination of stocks, convertible bonds, and straight debt securities. The unique feature of the fund is that its common stock portion is invested across a wide spectrum of companies including small-, mid-, and large-cap issues. While seeking the high growth potential offered by investment in smaller company stocks, management seeks to temper risk by investing not only in bonds, but in large-cap stocks that currently pay cash dividends. Because of the high growth prospects of its smaller company investments, we have chosen to include this fund in the growth fund category rather than the growth and income category. The fund's strategy has paid off handsomely for shareholders, who have garnered a better than 23-percent average annual return during the last five years.

**Annualized
Returns**

1-Year 14.1%
3-Year 14.4%
5-Year 23.5%

Portfolio Manager: Robert J. Milnamow since 1995. Previously, he served as a portfolio manager with the Phoenix Securities Group.

Suitability: This uniquely managed fund is suitable for both conservative and more aggressive growth-seeking investors.

Portfolio Implications: You are likely to find almost anything in this fund's portfolio. Recently, it contained both small- and large-company stocks, foreign stocks and bonds, investment-grade and lower-rate corporate bonds, and a few convertible securities. It can be considered a balanced investment program for investors who want the diversification that this fund provides.

Risk: Although it invests in relatively small growth stocks, the fund's bond investments have muted its risk. Its beta is a modest 0.92, and its share price declined by a modest 13 percent during the 1990 bear market.

Costs: The fund's class A shares are sold with a hefty 5.75-percent front-end load and an ongoing 0.24-percent 12b-1 fee. Its annual expense ratio is a below-average 1.07 percent, but its portfolio turnover ratio (101 percent) is above average.

Distributions: Income is paid in March, June, September, and December, and capital gains are distributed in December.

How to Buy and Sell: Class B shares (contingent deferred sales charge) and class C shares (available to institutional investors) are also available. Minimum initial investment $1,000; IRA $250; subsequent investments $25. Fund imposes a 1-percent redemption fee for shares held less than eighteen months.

PUTNAM VISTA CLASS A

Putnam Mutual Funds
One Post Office Square
Boston, MA 02109
800-225-1581

Inception: 1967
Total Assets: $1.3 Billion
Ticker Symbol: PVISX
Home Page: http://
www.putnaminv.com

Objective and Strategy: This fund pursues its capital appreciation objective by investing in companies that management believes are undervalued. Management stresses investment in companies that sell at a discount to their underlying growth rates and/or asset values. The fund's portfolio is packed with the stocks of mid-cap companies whose market value is between $399 million and $5 billion. These dynamic, innovative, and expanding companies may be among tomorrow's corporate leaders. Jennifer Silver took over the helm in 1991 and has improved the fund's performance considerably over the last few years, allowing this fund to maintain a five-year return that beats that of most of its competitors. Furthermore, the fund ranks 20th out of 156 growth funds for its ten-year performance.

Annualized Returns
1-Year 27.0%
3-Year 18.9%
5-Year 19.7%

Portfolio Manager: Jennifer K. Silver since 1991, C. Kim Goodwin since 1996, and Anthony C. Santosus since 1994. Silver joined Putnam in 1981 and Santosus in 1985.

Suitability: Because of its emphasis on smaller companies, this fund is suitable for more aggressive growth-seeking investors.

Portfolio Implications: Historically, the fund's portfolio has contained the stocks of about one hundred companies. Occasionally, you will find a handful drawn from the large-cap stock universe. Recently, these companies included Safety Kleen, Circus Circus, Dow Jones and Company, Office Depot, and Safeway.

Risk: Despite its emphasis on smaller, rapidly growing companies, this fund's portfolio contains only modestly above-average risk (beta 1.10). Its share price tumbled 17 percent during the 1990 bear market.

Costs: Detracting from this well-managed fund is its hefty 5.75-percent front-end load and ongoing 0.25-percent 12b-1 fee. Its expense ratio is below average (1.07 percent), but its 115-percent portfolio turnover ratio is on the high side.

Distributions: Both income and capital gains distributions are paid annually.

How to Buy and Sell: Class B shares (higher 12b-1 fee and contingent deferred sales charge) and class M (available to institutional investors) are also available. Minimum initial investment $500; IRA $500; subsequent investments $50.

SIT GROWTH

SIT Investment Associates, Inc.
4600 Norwest Center
Minneapolis, MN 55402
800-332-5580

Inception: 1982
Total Assets: $356 Million
Ticker Symbol: NBNGX
Home Page: http://
www.sitfunds.com

Objective and Strategy: One of eleven well-managed funds in the SIT fund family, this fund seeks maximum capital appreciation by investing primarily in the common stocks of small and medium-sized emerging growth companies before they become well recognized. The fund is capable of producing exceptional short-term returns as witnessed by its 44-percent return in 1985 and 66-percent return in 1991. Management seeks the stocks of companies which offer improved growth possibilities because of rejuvenated management, changes in product, or some other development that might stimulate earnings growth. To qualify for investment by the fund, a company must demonstrate long-term reasonable earnings growth. The fund may also invest up to 20 percent of its net assets in foreign corporate equity securities.

Portfolio Manager: Eugene C. Sit since the fund's inception in 1982 and Erik S. Anderson since 1990.

Suitability: Because of its emphasis on smaller, growth companies, this fund's shares are suitable for more aggressive growth-seeking investors.

**Annualized
Returns**

1-Year 19.2%

3-Year 17.4%

5-Year 14.6%

Portfolio Implications: The portfolio contains significant industry concentration. Recently, more than 80 percent of its assets were invested in stocks drawn from four industries: technology, health care, financial services, and business equipment.

Risk: The fund possess moderate risk. Its beta is 1.09, and the fund's share price declined by a hefty 18.6 percent during the 1990 bear market.

Costs: This is a cost-efficient fund. Its shares are sold with a no-load format. Its annual expense ratio is a low 0.83 percent, and its portfolio turnover ratio is slightly below average (75 percent).

Distributions: Both income and capital gains are distributed annually.

How to Buy and Sell: Minimum initial investment $2,000; no initial minimum IRA investment; subsequent investments $100. Telephone exchange with other SIT funds. Shares may also be obtained without transaction fees through Charles Schwab and Company.

SCUDDER LARGE COMPANY VALUE

Scudder Investor Services
175 Federal Street
Boston, MA 02110
800-225-2470

Inception: 1956
Total Assets: $1.6 Billion
Ticker Symbol: SCDUX
Home Page: http://
www.scudder.com

Objective and Strategy: This fund seeks to maximize long-term capital growth through a broad and flexible investment program. The fund may pursue companies that generate or apply new technologies, own or develop natural resources, benefit from changing consumer demands, are based in foreign countries with more growth than in the United States, may benefit from earnings growth projected at a pace well in excess of the average growth company, or are currently out of favor with investors because their earnings are temporarily depressed. Even though management focuses on "out of favor companies," there are many household names in its portfolio, including Philip Morris, Anheuser-Busch, Exxon, Chase Manhattan Corporation, and Dow Chemical. It has been an excellent performer during the last ten years.

Annualized Returns

1-Year 15.9%
3-Year 10.4%
5-Year 12.9%

Portfolio Manager: Kathleen T. Millard, portfolio manager since 1995, joined Scudder in 1991. Lois R. Friedman, portfolio manager since 1995, joined Scudder in 1990.

Suitability: This fund is for investors who are willing to accept above-average risk in exchange for the potential of above-average capital growth.

Portfolio Implications: The four largest investment sectors include financial services, consumer staples, manufacturing, and energy. The fund's portfolio is typical of that of a growth/value player and may result in duplication with other well-managed growth funds.

Risk: The fund sports a market beta (1.01), but contains significant short-run share price volatility as witnessed by its near 25-percent decline during the 1990 bear market.

Costs: This fund's shares are sold with a no-load format; its annual expense ratio is a modest 0.98 percent, but its portfolio turnover ratio is a hefty 154 percent.

Distributions: Both income and capital gains are distributed annually in December.

How to Buy and Sell: Minimum initial investment $1,000; IRA $500; subsequent investments $50. Telephone exchange with other Scudder funds. Shares may also be obtained without transaction costs through Charles Schwab and Company.

SCUDDER QUALITY GROWTH

Scudder Investor Services
175 Federal Street
Boston, MA 02110
800-225-2470

Inception: *1991*
Total Assets: *$220 Million*
Ticker Symbol: *SCQGX*
Home Page: *http://*
www.scudder.com

Objective and Strategy: The fund seeks long-term growth of capital by investing in the stocks of seasoned, financially strong medium- to large-sized growth companies located in the United States. Scudder targets companies that are recognized leaders in value-added businesses. These companies have demonstrated above-average long-term earnings growth, high levels of profitability, solid capital structures, and managements that are committed to the companies' shareholders. Stocks are sold when there is a deterioration in the quality or growth potential of a company, when the company is extremely overvalued, or when it fails to perform as expected. Management's recent strategy has been to maintain significant weightings in consumer staples, health care, and technology stocks and to focus on identifying companies that are not only market leaders but also have global franchises.

Portfolio Manager: Valerie F. Malter since joining Scudder in 1995, Bruce F. Beaty since the fund's inception, and Michael K. Shields since joining Scudder in 1992.

Suitability: Investment in this fund is suitable for both conservative and more aggressive growth-seeking investors. However, conservative investors should limit alloca-

Annualized Returns
1-Year 19.6%
3-Year 15.1%
5-Year 13.2%

tions to this fund to no more than 10 percent of portfolio assets.

Portfolio Implications: The fund has double-digit percentage weightings to consumer staples, health care, manufacturing, technology, and consumer discretionary spending sectors. Its household names include Philip Morris, General Electric, Procter & Gamble, PepsiCo, Merck, Johnson & Johnson, and Eli Lilly.

Risk: The fund's portfolio exhibits slightly above-average market risk (beta 1.08). This relatively young fund has yet to experience a major bear market. However, its share price will most likely decline by a greater percentage than the S&P 500 Index during a sharp stock market sell-off.

Costs: This is a modest-cost fund. Its shares are sold with a no-load format. Its annual expense ratio is a modest 1.17 percent, but its portfolio turnover ratio (97 percent) is above average.

Distributions: Both income and capital gains distributions are paid annually in December.

How to Buy and Sell: Minimum initial investment $1,000; IRA $500; subsequent investments $50. Telephone exchange with other Scudder funds.

SCUDDER VALUE

Scudder Investor Services
175 Federal Street
Boston, MA 02110
800-225-2470

Inception: 1992
Total Assets: $85 Million
Ticker Symbol: SCVAX
Home Page: http://
www.scudder.com

Objective and Strategy: This fund seeks capital appreciation through investment in equity securities that are believed to be undervalued in relation to current and estimated future earnings and dividends. Since its inception in December 1992, the fund has provided a 14.5-percent average annual return utilizing a computer model and combining systematic valuation techniques with intensive, traditional fundamental research. The model relies on Scudder's independent equity research effort for estimates of future earnings and dividend growth and proprietary quality ratings. Management's recent strategy has been to overweight financial service stocks, to underweight the health and consumer staples sectors, and to maintain a price-earnings discount to the market of at least 20 percent.

Annualized Returns
1-Year 17.2%
3-Year 13.9%
5-Year NA

Portfolio Manager: Donald E. Hall since the fund's inception in 1992. Hall joined Scudder in 1982. William J. Wallach joined Scudder in 1988 and has been portfolio manager of Value since 1992.

Suitability: This fund is suitable for investors who seek a value component to their portfolios, which may include both conservative and more aggressive investors.

Portfolio Implications: The fund can serve as a core component of an investment program that includes money market, bond, and specialized equity investments. Since growth portfolios generally do not move in tandem, the addition of this fund can lower overall portfolio risk.

Risk: Despite investments in mid-cap companies, this fund sports a modest 0.83 beta. This relatively young fund has yet to experience a major bear market.

Costs: The fund's shares are sold with a no-load format. Its 1.25-percent annual expense ratio is slightly below average, and its 98-percent portfolio turnover ratio is slightly above average.

Distributions: Both income and capital gains distributions are paid annually in December.

How to Buy and Sell: Minimum initial investment $1,000; IRA $500; subsequent investments $50. Telephone exchange with other Scudder funds.

SEVEN SEAS MATRIX EQUITY

The Seven Seas Series Funds
Two International Place, 35th Floor
Boston, MA 02110
617-654-6089

Inception: 1992
Total Assets: $255 Million
Ticker Symbol: SSNTX
Home Page: None

Objective and Strategy: This unique fund employs a sophisticated ranking system in the pursuit of returns that exceed those of the S&P 500 Index over long periods of time. Stocks are ranked by two uncorrelated measures: value and the momentum of Wall Street sentiment. The value measure compares a company's assets, projected earnings growth, and cash flow with its stock price. The Wall Street sentiment measure examines changes in Wall Street analysts' earnings estimates and ranks stocks by the strength and consistency of those changes. These two measures are combined to create a composite score of each stock's attractiveness. These scores are then plotted on a matrix according to their relative attractiveness. Sector weights are maintained at a similar level to that of the S&P 500 Index.

Annualized Returns
1-Year 16.2%
3-Year 13.5%
5-Year NA

Portfolio Manager: Douglas Holmes since the fund's inception in 1992. Holmes has been with State Street since 1984 and has managed State Street's matrix portfolios for the past seven years.

Suitability: This unique fund is suitable for both conservative and more aggressive growth-seeking investors.

Portfolio Implications: The fund's portfolio provides a way to own a portfolio with similar characteristics to the Standard & Poor's 500 Index but also gives investors an opportunity to outperform the Index over

time. The beauty is that if the model fails to perform as expected, the portfolio will still provide results similar to those of the S&P 500 Index, less operating costs.

Risk: Not too surprising is the fact that this fund's portfolio has a risk level about equal to that of the S&P 500 Index (beta 0.95). This relatively young fund has yet to experience a major bear market. However, its portfolio can be expected to decline in value at about the same percentage as the S&P 500 Index during a severe market sell-off.

Costs: The fund's shares are sold without either a front-end or a back-end sales fee but sport a modest 0.08-percent ongoing 12b-1 fee. Its 0.68-percent annual expense ratio is far below average, but its portfolio turnover ratio is an above-average 130 percent.

Distributions: Income is paid quarterly and capital gains are distributed annually in December.

How to Buy and Sell: Minimum initial investment $1,000; IRA $1,000; no subsequent minimum investment requirement. Telephone exchange with other Seven Seas funds. Shares may be obtained without transaction fees from Jack White and Company and Charles Schwab (institutional investors only).

STEIN ROE GROWTH STOCK

Stein Roe & Farnham
P.O. Box 804058
Chicago, IL 60680
800–338–2550

Inception: 1958
Total Assets: $408 Million
Ticker Symbol: SRFSX
Home Page: http://
www.steinroe.com

Objective and Strategy: This fund seeks long-term capital appreciation by investing in common stocks believed to possess long-term appreciation possibilities. Management emphasizes stocks they believe are quality growth companies with exceptional earnings growth, superior returns on investment, and above-average stability. Says portfolio manager Erik Gustafson, "We're bottom-up investors. We look for companies that fit specific criteria—including earnings growth and return on equity of at least 15 percent per year. We are owners of companies, not traders of paper. We want to own what we believe are the 50 best businesses we can find." These "best" firms include such names as Home Depot, General Electric, Coca-Cola, Johnson & Johnson, Gillette, Microsoft, Procter & Gamble, and Travelers Group.

Annualized Returns
1-Year 21.0%
3-Year 16.6%
5-Year 13.7%

Portfolio Manager: Erik P. Gustafson since 1994. He also manages the Young Investor Fund. He holds an M.B.A. and Juris Doctor degree from Florida State University.

Suitability: Everyone should have this fund's stocks in his or her portfolios. Thus, the fund is recommended for conservative as well as aggressive growth-seeking inves-

tors. Given the high quality of its investments, this is one fund you want to buy and hold.

Portfolio Implications: The portfolio is stuffed with the who's who of corporate America. You will probably find plenty of duplication with your other quality growth funds, but what the heck.

Risk: This growth fund possesses moderate risk with a beta of 1.08. Its share price declined about the same as the overall market (15.6 percent) during the 1990 bear market.

Costs: This fund sports quite reasonable fees. Its shares are sold with a no-load format. Annual operating expense ratio is a low 0.40 percent, but its recent portfolio turnover ratio (114 percent) is relatively high.

Distributions: Both income and capital gains distributions are paid annually in October.

How to Buy and Sell: Minimum initial investment $2,500; IRA $500; subsequent investments $100. Telephone exchange with other Stein Roe funds. Shares may also be obtained without transaction fees from Charles Schwab and Jack White and Company.

STEIN ROE SPECIAL

Stein Roe & Farnham
P.O. Box 804058
Chicago, IL 60680
800–338–2550

Inception: 1968
Total Assets: $1.1 Billion
Ticker Symbol: SRSPX
Home Page: http://
www.steinroe.com

Objective and Strategy: The Special fund seeks to achieve capital appreciation by investing in equity securities that are considered to have limited downside risk relative to their potential for above-average growth, including securities of undervalued, underfollowed, or out-of-favor companies. Management will go anywhere to find growth with value. It attempts to identify seasoned, established companies, as well as small and new companies, believed to exhibit quality management, strong balance sheets, and a competitive edge that will sustain above-average return on investment over the long run. Its affinity for these types of companies has resulted in Harley Davidson being the fund's largest single investment. Portfolio assets are invested in about sixty stocks that are equally distributed among companies with market caps less than $1 billion, market caps between $1 and $5 billion, and those over $5 billion.

Annualized Returns
1-Year 17.9%
3-Year 11.3%
5-Year 13.8%

Portfolio Manager: E. Bruce Dunn and Richard B. Peterson since 1991. They also have been managing the Special Venture fund since its inception in 1994. Both joined Stein Roe in the mid-1960s.

Suitability: The fund is suitable for both conservative and more aggressive growth-seeking investors. However, more conserva-tive investors should limit their allocations to this fund to no more than 10 percent of portfolio assets.

Portfolio Implications: Mid- and small-cap stocks account for about two-thirds of portfolio assets. About 75 percent of the fund's assets are invested in four industry sectors: consumer cyclicals, industrial, financial services, and consumer noncyclicals.

Risk: This fund sports a below-market beta (0.82). However, its share price tumbled 19 percent during the 1990 bear market.

Costs: This fund sports reasonable costs. Its shares are sold with a no-load format. Its 1.11-percent annual expense ratio is below average, but its 96-percent portfolio turnover ratio is above the average for the growth fund group.

Distributions: Both income and capital gains distributions are paid annually in December.

How to Buy and Sell: Minimum initial investment $2,500; IRA $500; subsequent investments $100. Telephone exchange with other Stein Roe funds. Shares may also be obtained without transaction fees through Charles Schwab, Fidelity Brokerage, and Jack White and Company.

STEIN ROE YOUNG INVESTORS

Stein Roe & Farnham
P.O. Box 804058
Chicago, IL 60680
800-338-2550

Inception: 1994
Total Assets: $257 Million
Ticker Symbol: SYRIX
Home Page: http://
www.steinroe.com

Objective and Strategy: Although this fund did not pass our three years in existence requirement, I just couldn't resist including this superb growth fund in this year's edition. If you want to feel like a kid again, this is the fund for you. It invests a substantial portion of its assets in companies that affect the lives of children or teenagers. Through its use of entertaining and educational communications, the fund creates a fun investing experience for young investors and their parents. However, you don't have to be young to take advantage of this growth-oriented fund. Management uses a bottom-up research strategy, seeking growth companies with dominant positions in their respective domestic markets. Their stock list reads like a who's who of fun companies: Nike, Disney, Wrigley, PetSmart, and McDonalds to name a few. Although it may seem like fun and games, the returns they have posted since inception are quite serious.

Portfolio Manager: Erik P. Gustafson since 1995, Dave Brady since 1995, and Art McQueen since 1996.

Suitability: If you want to get your children started out on the right financial foot, con-

sider making an initial investment for them in this fund and urge them to continue making periodic investments.

Portfolio Implications: This portfolio is packed with financially solid growth companies that should continue to prosper well into the twenty-first century.

Risk: This growth fund has modestly high risk. Its beta is an above-market 1.10. This relatively young fund has yet to experience a severe bear market.

Costs: This fund has reasonable costs. Its shares are sold with a no-load format. Its annual expense ratio is a modest 1.25 percent, and its 55-percent portfolio turnover ratio is below average.

Distributions: Both income and capital gains distributions are paid in October.

How to Buy and Sell: Minimum initial investment $2,500 (I wish it were lower); IRA $500; subsequent investment $100. Telephone exchange with other Stein Roe funds. Shares may also be obtained without transaction fees through Charles Schwab and Jack White and Company.

Annualized Returns

1-Year 40.3%

Inception (April 1994) 31.2%

STRATTON GROWTH FUND

Stratton Management Company
610 West German Town Pike, Suite 300
Plymouth Meeting, PA 19462-1050
800-634-5726

Inception: 1972
Total Assets: $42 Million
Ticker Symbol: STRGX
Home Page: None

Objective and Strategy: Stratton Growth pursues its primary objective of capital growth and secondary objective of current income through a conservative discipline that stresses both value and yield. Management invests the bulk of the fund's assets in common stocks that sell at low price-earnings multiples and pay above-market dividend yields and in high-yielding convertible bonds. Traditional yield sectors, such as energy, utilities, financial services, and industrial cyclicals, typically claim the bulk of the fund's assets. As a result, the fund is typically sensitive to interest rate movements. Although it is vulnerable to share price declines during periods of rising interest rates, it has produced competitive long-term results with moderate risk. Another plus: Jim Stratton has logged nearly a quarter century at the helm.

Portfolio Manager: James W. Stratton since the fund's inception in 1972.

Suitability: This moderate-risk growth vehicle is suitable for conservative growth-seeking investors.

Annualized Returns

1-Year 16.4%
3-Year 15.8%
5-Year 14.4%

Portfolio Implications: Combine this fund with a small- or mid-cap fund and one that invests in established, large companies and you will have a balanced equity fund portfolio.

Risk: The fund sports a modest 0.81 beta. Its shares are interest rate sensitive, but they declined by a very modest 10 percent during the severe 1990 bear market.

Costs: This fund possesses reasonable costs. Its shares are sold with a no-load format. Its 1.31-percent annual expense ratio is right at the group average, and its 43-percent portfolio turnover ratio is well below average.

Distributions: Both income and capital gains are distributed semiannually.

How to Buy and Sell: Minimum initial investment $2,000; IRA $2,000; subsequent investments $100. Telephone exchange with other Stratton funds.

STRONG OPPORTUNITY

Strong Funds
P.O. Box 2936
Milwaukee, WI 53201
800–368–3863

Inception: 1985
Total Assets: $1.7 Billion
Ticker Symbol: SOPFX
Home Page: http://
www.strong-funds.com

Objective and Strategy: This fund seeks capital growth by investing in the stocks of mid-cap companies. Stocks are selected under the umbrella of the following philosophy: Underfollowed stocks with low institutional ownership and low analyst coverage tend to be undervalued; small and mid-sized companies have historically outperformed larger-capitalization stocks and are often underfollowed; out-of-favor "quiet" sectors of the market tend to be undervalued; a company's stock price is likely to be more volatile than its underlying private market value. This philosophy has led management to produce market-topping returns during its ten-year existence, returning an annual average of 15.5 percent during that period. Its portfolio turnover ratio has been high historically due to management's willingness to invest in bonds and cash when it believes the market is overvalued.

Portfolio Manager: Richard T. Weiss since 1991. He also manages the Common Stock fund. Prior to joining Strong in 1991, Weiss was a portfolio manager with Stein Roe. He holds an M.B.A. from Harvard. He is assisted by Marina T. Carlson.

Suitability: Despite its below-market beta, the fund's emphasis on mid-cap companies

makes its shares suitable for more aggressive growth-seeking investors.

Portfolio Implications: Combine this fund with a contrarian fund and a large-cap vehicle for best results.

Risk: Although its portfolio is dominated by mid-cap growth stocks, it sports a modest 0.89 beta. Its share price declined by less than that of the market (14 percent) during the severe 1990 bear market.

Annualized Returns

1-Year 13.1%
3-Year 13.5%
5-Year 16.4%

Costs: This fund sports reasonable costs. Its shares are sold with a no-load format. Its 1.30-percent annual expense ratio is right at the group average. However, its 93-percent annual portfolio turnover ratio is above average.

Distributions: Both income and capital gains are distributed annually.

How to Buy and Sell: Minimum initial investment $1,000; IRA $250; subsequent investments $50. Telephone exchange with other Strong funds. Shares may also be obtained without transaction fees through Charles Schwab, Fidelity Brokerage, and Jack White and Company.

STRONG SCHAEFER VALUE

Strong Funds
P.O. Box 2936
Milwaukee, WI 53201
800-368-3863

Inception: 1985
Total Assets: $333 Million
Ticker Symbol: SCHVX
Home Page: http://
www.strong-funds.com

Objective and Strategy: This well-managed fund formed an alliance with the Strong family in January 1996. It continues to be managed by David Schaefer, using the same value-oriented, bottom-up investment approach it has used since the fund's inception in 1985. It continues to seek long-term capital appreciation with income as a secondary objective. Schaefer emphasizes simplicity and discipline in managing the portfolio. Each holding in the portfolio is approximately equally weighted, which keeps the manager's natural enthusiasm in check. In addition, the fund generally stays fully invested at all times. And when an attractive, new opportunity is found, Schaefer typically won't buy it unless he can use it to replace a less attractively valued stock. Because of his buy-and-hold strategy, portfolio turnover is very low.

Portfolio Manager: David K. Schaefer since the fund's inception in 1985. In 1981, Schaefer left INCO Ltd. to found Schaefer Capital Management.

Suitability: This superbly managed fund is suitable for conservative growth-oriented investors.

Annualized Returns

1-Year 13.0%
3-Year 14.2%
5-Year 18.0%

Portfolio Implications: The fund's portfolio is relatively compact with the stocks of about forty companies being represented. Because of its bottom-up approach to stock selection, the fund is seldom heavily invested in any one industry sector.

Risk: The fund sports a near-market beta (0.95). However, its share price plunged nearly 21 percent during the 1990 bear market, partly due to its full investment philosophy.

Costs: This is a cost-efficient fund. Its shares are sold with a no-load format; its 1.28-percent annual expense ratio is slightly below average, and its 33-percent portfolio turnover ratio is well below average.

Distributions: Income and capital gains are distributed annually.

How to Buy and Sell: Minimum initial investment $2,500; IRA $250; subsequent investments $50. Telephone exchange with other Strong funds. Shares may also be obtained without transaction fees through Charles Schwab and Fidelity Brokerage.

TOCQUEVILLE FUND

Tocqueville Asset Management
1675 Broadway
New York, NY 10019
212-698-0800

Inception: *1987*
Total Assets: *$43 Million*
Ticker Symbol: *TOCQX*
Home Page: *None*

Objective and Strategy: The fund's objective is long-term capital appreciation through investments in the common stocks of domestic companies. The fund has been alternately classified as a growth fund, a balanced fund, and a contrarian fund, depending on which media you read, but it is in fact a value fund. It invests in common stocks of companies whose securities represent outstanding, yet unrecognized value. To be considered attractive, a potential investment must be undervalued intrinsically, not merely relative to the market. These are companies with good finances, strong managements, and low stock prices relative to earnings, cash flow, or underlying assets. Because management is quite choosy, the fund tends to be invested in the stocks of about forty companies. The fund tends to perform reasonably well during up markets but saves considerable ground during down markets. As a result, its returns over a normal market cycle climb the rungs of the mutual fund performance ladder.

Annualized Returns

1-Year 13.9%
3-Year 15.2%
5-Year 16.4%

Portfolio Manager: The fund was established by Francois Sicart in 1987. Robert W. Kleinschmidt joined Tocqueville in 1991 and became president in 1994.

Suitability: This is an excellent fund for conservative growth-seeking investors.

Portfolio Implications: If you own this fund during a strong up market, you are not going to make as much money as with an earnings momentum fund. If you own this stock during a sharp market sell-off, you are going to lose money, albeit not as much as with the typical growth fund. However, if you hold the fund's shares during both up and down markets, you will earn enviable returns.

Risk: This is a low-risk growth vehicle. The fund's portfolio sports a 0.80 beta, and its share price declined by a very modest 8.8 percent during the severe 1990 bear market.

Costs: This is an average-cost fund. Its class A shares are sold with a 4.0-percent front-end load and an ongoing 0.25-percent 12b-1 fee. Its annual expense ratio is 1.54 percent, and its portfolio turnover ratio is 47 percent.

Distributions: Both income and capital gains are distributed annually.

How to Buy and Sell: Minimum initial investment $5,000; IRA $2,000; subsequent investments $1,000. Telephone exchange with other Tocqueville funds. Shares may be obtained through Jack White and Company.

T. ROWE PRICE BLUE CHIP GROWTH

T. Rowe Price Investment Services
100 East Pratt Street
Baltimore, MD 21202
800–225–5132

Inception: 1993
Total Assets: $223 Million
Ticker Symbol: TRBCX
Home Page: http://
www.troweprice.com

Objective and Strategy: This fund seeks growth of capital by investing what management believes are blue-chip stocks. In general, these are the stocks of large- and mid-cap companies with strong market franchises in industries that appear to be strategically poised for long-term growth. They are companies that have leading market positions that are expected to be maintained or enhanced over time. They have seasoned management teams with a track record of providing superior financial results. Specifically, these are companies that demonstrate faster earnings growth than their competitors and the market in general, they possess high profit margins relative to competitors, they have strong cash flow, a healthy balance sheet with relatively low debt, and a high return on equity with a comparatively low dividend payout ratio.

Annualized Returns
1-Year 25.3%
3-Year 20.1%
5-Year NA

Portfolio Manager: Larry J. Puglia has been chairman of the fund's investment committee since 1996. He joined T. Rowe Price in 1990 and has been managing investments since 1993.

Suitability: The fund is suitable for both conservative and more aggressive growth-seeking investors.

Portfolio Implications: Blue-chip stocks are what this fund promises, and it delivers on that promise. Its recent portfolio contained household names such as Chase Manhattan, Citicorp, American Express, AT&T, Coca-Cola, Sara Lee, Merck, Colgate-Palmolive, Home Depot, Intel, and IBM, just to name a few. The fund could provide duplication with other quality growth fund portfolios.

Risk: The fund's beta is a below-market 0.90. However, its growth stock strategy could result in significant short-term share price volatility. This relatively young fund has yet to experience a severe bear market.

Costs: Like most T. Rowe Price equity offerings, this is a cost-efficient fund. Its shares are sold with a no-load format. Its annual expense ratio is 1.25 percent, and its portfolio turnover ratio is a low 38 percent.

Distributions: Income and capital gains distributions are paid annually in December.

How to Buy and Sell: Minimum initial investment $2,500; IRA $1,000; subsequent investments $100. Telephone exchange with other Price funds. However, be aware that the company frowns on frequent switching.

T. ROWE PRICE CAPITAL APPRECIATION

T. Rowe Price Investment Services
100 East Pratt Street
Baltimore, MD 21202
800–225–5132

Inception: 1986
Total Assets: $906 Million
Ticker Symbol: PRWCX
Home Page: http://
www.troweprice.com

Objective and Strategy: This fund's goal is to provide long-term capital growth by investing primarily in common stocks, although it has the ability to invest in fixed-income securities as well. In general, it seeks common stocks believed to be undervalued in relation to various measures, such as assets or earnings. Specifically, it seeks the stocks of companies with above-average current dividend yield relative to the average yield of the S&P 500 Index, low price-earnings ratios relative to that Index, and low stock price relative to a company's underlying value measured by assets, earnings, cash flow, or business franchises. The fund differs from other growth vehicles in that its manager seeks to reduce risk. As a result, the fund may have a larger cash position at times than other funds, and its portfolio may include a significant investment in fixed-income securities when the risk-reward ratio becomes favorable relative to common stocks. The approach has worked exceptionally well, and this fund has one of the lowest risk-reward ratios in the growth fund category.

Portfolio Manager: Richard P. Howard has been chairman of the fund's investment committee since 1989. He joined T. Rowe Price in 1982.

Annualized Returns

1-Year 14.0%
3-Year 13.9%
5-Year 13.0%

Suitability: This fund is quite suitable for conservative investors. At times the portfolio will generate above-average current income.

Portfolio Implications: Sometimes this fund looks like an asset allocation fund with investments in stocks, bonds, and cash equivalents. Thus, its risk tends to be quite modest and current income relatively high. It may not be suitable for very aggressive investors who prefer capital gains over current dividend income.

Risk: With its mix of stocks, convertibles, and bonds, this is a low-risk growth vehicle. Its beta is a low 0.55, and its share price declined by a modest 13.7 percent during the 1990 bear market.

Costs: Like most T. Rowe Price equity offerings, this is a cost-efficient fund. Its shares are sold with a no-load format. Its annual expense ratio is a modest 0.97 percent, and its portfolio turnover ratio is a low 47 percent.

Distributions: Both income and capital gains distributions are paid in December.

How to Buy and Sell: Minimum initial investment $2,500; IRA $1,000; subsequent investments $100. Telephone exchange with other Price funds. However, be aware that the company frowns on frequent switching.

T. ROWE PRICE GROWTH STOCK

T. Rowe Price Investment
Services
100 East Pratt Street
Baltimore, MD 21202
800-225-5132

Inception: 1950
Total Assets: $3.1 Billion
Ticker Symbol: PRGFX
Home Page: http://
www.troweprice.com

Objective and Strategy: The original T. Rowe Price growth vehicle, this fund has been seeking capital appreciation by investing in the common stocks of large companies for nearly half a century. Management bases its investments on the belief that when a company's earnings outpace inflation and the general economy, eventually the market will reward success with higher prices for the stock. Most of the fund's companies show average growth in earnings and high profitability ratios. Management's desire to keep risk moderate, however, prevents it from paying high multiples. Consequently, the fund tends to overweight out-of-favor growth industries. Recently, its largest sector investments were in financial services, consumer nondurables, consumer services, business services, and capital equipment.

Annualized Returns

1-Year 18.6%
3-Year 16.8%
5-Year 15.4%

Portfolio Manager: John D. Gillespie has been the chairman of the fund's investment committee since 1994. He joined T. Rowe Price in 1986 and has managed investments since 1989.

Suitability: The fund's shares are suitable for both conservative and more aggressive long-term investors. The fund is appropriate for use in both regular and tax-deferred accounts such as IRAs.

Portfolio Implications: Because of its growing asset base, this fund invests in a few hundred reasonably priced growth stocks. Because of rising valuation multiples in the United States, the fund has increasingly raised its allocation to the stocks of companies domiciled outside the Unites States.

Risk: This is an average-risk growth fund. Its beta is 0.91, and its share price declined slightly less than 18 percent during the severe 1990 bear market.

Costs: Like most T. Rowe Price equity offerings, this is a cost-efficient fund. Its shares are sold with a no-load format. Its annual expense ratio is a low 0.80 percent, and its portfolio turnover ratio is a low 43 percent.

Distributions: Both income and capital gains are distributed annually in December.

How to Buy and Sell: Minimum initial investment $2,500; IRA $1,000; subsequent investments $100. Telephone exchange with other T. Rowe Price funds. However, be aware that the company frowns on frequent switching.

T. ROWE PRICE NEW AMERICA GROWTH

T. Rowe Price Investment Services
100 East Pratt Street
Baltimore, MD 21202
800–225–5132

Inception: 1985
Total Assets: $1.4 Billion
Ticker Symbol: PRWAX
Home Page: http://
www.troweprice.com

Objective and Strategy: This fund invests primarily in common stocks of service companies. It is designed for investors seeking aggressive long-term growth of capital and, secondarily, current income. The fund's investment program is based on the belief that growth in the service sector of the economy will outpace overall economic growth. Generally, the majority of the fund's assets will be in common stocks of companies deriving most of their revenues directly from service-related activities such as financial services, media, and information processing. Investments range from small, rapidly growing companies to larger blue-chip firms. This is one of the more aggressive Price equity funds. Its companies are growing at a 19-percent annual clip, have reported a 17-percent average return on equity, and are selling at slightly more than twenty-one times next year's estimated earnings.

Portfolio Manager: John H. Laporte has been chairman of the fund's investment committee since 1988. He joined Price in 1976 and has been managing investments since 1984.

Suitability: Because of its emphasis on rapidly growing companies and its willingness to pay higher price-earnings multiples to obtain stocks of those companies, the fund's shares are suitable for more aggressive growth-seeking investors.

Portfolio Implications: Although this is not a sector fund, its investments are concentrated in one type of business: services. Thus, the portfolio will not represent a complete investment program and should be coupled with other equity funds to produce portfolio balance.

Risk: This is one of the higher-risk growth fund offerings, with a beta of 1.12. Furthermore, its share price tumbled more than 25 percent during the 1990 bear market.

Costs: Like most T. Rowe Price equity offerings, this is a cost-efficient fund. Its shares are sold with a no-load format. Its annual expense ratio is a below-average 1.07 percent, as is its 56-percent portfolio turnover ratio.

Distributions: Both income and capital gains are distributed annually in December.

How to Buy and Sell: Minimum initial investment $2,500; IRA $1,000; subsequent investments $100. Telephone exchange with other Price funds. However, be aware that the company frowns on frequent switching.

Annualized Returns

1-Year 23.0%
3-Year 17.5%
5-Year 17.5%

T. ROWE PRICE NEW ERA

T. Rowe Price Investment Services
100 East Pratt Street
Baltimore, MD 21202
800-225-5132

Inception: *1969*
Total Assets: *$1.3 Billion*
Ticker Symbol: *PRNEX*
Home Page: *http://*
www.troweprice.com

Objective and Strategy: This fund seeks long-term growth of capital, but because of its investment focus on natural resource stocks, it also provides some current income. With nearly 82 percent of fund assets in natural resource companies, this fund provides a significant hedge against inflation. Even if another bout of inflation is not in the offing, the fund should perform well as long as the U.S. economy continues to expand. Energy stocks (oil exploration and development and energy services) now account for more than 20 percent of portfolio assets, and gold-mining stocks account for an additional 15 percent. Although its gold stock investments did not pay off in 1996, its energy stocks soared. The result was another banner year for a fund that experiences few down years and plenty of good upside performances.

Portfolio Manager: George A. Roche has been chairman of the fund's investment committee since 1988. He joined Price in 1968 and began working with the New Era fund the following year.

Suitability: I can't think of a single investor who wouldn't want to own a least a few shares of this well-managed fund.

Annualized Returns

1-Year 20.3%
3-Year 15.6%
5-Year 11.8%

Portfolio Implications: Aggressive growth investors will like the long-term performance of this fund. Conservative investors will appreciate the current dividends this fund pays while chalking up long-term capital gains. Even fixed-income investors will benefit from the fund's inflation offset.

Risk: With a portfolio packed with natural resource stocks, there is probably more risk here than meets the eye. Even so, its portfolio beta is a very low 0.52, and the fund's share price declined by a modest 14 percent during the severe 1990 bear market.

Costs: Like most T. Rowe Price equity funds, this is a very cost-efficient vehicle. Its shares are sold with a no-load format. Its 0.79-percent annual expense ratio is well below average, as is its 23-percent portfolio turnover ratio.

Distributions: Both income and capital gains distributions are paid annually in December.

How to Buy and Sell: Minimum initial investment $2,500; IRA $1,000; subsequent investments $100. Telephone exchange with other T. Rowe Price funds. However, be aware that the company frowns on frequent switching.

T. ROWE PRICE SPECTRUM GROWTH

T. Rowe Price Investment Services
100 East Pratt Street
Baltimore, MD 21202
800-225-5132

Inception: 1990
Total Assets: $1.8 Billion
Ticker Symbol: PRSGX
Home Page: http://
www.troweprice.com

Objective and Strategy: This recent addition to the Price family of funds invests in other T. Rowe Price funds to achieve long-term growth with income being a secondary consideration. (Its sibling seeks a high degree of current income by applying a similar investment strategy.) This all-weather vehicle may invest in domestic and international stock funds in the Price family plus money market funds. This fund offers wide diversification for the equity portion of one's portfolio and utilizes the superior management of T. Rowe Price. Recently, the fund held investments in the following Price funds: Equity-Income, Growth and Income, Growth Stock, New Era, International Stock, and New Horizons. Although relatively new to Price, this "fund of funds" should offer a fine risk-reward profile, and it has delivered respectable returns during its first five years in operation.

Portfolio Manager: Peter Van Dyke has been chairman of the fund's investment committee since its inception in 1990. He joined T. Rowe Price in 1985.

Suitability: This fund is suitable for new mutual fund investors who seek capital appreciation.

Annualized Returns

1-Year 19.6%
3-Year 16.9%
5-Year 14.5%

Portfolio Implications: If you are a growth-seeking investor and can invest in only one fund, this is the one. It offers a high degree of diversification across five Price growth funds. Additionally, it provides a way to invest a portion of your capital in New Horizons, which is closed to new investors.

Risk: Given its wide-diversification, this is a very modest-risk growth vehicle. Its beta is a modest 0.89. Although this young fund has yet to experience severe market turbulence, it should weather the storm quite well.

Costs: Shares are sold with a no-load format. The fund levies no additional fees. Investors assume the fees of the funds in which it invests. The weighted average of the underlying fund expense ratios is 0.79 percent.

Distributions: Income and capital gains are distributed annually.

How to Buy and Sell: Minimum initial investment $2,500; IRA $1,000; subsequent investments $100. Remember, when you invest in this fund, you are obtaining shares in six other equity funds. Thus this is an ideal starter fund for new investors or those beginning to fund an IRA.

USAA GROWTH

USAA Investment Management
Company
9800 Fredericksburg Road
San Antonio, TX 78288
800-531-8181

Inception: 1971
Total Assets: $1.2 Billion
Ticker Symbol: USAAX
Home Page: None

Objective and Strategy: This fund seeks growth of capital primarily by investing in common stocks of large, established companies. Secondary goals include the pursuit of current income and conservation of capital. An avowed contrarian investor, portfolio manager David Parsons becomes depressed when everyone else is happy. When investors become gloomy, Parsons perks up. He says, "When I go into an industry, people think I'm pretty stupid. I buy out-of-favor stocks, but I also want to know what can go right." When the prices of his favorite stocks go down, he is prone to buying more shares. He only sells when a company approaches bankruptcy or moves too far afield of its core business. Marching to a different drummer has served the shareholders of this "quiet" fund exceptionally well. Not only does the fund tend to perform reasonably well during bull markets, it cuts investor losses sharply during bear markets.

Portfolio Manager: David G. Parsons since 1994. He joined USAA in 1984 and has held various positions in equity investments. He received an M.B.A. from the University of Texas.

Annualized Returns

1-Year 14.9%
3-Year 14.0%
5-Year 13.8%

Suitability: This well-run fund is suitable for both highly conservative and more aggressive growth-seeking investors.

Portfolio Implications: If rummaging through flea markets in search of hidden treasures is your bag, this is the fund for you. Its investments are true out-of-favor companies that have performed remarkably well for shareholders over long periods of time.

Risk: True to its value style, this is a modest-risk fund. Its beta is a modest 0.85, and its share price declined a very modest 11 percent during the severe 1990 bear market.

Costs: This is a cost-efficient fund. Its shares are sold with a no-load format. Its 1.04-percent annual expense ratio is below-average, as is its 69-percent portfolio turnover ratio.

Distributions: Both income and capital gains are distributed annually in July.

How to Buy and Sell: Minimum initial investment $3,000; IRA $250; subsequent investments $50. Telephone exchange with other USAA funds.

VALUE LINE FUND

Value Line Securities
220 East 42nd Street
New York, NY 10017
800-223-0818

Inception: *1950*
Total Assets: *$376 Million*
Ticker Symbol: *VLIFX*
Home Page: *None*

Objective and Strategy: This fund seeks long-term growth of capital with income as a secondary objective. When selecting common stocks, management relies on the Value Line Timeliness Ranking System, which has evolved after many years of research and has been used in substantially its present form since 1965. It is based upon historical prices and reported earnings, recent earnings and price momentum, and the degree to which the last reported earnings deviated from estimated earnings. The Timeliness Rankings are published weekly in the Standard Edition of the Value Line Investment Survey for approximately 1,700 stocks. Stocks are ranked from one (most timely) to five (least timely) and compare the adviser's estimate of the probable market performance of each stock during the coming twelve months relative to all 1,700 stocks under review. The fund usually invests in the common stocks of the companies ranked either number one or two, but at times may invest in those ranked three.

Portfolio Manager: Mike Romanowsky since joining Value Line in October 1995. Previously, he was employed by Conning and Company and Monarch Capital. He received an M.B.A. from the University of Massachusetts.

Annualized Returns

1-Year 23.3%
3-Year 13.6%
5-Year 14.6%

Suitability: This fund's shares are suitable for modestly aggressive and highly aggressive growth-seeking investors.

Portfolio Implications: If you have ever been tempted to buy stocks according to the Value Line Ranking System but didn't possess sufficient capital to build a diversified portfolio of the companies ranked high for Timeliness, this fund provides the way to obtain those stocks with a very reasonable investment requirement.

Risk: The risk of this fund is typical of most growth vehicles. Its beta is 1.08, and its share price declined by an average 15.8 percent during the 1990 bear market.

Costs: This is a cost-efficient growth fund. Its shares are sold with a no-load format. Its 0.83-percent annual expense ratio is well below average, and its 78-percent portfolio turnover ratio is right at the group average.

Distributions: Income is paid in March, June, September, and December, and capital gains are distributed in December.

How to Buy and Sell: Minimum initial investment $1,000; IRA $1,000; subsequent investments $100. Shares may also be obtained through Jack White and Company without transaction fees.

WASATCH GROWTH

68 South Main Street
Salt Lake City, UT 84101
800–551–1700

Inception: *1986*
Total Assets: *$118 Million*
Ticker Symbol: *WGROX*
Home Page: *None*

Objective and Strategy: This fund seeks long-term growth of capital through investments in a diversified portfolio of reasonably valued stocks with superior growth potential. However, the fund's managers have shown an affinity for value stocks and tend to avoid the stocks of rapidly growing companies that command valuation multiples well above those of the market. This philosophy led management to avoid high-flying technology stocks during the last couple of years. The fund's largest holdings include a nursing home operator, a funeral home operator, and a dental lab. Says its portfolio managers, "We may not own the more recognizable names, but we do own the companies we believe in for the long term." The selection strategy is to find very stable companies with stable demand for their products. As a result, the fund performs reasonably well in both up and down markets.

Portfolio Manager: Samuel S. Stewart, Jr., Ph.D. and Jeff Cardon since the fund's inception in 1986. Dr. Stewart founded the Wasatch funds in 1975. Mr. Cardon joined the firm in 1990.

Annualized Returns
1-Year 12.4%
3-Year 17.7%
5-Year 14.1%

Suitability: This fund is suitable for conservative investors who can hold their shares over a complete stock market cycle.

Portfolio Implications: Most of the investments in this fund are unique. Thus, there is little possibility of overlap with your other growth fund holdings. If you want to broaden your stock holding base, consider adding this fund to your portfolio.

Risk: This is a modest-risk growth fund. Its beta is 0.86. Its share price declined by 16 percent during the 1990 bear market, but it finished the year with a 10-percent return.

Costs: This is a reasonable-cost fund. Its shares are sold with a no-load format. Its annual expense ratio is 1.50 percent, and its portfolio turnover ratio is 88 percent.

Distributions: Both income and capital gains distributions are paid annually in December.

How to Buy and Sell: Minimum initial investment $2,000; IRA $1,000; no subsequent minimum investment requirement. Telephone exchange with other Wasatch funds. Shares may also be obtained without transaction fees through Charles Schwab, Fidelity Brokerage, and Jack White and Company.

WILLIAM BLAIR GROWTH

William Blair & Company
135 South LaSalle Street
Chicago, IL 60603
800-742-7272

Inception: 1946
Total Assets: $514 Million
Ticker Symbol: WBGSX
Home Page: http://
www.wmblair.com

Objective and Strategy: This fund seeks capital appreciation by investing in companies that have demonstrated the ability to grow more rapidly than the U.S. economy from one business cycle to the next. Specifically, management seeks companies that are leaders in their field, possess a unique feature, produce quality products, have superior sales and service organizations, have maintained a high return on equity, and apply conservative accounting policies. The fund invests in large-, medium-, and small-cap stocks. Barber focuses on larger companies (market values above $1 billion) while Fuller concentrates on smaller firms. During their three-year tenure as comanagers, the fund has returned an enviable 19 percent per year. With low portfolio turnover and low expenses, the fund is one of the more efficient growth funds around.

Portfolio Manager: James (Rocky) Barber and Mark Fuller III. Barber joined Blair in 1986 after leaving Alliance Capital Management. Fuller, who joined Blair in 1983, was previously employed by IBM.

Annualized Returns
1-Year 17.9%
3-Year 12.1%
5-Year 10.8%

Suitability: This fund is suitable for both conservative and more aggressive growth-seeking investors.

Portfolio Implications: This fund is an excellent vehicle to use as the core of a long-term retirement program or for use in a child's education savings plan. You get a diverse group of growth companies selling at reasonable prices.

Risk: This fund sports a market beta (1.00), and its share price declined by slightly less than 17 percent during the 1990 bear market.

Costs: This is a cost-efficient fund. It is one of the few brokerage house–sponsored funds to sell its shares with a no-load format. Its expense ratio is 1.48 percent, and its portfolio turnover ratio is a very low 32 percent.

Distributions: Both income and capital gains distributions are paid annually.

How to Buy and Sell: Minimum initial investment $5,000; IRA $2,000; subsequent investments $1,000. Shares may also be obtained without transaction fees through Charles Schwab and Jack White and Company.

YACKTMAN FUND

The Yacktman Fund
303 West Madison Street
Chicago, IL 60606
800–525–8258

Inception: 1992
Total Assets: $608 Million
Ticker Symbol: YACKX
Home Page: None

Objective and Strategy: This fund seeks capital appreciation, although its emphasis on well-established companies selling at reasonable valuations produces a steady stream of dividend income as well. This fund is one of the more tame growth funds around. With a below-market price-earnings multiple and a 2.5-percent dividend yield, the portfolio reflects a strict value discipline. As is usually the case, the fund's portfolio is compact (less than thirty-five issues) and is packed with large-cap stocks. Portfolio cash has been building in recent months because Mr. Yacktman, the fund's portfolio manager, has admitted that he has had trouble finding stocks with suitable valuations. However, his penchant for buying high return on asset companies with reasonably priced stocks has led him into such value plays as Toys R Us, Reebok, and United Asset Management. After leaving Selected American Shares, which he piloted to the best ten-year record of any growth fund, he founded his namesake fund in 1992 and has never looked back.

Portfolio Manager: Donald A. Yacktman since the fund's inception in 1992. Previously, he managed Selected American Shares for ten years and spent fourteen years with Stein Roe and Farnham.

Annualized Returns

1-Year 19.0%
3-Year 20.2%
5-Year NA

Suitability: This fund's compact, value-based portfolio is suitable for both conservative and modestly aggressive investors.

Portfolio Implications: This fund's portfolio is rather compact. Thus, investors should combine investment in this fund with another fund or two to obtain required diversification. The fund fits well with either small-cap or mid-cap growth funds.

Risk: Because the fund will hold large cash balances at times, risk tends to be quite low. Its beta is 0.68. This young fund has yet to experience a severe bear market. However, its blue-chip stocks should hold up quite well during a prolonged bear market.

Costs: This is a very cost-efficient fund. Its shares are sold without either a front-end or a back-end load, but shareholders assume a modest 0.08-percent ongoing 12b-1 fee. Its annual expense ratio is a modest 0.99 percent, and its portfolio turnover ratio is a modest 55 percent.

Distributions: Income is paid quarterly and capital gains are distributed annually.

How to Buy and Sell: Minimum initial investment $2,500; IRA $500; subsequent investments $100. Shares may also be obtained without transaction fees through Charles Schwab and Fidelity Brokerage.

CHAPTER

THIRTY-NINE

Growth and Income Funds

Growth and income funds seek a high level of current income, some capital appreciation, and preservation of capital. This category includes balanced funds and equity-income funds.

Balanced funds (generally referred to as *total return funds* these days) invest in a portfolio of common stocks and bonds. The allocation may be either fixed by investment policy or may vary depending on which category of assets is expected to produce the greatest total return. Some balanced funds may invest in convertible bonds and preferred stocks. On average, balanced fund portfolios contain 60 percent common stocks and 40 percent bonds and convertible securities. Given the split allocation between common stocks and bonds, balanced funds tend to possess relatively low betas. While they provide some protection during periods of declining stock prices, they are highly sensitive to interest rate fluctuations, and their share prices can decline by significant amounts during periods of rising interest rates.

Equity-income funds invest primarily in common stocks that have higher dividend yields than the dividend yield of the Standard & Poor's 500 Index. In addition to higher-than-average dividend yields, the common stocks held by these funds tend to have relatively low betas, lower-than-average price-earnings (P-E) ratios, and relatively low price-to-book value ratios. As a consequence, the share prices of these funds fall less than the overall stock market in a decline. However, they usually rise less during bull markets as well.

Growth and income funds are suitable for conservative investors who are not willing to assume the full risk associated with the stock market. You can find a number of funds in this group whose portfolio managers follow a value stock selection strategy. Thus, their portfolios tend to be packed with common stocks with lower-than-average price-earnings and price-to-book value ratios. These funds also make suitable candidates for the portfolios of income-oriented investors because of their generous dividend yields. Furthermore, because these funds include common stocks in their portfolios, they offer a degree of capital appreciation and, thus, an offset against rising consumer prices. In other words, these funds offer income investors a degree of inflation protection that is not present in a pure fixed-income fund.

On average, growth and income funds possess about two-thirds to three-fourths the volatility of the market as a whole. And as you would expect, these funds have returned less than the S&P 500 Index over the past ten years.

AARP GROWTH & INCOME

160 Federal Street
Boston, MA 02110
800-322-2282

Inception: 1984
Total Assets: $3.9 Billion
Ticker Symbol: AGIFX
Home Page: http://
www.scudder.com

Objective and Strategy: This member of the AARP family seeks capital growth, current income, and growth of income as its investment objectives. The fund is managed by Scudder, Stevens and Clark, which was established in 1919 and is America's oldest independent investment counsel firm for individual investors. The fund invests in common stocks, securities convertible into common stocks, and preferred stocks. The fund emphasizes securities of companies that offer the opportunity for capital growth and growth of earnings while providing dividends. Its investments are spread across a variety of industries. However, like many income-oriented equity funds, it has established significant investments in financial stocks (banks, insurance companies, and real estate). Most of its common stock investments are in companies with household names.

Annualized Returns

1-Year 20.2%
3-Year 16.1%
5-Year 15.8%

Portfolio Manager: Robert I. Hoffman since 1991. Mr. Hoffman joined Scudder (the fund's subadviser) in 1990. He is assisted by Benjamin Thorndike, Kathleen Millard, and Lori Ensinger.

Suitability: The fund is suitable for investors who are seeking long-term growth of assets to keep ahead of inflation. Investors should invest for three years or more and be comfortable with some fluctuation in principal.

Portfolio Implications: This equity-income fund share price is impacted by changes in interest rates as well as general trends in the stock market. Adding a 30-percent allocation to this fund in a bond fund portfolio will provide a significant inflation offset. Coupling investment in this fund with a small gold fund allocation will reduce portfolio volatility.

Risk: The fund possesses a below-market beta (0.91). However, its share price can decline by a significant amount if interest rates rise dramatically. Its share price declined by slightly more than 11 percent during the 1990 bear market.

Costs: This is a very low-cost fund. Its shares are sold with a no-load format. Its 0.70-percent expense ratio is well below average as is its 30-percent portfolio turnover rate.

Distributions: Dividend income is distributed quarterly, and capital gains are distributed annually in December.

How to Buy and Sell: Shares available to AARP members only. Minimum initial investment $500; IRA $250; no subsequent minimum investment requirement. Telephone exchange with other AARP offerings.

ADDISON CAPITAL SHARES

Addison Capital Shares, Inc.
c/o Janney Montgomery Scott, Inc.
2 Bala Cynwyd Plaza
Bala Cynwyd, PA 19004
800–526–6397

Inception: 1986
Total Assets: $51 Million
Ticker Symbol: ADCSX
Home Page: None

Objective and Strategy: This value-oriented fund seeks long-term growth of capital by concentrating on out-of-favor stocks. It is one of a handful of funds that border the growth and income and growth categories. Its primary goal is growth of capital, but out-of-favor stocks tend to possess dividend yields greater than the S&P 500 Index, thereby giving the fund a growth and income flavor. Addison seeks stocks of companies which are attractively priced within their economic sector yet exhibit improving earnings per share and favorable market price momentum. The bulk of its assets are allocated across nine broad industry sectors and are concentrated in mid-cap and large-cap issues. The fund's shares are distributed by Janney Montgomery Scott.

Portfolio Manager: Team managed by Radcliffe Cheston (1986), Fred W. Thomas (1989), and James V. Kelly (1990).

Suitability: This fund should appeal to investors who seek long-term capital growth with some current income. It is ideally suited for conservative, growth-oriented investors.

Portfolio Implications: Out-of-favor companies can stay out of favor for long periods. Thus, this fund can experience long

Annualized Returns

1-Year 19.5%

3-Year 14.3%

5-Year 14.0%

periods of under- and overperformance. Investors who require a high level of current income from their investments should couple investment in this fund with bond funds or more generous income-paying growth and income funds.

Risk: This fund's portfolio sports a below-market beta (0.90), which indicates about 10 percent less risk than the stock market as a whole. Its share price declined by slightly more than 15 percent during the 1990 bear market.

Costs: Although sold without a front-end or back-end sales charge, shareholders assume a 0.40-percent ongoing 12b-1 fee, which balloons its expense ratio to a higher-than-average 2.06 percent. However, its portfolio turnover ratio is a modest 43 percent.

Distributions: Both income and capital gains distributions are paid semiannually in June and December.

How to Buy and Sell: Minimum initial investment $1,000; IRA $1,000; subsequent investments $50. The fund has no telephone exchange or automatic investment plans. It also discourages the actions of market timers.

AMERICAN BALANCED FUND

American Funds Distributors
Four Embarcadero Center
P.O. Box 7650
San Francisco, CA 94120
800-421-9900

Inception: 1933
Total Assets: $3.5 Billion
Ticker Symbol: ABALX
Home Page: None

Objective and Strategy: By investing in both stocks and bonds, this fund strives to meet three investment objectives: conservation of capital, current income, and long-term growth of capital and income. The fund is managed as though it constitutes a complete long-term investment program of a prudent investor. Management does not seek short-run trading profits, and changes in the fund's investments are generally gradual, as witnessed by its modest portfolio turnover ratio. Incorporated in 1932 (and a member of the American Funds Group since 1975), it is one of the oldest funds available to the public today. The fund's track record, coupled with a modest risk level, makes this fund a candidate for conservative growth and income investors. However, potential investors should note the 5.75-percent front-end sales load and the ongoing 12b-1 fee.

Portfolio Manager: Team managed by George A. Miller (1966), Abner D. Goldstine (1975), Robert G. O'Donnell (1986), and Eric S. Richter (1995).

Suitability: Given the fund's mixture of stocks, bonds, and cash, the fund is designed as a complete investment program for conservative investors. The fund is not suitable for more aggressive investors.

Annualized Returns
1-Year 13.4%
3-Year 11.6%
5-Year 12.2%

Portfolio Implications: Like most balanced funds that include both stocks and bonds in their portfolios, this fund will duplicate the holdings of investors who make their own asset allocation decisions. Its bond investments generally account for 30 to 40 percent of portfolio assets.

Risk: Despite its hefty investment in bonds, the fund's beta is a relatively high 0.87. During the severe 1990 bear market, this fund's share price declined by a modest 10 percent. However, its shares can be sensitive to changes in interest rates.

Costs: This fund's annual operating costs are quite low. Its 0.67-percent annual expense ratio (including 12b-1 fee) is very low, and its 39-percent portfolio turnover ratio is well below average. However, you must pay a hefty 5.75-percent front-end load to get aboard.

Distributions: Income distributions are paid quarterly in February, May, August, and December. Capital gains distributions are paid annually in December.

How to Buy and Sell: Minimum initial investment $500; IRA $100; subsequent investments $50. Class A shares carry a front-end load. Telephone exchange with twenty-seven other American funds. Sales charges reduced for large purchases.

AMERICAN CENTURY BALANCED

Twentieth Century Investors
4500 Main Street
P.O. Box 418210
Kansas City, MO 64111
800-345-2021

Inception: 1988
Total Assets: $846 Million
Ticker Symbol: TWBIX
Home Page: http://
www.americancentury.com

Objective and Strategy: A far cry from the typical balanced vehicle, this fund bears all the earmarks of the potent, earnings-momentum style that characterizes most Twentieth Century offerings. Rapid, high-growth stocks dominate the portfolio, with the balance being held in bonds and other fixed-income securities. Although a generally sizable bond position tempers some of this fund's share price volatility, the fund isn't for the risk wary. Moreover, investors who attempt to buy and sell shares at key intervals are likely to get badly whipsawed. Although returns have been muted in recent years, long-term investors have fared well given the fund's 12-percent average annual return since its inception in October 1988.

Portfolio Manager: Charles M. Duboc since 1993, Nancy B. Prial since 1994, and Norman E. Hoops since 1989. Duboc and Prial specialize in the equity portion and Hoops manages the income portion of the fund's portfolio.

Suitability: The fund is suitable for risk-tolerant investors with the discipline to buy and hold. The fund is definitely not for the timid.

Portfolio Implications: Twentieth Century is known for its earning momentum,

Annualized Returns

1-Year 11.4%

3-Year 9.5%

5-Year 9.1%

growth company stock selection philosophy. You get that here, but limited volatility due to a hefty bond allocation. The fund could be considered a complete investment program for conservative investors.

Risk: The fund's beta (0.96) is relatively high for a fund that invests in both stocks and bonds. However, during the 1990 bear market the fund's share price declined by a very modest 9.7 percent.

Costs: This fund sports a very reasonable cost. Its shares are sold with a no-load format, its annual expense ratio is fixed at 1.00 percent, and its portfolio turnover ratio is an average 85 percent.

Distributions: Both net investment income and capital gains are distributed annually, usually in December.

How to Buy and Sell: Minuimum initial investment $2,500 ($50 if you establish a monthly investment program); no minumum IRA or subsequent investment requirement. Telephone exchange with other Twentieth Century/Benham funds. Shares may also be obtained through Charles Schwab without transaction fees.

AMERICAN CENTURY INCOME & GROWTH

The Benham Group
1665 Charleston Road
Mountain View, CA 94043
800-321-8321

Inception: 1990
Total Assets: $537 Million
Ticker Symbol: BIGRX
Home Page: http://
www.americancentury.com

Objective and Strategy: This is one of the best growth and income vehicles around. Stock selection begins with a list of the 1,400 largest companies whose shares are traded in the United States. A proprietary quantitative model is then employed to locate stocks that possess four characteristics: low valuations relative to the S&P 500 Index, attractive growth potential, a high degree of correlation with the S&P 500 Index, and higher-than-average dividend yields. Although the model tends to produce a portfolio heavily laden with utility, energy, financial, and industrial cyclical stocks, the portfolio may include significant allocations to health care and technology stocks when valuations are reasonable. The fund may invest up to 35 percent of its assets in bonds. However, during the fund's six-year operating history it has been nearly fully invested in equities.

Annualized Returns

1-Year 20.6%
3-Year 15.4%
5-Year 15.4%

Portfolio Manager: Steve Colton since the fund's inception in December 1990. He joined Benham in 1987 and has also managed the Utilities Index fund since its inception in March 1993.

Suitability: This is one of the few funds whose shares are suitable for both conservative and aggressive growth-oriented investors.

Portfolio Implications: The fund performs best in a falling or stable interest rate environment. Because of large allocations to utility, financial, and energy stocks, its share price is highly interest rate sensitive. Can be combined with a bond fund to form a complete investment program.

Risk: This relatively young fund has yet to experience a major bear market. In fact, it began selling shares at the market's bottom in 1990. Given its recent returns, portfolio risk may be a bit higher than indicated by its below-market beta (0.91).

Costs: This is a very low-cost fund. Its shares are sold with a no-load format and its annual expense ratio (0.69) is well below those of other actively managed equity funds. Its 70-percent portfolio turnover ratio is also slightly below average.

Distributions: Income is distributed monthly, and capital gains are distributed annually in December.

How to Buy and Sell: Minimum initial investment $1,000; IRA $1,000; subsequent investments $100. Telephone exchange with other Benham/Twentieth Century funds. Shares may also be obtained with no transaction fees from Charles Schwab and Jack White and Company.

BARTLETT BASIC VALUE

Bartlett & Company
36 East Fourth Street
Cincinnati, OH 45202-3896
800-800-3609

Inception: 1983
Total Assets: $127 Million
Ticker Symbol: MBBVX
Home Page: http://
www.leggmason.com

Objective and Strategy: Although there are many "value" funds around these days, this one is true to its colors. As a company, Bartlett embraced a value strategy based on the teachings of Benjamin Graham in the mid-1970s. Portfolio manager Jim Miller's approach to value investing is not to have a portfolio with less than a market multiple, but to own a diverse group of stocks of good companies that have been acquired at reasonable prices. Jim says there's a world of difference between cheapness and reasonableness. He concentrates his attention on companies with strong franchises that have joined the ranks of the fallen angles. He uses a strict bottom-up approach in searching for new additions and tries to avoid large sector bets. In addition, he tends to favor smaller companies.

Portfolio Manager: James A. Miller since 1990 and Woodrow H. Uible since 1993. They have been employed by Bartlett and Company since 1977 and 1980, respectively.

Suitability: The fund is ideally suited for conservative, patient, growth-oriented investors. Remember, it takes time for out-of-favor companies to return to favor.

Annualized Returns
1-Year 13.0%
3-Year 13.6%
5-Year 12.7%

Portfolio Implications: This is an equity-income portfolio and investors can expect a combination of both capital appreciation and current income. The fund holds a relatively large investment in the small-cap–dominated Royce Value Trust.

Risk: The fund sports a relatively low beta (0.77) for a diversified equity fund. However, its share price can be somewhat volatile during the short run as witnessed by its near 20-percent decline during the 1990 bear market.

Costs: This is a below-average cost fund. Its shares are sold with a no-load format. Its 1.20-percent annual expense ratio is a below average, as is its 26-percent portfolio turnover ratio.

Distributions: Income distributions are paid quarterly in May, July, October, and December, and capital gains are distributed annually, usually in late December.

How to Buy and Sell: Minimum initial investment $5,000; IRA $250; subsequent investments $100. Telephone exchange with other Bartlett funds. Shares may also be obtained without transaction fees from Jack White and Company.

BERGER GROWTH & INCOME

Berger Associates
P.O. Box 5005
Denver, CO 80217
800-333-1001

Inception: 1966
Total Assets: $324 Million
Ticker Symbol: BEOOX
Home Page: None

Objective and Strategy: Although this fund is called a growth and income fund, its primary objective is capital appreciation. A secondary goal is to provide some current income. However, during periods of low interest rates and security yields, the income portion of total return can be substantially reduced or even eliminated. In selecting securities, management places primary emphasis on those it believes offer favorable growth prospects. Common stocks of companies with mid-sized to large market capitalizations usually constitute the majority of the fund's investment portfolio. The fund also invests in senior securities such as convertible bonds, preferred stocks, and corporate bonds. For defensive purposes the fund may sell S&P futures contracts, as it has done recently.

Portfolio Manager: Rodney L. Linafelter since January 1990. Since joining Berger in 1990, he has also managed the Berger 100 Fund.

Suitability: The fund is suitable for conservative growth-seeking investors. Investors who demand a high level of current income should probably look elsewhere.

Portfolio Implications: Unlike most growth and income portfolios, this fund has at times allocated a significant portion of portfolio assets to technology and health care stocks.

Annualized Returns
1-Year 10.7%
3-Year 9.0%
5-Year 12.1%

This fund has a lower interest rate sensitivity than most growth and income vehicles.

Risk: The portfolio possesses a surprisingly modest beta (0.89), given its affinity for growth company stocks. Its ability and inclination to hedge the portfolio using S&P futures is most likely the cause of its relatively low volatility. The fund's share price declined by slightly less than 14 percent during the 1990 bear market.

Costs: This is an average-cost growth and income fund. Its shares are sold without either a front-end or a back-end load. Its expense ratio (1.62 percent) is slightly above average, most likely because it includes a 0.25-percent 12b-1 fee. Its 85-percent portfolio turnover ratio is about average for the group.

Distributions: Income (when earned) is distributed quarterly in March, June, September, and December. Capital gains are distributed annually in December.

How to Buy and Sell: Minimum initial investment $2,000 (recently raised from $500); IRA $500; subsequent investments $50. Telephone exchange with other Berger funds. Shares may also be obtained through Charles Schwab, Fidelity Brokerage, and Jack White without transaction fees.

CGM MUTUAL

Capital Growth Management
One International Place
Boston, MA 02110
800-345-4048

Inception: 1932
Total Assets: $1.2 Billion
Ticker Symbol: LOMMX
Home Page: http://
www.cgmfunds.com

Objective and Strategy: The fund has as its investment objective reasonable long-term capital appreciation with a prudent approach to protection of capital from undue risks. While consideration is given to current income in the selection of the fund's portfolio securities, it is not a controlling factor. The fund is "flexibly managed;" it sometimes will be more heavily invested in equity securities and at other times will be more heavily invested in debt of fixed-income securities, depending on portfolio manager Ken Heebner's view of the economic and investment outlook. Mr. Heebner's style is to make large bets on a few stocks. In fact, this portfolio is concentrated in fewer than two dozen stocks. Thus, annual portfolio returns tend to be either well above or well below the market averages. However, Mr. Heebner has build a solid reputation for being right far more often than being wrong.

Portfolio Manager: G. Kenneth Heebner since 1981. He is also portfolio manager for the Capital Development and Realty Fund. He says he will be at the helm until he dies.

Suitability: This is an aggressively managed growth and income vehicle. It is not suitable for highly conservative investors who prefer a combination of income and capital appreciation and below-market risk.

Annualized Returns

1-Year 11.0%
3-Year 7.2%
5-Year 11.5%

Portfolio Implications: This portfolio is quite compact. Frequently it contains less than two dozen stock issues with only two or three in a single industry. From time to time it invests in below investment grade bonds.

Risk: Its beta is well above average for a growth and income vehicle. However, if you know Ken Heebner's investment style, this should be no surprise. However, it is a surprise to find that the fund's share price declined by a very modest 9 percent during the 1990 bear market.

Costs: This is a very modest-cost fund. Its shares are sold with a no-load format. Its 0.91-percent expense ratio is below average. However, like most CGM offerings, its portfolio turnover ratio is a high 291 percent.

Distributions: Income is distributed quarterly, and capital gains are distributed annually in December.

How to Buy and Sell: Minimum initial investment $2,500; IRA $1,000; subsequent investments $50. Telephone exchange with Fixed Income, American Tax Free, New England Funds (money market funds), and CGM Realty Fund.

CLOVER CAPITAL EQUITY VALUE

680 East Swedesford Road
Wayne, PA 19087
800-932-7781

Inception: 1991
Total Assets: $76 Million
Ticker Symbol: CCEVX
Home Page: None

Objective and Strategy: This fund seeks high total return by employing a price-sensitive, analytical approach to equity investing known as "value investing." The search process begins by identifying attractively priced stocks that possess low price/cash flow, price-earnings, price-revenue and price-to-book value ratios. The price-earnings and price/cash flow ratios are then further refined by adjusting the earnings and cash flow margins to levels that should be attained under normal business conditions. The adviser also looks for companies that have the ability to generate significant excess cash flow beyond what is needed for maintenance of business capital spending. Quite often this search for value leads to out-of-favor, unglamourous industry groups. The stocks it eventually selects are generally characterized by low valuation and the expectation of business fundamentals. Historically, the portfolio has been quite compact with less than three dozen companies being represented.

Annualized Returns
1-Year 11.0%
3-Year 19.0%
5-Year NA

Portfolio Manager: Michael Jones since the fund's inception in 1991. Mr. Jones, age 41, is the founder of the fund's investment adviser. He is assisted by Paul W. Spindler.

Suitability: The fund is suitable for conservative, growth-oriented investors.

However, patience is required since out-of-favor stocks require time to show improving fundamentals.

Portfolio Implications: The fund invests in a very compact portfolio of value stocks. Thus, it should not be considered a complete investment program. It works well when combined with growth and small-cap funds.

Risk: This relatively new fund has yet to experience a major bear market. However, its affinity for the "unloved" and its low beta (0.64) indicate that its shares may not be as sensitive to a market sell-off as other growth and income funds.

Costs: This is a modest-cost fund. Its shares are sold with a no-load format. Its 1.10-percent annual expense ratio is well below average, and its 85-percent portfolio turnover ratio is right at the group average.

Distributions: Income is distributed quarterly and capital gains are distributed annually, usually in December.

How to Buy and Sell: Minimum initial investment $2,000 (recently reduced from $5,000); IRA $2,000; subsequent investments $100. Shares may also be obtained through Jack White and Company without transaction fees.

COLUMBIA BALANCED

Columbia Financial Center, Inc.
1301 South West Fifth Avenue
P.O. Box 1350
Portland, OR 97207-1350
800-547-1707

Inception: 1991
Total Assets: $574 Million
Ticker Symbol: CBALX
Home Page: None

Objective and Strategy: This fund, which began offering shares to the public on October 1, 1991, seeks to provide shareholders with a high total return by investing in common stocks and fixed-income securities. The adviser uses a top-down approach to determining appropriate weightings between common stocks and fixed-income securities, based on expected relative returns for those two classes of assets. Management does not attempt to time the markets, and changes between the asset classes normally are made gradually. Management usually allocates 35 to 65 percent of portfolio assets to common stocks with the balance invested in government and corporate bonds. At least 25 percent of assets are invested at all times in nonconvertible fixed-income securities. Its common stocks are usually those of larger companies that are well established. Many of these issues are those of companies with a history of paying level or rising dividends.

Portfolio Manager: Michael W. Powers since the fund's inception. He previously managed the Growth Fund and has been employed by Columbia since 1979. He obtained an M.B.A. from the University of California.

Suitability: The fund is designed as a complete investment program. It is suitable for conservative investors, especially those with limited resources who wish to allocate their assets to both stocks and bonds.

Portfolio Implications: Bonds and high yield common stocks make for a portfolio sensitive to interest rate fluctuations. The fund can invest up to one-third of its assets in companies located in foreign countries, although it has allocated a much smaller percentage of assets to these companies.

Annualized Returns

1-Year 12.6%
3-Year 10.5%
5-Year NA

Risk: Although its beta (0.84) is below that of the market, the fund's share price can be highly interest rate sensitive due to its large allocation to long-term bonds. This relatively young fund has yet to experience a severe bear market.

Costs: Like all Columbia offerings, this fund's shares are sold with a no-load format. Its 0.69-percent annual expense ratio is well below the group average. However, its 108-percent portfolio turnover ratio is above the norm.

Distributions: Income distributions are paid quarterly, and capital gains are paid in December.

How to Buy and Sell: Minimum initial investment $1,000; IRA $1,000; subsequent investments $100. Telephone exchange with other Columbia funds.

COLUMBIA COMMON STOCK

Columbia Financial Center, Inc.
1301 South West Fifth Avenue
P.O. Box 1350
Portland, OR 97207-1350
800-547-1707

Inception: 1991
Total Assets: $440 Million
Ticker Symbol: CMSTX
Home Page: None

Objective and Strategy: The objective of this fund, which began selling shares to the public in October 1991, is to provide growth of capital and dividend income. The fund invests primarily in larger companies that are well established. Many of these companies are expected to or have a history of paying level or rising dividends. The fund may invest up to one-third of its portfolio in common stocks issued by companies located in developed foreign countries located in Western Europe or Asia but historically has maintained a much smaller allocation to foreign stocks. Its portfolio tends to include from eighty to one hundred different stocks spread across nearly two dozen industry sectors. Recently, its largest sector holdings were banking and finance, consumer nondurables and consumer staples, health care, and technology.

Annualized Returns
1-Year 20.5%
3-Year 15.5%
5-Year NA

Portfolio Manager: Alan J. Folkman since 1996. He joined Columbia in 1975 and has served as portfolio manager of the Growth Fund and the Special Fund.

Suitability: The fund's shares are suitable for both aggressive growth and conservative growth investors.

Portfolio Implications: This fund's portfolio is packed with household-name companies and contains many of the stocks included in the Dow Jones Industrial Average. As a result, its portfolio's returns tend to correlate highly with the major stock market averages.

Risk: This relatively young fund has yet to experience a severe bear market. However, its affinity for established large-cap companies and its near-market beta (0.88) suggest that its share price will follow that of the market during a prolonged bear market.

Costs: This fund has very reasonable costs. Its shares are sold with a no-load format. Its 0.80-percent annual expense ratio is well below the group average. Its portfolio turnover ratio (75 percent) is slightly below average for a pure equity fund.

Distributions: Income distributions are paid quarterly, and capital gains are distributed annually in December.

How to Buy and Sell: Minimum initial investment $1,000; IRA $1,000; subsequent investments $100. Telephone exchange with other Columbia funds. Shares are also available through Charles Schwab without transaction fees.

CRABBE HUSON ASSET ALLOCATION

Crabbe Huson Funds
P.O. Box 8413
Boston, MA 02266-8413
800-638-3148

Inception: 1989
Total Assets: $145 Million
Ticker Symbol: CHAAX
Home Page: http://
www.contrarian.com

Objective and Strategy: This fund, which began operations in late January 1989, seeks long-term capital appreciation and a modest amount of income by investing in a combination of common stocks, fixed-income securities, and cash equivalents. The fund may invest as little as 20 percent or as much as 75 percent of its entire portfolio in common stocks. Since its inception, the fund has invested 45 to 55 percent of its net assets in fixed-income securities, 25 to 45 percent in common stocks, and 5 to 30 percent in cash equivalents. When selecting common stocks the adviser employs a basic value, contrarian approach that emphasizes income and balance sheet analysis and the relationship between the market price of a security and the adviser's opinion of its underlying value. Generally, this leads to investments in companies that are out of favor with the investment community.

Annualized Returns
1-Year 6.6%
3-Year 9.0%
5-Year 11.3%

Portfolio Manager: James E. Crabbe and Richard S. Huson since the fund's inception in 1989. Both Crabbe and Huson have served in various management positions since founding their advisory firm in 1980.

Suitability: Because of its allocation to fixed-income securities and cash equivalents, this fund is not recommended for growth-oriented investors. However, it represents a solid investment program for conservative investors seeking a combination of current income and capital growth.

Portfolio Implications: This fund will never beat the market during a strong bull market because of its allocations to bonds and cash. To garner this fund's full return potential you must hold its shares over an entire market cycle.

Risk: Because of its diversity, this is a low-risk fund. Its beta is a bit higher than expected (0.88), given that its share price declined by a very modest 7 percent during the severe 1990 bear market.

Costs: The fund's shares are sold without either a front-end or a back-end load. However, its 0.25-percent ongoing 12b-1 fee has increased its annual expense ratio to 1.48 percent, slightly above average for the group. Its portfolio turnover ratio (226 percent) is well above average for a growth and income fund.

Distributions: Income distributions are paid quarterly, and capital gains are paid in December.

How to Buy and Sell: Minimum initial investment $2,000; IRA $2,000; subsequent investments $500. Shares may also be obtained without transaction fees from Charles Schwab and Jack White and Company.

DODGE & COX BALANCED

Dodge & Cox Investment Managers
One Sansome Street
San Francisco, CA 94104
800-621-3979

Inception: 1931
Total Assets: $2.8 Billion
Ticker Symbol: DODBX
Home Page: None

Objective and Strategy: This is one of three funds in the Dodge & Cox family that, despite its phenomenal success, is one of the industry's best-kept secrets. The fund, which seeks a combination of growth and income, owns a mix of bonds and blue-chip stocks, and hasn't suffered a calender-year loss since 1981. Even in 1994, a horrible year for bonds, its portfolio eked out a 2-percent gain. The fund, which has been offering shares to the public since 1931, holds a portfolio containing a mix of about 60 percent stocks and 40 percent bonds. The bond portion of its portfolio is largely invested in mortgages and corporates with a duration of about five years. Its common stocks are those of well-established, large capitalization companies. If you were only allowed to invest in one fund, this fund would be an excellent choice.

Portfolio Manager: The fund's investments are managed by Dodge & Cox's Investment Policy Committee, and no one person is primarily responsible for making investment recommendations to the committee.

Suitability: If you are looking for a core fund for college savings, this fund is it. It is suitable for all modestly aggressive and con-

servative investors who desire a combination of income and capital growth.

Portfolio Implications: With a very conservative stock/bond mix, this fund's portfolio can be considered a complete investment program. If you are more aggressive, consider investing in this company's stock fund instead.

Risk: Despite its relatively high beta (0.97), this is a very low-risk fund. Its share price declined by a modest 10.6 percent during the 1990 bear market.

Costs: This is one of the lowest cost, actively managed funds around. Its shares are sold with a no-load format. Its annual expense ratio is a very low 0.57 percent, and its portfolio turnover ratio (20 percent) is one of the lowest you'll find in the growth and income category.

Distributions: Income is distributed quarterly, and capital gains are paid annually in December.

How to Buy and Sell: Minimum initial investment $2,500; IRA $1,000; subsequent investments $100. Telephone exchange with other Dodge & Cox funds. However, frequent switching is not tolerated.

Annualized Returns

1-Year 12.1%
3-Year 12.5%
5-Year 13.5%

DODGE & COX STOCK

Dodge & Cox Investment Managers
One Sansome Street
San Francisco, CA 94104
800-621-3979

Inception: 1965
Total Assets: $1.8 Billion
Ticker Symbol: DODGX
Home Page: None

Objective and Strategy: This is the most aggressively managed of the three funds offered by Dodge & Cox. However, its volatility is less than that of the overall market. The fund's objective is to provide long-term growth of principal with some income. Diversification in the types of common stocks held in the portfolio receives heavy emphasis. Individual securities are chosen based on their financial strength, underlying asset values, and prospective earnings and dividend growth. Moreover, management employs a long-term, buy-and-hold strategy, reflected in the fund's incredibly low portfolio turnover ratio. While other fund managers scurry in and out of "hot" stocks in an effort to boost performance, this fund's investment committee seeks the shares of financially sound, well-established companies and sticks around for the rewards they are capable of producing. You can't go wrong investing in this fund for the long term.

Annualized Returns

1-Year 16.5%
3-Year 16.8%
5-Year 16.4%

Portfolio Manager: The fund's investments are managed by Dodge & Cox's Investment Policy Committee, and no one person is primarily responsible for making investment recommendations to the committee.

Suitability: Aggressive or conservative, you probably will want to own some of this fund's shares. Its shares make an excellent

vehicle for funding a child's education or a retirement program.

Portfolio Implications: This is an actively managed fund, but you wouldn't know it by looking at its turnover ratio. If you want to own shares in some of America's largest and best run companies, this is the fund of choice.

Risk: With the fund's stellar returns, you'd expect risk to be high. However, its share price volatility is about equal to that of the market generally. Its beta is 0.97 and its share price tumbled slightly less than 19 percent during 1990 severe bear market.

Costs: Like the other two Dodge & Cox funds, the costs of investing here are very low. Its shares are sold with a no-load format. Its expense ratio is a very low 0.60 percent, and its portfolio turnover ratio (13 percent) rivals that of most index funds.

Distributions: Income is paid quarterly and capital gains are distributed annually in December.

How to Buy and Sell: Minimum initial investment $2,500; IRA $1,000; subsequent investments $100. Telephone exchange with other Dodge & Cox funds. However, frequent switching is not tolerated.

DREYFUS BALANCED

Dreyfus Balanced Fund, Inc.
200 Park Avenue
New York, NY 10166
800-645-6561

Inception: 1992
Total Assets: $279 Million
Ticker Symbol: DRBAX
Home Page: http://
www.dreyfus.com

Objective and Strategy: This fund seeks a combination of current income and capital appreciation by investing in a portfolio of both stocks and bonds. Although its long-term target allocations are 50 percent stocks and 50 percent bonds, management has wandered far from these targets during the fund's relatively young life. This is another one of the ho-hum balanced funds that offers a conservative asset mix. Although you can't expect a balanced portfolio to keep pace with a runaway stock market, you can expect this fund's portfolio to provide solid double-digit returns over the long run. The stock portion of its portfolio is relatively compact, but quite diverse, ranging from billion-dollar giants to small-cap stocks. Its fixed-income investments are high quality, with a large proportion of government issues being represented.

Annualized Returns
1-Year 6.7%
3-Year 11.7%
5-Year NA

Portfolio: Timothy M. Ghriskey since March 1996. Prior to joining Dreyfus in July 1995, Ghriskey was a managing partner of Loomis, Sayles and Company.

Suitability: The fund is suitable for conservative investors who are seeking a complete investment program in a single fund. However, aggressive investors should look elsewhere, because the fund's significant investment in bonds will mute long-term returns.

Portfolio Implications: With a hefty fixed-income allocation this fund's share price will be heavily influenced by changes in interest rates. In addition, management has a great deal of latitude in changing the fund's composition, which could cause returns to suffer if a large bet on either stocks or bonds fails to pay off.

Risk: As you might expect, this is a modest-risk fund with a beta of 0.73. It is a relatively young fund and has yet to experience a severe bear market. However, its bond investments can be expected to shore up its value during a bear market set off by an unexpected economic recession.

Costs: This is a modest-cost fund. Its shares are sold with a no-load format. Its 1.04-percent annual expense ratio is well below the group average. Its portfolio turnover ratio has ballooned at bit (160 percent) due to recent changes in the fund's ratio of stocks to bonds.

Distributions: Income distributions are paid quarterly and capital gains are distributed in December.

How to Buy and Sell: Minimum initial investment $2,500; IRA $750; no minimum subsequent investment requirement. Telephone exchange with other Dreyfus funds. Shares are also available without transaction fees from Charles Schwab and Jack White and Company.

DREYFUS GROWTH & INCOME

Dreyfus Growth & Income Fund
200 Park Avenue
New York, NY 10166
800-645-6561

Inception: 1991
Total Assets: $2.0 Billion
Ticker Symbol: DGRIX
Home Page: http://
www.dreyfus.com

Objective and Strategy: This fund seeks to provide long-term capital growth, current income, and growth of income, consistent with reasonable investment risk. Although the fund may invest in both stocks and bonds, its portfolio has been largely composed of stocks, convertible bonds, and convertible preferred stocks. The fund's stellar performance in 1996 resulted in part from its avoidance of straight bonds and a very low weighting in interest rate–sensitive sectors such as electric utilities. On the plus side, its performance benefitted from investment in several cyclical industries, notably chemicals. At midyear, 60 percent of portfolio assets were invested in common stocks with the balance invested in convertible securities and cash equivalents. The fund's conservative position may limit upside gains, but provides significant downside protection.

Annualized Returns
1-Year 16.4%
3-Year 11.2%
5-Year NA

Portfolio Manager: Richard Hoey since the fund's inception in 1991. Prior to joining Dreyfus in April 1991, Hoey was chief economist and managing director of Barclays de Zoete Wedd.

Suitability: This fund is suitable for conservative investors who seek a combination of current income and capital growth.

Portfolio Implications: Although the fund can invest in straight debt, management has opted for a fully invested position in equity securities (including convertibles). As a result, the fund possesses a much lower sensitivity to interest rate changes than most balanced funds.

Risk: This relatively young fund has yet to experience a major bear stock market. Its affinity for equities and a 0.88 beta suggest that its shares are vulnerable to a market sell-off.

Costs: This is a relatively low-cost fund. Its shares are sold with a no-load format and its 1.06-percent annual expense ratio is well below average for the group. However, since inception its portfolio turnover ratio has averaged more than 100 percent, which is well above the group average.

Distributions: Income distributions are paid quarterly, and capital gains are distributed annually in December.

How to Buy and Sell: Minimum initial investment $2,500; IRA $750; no minimum subsequent investment requirement. Telephone exchange with other Dreyfus funds. Shares may also be obtained without transaction costs from Charles Schwab and Jack White and Company.

ECLIPSE BALANCED

P.O. Box 2196
Peachtree City, GA 30269
800-872-2710

Inception: 1989
Total Assets: $85 Million
Ticker Symbol: EBALX
Home Page: http://
www.eclipsefund.com

Objective and Strategy: The investment objective of this fund is to seek a high total return from a combination of equity and fixed-income securities. Although a minimum of 25 percent of assets must be invested in fixed-income securities, the fund has targeted a 60-percent allocation to stocks and a 40-percent allocation to bonds. Its bond strategy is to invest in bonds with very short-term maturities. This strategy protects investors in a stock and bond market downturn, although it also limits gains when interest rates are tumbling. Its equity strategy is to invest in the stocks of companies whose equity capitalizations are similar to the average total market capitalization of stocks making up the Standard & Poor's 500 Index. Since inception, this very conservative strategy has allowed the fund to provide about the same return as the typical balanced fund but with less volatility.

Annualized Returns

1-Year 10.2%
3-Year 9.4%
5-Year 12.2%

Portfolio Manager: Dr. Wesley G. McCain since the fund's inception. Dr. McCain holds a doctoral degree from Stanford University and master's degrees from Stanford and Columbia Universities.

Suitability: This is an excellent vehicle for conservative investors who seek a combination of current income, capital preservation, and long-term growth of capital.

Portfolio Implications: Because of the fund's strategy of investing in both common stocks and bonds, it can be considered a complete investment program. Its strategy of investing in S&P 500 Index-type stocks and bonds with very short maturities makes its portfolio composition somewhat unique.

Risk: The fund's 0.83 beta indicates a modest-risk portfolio. However, management's strategy of investing 40 percent of assets in short-term bonds produces a very low-risk fund as witnessed by its very modest 4.6-percent decline during the 1990 bear market.

Costs: This is a very modest-cost fund. Its shares are sold with a no-load format. Both its 0.81-percent annual expense ratio and its 75-percent portfolio turnover ratio are below average for the group.

Distributions: Net investment income is distributed quarterly, and capital gains are distributed annually.

How to Buy and Sell: Minimum initial investment $1,000; IRA $1,000; no minimum subsequent investment requirement. Telephone exchange with the other three funds in the Eclipse Financial Asset Trust. Shares may also be obtained without transaction fees from Jack White and Company.

FIDELITY EQUITY INCOME

Fidelity Distributors
82 Devonshire Street
Mail Zone L7B
Boston, MA 02109
800-752-2347

Inception: 1966
Total Assets: $12.8 Billion
Ticker Symbol: FEQIX
Home Page: http://
www.fidelity.com

Objective and Strategy: This fund seeks a combination of current income and capital appreciation by investing primarily in income-producing equity securities. When choosing these securities, management looks for a yield that exceeds the composite yield of stocks composing the Standard & Poor's 500 Index and securities that also offer some capital appreciation potential. The fund has historically sported an above-average current yield and still has produced enviable returns during the past five years. Although overshadowed by more glitzy Fidelity offerings, this fund has been producing solid returns (14.2-percent annual average) for three decades. Giving the fund additional appeal is the fact that it dropped its 2-percent front-end sales charge in January 1996.

Annualized Returns

1-Year 18.2%
3-Year 15.1%
5-Year 16.6%

Portfolio Manager: Stephen Peterson since August 1993. He joined Fidelity in October 1980 and also is senior vice president of Fidelity Management Trust Company.

Suitability: This is an excellent fund for both conservative and aggressive growth-seeking investors.

Portfolio Implications: This is a huge fund that must invest in huge, well-established companies. Nearly half its portfolio is invested in finance, energy, and utility stocks. Thus, it exhibits a degree of interest rate sensitivity.

Risk: This is a modest-risk equity fund. Its 0.89 beta is slightly below that of the market. However, its interest rate sensitivity gives its risk a boost as witnessed by its near 18-percent decline during the 1990 bear market.

Costs: This is one of Fidelity's more cost-efficient funds. Its shares are sold with a no-load format. Its 0.68-percent annual expense ratio and 40-percent portfolio turnover ratio are well below average for an equity fund.

Distributions: Income is distributed in March, June, September, and December. Capital gains are distributed in March and December.

How to Buy and Sell: Minimum initial investment $2,500; IRA $500; subsequent investments $250. Telephone exchange with other Fidelity offerings. Shares may be obtained through Fidelity Brokerage without transaction fees.

FIDELITY EQUITY INCOME II

Fidelity Distributors
82 Devonshire Street
Mail Zone L7B
Boston, MA 02109
800-752-2347

Inception: 1990
Total Assets: $14.4 Billion
Ticker Symbol: FEQTX
Home Page: http://
www.fidelity.com

Objective and Strategy: Like Fidelity's Growth and Income fund, this fund seeks a combination of current income and growth of capital. It was organized when the assets of Growth and Income ballooned to $5 billion in 1989. However, considering the money pouring into the mutual fund industry these days and the growing size of Fidelity funds in general, one might question the cloning of Equity Income. Even so, this fund has produced handsome returns during its six-year life. Falling interest rates and soaring blue-chip stock prices have treated this fund exceptionally well. Its return since inception is an enviable 20.6 percent. Like its sibling, its largest industry allocations include finance and energy. Foreign investments comprise about 12 percent of portfolio assets.

Portfolio Manager: Brian Posner since April 1992. Since joining Fidelity in 1987, he has managed Value, Select Energy, and Property and Casualty Insurance funds.

Suitability: This fund's shares are suitable for both aggressive and somewhat conservative, growth-seeking investors. It's an excellent fund for use in a child's education savings program.

Annualized Returns

1-Year 15.9%
3-Year 14.2%
5-Year 16.8%

Portfolio Implications: What you get here is plenty of well-established, large blue-chip stocks. Some degree of interest rate sensitivity is present because of a large allocation to financial stocks.

Risk: This relatively young fund has yet to experience a bear market. In fact, since inception, the stock market has marched steadily higher. Thus, its 0.86 beta probably masks some of its short-term volatility.

Costs: This is another one of Fidelity's cost-efficient funds. Its shares are sold with a no-load format. Its annual expense ratio is a low 0.74 percent as is its 47-percent portfolio turnover ratio.

Distributions: Income is distributed in March, June, September, and December. Capital gains are distributed in January and December.

How to Buy and Sell: Minimum initial investment $2,500; IRA $500; subsequent investments $250. Telephone exchange with other Fidelity funds. Shares may also be obtained through Fidelity Brokerage without transaction fees.

FIDELITY GROWTH AND INCOME

Fidelity Distributors
82 Devonshire Street
Mail Zone L7B
Boston, MA 02109
800-752-2347

Inception: *1985*
Total Assets: *$21.4 Billion*
Ticker Symbol: *FGRIX*
Home Page: *http://www.fidelity.com*

Objective and Strategy: This fund seeks long-term capital growth, current income, and growth of income, consistent with reasonable investment risk. The fund invests in securities of firms with growth potential that currently are paying regular cash dividends. The fund will generally sell those stocks whose yields fall to less than the yield of the Standard & Poor's 500 Index. Despite holding a large portion of assets in interest rate–sensitive finance and natural resources stocks, the fund has done a remarkable job over its lifetime, during which it posted an 18.5-percent average annual return. Although investors should not expect a repeat performance of these stellar numbers, the fund's above-average performance record, below-average operating expenses, and low volatility make this an excellent growth and income vehicle.

Annualized Returns

1-Year 20.8%
3-Year 16.5%
5-Year 18.5%

Portfolio Manager: Steven Kaye since January 1993. Previously he managed Blue Chip Growth, Select Biotechnology, Select Energy, and Select Health Care. He joined Fidelity in 1985.

Suitability: This fund's shares are suitable for both aggressive and more conservative growth-oriented investors. It is an ideal fund for use in a retirement program for younger investors or as the core of a portfolio designed to provide for a child's college education.

Portfolio Implications: What you get here are the stocks of large, well-established, dividend-paying companies. This fund is true blue. Its high-yield sectors (finance, energy, and utilities) are balanced with hefty investments in health care and technology.

Risk: This fund's beta is a modest 0.90 percent. However, considering its exceptional returns, there is probably more risk here than first meets the eye. The fund's share price tumbled 15 percent during the 1990 bear market.

Costs: This is a very cost-efficient fund. Its shares are sold with a no-load format, and both its annual expense ratio (0.75 percent) and portfolio turnover ratio (41 percent) are below the average of all equity funds.

Distributions: Income distributions are paid in March, June, September, and December. Capital gains are distributed in September and December.

How to Buy and Sell: Minimum initial investment $2,500; IRA $500; subsequent investments $250. Telephone exchange with other Fidelity funds. Shares may also be obtained through Fidelity Brokerage without transaction fees.

FIDELITY PURITAN

Fidelity Distributors
82 Devonshire Street
Mail Zone L7B
Boston, MA 02109
800-752-2347

Inception: 1947
Total Assets: $17.5 Billion
Ticker Symbol: FPURX
Home Page: http://www.fidelity.com

Objective and Strategy: One of Fidelity's oldest funds, it seeks a combination of current income and capital appreciation by maintaining a portfolio that generally consists of 40 percent bonds and 60 percent common stocks. During its lifetime, which spans nearly five decades, the fund has returned an average of 12.3 percent per year. This, I believe, is an exceptional feat considering the fact that the S&P 500 Index returned 12.4 percent and government bonds returned 5.5 percent during the same period. Utility and basis industry stocks make up the largest equity portions, and the fund's bond stake keeps the fund alive during bear markets. The fund usually sports an impressive current yield and is a decent holding for income-oriented investors since its common stock component provides a significant inflation offset.

Annualized Returns

1-Year 13.3%
3-Year 11.5%
5-Year 14.4%

Portfolio Manager: Bettina Doulton since March 1996. She also manages the Advisor Annuity Income & Growth and Advisor Income & Growth funds. Previously, she managed the Value Fund and Advisor Equity and assisted in managing Magellan.

Suitability: This fund is suitable for conservative investors. Its bond component makes it unsuitable for more aggressive investors who seek capital appreciation.

Portfolio Implications: At times this fund will be invested in stocks, bonds, and some cash equivalents. Thus, it could be considered a complete investment program for conservative investors. It experiences a degree of interest rate sensitivity but provides plenty of protection during a bear market driven by an economic recession.

Risk: This is a low-risk offering, with a beta of 0.68. However, its share price is sensitive to changes in interest rates. Its share price declined by slightly more than 13 percent during the 1990 bear market.

Costs: The fund dropped its 2-percent front-end load in 1996, and thus became a very cost-efficient fund. Its 0.74-percent expense ratio is well below average. However, its recent portfolio turnover ratio (139 percent) is well above average.

Distributions: Net investment income is distributed in March, June, September, and December. Capital gains are distributed in September and December.

How to Buy and Sell: Minimum initial investment $2,500; IRA $500; subsequent investments $250. Telephone exchange with other Fidelity funds.

FOUNDERS BALANCED

Founders Asset Management
2930 East Third Avenue
Denver, CO 80206
800–525–2440

Inception: 1963
Total Assets: $223 Million
Ticker Symbol: FRINX
Home Page: http://
www.networth.galt.com/founders

Objective and Strategy: This fund's objective is current income and capital appreciation. To achieve its objective, the fund invests in a balanced portfolio of dividend-paying common stocks, U.S. and foreign government obligations, and a variety of corporate fixed-income securities. The fund emphasizes investment in common stocks with the potential for increased dividends as well as capital appreciation. It will maintain a minimum of 25 percent of its total assets in fixed-income, investment-grade securities rated Baa or better by Moody's. Recently, the fund adopted a highly conservative strategy with 43 percent of assets allocated to common stocks, 11 percent to preferred stocks and convertible securities, 34 percent to government and corporate bonds, and 12 percent to cash equivalents. Under the capable leadership of Brian Kelly, look for this fund to perform well during both up and down markets.

Annualized Returns
1-Year 26.5%
3-Year 16.1%
5-Year 15.5%

Portfolio Manager: Brian Kelly since July 1996. Prior to joining Founders, Mr. Kelly was the lead portfolio manager of Invesco's Balanced, Strategic Utilities, and Worldwide Communications funds.

Suitability: The fund's shares are suitable for investors who seek to participate in both the equity and fixed-income sectors of the market with one investment. Because of its bond component this fund is not suitable for those who seek long-term growth of capital.

Portfolio Implications: If you make your own portfolio allocation decisions, this fund is not for you. Depending on market conditions, this fund holds varying percentages of stocks, bonds, and cash in its portfolio.

Risk: This fund has provided high returns with low risk. During the last five years, the fund has produced high double-digit returns while sporting a very modest beta of 0.66. In addition, its share price declined by a very modest 6.5 percent during the 1990 bear market.

Costs: This is a modest-cost fund. Its shares are sold without either a front-end or a back-end load, although shareholders pay a 0.25-percent ongoing 12b-1 fee. Its expense ratio is a modest 1.23 percent, but its portfolio turnover ratio is a hefty 286 percent.

Distributions: Income distributions are paid in March, June, September, and December. Capital gains are distributed in December.

How to Buy and Sell: Minimum initial investment $1,000; IRA $500; subsequent investments $100. Telephone exchange with other Founders funds. Shares may also be obtained without transaction charges from Charles Schwab and Fidelity Brokerage.

GREENSPRING FUND

Greenspring Fund, Inc.
2330 West Joppa Road
Suite 110
Lutherville, MD 21093-4641
800-366-3863

Inception: 1983
Total Assets: $74 Million
Ticker Symbol: GRSPX
Home Page: None

Objective and Strategy: This relatively small, stand-alone fund has benefitted from the wizardry of Chip Carlson, who took over the fund's management responsibilities in early 1987. Consider the fact that this fund has managed to keep pace with the return of the S&P 500 Index while maintaining a risk level equal to about half that of the index. Furthermore the fund has not had a down quarter since Carlson took over. How does he do it? He implements a unique strategy which couples investment in smaller company stocks with small, undiscovered discounted bonds, many of which are unrated by Standard & Poor's and Moody's. Says Carlson, "I can usually buy [these issues] so cheap that it's difficult not to make money, no matter what the market does." His affinity for the unloved has paid off big time for the fund's loyal shareholders.

Annualized Returns

1-Year	14.8%
3-Year	11.4%
5-Year	13.6%

Portfolio Manager: Charles Carlson since January 1987. He has been president of the fund since March 1993 and serves as president for Key Equity Management, the fund's adviser.

Suitability: This fund's shares are suitable for both aggressive and modestly aggressive investors who don't mind a combination of current income and capital appreciation.

Portfolio Implications: Because of the fund's unique strategy of coupling small firm stocks with bonds drawn from the same universe, you won't find any other growth and income funds with similar investments. This is an excellent fund to combine with your other growth and income vehicles.

Risk: The fund looks more like a growth vehicle than a growth and income fund. However, you won't find many other equity funds with a 0.37 beta. However, during sharp stock market declines, its share price will exhibit some volatility because of the limited markets for its holdings as witnessed by its 12-percent decline during the 1990 bear market.

Costs: For a small fund it has a very reasonable cost structure. Its shares are sold with a no-load format, and its 1.06-percent annual expense ratio and 65-percent portfolio turnover ratio are below average.

Distributions: Both income and capital gains are distributed in July and December.

How to Buy and Sell: Minimum initial investment $2,000; IRA $1,000; subsequent investments $100.

HARBOR VALUE

Harbor Funds
One Seagate
Toledo, OH 43666
800-422-1050

Inception: 1987
Total Assets: $108 Million
Ticker Symbol: HAVLX
Home Page: None

Objective and Strategy: The fund seeks maximum long-term total return from a combination of capital growth and income through investment in a portfolio of dividend-paying common stocks. The fund's portfolio has a yield strategy of maintaining a current yield greater than or equal to 1.5 times the S&P 500 Index yield. Management responsibilities are divided between two subadvisers, DRZ, which actively manages 75 percent of portfolio assets, and Richards & Tierney, which manages the balance. Before buying or selling a stock, DRZ analyzes current yield and relative valuation by comparing a stock's twenty-year history of yield, price-earnings ratios, and price-cash flow ratios to that of the S&P 500 Index. Those with relatively low ratios are investment candidates. The balance of the portfolio is more passively managed using high-yield stocks.

Annualized Returns
1-Year 20.4%
3-Year 15.8%
5-Year 12.8%

Portfolio Manager: Gregory DePrince (since 1994) is principal and partner of DRZ, and David Tierney since 1993 is managing partner and founder of Richards & Tierney.

Suitability: This fund's shares are suitable for aggressive or modestly aggressive investors.

Portfolio Implications: The use of two subadvisers gives the fund a degree of diversification not usually found in funds that employ a single adviser. On the other hand, a large number of its holdings will be found in other equity-income portfolios. Thus, before purchase, check for possible duplication with your other growth and income funds.

Risk: Because of its preference for growth of capital, this fund has a bit more risk than the typical equity-income fund. It sports a near-market beta (0.91), and its share price tumbled more than 17 percnt during the 1990 bear market.

Costs: This is a modest-cost fund. Its shares are sold with a no-load format, and its annual expense ratio is a low 0.90 percent. However, it sports an above-average 136-percent portfolio turnover ratio.

Distributions: Both income and capital gains are distributed in December.

How to Buy and Sell: Minimum initial investment $2,000; IRA $500; subsequent investments $100. Telephone exchange with other Harbor funds (except Harbor International).

IAI VALUE FUND

IAI Mutual Funds
3700 First Bank Place
P.O. Box 357
Minneapolis, MN 55440-0357
800-945-3863

Inception: 1983
Total Assets: $42 Million
Ticker Symbol: IAAPX
Home Page: http://
networth.galt.com/iai

Objective and Strategy: This fund seeks capital appreciation by investing in what are known as value stocks. The fund's portfolio is a cross between a growth vehicle and a growth and income fund. Its affinity for rapidly growing companies (the stocks of companies with 20-percent annual earnings growth and 15-percent return on equity are preferred) would normally put it in the growth category. However, management seeks out-of-favor companies whose stocks are selling at low multiples of revenues, earnings, and book values. That usually leads it to stocks that also provide decent dividend yields. In addition, management has no hesitancy in holding a large cash balance when value is difficult to fund. As a result, the fund, at times, also provides current income.

Annualized Returns
1-Year 8.1%
3-Year 9.1%
5-Year 11.5%

Portfolio Manager: Douglas Platt since 1991 and Donald Hoelting since August 1996. Platt has served as a portfolio manager of various IAI funds since he joined the company in 1967. Hoelting also manages the IAI Growth and Income fund.

Suitability: Because of its pursuit of capital appreciation, this fund's shares are suitable for modestly aggressive investors who desire a combination of current income and capital growth.

Portfolio Implications: You are likely to find nearly anything in this fund's portfolio, provided it is modestly valued. Recently, management began adding smaller company stocks to the portfolio because of high valuation multiples in the large-cap sector of the market.

Risk: This is one of the higher-risk entries in the growth and income category. Although its beta is a modest 0.79, its share price plunged nearly 23 percent during the 1990 bear market.

Costs: This is a very cost-efficient equity fund. Its shares are sold with a no-load format. Its 1.25-percent annual expense ratio is below average for the group as is its 73-percent portfolio turnover ratio.

Distributions: Both income and capital gains distributions are paid in June.

How to Buy and Sell: Minimum initial investment $5,000; IRA $2,000; subsequent investments $100. Telephone exchange with other IAI funds. Shares may also be obtained without transaction costs from Charles Schwab, Fidelity Brokerage, and Jack White and Company.

IDS STOCK FUND

IDS Financial Services
IDS Tower 10
Minneapolis, MN 55440
800-328-8300

Inception: 1945
Total Assets: $2.3 Billion
Ticker Symbol: INSTX
Home Page: http://
www.americanexpress.com/advisors

Objective and Strategy: If you're scared off by the high price-earnings ratios and high-risk strategies of other IDS stock funds, this moderate-risk vehicle may be to your liking. And if you desire decent returns and a below-market beta, you'll like this fund even more. It concentrates its investments in large-capitalization stocks that offer both growth and modest income. The fund's low portfolio turnover ratio, low expense ratio, and below-average volatility are just a few of the reasons why management has turned in a decent performance track record. Investors should note, however, that the fund's class A shares carry a hefty 5-percent front-end load, and its class B shares are sold with a contingent deferred sales charge and carry a higher annual expense ratio.

Portfolio Manager: Richard Warden since January 1995. Previously, he managed the IDS Precious Metals fund and has assisted with the IDS Progressive fund. He joined American Express Financial in 1962.

Suitability: This fund's shares are suitable for modestly aggressive investors who desire a combination of capital appreciation and current income.

Annualized Returns
1-Year 16.5%
3-Year 13.0%
5-Year 13.3%

Portfolio Implications: You'll find a number of this equity-income fund's holdings in your other growth and income funds. Because of the possibility of duplication, consider combining this fund with funds that invest in smaller-company stocks.

Risk: Although one of the lower-risk IDS equity offerings, the fund sports a near-market beta of 0.96. However, its share price declined by a modest 9 percent during the 1990 bear market.

Costs: The fund sports a relatively high front-end sales fee. However, once a shareholder, operating costs are quite modest. Its 0.86-percent annual expense ratio and 69-percent portfolio turnover ratio are both below average for the group.

Distributions: Income is distributed in March, June, September, and December. Capital gains are distributed in December.

How to Buy and Sell: Minimum initial investment $2,000; IRA $2,000; subsequent investments $100. Telephone exchange with other IDS funds. Class B shares (contingent deferred sales charge) and class Y shares (institutional investors only) are also available.

INVESCO INDUSTRIAL INCOME

Invesco Funds Group
P.O. Box 173706
Denver, CO 80217-3706
800-525-8085

Inception: 1960
Total Assets: $4.2 Billion
Ticker Symbol: FIIIX
Home Page: http://
www.invesco.com

Objective and Strategy: There are plenty of equity funds that go up like a rocket and come down like the stick. If you don't want to get taken on a ride by these funds, consider Industrial Income, an income and growth fund that has been delivering solid returns for more than three and a half decades. The fund normally invests between 60 and 75 percent of its assets in dividend-paying common stocks, with the balance invested in corporate bonds. The exact mix is adjusted according to shifts in the stock and bond markets. While income levels are not guaranteed, this well-run fund has paid an income dividend to shareholders every quarter since its introduction in 1960. Unlike many other growth and income funds, you'll find this fund's portfolio packed with consumer cyclicals, capital goods, consumer staples, and energy stocks.

Portfolio Manager: Charles Mayer since 1993 and Donovan Paul since 1994. Mayer focuses on equity investments and Paul focuses on fixed-income investments. Paul also manages the High Yield and Select Income funds.

Suitability: This fund is right for all kinds of investors, whether young or old, experienced or novices. The fund makes an excellent core holding for a growth and income

portfolio and is well-suited for use in a child's education savings program.

Portfolio Implications: This fund's portfolio will provide significant duplication with other growth and income fund offerings. It seems to work best when combined with international equity funds and funds that invest in smaller company stocks.

Risk: The stability of this fund, given its long-run, double-digit returns, is remarkable. Its beta is a modest 0.74, and its share price declined by a modest 11 percent during the 1990 bear market.

Costs: Shares are sold without either a front-end or a back-end load. Although it possesses a 0.25-percent ongoing 12b-1 fee, its annual expense ratio is a modest 0.94 percent, as is its 54-percent portfolio turnover ratio.

Distributions: Income distributions are paid quarterly and capital gains are distributed annually in December.

How to Buy and Sell: Minimum initial investment $1,000; IRA $250; subsequent investments $50. Telephone switch with other Invesco funds. Shares may also be obtained without transaction fees from Charles Schwab, Fidelity Brokerage, and Jack White and Company.

Annualized Returns

1-Year 14.6%
3-Year 11.3%
5-Year 11.5%

INVESCO TOTAL RETURN

Invesco Funds Group
P.O. Box 173706
Denver, CO 80217-3706
800-525-8085

Inception: 1987
Total Assets: $1.0 Billion
Ticker Symbol: FSFLX
Home Page: http://www.invesco.com

Objective and Strategy: This fund balances investments in stocks and bonds with the objective of providing shareholders with quarterly income plus capital appreciation over the long term. Normally, at least 30 percent of the fund's assets are invested in common stocks and 30 percent in fixed- and variable-income securities. The remaining 40 percent is allocated between stocks and bonds, depending on management's assessment of their prospects given current business, economic, and market conditions. Above all, management seeks reasonably consistent total returns over up and down market cycles. Equity securities are chosen using a value-oriented strategy that emphasizes a company's consistent dividend history and solid, current financial situation. The income side of the portfolio is usually invested in government bonds.

Portfolio Manager: Edward C. Mitchell, Jr. since 1987. He also manages the EBI Flex fund and has been a director of Invesco Capital since 1979. He has a B.A. from the University of Virginia and an M.B.A. from the University of Colorado.

Suitability: Whether you're saving for retirement, your children's education, or the purchase of a house, this fund's balanced

Annualized Returns
1-Year 12.3%
3-Year 13.5%
5-Year 13.2%

approach to the pursuit of high total returns may fit well with your investment goals.

Portfolio Implications: This fund's portfolio looks like Invesco's growth and income fund offerings. Its biggest stock holdings are in the financial, consumer staples, and consumer cyclical industries. Its bond portion has an average maturity of about six years and a duration of about four years.

Risk: Although the fund sports a near-market beta (0.93), its affinity for value stocks and allocation to relatively short maturity government bonds gives this fund plenty of stability as witnessed by its less than 9-percent share price decline during the 1990 bear market.

Costs: This is a very cost-efficient fund. Its shares are sold with a no-load format, and its annual expense ratio (0.95 percent) and portfolio turnover ratio (30 percent) are well below average for the growth and income fund category.

Distributions: Income is distributed quarterly, and capital gains are distributed annually in December.

How to Buy and Sell: Minimum initial investment $1,000; IRA $250; subsequent investments $50. Telephone exchange with other Invesco funds.

INVESCO VALUE EQUITY

Invesco Funds Group
P.O. Box 173706
Denver, CO 80217-3706
800-525-8085

Inception: 1986
Total Assets: $196 Million
Ticker Symbol: FSEQX
Home Page: http://www.invesco.com

Objective and Strategy: If you prefer investing in common stocks with stable dividends and strong fundamentals, consider sending some of your capital in the direction of this fund. Asset selection begins with a rigorous application of quantitative screens that retains medium- to large-cap stocks that have low price-earnings ratios, low price-to-book value ratios, and high dividend yields. This list of stocks is intensively scrutinized through the application of qualitative factors such as quality of management, business strategy, and available resources, in an attempt to determine if a particular company is likely to repeat its past successes. Final stock selections are made from a universe that has been narrowed to approximately one hundred firms. The fund's portfolio has been tilted heavily in favor of consumer cyclicals and staples, financial, and technology stocks.

Portfolio Manager: Michael C. Harhai since he joined Invesco in 1993. He is assisted by Terrence Irrgang, who joined Invesco in 1992.

Suitability: This fund's shares are suitable for modestly aggressive and aggressive in-

Annualized Returns
1-Year 18.7%
3-Year 17.2%
5-Year 14.1%

vestors who seek a balance between capital appreciation and current dividend income.

Portfolio Implications: The fund looks much like other Invesco growth and income fund offerings. Its portfolio will duplicate the holdings of other funds that use a value-based investment selection strategy.

Risk: This fund sports a modest 0.88 beta. However, its share price plunged by a slightly more than the S&P 500 Index (17 percent versus 15 percent) during the 1990 bear market.

Costs: This is a very cost-efficient fund. Its shares are sold with a no-load format, and its 0.97-percent annual expense ratio and 34-percent portfolio turnover ratio are both below average for equity-income funds.

Distributions: Income is distributed quarterly, and capital gains are distributed annually in December.

How to Buy and Sell: Minimum initial investment $1,000; IRA $250; subsequent investments $50. Telephone exchange with other Invesco funds.

JANUS BALANCED

Janus Fund, Inc.
100 Fillmore Street
Denver, CO 80206-4923
800-525-3713

Inception: 1992
Total Assets: $162 Million
Ticker Symbol: JABAX
Home Page: http://www.janus.com

Objective and Strategy: This diversified fund seeks long-term growth of capital and capital preservation balanced by current income. The fund normally invests 40 to 60 percent of its assets in securities selected primarily for their growth potential (i.e., common stocks) with the balance invested in preferred stocks and bonds of all types. When selecting stocks, management takes a bottom-up approach to building the fund's portfolio. That is, they seek to identify individual companies with earnings growth potential that may not be recognized by the market. Securities are generally selected without regard to any defined industry sector. Unlike a number of balanced funds that invest heavily in financial, energy, and utility stocks, this fund has committed no more than 5 percent of portfolio assets to any one sector.

Portfolio Manager: Blaine P. Rollins since January 1996. He joined Janus Capital in 1990 and has served as a fixed-income trader and equity research analyst before taking the helm of the Balanced fund.

Suitability: This fund is suitable for conservative investors who seek a balance between current income and capital appreciation.

Annualized Returns

1-Year 19.2%
3-Year 13.6%
5-Year NA

Portfolio Implications: This fund differs from Janus Growth and Income in that it places more stress on income. Its fixed-income component is invested across a wide spectrum of bonds and thus is less interest rate sensitive than those balanced funds that invest in government or corporate bonds only.

Risk: The 40-percent allocation to bonds has resulted in a modest 0.70 beta. However, interest rate sensitivity could drive the share price lower than indicated by the beta in an environment marked by falling stock prices and rising interest rates.

Costs: This is an average-cost growth and income vehicle. Its shares are sold with a no-load format, and its annual expense ratio is right at the group average (1.35 percent). However, its portfolio turnover ratio is a hefty 185 percent.

Distributions: Net investment income is distributed in March, and capital gains are distributed in December.

How to Buy and Sell: Minimum initial investment $2,500; IRA $500; subsequent investments $100. Telephone exchange with other Janus funds. Shares may also be obtained through Charles Schwab and Fidelity Brokerage with no transaction fees.

JANUS GROWTH & INC

Janus Fund, Inc.
100 Fillmore Street
Denver, CO 80206-4923
800-525-3713

Inception: 1991
Total Assets: $853 Million
Ticker Symbol: JAGIX
Home Page: http://www.janus.com

Objective and Strategy: This fund seeks long-term capital growth and current income by investing up to 75 percent of its assets in common stocks with at least 25 percent invested in securities selected for their income potential. Emphasis is placed on the growth component, which differentiates this fund's portfolio from Janus Balanced. Like all Janus equity funds, management selects individual common stocks using a bottom-up approach. That is, management seeks to identify companies with earnings growth potential that may not be recognized by the market generally. Recently, a combination of growth stocks and income-producing stocks represented more than 90 percent of portfolio assets. Its largest sector investments included pharmaceuticals, financial services, and chemicals. Because of its aggressive style, this fund is capable of producing exceptional returns at times.

Annualized Returns

1-Year 23.2%
3-Year 15.6%
5-Year 14.9%

Portfolio Manager: Thomas Marisco since the fund's inception in 1991. He has also managed the Janus Twenty fund since March 1988. He has an M.B.A. in finance from the University of Denver.

Suitability: This growth and income fund's shares are suitable for both modestly aggressive and aggressive investors. More conservative investors should consider Janus Balanced.

Portfolio Implications: This is a growth and income fund that looks more like a growth vehicle. Heavy investment in common stocks and the presence of a number of growth issues give this portfolio an extra boost during bull markets.

Risk: This is one of the few growth and income funds you will find with a greater-than-market beta (1.16). That's plenty of risk for a fund categorized as conservative. Although it has yet to experience a major bear market, its shares could get hit hard during a market sell-off.

Costs: This is a modest-cost fund. Its shares are sold with a no-load format, and its 1.19-percent expense ratio is below average for the group. However, like a number of Janus funds, its portfolio turnover ratio is a hefty 195 percent.

Distributions: Income distributions are paid quarterly in March, June, September, and December. Capital gains are distributed in December.

How to Buy and Sell: Minimum initial investment $2,500; IRA $500; subsequent investments $100. Telephone exchange with other Janus funds. Shares also available without transaction fees from Charles Schwab and Fidelity Brokerage.

...PER DREMAN HIGH RETURN

...er Services
Fund Plan...
10 Ex... ...ge Place
S... ...e 2050
Jersey City, NJ 07302
800–533–1608

Inception: *1988*
Total Assets: *$167 Million*
Ticker Symbol: *KDHAX*
Home Page: *http://*
www.kemper.com

Objective and Strategy: If you buy mittens in the summer and love to get your exercise by swimming upstream, you'll love this fund. While many fund managers give lip service to the concept of value investing, David Dreman has been recommending highly out-of-favor stocks for decades. His philosophy, outlined in his best-selling book *Contrarian Investing*, is strictly practiced by this fund. The portfolio maintains a rather compact portfolio of the downtrodden. A few large bets on beaten-up stocks have paid off handsomely for this fund's shareholders. However, as a contrarian investor, you must have patience to allow your picks time to return to favor, and Dreman does just that, as witnessed by the funds low portfolio turnover ratio. However, its compact portfolio boosts short-term share price volatility.

Annualized Returns
1-Year 30.6%
3-Year 21.2%
5-Year 18.7%

Portfolio Manager: David Dreman since the fund's inception. He is chairman of Dreman Value Advisors and has more than thirty years experience as an investment analyst, adviser, and manager.

Suitability: Both aggressive and conservative investors should consider an investment in this fund. However, if you can't stick around for a few years, invest somewhere else.

Portfolio Implications: The last time we surveyed this fund's portfolio, it contained fifty different stocks. However, its top ten holdings accounted for more than 40 percent of portfolio assets. In short, you don't get the full benefit of diversification when you invest in this fund.

Risk: The risks here are large for a growth and income fund. Its beta is a hefty 1.10, and its share price plunged more than 26 percent during the 1990 bear market. Its concentrated portfolio adds to its risk.

Costs: If it weren't for the hefty 5.75-percent front-end load, this would be an average-cost fund. Its 1.57-percent annual expense ratio is slightly above average, but its 18-percent portfolio turnover ratio is one of the lowest in the growth and income category.

Distributions: Net investment income is paid quarterly, and capital gains are distributed annually, usually in mid-December.

How to Buy and Sell: Class A shares carry a front-end load. Class B and C shares are also available. Minimum initial investment $1,000; IRA $250; subsequent investments $50. Telephone exchange with other Kemper funds.

LEXINGTON CORPORATE LEADERS TRUST

Lexington Management Corporation
P.O. Box 1515
Park 80 West Plaza Two
Saddle Brook, NJ 07663
800-526-0057

Inception: 1935
Total Assets: $326 Million
Ticker Symbol: LEXCX
Home Page: None

Objective and Strategy: This unique fund was created in 1935 with the objective of seeking long-term capital growth and income through investment in an equal number of shares of the common stocks of American blue-chip corporations. Currently, the trust is invested in twenty-three such corporations, including AT&T, Allied Signal, American Brands, Burlingtron Northern, Chevron, Columbia Gas, Consolidated Edison, DuPont, Eastman Kodak, Exxon, General Electric, Mobil, Pacific Gas & Electric, Praxair, Procter & Gamble, Sears, Travelers Group, USX Marathon, Union Carbide, Union Electric, Union Pacific, Westinghouse, and Woolworth. Add an exceptionally low expense ratio and no active trading and you get a superb blue-chip portfolio with extremely low costs. If you are a "buy it and forget it investor," this is the fund for you.

Portfolio Manager: Lawrence Kantor since 1988. He is executive vice president and managing director of Lexington Management Corporation.

Suitability: This fund is suitable for any investor who seeks capital appreciation with some growth. With its low cost structure and buy-and-hold policy it is ideally suited for a child's education savings program or as a core holding in a retirement portfolio.

Annualized Returns

1-Year	21.5%
3-Year	15.6%
5-Year	16.3%

Portfolio Implications: This is the ultimate buy-and-hold portfolio. As goes the Dow Jones Industrial Average, so goes the fortunes of this fund. This fund could easily provide the core of any investment program you can create. Can be used as a large-cap index fund.

Risk: Given its large-cap blue-chip holdings, it's no surprise to find this fund sporting a near-market beta (1.04). However, its dividend-paying stocks can shore up its share price during a severe bear market as witnessed by its modest 10-percent decline during the 1990 bear market.

Costs: This is one of the lowest cost equity funds we have ever seen. Its annual expense ratio is a minuscule 0.58 percent, and it possesses a zero portfolio turnover ratio, thus it has no brokerage costs.

Distributions: Income is distributed in June and December, and capital gains (if any) are distributed in December. This is a very tax-efficient fund.

How to Buy and Sell: Minimum initial investment $1,000; IRA $1,000; subsequent investments $50. Shares may also be obtained without transaction fees from Charles Schwab, Fidelity Brokerage, and Jack White and Company.

LINDNER DIVIDEND

Ryback Management
7711 Corondelet Avenue
Suite 700, P.O. Box 11208
St. Louis, MO 63105
314-727-5305

Inception: 1976
Total Assets: $1.4 Billion
Ticker Symbol: LDDVX
Home Page: http://
www.lindnerfunds.com

Objective and Strategy: This growth and income fund stresses a high level of current income. Thus, the portfolio generally contains only a few common stocks, the bulk of its assets being invested in convertible preferred stocks, convertible bonds, and straight-debt instruments such as corporate bonds, government bonds, and preferred stocks. As a result, the fund's share price is considerably more stable than that of the typical growth and income fund. During the declining interest rate environment of the 1980s, for example, the fund delivered a better-than-average 20.5-percent compound annual rate of return. Indeed, the 1990s are turning out to be excellent years for the fund as well. If you're looking for a high-quality growth and income fund, look no further.

Portfolio Manager: Eric E. Ryback since 1984. He has also managed the Lindner Utility fund and Lindner Small Cap since their inceptions. He is also comanager of other Lindner funds.

Suitability: If you are a highly conservative investor and favor income over growth, this is the fund of choice. Because of its high income distributions, this fund works best in a tax-deferred portfolio.

Annualized Returns

1-Year 17.3%
3-Year 12.7%
5-Year 13.8%

Portfolio Implications: The bulk of this fund's common stocks have been drawn from the public utility industry. It's no utility index fund, but its high allocations to this sector and hefty investments in preferred stocks and convertible bonds make this fund highly sensitive to interest rate fluctuations.

Risk: Whenever you get high returns accompanied by a low beta (0.57), you know there are risks hidden somewhere. The hidden risk here is the fund's extreme interest rate sensitivity. Even so, its share price declined by a modest 14 percent during the 1990 bear market.

Costs: This is a very cost-efficient fund. Its shares are sold with a no-load format, and both its annual expense ratio (0.61 percent) and its portfolio turnover ratio (30 percent) are well below average.

Distributions: Income is distributed annually in September and capital gains are paid in December.

How to Buy and Sell: Minimum initial investment $2,000; IRA $250; subsequent investments $100. Telephone exchange with other Lindner funds. Shares may also be obtained without transaction fees from Charles Schwab, Fidelity Brokerage, and Jack White and Company.

LOOMIS SAYLES GROWTH & INCOME

Loomis Sayles & Co., L.P.
One Financial Center
Boston, MA 02111
800-633-3330

Inception: 1991
Total Assets: $39 Million
Ticker Symbol: LSGIX
Home Page: None

Objective and Strategy: In pursuing its objective of long-term growth of capital and income, this relatively small fund invests almost exclusively in common stocks that management considers to be undervalued in relation to earnings, dividends, assets, and growth prospects. Its portfolio contains a well-diversified list of mostly large-cap and mid-cap companies. No one industry sector claims more than 7 percent of its assets, but the fund does have a banking and financial services bent. Additionally, this fund tends to favor higher-growth sectors such as telecommunications, health care, and retail. This is a relatively young fund, but it has performed well right out of the box. One big plus is that it is a relatively small fund that can easily handle a flood of cash, should it occur.

Portfolio Manager: Jeffrey W. Wardlow, vice president of the trust and of Loomis Sayles, has served as portfolio manager since the fund's inception in 1991.

Suitability: This fund is suitable for investors who prefer a combination of capital appreciation and current income but place a greater emphasis on capital growth.

Annualized Returns

1-Year 12.7%
3-Year 14.8%
5-Year 14.1%

Portfolio Implications: This is a typical equity-income portfolio filled with the usual suspects. Thus, there is little reason to combine this fund with any other equity-income offering.

Risk: This relatively young fund has yet to experience a major bear market. However, its near-market beta (0.96) and its nearly fully invested position in dividend-paying common stocks insures that its share price will rise and fall in concert with the S&P 500 Index.

Costs: This is a very cost-efficient fund. Its shares are sold with a no-load format and both its 1.20-percent annual expense ratio and 60-percent portfolio turnover ratio are below average.

Distributions: Both income and capital gains distributions are paid annually in September.

How to Buy and Sell: Minimum initial investment $2,500; IRA $250; subsequent investments $50. Telephone exchange with other Loomis Sayles funds. Shares may also be obtained with no transaction fees from Charles Schwab and Jack White and Company.

MANAGERS INCOME EQUITY

The Managers Funds, L.P.
40 Richards Avenue
Norwalk, CT 06854–2325
800-835-3879

Inception: 1984
Total Assets: $47 Million
Ticker Symbol: MGIEX
Home Page: None

Objective and Strategy: This fund, one of ten portfolios in the Managers Trust, seeks a combination of capital appreciation and current income by investing in income-producing securities, such as common stocks, preferred stocks, and convertible bonds. The fund also may invest in debt securities with a maximum maturity of fifteen years. It seeks securities that possess current yields that are at least 20 percent greater than the yield offered by the Standard & Poor's 500 Index. The security issuers must also have a strong cash flow and good growth prospects. The fund is unique in that it hires subadvisers to manage fund portfolios. This portfolio is comanaged by Scudder, Stevens and Clark and Spare, Kaplan, Bischel and Associates.

Annualized Returns

1-Year 16.4%
3-Year 14.3%
5-Year 13.8%

Portfolio Manager: Robert T. Hoffman of Scudder, Stevens & Clark and Anthony E. Spare of SKB.

Suitability: The fund's shares are suitable for moderately aggressive investors who desire a combination of capital appreciation and current income.

Portfolio Implications: This is a highly diverse fund with investments spread across fifteen broad industry sectors with no sector dominating. Its portfolio can be characterized as a plain-vanilla equity-income offering.

Risk: This fund's risk is typical of those in the equity-income category. Its beta is a modest 0.86, and its share price declined by 20 percent during the 1990 bear market.

Costs: This fund possesses modest costs. Its shares are sold with a no-load format. Its 1.45-percent expense ratio is about at the group average while its 36-percent portfolio turnover ratio is below average.

Distributions: Income is distributed monthly and capital gains are distributed annually in December.

How to Buy and Sell: Minimum initial investment $2,000 (recently reduced from $10,000); IRA $500; no subsequent minimum investment requirement. Telephone exchange with other funds in the Managers trust. Shares may also be obtained without transaction fees from Charles Schwab and Jack White and Company.

MUTUAL BEACON

Mutual Series Fund, Inc.
51 John F. Kennedy Parkway
Short Hill, NJ 07078
800-448-3863

Inception: 1961
Total Assets: $4.4 Billion
Ticker Symbol: BEGRX
Home Page: None

Objective and Strategy: This fund is managed by the same portfolio manager as the highly acclaimed Mutual Shares fund. Michael Price's style is to buy a dollar's worth of assets for fifty or sixty cents. He takes a patient, long-term approach to investing in stocks that sell at substantial discounts to their underlying asset values. Most of its cheap stocks are those of companies that are experiencing severe difficulties, but their low valuations leave little room for further stock price deterioration. Also reducing risk is the fund's wide diversification; its portfolio consists of more than two hundred stocks. Although the fund lagged in the early 1990s, management's value discipline has begun to pay off for shareholders. At press time, the fund was sold to Franklin Resources, who plans to distribute Class One and Class Two shares that will possess sales loads. Current shareholders can make new purchases without paying sales fees.

Portfolio Manager: Michael Price since 1985. Mr. Price has agreed to remain portfolio manager of the fund for five years after the sale of his advisory firm to Franklin Resources.

Suitability: The fund is suitable for both conservative and more aggressive investors who have the patience to reap the rewards of a contrarian investment strategy.

Portfolio Implications: There's a lot of stuff in this portfolio that other fund managers would never consider. But that's the nature of trying to buy a dollar's worth of assets at half the price. The fund works well with most other growth and income funds.

Risk: To get big rewards, you must take big risks. The risk here is that Mr. Price's value bets will not pay off. However, they usually do. The fund sports a 0.70 beta, and its share price declined by a modest 13 percent during the 1990 bear market.

Costs: Prior to its sale to Franklin, this was a very cost-efficient fund. However, Class One shares will now sport a 4.5-percent front-end load. Annual expenses are a low 0.72 percent and the turnover ratio (73 percent) is modest.

Distributions: Income and capital gains are distributed annually in June.

How to Buy and Sell: Class One and Two shares are now available from Franklin Resources. Minimum initial investment $5,000; IRA $2,000; subsequent investments $100.

Annualized Returns

1-Year 15.0%
3-Year 15.9%
5-Year 17.9%

MUTUAL DISCOVERY

Mutual Series Fund, Inc.
51 John F. Kennedy Parkway
Short Hills, NJ 07078
800-448-3863

Inception: 1992
Total Assets: $2.3 Billion
Ticker Symbol: MDISX
Home Page: None

Objective and Strategy: This fund seeks long-term capital appreciation by investing in the stocks of smaller companies. It appears in the growth and income section because of the portfolio manager's affinity for the beaten-up stocks of companies that are having difficulties. Portfolio manager Price attempts to buy a dollar's worth of assets for fifty to sixty cents. As a result, the stocks held in the portfolio usually possess relatively low price-earnings multiples and, at times, lofty dividend yields. The search for extreme values has led the fund to invest in a number of unlikely places. In fact, more than 40 percent of the fund's investments are in companies domiciled outside the United States. At press time, the fund was sold to Franklin Resources, who plans to distribute Class One and Class Two shares that will possess sales loads. Current shareholders can make new purchases in the fund without paying sales fees.

Annualized Returns
1-Year 18.5%
3-Year 19.7%
5-Year NA

Portfolio Manager: Michael Price since the fund's inception in 1992. Mr. Price has agreed to remain portfolio manager of the fund for five years after the sale of his advisory firm to Franklin.

Suitability: This fund's shares are suitable only for more aggressive investors who can tolerate the additional volatility that accompanies small company investing.

Portfolio Implications: What you get here are both domestic and foreign, small firm stocks as well as some bonds and notes in reorganization. This fund can be characterized as a junk fund. You won't find many of this portfolio's holdings anywhere else. Thus, the fund provides added diversification to nearly any portfolio you may construct.

Risk: Although the fund's beta is a modest 1.07, high returns are usually accompanied by high risks. The risks here are a lack of liquidity for many of its holdings, which could cause their share prices to tumble during a sharp stock market decline.

Costs: Prior to its sale to Franklin, this was a very cost-efficient small-cap fund. However, Class One shares now sport a 4.5-percent front-end load. Annual expenses are a low 0.99 percent and the turnover ratio (73 percent) is modest.

Distributions: Income and capital gains are distributed annually.

How to Buy and Sell: Class One and Two shares are now available from Franklin Resources. Minimum initial investment $5,000; IRA $2,000; subsequent investments $100. Telephone exchange with other Franklin/Templeton funds.

MUTUAL QUALIFIED

Mutual Series Fund, Inc.
51 John F. Kennedy Parkway
Short Hills, NJ 07078
800-448-3863

Inception: 1980
Total Assets: $3.8 Billion
Ticker Symbol: MQUEX
Home Page: None

Objective and Strategy: This fund's primary investment objective is capital appreciation, with income a secondary consideration. Investments are made in common stocks, preferred stocks, and bonds that management believes are undervalued by the market relative to the firm's asset values, takeover potential, etc. This may include investment in companies involved in mergers, consolidations, liquidations, or reorganizations. The fund's value and special situation posture provide special risks, but have also provided investors with stellar returns for a decade and a half. This fund's long-term track record of continued success should continue to serve shareholders well. At press time, the fund was sold to Franklin Resources, who plans to distribute Class One and Class Two shares that will possess sales loads. Current shareholders can make new purchases in the fund without paying sales fees.

Annualized Returns

1-Year 14.2%
3-Year 16.2%
5-Year 18.0%

Portfolio Manager: Michael Price since the fund's inception in 1980. Mr. Price has agreed to remain the portfolio manager of the fund for five years after the sale of his advisory firm to Franklin Resources.

Suitability: This fund is suitable for aggressive and modestly aggressive investors only. Because of the nature of out-of-favor investments, shareholders must exhibit extreme patience.

Portfolio Implications: This is another portfolio in the Mutual series of funds that contains plenty of what other investors might call junk. In addition, one-third of portfolio assets have been allocated to foreign securities. From time to time you will also find a hefty investment in government securities and some currency hedges.

Risk: If you want large returns, you must take large risks, and this fund is no exception. It possesses a modest beta (0.75), but the limited liquidity of some of its investments introduces an additional element of risk. Its share price declined by slightly more than 14 percent during the 1990 bear market.

Costs: Prior to its sale to Franklin, this was a very cost-efficient fund. However, Class One shares now sport a 4.5-percent front-end load. Annual expenses are a low 0.72 percent, and the turnover ratio is a modest 75 percent.

Distributions: Income and capital gains distributions are paid annually.

How to Buy and Sell: Minimum initial investment $1,000; IRA $1,000; subsequent investments $50. Telephone exchange with other Franklin/Templeton funds. Class One and Two shares are now available from Franklin Resources.

MUTUAL SHARES

Mutual Series Fund, Inc.
51 John F. Kennedy Parkway
Short Hills, NJ 07078
800-448-3863

Inception: 1987
Total Assets: $5.9 Billion
Ticker Symbol: MUTHX
Home Page: None

Objective and Strategy: This is another portfolio in the Mutual Series Fund run by superstar portfolio manager Michael Price. Mr. Price is fond of telling shareholders that his objective is to provide growth of capital by purchasing a dollar's worth of assets for fifty or sixty cents and then selling those assets when they become fully valued. Historically, the fund has profited handsomely by investing in companies involved in bankruptcy proceedings or those in takeover situations. Generally, you won't find too many of this funds holdings in other funds. That's because Mr. Price prides himself on buying the unpopular. His stock search has led him to investments in Sweden, the United Kingdom, the Netherlands, and Canada in addition to those based here at home. At press time, the fund was sold to Franklin Resources, who plans to distribute Class One and Class Two shares that will possess sales loads. Current shareholders can make new purchases in the fund without paying sales fees.

Annualized Returns

1-Year 13.6%
3-Year 16.0%
5-Year 17.5%

Portfolio Manager: Michael F. Price since inception. Mr. Price has agreed to remain the fund's portfolio manager for five years after the sale of his advisory firm to Franklin in October 1996.

Suitability: This fund's shares are suitable for aggressive and modestly aggressive investors who can afford to exercise the patience required to profit from investing in out-of-favor stocks.

Portfolio Implications: Given the mandate to buy assets for fifty cents on the dollar, you won't find many of this fund's holdings in other growth or growth and income vehicles. Thus, the fund works exceptionally well when coupled with other equity funds.

Risk: Despite a beta of 0.82, there are substantial risks here. The fund invests in out-of-favor stocks that may not return to favor for some time. During the 1990 bear market the fund's share price declined by nearly 15 percent.

Costs: Prior to its sale to Franklin, this was a very cost-efficient fund. However, Class One shares now sport a 4.5-percent front-end sales load. Annual expenses are a low 0.69 percent, and the turnover ratio (79 percent) is about average for the group.

Distributions: Income and capital gains distributions are paid annually.

How to Buy and Sell: Class One and Two shares are now available from Franklin Resources. Minimum initial investment $5,000; IRA $2,000; subsequent investments $100. Telephone exchange with other Franklin/Templeton funds.

NEUBERGER & BERMAN GUARDIAN

Neuberger & Berman Management,
    Inc.
605 Third Avenue, 2nd Floor
New York, NY 10158-0180
800-877-9700

Inception: 1950
Total Assets: $5.0 Billion
Ticker Symbol: NGUAX
Home Page: http://
www.nbfunds.com

Objective and Strategy: This is a growth and income fund that emphasizes investments stocks of established, high-quality companies considered to be undervalued. It was one of the first no-load funds in the country and has paid quarterly income dividends and annual capital gain distributions every year since its inception in 1950. Since inception, the fund has returned an average of 13.1 percent annually, an exceptional feat considering the dull stock market of the 1970s. Management has a preference for stocks with price-earnings multiples lower than those of the market as a whole, high dividend yields, strong balance sheets, and a catalyst that would allow the company to capitalize on hidden values. Interestingly, its recent portfolio included large allocations to financial and technology stocks, which usually reside on opposite ends of the value spectrum.

**Annualized
Returns**

1-Year 7.2%
3-Year 14.3%
5-Year 16.2%

Portfolio Manager: Kent C. Simons since 1983 and Lawrence Marx III since 1988. Both are vice presidents of Neuberger and Berman Management and general partners of Neuberger and Berman.

Suitability: The fund is suitable for aggressive and modestly aggressive investors who have a preference for growth of capital but also want some current income. The fund is ideal for use as the core of a retirement or child's education portfolio.

Portfolio Implications: This value-based, equity-income fund's portfolio, not too surprisingly, looks similar to many other funds that practice the same style of investing. Thus, potential investors should compare this fund's investments to those in their other funds before making a significant purchase.

Risk: Despite an affinity for undervalued, out-of-favor stocks, this fund sports a near-market beta of 1.01. Thus, there is a bit of risk here, as witnessed by the 19-percent decline in the fund's share price during the 1990 bear market.

Costs: Like all Neuberger and Berman offerings, this is a very cost-efficient fund. Its shares are sold with a no-load format. Its annual expense ratio is a very low 0.84 percent, but its portfolio turnover ratio (98 percent) is slightly above average for the group.

Distributions: Both net investment income and capital gains distributions are paid in December.

How to Buy and Sell: Minimum initial investment $1,000; IRA $250; subsequent investments $100. Telephone switch with other Neuberger and Berman funds. Shares can also be obtained without transaction fees from Charles Schwab and Fidelity Brokerage.

PARNASSUS BALANCED PORTFOLIO

Parnassus Investments
One Market–Steuart Tower #1600
San Francisco, CA 94105
800-999-3505

Inception: *1992*
Total Assets: *$30 Million*
Ticker Symbol: *PRBLX*
Home Page: *None*

Objective and Strategy: The primary objective of this fund is income and capital preservation. At least 25 percent of its assets are invested in fixed-income securities at all times. In addition, its common stocks must pay a dividend at least equal to that paid by the average stock in the S&P 500 Index. The fund's adviser also looks for certain social policies in the companies in which its invests. These are treating employees fairly, sound environmental protection policies, a good equal opportunity employment policy, quality products and services, sensitivity to the communities where they operate, and ethical business practices. Excluded from the fund's portfolio are companies that manufacture alcohol or tobacco products, those that are involved in gambling, weapons contractors, and those that generate electricity from electric power.

Portfolio Manager: Jerome L. Dodson since the fund's inception in September 1992. He is also president of the fund and of Parnassus Investments, the fund's adviser.

Suitability: This fund's shares are suitable for investors who wish to invest their capital in "socially responsible" companies. Its portfolio is conservatively managed and thus may have appeal to conservative investors generally.

Annualized Returns
1-Year 11.2%
3-Year 8.5%
5-Year NA

Portfolio Implications: Run as a "socially responsible" fund, by definition, investments in a number of companies with high return potential are automatically excluded from consideration by the fund's adviser. Although the adviser believes that it can find suitable investments given these exclusions, the fund's return might suffer because of its restrictive investment policies.

Risk: The fund's bond investments have lowered the portfolio beta to 0.88. Its restriction of certain types of investments may add an additional element of risk. This relatively young fund has yet to experience a severe bear stock market.

Costs: This is a very cost-efficient fund. Its shares are sold with a no-load format. Its 0.72-percent annual expense ratio is well below average, and its portfolio turnover ratio (15 percent) is extremely low.

Distributions: Net investment income is paid quarterly, and capital gains are distributed annually, usually in December.

How to Buy and Sell: Minimum initial investment $2,000; IRA $500; subsequent investments $50. Shares may also be obtained through Jack White and Company with no transaction fees.

PENN SQUARE MUTUAL

Penn Square Management
2650 Westview Drive
Wyomissing, PA 19610
800-523-8440

Inception: 1958
Total Assets: $314 Million
Ticker Symbol: PESQX
Home Page: None

Objective and Strategy: Seeking long-term capital growth and current income, the fund invests in large, well-established Standard & Poor's 500 Index companies that pay dividends. Although the yield is lower than that of the average growth and income fund, the growth aspect of the portfolio has more than compensated for the lack of generous current income. Given the modest level of risk assumed, the fund has performed adequately in both up and down markets. Additionally, portfolio manager James Jordon is a patient investor, which is proven by the fund's low portfolio turnover ratio. Once selected, stocks tend to stay in this portfolio for an average of three years. Once, this fund's shares were available without sales charges, but about a decade ago the fund added a front-end sales charge and an annual 12b-1 distribution fee.

Portfolio Manager: James E. Jordon, chairman of the fund and president of the fund's adviser, since 1986. Emmett M. Murphy, who has been on the fund's investment committee since 1987, became comanager in January 1996.

Suitability: This fund is suitable for modestly aggressive investors who prefer some current income to complement appreciation of capital. This is an excellent fund for use as the core of a retirement or child's education portfolio.

Annualized Returns
1-Year 18.9%
3-Year 15.5%
5-Year 14.1%

Portfolio Implications: Although this is not an index fund, its use of the Standard & Poor's 500 Index as a selection universe and its affinity for dividend-paying stocks drawn from this universe make its portfolio characteristics very similar to the BARRA/Value Index.

Risk: This fund's risk is slightly less than that of the overall market (as measured by the S&P 500 Index). It has a 0.89 beta and its share price declined by less than 15 percent during the 1990 bear market.

Costs: Its front-end sales load aside, this fund possesses very modest operating expenses. Its annual expense ratio is a below-average 0.96 percent, and its 38-percent portfolio turnover ratio is below average for the growth and income group.

Distributions: Net investment income is distributed in January, April, July, and October, and capital gains are distributed in December.

How to Buy and Sell: Minimum initial investment $500; IRA $250; subsequent investments $100. Class C shares are also available. These shares are sold without a front- or back-end sales charge, but carry an annual 1-percent 12b-1 fee.

PREFERRED VALUE FUND

P.O. Box 8320
Boston, MA 02266
800-662-4769

Inception: 1992
Total Assets: $267 Million
Ticker Symbol: PFVLX
Home Page: None

Objective and Strategy: This fund seeks capital appreciation and current income by investing at least 65 percent of its assets in equity securities that Oppenheimer (the fund's subadviser) believes are undervalued and offer above-average potential for capital appreciation. Equity securities are those that have high return on equity and assets, large undedicated cash flows, significant prospects for dividend growth, and reasonable prices in relation to their book values. The key considerations in evaluating a security are financial strength of the balance sheet, industrial position, current and future profitability, effectiveness of management, and attractive valuation. Since inception, this fund has produced a return slightly higher than the unmanaged S&P 500 Index. Its largest allocations are to the high-tech sector (computers, computer software, and electronics).

Portfolio Manager: John G. Lindenthal since the fund's inception on July 1, 1992. Mr. Lindenthal is managing director of Oppenheimer (the fund's subadviser) and has an M.B.A. from the University of Santa Clara.

Suitability: Although this fund is a growth and income seeker, its emphasis is squarely on growth of capital and thus its shares are only suitable for more aggressive investors.

Portfolio Implications: This is a growth and income fund with about half its investments in the technology sector. Although emphasizing larger companies in this sector, this fund looks like some growth and even aggressive growth funds.

Risk: This fund possesses a beta slightly less than that of the market (0.97). However, its large allocation to technology stocks masks its potential share price volatility. This young fund has yet to experience a major bear market, but should participate fully when one eventually occurs.

Costs: This is a very cost-efficient fund. Its shares are sold with a no-load format. Its annual expense ratio is a low 0.89 percent, and its portfolio turnover ratio is also an exceptionally low 29 percent.

Distributions: Both income and capital gains distributions are paid annually.

How to Buy and Sell: Minimum initial investment $1,000; IRA $250; subsequent investments $50. Telephone switch with eight other Preferred funds.

Annualized Returns

1-Year 21.3%
3-Year 17.3%
5-Year NA

QUANTITATIVE GROWTH & INCOME

Lincoln North
Lincoln, MA 01773
800-331-1244

Inception: 1985
Total Assets: $42 Million
Ticker Symbol: USBOX
Home Page: None

Objective and Strategy: This fund seeks long-term growth of capital and income by investing primarily in common stocks of larger companies that have substantial equity capital and are currently paying dividends. The six funds in the Quantitative group employ a "quantitative" investment approach to selecting investments in that they rely on computer technology and financial databases to assist in the stock selection process. Potential investments are ranked on the basis of cash flow, earnings growth, and price-earnings ratios. Stocks are selected for this fund that are rapidly growing, yet pay some cash dividends. Its current portfolio contains stocks with an average return on equity of nearly 21 percent and have been growing at a 15-percent annual rate for five years. Thus, the portfolio, by growth and income fund standards, is very aggressively managed.

Annualized Returns
1-Year 12.5%
3-Year 12.5%
5-Year 12.5%

Portfolio Manager: The portfolio is managed by an investment committee of its subadviser, State Street Global Advisors.

Suitability: This fund is suitable for only aggressive investors who wish to capitalize on a security's total return.

Portfolio Implications: Plenty of high-growth companies are represented in this fund's portfolio. All are large, and most are household names such as Ameritech, BankAmerica, Chrysler, Exxon, Merck, Philip Morris, etc. Although classified as a growth and income fund, this is more of a straight blue-chip growth offering.

Risk: This high-growth portfolio has more risk than meets the eye. Its beta is a modest 0.87, but its share price could suffer during a prolonged stock market decline. However, its share price declined by a modest 13 percent during the 1990 bear market.

Costs: Shares are sold without a front-end load but carry a 1-percent deferred sales charge and a 0.50-percent ongoing 12b-1 fee. Because of the 12b-1 fee, annual operating expenses (1.73 percent) are above average as is its 152-percent portfolio turnover ratio.

Distributions: Income and capital gains distributions are paid annually in December.

How to Buy and Sell: Minimum initial investment $5,000; IRA $1,000; no minimum subsequent investment. Telephone exchange with five other Quantitative funds. Shares also available without transaction fees through Jack White and Company.

ROYCE EQUITY INCOME

Quest Distributors
1414 Avenue of the Americas
New York, NY 10019
800-221-4268

Inception: 1990
Total Assets: $37 Million
Ticker Symbol: RYEQX
Home Page: http://
www.roycefunds.com

Objective and Strategy: This fund offers a conservative approach to small-cap stock investing. Management first selects securities that provide an income stream above that of the broader market averages. Securities are purchased if they meet a strict valuation parameter, such as low price-earnings multiple or low price-to-book value multiple. This strict approach often forces the fund to miss some interesting opportunities as well as leading it to sell a stock too soon. However, the fund was created to minimize risk, and management just won't hold a stock in the portfolio if it attains a lofty valuation multiple. This fund's returns are below those of most small-cap funds, but it measures up well on a risk-adjusted basis. This is an ideal way for conservative investors to play the small-cap sector of the market.

Annualized Returns
1-Year 9.0%
3-Year 8.1%
5-Year 11.5%

Portfolio Manager: Charles M. Royce, the adviser's founder, since the fund's inception in 1990. Mr. Royce also directs the firm's other portfolios. He is assisted by Jack E. Fockler, Jr.

Suitability: Investors who seek a small-cap fund but are afraid of the volatility that these stocks usually present, will find this an ideal addition to their growth and income portfolios.

Portfolio Implications: This fund will soon be dubbed a "micro-cap" fund by industry followers. It is one of only a handful of funds that invests in tiny companies (those with market values below $300 million). If you want a spectrum of growth and income stocks, consider combining this fund with one of the more traditional growth and income vehicles.

Risk: This is an exceptionally low-risk small-cap fund, with a beta of only 0.47. However, small-cap stocks suffer from limited liquidity and their share prices can tumble in a severe bear market as witnessed by their 20-percent decline during the 1990 bear market.

Costs: This is a very cost-efficient fund. Its shares are sold with a no-load format. Its 1.24-percent annual expense ratio is below average as is its 29-percent portfolio turnover ratio.

Distributions: Net investment income is paid quarterly, and capital gains are distributed annually in December.

How to Buy and Sell: Minimum initial investment $2,000; IRA $500; subsequent investments $50. The fund charges a 1-percent redemption fee for shares held less than twelve months. Shares are also available without transaction fees through Charles Schwab, Fidelity Brokerage, and Jack White and Company.

SAFECO EQUITY

Safeco Mutual Funds
P.O. Box 34890
Seattle, WA 98124-1890
800-426-6730

Inception: 1932
Total Assets: $685 Million
Ticker Symbol: SAFQX
Home Page: http://
networth.galt.com/safeco

Objective and Strategy: This fund, which was founded in 1932 and previously managed by the Pacific Northwest Company and Fidelity Management, seeks long-term growth of capital and reasonable current income. Had you invested $2,000 in this fund back in 1932, and reinvested all dividends and capital gains, you'd have more than $3.8 million as of September 1996. The only bet portfolio manager Rich Meagley likes to make is on quality. And that describes the fund's holdings to a T. Among its dividend-paying common stocks, you'll find names such as Chase Manhattan, Federal National Mortgage, Salomon, AT&T, Mobil, and Citicorp. Once acquired, the quality stocks of large companies are held unless their growth stalls or they become too pricey. Following the philosophy of its manager, this is a fund you want to buy and hold.

Portfolio Manager: Richard D. Meagley since 1995. Prior to joining Safeco, he served as portfolio manager for Kennedy Associates, Inc. In a prior stint with Safeco, he managed the Northwest fund in 1991 and 1992.

Suitability: You can't argue with a successful fund that has been around for more than six decades. This fund is suitable for all investors, young and old, conservative and more aggressive.

Annualized Returns

1-Year 18.0%
3-Year 18.7%
5-Year 18.9%

Portfolio Implications: Large-cap, dividend-paying companies is what you'll find in this fund's portfolio. Although there is a lot to like here, check the holdings of your current equity-income funds before adding this one to your portfolio to avoid possible duplication of investments.

Risk: Although there is little risk in holding this fund long-term, its 0.83 beta suggests a bit of short-term share price volatility. Its share price tumbled slightly more than 18 percent during the 1990 bear market.

Costs: This is a very cost-efficient fund. Its shares are sold with a no-load format, and its 0.84-percent annual expense ratio and 56-percent portfolio turnover ratio are both below average.

Distributions: Income is distributed quarterly, and capital gains are paid annually in December.

How to Buy and Sell: Minimum initial investment $1,000; IRA $250; subsequent investments $100. Telephone exchange with other funds in the series. Shares may also be obtained through Charles Schwab and Jack White and Company with no transaction fees.

SAFECO INCOME

Safeco Mutual Funds
P.O. Box 34890
Seattle, WA 98124–1890
800–426–6730

Inception: 1969
Total Assets: $244 Million
Ticker Symbol: SAFIX
Home Page: http://
networth.galt.com/safeco

Objective and Strategy: Tom Rath assumed the helm of this well-managed growth and income provider in March 1996. He fills the well-worn shoes of Arley Hudson, who had been at the helm for eighteen years, during which time the fund recorded a remarkable performance history. During those years, the fund did not hit very many home runs. (Its yearly returns never topped 35 percent.) However, it did hit plenty of singles. The fund posted only three yearly declines (1987, 1990, and 1994) and a dozen years of double-digit percentage share price increases. The secret to the fund's success has been a stable allocation to dividend-paying, blue-chip stocks and a hefty stake in convertible bonds and preferred stocks (which accounted for about 30 percent of fund assets in recent years). Since taking over, Rath has continued along these lines, and you can expect a continuation of its winning ways.

Annualized Returns

1-Year 19.0%
3-Year 14.0%
5-Year 13.6%

Portfolio Manager: Thomas E. Rath since March 1996. He has served as a portfolio manager and analyst with Safeco since 1994. Prior to that he managed portfolios at Meridian Capital Management and First Interstate Bank.

Suitability: This fund's shares are suitable for both conservative and aggressive investors who prefer total return to either current income or capital appreciation exclusively.

An excellent core holding for a retirement program or child's education savings plan.

Portfolio Implications: The "income" name is somewhat a misnomer. Income is derived from convertible bonds, preferred stocks, and dividend-paying common stocks. With 30 percent of assets in the former two categories, the fund possesses a degree of interest rate risk.

Risk: Investment in convertibles and preferreds has tempered portfolio risk. Its beta is a modest 0.80, and its share price declined slightly more than 15 percent during the 1990 bear market.

Costs: This is another cost-efficient Safeco fund. Its shares are sold with a no-load format, and both its annual expense ratio (0.87 percent) and portfolio turnover ratio (31 percent) are well below average.

Distributions: Net investment income is distributed quarterly and capital gains are paid annually.

How to Buy and Sell: Minimum initial investment $1,000; IRA $250; subsequent investments $100. Telephone exchange with other funds in the series. Shares may also be obtained without transaction fees from Charles Schwab and Jack White and Company.

SCUDDER GROWTH AND INCOME

Scudder Investor Services
175 Federal Street
Boston, MA 02110
800-225-2470

Inception: 1984
Total Assets: $3.6 Billion
Ticker Symbol: SCDGX
Home Page: http://
www.scudder.com

Objective and Strategy: The fund seeks long-term growth of capital, current income, and growth of income. The fund helps to reduce risk by actively investing in stocks with above-average dividend yields and the potential for capital appreciation and rising dividends. At the time of purchase, a stock typically has a current dividend yield at least 20 percent higher than that of the S&P 500 Index and a current yield above the stock's historical average. Recently, the fund has maintained an overweight position in REITs, auto stocks, forest products, and consumer-oriented stocks whose prices discount during a recession. It has scaled back its investments in pharmaceuticals and other consumer staples issues. Even so, its largest industry concentrations include financial, manufacturing, health care, and consumer staples.

Annualized Returns
1-Year 20.1%
3-Year 15.8%
5-Year 15.8%

Portfolio Manager: Robert T. Hoffman (lead manager) since 1991. He joined Scudder in 1990. Also managing the fund are Kathleen Millard, Benjamin Thorndike, Lori Ensinger, and G. Todd Silva.

Suitability: The fund is designed for investors seeking an income-oriented approach to common stock investing. It may be more appropriate for the conservative portion of an investor's equity portfolio because of its emphasis on income.

Portfolio Implications: This is another well-managed equity-income fund. As such, its holding will most likely duplicate those of other well-managed funds in the same category. In short, you only need one fund from this category in your conservative growth and income portfolio.

Risk: The fund's portfolio volatility is slightly less than that of the market as a whole (beta 0.92). However, it weathered the 1990 bear market quite well as its share price declined a modest 7.5 percent.

Costs: Like most Scudder offerings, this is a very cost-efficient fund. Its shares are sold with a no-load format, and its 0.80-percent annual expense ratio and 27-percent portfolio turnover ratio are well below average.

Distributions: Income is paid in April, July, October, and December. Capital gains are distributed in December.

How to Buy and Sell: Minimum initial investment $1,000; IRA $500; subsequent investments $50. Telephone exchange with other Scudder funds.

SELECTED AMERICAN SHARES

Selected Funds
124 East Marcy Street
Santa Fe, NM 87501
800–243–1575

Inception: 1933
Total Assets: $1.1 Billion
Ticker Symbol: SLASX
Home Page: None

Objective and Strategy: This fund, founded in 1933, is one of the oldest no-load growth and income mutual funds in the United States. It seeks to provide shareholders with an opportunity to increase the value of their investments through a combination of capital growth and current income. Management emphasizes blue-chip firms that have market capitalizations of more than $1 billion and long records of earnings growth and dividends. The fund has established a solid record of superior performance (12.4-percent average annual return for more than sixty-two years). The portfolio managers pay close attention to demographics in order to identify long-term investment opportunities. One such opportunity the fund seeks to capitalize on is the number of baby boomers and their retirement worries. Thus, the fund has assumed a large investment position in financial services companies, insurance companies, and banks.

Annualized Returns
1-Year 19.5%
3-Year 14.9%
5-Year 13.9%

Portfolio Manager: Shelby Davis since 1993 and Christopher Davis since 1995. Shelby also manages the Davis New York Venture Fund and has been a general partner of the adviser since 1968.

Suitability: Like its forward-thinking portfolio managers, conservative investors who invest in this fund should assume a long-term posture to reap the fund's best returns.

Portfolio Implications: With about eighty stock holdings spread among twenty industries, this is a relatively compact fund, given its billion-dollar asset base. The fund's few large company bets could either propel performance to new heights or cause the fund to lag the market. Thus, you want to combine this fund with several others to obtain the maximum benefits of diversification.

Risk: The fund's beta (1.03) is above average for a growth and income fund. In addition, its large allocation to financial services companies gives it a bit of interest rate sensitivity. Its share price declined by slightly more than the market (17.8 percent) during the 1990 bear market.

Costs: The fund's shares are sold without either a front-end or a back-end load. However, its ongoing 0.25-percent 12b-1 fee has caused its expense ratio to expand to 1.09 percent. Even so, it is below average for the group, as is its modest 27-percent portfolio turnover ratio.

Distributions: Income is distributed quarterly and capital gains are distributed annually.

How to Buy and Sell: Minimum initial investment $1,000; IRA $250; subsequent investments $100. Shares may also be obtained through Charles Schwab and Jack White and Company without transaction fees.

SIT GROWTH AND INCOME

SIT Investment Associates, Inc.
4600 Norwest Center
Minneapolis, MN 55402
800-332-5580

Inception: 1982
Total Assets: $53 Million
Ticker Symbol: SNIGX
Home Page: http://
www.sitfunds.com

Objective and Strategy: This fund seeks long-term capital appreciation and, secondarily, current income by investing exclusively in common and preferred stocks and securities convertible into common stock. In making common stock investments, effort is directed toward the selection of blue-chip common stocks that pay dividends, particularly those that have provided stable and growing dividend rates on a historical basis. At the center of the stock selection is the investment philosophy of James Sit, the fund's founder, namely, that "companies with superior earnings growth produce superior long-term stock performance." Thus, the portfolio is packed with leading companies with extraordinary growth opportunities that are on the cutting edge of change and possess consistent earnings-growth rates in large and growing markets.

Annualized Returns
1-Year 19.5%%
3-Year 17.3%
5-Year 13.8%

Portfolio Manager: Peter L. Mitchelson (senior portfolio manager) and Ronald D. Sit.

Suitability: The fund is suitable for more aggressive investors who prefer capital appreciation over current income. The fund is suitable for those saving for retirement or a child's education and have long investment horizons.

Portfolio Implications: Given the adviser's philosophy, it shouldn't be a big surprise to find this portfolio packed with technology stocks and other high profile, high growth, blue-chip stocks.

Risk: This fund's shares contain higher-than-average risk, considering its twin objectives of capital growth and current income. Its beta is 1.07. However, its share price declined by a modest 11 percent during the 1990 bear market.

Costs: This is a cost-efficient fund. Its shares are sold with a no-load format. Its annual expense ratio is a modest 1.00 percent, and its portfolio turnover ratio (67 percent) is slightly below average for the group.

Distributions: Income and capital gains are distributed annually.

How to Buy and Sell: Minimum initial investment $2,000; IRA no minimum requirements; subsequent investments $100. Shares can also be obtained through Charles Schwab and Jack White and Company without transaction fees.

STEIN ROE GROWTH & INCOME

Stein Roe & Farnham
P.O. Box 804058
Chicago, IL 60680
800–338–2550

Inception: 1987
Total Assets: $177 Million
Ticker Symbol: SRPEX
Home Page: http://
www.steinroe.com

Objective and Strategy: The fund seeks long-term capital appreciation by investing primarily in large, well-established companies—companies with improving fundamentals, solid earnings and healthy cash flows, broadly diversified product lines and services, strong competitive advantages, sound balance sheets, and proven management capabilities. These are often companies you'll recognize. They are typically key players in their respective industries, and their stocks offer liquidity and long-term growth potential. Total return is management's overriding objective, and that's a function of an emphasis on growth combined with a nearly equal emphasis on income. The fund is managed to be an all-weather fund, with the objective of performing well in bull and bear markets alike.

Portfolio Manager: Daniel Cantor since 1995 and Jeffrey Kinzel since April 1996. Cantor, who joined Stein Roe in 1985, also manages the family's Young Investor fund.

Suitability: This fund is suitable for both conservative and aggressive investors who prefer to take a total return approach to wealth building.

Annualized Returns

1-Year 22.7%

3-Year 15.6%

5-Year 15.8%

Portfolio Implications: The fund's portfolio is packed with the who's who of corporate America. It's a value/growth player that concentrates its investments in blue-chip stocks. Thus, its portfolio holdings will most likely provide duplication with other well-managed equity-income funds.

Risk: Surprisingly, this fund possesses a very modest beta (0.76) given its emphasis on growth stocks. Furthermore, its share price declined by a modest 12.5 percent during the 1990 bear market.

Costs: This is a modest-cost offering. Its shares are sold with a no-load format, and its 1.15-percent annual operating expense ratio and 70-percent portfolio turnover ratio are slightly below the equity fund average.

Distributions: Net investment income is distributed quarterly, and capital gains are paid in December.

How to Buy and Sell: Minimum investment requirement $2,500; IRA $500; subsequent investments $100. Telephone exchange with other Stein Roe funds. Shares may also be obtained without transaction fees from Charles Schwab and Jack White and Company.

STRONG TOTAL RETURN

Strong Funds Distributors
100 Heritage Reserve
P.O. Box 2936
Milwaukee, WI 53201
800-368-3863

Inception: 1981
Total Assets: $737 Million
Ticker Symbol: STRFX
Home Page: http://www.strong-funds.com

Objective and Strategy: The fund seeks high total return by investing for capital growth and income. Management emphasizes large- and medium-sized companies with superior earnings or dividend growth potential. These companies often benefit from favorable secular trends, which currently include services and technologies that enhance productivity and provide solutions, greying of America, and consolidating industries. The vast majority (85 percent) of the fund's assets are invested in common stocks. Following investment themes has served shareholders well. The fund has returned an average of 15.6 percent annually since its inception in December 1981. This is a highly diversified vehicle with more than one hundred different companies and forty-five industries being represented.

Portfolio Manager: Ronald C. Ognar since 1993 and Ian J. Rogers since 1994. Ognar also manages the family's Asset Allocation and Growth funds. Rogers has worked with Ognar as an equity analyst since joining Strong in August 1993.

Suitability: This fund is suitable for modestly or highly aggressive investors who prefer a total return strategy to increasing wealth.

Annualized Returns

1-Year 12.7%
3-Year 11.6%
5-Year 13.1%

Portfolio Implications: Although this is a total return fund, management places more of its emphasis on growth. Thus, you can expect this fund to produce market-topping returns over the long run. However, many of its holdings will duplicate those of other well-managed equity-income funds.

Risk: This fund is near the high end of the growth and income fund risk spectrum with a beta of 1.06. However, its share price declined by a surprisingly modest 8.5 percent during the 1990 bear market.

Costs: This fund's shares are sold with a no-load format. Its annual operating expense ratio (1.14 percent) is below average, but its portfolio turnover ratio (like those of most Strong funds) is a hefty 299 percent, which increases portfolio transaction costs.

Distributions: Net investment income is paid quarterly and capital gains are distributed annually.

How to Buy and Sell: Minimum initial investment $250; IRA $250; subsequent investments $50. Telephone exchange with other Strong funds. Shares may also be obtained through Charles Schwab, Fidelity Brokerage, and Jack White and Company without transaction fees.

T. ROWE PRICE BALANCED

T. Rowe Price Investment Services
100 East Pratt Street
Baltimore, MD 21202
800-225-5132

Inception: 1939
Total Assets: $788 Million
Ticker Symbol: RPBAX
Home Page: http://
www.troweprice.com

Objective and Strategy: This fund, which began selling shares in 1939, was acquired by T. Rowe Price from USF&G in September 1992. It was previously known as the Axe-Houghton Fund. It seeks to conserve capital while providing some current income and long-term capital growth. Assets are invested in common stocks, bonds, and preferred stocks. Management will adjust the weight of each asset class with accommodating market conditions. No more than 75 percent of the fund's assets may be invested in common stocks. The fund also invests in foreign bonds and equities. Since being guided by T. Rowe Price managers, the fund has posted enviable returns. Of course, falling interest rates and rising stock prices provided a favorable environment. The fund is highly diversified, with no single common stock accounting for more than 1 percent of portfolio assets.

Portfolio Manager: Richard T. Whitney has been chairman of the fund's management committee since 1994. He joined T. Rowe Price in 1985.

Suitability: This fund could be considered to be a complete investment program for conservative investors. Modestly aggressive investors who prefer a balance between capital appreciation and current income will also be attracted to this well-managed fund.

Annualized Returns

1-Year 13.4%
3-Year 11.0%
5-Year 12.0%

Portfolio Implications: This fund is exceptionally well diversified with the stocks of more than four hundred companies being represented. In addition, its bond holdings include both domestic and foreign issues. If you are a conservative investor with limited resources, this is the fund for you.

Risk: This fund's beta is a bit high for a balanced fund (0.92). However, its numerous holdings provide plenty of risk protection. Its share price declined by a very modest 2.4 percent during the 1990 bear market.

Costs: Like all T. Rowe Price offerings, this is a very cost-efficient fund. Its shares are sold with a no-load format; its annual expense ratio is a low 0.95 percent, and its portfolio turnover ratio is an extremely low 13 percent.

Distributions: Income distributions are paid quarterly and capital gains are distributed in December.

How to Buy and Sell: Minimum initial investment $2,500; IRA $1,000; subsequent investments $100. Telephone exchange with other T. Rowe Price funds. However, the company frowns on frequent switching and will not accommodate market timers.

T. ROWE PRICE DIVIDEND GROWTH

T. Rowe Price Investment Services
100 East Pratt Street
Baltimore, MD 21202
800–225–5132

Inception: 1992
Total Assets: $112 Million
Ticker Symbol: PRDGX
Home Page: http://
www.troweprice.com

Objective and Strategy: This fund's objective is to provide increasing dividend income over time, long-term capital appreciation, and reasonable current income through investments in dividend-paying stocks. The fund looks for stocks with both above-average earnings and dividend growth potential, and attempts to buy them when they are temporarily out of favor or undervalued by the market. Management seeks stocks that possess one or more of the following characteristics: a track record of above-average dividend growth, competitive current dividend yield, sound balance sheet and solid cash flow, a sustainable competitive advantage and leading market position, and attractive valuations evidenced by a relatively high dividend yield. Since the fund's inception in late 1992, it has returned an average of more than 17 percent a year.

Portfolio Manager: William J. Stromberg has been chairman of the fund's management committee since 1992. Stromberg joined Price in 1987.

Suitability: This fund is suitable for conservative investors of all kinds. If you are primarily a fixed-income (bond) fund investor, this portfolio adds the inflation offset that you need. If you are interested in quality growth stocks, you won't find many better portfolios than this.

Annualized Returns
1-Year 23.1%
3-Year 17.3%
5-Year NA

Portfolio Implications: What you get here is a pot of large-cap, blue-chip, dividend-paying stocks. For maximum diversification benefit, add an international equity and a small-cap fund to an investment in this fund.

Risk: The fund boasts a modest beta (0.70) for an equity fund. This relatively young fund has yet to experience a severe bear market, but we expect it will weather financial storms quite well.

Costs: Like all T. Rowe Price offerings, this is a very cost-efficient fund. Its shares are sold with a no-load format, its annual expense ratio is a modest 1.10 percent, and its portfolio turnover ratio is a below-average 56 percent.

Distributions: Net investment income is paid quarterly, and capital gains are distributed annually in late December.

How to Buy and Sell: Minimum initial investment $2,500; IRA $1,000; subsequent investments $100. Telephone exchange with other T. Rowe Price funds. However, the company frowns on frequent switching and will not accommodate market timers.

T. ROWE PRICE EQUITY INCOME

T. Rowe Price Investment Services
100 East Pratt Street
Baltimore, MD 21202
800-225-5132

Inception: 1985
Total Assets: $6.3 Billion
Ticker Symbol: PRFDX
Home Page: http://
www.troweprice.com

Objective and Strategy: This fund, which seeks a combination of capital appreciation and current income by investing in dividend-paying common stocks, is one of the best funds in the growth and income group. In fact, the fund has posted the best returns of any equity-income fund over the last ten years, and there is no reason to suspect that its stellar performance won't continue. This fact is somewhat surprising in that this fund leans toward the conservative in stressing a higher dividend yield rather than capital growth. However, most investors forget that 40 percent of the stock market's average return during the last half-century has been supplied by dividend yield. This is not a stop-and-go fund, reporting a spectacular return one year and a mediocre return the next. It is a steady performer, year after year. In fact, it has experienced only one down year in its history—a 6.8-percent decline in 1990.

Portfolio Manager: Brian C. Rogers has been chairman of this fund's management committee since 1993. He joined Price in 1982.

Suitability: This is a fund for one and all. If you are an aggressive investor, you'll like the total returns this fund provides. If you are a conservative investor, you'll like the safety as well as the current income.

Annualized Returns

1-Year 20.5%
3-Year 17.2%
5-Year 16.3%

Portfolio Implications: This portfolio is packed with solid dividend-paying companies. Invest in this fund and add a few other well-managed funds and you can't go wrong. It is the ideal fund to use as the core of a retirement program or a child's education savings plan.

Risk: This fund sports a modest 0.75 beta, but its share price can be volatile when interest rates gyrate wildly. Its share price declined by slightly more than 16 percent during the 1990 bear market.

Costs: Like all T. Rowe Price offerings, this is a very cost-efficient fund. Its shares are sold with a no-load format, its annual expense ratio is a low 0.85 percent, and its portfolio turnover ratio is a very low 21 percent.

Distributions: Net investment income is paid quarterly, and capital gains are distributed annually in December.

How to Buy and Sell: Minimum initial investment $2,500; IRA $1,000; subsequent investments $100. Telephone exchange with other T. Rowe Price funds. However, the company frowns on frequent switching and will not accommodate market timers.

T. ROWE PRICE GROWTH & INCOME

T. Rowe Price Investment Services
100 East Pratt Street
Baltimore, MD 21202
800-225-5132

Inception: 1982
Total Assets: $2.1 Billion
Ticker Symbol: PRGIX
Home Page: http://
www.troweprice.com

Objective and Strategy: As its name implies, the fund seeks to provide both capital growth and current income. Investments include dividend-paying common stocks, preferred stocks, and convertible bonds. Stocks are selected that have good prospects for growth of capital and increasing dividends. The fund has maintained an above-average current yield and lower-than-average risk and has provided investors with a ten-year return above the average of its growth and income counterparts. A strict value strategy helps bolt this fund to the top of the performance charts in appropriate market environments. Give this fund a try. You'll get a diversified portfolio containing more than 120 carefully selected common stocks.

Portfolio Manager: Stephen W. Boesel has been chairman of the fund's management committee since 1987. He joined Price in 1973.

Suitability: This fund is suitable for conservative investors who prefer a combination of capital appreciation and current dividend income.

Annualized Returns

1-Year 21.1%

3-Year 16.1%

5-Year 15.2%

Portfolio Implications: This well-managed fund is packed with large-cap, blue-chip, dividend-paying stocks. It looks like many other growth and income funds. Thus, there is the potential for portfolio duplication if this fund is added to a portfolio packed with other growth and income funds.

Risk: If you want to earn exceptional returns, you have to assume appropriate risks. Although the beta of this fund is a modest 0.79, its share price tumbled nearly 20 percent during the 1990 bear market.

Costs: Like all T. Rowe Price offerings, this is a very cost-efficient fund. Its shares are sold with a no-load format, its annual expense ratio is a low 0.84 percent, and its portfolio turnover ratio is a low 26 percent.

Distributions: Net investment income is paid quarterly, and capital gains are distributed annually in late December.

How to Buy and Sell: Minimum initial investment $2,500; IRA $1,000; subsequent investments $100. Telephone exchange with other T. Rowe Price funds. However, the company frowns on frequent switching and will not accommodate active market timers.

USAA CORNERSTONE STRATEGY

USAA Investment Management Co.
9800 Fredericksburg Road
San Antonio, TX 78288
800-531-8181

Inception: 1984
Total Assets: $1.0 Billion
Ticker Symbol: USCRX
Home Page: None

Objective and Strategy: This is an asset allocation fund that produces a combination of capital appreciation and current income. Its investment objective is the preservation of shareholders' purchasing power against inflation and the achievement of a stable net asset value with a positive real (after inflation) return. The fund divides its assets among five investment categories (domestic stocks, foreign stocks, gold equities, U.S. government bonds, and real estate related securities) to meet its objective. While maintaining low share price volatility and a reasonable expense ratio, the fund has continuously provided investors with double-digit, long-term returns. It you are seeking the ultimate in portfolio balance and are willing to sacrifice some return during a bull market for plenty of protection during a bear market, consider sending some of your capital in the direction of this fund.

Portfolio Manager: Harry Miller since 1987 is the fund's asset allocation manager and focuses on basic value stocks. John Saunders manages the portfolio's bond portion, David Peebles manages foreign stocks, and Mark Johnson manages the gold and real estate portions.

Suitability: We can't think of an investor that couldn't benefit from investment in this

Annualized Returns

1-Year 14.3%
3-Year 10.0%
5-Year 12.3%

fund. If you are seeking a complete investment program and want to invest in a single fund, this is the one.

Portfolio Implications: You can't judge this fund by its return relative to that of the stock market because it contains diverse asset categories that mute both returns and risk. Its allocation to gold mining stocks gives it plenty of inflation protection.

Risk: Although the fund sports a 0.89 beta, this is one of the lowest risk funds you'll find that invests in equity securities. Its share price declined a modest 9.4 percent during the 1990 bear market, which devastated most equity funds.

Costs: This fund provides diversification at a reasonable cost. Its shares are sold with a no-load format, its annual expense ratio is a modest 1.15 percent, and its portfolio turnover ratio is a low 36 percent.

Distributions: Both income and capital gains are distributed annually, usually in November.

How to Buy and Sell: Minimum initial investment $3,000; IRA $250; subsequent investments $50. Telephone exchange with other USAA funds.

USAA GROWTH & INCOME

USAA Investment Management Co.
9800 Fredericksburg Road
San Antonio, TX 78288
800-382-8722

Inception: 1993
Total Assets: $381 Million
Ticker Symbol: USGRX
Home Page: None

Objective and Strategy: The fund's investment objective is capital growth and current income. The fund's manager pursues this objective by investing at least 65 percent of the fund's assets in dividend-paying common stocks or in securities convertible into common stocks. Up to 30 percent of the fund's assets may be invested in American Depository Receipts or similar forms of ownership interest in securities of foreign issuers. In recent months, the fund's manager reduced the weighting in health care and utility stocks. Adherence to its value-oriented investment philosophy resulted in the addition of various investments in chemicals, aerospace, and selected retailing sectors. The purchases and sales over the year continued to comply with the fund's philosophy of focusing on value, as defined by earnings, cash flow, book value, and yield.

Annualized Returns
1-Year 18.8%
3-Year 15.5%
5-Year NA

Portfolio Manager: R. David Ullom since the fund's inception in June 1993. He joined USAA in 1986 and has held various positions in the equity investment side of the business. He received an M.B.A. from Washington University, St. Louis.

Suitability: The fund is suitable for both conservative and more modestly aggressive

investors who prefer a total return investment strategy.

Portfolio Implications: The fund's value-oriented, equity-income approach to providing total return has resulted in a portfolio with characteristics quite similar to those of other equity-income funds. Thus, you only need one of these vehicles in your conservative growth and income portfolio.

Risk: This relatively young fund has yet to experience a major bear stock market. Its near-market beta (0.94) suggests that it will fully participate on the downside during a sharp stock market sell-off.

Costs: The fund possesses a modest cost structure. Its shares are sold with a no-load format, and its 1.01-percent expense ratio is below average, as is its 20-percent annual portfolio turnover ratio.

Distributions: Income is paid quarterly and capital gains are distributed annually.

How to Buy and Sell: Minimum initial investment $3,000; IRA $250; subsequent investments $50. Telephone exchange with other USAA funds.

USAA INCOME STOCK

USAA Investment Management Co.
9800 Fredericksburg Road
San Antonio, TX 78288
800-531-8181

Inception: 1987
Total Assets: $1.8 Billion
Ticker Symbol: USISX
Home Page: None

Objective and Strategy: Yield calls the tune at this conservative growth and income fund. The goals of this fund are to provide a high cash dividend yield, increase cash payments to shareholders every year, and maintain a portfolio that doesn't have a great deal of volatility. To maintain a high yield (the highest of any diversified equity fund), management has turned to investing in real estate investment trusts, electric utility stocks, and convertible bonds. Focus is placed on stocks with a history of dividend increases and those of "turnaround" companies. Portfolio turnover is relatively low and would be virtually non-existent except for the reinvestment of cash dividends and periodic profit taking.

Portfolio Manager: Harry Miller since 1989. He has worked for USAA for twenty-one years. He received an M.B.A. from the University of Southern California.

Suitability: This is an ideally suited fund for conservative investors who desire a greater-than-average dividend yield from their equity investments.

Annualized Returns
1-Year 12.7%
3-Year 10.7%
5-Year 12.4%

Portfolio Implications: Although the fund is interest rate sensitive, it declines by far less than the market during sell-offs, and its steady dividend income is used to buy additional shares of well-managed companies that have declined with the market.

Risk: The fund sports a modest 0.82 beta. Because of its emphasis on high-yield common stocks, its shares can be highly interest rate sensitive. However, its share price declined by a very modest 6.4 percent during the 1990 bear market.

Costs: This is a very cost-efficient fund. Its shares are sold with a no-load format and both its 0.75-percent annual expense ratio and 35-percent portfolio turnover ratio are below average for equity funds.

Distributions: Income is paid quarterly and capital gains are distributed annually.

How to Buy and Sell: Minimum initial investment $3,000; IRA $250; subsequent investments $50. Telephone exchange with other USAA funds.

VANGUARD EQUITY INCOME

Vanguard Group
Vanguard Financial Center
P.O. Box 2600
Valley Forge, PA 19482
800-635-1511

Inception: 1988
Total Assets: $1.3 Billion
Ticker Symbol: VEIPX
Home Page: http://
www.vanguard.com

Objective and Strategy: This pure no-load fund seeks a high level of income by investing in a broad array of dividend-paying equity securities. Capital appreciation is a secondary investment objective. Management hopes to maintain an income yield at least 50 percent greater than that of the Standard & Poor's 500 Index. Lead portfolio manager Roger Newell has done an excellent job of following the guidelines set by the fund's investment objective. The fund has provided generous yields and competitive total returns. Benefitting long-term return is Vanguard's philosophy of keeping investment expenses low. This fund has an exceptionally low expense and portfolio turnover ratio. Thus, its shareholders get to keep most of what this well-managed fund earns.

Portfolio Manager: Managed by three investment advisers: Newell Associates (Roger Newell), Spare, Kaplan, Bischell (Anthony Spare), and John Al Levin (Jeffrey Kigner and Melody Sarnell).

Suitability: The fund is suitable for cost-conscious, conservative investors who prefer to balance total returns between current income and capital appreciation. This fund works best in tax-deferred accounts.

Annualized Returns

1-Year 18.2%
3-Year 13.0%
5-Year 14.1%

Portfolio Implications: The fund's portfolio is packed with the who's who of dividend-paying corporations. Its portfolio will probably provide significant duplication with other well-managed equity-income funds.

Risk: This fund's fully-invested posture adds a bit of risk. Its beta is below that of the market (0.88). However, its share price declined by a hefty 19 percent during the 1990 bear market.

Costs: You won't find many funds that are more cost-efficient than those offered by Vanguard. The fund's shares are sold with a no-load format. Its annual expense ratio is a phenomenally low 0.47 percent, and its 31-percent portfolio turnover ratio is well below average.

Distributions: Income is paid quarterly and capital gains are distributed annually in December.

How to Buy and Sell: Minimum initial investment $3,000; IRA $1,000; subsequent investments $100. Telephone exchange with other Vanguard funds. However, frequent switchers will be asked to invest somewhere else.

VANGUARD QUANTITATIVE

Vanguard Group
Vanguard Financial Center
P.O. Box 2600
Valley Forge, PA 19482
800-662-7447

Inception: 1986
Total Assets: $1.1 Billion
Ticker Symbol: VQNPX
Home Page: http://
www.vanguard.com

Objective and Strategy: This fund seeks to realize a total return (dividend income plus capital appreciation) greater than the return of the aggregate U.S. stock market, as measured by the Standard & Poor's 500 Composite Index. The fund holds a broadly diversified portfolio of common stocks that in aggregate exhibit the investment characteristics of the S&P 500 Index. These characteristics include such measures as dividend yield, price-earnings ratio, beta, return on equity, and market price-to-book value ratio. To select stocks, the adviser first ranks a broad universe of common stocks using several quantitative investment models. These models are based on such factors as measures of changes in earnings and of relative value based on present and historical P-E ratios and yields, as well as dividend discount calculations based on corporate cash flow.

Annualized Returns
1-Year 17.7%
3-Year 15.7%
5-Year 15.0%

Portfolio Manager: John J. Nagorniak since the fund's inception in 1986. He oversees the application of Franklin's quantitative techniques and the ongoing development and enhancement of these techniques.

Suitability: The fund is designed for investors whose objective is to achieve a total return marginally superior to the return from the S&P 500 Index with reasonable consistency over time.

Portfolio Implications: This is an interesting portfolio. Its financial characteristics are quite similar to the S&P 500 Index portfolio, yet its emphasis on earnings momentum and relative value produce marginally market-topping returns. However, these returns must be measured over long time periods, since the fund will underperform during some short-run periods.

Risk: This fund has marginally higher risk than that of the market as indicated by its 1.02 beta. Its share price declined about as much as the market (about 15 percent) during the 1990 bear market.

Costs: You won't find many funds that are more cost-efficient than those offered by Vanguard. The fund's shares are sold with a no-load format. Its annual expense ratio is a phenomenally low 0.47 percent, and its portfolio turnover ratio is a below average 59 percent.

Distributions: Income is paid quarterly and capital gains are distributed annually in December.

How to Buy and Sell: Minimum initial investment $3,000; IRA $1,000; subsequent investments $100. No telephone exchanges in regular accounts into or out of this fund.

VANGUARD STAR

Vanguard Group
Vanguard Financial Center
P.O. Box 2600
Valley Forge, PA 19482
800-635-1511

Inception: 1985
Total Assets: $5.3 Billion
Ticker Symbol: VGSTX
Home Page: http://
www.vanguard.com

Objective and Strategy: This fund uses a "fund of funds" concept in seeking maximum total investment returns. The portfolio consists of 60 to 70 percent of its assets invested in seven Vanguard funds that primarily invest in equities (Windsor, Windsor II, Explorer, Morgan Growth, U.S. Growth, PRIMECAP, and S&P 500 Index Portfolio). Twenty to thirty percent of its assets are allocated to two Vanguard bond funds (GNMA Portfolio and Long-Term Corporate Bond Portfolio), and the balance (10 to 20 percent) is allocated to Vanguard's Prime money market fund. The portfolio's investment in equity funds has been targeted at 62.5 percent of assets, its bond fund target is 25 percent, and its money market fund target is 12.5 percent. Management believes this allocation strategy will provide more favorable returns with moderate risk than continual rebalancing.

Annualized Returns
1-Year 14.0%
3-Year 12.2%
5-Year 12.7%

Portfolio Manager: This fund has no designated portfolio manager. Its allocations to other Vanguard funds are fixed by policy.

Suitability: The Star portfolio was designed primarily for tax-advantaged retirement accounts and other long-term investment savings. If you want asset allocation at a reasonable cost and prefer a total return approach to investing, this is the fund of choice.

Portfolio Implications: The expense ratio of this fund is zero. However, investors assume a pro rata share of the expenses of the underlying funds. This is the ultimate version of a diversified portfolio, a mutual fund that consists of investment in other mutual funds.

Risk: Because of the fund's large allocation to money market and bond funds, its beta is a very modest 0.69 percent. During the severe 1990 bear market, the fund's share price declined by a modest 11.9 percent.

Costs: Although the annual expense ratio of this fund is officially 0.0 percent, shareholders assume the expenses of the underlying funds. The average of those expenses is less than 0.50 percent. Portfolio turnover is an exceptionally low 13 percent. This is a very cost-efficient asset allocation fund.

Distributions: Income is distributed semi-annually and capital gains are distributed annually.

How to Buy and Sell: Minimum initial investment $1,000; IRA $1,000; subsequent investments $100. Telephone exchange with other Vanguard funds. However, frequent switchers will be asked to invest somewhere else.

VANGUARD WELLESLEY INCOME

Vanguard Group
Vanguard Financial Center
P.O. Box 2600
Valley Forge, PA 19482
800-635-1511

Inception: 1970
Total Assets: $6.9 Billion
Ticker Symbol: VWINX
Home Page: http://
www.vanguard.com

Objective and Strategy: By investing in a balanced portfolio of corporate bonds and high-yielding common stocks, this no-load fund seeks to achieve current income with moderate capital growth. When selecting corporate bonds for the portfolio, management prefers AAA-rated debentures. Over the past seven years, the fund managed to match the market's return, with a risk level significantly lower than that of the Standard & Poor's 500 Index. Furthermore, the fund sports one of the better current yields in the growth and income group. This fund has all the makings of an excellent growth and income vehicle. However, its high exposure to utility stocks and longer-term bonds makes it more sensitive than many of its peers to interest rate fluctuations.

Portfolio Manager: Earl E. McEvoy since 1982. McEvoy is assisted by John R. Ryan, who has managed the fund's equity investments since 1986.

Suitability: This very conservatively managed fund is an ideal investment for timid investors who wish to dodge the extreme volatility of the stock market but wish to earn long-term returns greater than those available in the bond or money markets.

**Annualized
Returns**

1-Year 9.2%

3-Year 7.8%

5-Year 11.0%

Portfolio Implications: This is a ho-hum portfolio, but it delivers the goods. If you are seeking a well-managed balanced fund and want exposure to both the stock and bond markets, this portfolio will fill the bill.

Risk: The returns of this conservatively managed fund are somewhat muted, but so is risk. The fund sports a low 0.58 beta, and its share price declined by less than 2 percent during the 1990 bear market.

Costs: You won't find many funds that are more cost-efficient than those offered by Vanguard. The fund's shares are sold with a no-load format. Its 0.35-percent annual expense ratio is exceptionally low, as is its 32-percent portfolio turnover ratio.

Distributions: Income is paid quarterly and capital gains are distributed annually in December.

How to Buy and Sell: Minimum initial investment $3,000; IRA $1,000; subsequent investments $50. Telephone exchange with other Vanguard funds. However, frequent switchers will be asked to invest somewhere else.

VANGUARD WELLINGTON

Vanguard Group
Vanguard Financial Center
P.O. Box 2600
Valley Forge, PA 19482
800-635-1511

Inception: 1929
Total Assets: $14.1 Billion
Ticker Symbol: VWELX
Home Page: http://
www.vanguard.com

Objective and Strategy: This fund's objective is to provide investors with preservation of principal, reasonable income, and capital growth without assuming undue risk. The fund performed well during the 1980s and, considering its low beta, it has more than accomplished its multiple objectives during the 1990s as well. The fund's performance has not gone unnoticed by investors as the fund's assets nearly doubled to more than $14 billion during the last two years. Such a flood of fresh capital might have hampered other funds in obtaining their objectives. However, this fund's low portfolio turnover ratio, large commitment to bonds of all kinds (i.e., government, corporate, and foreign), and investment in billion-dollar capitalization stocks has allowed it to easily invest new cash.

Portfolio Manager: Ernst H. von Metzsch since 1995. He previously served as the fund's assistant portfolio manager for twenty years. Paul D. Kaplan began managing the fund's fixed-income investments in 1994.

Suitability: This fund is suitable for conservative investors who wish to invest in a combination of quality stocks and bonds. Because of the high yield component of its total return, the fund works best in tax-deferred accounts.

Annualized Returns

1-Year 15.4%
3-Year 13.7%
5-Year 13.4%

Portfolio Implications: Given this fund's gigantic size, its portfolio is relatively compact, containing the common stocks of less than one hundred companies. Most Dow Jones Industrial Average stocks are represented, as are some of the largest stocks in the Standard & Poor's 500 Index.

Risk: The fund possesses a surprisingly high beta (1.11), given its commitment to both stocks and bonds. However, its share price declined by a modest 10.7 percent during the 1990 bear market.

Costs: You won't find many funds that are more cost-efficient than those offered by Vanguard. The fund's shares are sold with a no-load format. Its 0.35-percent annual expense ratio is exceptionally low, as is its 24-percent portfolio turnover ratio.

Distributions: Net investment income is paid quarterly, and capital gains are distributed annually in December.

How to Buy and Sell: Minimum initial investment $3,000; IRA $1,000; subsequent investments $100. Telephone exchange with other Vanguard funds. However, frequent switchers will be asked to invest somewhere else.

VANGUARD WINDSOR II

Vanguard Group
Vanguard Financial Center
P.O. Box 2600
Valley Forge, PA 19482
800-635-1511

Inception: 1985
Total Assets: $13.3 Billion
Ticker Symbol: VWNEX
Home Page: http://
www.vanguard.com

Objective and Strategy: This no-load fund was created to cash in on the success of the highly popular Windsor fund, which closed its doors to new investors in 1985. Windsor II, like its namesake, is a growth and income fund. However, it is not a clone. The fund emphasizes income-producing common stocks that are largely characterized by above-average income yields and below-average price-earnings ratios. Stocks are selected based upon assessments of statistical measures of current value (such as low price-earnings ratios and low price-to-book ratios) and future earnings prospects. During the last ten years, the fund has produced a very respectable 13.3-percent average annual return. As might be expected, financial stocks make up a significant portion of the fund's equity holdings. Its emphasis on low valuations and high dividend yields give this fund full equity exposure, yet provides some protection during stock market declines.

Annualized Returns
1-Year 20.6%
3-Year 16.1%
5-Year 16.0%

Portfolio Manager: The fund is managed by three outside advisers: Barrow, Hanley, Mewhinney & Strauss (James Barrow), Equinox Capital Management (Ron Ulrich), and Tukman Capital Management (Melvin Tukman).

Suitability: The fund is intended for investors who are seeking growth of capital and income. However, the fund should not be considered a substitute for fixed-income investments.

Portfolio Implications: This fund's portfolio is packed with the stocks that traditionally rank high on value and income—financials, energy, and public utilities. In fact, in total, these three sectors account for more than half of the fund's portfolio. Thus, there is plenty of interest rate sensitivity here.

Risk: The fund possesses a near-market beta (0.96). However, its interest rate exposure can create more share price volatility during turbulent periods in the financial markets as witnessed by its 17.7-percent share price decline during the 1990 bear market.

Costs: You won't find many funds that are more cost-efficient than those offered by Vanguard. The fund's shares are sold with a no-load format. Its 0.40-percent annual expense ratio is exceptionally low, as is its 40-percent portfolio turnover ratio.

Distributions: Income is paid semi-annually and capital gains are distributed in December.

How to Buy and Sell: Minimum initial investment $3,000; IRA $1,000; subsequent investments $100. Telephone exchange with other Vanguard funds. Frequent switching is not permitted.

WPG GROWTH AND INCOME

WPG Mutual Funds
One New York Plaza
New York, NY 10004
800-223-3332

Inception: 1979
Total Assets: $69 Million
Ticker Symbol: WPGFX
Home Page: None

Objective and Strategy: As one of the more aggressive growth and income vehicles, this fund seeks long-term growth of capital, a reasonable level of current income, and an increase in future income through investments in primarily income-producing equity securities. The fund invests in common stocks and convertible securities of companies believed to have better-than-average growth prospects and investment-grade fixed-income securities. This fund has a greater portion of assets committed to small company stocks than most growth and income vehicles, giving it a more aggressive stance. Of course, this posture gives the fund a better-than-average return potential, and it has delivered on that potential. The fund has its share of household names, too. Included are the stocks of such companies as Philip Morris, General Electric, Merck, and Exxon.

Portfolio Manager: A. Roy Knutsen since 1992. Mr. Knutsen has been a principal of WPG for over five years.

Suitability: The fund is ideally suited for investors who can handle management's aggressive touch. This includes both modestly aggressive and aggressive investors

Annualized Returns
1-Year 20.2%
3-Year 12.4%
5-Year 14.4%

who seek a total return approach to wealth enhancement.

Portfolio Implications: This fund actually lies somewhere between the growth and income and growth categories. Thus, its performance usually stacks up well when compared to more tame growth and income funds.

Risk: This is one of the more aggressive growth and income entrants. Its beta is about equal to that of the market (0.99). However, its share price tumbled more than 24 percent during the 1990 bear market.

Costs: This is an average-cost growth and income fund. Its shares are sold with a no-load format, its annual expense ratio is 1.22 percent, and its portfolio turnover ratio is 79 percent.

Distributions: Both income and capital gains are distributed annually.

How to Buy and Sell: Minimum initial investment $2,500; IRA $250; subsequent investments $100. Telephone exchange with other WPG funds.

WPG QUANTITATIVE EQUITY

WPG Mutual Funds
One New York Plaza
New York, NY 10004
800-223-3332

Inception: 1993
Total Assets: $156 Million
Ticker Symbol: WPGQX
Home Page: None

Objective and Strategy: If you want to own stocks contained in the S&P 500 Index, yet possess the potential to outperform the index, try investing in this fund. It seeks to outperform the S&P 500 Index by beginning with the five hundred stocks in the index and applying a sophisticated quantitative model that balances risk against return. The object of the exercise is to develop a so-called efficient portfolio in the Capital Asset Pricing Model sense that contains an optimal balance between risk and return. The portfolio selected for the fund consists of S&P 500 Index stocks with the appropriate weights to produce a portfolio with a level of risk equivalent to that of the S&P 500 Index, yet possess greater long-term potential. Every six months, WPG repeats the entire optimization process and readjusts the fund's portfolio to conform to the requirements of the most recent statistical application.

Annualized Returns
1-Year 19.1%
3-Year 14.4%
5-Year NA

Portfolio Manager: Joseph N. Pappo since the fund's inception in 1993. Prior to joining WPG, Pappo was founder and president of Eden Financial Group, which was acquired by WPG in 1991.

Suitability: This fund's shares are suitable for more aggressive investors who prefer a mix of capital appreciation and some current income.

Portfolio Implications: The fund's portfolio is drawn from stocks contained in the S&P 500 Index and thus contains only large-capitalization issues. However, not all 500 stocks are included. Its recent portfolio contained about 150 of the Index's 500 stocks.

Risk: This fund's risk level, by definition, will parallel that of the Standard & Poor's 500 Index, and its beta (currently 0.98) will average about 1.00. This relatively young fund has yet to experience a major bear market. However, its share price will decline by a percentage similar to the S&P 500 Index.

Costs: This is a very cost-efficient fund. Its shares are sold with a no-load format. Its annual expense ratio is a modest 1.00 percent, and its portfolio turnover ratio (26 percent) is well below average.

Distributions: Both income and capital gains are distributed annually.

How to Buy and Sell: Minimum initial investment $5,000; IRA $250; subsequent investments $500 ($100 IRA).

WARBURG PINCUS BALANCED

Warburg Pincus Funds
466 Lexington Avenue
New York, NY 10017
800-257-5614

Inception: 1989
Total Assets: $29 Million
Ticker Symbol: WAPBX
Home Page: None

Objective and Strategy: This somewhat unique balanced fund seeks to maximize total return through a combination of long-term growth of capital and current income consistent with preservation of capital. What makes this fund unique is that it uses four equity portfolio managers to oversee an allocated portion of the fund's equity holdings. Each manager acts independently of the others and invests in a particular sector of the global equities markets. The four sectors include U.S. value sector (consisting of large-cap stocks with valuations below that of the S&P 500), U.S. small-company sector (consisting of small- and mid-cap companies that have passed their start-up phase and exhibit exceptional growth), U.S. mid-cap sector (consisting of growth companies with equity capitalizations between $600 million and $13.8 billion), and international equity sector (consisting of foreign-domiciled companies of varying sizes). The balance of the portfolio is invested in both investment-grade and junk bonds.

Portfolio Manager: The fund uses a multiple manager approach. Anthony G. Orphanos and Dale C. Christensen oversee the portfolio strategy and sector allocation. Orphanos joined Warburg in 1977 and Christensen in 1989.

Suitability: Given the fund's diverse group of equity investments coupled with an allocation to bonds, this fund can represent a

Annualized Returns:

1-Year 12.0%
3-Year 13.8%
5-Year 12.7%

complete investment program. It is ideally suited for conservative investors who desire a balance between current income and capital growth.

Portfolio Implications: With all major sectors of the equity market being represented, investors with limited resources can obtain a highly diverse portfolio with an initial investment as low as $1,000. The fund's portfolio provides little duplication with other growth and income funds.

Risk: Risk is somewhat muted because of the fund's wide diversification. Its beta is a modest 0.87, and its share price declined by a very modest 5.2 percent during the 1990 bear market.

Costs: This is an average-cost fund. Its shares are sold without either a front-end or back-end sales charge, but carry an ongoing 12b-1 fee (0.25 percent). Its 1.53-percent expense ratio is slightly above average as is its 107-percent portfolio turnover ratio.

Distributions: Net investment income is paid quarterly, and capital gains are distributed annually in either November or December.

How to Buy and Sell: Minimum initial investment $1,000; IRA $500; subsequent investments $100. Telephone exchange with other Warburg funds. Shares may also be obtained through Charles Schwab, Fidelity Brokerage, and Jack White and Company.

WARBURG PINCUS GROWTH & INCOME (COM)

Warburg Pincus Funds
466 Lexington Avenue
New York, NY 10017
800-257-5614

Inception: 1989
Total Assets: $897 Million
Ticker Symbol: RBEGX
Home Page: None

Objective and Strategy: This fund seeks growth of capital and income and a reasonable current return by investing primarily in equity securities. However, the fund has a high degree of flexibility and can invest in bonds and cash equivalents as well. In recent years, the fund has been packed with equity securities, primarily those of companies involved in the development of industrial materials (paper products, steel, etc.), energy and energy service companies, and banks and savings and loans. These are secular themes that the fund's portfolio manager plans to pursue in the future. He hopes to continue to capitalize on consolidation in the banking community, the heightened demand for industrial products resulting from the spread of capitalism to the former Soviet Union and China, and a heightened demand for energy as emerging economies expand their productive capabilities.

Annualized Returns

1-Year -3.6%
3-Year 9.6%
5-Year 13.6%

Portfolio Manager: Anthony G. Orphanos since 1991. He has been with Warburg since 1977 and also oversees the strategy for the Balanced fund.

Suitability: This fund is suitable for more aggressive investors who desire a greater portion of their total return from capital appreciation rather than income.

Portfolio Implications: The fund's portfolio is heavily influenced by the twin engines of low interest rates and global economic expansion. Its heavy investments in three sectors gives this fund a more concentrated portfolio than most other growth and income vehicles.

Risk: Big sector bets lead to big risks. Although the fund's beta is a modest 0.71 and its share price declined by a very modest 5 percent during the 1990 bear market, the risk in this fund is that its large sector bets may not pay off during a robust bull market.

Costs: This is an average-cost fund. Its shares are sold with a no-load format. Its 1.22-percent annual expense ratio is slightly below average, but its 109-percent portfolio turnover ratio is above average.

Distributions: Income is paid quarterly, and capital gains are distributed annually in either November or December.

How to Buy and Sell: Minimum initial investment $1,000; IRA $500; subsequent investments $100. Shares may also be obtained without transaction fees from Charles Schwab, Fidelity Brokerage, and Jack White and Company.

FORTY

International Equity Funds

This chapter contains descriptions of top-rated equity funds that invest around the world. Included are both *global funds,* which invest in both U.S. and foreign securities and *foreign funds,* which restrict their security holdings to companies domiciled outside the United States. Table 29 in section II lists financial statistics for regional funds (which invest in countries in a specific geographic region such as Europe, Latin America, or the Pacific Basin), while table 30 lists statistics of funds that concentrate their investments in so-called emerging markets.

Investment risk in international equity funds tends to parallel the fund's degree of diversification, with the most diversified (global funds) possessing the least risk and the most concentrated (single-country funds) possessing the most risk. Returns from foreign securities tend to have relatively low correlations with returns from U.S. securities. Thus, a portfolio consisting of investment in both U.S. and comparable foreign securities tends to possess less variability (risk) than a portfolio whose assets are concentrated in a single country. Some academic studies indicate that the optimally balanced portfolio allocates two-thirds of its assets to stocks of U.S.-domiciled companies and one-third to foreign stocks. This mix delivers the greatest equity return for the least amount of volatility or risk.

On average international and global funds possess greater expense ratios than do funds that specialize in U.S. equities. In addition, international and global funds tend to pay relatively modest income distributions. Furthermore, since investing activities take place in foreign markets, fund profits are taxed by the countries in which those profits were derived. However, U.S. investors can obtain an income tax credit for their pro rata share of the foreign taxes paid by international mutual funds.

During most of the 1980s, international equity returns were above average as a result of both a runaway stock market in Japan and the falling value of the U.S. dollar. Thus, it is not surprising to find that, on average, funds that invested internationally have posted enviable track records over the past fifteen years. However, beginning in 1990, the value of the U.S. dollar began to stabilize against most international currencies and in some cases showed considerable strength. In addition, stock prices on most international exchanges hit the skids. At one point during 1992, for example, the Nikkei Index on the Tokyo stock exchange was trading 50 percent below its 1986 level. Although international equity markets made an abrupt about-face in 1993, the returns of foreign stocks, on average, have not kept pace with the returns from U.S. stocks in recent years.

With an average beta of about 0.80, these funds may appear to possess lower risk than domestic growth funds. However, the beta is somewhat misleading in that it results from the relatively low correlation of returns between U.S. and foreign securities and not from a low level of volatility of international equities. In fact, the returns of foreign stocks tend to be more volatile than those of U.S. stocks because of changing rates of exchange between the U.S. dollar and major foreign currencies. When the value of the dollar is rising, returns from international securities (restated in dollar terms) tend to fall. On the other hand, when the value of the dollar is falling, returns of international securities are enhanced. Finally, be aware that investing internationally entails the assumption of political risk. For example, a change in government can result in a change in laws governing investment by foreigners. At the extreme, such changes can result in the confiscation of assets owned by nonnationals. Thus, international investments suffer the compound effects of economic, foreign exchange, and political risks.

ACORN INTERNATIONAL

Acorn Funds
P.O. Box 8502
Boston, MA 02266-8502
800-922-6769

Inception: 1992
Total Assets: $1.6 Billion
Ticker Symbol: ACING
Home Page: None

Objective and Strategy: This fund seeks long-term capital appreciation by investing in small and medium-sized companies based abroad. It is particularly interested in companies with strong growth prospects, strong balance sheets, and whose shares provide fundamental value. Rather than emphasize country or region weightings, the fund's portfolio manager will invest anywhere in the world where value can be found. The fund tends to be loaded with rapidly growing companies domiciled in so-called emerging markets, especially those located in the Pacific Rim. Even so, it maintains significant investments in mature economies such as those found in Europe. As a result, the fund is highly diversified, which provides a degree of safety. At times management has hedged the fund against currency risk but with little success.

Annualized Returns
1-Year 16.1%
3-Year 12.0%
5-Year NA

Portfolio Manager: Ralph Wanger since inception. He is assisted by his wife, Leah Zell. Mr. Wanger has also been portfolio manager of the Acorn Fund since its inception. He is profiled in John Train's *The New Money Masters*.

Suitability: Recommended for all growth and growth and income oriented investors. Ideally suited for conservative investors who desire exposure to foreign stock markets. Conservative investors should limit their investment in this fund to 20 percent of portfolio assets.

Portfolio Implications: Investment in this fund, when coupled with domestic growth funds, can lower overall portfolio volatility (risk). Returns are enhanced during periods marked by a falling value of the U.S. dollar.

Risk: Like all international funds, investors are exposed to both currency and political risks in addition to the risk normally experienced by equity investors. Although the fund did not exist during 1990's sharp sell-off in international stocks, its share price declined by a modest 4 percent during 1994.

Costs: This is a very low-cost international offering. Management fees are 0.85 percent of assets, its annual expense ratio is a low 1.24 percent, and portfolio turnover is a very low 20 percent annually.

Distributions: Income distributions occur in both June and December, and capital gains distributions are usually made in late December.

How to Buy and Sell: The fund is sold with a no-load format. The minimum initial investment is a modest $1,000; IRA $200; subsequent investments $100. The fund's shares may also be obtained through Charles Schwab.

ALLIANCE INTERNATIONAL CLASS A

Alliance Fund Distributor
500 Plaza Drive, 3rd Floor
P.O. Box 1520
Secaucus, NJ 07096–1520
800–227–4618

Inception: 1981
Total Assets: $196 Million
Ticker Symbol: ALIFX
Home Page: http://
www.alliancecapital.com

Objective and Strategy: This fund seeks capital appreciation by investing in the equity securities of relatively large-capitalization companies domiciled outside the United States. Although the fund can invest anywhere, the vast majority of its investments have been drawn from the industrialized world. Management does not intend to invest more than 10 percent of its total assets in companies located in developing countries. Traditionally it has maintained a hefty investment in Japanese stocks. In addition, it generally has maintained a relatively large commitment to European stocks including those domiciled in the United Kingdom, France, and Germany. At times, management attempts to mitigate the negative impact of a rising dollar on investment returns by engaging in currency hedges.

Annualized Returns
1-Year 9.6%
3-Year 7.7%
5-Year 8.2%

Portfolio Manager: A. Rama Krishna since 1993. Prior to joining Alliance in 1993, he served as Chief Investment Strategist and Director of Equity Research for CS First Boston.

Suitability: Recommended for all growth and growth and income investors. Ideally suited for conservative investors who desire exposure to foreign stock markets. Conservative investors should limit their investment in this fund to 20 percent of portfolio assets.

Portfolio Implications: Investment in this fund, when coupled with domestic growth funds, can lower overall portfolio volatility (risk). Returns are enhanced during periods marked by a falling value of the U.S. dollar.

Risk: As with all international funds, investors are exposed to foreign currency fluctuations and, to a lesser extent, political risk in addition to the risk normally experienced by equity investors. The fund's share price plunged 21 percent during the bear market of 1990 but gained approximately 6 percent during the weak international market in 1994.

Costs: Class A shares are sold with a 4.25-percent front-end sales charge and an annual 0.17-percent 12b-1 fee. Annual expense ratio is 1.72 percent, and portfolio turnover is 78 percent.

Distributions: Income and capital gains are distributed annually, usually in early December.

How to Buy and Sell: Minimum initial investment is $250; IRA $250; subsequent investments $50. Class B and C shares are also available. The fund's shares may also be purchased through Fidelity Brokerage.

AMERICAN EUROPACIFIC GROWTH FUND

American Funds Distributors
333 South Hope Street
Los Angeles, CA 90071
800-421-9900

Inception: 1984
Total Assets: $13.6 Billion
Ticker Symbol: AEPGX
Home Page: None

Objective and Strategy: This fund seeks long-term growth of capital by investing in a carefully chosen selection of more than 280 companies based outside the United States (primarily in the Pacific Basin and Europe). These include both small firms and large corporations located in major world markets as well as in smaller, developing countries. The Pacific Basin is defined as those countries bordering the Pacific Ocean including Australia, Canada, Japan, Malaysia, and Singapore. Developing-country investments are limited to 20 percent of portfolio assets. The fund's assets have soared in recent years as a result of a combination of one of the best long-term returns and one of the lowest risk scores among international equity funds. Backed by solid research, allocations are based on a consensus opinion of a six-person management team.

Portfolio Manager: Team managed. Led by Thierry Vandeventer who has been overseeing the fund's portfolio since it began operations in 1984. He has thirty-three years experience with the fund's adviser.

Suitability: Suitable for both aggressive and conservative growth-oriented investors. Limit investment in this fund to the lesser of 10 percent of portfolio assets or one-third of your total allocation to international equity funds.

Annualized Returns

1-Year	13.0%
3-Year	12.1%
5-Year	13.0%

Portfolio Implications: Investment in this fund, when coupled with domestic growth funds, can lower overall portfolio volatility (risk). Returns are enhanced during periods marked by a falling value of the U.S. dollar.

Risk: As with all international funds, investors are exposed to political and currency risk. However, the fund's share price experienced a very modest 6-percent decline during the severe 1990 bear market, and it rose slightly more than 1 percent during the weak 1994 market.

Costs: This is a relatively low-cost fund once you get by the steep 5.75-percent front-end load. Its expense ratio is a very low 0.95 percent, and its portfolio turnover ratio is a low 22 percent.

Distributions: Income distributions are paid in June and December, and capital gains distributions are paid annually, usually in late December.

How to Buy and Sell: The fund is sold by brokers and financial planners with a 5.75-percent front-end load and an ongoing 0.24-percent 12b-1 fee. Minimum initial investment $250; IRA $250; subsequent investments $50. Telephone exchange with other American funds without payment of sales fee.

BABSON STEWART IVORY INTERNATIONAL FUND

Jones and Babson
3 Crown Center
2440 Pershing Road
Kansas City, MO 64108
800-422-2766

Inception: 1988
Total Assets: $80 Million
Ticker Symbol: BAINX
Home Page: http://
www.jbfunds.com

Objective and Strategy: The fund seeks capital appreciation by investing in a core portfolio of high-quality stocks of companies in Western Europe and Japan, plus small and medium-sized companies in faster growing countries such as Hong Kong, Korea, and Singapore. Emerging market exposure is limited to approximately 10 percent of the total portfolio. The fund searches for smaller companies with growing earnings, mainly in economically developed areas. When selecting particular investments, the fund looks for securities of "seasoned" companies that are listed on foreign stock exchanges and those that the adviser considers attractive in terms of profitability, growth, and financial resources. The adviser defines "seasoned" companies as those that are known for their quality and the acceptance of their products and services.

Annualized Returns

1-Year 10.8%
3-Year 10.6%
5-Year 10.8%

Portfolio Manager: John Wright since the fund's inception in 1988. He lives and works outside the United States. Educated at Oxford University, he joined Stewart Ivory Ltd in 1971.

Suitability: Recommended for all growth and growth and income investors. Ideally suited for conservative investors who desire exposure to foreign stock markets. Conservative investors should limit their allocation to this fund to 20 percent of portfolio assets.

Portfolio Implications: Investment in this fund, when coupled with domestic growth funds, can lower overall portfolio volatility (risk). Returns are enhanced during periods marked by a falling value of the U.S. dollar.

Risk: This is a relatively low-risk international equity fund. Its share price declined by less than 10 percent during the severe bear market in 1990 and rose slightly more than 1 percent during the bull market in 1994. However, like all international funds, investors are exposed to currency risk and, to a lesser extend, political risk.

Costs: This is a very low-cost international fund. The fund is sold with a no-load format. The annual expense ratio is a low 1.30 percent, and portfolio turnover is also a low 37 percent.

Distributions: Both income and capital gains distributions occur in June.

How to Buy and Sell: Minimum initial investment $2,500; IRA $250; subsequent investments $100. Shares are purchased and redeemed at net asset value. Telephone exchange with other Babson funds (except Enterprise). Shares are also available with no transaction fees from Fidelity Brokerage, Charles Schwab, and Jack White and Company.

BARTLETT VALUE INTERNATIONAL

Bartlett Capital Trust
36 East Fourth Street, 5th Floor
Cincinnati, OH 45202
513-345-6212

Inception: 1989
Total Assets: $79 Million
Ticker Symbol: BVLIX
Home Page: None

Objective and Strategy: This fund seeks capital appreciation as its primary investment objective by investing in foreign securities that management believes are undervalued relative to their intrinsic value. Income is a secondary consideration. Some of the intrinsic value measures that management uses are price-earnings ratios, price-to-book ratios, and dividend yields. The fund also invests in American Depository Receipts and, at times, may invest in closed-end investment companies that hold foreign equity securities in their portfolios. Although the fund is not restricted as to where in the world it may invest, its portfolio tends to be packed with the stocks of companies domiciled in developed countries. In mid-1996, its largest country allocations included Australia, France, Italy, Japan, and the United Kingdom.

Portfolio Manager: Madelynn Matlock since 1992. She joined the adviser in 1981 and currently serves as director of international investment for the adviser.

Suitability: Recommended for all growth and growth and income investors. Ideally suited for conservative investors who desire exposure to foreign stock markets. Conservative investors should limit their investment in this fund to 20 percent of portfolio assets.

Annualized Returns
1-Year 8.9%
3-Year 9.0%
5-Year 9.6%

Portfolio Implications: Investment in this fund, when coupled with domestic growth funds, can lower overall portfolio volatility (risk). Returns are enhanced during periods marked by a falling value of the U.S. dollar.

Risk: As with all international funds, investors are exposed to currency risk and, to a lesser extent, political risk. During the 1990 bear market, the share price of this fund declined 15 percent, and it posted a minor 0.6-percent decline during the weak market in 1994.

Costs: This is a relatively low-cost fund, sold with a no-load format. Expense ratio is 1.83 percent, and portfolio turnover is a low 24 percent.

Distributions: Income distributions occur quarterly, and capital gains distributions are made annually, usually near year-end.

How to Buy and Sell: Minimum initial investment is a relatively high $5,000; IRA $250; subsequent investments $100. Sold without front-end, back-end, or ongoing 12b-1 fees. Telephone exchange with other Bartlett funds. Shares may also be obtained from Charles Schwab and Jack White (no transaction fees).

BT INVESTMENT INTERNATIONAL EQUITY

6 St. James Avenue
Boston, MA 02116
800-730-1313

Inception: 1992
Total Assets: $141 Million
Ticker Symbol: BTEQX
Home Page: None

Objective and Strategy: This fund seeks capital appreciation by investing in foreign stocks believed to offer good long-term earnings growth at a reasonable price. Fundamental analysis of individual securities forms the basis of stock selection. Although individual markets are screened for relative attractiveness, regional allocation preferences are ultimately driven by what management believes to be the availability of undervalued stocks with outstanding growth characteristics, which, for example, resulted in a significant underweighting of Japanese stocks in recent years. The fund targets high-quality, undervalued mid- and large-cap stocks that exhibit strong earnings and cash flow potential. Management emphasizes cash flow rather than traditional price-earnings valuation. It also looks for stocks that have received earnings upgrades by analysts.

Annualized Returns
1-Year 13.5%
3-Year 14.8%
5-Year NA

Portfolio Manager: Michael Levy since August 1995. Joined Bankers Trust in 1993 and has fourteen years experience in the investment industry.

Suitability: Recommended for all growth and growth and income investors. Ideally suited for conservative investors who desire exposure to foreign stock markets. Conservative investors should limit their invest-

ment in this fund to 20 percent of portfolio assets.

Portfolio Implications: Investment in this fund, when coupled with domestic growth funds, can lower overall portfolio volatility (risk). Returns are enhanced during periods marked by a falling value of the U.S. dollar.

Risk: As with all international funds, investors are exposed to currency risk and, to a lesser extent, political risk in addition to the normal risks assumed by equity investors. The fund did not exist at the time of the 1990 bear market, and posted a modest 4-percent gain during the weak 1994 market.

Costs: This is a low-cost international equity fund. Sold with a no-load format, its expense ratio is a low 1.5 percent, and its portfolio turnover ratio is an extremely low 15 percent.

Distributions: Income and capital gains distributions are made annually, usually in late October.

How to Buy and Sell: Minimum initial investment $2,500; IRA $500; subsequent investments $100. Telephone exchange with other BT funds. Shares may also be obtained from Charles Schwab and Company.

FIDELITY DIVERSIFIED INTERNATIONAL

Fidelity Distributors
82 Devonshire Street
Mail Zone L7B
Boston, MA 02109
800-752-2347

Inception: *1991*
Total Assets: *$621 Million*
Ticker Symbol: *FDIVX*
Home Page: *http://www.fidelity.com*

Objective and Strategy: The management of this fund has chosen to invest mostly in countries that are included in the Morgan Stanley EAFE (Europe, Australia, Far East) Index. By investing in securities of companies with market capitalizations greater than $100 million, the fund strives for a rate of return higher than that of the GDP-weighted EAFE Index. Management uses a disciplined approach that involves computer-aided, quantitative analysis supported by fundamental research. Thousands of foreign stocks are evaluated using historical earnings and dividend yield and fundamental value criteria related to a company's estimated growth potential. This relatively new fund has bested the average international equity fund's returns over the last one and three years.

Annualized Returns
1-Year 16.4%
3-Year 12.4%
5-Year NA

Portfolio Manager: Greg Fraser since December 1991. Previously, he managed Select Defense and Aerospace and Select Environmental Services. He joined Fidelity in 1986.

Suitability: Recommended for all growth and growth and income investors. Ideally suited for conservative investors who desire exposure to foreign stock markets. Conservative investors should limit their investment in this fund to 20 percent of portfolio assets.

Portfolio Implications: Investment in this fund, when coupled with domestic growth funds, can lower overall portfolio volatility (risk). Returns are enhanced during periods marked by a falling value of the U.S. dollar.

Risk: As with all international funds, investors are exposed to currency risk and, to a lesser extent, political risk in addition to the normal risk experienced by equity investors. This fund was not in existence during the severe 1990 bear market. However, its share price rose slightly more than 1 percent during the weak market in 1994.

Costs: The fund is sold with a no-load format. Its expense ratio is a very low 1.13 percent, but its 101-percent portfolio turnover ratio is slightly above average.

Distributions: Income and capital gains distributions are paid annually, usually in mid- to late December.

How to Buy and Sell: Minimum initial investment $2,500; IRA $500; subsequent investments $250. Telephone exchange with other Fidelity funds. Shares are also available at Charles Schwab and Fidelity Brokerage (no transaction fees).

FIDELITY EMERGING MARKETS

Fidelity Distributors
82 Devonshire Street
Mail Zone L7B
Boston, MA 02109
800-752-2347

Inception: 1990
Total Assets: $1.4 Billion
Ticker Symbol: FEMKX
Home Page: http://www.fidelity.com

Objective and Strategy: This highly aggressive fund seeks capital appreciation by investing in the world's emerging markets. In pursuit of its goal, the fund emphasizes countries with relatively low gross national product per capita compared to the world's major economies and with the potential for rapid economic growth. The fund normally invests in at least six different countries, although it may invest all of its assets in a single country. In mid-1996 one-half of the fund's assets were invested in three countries: Malaysia (25%), Thailand (13%), and Brazil (12%). Other significant country allocations include South Africa, the Philippines, India, Indonesia, South Korea, and Mexico. Top industry sectors include finance, utilities, basic industries, and construction and real estate. Its assets are spread over more than four hundred different companies.

Portfolio Manager: Richard Hazelwood since July 1993. Previously, he assisted on Low-Priced Stock and Contrafund. He joined Fidelity in March 1991 after leaving Sassoon Ltd. in Tokyo.

Suitability: This fund is suitable for aggressive growth investors only. Because of the fund's extreme volatility, investors should limit their allocations to no more than 10 percent of portfolio assets.

Annualized Returns
1-Year 6.9%
3-Year 6.5%
5-Year 11.2%

Portfolio Implications: This fund complements investment in global and diversified international equity funds. Its return has a low correlation with the returns of domestic growth and aggressive growth funds. Thus, it provides diversification benefits to aggressive growth-oriented investors.

Risk: Emerging markets are small, political risk is usually high, and currency fluctuations can exert a significant impact on returns. Although the fund was not in existence during the 1990 bear market, its share price plummeted nearly 18 percent during 1994.

Costs: Like many Fidelity funds, this fund is sold with a 3-percent front-end sales charge. Once past that fee, expenses are relatively modest. The fund's expense ratio is a relatively low 1.34 percent, and its portfolio turnover is 80 percent.

Distributions: Income and capital gains distributions are usually paid in mid- to late December.

How to Buy and Sell: The sales fee is waived for telephone transfers from other Fidelity funds that levy a 3-percent sales fee. Investors must pay a 1.5-percent redemption fee for shares held less than ninety days. Minimum initial investment $2,500; IRA $500; subsequent investment $250. Shares may also be obtained from Charles Schwab and Fidelity Brokerage.

FIDELITY EUROPE

Fidelity Distributors
82 Devonshire Street
Mail Zone L7B
Boston, MA 02109
800-752-2347

Inception: 1986
Total Assets: $667 Million
Ticker Symbol: FIEUX
Home Page: http://www.fidelity.com

Objective and Strategy: This fund seeks growth of capital over the long term by investing in securities of issuers that have their principal activities in Western Europe. Western European countries include Austria, Belgium, Denmark, Germany, Finland, France, Greece, Ireland, Italy, Luxembourg, the Netherlands, Norway, Portugal, Spain, Sweden, Switzerland, and the United Kingdom. At times, the fund will also invest in companies domiciled in the United States that derive a significant portion of their revenues from Europe. In mid-1996, nearly one-third of its assets were invested in the United Kingdom. Its largest sectors include finance, media and leisure, and health care. Given the problems that have plagued European markets since this fund's inception, it has performed admirably.

Annualized Returns

1-Year 12.9%
3-Year 15.5%
5-Year 12.0%

Portfolio Manager: Sally Walden since July 1992. She also manages European Opportunities and U.K. Growth Trust for Fidelity. She joined the company in 1984.

Suitability: This fund is suitable for both aggressive and conservative growth-oriented investors. Limit investment in this fund to the lesser of 10 percent of portfolio assets or one-third of your total allocation to international equity funds.

Portfolio Implications: This fund is not a substitute for a global or diversified international fund. It should be used to complement investments in other international equity funds by investors who wish to boost their allocation to European markets.

Risk: In addition to the risks associated with equity investing, investors are exposed to currency and, to a lesser extent, political risks. However, volatility is relatively modest. For example, the fund's share price only declined by about 5 percent during the severe 1990 bear market.

Costs: Sold with a 3-percent front-end sales fee. However, operating expenses are relatively modest. It possesses a low expense ratio of 1.26 percent and a modest 52-percent portfolio turnover ratio.

Distributions: Income and capital gains distributions are paid in mid- to late December.

How to Buy and Sell: New shareholders pay a 3-percent front-end load. Sellers pay a 1-percent redemption fee for shares held less than ninety days. Minimum initial investment $2,500; IRA $500; subsequent investments $250. Shares also available from Charles Schwab and Fidelity Brokerage.

FIDELITY INTERNATIONAL GROWTH & INCOME

Fidelity Distributors
82 Devonshire Street
Mail Zone L7B
Boston, MA 02109
800-752-2347

Inception: 1986
Total Assets: $1.0 Billion
Ticker Symbol: FIGRX
Home Page: http://www.fidelity.com

Objective and Strategy: This relatively tame international offering seeks capital growth, current income, and growth of income by investing in a combination of equity and fixed-income securities. Typically, investments in fixed-income securities are limited to 25 percent to 35 percent of total assets. By investing in a combination of fixed-income securities and equities, volatility is lessened. Good defensive abilities of the fund's manager in limiting the losses in 1994 when most international funds were taking a licking suggest the possibility of highly competitive long-term results. Although geographically diverse, one-half of its assets are invested in four countries: Japan, Germany, the United Kingdom, and France.

Annualized Returns
1-Year 9.4%
3-Year 6.9%
5-Year 8.6%

Portfolio Manager: John Hickling since March 1996. He is also portfolio manager of Fidelity Overseas and has managed several of Fidelity's international offerings. He joined the firm in 1982.

Suitability: This fund is suitable for conservative growth and income investors. Ideally suited for conservative investors who desire exposure to foreign stock markets. Conservative investors should limit their investment in this fund to 30 percent of portfolio assets.

Portfolio Implications: Investment in this fund, when coupled with investment in domestic growth and income funds, can lower overall portfolio volatility (risk) while enhancing long-term investment returns. This fund performs exceptionally well when the U.S. dollar is declining in value against the world's major currencies.

Risk: You won't find an international fund with lower risk than this one. As with all international funds, investors experience both currency and political risk. However, the combination of both bonds and stocks reduces portfolio volatility significantly. For example, the fund lost only about 3 percent during the severe 1990 bear market.

Costs: This is one of the few Fidelity funds with a no-load format. Its expense ratio is a very low 1.17 percent, although portfolio turnover of 135 percent is on the high side. On balance, this is a very low-cost way to invest internationally.

Distributions: Both income and capital gains are distributed in mid- to late December.

How to Buy and Sell: Minimum initial investment $2,500; IRA $500; subsequent investments $250. Telephone exchange with other Fidelity funds. Shares also available through Charles Schwab and Fidelity Brokerage.

FIDELITY OVERSEAS FUND

Fidelity Distributors
82 Devonshire Street
Mail Zone L7B
Boston, MA 02109
800-752-2347

Inception: 1984
Total Assets: $3.0 Billion
Ticker Symbol: FOSFX
Home Page: http://www.fidelity.com

Objective and Strategy: This fund mixes investments in U.S. equities with those of companies domiciled around the world. In selecting individual stocks, management focuses on both cash flow and balance items. The goal is to identify investments that have two or three times as much upside potential as downside risk. Traditionally, the fund has allocated a relatively large percentage of assets to Japanese stocks. Prior to 1990 this strategy enhanced returns. However, with the dismal showing of the Japanese stock market in recent years, the strategy has been a drag on returns. During 1996 management trimmed its investments in emerging markets and beefed up its European holdings. Aside from Japan, the fund's other large country holdings include the United States (20%), the United Kingdom (12%), and France (6%).

Annualized Returns

1-Year 10.4%
3-Year 8.4%
5-Year 8.2%

Portfolio Manager: Richard Mace since March 1996. He also manages International Value and has participated in managing Fidelity's other international offerings. He joined Fidelity in 1987.

Suitability: This fund is recommended for all growth and growth and income investors. It is ideally suited for conservative investors who desire some exposure to foreign stock markets. Conservative investors should limit their investment in this fund to 30 percent of portfolio assets.

Portfolio Implications: Since this fund invests in U.S. stocks in addition to foreign equities, a portion of its portfolio may duplicate the investments of domestic growth funds. The fund is an excellent fit with domestic small- and mid-cap funds.

Risk: Although shareholders are subject to both currency and political risk as is the case with all international funds, the combination of U.S. stocks and emphasis on developed economies mitigate both of these risks. In addition, its global strategy limits portfolio volatility as witnessed by its modest 6-percent decline during the 1990 bear market.

Costs: The fund is sold with a no-load format, which is a big plus. Its expense ratio is a very low 1.12 percent, and its portfolio turnover ratio is a moderate 88 percent.

Distributions: Both income and capital gains distributions occur in mid- to late December.

How to Buy and Sell: The fund's front-end load was eliminated in July 1995. Minimum initial investment $2,500; IRA $500; subsequent investments $250. Telephone exchange with other Fidelity funds. Shares also available through Charles Schwab and Fidelity Brokerage.

FIDELITY PACIFIC BASIN FUND

Fidelity Distributors
82 Devonshire Street
Mail Zone L7B
Boston, MA 02109
800-752-2347

Inception: 1986
Total Assets: $630 Million
Ticker Symbol: FPBFX
Home Page: http://www.fidelity.com

Objective and Strategy: The fund seeks growth of capital over the long term by investing in securities of issuers that have their principal activities in the Pacific Basin (i.e., Australia, Hong Kong, Indonesia, Japan, Korea, Malaysia, New Zealand, China, the Philippines, Singapore, Taiwan, and Thailand). When selecting individual stocks, management looks for companies that can achieve a high return on equity and assets on a consistent basis, companies with barriers to entry, strong pricing power, high profit margins, shareholder-oriented management, and strong cash flow. Because economies in this region are the fastest growing in the world, most of the attractive investments fall into the growth stock camp and ordinarily sell at high price-earnings multiples. Although the reward potential is high, the combination of political uncertainties and high multiple stocks give this fund a high risk profile.

Annualized Returns
1-Year -3.5%
3-Year 2.1%
5-Year 6.4%

Portfolio Manager: Shigeki Makino since May 1996. He previously managed Fidelity's Japan fund. He joined the firm in 1990.

Suitability: This fund is suitable for both aggressive and conservative growth-oriented investors. However, investment should be limited in this fund to the lesser of 10 percent of portfolio assets or one-third of the total allocation to international equity funds.

Portfolio Implications: This fund is not a substitute for a global or diversified international equity fund. It should be used to complement investments in other international equity funds by investors who wish to boost their allocation to markets in the Pacific Basin.

Risk: By concentrating its investments in the Pacific Basin, this fund exposes investors to a high level of both currency and political risk. As one might expect, share price volatility is extremely high. The fund suffered a whopping 27-percent loss during the 1990 bear market.

Costs: Sold with a 3-percent front-end load and sporting a hefty 133-percent portfolio turnover ratio, this fund is not one of the cheaper Pacific Basin funds around. However, the fund's 1.23-percent annual expense ratio is well below average.

Distributions: Both income and capital gains distributions are paid in mid- to late December.

How to Buy and Sell: Investors pay 3 percent up front. Minimum initial investment $2,500; IRA $500; subsequent investments $250. Telephone exchange with other Fidelity funds. Shares also available through Charles Schwab and Fidelity Brokerage.

FIDELITY WORLDWIDE FUND

Fidelity Distributors
82 Devonshire Street
Mail Zone L7B
Boston, MA 02109
800-752-2347

Inception: 1990
Total Assets: $855 Million
Ticker Symbol: FWWFX
Home Page: http://www.fidelity.com

Objective and Strategy: Investing in issues anywhere in the world, this global fund strives for strong growth of capital by focusing mainly on companies based in North America, Europe, and the Pacific Basin. The fund has been a stellar performer since its inception in 1990, providing positive returns in every year including the bear market which struck most foreign stock markets in 1994. Management's bottom-up approach in selecting investments and searching for bargains, coupled with a positive economic outlook for most of the world's economies should keep this fund on track to deliver above-average returns. Low expenses and a relatively low level of share price volatility make this fund a good vehicle for those seeking equity exposure in the world's developed countries.

Annualized Returns
1-Year 10.2%
3-Year 10.2%
5-Year 12.2%

Portfolio Manager: Penelope Dobkin since May 1990. Previously, she managed Fidelity's Europe Fund, Overseas, and Select Financial Services. She joined Fidelity in 1981.

Suitability: This fund is recommended for all growth and growth and income investors. It is ideally suited for conservative investors who desire exposure to foreign stock markets. Conservative investors should limit their investment in this fund to 30 percent of portfolio assets.

Portfolio Implications: Since this fund can invest in U.S. stocks in addition to foreign equities, a portion of its portfolio may duplicate the investments of domestic growth funds. The fund is an excellent fit with domestic small- and mid-cap funds.

Risk: With investments in several continents and emphasis on developed economies, the fund possesses a modest degree of currency and political risk. However, its share price can be volatile at times as witnessed by the fund's 10-percent decline during the 1990 bear market.

Costs: This is one of the lowest-cost international funds around. It is sold with a no-load format; it possesses a low 1.2-percent annual expense ratio and a below-average 43-percent portfolio turnover ratio.

Distributions: Both income and capital gains distributions, if any, are paid in December.

How to Buy and Sell: This is one of the Fidelity no-load funds. Minimum initial investment $2,500; IRA $500; subsequent investments $250. Telephone exchange with other Fidelity funds. Shares also available through Charles Schwab and Fidelity Brokerage.

FOUNDERS WORLDWIDE GROWTH FUND

Founders Asset Management
2930 East Third Avenue
Denver, CO 80206
800-525-2440

Inception: 1990
Total Assets: $343 Million
Ticker Symbol: FWWGX
Home Page: http://
www.networth.galt.com/founders

Objective and Strategy: The fund seeks long-term capital appreciation using a global strategy, which allows it to pick stocks based in any country including the United States. In fact, a large reason why this international fund sports one of the best performance records in its category has been its hefty allocation to U.S. stocks. When selecting investments, management primarily focuses on company fundamentals, which minimizes emphasis on geographical allocations. Management notes that many companies abroad are following the U.S. model of downsizing and increasing their competitiveness. As a result, management reports finding many companies in the technology, telecommunications, and data-processing industries that are meeting global demand.

Annualized Returns
1-Year 9.9%
3-Year 14.1%
5-Year 13.3%

Portfolio Manager: Michael Gerding since 1990. He has served as lead portfolio manager for International Equity and Passport. He joined Founders in 1990 and holds an M.B.A from Texas Christian University.

Suitability: This fund is recommended for all growth and growth and income investors. It is ideally suited for conservative investors who desire exposure to foreign stock markets. Conservative investors should limit their investment in this fund to 30 percent of portfolio assets.

Portfolio Implications: Since this fund can also invest in U.S. stocks in addition to foreign stocks, a portion of its portfolio may duplicate the investments of domestic growth funds. The fund is an excellent fit with domestic small- and mid-cap funds.

Risk: Although the fund contains elements of both currency and political risk, its large allocation to U.S. stocks mitigates both of these risks. Its global aspect has also led to an unusually low level of volatility as witnessed by its near 7-percent gain during the severe 1990 bear market.

Costs: The fund is sold with a no-load format. Its annual expense ratio of 1.58 percent is slightly below average for the group, as is its 60-percent portfolio turnover ratio. On balance portfolio maintenance costs are quite modest.

Distributions: Both income and capital gains distributions are paid in late December.

How to Buy and Sell: Shares are bought and redeemed at net asset value. Minimum initial investment $1,000; IRA $500; subsequent investments $100. Telephone exchange with other Founders funds ($100 minimum). Shares also available through Charles Schwab and Fidelity Brokerage.

IAI INTERNATIONAL FUND

IAI Securities
3700 First Bank Place
P.O. Box 357
Minneapolis, MN 55440
800-945-3863

Inception: 1987
Total Assets: $140 Million
Ticker Symbol: IAINX
Home Page: http://
networth.galt.com/iai

Objective and Strategy: Similar to its domestic siblings, this fund is guided by a value orientation. Its country exposures are a reflection of individual companies' strength and potential earnings growth, not a reflection of top-down views. Its investments are drawn primarily from markets in developed countries such as Japan, the United Kingdom, France, Spain, and Germany. As opposed to the average international fund, this fund is likely to have greater exposure to unpopular countries at the expense of high-expectation markets. Such contrarian tactics may prevent it from leading the charge in a speculative bull market, but they should allow the fund to build a solid track record over time with less volatility than more conventional rivals.

Portfolio Manager: Roy Gillson since 1990. He joined IAI International in 1983 and also manages the Developing Countries fund.

Suitability: This relatively tame fund is recommended for both conservative growth and income and aggressive growth-oriented investors. It is ideally suited for conservative investors who desire exposure to foreign stock markets. Conservative investors should limit their investment in this fund to 20 percent of portfolio assets.

Annualized Returns

1-Year 7.1%
3-Year 8.2%
5-Year 9.1%

Portfolio Implications: Investment in this fund, when coupled with investment in domestic growth funds, can lower overall portfolio volatility (risk). Returns are enhanced during periods marked by a falling value of the U.S. dollar.

Risk: As with all international funds, investors are exposed to currency and, to a lesser extent, political risks. Even so, the fund experienced a better than 13-percent decline during the 1990 bear market.

Costs: On balance this is a modest-cost fund. It is sold with a no-load format and its portfolio turnover ratio is a below-average 40 percent. On the other hand, its 1.7-percent annual expense ratio is slightly above average.

Distributions: Income distributions are paid in June and December, and capital gains distributions are paid annually in December.

How to Buy and Sell: This no-load fund has a higher than average $5,000 minimum initial investment; IRA $2,000; subsequent investments $100. Telephone exchange with other IAI funds. The fund's shares may also be purchased with no transaction fee from Charles Schwab, Fidelity Brokerage, and Jack White and Company.

INVESCO EUROPEAN

Invesco Funds Group
P.O. Box 173706
Denver, CO 80217-3706
800-525-8085

Inception: 1986
Total Assets: $256 Million
Ticker Symbol: FEURX
Home Page: http://
www.invesco.com

Objective and Strategy: The assets of this fund are primarily invested in securities of large-capitalization, well-established companies domiciled in Europe. There are no restrictions on how much can or cannot be invested in a specific country or specific industry, so management can exercise a great deal of flexibility. Stock selection is made through a bottom-up approach. Management develops themes based on economic fundamentals and then performs detailed analyses on individual companies. The fund is a great vehicle for those interested in a long-term bet on a continued European economic recovery, the benefits of an increasingly unified Europe, and/ or potential economic growth in the Eastern Bloc. In recent years, this has been one of the better-performing funds in the international equity sector.

Annualized Returns
1-Year 18.5%
3-Year 14.3%
5-Year 9.8%

Portfolio Manager: Team managed. Steve Chamberlin, team leader, joined Invesco in August 1990.

Suitability: The fund is suitable for both aggressive and conservative growth-oriented investors. Because of its regional concentration, investors should limit their investment in this fund to the lesser of 10 percent of portfolio assets or one-third of their total allocation to international equity funds.

Portfolio Implications: This fund is not a substitute for a global or diversified international equity fund. It should be used to complement investments in other international equity funds by investors who wish to boost their allocation to European stock markets.

Risk: Although investors are exposed to currency and political risks as is the case with all international funds, this is a very modest-risk fund. During the severe 1990 bear market it actually posted a small gain, although its share price declined by about 3 percent during the weak 1994 market.

Costs: The fund is sold with a no-load format. Its expense ratio is a below-average 1.48 percent, although its 96-percent portfolio turnover ratio is a bit above average. On balance it is a very low-cost international equity fund.

Distributions: Both income and capital gains distributions are paid annually in late December.

How to Buy and Sell: Shares are purchased and redeemed at net asset value. Minimum initial investment $1,000; IRA $250; subsequent investments $50. Telephone exchange with other Invesco funds. Shares also available through Charles Schwab (no transaction fee) and Fidelity Brokerage.

INVESCO EUROPEAN SMALL COMPANY FUND

Invesco Funds Group
P.O. Box 173706
Denver, CO 80217-3706
800-525-8085

Inception: 1995
Total Assets: $33 Million
Ticker Symbol: IVECX
Home Page: http://
www.invesco.com

Objective and Strategy: This aggressive growth fund has been around for only two years. However, because it is the only fund selling shares to individual investors that specializes in European small-company investments, I was compelled to include it in this book. What's even better is that this fund is guided by two excellent portfolio managers, one specializing in the United Kingdom and the other in Continental Europe. Given the low valuations in European stock markets in general and in the small-cap sector specifically, it was no surprise to see this fund among the international fund return leaders. Even better is the fact that an economic recovery spreading across Europe promises that the fund's stellar returns will continue. If European stocks belong in your portfolio, you will want to own this well-positioned fund.

Portfolio Manager: Andy Crossley and Clair Griffiths since inception in 1995. Both work in the company's London office and have also managed the Invesco Asset Management Limited portfolio since 1991.

Suitability: This fund is suitable for aggressive growth-oriented investors. Limit investment in this fund to the lesser of 10 percent of portfolio assets or one-third of your total allocation to international equity funds.

Annualized Returns
1-Year 25.7%
3-Year NA
5-Year NA

Portfolio Implications: This fund makes an excellent addition to a portfolio containing large-cap international stocks. It is also an excellent complement to domestic small-cap funds. In fact, this fund provides little duplication with any other types of equity funds. Resist the urge to trade this fund as over-performance cycles can be relatively long.

Risk: With investments concentrated in Europe, the fund possesses little political risk but substantial currency risk. In addition, small-cap stocks are more volatile than those of larger, well-established companies.

Costs: The fund is sold without a front-end load or redemption fee, but possesses a 0.25-percent annual 12b-1 fee. Portfolio turnover is extremely low, but its annual expense ratio is a hefty 2 percent. However, look for this ratio to plummet as the fund attracts additional shareholders.

Distributions: Income distributions (if any) and capital gains are paid in December.

How to Buy and Sell: Shares are purchased and redeemed at net asset value. Minimum initial investment $1,000; IRA $250; subsequent investments $250. Telephone exchange with other Invesco funds. Shares also available at both Charles Schwab and Jack White with no transaction fees.

IVY INTERNATIONAL FUND A

Mackenzie Funds Distribution
P.O. Box 5007
Boca Raton, FL 33431
800-777-6472

Inception: 1986
Total Assets: $699 Million
Ticker Symbol: IVINX
Home Page: None

Objective and Strategy: This fund proves that slow and steady wins the race. The fund selects investments from the bottom-up and takes a patient, long-term approach to investing. In fact, you won't find another international equity fund with a portfolio turnover ratio as low as that sported by Ivy. Its search for stocks that sell at a discount to their underlying fundamentals prevents the fund from chasing hot markets and sectors. The fund has performed quite well since its inception in 1986 by overweighting cheaper bourses, including the United Kingdom, France, and Spain. So far, these tactics have produced highly competitive results. However, its hefty front-end load will cut into profits.

Portfolio Manager: Hakan Castegren since the fund's inception in 1986. He has thirty-six years of investment experience and earned an M.B.A. from the Stockholm School of Economics.

Suitability: This fund is recommended for all growth and growth and income investors. It is ideally suited for conservative investors who desire exposure to foreign stock markets. Conservative investors should limit their investment in this fund to no more than 20 percent of portfolio assets.

Annualized Returns
1-Year 14.7%
3-Year 13.7%
5-Year 14.0%

Portfolio Implications: Investment in this fund, when coupled with investments in domestic growth funds, can lower overall portfolio volatility (risk). Returns are enhanced during periods in which the value of the U.S. dollar is declining against major foreign currencies.

Risk: Like all international funds, shareholders are exposed to currency and political risks in addition to the normal risks assumed by equity investors. The fund's share price declined by 13 percent during the 1990 bear market.

Costs: The fund is sold with a hefty 5.75-percent front-end load. However, annual maintenance costs are modest. Its 1.52-percent expense ratio is about average for the group, and its 6-percent portfolio turnover ratio is about the lowest you will find among international equity funds.

Distributions: Both income and capital gains distributions are paid annually, usually in late December.

How to Buy and Sell: Minimum initial investment $1,000; IRA $25; subsequent investments $100. The fund's shares are available at both Fidelity Brokerage and Charles Schwab. It is sold without transaction fees to institutional clients at Schwab.

JANUS WORLDWIDE

100 Fillmore Street
Denver, CO 80206–4923
800-525-3713

Inception: 1991
Total Assets: $3.5 Billion
Ticker Symbol: JAWWX
Home Page: http://www.janus.com

Objective and Strategy: With Janus on the door, can you ask for more? This fund, like many other in the Janus family, has an excellent long-term performance track record. It seeks growth of capital primarily by investing in common stocks of both foreign and domestic issuers of any size, although the portfolio tends to be packed with large-cap firms. When selecting individual securities, management follows four themes: pharmaceuticals, information technology, outsourcing vendors, and telecommunications. The fund owes its spectacular returns to good stock picking rather than to bets placed with individual countries or geographic areas. At last glance, the fund was diversified across about two hundred companies domiciled in about three dozen countries.

Portfolio Manager: Helen Young Hayes since the fund's inception in 1991. She joined Janus in 1987 and also manages the Janus Overseas Fund. She received a B.A. in economics from Yale University.

Suitability: This fund is highly recommended for all growth and growth and income investors. It is ideally suited for conservative investors who desire exposure to foreign stock markets. Conservative investors should limit their investment in this fund to no more than 30 percent of portfolio assets. This is an excellent choice for in-

Annualized Returns
1-Year 27.5%
3-Year 20.0%
5-Year 18.7%

vestors with limited funds who want global diversification.

Portfolio Implications: Since this fund invests in U.S. stocks in addition to foreign equities, a portion of its portfolio may duplicate the investments of other domestic stock funds. The fund is an excellent fit with domestic small- and mid-cap funds.

Risk: Although shareholders are subject to both currency and political risks, the fund's exposure to domestic stocks reduces risk substantially. The fund did not exist during the 1990 bear market and posted a modest 3.6-percent gain during the weak 1994 market.

Costs: This is a modest-cost fund. It is sold with a no-load format and has a below-average 1.24-percent expense ratio. However, its 142-percent portfolio turnover ratio is relatively high.

Distributions: Both income and capital gains distributions are paid annually, usually in late December.

How to Buy and Sell: Minimum initial investment $2,500; IRA $500; subsequent investments $100. Four free telephone switches with other Janus funds annually. Shares are also available without transaction fees at both Fidelity Brokerage and Charles Schwab.

LEXINGTON WORLDWIDE EMERGING MARKETS

Lexington Management Corporation
P.O. Box 1515
Park 80 West Plaza Two
Saddle Brook, NJ 07663
800-526-0056

Inception: 1969
Total Assets: $331 Million
Ticker Symbol: LEXGX
Home Page: None

Objective and Strategy: The fund, which changed its objective in 1991, seeks long-term capital appreciation by investing in the stocks of companies domiciled in, or doing business in, emerging countries and emerging markets. Countries are designated as emerging by the World Bank or the United Nations. Currently, the fund has developed an eligible country list that contains fifty-five different economies. In mid-1996, the fund held investments in two dozen of those countries. Its largest country allocations include Brazil, Chile, the Philippines, Poland, and South Africa. To gain instant exposure to some developing countries, the fund will invest in closed-end single-country emerging markets funds. Its top five sector holdings include banking, capital equipment, consumer nondurables, materials, and telecommunications. Because of its orientation to thinly traded markets, this fund has exhibited extreme share price volatility.

Annualized Returns
1-Year 6.9%
3-Year 5.6%
5-Year 9.4%

Portfolio Manager: Richard T. Saler since 1992. He returned to Lexington after a stint with Nomura Securities. He received a B.S. and M.B.A. from New York University.

Suitability: This fund is suited for aggressive growth-oriented investors only. Because of the fund's extreme volatility, investors should limit their allocations to this fund to no more than 10 percent of portfolio assets.

Portfolio Implications: This fund complements investments in global and diversified international equity funds. Its return has a low correlation with the returns of domestic equity funds. Thus, it provides diversification benefits (in addition to return enhancement) to aggressive growth-oriented investors.

Risk: Emerging markets investing has special risks, including currency, political, and liquidity risks. Share price can be extremely volatile as witnessed by its 23-percent plunge during the 1990 bear market.

Costs: The fund is sold with a no-load format. Its 1.88-percent annual expense ratio and 93-percent portfolio turnover ratio are slightly above average for the group.

Distributions: Both income and capital gains distributions are paid in late December.

How to Buy and Sell: Minimum initial investment $1,000; IRA $1,000; subsequent investments $50. Shares held less than 365 days are subject to a 2-percent redemption fee. Shares are also available with no transaction fees at Fidelity Brokerage, Charles Schwab, and Jack White.

LOOMIS SAYLES INTERNATIONAL EQUITY

Loomis Sayles and Company, L.P.
One Financial Center
Boston, MA 02111
800-633-3330

Inception: 1991
Total Assets: $86 Million
Ticker Symbol: LSIEX
Home Page: None

Objective and Strategy: The fund's investment objective is high total investment return through a combination of capital appreciation and current income. It seeks its objective by investing in cash dividend-paying equity securities of companies organized or headquartered outside the United States. Although the fund invests in both developed and emerging economies, its emphasis on yield as well as capital appreciation should give this fund more stability than similar funds seeking primarily growth of capital. In addition, its emphasis on dividend-paying firms has led it to invest in some of the largest and financially strongest corporations in the world. Interestingly, management tends to invest the fund's assets about equally among eight countries with highly developed economies. More than half its investments have been allocated to European markets.

Portfolio Manager: Paul H. Drexler since July 1996. Prior to joining Loomis Sayles he was an economist and portfolio manager at Brown Brothers Harriman and Company.

Suitability: This fund is recommended for all growth and growth and income investors. It is ideally suited for conservative investors who desire exposure to foreign stock markets. Conservative investors should limit their investments in this fund to no more than 20 percent of portfolio assets.

Annualized Returns

1-Year 7.8%
3-Year 9.5%
5-Year 9.0%

Portfolio Implications: Investment in this fund, when coupled with domestic growth funds, can lower overall portfolio volatility (risk). Returns are enhanced during periods marked by a falling value of the U.S. dollar, especially against the currencies of European economies.

Risk: Since its inception in 1991, the fund's share price has experienced only modest volatility. However, this young fund has yet to experience a severe bear market. Share price declined by a modest 1.8 percent during the weak 1994 market.

Costs: Except for a higher-than-average 133-percent portfolio turnover ratio, this is a very modest-cost fund. Its 1.45-percent annual expense ratio is below average for the group, and its shares are sold with a no-load format.

Distributions: Both income and capital gains distributions are paid in late December.

How to Buy and Sell: Minimum initial investment $2,500; IRA $250; subsequent investments $50. Telephone exchange with other Loomis Sayles funds. Shares also available without transaction fees at Charles Schwab and Jack White.

MANAGERS INTERNATIONAL EQUITY

The Managers Fund, L.P.
40 Richards Avenue
Norwalk, CT 06854-2325
800-835-3879

Inception: 1985
Total Assets: $208 Million
Ticker Symbol: MCITX
Home Page: None

Objective and Strategy: The fund seeks capital appreciation by investing in stocks that it believes are undervalued and are traded in undervalued markets. It invests only in undervalued markets according to the firm's value indicator which compares the relationship of each market's aggregate return on equity and price-to-book value with that of the world index. The firm seeks to identify companies that are financially productive and inexpensively priced. Allocation of assets by country is a residual of the stock selection process. Though country weightings may deviate significantly from the appropriate benchmark, upper limits are in place to ensure adequate diversification. During the last five years the fund has performed among the top third of all international equity funds.

Annualized Returns
1-Year 8.7%
3-Year 11.8%
5-Year 13.4%

Portfolio Manager: Team managed. Team includes William Holzer, managing director of Scudder since 1980, and John Reinsberg, general partner of Lazard since 1992.

Suitability: This fund is recommended for all growth and growth and income investors. It is ideally suited for conservative investors who desire exposure to foreign stock markets. Conservative investors should limit their investments in this fund to no more than 20 percent of portfolio assets.

Portfolio Implications: Investment in this fund, when coupled with investment in domestic growth funds, can lower overall portfolio volatility (risk). The fund's returns are enhanced during periods marked by a falling value of the U.S. dollar against major foreign currencies.

Risk: As with all international funds, shareholders assume currency and political risks. However, share price volatility has been modest as witnessed by its below-average 11-percent decline during the 1990 bear market.

Costs: Sold with a no-load format, this is a modest-cost international equity fund. Its 1.58-percent annual expense ratio is about average for the group, as is its 73-percent portfolio turnover ratio.

Distributions: Both income and capital gains distributions are paid annually in December.

How to Buy and Sell: Minimum initial investment $2,000; IRA $500; no minimum subsequent investment. Telephone exchange with other Managers funds. Shares are also available without transaction fees at both Charles Schwab and Jack White and Company.

MONTGOMERY EMERGING MARKETS CLASS R

The Montgomery Funds
600 Montgomery Street, 15th Floor
San Francisco, CA 94111-9361
800-572-3863

Inception: *1992*
Total Assets: *$994 Million*
Ticker Symbol: *MNEMX*
Home Page: *http://*
www.xperts.montgomery.com

Objective and Strategy: While not for the faint of heart, this fund should not be overlooked by any growth-seeking investor. Under the direction of Josephine Jimenez, the fund employs a mean-variance optimization technique drawn from modern portfolio theory, which assists in determining the percentage of assets to invest in each of thirty-three emerging markets countries. After optimization (targeting the highest returns for given levels of risk), management spends a great deal of time selecting individual securities, including making company visits. Although the fund has performed dismally during the last three years, Jimenez believes emerging markets are a compelling investment due to the overall demographics, and I agree. As emerging markets rebound from their 1994 disasters, this fund should perform exceptionally well.

Annualized Returns
1-Year 7.5%
3-Year 6.5%
5-Year NA

Portfolio Manager: Josephine S. Jimenez since the fund's inception in 1992. Prior to joining Montgomery in 1992, she was a portfolio manager and senior analyst with Emerging Markets Investors Corp. in Washington, D.C.

Suitability: This fund is suitable for aggressive investors only. Because of the fund's extreme share price volatility, investors should limit their allocations to no more than 10 percent of portfolio assets.

Portfolio Implications: This fund complements investments in global and diversified international funds. Its return has a low correlation with the returns of other domestic equity funds. Thus, it provides significant diversification benefits (while enhancing long-term returns) to aggressive growth-oriented investors.

Risk: Emerging markets funds are the most volatile around. In addition to the normal risks faced by equity fund investors, emerging markets funds add currency, political, and liquidity risks. However, this is one of the more tame versions, with investments in thirty-three emerging economies.

Costs: This is an average-cost fund. It is sold with a no-load format, possesses a 1.80-percent annual expense ratio (which should decline as assets grow), and an average 92-percent portfolio turnover ratio.

Distributions: Income and capital gains distributions are paid in late December.

How to Buy and Sell: Minimum initial investment $1,000; IRA $1,000; subsequent investments $100. Telephone exchange with other Montgomery funds. Shares are also available at Fidelity Brokerage, Charles Schwab, and Jack White with no transaction fees.

NOMURA PACIFIC BASIN FUND

Nomura Securities International
180 Maiden Lane
New York, NY 10038
800-833-0018

Inception: 1985
Total Assets: $33 Million
Ticker Symbol: NPBFX
Home Page: None

Objective and Strategy: This fund seeks long-term capital appreciation through investments in equity securities of corporations domiciled in Japan and other Far Eastern and Western Pacific countries, including Australia, Hong Kong, Indonesia, Malaysia, New Zealand, Singapore, South Korea, Taiwan, Thailand, and the Philippines. The fund attempts to maximize opportunities and reduce risk by investing in a diversified portfolio of companies in different stages of development, ranging from large, well-established companies to smaller, less-seasoned companies in earlier stages of development. Traditionally, the fund has maintained a hefty investment in Japan, and its returns have been heavily dependent on the state of the Japanese economy and its stock market.

Annualized Returns
1-Year 6.3%
3-Year 3.5%
5-Year 5.7%

Portfolio Manager: Iwao Komatsu since becoming president of the fund in 1995.

Suitability: Investment in this fund is suitable for both aggressive and conservative growth-oriented investors. However, because of the unique risks associated with regional investing, investors should limit their investments in this fund to the lesser of 10 percent of portfolio assets or one-third of the total allocation to international equity funds.

Portfolio Implications: This fund is not a substitute for a global or diversified international equity fund. It should be used to complement investments in other international equity funds by investors who wish to boost their allocation to the Pacific Rim.

Risk: As with all international funds, shareholders are exposed to political and currency risks. Its returns are vulnerable to the dollar-yen exchange rate. A weak dollar buoyed the fund's share price during the 1990 bear market, and it declined a very modest 2.6 percent.

Costs: This is a modest-cost fund. Its shares are sold with a no-load format. Its management fee is a modest 0.75 percent, its 1.78-percent expense ratio is about average for the group, and its portfolio turnover ratio is a low 45 percent.

Distributions: Income distributions are paid in May and November, and capital gains are usually distributed in late November.

How to Buy and Sell: Minimum initial investment $1,000; no minimum subsequent investment requirement.

OAKMARK INTERNATIONAL

Harris Associates, L.P.
2 North LaSalle Street
Chicago, IL 60602
800–625–6275

Inception: *1992*
Total Assets: *$1.2 Billion*
Ticker Symbol: *OAKIX*
Home Page: *None*

Objective and Strategy: This fund seeks capital appreciation by investing internationally in stocks that management believes are fundamentally undervalued. Although it may invest anywhere, more than half of the fund's assets have traditionally been spread across European countries. In addition, management has demonstrated a penchant for investing in smaller companies that possess much higher growth potential than in large, established companies. Although the emphasis on smaller companies adds to portfolio risk, aggressive international investors should be well rewarded over the long term. Also, the fund tends to hold a compact portfolio consisting of the stocks of approximately fifty to sixty companies. The fund has traditionally underweighted Japanese stocks, which has led the fund to above-average returns in recent years.

Portfolio Manager: David G. Herro since inception and Mike Welsh since 1995. Both joined the fund at its inception. Herro earned an M.A. in economics from the University of Wisconsin, and Welsh holds a M.M. Finance from Northwestern University.

Suitability: This fund is recommended for all growth and growth and income investors. It is ideally suited for conservative investors

who desire exposure to foreign stock markets. Conservative investors should limit their investments in this fund to 20 percent of portfolio assets.

Portfolio Implications: Investment in this fund, when coupled with domestic growth funds, can lower overall portfolio volatility (risk). Returns are enhanced during periods marked by a declining value of the U.S. dollar against the world's major currencies.

Annualized Returns
1-Year 18.3%
3-Year 11.1%
5-Year NA

Risk: Although this fund did not exist during the 1990 bear market, its share price can be extremely volatile as witnessed by its 9-percent decline during the weak 1994 market. It contains currency and political risk.

Costs: This is a relatively low-cost international equity fund. Its shares are sold with a no-load format. It possesses a below-average 1.40-percent annual expense ratio, and its 27-percent portfolio turnover ratio is well below average.

Distributions: Both income and capital gains distributions are paid in mid-December.

How to Buy and Sell: Minimum initial investment $2,500; IRA $1,000; subsequent investments $100. Telephone exchange with other Oakmark funds. Shares also available without transaction fees at Charles Schwab.

SCHRODER INTERNATIONAL

Schroder Capital Management
480 Seventh Avenue
New York, NY 10019
800-344-8332

Inception: 1989
Total Assets: $226 Million
Ticker Symbol: SCINX
Home Page: None

Objective and Strategy: The fund seeks long-term growth of capital by investing in foreign equity securities. At times the fund may invest up to 20 percent of its assets in fixed-income securities. Management employs a top-down approach in determining country allocations. Rigorous fundamental analysis, including company visits, is used in individual security selection. The portfolio is quite diverse, with the number of holdings ranging from one hundred to two hundred different stocks. Since its inception in 1989, the fund has exhibited mildly lower volatility than its peers. Although assets are invested across geographically diverse regions, the fund has traditionally invested about one-third of its assets in the Japanese stock market. Consistent returns and relatively low volatility should attract the attention of investors seeking some foreign exposure.

Portfolio Manager: Laura Luckyn-Malone since March 1995 and Mark J. Smith since the fund's inception. Ms. Malone has been a director since 1990. Smith has been employed by Schroder since 1983.

Suitability: Investment in this fund is recommended for all growth and growth and income investors. It is ideally suited for conservative investors who desire to gain exposure to foreign stock markets. Conservative investors should limit their investments in this fund to no more than 20 percent of portfolio assets.

Portfolio Implications: High investment in the Japanese stock market could duplicate investments of other international funds with Japanese exposure. Investment in this fund can reduce overall portfolio volatility when coupled with domestic equity growth funds.

Risk: As with all international funds, shareholders are exposed to both currency and political risks.

Costs: This is a very modest-cost international equity fund. Its shares are sold with a no-load format. Its annual expense ratio is a below-average 0.99-percent, as is its 66-percent portfolio turnover ratio.

Distributions: Both income and capital gains distributions are paid in late December.

How to Buy and Sell: Minimum initial investment a very high $10,000; IRA $2,000; subsequent investments $2,500 ($250 IRA). Shares also available without transaction fees from Jack White and Company.

Annualized Returns

1-Year 10.4%
3-Year 11.0%
5-Year 10.8%

SCUDDER GLOBAL

Scudder Investor Services
175 Federal Street
Boston, MA 02110
800-225-2470

Inception: 1986
Total Assets: $1.37 Billion
Ticker Symbol: SCOBX
Home Page: http://
www.scudder.com

Objective and Strategy: This international fund seeks long-term growth by investing primarily in the equity securities of both domestic and foreign firms. The bulk of the fund's portfolio is concentrated in established companies whose stocks are listed on major stock exchanges. The fund also has a small exposure to emerging markets where its focus is on companies with the ability to be among the world's low-cost producers rather than those in specific industries. The fund has performed well during the last five years, thanks to a hefty investment in the U.S. stock market, whose returns have outstripped markets abroad. Its largest exposure has been in Europe where it has established hefty allocations to manufacturing and financial companies. The fund has also assumed a 10-percent position in gold-mining companies, based on the belief that prices for gold and platinum are at an historic low in yen terms.

Annualized Returns
1-Year 10.1%
3-Year 10.1%
5-Year 12.0%

Portfolio Manager: William E. Holzer since inception in 1986. Holzer has been with Scudder since 1980. The fund is also managed by Nicholas Bratt and Alice Ho.

Suitability: This fund is recommended for all growth and growth and income investors. It is ideally suited for conservative investors who desire to gain exposure to foreign stock markets. Investors should limit their investments in this fund to no more than 25 percent of portfolio assets.

Portfolio Implications: Since this fund invests in U.S. stocks in addition to foreign equities, a portion of its portfolio may duplicate the investments of domestic growth funds. The fund is an excellent fit with domestic small- and mid-cap funds.

Risk: Although currency and political risks are present, investment in domestic stocks reduces the impact of these two variables. Share price volatility is modest as witnessed by its 6.4-percent decline during the severe 1990 bear market.

Costs: This is a low-cost global fund. It is sold with a no-load format. Its annual expense ratio is a modest 1.38 percent ,and its 44-percent portfolio turnover ratio is below average for the group.

Distributions: Both income and capital gains distributions are paid in either late November or early December.

How to Buy and Sell: Minimum initial investment $1,000; IRA $500; subsequent investments $100 ($50 IRA). Telephone exchange with other Scudder funds. Shares may also be purchased through Charles Schwab and Fidelity Brokerage.

SCUDDER GLOBAL DISCOVERY

Scudder Investor Services
175 Federal Street
Boston, MA 02110
800-225-2470

Inception: 1991
Total Assets: $322 Million
Ticker Symbol: SGSCX
Home Page: http://
www.scudder.com

Objective and Strategy: Formerly called the Global Small Company Fund, this fund seeks above-average, long-term capital appreciation by investing in the equity securities of small, rapidly growing companies located throughout the world, including the developed markets of the United States, Japan, and Western Europe. However, its focus tends to be on emerging markets in the Far East, Latin America, and Europe. When selecting individual securities, management uses a bottom-up approach (i.e., selecting good companies rather than emphasizing regional diversification). In addition to strong growth prospects, management looks for companies with solid management, good balance sheets, and dominant positions in local markets. The fund's domestic small-firm investments have contributed significant gains since the fund's inception in 1991.

Portfolio Manager: Gerald J. Moran since inception in 1991. He joined Scudder in equity research in 1968 and has been a portfolio manager since 1985.

Suitability: The fund is designed for aggressive growth-oriented investors who can accept the share price fluctuations and greater risks of small-company investing

and international investing including currency fluctuations, in exchange for potentially greater rewards.

Portfolio Implications: Because of its small-company orientation, this fund works best when combined with funds (both domestic and international) that are packed with the stocks of large, established companies.

Risk: This fund's investments in smaller companies add an element of liquidity risk to the currency and political risks assumed by international investors. Its investment in U.S. stocks offset a degree of both currency and political risk. The fund has yet to experience a severe bear market.

Annualized Returns
1-Year 18.0%
3-Year 11.5%
5-Year 12.7%

Costs: This is a very low-cost global fund. Its shares are sold with a no-load format, its expense ratio is a low 1.69 percent, as is its 44-percent portfolio turnover ratio.

Distributions: Both income and capital gains distributions occur in December.

How to Buy and Sell: Minimum initial investment $1,000; IRA $500; subsequent investments $100 ($50 IRA). Telephone exchange with other Scudder funds. Shares may also be obtained at Charles Schwab and Fidelity Brokerage.

SCUDDER INTERNATIONAL FUND

Scudder Investor Services
175 Federal Street
Boston, MA 02110
800-225-2470

Inception: 1953
Total Assets: $2.6 Billion
Ticker Symbol: SCINX
Home Page: http://
www.scudder.com

Objective and Strategy: This fund, the first international fund available to U.S. investors, seeks capital growth by investing in foreign markets. The portfolio focuses on large, well-capitalized companies and markets worldwide. The fund has sought to benefit from sector consolidation and corporate restructuring in Europe where it has invested more than half of the fund's assets. In addition, it seeks Japanese companies that are beneficiaries of the weaker yen or are likely to respond to a strengthening economy (i.e., cyclical stocks). The fund has been steadily increasing its weighting in Japan and has hedged approximately half of its exposure to the yen. Wide diversification, emphasis on developed economies, and a large-company orientation make this fund an ideal vehicle for all investors who want to participate in the international equities markets.

Annualized Returns
1-Year 8.4%
3-Year 8.7%
5-Year 9.6%

Portfolio Manager: Carol L. Franklin since 1986. She joined Scudder in 1981. Fund team also includes Nicholas Bratt, Irene Cheng, Francisco Rodrigo III, and Joan Gregory.

Suitability: This fund is highly recommended for all growth-oriented investors. It is ideally suited for conservative investors who desire to gain exposure to foreign equity markets. Conservative investors should limit their investments in this fund to no more than 20 percent of portfolio assets.

Portfolio Implications: Investment in this fund, when coupled with domestic growth funds, can lower overall portfolio volatility without compromising long-term return potential. Returns are enhanced during periods marked by a declining value of the U.S. dollar against the world's major currencies.

Risk: This is one of the lowest-risk international funds you can find. Although investors are exposed to both political and currency risks in addition to the normal risks experienced by equity fund investors, share price volatility is low, as witnessed by its modest 9-percent decline during the 1990 bear market.

Costs: This is also one of the lowest-cost international funds around. Its shares are sold with a no-load format; its 1.14-percent annual expense ratio is well below average as is its 45-percent portfolio turnover ratio.

Distributions: Income and capital gains distributions are paid in either late November or December.

How to Buy and Sell: Minimum initial investment $1,000; IRA $500; subsequent investments $100 ($50 IRA). Telephone exchange with other Scudder funds.

SCUDDER LATIN AMERICA FUND

Scudder Investor Services
175 Federal Street
Boston, MA 02110
800-225-2470

Inception: 1992
Total Assets: $646 Million
Ticker Symbol: SLAFX
Home Page: http://
www.scudder.com

Objective and Strategy: This relatively new fund seeks above-average growth by investing in Latin American stocks, focusing on those in Argentina, Brazil, Chile, Colombia, Mexico, and Peru. The fund seeks to capitalize on opportunities created by political and economic reforms taking place throughout the region. Although the dismal performance of Latin American stock markets, especially that of Mexico, has soured many investors on investing south of the border, there are compelling reasons to invest in rapidly growing Latin American economies. By the year 2000, Latin America will have a $2 trillion economy and will trade more than $600 billion in goods and services. Its total population will be almost twice that of the United States and will be growing twice as fast. This well-managed fund is well positioned to participate in that growth.

Annualized Returns
1-Year 19.5%
3-Year 8.3%
5-Year NA

Portfolio Manager: Edmund B. Games, Jr. since the fund's inception in 1992. He joined Scudder's equity research in 1960 and has focused on Latin American stocks since 1988.

Suitability: This fund is suitable for aggressive growth investors who wish to capture the above-average return potential offered by Latin American economies. Because of its extreme share price volatility, investors should limit their investment in this fund to no more than 5 percent of portfolio assets.

Portfolio Implications: This fund is not a substitute for a diversified international equity fund. It should be used to complement investments in other international equity funds by investors who wish to boost their allocation to Latin American markets.

Risk: This is a very high-risk fund. Shareholders are exposed to currency, political, and liquidity risks. The fund's share price plunged nearly 40 percent during the meltdown in Latin American stock markets that occurred in late 1994 and early 1995.

Costs: The fund is sold with a no-load format. Its annual expense ratio is a relatively high 2.08 percent, but its portfolio turnover ratio is a below-average 40 percent.

Distributions: Both income and capital gains distributions are paid in late December.

How to Buy and Sell: Minimum initial investment $1,000; IRA $500; subsequent investments $100 ($50 IRA). Telephone exchange with other Scudder funds. Fund recently repealed its 2-percent redemption fee.

SIT INTERNATIONAL GROWTH

SIT Investment Associates, Inc.
4600 Norwest Center
Minneapolis, MN 55402
800-332-5580

Inception: 1991
Total Assets: $89 Million
Ticker Symbol: SNGBX
Home Page: http://www.sitfunds.com

Objective and Strategy: This fund's charter is a bit more strict than many of its international fund peers. At least 90 percent of its assets will normally be invested in companies outside the United States, and the fund may invest up to 50 percent of its assets in small-cap companies in both developed and emerging markets. To mitigate risk, the fund attempts to buy only the highest-quality issues from different parts of the world. Recently, management has been seeking stocks in dynamic, high-growth industries such as telecommunications. To be added to the fund's portfolio (which contains about sixty-five companies), a company must show sustained annual earnings growth of 15 percent or more and a return on equity in the high teens. Recently, one-quarter of the fund's assets were invested in Japan with another one-quarter invested in other Asian nations.

Portfolio Manager: Eugene C. Sit and Andy B. Kim since the fund's inception in 1991. Sit has been CEO since 1981 after leaving a job as portfolio manager at IDS Funds.

Suitability: This fund is recommended for growth-oriented investors who can assume above-average risks. If you desire an exposure to foreign stock markets, this fund is

Annualized Returns

1-Year 5.0%
3-Year 9.9%
5-Year NA

an excellent vehicle. However, because of its above-average risk, investors should limit their investment in this fund to no more than 15 percent of portfolio assets.

Portfolio Implications: Investment in this fund, when coupled with domestic growth funds, can lower overall portfolio volatility without compromising long-term return potential. Returns are enhanced during periods marked by a decline in the value of the U.S. dollar against the world's major foreign currencies.

Risk: As with all international funds, shareholders assume a degree of both currency and political risk in addition to the normal risks assumed by equity fund investors. The fund did not exist during the 1990 bear market.

Costs: This is a low-cost international equity fund. Its shares are sold with a no-load format, its annual expense ratio, 1.50 percent, is below average, as is its 40-percent portfolio turnover ratio.

Distributions: Both income and capital gains distributions are paid in mid-December.

How to Buy and Sell: Minimum initial investment $2,000; subsequent investments $100. Shares are also available from Charles Schwab and Jack White without transaction fees.

SOGEN INTERNATIONAL FUND

Societe Generale Securities
1221 Avenue of the Americas
8th Floor
New York, NY 10020
800-334-2143

Inception: 1970
Total Assets: $3.3 Billion
Ticker Symbol: SGENX
Home Page: None

Objective and Strategy: This fund emphasizes low price-earnings and price-to-book value stocks, an investment style which helps to shield its position in "hot markets." The portfolio allocation of this fund barely resembles the prototypical international portfolio. More often than not you are apt to find investments in U.S. stocks, bonds, and some gold-mining exposure in addition to investments in foreign markets. Superior defensive characteristics have in the past provided enviable protection from severe market corrections that have plagued other growth-seeking international equity funds. However, its penchant for small-cap stocks has en-abled it to take advantage of strong, growth-oriented issues throughout the world. An initial $10,000 investment in this fund at its inception in 1970 would now be worth more than $300,000.

Annualized Returns
1-Year 12.1%
3-Year 11.4%
5-Year 13.0%

Portfolio Manager: Jean-Marie Eveillard since 1979. He was the fund's original analyst when the fund began operations in 1970 and has been with Societe Generale since 1962.

Suitability: This fund is recommended for all growth and growth and income investors. It is ideally suited for conservative investors who desire some exposure to foreign stock markets. Conservative investors should limit their investments in this fund to no more than 25 percent of portfolio assets.

Portfolio Implications: Since this fund invests in U.S. stocks in addition to foreign equities, a portion of its portfolio may duplicate the investments of domestic equity funds. The fund is an excellent fit with domestic small- and mid-cap funds.

Risk: As with all international funds, shareholders are exposed to both political and currency risks. Share price volatility, at times, can be relatively high.

Costs: The fund is sold with a 3.75-percent front-end load and ongoing 0.24-percent 12b-1 fee. However, its 1.25-percent annual expense ratio is below average for the group, and its portfolio turnover ratio, 10 percent, is extremely low.

Distributions: Both income and capital gains distributions are paid in late December.

How to Buy and Sell: Front-end load declines to 2.75-percent for purchases in excess of $50,000. Available without sales load for Schwab institutional clients. Minimum initial investment $1,000; subsequent investments $100.

STRONG INTERNATIONAL STOCK

P.O. Box 2936
Milwaukee, WI 53201
800-368-1030

Inception: 1992
Total Assets: $337 Million
Ticker Symbol: STISX
Home Page: http://www.strong-funds.com

Objective and Strategy: This fund aggressively seeks capital appreciation by investing internationally. Rather than concentrate on specific countries, the fund's management favors a bottom-up, stock-by-stock approach to uncover opportunities worldwide. The fund seeks financially sound, well-managed companies with a focused business strategy, growing earnings, and sustainable competitive advantages. The fund attempts to locate outstanding growth prospects, even if those firms happen to be in underperforming markets. Its largest allocations by country include Japan, Australia, the United Kingdom, New Zealand, and Singapore. Recently, the fund has benefitted from selective bets in emerging markets including Poland and India. If international markets outperform the U.S. market during the next couple of years as expected, look for this fund to shine.

Annualized Returns
1-Year 10.1%
3-Year 10.8%
5-Year NA

Portfolio Manager: Anthony L. T. Cragg since 1993. He also manages Strong Asia Pacific. A graduate of Christ Church, Oxford University, he began his investment career in 1980.

Suitability: This fund is recommended for all growth and growth and income investors. It is ideally suited for conservative investors who desire to gain some exposure to foreign stock markets. Aggressive investors may wish to allocate up to 30 percent of portfolio assets to this fund. Conservative inves-

tors should limit their allocations to no more than 20 percent of portfolio assets.

Portfolio Implications: Investment in this fund, when coupled with investment in domestic equity funds, can lower overall portfolio volatility without compromising long-term return potential. Returns are enhanced during periods marked by a declining value of the U.S. dollar against the world's major currencies.

Risk: As with all international funds, shareholders are exposed to currency and political risks in addition to the normal risks borne by equity fund investors. The fund's emerging markets investments pose additional risks. The fund has yet to experience a severe bear market.

Costs: The fund's shares are sold with a no-load format. Its 1.77-percent annual expense ratio is about average for the international group. Its 102-percent portfolio turnover ratio is slightly above the group average.

Distributions: Income distributions are paid quarterly. Capital gains are distributed in December.

How to Buy and Sell: Minimum initial investment $1,000; IRA $250; subsequent investments $50. Telephone exchange with other Strong funds. Shares are available without transaction fees from Charles Schwab, Jack White and Company, and Fidelity Brokerage.

TEMPLETON DEVELOPING MARKETS TRUST I

Franklin/Templeton Distributors
500 West Broward Boulevard
Suite 2100
Fort Lauderdale, FL 33394
800-237-0738

Inception: 1991
Total Assets: $2.98 Billion
Ticker Symbol: TEDMX
Home Page: http://www.frk.com

Objective and Strategy: This fund invests in developing nations all over the globe, primarily in Europe, Latin America, and the Pacific Rim. Fund management uses a careful bottom-up approach when choosing investments and does not make off-the-cuff decisions. Instead, Mark Mobius uses a hands-on approach, which relies heavily on company visits and conversations with management. The fund has in the past used leverage to enhance performance, thus increasing risks, but its low turnover and heavy emphasis on holding cash for defensive purposes helps to mitigate this risk. Recently, the fund began to build positions in markets that experienced severe corrections in 1990 (i.e., Mexico, Hong Kong, and Turkey). Because of the hefty front-end load, investors in this fund should plan to stick around for a long time. Although I prefer no-load funds, the Templeton philosophy and Dr. Mobius's guidance are compelling reasons to invest in this fund.

Annualized Returns
1-Year 12.0%
3-Year 8.6%
5-Year NA

Portfolio Manager: Dr. Mark Mobius since 1991. He has a Ph.D. in economics from the Massachusetts Institute of Technology and joined Templeton in 1987.

Suitability: This fund is suitable for aggressive investors only. Because of the fund's extreme share price volatility, investors should limit their allocations to this fund to no more than 10 percent of portfolio assets.

Portfolio Implications: This fund complements investment in global and diversified international equity funds. Its return has a low correlation with the returns of growth and aggressive growth funds. Thus, it provides considerable diversification benefits to growth and aggressive growth-oriented investors.

Risk: This is the highest-risk fund in the Templeton group. Investors are exposed to currency and political risks as well as the risk stemming from the illiquidity in tiny emerging markets.

Costs: Shares are sold with a relatively hefty 5.75-percent front-end load. Its annual expense ratio is a hefty 2.10 percent. However, its 10-percent portfolio turnover ratio is extremely low.

Distributions: Both income and capital gains distributions are paid in February.

How to Buy and Sell: Shares are sold with a front-end sales charge. Minimum initial investment $100; subsequent investments $50. Shares redeemed within one year are assessed a 1-percent redemption fee.

TEMPLETON FOREIGN FUND I

Franklin/Templeton Distributors
500 West Broward Boulevard
Suite 2100
Fort Lauderdale, FL 33394
800-237-0738

Inception: 1982
Total Assets: $9.3 Billion
Ticker Symbol: TEMFX
Home Page: http://www.frk.com

Objective and Strategy: This fund seeks long-term capital growth by investing solely in securities issued by companies and governments outside the United States. Like all of the Templeton funds, management of this fund takes a disciplined approach to global investing. It hunts for bargains, searches for good investments worldwide, and holds those investments over the longer term. Since 1987, this fund is nine for nine, having ended every calendar your in the top half of the foreign stock fund group. The fund's investment strategy does not follow typical top-down analysis in allocating assets to countries, nor does it stick safely to the EAFE Index. Its country allocations are simply the result of the manager's search for companies that are cheap relative to assets or projected long-term earnings.

Annualized Returns
1-Year 10.1%
3-Year 11.1%
5-Year 11.4%

Portfolio Manager: Mark Holowesko since 1985. He joined Templeton in 1985 and also manages both the World and Growth funds for Templeton.

Suitability: This fund is recommended for all growth and growth and income investors. It is ideally suited to conservative investors who desire exposure to foreign stock markets. Conservative investors should limit their investments in this fund to no more than 20 percent of portfolio assets.

Portfolio Implications: Investment in this fund, when coupled with investment in domestic equity funds, can lower overall portfolio volatility without compromising long-term return potential. Returns are enhanced during periods marked by a declining value of the U.S. dollar against the world's major currencies.

Risk: As with all international funds, investors are exposed to currency and political risks in addition to the normal risks assumed by equity fund investors. However, this fund has demonstrated very low volatility as witnessed by its modest 3-percent decline during the 1990 bear market.

Costs: Shares are sold with a 5.75-percent front-end sales fee. However, annual operating costs are relatively low. Its 1.15-percent annual expense ratio is below average as is its 22-percent portfolio turnover ratio.

Distributions: Income and capital gains distributions are paid annually in mid-October.

How to Buy and Sell: Shares are sold with a hefty front-end load. Minimum initial investment a low $100; subsequent investments $50. Shares redeemed within one year are assessed a 1-percent redemption fee.

TEMPLETON GLOBAL OPPORTUNITIES TRUST I

Franklin/Templeton Distributors
500 West Broward Boulevard
Suite 2100
Fort Lauderdale, FL 33394
800-237-0738

Inception: 1990
Total Assets: $575 Million
Ticker Symbol: TEGOX
Home Page: http://www.frk.com

Objective and Strategy: Like other Templeton funds, this fund adheres to a characteristic, stock-picking investment style. Price markets are absent from this value-oriented portfolio, which chooses stocks for the combination of fundamental strengths and low prices. Thus the U.S. and European markets are typically prominent. Essentially, this fund is just like all the other Templeton funds but with a heavier emphasis on small- to mid-cap issues. Assets may go to emerging market holdings, or they may be invested in higher-grade international bonds. Overall, long-term success and stock-picking discipline make this fund a good choice for fairly aggressive global investors.

Portfolio Manager: Howard Leonard since 1993. Prior to joining Franklin in 1989, he was director of investment research at First Pennsylvania Bank

Suitability: This fund is recommended for aggressive and modestly aggressive growth-oriented investors. It is ideally suited for growth investors who desire exposure to foreign stock markets. Conservative investors should limit their investments in this fund to no more than 15 percent of portfolio assets.

Annualized Returns

1-Year 11.0%
3-Year 10.8%
5-Year 13.4%

Portfolio Implications: Investment in this fund, when coupled with investment in domestic equity funds, can lower overall portfolio volatility without compromising long-term return potential. Returns are enhanced during a period marked by a declining value of the U.S. dollar against the world's major currencies.

Risk: Because of substantial investments in domestic stocks, currency and political risks are lower than those of most international funds. This relatively young fund has yet to experience a major bear market.

Costs: The fund is sold with a maximum 5.75-percent front-end load, and thus is somewhat pricey. Expense ratio is a low 1.27 percent. Portfolio turnover, 16 percent, is also low.

Distributions: Income and capital distributions are paid in mid-December.

How to Buy and Sell: Sold by financial planners and brokers with a front-end load. Minimum initial investment a low $100; subsequent investments $50. One-percent redemption fee imposed for shares redeemed within one year.

TEMPLETON GROWTH FUND I

Franklin/Templeton Distributors
500 West Broward Boulevard
Suite 2100
Fort Lauderdale, FL 33394
800-237-0738

Inception: 1986
Total Assets: $8.4 Billion
Ticker Symbol: TEPLX
Home Page: http://www.frk.com

Objective and Strategy: This global fund seeks long-term growth of capital through investments in equity securities both in the United States and abroad. Management uses a strict value discipline when selecting portfolio securities. On the whole, this fund is a relatively safe bet, producing above-average results over the past one, three, and five years, with lower than average volatility among global stock funds. The manager of this fund is a familiar face at Templeton, and his experience gives him the know-how to pick winning stocks. Investors not put off by finding their money invested in Mexico, Hong Kong, and China should explore this fund since it is one of the least risky ways to enter these markets. However, like all Templeton funds, you must pay a hefty access fee in terms of a front-end load.

Annualized Returns
1-Year 10.6%
3-Year 13.5%
5-Year 14.2%

Portfolio Manager: Mark G. Holowesko since the fund's inception in 1986. He joined Templeton in 1985 and also manages the Foreign Fund and the World Fund.

Suitability: This fund is recommended for all growth and growth and income investors. It is ideally suited for conservative investors who desire exposure to foreign stock markets. Conservative investors should limit their investment in this fund to no more than 25 percent of portfolio assets.

Portfolio Implications: Since this fund invests in U.S. stocks in addition to foreign equities, a portion of its portfolio may duplicate the investments of large-cap domestic equity funds. The fund is an excellent fit with domestic small- and mid-cap funds.

Risk: Although shareholders are exposed to both currency and political risk, as is the case with all international funds, the fund's share price volatility is relatively low as witnessed by its modest 9-percent decline during the 1990 bear market.

Costs: Like all Templeton funds, shares are purchased with a 5.75-percent front-end load. However, once you get past the entry fee, operating costs are modest. Its 1.12-percent annual expense ratio is below average, as is its 35-percent portfolio turnover ratio.

Distributions: Income and capital gains distributions are paid in mid-October.

How to Buy and Sell: Shares sold with hefty front-end load. Minimum initial investment is a low $100; subsequent investments $50. A 1-percent redemption fee is imposed on shares redeemed within one year.

TEMPLETON WORLD FUND I

Franklin/Templeton Distributors
500 West Broward Boulevard
Suite 2100
Fort Lauderdale, FL 33394
800-237-0738

Inception: 1978
Total Assets: $6.5 Billion
Ticker Symbol: TEMWX
Home Page: http://www.frk.com

Objective and Strategy: This fund has a flexible policy of investing in companies and governments of any nation, including the United States. Like all Templeton funds, management searches worldwide for bargain-priced stocks and holds them for an average of five years. Its enviable five-year returns and a manager that has a proven track record make this fund one to consider. The fund has been building its Latin American investments, especially in Mexico, and has been adding exposure to the Chinese economy. The value-based fund now holds a historically high two hundred companies, thus providing needed diversification. This fund has been providing solid returns for nearly twenty years, and there is no indication that the future holds anything less.

Portfolio Manager: Mark G. Holowesko since 1985. He joined Templeton in 1985 and also manages the Foreign Fund and the Growth Fund.

Suitability: This fund is highly recommended for all growth and growth and income investors. It is ideally suited for conservative investors who desire exposure to foreign stock markets. With one-third of assets invested in the United States and two-thirds in thirty-five other countries, this fund represents a balanced investment program and is an ideal starter fund for investors with limited resources.

Portfolio Implications: Since this fund invests in U.S. stocks in addition to foreign stocks, a portion of its portfolio may duplicate the investments of domestic large-cap equity funds. The fund provides an excellent addition to a portfolio dominated by small- and mid-cap funds.

Annualized Returns

1-Year 11.5%
3-Year 14.5%
5-Year 14.8%

Risk: As with all international funds, shareholders are exposed to both currency and political risks. Share price volatility can be high at times as witnessed by the fund's 16-percent decline during the 1990 bear market.

Costs: Like all Templeton funds, the fund's shares are sold with a 5.75-percent front-end sales fee. However, annual operating costs are relatively low. Its expense ratio is modest at 1.05 percent, as is its 34-percent portfolio turnover ratio.

Distributions: Both income and capital gains distributions are paid in mid-October.

How to Buy and Sell: Investors must pay a hefty front-end sales fee. Minimum initial investment $100; subsequent investments $50. Shares redeemed within one year are assessed a 1-percent redemption fee.

T. ROWE PRICE EUROPEAN STOCK

T. Rowe Price Investment Services
100 East Pratt Street
Baltimore, MD 21202
800-225-5132

Inception: 1990
Total Assets: $644 Million
Ticker Symbol: PRESX
Home Page: http://
www.troweprice.com

Objective and Strategy: Consistency and an eye for minimization of volatility are the key phrases in describing this offering. The portfolio generally consists of small- and mid-cap stocks with a smattering of blue chips thrown in for good measure. The fund seeks capital appreciation by emphasizing investments in France, Germany, the Netherlands, Italy, Spain, Sweden, Switzerland, and the United Kingdom. Although the vast majority of the fund's investments are made in companies located in developed economies, the fund generally invests 5 to 10 percent of its assets in the developing markets of Eastern Europe and Russia. However, the fund's conservative orientation and a penchant for gradually changing investment positions make this one of the tamest international funds around.

Portfolio Manager: Martin G. Wade since the fund's inception in 1990 in conjunction with "Advisor Group." He also advises other T. Rowe Price international funds.

Suitability: This fund is suitable for both aggressive and conservative growth-oriented investors. Because of its regional orientation, investors should limit their allocations to this fund to the lesser of 10 percent of

portfolio assets or one-third of their total allocation to international equity funds.

Portfolio Implications: This fund is not a substitute for a global or diversified international equity fund. It should be used to complement investments in other international equity funds by investors who wish to boost their allocation to European stocks.

Risk: The fund possesses modest currency and political risks in addition to the normal risks assumed by equity fund investors. The fund has yet to experience a severe bear market, and it posted a modest 4-percent gain during the weak 1994 market.

Costs: This is a very low-cost fund. Its shares are sold with a no-load format. Its annual expense ratio is a low 1.20 percent as is its 17-percent portfolio turnover ratio.

Distributions: Both income and capital gains distributions are paid in late December.

How to Buy and Sell: Minimum initial investment $2,500; IRA $1,000; subsequent investments $100. Telephone switch with other Price funds, but management frowns on frequent switching.

Annualized Returns
1-Year 19.4%
3-Year 17.0%
5-Year 12.4%

T. ROWE PRICE INTERNATIONAL DISCOVERY

T. Rowe Price Investment Services
100 East Pratt Street
Baltimore, MD 21202
800-225-5132

Inception: 1989
Total Assets: $347 Million
Ticker Symbol: PRIDX
Home Page: http://
www.troweprice.com

Objective and Strategy: In seeking long-term capital appreciation by investing in issues of small- to mid-sized companies, this fund presents itself with a little more volatility than the average international fund. Diversification across approximately five hundred companies provides some relief from the risks posed by small, rapidly growing foreign companies; however, its shares are subject to wide swings caused by changing economic fortunes that have a much more pronounced effect on smaller firms than on large ones. The fund performs exceptionally well when international markets are in an up trend. At present, positive developments in most of the world's economies bode well for the prospects of this fund. In mid-1996 its largest allocations were made to markets in Europe (40%), the Far East (26%) Japan (15%), and Latin America (9%).

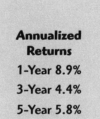

**Annualized
Returns**
1-Year 8.9%
3-Year 4.4%
5-Year 5.8%

Portfolio Manager: Martin G. Wade since inception, in conjunction with "Advisory Group." He also advises other T. Rowe Price international funds.

Suitability: This fund is recommended for growth-oriented investors who can assume an above-average level of risk. Although geographically diversified, the fund's concentration on smaller companies increases both return potential and share price volatility.

Portfolio Implications: Investment in this fund complements investments in funds that invest in large- and small-cap funds. If you currently have an investment in a U.S. small-cap fund, you should consider investing in this fund. Because small-caps have long-term performance cycles, you want to be patient with your investment in this fund.

Risk: Share price volatility is enhanced by the fund's investment in the stocks of relatively small foreign companies. In addition, investors are exposed to both currency and political risks. The fund's share price declined by approximately 13 percent during the 1990 bear market.

Costs: Like most T. Rowe Price funds, this is a low-cost international fund. It is sold with a no-load format and possesses an average 1.46-percent annual expense ratio and a low 44-percent portfolio turnover ratio.

Distributions: Both income and capital gains distributions are paid in late December.

How to Buy and Sell: Minimum initial investment $2,500; IRA $1,000; subsequent investments $50. Telephone exchange with other Price funds, but company frowns on frequent switching. A 2-percent redemption fee is imposed on shares held less than one year.

T. ROWE PRICE INTERNATIONAL STOCK

T. Rowe Price Investment Services
100 East Pratt Street
Baltimore, MD 21202
800-225-5132

Inception: 1980
Total Assets: $8.3 Billion
Ticker Symbol: PRITX
Home Page: http://
www.troweprice.com

Objective and Strategy: This pure international fund invests exclusively in foreign securities. Typically, the fund is well diversified and has a presence in at least twenty countries at any given time. It stresses macroeconomic themes and above-average growth markets. Management's price consciousness, however, prevents the fund from being heavily invested in markets or sectors that it considers speculative. Despite its pure foreign exposure, which makes the fund more sensitive to exchange-rate fluctuations than its global fund rivals, the fund has not exhibited excessive volatility and has outperformed most international funds over the long haul. The fund was one of the pioneers in international investing and has more than fulfilled its objective of providing capital appreciation to shareholders wishing international exposure.

Portfolio Manager: Martin G. Wade since the fund's inception in 1980 in conjunction with "Advisory Group." He also advises other T. Rowe Price international funds.

Suitability: This is one of the tamest diversified international equity funds around. It is ideally suited for both conservative and aggressive growth-oriented investors who wish to diversify globally. An investment in this fund, when coupled with investments in domestic equity funds, reduces overall portfolio volatility (risk).

Annualized Returns

1-Year 13.6%
3-Year 11.1%
5-Year 11.1%

Portfolio Implications: This fund makes an ideal addition to any growth-oriented portfolio. Its investments are drawn from countries all over the world (except the United States) and it invests in both developed and developing economies. This is one international fund you want to buy and hold.

Risk: As with all international funds, shareholders are exposed to currency and political risks. However, this fund is well diversified and its share price volatility is below that of most international equity funds. Its share price declined by less than 9 percent during the 1990 bear market.

Costs: You won't find many international equity funds with lower costs. Its shares are sold with a no-load format. It possesses a very low 0.91-annual expense ratio and a modest 18-percent portfolio turnover ratio.

Distributions: Both income and capital gains distributions are paid in late December.

How to Buy and Sell: Minimum initial investment $2,500; IRA $1,000; subsequent investments $100. Telephone exchange with other Price funds. Shares may also be obtained through Charles Schwab and Fidelity Brokerage.

T. ROWE PRICE LATIN AMERICA

T. Rowe Price Investor Services
100 East Pratt Street
Baltimore, MD 21202
800-225-5132

Inception: 1993
Total Assets: $26 Million
Ticker Symbol: PRLAX
Home Page: http://
www.troweprice.com

Objective and Strategy: This regional international equity fund was founded at a most inopportune time. Shortly after it began selling shares, the Mexican stock market collapsed, which in turn led to sharp declines in most Latin American stock markets. In 1995, the fund's share price declined a whopping 37 percent. However, since then, Latin American economies have been on the mend. A bet on this fund is a bet that a growing middle class in Latin America will spur above-average economic growth for the next couple of decades. Although the long-term potential of these economies is robust, their stock markets are small and highly susceptible to investor mood swings. However, these markets and this fund should provide handsome returns over the longer term. Countries with the largest allocations include Brazil (37%), Mexico (28%), Argentina (13%), and Chile (10%).

Annualized Returns
1-Year 18.5%
3-Year NA
5-Year NA

Portfolio Manager: Martin G. Wade since the fund's inception in 1993 in conjunction with "Advisory Group." He also advises other T. Rowe Price international funds.

Suitability: This fund is ideally suited for aggressive growth-oriented investors who wish to boost overall portfolio returns. However, because of the extreme volatility that exists in tiny Latin American stock markets, investors should limit their investment in this fund to between 5 and 10 percent of portfolio assets.

Portfolio Implications: This fund is not a substitute for a global or diversified international equity fund. It should be used to complement investments in other international equity funds by investors who want to boost their allocation to Latin American markets.

Risk: In addition to both currency and political risks, shareholders are exposed to extreme volatility that results from tiny markets such as those located in South America. The fund did not exist during the 1990 bear market but suffered during the emerging market meltdown in 1994-1995.

Costs: This is one of the lowest-cost emerging markets funds. Its shares are sold with a no-load format. Its 1.82-percent annual expense ratio is about average, and it possesses a very low 20 percent portfolio turnover ratio.

Distributions: Both income and capital gains distributions are paid in late December.

How to Buy and Sell: Minimum initial investment $2,500; IRA $1,000; subsequent investments $100. Telephone exchange with other Price funds. A 2-percent redemption fee is imposed for shares held less than one year.

T. ROWE PRICE NEW ASIA FUND

T. Rowe Price Investment Services
100 East Pratt Street
Baltimore, MD 21202
800-225-5132

Inception: 1990
Total Assets: $2.3 Billion
Ticker Symbol: PRASX
Home Page: http://
www.troweprice.com

Objective and Strategy: In pursuit of capital appreciation, this fund will invest primarily in equities of both large-cap and small-cap companies domiciled in, or with primary operations in Asia and the Pacific Basin, excluding Japan. Its portfolio tends to be concentrated in investments in the following countries: Australia, Hong Kong, India, Indonesia, Malaysia, New Zealand, the Philippines, Singapore, South Korea, Taiwan, and Thailand. These are among the fastest growing economies in the world, with GDP growth rates more than twice those experienced in Europe, Japan, and the United States. Investments in Hong Kong account for the largest portion (26%) of portfolio assets. Significant allocations have also been made to Malaysia and Singapore markets. Because of the geographic location of its investments and its strong management, this fund is poised to deliver exceptional long-term returns

Portfolio Manager: Martin G. Wade since the fund's inception in 1990 in conjunction with "Advisory Group." He also advises other T. Rowe Price international funds.

Suitability: This fund is suitable for aggressive growth-oriented investors only. Because it excludes investment in Japan, the bulk of its investments are in emerging markets, which are small and highly volatile.

Portfolio Implications: This portfolio will nearly duplicate those of most emerging markets funds. Investment in the fund complements investments in other diversified international equity funds. Limit holdings in this fund to one-third of the total allocation made to international equity funds.

Annualized Returns
1-Year 6.9%
3-Year 6.4%
5-Year 13.0%

Risk: With its investments in the Pacific Rim in rapidly expanding economies, this fund could experience extreme share price volatility at times. Investors also face currency and political risks.

Costs: This is one of the lowest-cost funds in its category. Sold with a no-load format, its annual expense ratio is a very low 1.15 percent, and its portfolio turnover ratio is a below-average 64 percent.

Distributions: Both income and capital gains distributions occur in late December.

How to Buy and Sell: Minimum initial investment $2,500; IRA $1,000; subsequent investments $100. Telephone exchange with other Price funds with no fee. However, management frowns on frequent switches. Shares also available at Charles Schwab.

TWENTIETH CENTURY INTERNATIONAL GROWTH

Twentieth Century Investors
4500 Main Street
P.O. Box 418210
Kansas City, MO 64111
800-345-2021

Inception: 1991
Total Assets: $1.3 Billion
Ticker Symbol: TWIEX
Home Page: http://
www.americancentury.com

Objective and Strategy: In seeking capital appreciation, this fund uses a somewhat contrarian approach to international investing by selecting stocks that have high fundamental and technical standards first, and analyzing the economic and political situation of the issuer's country second. Such bottom-up strategies have often led to geographical weightings different from the group norm. The fund has managed to hold its own, typically through underweighting the hot, but volatile emerging markets. Investors should not, however, discount the possibility of an increase in emerging markets exposure, which would correspondingly increase portfolio risk. Nevertheless, this fund has maintained somewhat less volatility than the typical international equity fund.

**Annualized
Returns**
1-Year 11.6%
3-Year 10.6%
5-Year 12.6%

Portfolio Manager: Robert C. Puff since the fund's inception in 1991. He joined Investors Research in 1983 and is assisted by Theodore Tyson and Henrik Strabo.

Suitability: This fund is recommended for all growth and growth and income investors. It is ideally suited for conservative investors who desire exposure to foreign stock markets. Conservative investors should limit their investment in this fund to 20 percent of portfolio assets.

Portfolio Implications: Investment in this fund, when coupled with domestic growth funds, can lower overall portfolio volatility (risk). Returns are enhanced during periods marked by a falling value of the U.S. dollar.

Risk: In addition to the normal risks assumed by all equity investors, investment in this fund is accompanied by currency risk and, to a lesser extent, political risk. Its share price declined by about 5 percent during 1994, and it was not in business during 1990 severe bear market.

Costs: This is a modest-cost international equity offering. It is sold without sales charges of any kind, possesses a 1.9-percent expense ratio, but a relatively high 169-percent annual portfolio turnover ratio.

Distributions: Income and capital gains distributions are paid annually, usually in mid-December.

How to Buy and Sell: Minimum initial investment $2,500; IRA $1,000; subsequent investments $50. Sold with a no-load format. Telephone exchange with other Twentieth Century/Benham funds. Shares also available through Fidelity and Charles Schwab (no transaction fees).

USAA INTERNATIONAL

USAA Investment Management Co.
9800 Fredericksburg Road
San Antonio, TX 78288
800-531-8181

Inception: 1988
Total Assets: $434 Million
Ticker Symbol: USIFX
Home Page: None

Objective and Strategy: The fund's objective is capital appreciation with income as a secondary consideration. Investment selection is not conducted under "hard-and-fast" rules and can consist of both a bottom-up and a top-down approach. Generally, the fund is geographically diverse with investments spread across nearly forty countries. Its largest asset allocation is to Japan (14%) followed by approximately 5-percent allocations to the Netherlands, France, Canada, and Sweden. Although it also invests in about a dozen so-called developing markets, its allocation to this sector is relatively light. Because of its wide diversification, the fund's exposure to foreign currency fluctuations is less than many other international funds. With the exception of 1989, this fund has scored above the group average in every year of its existence.

Portfolio Manager: David G. Peebles since 1988. He has worked for USAA since 1984 and obtained his B.S. and M.B.A. from Texas Christian University.

Suitability: This fund is recommended for growth and growth and income investors who desire to obtain some exposure to foreign stock markets. Conservative investors should limit their investment in this fund to no more than 20 percent of portfolio assets.

**Annualized
Returns**

1-Year 15.0%
3-Year 12.6%
5-Year 12.7%

Portfolio Implications: Investment in this fund, when coupled with investment in domestic equity funds, can lower over portfolio volatility without compromising long-term return potential. Returns tend to be enhanced during periods marked by a decline in the value of the U.S. dollar against the world's major currencies.

Risk: Shareholders are exposed to both currency and political risks. Share price volatility is higher than that of diversified domestic equity funds. However, the fund's share price declined by a modest 9.3 percent during the 1990 bear market.

Costs: The fund is sold with a no-load format. Operating expenses are also low. Its 1.19-percent expense ratio is below average as is its 70-percent portfolio turnover ratio. On balance, this is a low-cost international equity fund.

Distributions: Income and capital gains distributions during 1996 were paid in May.

How to Buy and Sell: Minimum initial investment $3,000; IRA $250; subsequent investments $50. Telephone exchange with other USAA funds.

UNITED INTERNATIONAL GROWTH FUND A

Waddell & Reed
6300 Lamar Avenue
P.O. Box 29217
Shawnee Mission, KS 66201
913-236-2000

Inception: 1970
Total Assets: $771 Million
Ticker Symbol: UNCGX
Home Page: http://
www.waddell.com

Objective and Strategy: This fund seeks capital appreciation by investing in equity securities issued by companies located anywhere in the world, including the United States. Although the fund invests in emerging markets, its allocations to these markets has rarely exceeded 20 percent of portfolio assets. Instead, it tends to concentrate its investments in large-capitalization firms operating in highly developed economies. Its portfolio tends to be geographically compact as well, with about two dozen countries being represented. Unlike a number of global funds, it has also tended to significantly underweight Japan. Far and away, European economies tend to dominate the portfolio. The fund provides a blend of both large and small markets and is suitable for conservative investors who desire some international diversification.

Portfolio Manager: Thomas A. Mengel since May 1996. He has ten years previous experience in securities and banking. He recently replaced Mark L. Yockey.

Suitability: This fund is recommended for growth and growth and income investors who can assume modest risks. It is ideally suited for conservative investors who desire some exposure to foreign stock markets. Conservative investors should limit invest-

ment in this fund to no more than 20 percent of portfolio assets.

Portfolio Implications: Since this fund may invest in U.S. stocks in addition to foreign equities, a portion of its portfolio may duplicate the investments of domestic growth funds. The fund is an excellent fit with domestic small- and mid-cap funds.

Risk: As with all international funds, shareholders are exposed to both political and currency risks in addition to the normal risks assumed by all equity fund investors. Portfolio volatility tends to be higher than that of most diversified domestic equity funds. Its share price declined by about 14 percent during the 1990 bear market.

Costs: Share purchases less than $100,000 are accompanied by a hefty 5.75-percent front-end load. However, annual operating costs tend to be relatively modest. Its annual expense ratio is a below-average 1.24 percent as is its 57-percent portfolio turnover ratio.

Distributions: Income distributions are paid in June and December. Capital gains are distributed in December.

How to Buy and Sell: Investors pay a front-end sales fee. Minimum initial investment $500; IRA $50; subsequent investments $25.

**Annualized
Returns**
1-Year 5.5%
3-Year 12.6%
5-Year 13.1%

VANGUARD INTERNATIONAL GROWTH

Vanguard Group
Vanguard Financial Center
P.O. Box 2600
Valley Forge, PA 19482
800-635-1511

Inception: 1981
Total Assets: $4.9 Billion
Ticker Symbol: VWIGX
Home Page: http://
www.vanguard.com

Objective and Strategy: The fund aggressively seeks capital growth by investing in above-average growth companies domiciled outside the United States. The portfolio is under the supervision of Schroder Capital Management, an investment advisory firm based in London with operations conducted from eleven offices worldwide. Core securities, which normally constitute about two-thirds of portfolio assets, are small to medium-sized growth companies with sustainable competitive advantages. The fund's noncore securities are large-cap stocks that have historically exhibited high correlation with their local markets. These stocks are used to supplement the weightings in local markets where Schroder's short-term view is optimistic. The fund has outperformed the EAFE Index during the last one-, three-, five-, and ten-year periods.

Portfolio Manager: Richard Folkes since the fund's inception in 1981. Folkes has twenty-eight years investment experience with Schroder. He was educated at the Sorbonne, France and obtained his M.A. from Cambridge University.

Suitability: This low-cost fund is highly recommended for all growth and growth and income investors. It is ideally suited for conservative investors who desire exposure to foreign equity markets. Conservative investors should limit their investments in

this fund to no more than 20 percent of portfolio assets.

Portfolio Implications: Investment in this fund, when coupled with domestic equity fund investments, can lower overall portfolio volatility without compromising long-term return potential. Returns are enhanced during periods marked by a decline in the value of the U.S. dollar against the world's major currencies.

Annualized Returns

1-Year 12.3%
3-Year 12.7%
5-Year 11.4%

Risk: Shareholders experience both currency and political risks in addition to the normal risks experienced by equity fund investors. The fund's share price declined by slightly more than 12 percent during the 1990 bear market.

Costs: This is a very low-cost vehicle. The management fee is a low 0.32 percent, and its annual expense ratio is also a low 0.59 percent. Portfolio turnover is a modest 30 percent annually.

Distributions: Both capital gains and income distributions are paid in late December.

How to Buy and Sell: Shares are sold without a sales charge of any kind. Minimum initial investment $3,000; IRA $1,000; subsequent investments $100. Telephone exchange with other Vanguard funds, however management frowns on frequent switching.

WARBURG PINCUS INTERNATIONAL EQUITY FUND

Counselors Securities
466 Lexington Avenue, 10th Floor
New York, NY 10017
800-888-6878

Inception: 1989
Total Assets: $2.9 Billion
Ticker Symbol: CUIEX
Home Page: None

Objective and Strategy: This fund seeks capital appreciation by investing in companies domiciled outside the United States. Not only did the fund garner exceptional returns during 1994, when most foreign markets were soaring, it also managed to dodge the carnage during 1995 when the devaluation of the Mexican peso sent shock waves throughout the world's markets. As a result, its assets soared. Richard King has the knack for being in the right place at the right time, for he has built one of the finest performance track records in the business. Investment selections demand exceptional intrinsic value and strong cash flows, in addition to a low price and strong underlying macroeconomic fundamentals. Richard's crystal ball seems to be working overtime, as he has managed to strategically enter and exit various global markets.

Annualized Returns
1-Year 9.3%
3-Year 11.4%
5-Year 11.4%

Portfolio Manager: Richard King since the fund's inception in 1989. Prior to joining Warburg Pincus in 1989, he worked in London for Fiduciary Trust Company International.

Suitability: This fund is recommended for all growth-oriented investors. It is ideally suited for conservative growth-oriented investors who desire to gain some exposure to foreign equity markets. Conservative investors should limit their investments in this fund to no more than 20 percent of portfolio assets.

Portfolio Implications: Investment in this fund, when coupled with investments in domestic equity funds, can lower overall portfolio volatility without compromising long-term return potential. The fund tends to perform exceptionally well during periods marked by a slight decline in the value of the U.S. dollar against most of the world's major currencies.

Risk: As with all international funds, shareholders are exposed to both political and foreign currency risks. Although the volatility of international equity funds tends to be high, this fund managed to dodge the 1990 bear market when it experienced a modest 4.6-percent share price decline.

Costs: The fund is sold with a no-load format. Its operating expenses are quite modest: 1.39-percent annual expense ratio and a below-average 39-percent portfolio turnover ratio.

Distributions: Income and capital gains distributions are paid in either late November or early December.

How to Buy and Sell: Minimum initial investment $2,500; IRA $500; subsequent investments $500 ($50 IRA). The fund's shares are also available with no transaction fees at Charles Schwab, Fidelity Brokerage, and Jack White and Company.

WILLIAM BLAIR INTERNATIONAL GROWTH

William Blair & Company
135 South LaSalle Street
Chicago, IL 60603
800-742-7272

Inception: 1992
Total Assets: $101 Million
Ticker Symbol: WBIGX
Home Page: http://
www.wmblair.com

Objective and Strategy: This fund invests in common stocks issued by companies domiciled outside the United States. Current income is not a significant factor in investment selection although the fund can be counted on to generate modest investment income. Its focus is on well-managed companies in growing industries. Its investments tend to be spread across about two dozen countries with investments in Germany, Japan, and the United Kingdom dominating. When selecting individual securities management emphasizes several broad themes: companies implementing efficiencies, niche competitors, low-cost producers in emerging markets, and rising returns to shareholders in areas where private equity capital is playing an expanding role. In short, these are consistent growth companies with coherent strategies and strong management disciplines.

Annualized Returns
1-Year 8.7%
3-Year 7.8%
5-Year NA

Portfolio Manager: Norbert W. Truderung since the fund's inception in 1992. He is assisted by Michael Vogel and Simon Key, who are employed by a subadviser domiciled in London.

Suitability: This fund is recommended for growth-oriented investors. It is ideally suited for conservative investors who desire to gain some exposure to foreign equity markets. Conservative investors should limit their investments in this fund to no more than 20 percent of portfolio assets.

Portfolio Implications: Investment in this fund, when coupled with investments in domestic equity funds, can lower overall portfolio volatility without compromising long-term return potential. Returns tend to be enhanced during periods marked by a declining value of the U.S. dollar against the world's major currencies.

Risk: As with all international funds, shareholders experience currency and political risks in addition to the normal risks assumed by all equity fund investors. This relatively young fund has yet to experience a major bear market.

Costs: This is one of the few brokerage-sponsored funds sold with a no-load format. Operating expenses are also low: 1.48-percent annual expense ratio and 77-percent portfolio turnover ratio.

Distributions: Income and capital gains distributions are paid in December.

How to Buy and Sell: Minimum initial investment $5,000; IRA $2,000; subsequent investments $1,000. Exchange with other Blair funds. Shares may also be obtained with no transaction fees from Charles Schwab and Jack White and Company.

WRIGHT INTERNATIONAL BLUE CHIP

1000 Lafayette Boulevard
Bridgeport, CT 06604
800-888-9471

Inception: 1989
Total Assets: $226 Million
Ticker Symbol: WIBCX
Home Page: http://www.wisi.com

Objective and Strategy: This fund offers an internationally diversified portfolio covering nineteen nations (including the United States) and twenty-two major industry sectors. Its objective is to provide long-term growth of capital and at the same time earn reasonable current income. At present the fund has invested in approximately 125 companies that meet Wright's high quality standards. Focus is on high-quality companies that have demonstrated they can consistently deliver high rates of return to shareholders. Rather than weight the fund on a geographical basis, the fund's manager will overweight those markets, regardless of size, that are believed to offer the best potential. As a result, this fund has benefitted from a significant underweighting to Japan and an overweighting of strong markets such as the United Kingdom, Denmark, Sweden, and Hong Kong.

Annualized Returns

1-Year 14.3%
3-Year 11.7%
5-Year 10.3%

Portfolio Manager: Managed by committee headed by Peter Donovan, who joined Wright in 1996.

Suitability: This fund is recommended for all growth-oriented investors. It is ideally suited for conservative investors who desire to obtain some exposure to foreign equity markets. Conservative investors should limit their investments in this fund to no more than 20 percent of portfolio assets.

Portfolio Implications: Investment in this fund, when coupled with investments in domestic equity funds, can lower overall portfolio volatility without compromising long-term return potential. The fund tends to perform exceptionally well during periods marked by a slightly declining value of the U.S. dollar against the world's major currencies.

Risk: Shareholders experience both currency and political risks in addition to the normal risks experienced by all equity fund investors. Interestingly, the fund has exhibited relatively tame share price volatility as witnessed by its modest 6.9-percent decline during the 1990 bear market.

Costs: Shares are sold without a front-end or back-end load but carry an ongoing 0.20-percent 12b-1 distribution fee. Operating costs are quite modest: 1.29-percent annual expense ratio and a very low 12-percent portfolio turnover ratio.

Distributions: Income distributions are paid quarterly, and capital gains are distributed in late December.

How to Buy and Sell: Minimum initial investment $1,000; IRA $50; no minimum subsequent investments. Telephone exchange with other Wright funds. Shares may also be obtained through Jack White and Company and Fidelity Brokerage with no transaction fees.

CHAPTER

FORTY-ONE

Precious Metals Funds

Table 28 in Section II contains financial statistics for the funds that invest in precious metals. Some of the funds invest in gold bullion and the shares of gold-mining companies only; others expand their portfolios to include investments in silver and platinum. A few funds restrict their investments to specific geographic areas such as South Africa or North America.

On average, the share prices of precious metals funds tend to be more volatile than the underlying prices of gold or silver bullion. That is because most funds invest heavily in mining stocks, whose earnings and share prices possess high volatility as a result of doing business in a high-fixed-cost industry. As a result of a high degree of operating leverage, small percentage changes in the price of gold can lead to large percentage changes in mining profits. For example, suppose that it costs a mining company $200 million to mine six hundred thousand ounces of gold annually. When the price of gold is $360 an ounce, revenues total $216 million and operating profits are $16 million. Now suppose the price of gold rises 20 percent to $432 an ounce. Revenues rise to $259 million, and, since operating costs are unaffected, operating profits rise to $59 million, a gain of 268 percent.

One basic force drives the price of gold: fear (or the lack of it). Political instability, the prospect of higher inflation, and a falling value of the U.S. dollar tend to drive the price of gold higher. Thus, the return from investing in a precious metals fund tends to fluctuate in an opposite direction to the returns of most financial assets. As a result, investment in gold tends to lower portfolio variability (that is, investment risk) when combined with other investments such as stocks and bonds. However, to the extent that many precious metals funds invest in gold mining shares of companies doing business outside of the United States, there are also elements of political and foreign exchange risk inherent in these investments.

The price of gold bullion rose nearly every year during the inflation years of the 1970s, rising from $32 per ounce in 1972, when U.S. citizens were again allowed to speculate in this precious metal, to nearly $800 an ounce for a brief instant in 1980. During the double-digit inflation years (1978–1980), the price of gold bullion nearly quadrupled. However, after rising by nearly 92 percent during 1980, the price of gold bullion has been on the decline ever since.

Given the depressed conditions that have existed in the gold and silver bullion markets in recent years, it is not surprising that precious metals funds as a group have been among the industry's poorest performers during the past fifteen years.

Although precious metals funds sport relatively low average betas, their share prices are extremely volatile. The low beta results from a very low correlation with returns from equities. On average, these funds pay very little current income, the exception being funds specializing in South African gold mining shares.

AMERICAN CENTURY GLOBAL GOLD

1665 Charleston Road
Mountain View, CA 94043
800-345-2021

Inception: 1988
Total Assets: $515 Million
Ticker Symbol: BGEIX
Home Page: http://
www.americancentury.com

Objective and Strategy: In early 1996, this fund changed both its name and investment strategy. Formerly, this gold index fund tracked a North American gold index. It now tracks the FT-SE Gold Mines Index (a widely recognized measure of the global gold industry). As a result, it has reduced its allocation to North American gold mining stocks from 100 percent of portfolio assets to 60 percent and has added a 25 percent allocation to South African gold stocks and a 15 percent allocation to Australian gold stocks. The fund is designed as an inflation hedge. Although gold stock prices can be extremely volatile in the short term, they help reduce overall portfolio volatility since their prices tend to run counter to bond prices and the stock market generally.

Portfolio Manager: William Martin has been managing this fund since its inception in August 1988. He also serves as portfolio manager of the Benham Natural Resources Fund.

Suitability: Because of its inherent volatility, the fund is most suitable for investors who seek to reduce overall portfolio volatility through a long-term diversification strategy. The fund does not constitute a balanced investment plan by itself.

Annualized Returns

1-Year	3.2%
3-Year	5.1%
5-Year	9.7%

Portfolio Implications: Income investors can reduce interest rate risk by combining a 5 to 10 percent allocation in this fund with their bond portfolios. A small allocation can also reduce the volatility of a portfolio crammed with aggressive equity funds.

Risk: Share price is highly volatile, as with most gold funds. Because of this fund's international diversification, investors are also exposed to currency and political risk.

Costs: This is one of the lowest-cost gold funds around. The management fee is a low 0.3 percent, and the fund's total expense ratio is a very low 0.64 percent. Sold with a no-load format and with a modest 35 percent turnover ratio, this is a very efficient fund.

Distributions: Late December. Given the poor performance of gold in recent years, this fund has little unrealized capital gains exposure.

How to Buy and Sell: The initial investment requirement was recently raised to $2,500; subsequent investments $250. There are free telephone exchanges with other Benham or Twentieth Century funds. Shares can also be purchased without transaction fees from Schwab, Jack White, and Fidelity.

FIDELITY SELECT AMERICAN GOLD

82 Devonshire Street
Boston, MA 02109
800-544-8888

Inception: 1985
Total Assets: $416 Million
Ticker Symbol: FSAGX
Home Page: http://www.fidelity.com

Objective and Strategy: This fund attempts to temper the risk inherent in gold investing by shifting assets among gold stocks, bullion, and cash, although under normal circumstances 80 percent of the portfolio will be invested in gold bullion or gold mining stocks. South African investments have claimed less than 10 percent of its assets in recent years. Its large allocation to North American mining operations has allowed the fund to post enviable returns relative to internationally diversified gold funds in recent years. Because of its emphasis on non-dividend-paying development-type gold mining stocks, the fund is extremely volatile. However, during periods marked by rapidly rising gold prices, this fund's return will lead funds in its category.

**Annualized
Returns**

1-Year 23.6%
3-Year 13.5%
5-Year 16.7%

Portfolio Manager: Larry Rakers has been managing this fund since July 1995. He also manages the Select Paper and Forest Products portfolio. He joined Fidelity in 1993 as precious metals research analyst.

Suitability: Like all gold funds, this fund is suitable for investors seeking an inflation hedge or those who wish to temper overall portfolio volatility by staying well diversified. Because of its extreme volatility, when used alone, the fund is a highly speculative vehicle.

Portfolio Implications: This fund can be used for speculative purposes, but it is a costly proposition considering its front-end load and redemption fee. It is best used to temper portfolio volatility of bond fund or aggressive equity portfolios. Allocations should be limited to 10 percent of portfolio assets.

Risk: As with all gold funds, this fund does not represent a balanced portfolio. It possesses limited foreign exchange and political risks. Volatility is extremely high. However, returns have low correlation with those of diversified equity and bond funds.

Costs: The fund levies a 3-percent front-end load and a 0.75-percent redemption charge for shares held less than one month. Its expense ratio (1.39 percent) is below average for its category, as is its 56-percent portfolio turnover ratio.

Distributions: Capital gains and income distributions occur in December. The fund has considerable unrealized capital gains tax exposure at the current time.

How to Buy and Sell: It can be purchased without transaction fees from Fidelity Brokerage. The minimum investment requirement is $2,500; subsequent investments $250. There is a front-end load of 3-percent; a 0.75-percent redemption fee; and unlimited exchanges with other Select Portfolios, with a $7.50 trading fee.

FIDELITY SELECT PRECIOUS METALS AND MINERALS

82 Devonshire Street
Boston, MA 02109
800-544-8888

Inception: 1981
Total Assets: $309 Million
Ticker Symbol: FDPMX
Home Page: http://www.fidelity.com

Objective and Strategy: This fund's geographic diversification makes it a much riskier investment than sibling Fidelity Select American Gold. Specifically, a 65-percent stake in South African and Australian gold mining stocks makes the fund vulnerable to the large price swings that accompany those positions. Its foreign mining investments also add an element of foreign currency exposure. In all parts of the world, the fund stresses top quality and major gold producers, and it avoids secondary gold stocks and exploration plays. Considering the fund's South African and Australian investments, its returns have been not only relatively steady, but also, on average, well above those of its competitors.

Annualized Returns

1-Year 5.1%
3-Year 11.3%
5-Year 12.6%

Portfolio Manager: Malcolm MacNaught has been managing the fund since 1981. He also has managed Fidelity Advisor Global Resources since 1988. He joined Fidelity in 1968.

Suitability: The fund does not represent a balanced investment program. It can be used as a speculative vehicle, but sales fees reduce trading returns. It is not recommended for conservative investors except as a volatility or inflation hedge.

Portfolio Implications: As with all gold funds, a small allocation to this fund can reduce the volatility of aggressive equity or bond fund portfolios. Because of the leverage in gold mining stocks, portfolio allocations above 10 percent of assets are not recommended.

Risk: Share price volatility is extremely high. The fund also possesses a modest amount of political and foreign exchange risk due to its exposure to South African stocks.

Costs: Once you get beyond the 3-percent front-end load, expenses are quite modest. The management fee is 0.61 percent; annual expense ratio, 1.43 percent; turnover ratio, 53 percent. You have unlimited exchanges to other Select funds with payment of a $7.50 fee.

Distributions: Capital gains and income distributions are paid in early April.

How to Buy and Sell: The minimum initial investment is $2,500; subsequent investments $250. It can be purchased without transaction fees from Fidelity Brokerage. There are plans to add Internet trading capability in early 1996.

INVESCO STRATEGIC GOLD

INVESCO Funds Group
P.O. Box 173706
Denver, CO 80217-3706
800-525-8085

Inception: 1984
Total Assets: $244 Million
Ticker Symbol: FGLDX
Home Page: http://www.invesco.com

Objective and Strategy: This pure gold fund invests nearly all of its assets in North American gold mining stocks (mostly Canadian producers). It purchases no gold bullion and few diversified metals stocks. Like some other funds, it will not raise much cash when the prospects for gold are unfavorable. This, coupled with its willingness to invest up to 10 percent of its assets in leveraged, secondary gold mining stocks, makes the fund sensitive to gold price movements. It promises significant upside performance in the face of a rising gold price, but it may also underperform its tamer rivals during periods when the price of gold is declining. It is one of a handful of pure no-load funds in its category.

Portfolio Manager: Dan Leonard has been managing the fund since 1989. He also serves as co-portfolio manager of the Technology portfolio. He began his investment career in 1960, joined Invesco in 1975, and became a portfolio manager in 1977. He holds a B.A. degree from by Washington and Lee University.

Suitability: The fund does not represent a balanced investment program. Unless used as part of a diversified portfolio as an inflation hedge, this fund is not suitable for conservative investors. Speculators get the full

Annualized Returns

1-Year 44.9%
3-Year 16.4%
5-Year 15.6%

benefit of trading returns because of the no-load format.

Portfolio Implications: This fund works best when coupled with an aggressive equity or bond portfolio. Because the fund's shares are inflation sensitive, they can offset a considerable degree of interest rate risk present in bond fund portfolios.

Risk: This is a highly volatile fund, near the top of its category. It has limited foreign exchange and political risk because of its concentration in North American gold mining stocks.

Costs: It is sold in a 100-percent no-load format. Management fees are 0.75 percent; total expense ratio, a modest 1.42 percent; portfolio turnover, 53 percent. On balance, it is a low-cost vehicle.

Distributions: Capital gains are paid in October. Little or no income distributions are anticipated. Unrealized capital gains exposure is relatively low.

How to Buy and Sell: The initial investment requirement is a modest $1,000; subsequent investments $50. There is no minimum investment with EasiVest automatic investment plan. Shares can be purchased without transaction fees from Schwab, Fidelity, and Jack White.

LEXINGTON GOLD FUND

P.O. Box 1515
Park 80 West Plaza Two
Saddle Brook, NJ 07663
800-526-0056

Inception: 1975
Total Assets: $136 Million
Ticker Symbol: LEXMX
Home Page: None

Objective and Strategy: Among the more tame precious metals funds, this no-load fund attempts to temper the volatility associated with gold investing by adjusting its asset mix in response to market conditions. Besides raising the portfolio's level of cash and bullion when the prospects for gold seem unfavorable, it reduces risk by stressing top-quality gold stocks and avoiding smaller, leveraged mines. Modest stakes in platinum and diversified metals stocks also help keep risk moderate relative to other precious metals funds. While the majority of its holdings consist of North American gold equities, the fund also has considerable positions in South African and Australian mining stocks. Although it's unlikely that you'll find this fund at the top of the performance charts in its category, it will not reside near the bottom either.

Annualized Returns
1-Year 11.7%
3-year 10.7%
5-Year 9.4%

Portfolio Manager: Robert Radsch took over the helm in 1992. Prior to that, he was a gold fund manager with the Bull and Bear Group. He has thirteen years experience managing precious metals on an international basis. He has a B.A degree from Yale and an M.B.A (finance) from Columbia University.

Suitability: The fund is not meant to be a balanced investment plan. It is highly speculative when used alone and not recommended for conservative investors. It is rec-

ommended that allocations not exceed 10 percent of portfolio assets.

Portfolio Implications: Because the returns of this highly volatile fund possess a very low correlation with equity funds and a negative correlation with bond funds, it is best used to reduce portfolio volatility. A 10-percent allocation can offset significant interest rate risk in bond portfolios.

Risk: Although its share price volatility is high, this is one of the more tame funds in the gold fund category. Investments in South Africa introduce an element of foreign exchange and political risk.

Costs: The management fee is 0.83 percent; the annual expense ratio, 1.70 percent; turnover ratio, a modest 40 percent. The fund is sold without a front-end or back-end load but levies a 0.25 percent annual 12b-1 charge. On balance, it is one of the lower-cost gold funds around.

Distributions: Capital gains and income distributions are paid annually in October. There is minimal unrealized capital gains tax exposure.

How to Buy and Sell: The minimum initial investment requirement is $1,000; subsequent investments $50. Telephone transfers are permitted to other Lexington funds. Shares can be purchased with no transaction fee from Schwab and Jack White.

MIDAS FUND

11 Hanover Square
New York, NY 10005
800-400-6432

Inception: 1986
Total Assets: $176 Million
Ticker Symbol: EMGSX
Home Page: None

Objective and Strategy: This fund invests worldwide in the equity securities of established mining companies. It also invests a smaller proportion of its assets in developing companies that offer strong growth potential. When investing in gold mining shares, management painstakingly evaluates three factors: people, projects, and pricing. The goal is to have a mix of investments with two dimensions. The fund's core portfolio is invested in quality mining companies with established records of operational success. Stocks are accumulated when they are out of favor and undervalued and held for long-term appreciation. Under the guidance of portfolio manager Kjeld Thygesen, this fund truly has "the golden touch." Its returns have been nothing short of phenomenal, averaging more than 20 percent a year during the last one-, three-, and five-year periods.

Portfolio Manager: Kjeld Thygesen has been managing this fund since 1992. Born and educated in South Africa, he is a former geologist and mining analyst. His background partially explains his uncanny ability to spot winners in their early stages.

Suitability: This fund is not meant to be a balanced investment program. It provides an excellent inflation hedge for income-oriented investors. An allocation of more than 10 percent of portfolio assets is not recommended.

Portfolio Implications: Because of a negative correlation with the stock and bond markets, a small allocation in this fund can reduce overall portfolio volatility. It works best when coupled with income-type investments.

Risk: Share price volatility is extremely high. International investments introduce an element of foreign exchange and political risk. In addition, the fund may invest in illiquid private placements.

Costs: The fund recently dropped its sales charges and is now available in a no-load format. The annual expense ratio is a very low 1.36 percent; portfolio turnover, 47 percent. Dollar per pound, this is the cheapest gold fund around.

Distributions: Income and capital gains distributions are paid in late December. The fund currently possesses no unrealized capital gains tax liabilities.

How to Buy and Sell: The minimum initial investment is $500; subsequent investments $100; IRA $100. Shares can also be purchased through Schwab, Bull and Bear, Fidelity, Jack White (no transaction fees), and Waterhouse Securities.

Annualized Returns

1-Year 22.3%
3-Year 22.1%
5-Year 23.5%

SCUDDER GOLD

Scudder Investor Services
175 Federal Street
Boston, MA 02110
800-225-2470

Inception: 1988
Total Assets: $175 Million
Ticker Symbol: SCGDX
Home Page: http://
www.scudder.com

Objective and Strategy: By precious metals fund standards, Scudder Gold is quite tame. The fund's relative low volatility has been due to its constant 15 percent to 25 percent bullion stake. Cash reserves, which may make up as much as 15 percent of assets, also have helped minimize losses in recent years, as have the fund's neglect of South African gold stocks and its relatively low exposure to Australian shares. Although most of its stocks are large, liquid shares of quality gold producers with low to medium production costs, it has recently begun to build a hefty position in highly leveraged secondary gold stocks and exploration/development companies. With nearly one-third of its portfolio invested in these higher-risk, but higher-return-potential stocks, this fund has markedly changed its operating characteristics.

Portfolio Manager: The fund has been team managed under leader Douglas Donald since 1988. He joined Scudder in 1964, and has more than forty years experience with investments in precious metals and mining.

Suitability: Like gold funds in general, this is a highly speculative investment and is not meant to represent a complete investment program. It is not suitable for conservative investors unless part of a well-diversified portfolio. It is best suited as an inflation hedge.

Portfolio Implications: Because of the low correlation of returns with both equity and bond funds, a small allocation to this fund (10 percent of assets or less) can reduce overall portfolio volatility. The fund can produce huge gains for speculators, but at considerable risk.

Risk: Like all gold funds, this fund is subject to wide swings in share price. The fund's international investments also introduce an element of currency and political risk.

Costs: This is a pure no-load mutual fund. The annual expense ratio is 1.50 percent; the turnover ratio of 37 percent is very modest. This is one of the most efficient gold funds you will find anywhere.

Distributions: Income and capital gains distributions occur in September. Given its recent payment, the fund possesses little unrealized capital gains tax liability.

How to Buy and Sell: The minimum initial investment is $1,000; subsequent investments $100; IRA $500. You can exchange a minimum of $100 with other Scudder funds. Shares can also be purchased with a small transaction fee from Fidelity, Schwab, and Jack White.

Annualized Returns

1-Year 40.5%
3-Year 20.7%
5-Year 16.4%

USAA GOLD FUND

USAA Investment Management
USAA Building
San Antonio, TX 78288
800-382-8722

Inception: 1984
Total Assets: $140 Million
Ticker Symbol: USAGX
Home Page: None

Objective and Strategy: Holding neither gold bullion nor significant amounts of cash, the fund maintains a fairly pure gold equity portfolio. North American gold stocks predominate, but the fund also keeps some exposure to major South African and Australian gold producers. While the fund is far from the tamest entrant in the precious metals group, its strategy is to emphasize low-cost producers with good production or reserve growth potential that sell at reasonable valuations on a risk-adjusted basis. Management continually upgrades the fund's investments, eliminating those that don't meet its criteria and adding those that do. The fund now carries most of the prominent North American gold producers. On balance, the fund's return should parallel that of the average gold mining stock.

Annualized Returns

1-Year 1.2%
3-Year 5.0%
5-Year 7.9%

Portfolio Manager: Mark W. Johnson has managed the fund since January 1994. He has twenty-two years investment management experience and holds an M.B.A. and B.B.A. from the University of Michigan.

Suitability: Because of its concentration in one industry, this fund should not be considered a complete investment program. It is best used as part of a well-diversified investment portfolio or as an inflation hedge. It is not suitable for conservative investors unless used as a volatility or inflation hedge.

Allocation in excess of 10 percent of portfolio assets is not recommended.

Portfolio Implications: Because this fund's returns do not move in lockstep with stock or bond market returns, a small allocation can reduce overall portfolio volatility. A 5 to 10 percent allocation can significantly reduce interest rate risk for bond portfolios.

Risk: Share price volatility is extremely high. Foreign investments also introduce an element of currency and political risk. When the fund is held alone, portfolio risk can be excessive.

Costs: Management fees are 0.75 percent; annual expense ratio, 1.28 percent. It is sold as a 100-percent no-load fund. The turnover ratio is a very modest 35 percent. Overall, a highly efficient fund.

Distributions: Income and capital appreciation distributions occur in late December. There is minimal unrealized gain tax liability at the current time.

How to Buy and Sell: The initial minimum investment requirement was raised to $3,000 beginning January 31, 1993, with a $100 subsequent investment minimum; IRA minimum $1,000. Telephone switches with other USAA funds are permitted.

UNITED SERVICES WORLD GOLD

United Services Advisors
P.O. Box 29467
San Antonio, TX 78229
800-873-8637

Inception: 1985
Total Assets: $251 Million
Ticker Symbol: UNWPX
Home Page: None

Objective and Strategy: Previously known as New Prospector Fund, this fund is among the precious metals category's most volatile offerings. Its volatility stems from its pure gold equity focus, its practice of staying fully invested at all times, and its relatively large exposure to intermediate gold stocks. Although the fund does not invest in South Africa, its exposure to smaller mining companies gives it enormous leverage to a rising gold price. But the fund is equally vulnerable to sharp price corrections when the gold price declines. It is best suited to the most aggressive goldbugs who wish to sidestep South African gold mining stocks. Its bet on small Canadian exploration/development companies in recent years has paid off handsomely. Should the price of gold break $400 an ounce, look for the share price of this fund to soar.

Portfolio Manager: Victor Flores has managed the fund since December 1989. He is also manager of the Gold Shares fund, which specializes in South African gold stock investments. He served as investment analyst prior to becoming portfolio manager of both funds.

Suitability: This fund is not meant to be a complete investment program, and it is not suitable for conservative investors unless part of a well-diversified portfolio. It can be used as a speculative bet on the price of gold, but that is not recommended.

Portfolio Implications: As with all gold funds, this fund's returns have a low correlation with the returns of the stock and bond markets. Thus, it can be used to reduce portfolio volatility. It works best when used to reduce interest rate risk of bond portfolios.

Risk: Share price is highly volatile. Although the fund has minimal exposure to foreign currency or political risk, its large allocation to secondary gold mining companies adds to portfolio volatility.

Costs: The annual expense ratio 1.55 percent. The fund has always maintained a lower than average turnover ratio, thus transaction costs tend to be well below average.

Distributions: Capital gains and income distributions occur in late June.

How to Buy and Sell: The minimum initial investment is $1,000; subsequent investments $100. Telephone exchanges with other United Services funds are permitted with a $5 exchange fee. The automatic investment plan is as follows: $100 initial, $30 per month. Shares can be purchased with no transaction fees through Fidelity, Schwab, and Jack White.

Annualized Returns

1-Year	28.7%
3-Year	16.1%
5-Year	18.9%

VANGUARD SPECIALIZED GOLD

Vanguard Group
Vanguard Financial Center
P.O. Box 2600
Valley Forge, PA 19482
800-635-1511

Inception: 1984
Total Assets: $582 Million
Ticker Symbol: VGPMX
Home Page: http://
www.vanguard.com

Objective and Strategy: Typically, Vanguard's entrant in the precious metals arena is among the best of its kind, and the fund is among the category's most consistent performers. Its ability to outpace its average rival in most markets over the longer run is due in part to Vanguard's usual low expenses. Also responsible is the fund's quality focus and its neglect of highly volatile, secondary gold stocks. Some exposure to diversified metals and minerals producers and to gold bullion also helps mitigate risk. However, recently, its performance has suffered because of an underweighting in North American gold mining companies, which have been the best performers in the gold group during the last year. That shortcoming aside, this no-load fund is an excellent choice for investors seeking exposure to each of the free world's major gold mining regions.

Portfolio Manager: Like most Vanguard funds, this portfolio is managed by an outside adviser. For this fund it's M&G Investment Management Limited of London, England. David J. Hutchins, an investment manager of M&G, has served as portfolio manager since January 1987.

Suitability: The fund is not meant to be a complete investment program. It cannot be used as a trading portfolio because of Vanguard limitations. It is best used to reduce portfolio volatility as part of a well-diversi-

**Annualized
Returns**

1-Year 1.0%

3-Year 7.2

5-Year 8.2

fied portfolio. Investment of more than 10 percent of assets is not recommended.

Portfolio Implications: Because of the low correlation of return with the returns of diversified equity and bond fund portfolios, a small investment in this fund can reduce overall portfolio volatility. It can be used to offset a significant portion of interest rate risk contained in bond fund portfolios.

Risk: Share price volatility is high. The fund's international gold mining stock investments add an element of foreign exchange and political risk. Its emphasis on large producers mitigates volatility a bit.

Costs: Like most Vanguard funds, this fund is highly efficient. The annual expense ratio is 0.60 percent; portfolio turnover, an extremely low 5 percent.

Distributions: Capital gains and income distributions occur in late December. Vanguard usually estimates the amount of intended distribution in late October. Call for details.

How to Buy and Sell: The minimum initial investment in this fund is $3,000; subsequent investments $100. There is a redemption fee of 1 percent if shares are redeemed within one year. Free telephone exchanges with other Vanguard funds are permitted. Shares can also be purchased through Schwab and Jack White with a small transaction charge.

FORTY-TWO

Sector Funds

Sector funds invest in very concentrated portfolios of common stocks, usually drawing their selections from a single industry. Although most sector funds got their start during the past decade, this investment strategy is not new to the mutual fund industry. For example, Century Shares Trust, which invests the vast majority of its assets in insurance stocks, began operations in 1931. In 1981, Fidelity Management and Research opened the floodgates to sector investing with the initiation of the Fidelity Select Portfolios Fund, which gave investors the opportunity to concentrate in, and switch between, one or more of the following industries: technology, utilities, health care, energy, precious metals, and financial services. INVESCO Funds and the Vanguard Group shortly followed suit, establishing funds with similar group portfolios. Except with popular industries such as technology, health care, utilities, and energy, fund distributors have had a difficult time attracting large numbers of investors to industry-concentrated funds in recent years. Thus, growth in the number of sector funds has been virtually nonexistent during the past three years; and, in fact, a few sector funds have merged with other funds in this period.

One of the benefits of investing in mutual funds is the risk reduction that investors receive by holding a highly diversified portfolio of common stocks. On average, the typical diversified common stock fund contains one-third the risk of a portfolio consisting of a single stock. Industry-concentrated portfolios, on the other hand, contain significantly more risk than the typical equity fund. That's because the factors that affect one stock in an industry-concentrated portfolio tend to affect all stocks in the industry. Thus, sector fund share prices can be highly volatile.

Sector funds appeal to three types of investors. First, investors who seek above-average current yields from their equity portfolios might seek investment in funds that concentrate their investments in utility, bank, or insurance stocks. Second, aggressive-growth investors may wish to include investments in rapid-growth industries such as biotechnology, health care, or technology in their portfolios. Finally, investors who attempt to time the economic cycle by practicing "sector rotation" will find these funds of interest. Sector rotation is an attempt to continually allocate assets among industries that are affected differently by changes in the business cycle; for example, investing in interest-rate-sensitive industries during an economic downturn, cyclical stocks during the early stages of an economic turnaround, and consumer stocks during a period of robust economic growth.

Because of the high degree of concentration of assets and the extreme volatility contained in their shares, sector funds are not for the faint of heart. Although some of the best-performing funds in recent years concentrate their investments in a single industry, a much larger number of sector funds tend to reside at the bottom of the performance charts. So, approach this category of mutual funds with a high degree of caution.

ALLIANCE TECHNOLOGY A

Alliance Fund Distributor
500 Plaza Drive, 3rd Floor
P.O. Box 1520
Secaucus, NJ 07096–1520
800-221-5672

Inception: 1980
Total Assets: $424 Million
Ticker Symbol: ALTFX
Home Page: http://
www.alliancecapital.com

Objective and Strategy: This fund seeks capital growth by investing primarily in companies that are expected to benefit from technological advances and improvements (that is, companies that use technology extensively in the development of new or improved products or processes). When selecting individual securities, the adviser considers such factors as the economic and political outlooks, the value of individual securities relative to other investment alternatives, trends in the determinants of corporate profits, and management capability and practices. In general, the philosophy of management is to identify innovators, anticipate trends, and invest very aggressively.

Portfolio Manager: Peter Anastos and Gerald Malone have been managing this fund since 1992.

Suitability: This fund is suitable for aggressive investors with a long-term investment horizon (five years or more). It is not suitable for conservative investors or those with short-term investment horizons.

Annualized Returns

1-Year	7.5%
3-Year	30.3%
5-Year	29.9%

Portfolio Implications: As an industry-sector fund, this fund should be used as a small component of a diversified equity portfolio. Limit allocations to no more than 10 percent of portfolio assets.

Risk: With a beta of 1.13, this fund looks more tame than it is. During the 1990 bear market, this fund's share price declined by slightly more than 33 percent.

Costs: This is one of the higher-cost technology-sector funds. It is sold with a 4.25 percent front-end load and a 0.30-percent 12b-1 annual marketing fee. It has an expense ratio of 1.75 percent, a modest (55 percent) portfolio turnover ratio, and a management fee of 1 percent.

Distributions: Both income and capital gains distributions are paid in late December.

How to Buy and Sell: Fund shares are sold by financial planners and broker/dealers with a front-end sales charge. Minimum initial investment $250; subsequent investments $50; IRA $100. Shares are also available through Fidelity Brokerage.

AMERICAN CENTURY UTILITIES

Twentieth Century Mutual Funds
4500 Main Street
P.O. Box 419200
Kansas City, MO 64141-6200
800-345-2021

Inception: 1993
Total Assets: $163 Million
Ticker Symbol: BULIX
Home Page: http://
www.americancentury.com

Objective and Strategy: This fund invests in companies that derive at least 50 percent of their revenues from the ownership or operation of facilities used to provide electricity, natural gas, telecommunications services, cable television, water, or sanitary services to the public. The unique feature of this utilities fund is that it attempts to provide investors with a consistent level of monthly dividend income. At times, the fund will invest up to 25 percent of its assets in bonds to enhance dividend income or support share price stability. Management seeks to maximize the benefits from increased competition and expanded growth prospects that have resulted from deregulation in the utilities industry. This well-managed fund possesses a low expense ratio and low portfolio turnover, thus minimizing costs. However, as with its peers, the fund's share price is sensitive to interest rate changes, and its returns have suffered in recent years due to increasing interest rates. However, the fund is positioned to deliver solid returns in a stable or declining interest rate environment.

Portfolio Manager: Steven Colton has been manager since inception. He has been with Benham since 1987, and he also manages the Benham Income and Growth Fund.

Suitability: The fund is suitable for conservative growth investors. It is also suitable for investors who prefer regular monthly income.

Annualized Returns

1-Year	5.1%
3-Year	3.4%
5-Year	NA%

Portfolio Implications: Like bond funds, this fund is highly interest rate sensitive and provides little diversification benefits for bond fund investors. A small gold fund investment can be used to reduce interest rate sensitivity. It should be used with other growth and growth and income funds.

Risk: This fund has a higher-than-average beta (0.91) compared to its peers because of telecommunications investments. The share price is subject to erosion during a rising interest rate environment.

Costs: The fund has no sales fees, and a low management fee (0.30 percent) and expense ratio (0.74 percent). These rates coupled with a low portfolio turnover make this a very cost-efficient fund.

Distributions: Dividend income is distributed monthly; capital gains are distributed in late December.

How to Buy and Sell: Fund shares are sold without sales charges of any kind. The minimum initial investment is $2,500; subsequent investments $100; IRA $1,000. Shares may also be purchased through Fidelity, Schwab, and Jack White, the latter two without transaction charges. Telephone switches are permitted with other Benham and Twentieth Century funds.

CENTURY SHARES TRUST

2 Heritage Drive
North Quincy, MA 02171
800-321-1928

Inception: 1928
Total Assets: $244 Million
Ticker Symbol: CENSX
Home Page: None

Objective and Strategy: This fund, which began selling its shares in 1928, is the tenth oldest mutual fund in the country and the earliest sector fund offering. It seeks capital appreciation by investing primarily in insurance and bank stocks. Although sector funds are more risky than diversified funds, insurance stocks tend to have below-average volatility. Rising interest rates, however, tend to affect insurance stocks more than the typical industrial stock. Because insurance companies hold large portfolios of bonds, rising interest rates cause insurance company assets (and book values) to decline. Providing a better-than-average current yield for a fund that seeks capital appreciation, this no-load fund is ideal for investors seeking a position in the insurance industry.

Portfolio Manager: Allan Fulkerson has been guiding this fund since 1976. He is one of only a handful of fund managers who have been guiding the same fund for more than twenty years.

Suitability: Because insurance and bank stocks tend to pay hefty cash dividends, this fund is suitable for investors seeking a combination of growth and income. However, remember it is an industry-sector fund and therefore does not represent a balanced portfolio.

Annualized Returns

1-Year	11.1%
3-Year	7.4%
5-Year	14.2%

Portfolio Implications: It makes an excellent addition to a growth and income portfolio containing utility funds and equity-income funds. Interest rate risk can be moderated when the fund is combined with a small investment in a gold fund.

Risk: The fund possesses a modest beta (0.89) but can suffer during a sharp market sell-off accompanied by rising interest rates, as was the case during the 1990 bear market when the fund's share price declined by about 24 percent.

Costs: This is a very cost-efficient fund. It is sold with a no-load format and does not have a 12b-1 fee. The annual expense ratio is a modest 0.94 percent, and it has an extremely low (5 percent) portfolio turnover ratio.

Distributions: Income distributions are paid twice a year, and capital distributions are paid once a year, usually in December.

How to Buy and Sell: The minimum initial investment is $500; subsequent investments $50; IRA $500. Shares may be purchased without transaction fees from Schwab, Jack White, Fidelity Brokerage, and Waterhouse.

FIDELITY SELECT BIOTECHNOLOGY

Fidelity Distributors
82 Devonshire Street
Boston, MA 02109
800–752–2347

Inception: 1985
Total Assets: $664 Million
Ticker Symbol: FBIOX
Home Page: http://www.fidelity.com

Objective and Strategy: This fund seeks capital appreciation by investing in a relatively diversified portfolio of biotechnology stocks. In addition, the fund's holdings include a smattering from such industries as drugs and pharmaceuticals, medical equipment and supplies, and medical facilities management. The fund offers indexlike exposure to both small and large firms and the relative stability that comes with diversification. In recent years, biotechnology stocks have gone through periods of boom and bust. However, this industry is capable of growing at double-digit annual rates for decades.

Portfolio Manager: Karen Firestone has managed this fund since July 1992. She also manages Select Health Care. Previously, she managed Select Air Transport. She joined Fidelity in 1983.

Suitability: The fund's shares are suitable for highly aggressive investors only. This fund is recommended for long-term-oriented investors who plan to hold for five or more years. Avoid the urge to trade this fund.

Annualized Returns
1-Year 10.9%
3-year 9.8%
5-Year 5.7%

Portfolio Implications: Because the portfolio is industry-concentrated, the fund should be combined with other growth and aggressive growth funds.

Risk: This portfolio has a very high beta (1.29). In addition, it contains significant non-market-related volatility. However, the fund managed to dodge the 1990 bear market.

Costs: There is an initial 3-percent front-end load; no sales charges (except a $7.50 exchange fee) when exchanging with other Select portfolios; modest expense ratio (1.44 percent) and modest portfolio turnover ratio (67 percent).

Distributions: Income and capital gains distributions are paid in December.

How to Buy and Sell: The minimum initial investment is $2,500; subsequent investments $250; IRA $500. Unlimited telephone exchanges are allowed with other Select portfolios with a $7.50 exchange fee and 0.75 percent for shares held less than thirty days. Shares are also available through Schwab and Fidelity Brokerage (no transaction fees).

FIDELITY SELECT COMPUTERS

Fidelity Distributors
82 Devonshire Street
Mail Zone L7B
Boston, MA 02109
800-752-2347

Inception: 1985
Total Assets: $52 Million
Ticker Symbol: FDCPX
Home Page: http://www.fidelity.com

Objective and Strategy: This fund invests in common stocks of companies engaged in the research, design, development, manufacture, or distribution of products, processes, and services used in the computer industry. Management invests in a variety of high-technology companies, including major personal computer producers, semiconductor manufacturers, networking systems, and software with relatively strong earnings momentum. A lack of industry diversification implied by this fund's sector mandate and the volatile nature of technology stocks suggest significant share price fluctuations. The fund has, however, provided investors with strong long-term returns, and the odds are high that rapid industry growth will continue into the twenty-first century.

Portfolio Manager: Jason Weiner has managed the fund since March 1996. He is also portfolio manager of Select Air Transportation. He joined Fidelity as a research associate in 1991, after receiving a B.A. from Swarthmore College.

Suitability: The fund's shares are suitable for highly aggressive investors only. Recommended for long-term-oriented investors. Avoid the urge to trade this fund.

Annualized Returns

1-Year	4.1%
3-Year	29.2%
5-Year	26.5%

Portfolio Implications: Because its portfolio is industry concentrated, the fund should be combined with other growth and aggressive growth funds. Limit allocations to 20 percent of portfolio assets.

Risk: The portfolio has a modest beta (0.94); however, it also contains significant non-market-related volatility. The fund's share price plunged 23 percent during the 1990 bear market.

Costs: There is an initial 3-percent front-end load; no sales charge (except a $7.50 exchange fee) to exchange with other Select portfolios. It has a modest expense ratio (1.40 percent) but a relatively high portfolio turnover ratio (129 percent).

Distributions: Income and capital gains distributions are paid in December.

How to Buy and Sell: The minimum initial investment is $2,500; subsequent investments $250; IRA $500. Unlimited telephone exchanges with other Select portfolios are permitted with a $7.50 exchange fee and 0.75-percent fee for shares held less than thirty days. Shares are also available through Schwab and Fidelity Brokerage (no transaction fees).

FIDELITY SELECT CONSUMER PRODUCTS

Fidelity Distributors
82 Devonshire Street
Mail Zone L7B
Boston, MA 02109
800-752-2347

Inception: 1990
Total Assets: $23 Million
Ticker Symbol: FSCPX
Home Page: http://www.fidelity.com

Objective and Strategy: Among the newer additions to the Fidelity Select portfolios, the Select Consumer Products portfolio seeks capital appreciation through investments in equity securities of companies engaged in the manufacture and distribution of consumer products. Major industries include food, beverages, pharmaceuticals, soaps and detergents, and tobacco. Although the fund owns a few young companies, most of the companies are mature and well known. While the fund's nondiversified character suggests additional risk, the stable growth characteristics of most consumer products companies tend to temper some of this added volatility. Because of their relatively stable earnings and revenue growth, consumer stocks provide a heaven for equity investors during prolonged bear markets.

Portfolio Manager: Mary English has managed the fund since February 1994. She joined Fidelity in 1991 and previously managed Select Retailing. She received an M.B.A. from the University of Virginia.

Suitability: This fund is an ideal investment for all growth-oriented investors who possess a long-term view (five years or more).

Annualized Returns	
1-Year	16.3%
3-Year	10.1%
5-Year	14.0%

Portfolio Implications: Because of its industry concentration, this fund should be combined with other growth and aggressive growth funds. Limit portfolio allocations to 25 percent of assets.

Risk: The fund's portfolio has an above-average beta (1.14). In addition, it contains significant non market-related volatility. This relatively new fund has yet to experience a bear stock market.

Costs: There is an initial 3-percent front-end load; no sales charges (except a $7.50 exchange fee) to exchange with other Select portfolios. The fund has a higher-than-average expense ratio (1.53 percent) and an astronomical portfolio turnover ratio (601 percent).

Distributions: Income and capital gains distributions are paid in December.

How to Buy and Sell: The minimum initial investment is $2,500; subsequent investments $250; IRA $500. Unlimited telephone exchanges with other Select portfolios are permitted with a $7.50 exchange fee and 0.75-percent fee for shares held less than thirty days. Shares are also available through Schwab and Fidelity Brokerage (no transaction fees).

FIDELITY SELECT DEVELOPING COMMUNICATIONS

Fidelity Distributors
82 Devonshire Street
Mail Zone L7B
Boston, MA 02109
800-752-2347

Inception: 1990
Total Assets: $324 Million
Ticker Symbol: FSDCX
Home Page: http://www.fidelity.com

Objective and Strategy: Focusing on one of the most promising growth industries of the 1990s, this fund seeks to capitalize on emerging technologies in the communications industry and the expansion of global telecommunications networks. Since its inception, the fund's investments have been concentrated in four industry sectors: cellular communications, cable systems, telephone equipment, and international telephone systems. Its 23.4-percent average annual return during the last five years is a feat that may prove difficult to duplicate. However, this fund's long-term potential continues to appear bright.

Portfolio Manager: Paul Antico has managed the fund since March 1996. He joined Fidelity in 1991, after receiving a B.S. from the Massachusetts Institute of Technology. He also has managed Fidelity Select Developing Communications since 1993.

Suitability: The fund's shares are suitable for highly aggressive, growth-seeking investors only. This fund is recommended for investors with a long-term orientation (five years or more).

Portfolio Implications: Because of its industry concentration, this fund should be combined with other growth and aggressive growth funds. Limit allocations to 20 percent of portfolio assets.

Risk: The fund's portfolio has an extremely high beta (1.42). In addition, it contains significant non-market-related volatility. This relatively new fund has yet to experience a bear market.

Costs: There is an initial 3-percent front-end load; no sales charge (except a $7.50 exchange fee) to exchange with other Select portfolios. The fund has a higher-than-average expense ratio (1.53 percent) and a very high portfolio turnover ratio (249 percent).

Distributions: Income and capital gains distributions are paid in December.

How to Buy and Sell: The minimum initial investment is $2,500; subsequent investments $250; IRA $500. Unlimited telephone exchanges with other Select portfolios are permitted with a $7.50 exchange fee and 0.75-percent fee for shares held less than thirty days. Shares are also available through Schwab and Fidelity Brokerage (no transaction fees).

Annualized Returns

1-Year	-2.6%
3-Year	15.6%
5-Year	21.1%

FIDELITY SELECT ELECTRONICS

Fidelity Distributors
82 Devonshire Street
Mail Zone L7B
Boston, MA 02109
800-752-2347

Inception: 1985
Total Assets: $1.26 Billion
Ticker Symbol: FSELX
Home Page: http://www.fidelity.com

Objective and Strategy: This fund seeks capital appreciation primarily through investments in companies engaged in the design, manufacture, or sale of electronic components, including electronic component manufacturers, equipment vendors, and electronic component distributors. Its largest industry bets include semiconductors, computers, and data communications equipment. Started in 1986, the fund was launched at a difficult time. A fiercely competitive pricing environment followed by a weak economy led to severe earnings disappointment in the electronics industry, causing the fund to lose money in four out of its first five years in operation. However, a rebound in the technology sector of the market has helped the fund to produce strong returns during the last five years.

Annualized Returns

1-Year	5.0%
3-Year	33.4%
5-Year	34.3%

Portfolio Manager: Andrew Kaplan has led the fund since August 1996. The portfolio was managed by Marc Kaufman from March 1995 to August 1996.

Suitability: The fund's shares are suitable for highly aggressive, growth-oriented investors only. The fund is recommended for investors with a five-year or greater investment horizon. Limit allocations to 20 percent of portfolio assets.

Portfolio Implications: Because of industry concentration, the fund should be combined with other growth and aggressive growth funds. The fund's portfolio may duplicate that of other technology-oriented funds.

Risk: The fund's portfolio has a high beta (1.28), and it contains significant non-market-related volatility. The fund's share price plunged slightly more than 33 percent during the 1990 bear market.

Costs: There is an initial 3-percent front-end load; no sales charge (except a $7.50 exchange fee) when exchanging with other Select portfolios. The fund has a low expense ratio (1.25 percent) but a very high portfolio turnover ratio (366 percent).

Distributions: Income and capital gains distributions are paid in December.

How to Buy and Sell: The minimum initial investment is $2,500; subsequent investment $250; IRA $500. Unlimited telephone exchanges with other Select portfolios are permitted with a $7.50 exchange fee and 0.75-percent fee for shares held less than thirty days. Shares are also available through Schwab and Fidelity Brokerage (no transaction fees).

FIDELITY SELECT FINANCIAL SERVICES

Fidelity Distributors
82 Devonshire Street
Mail Zone L7B
Boston, MA 02109
800-752-2347

Inception: 1981
Total Assets: $252 Million
Ticker Symbol: FIDSX
Home Page: http://www.fidelity.com

Objective and Strategy: This fund invests in the 1990s version of a growth industry: financial services. Banks, savings and loans, finance companies, brokerage firms, and money management companies are included in its holdings. This makes the fund a bit less sensitive to the gyrations of the market. The fund offers some diversification (relative to other Select portfolios). Its dismal performance during the late 1980s is directly related to a beleaguered banking industry. However, falling interest rates during the early 1990s has produced stellar recent returns. Normally this fund should rally in an environment of falling interest rates and sustain losses in the opposite environment. Unlike a number of the Select portfolios, this fund provides a combination of current income and capital growth.

Portfolio Manager: Louis Salemy has managed this fund since December 1994. He also manages the Select Brokerage and Investment portfolio. He joined Fidelity in 1992 and has previously managed Select Industrial Materials, Medical Delivery, and Regional Bank portfolios.

Suitability: The fund is suitable for both growth and growth and income seeking investors who possess a long-term view. Conservative investors should limit portfolio allocations to no more than 15 percent of portfolio assets.

Annualized Returns

1-Year	19.2%
3-Year	15.8%
5-Year	24.2%

Portfolio Implications: Because of its industry concentration, this fund should be combined with other growth and growth and income funds. A small gold fund allocation can be used to offset some interest rate risk.

Risk: The fund's portfolio has a high beta (1.25). In addition, it contains significant non-market-related volatility, including a high degree of sensitivity to interest rate changes. The fund's share price plummeted nearly 38 percent during the 1990 bear market.

Costs: There is an initial 3-percent front-end load; no sales charge (except a $7.50 exchange fee) when exchanging with other Select portfolios. The fund has a modest expense ratio (1.42 percent) but a high portfolio turnover ratio (125 percent).

Distributions: Income and capital gains distributions are paid in December.

How to Buy and Sell: The minimum initial investment is $2,500; subsequent investments $250; IRA $500. Unlimited telephone exchanges with other Select portfolios are permitted with a $7.50 exchange fee and 0.75-percent fee for shares held less than thirty days. Shares are also available through Schwab and Fidelity Brokerage (no transaction fees).

FIDELITY SELECT FOOD AND AGRICULTURE

Fidelity Distributors
82 Devonshire Street
Mail Zone L7B
Boston, MA 02109
800-752-2347

Inception: 1985
Total Assets: $298 Million
Ticker Symbol: FDEAX
Home Page: http://www.fidelity.com

Objective and Strategy: Capital appreciation is this fund's investment objective. As the name implies, the fund invests in food- and agriculture-related products. Management may also look for opportunities anywhere from food processing, farm equipment, and forest product companies, to restaurants, vitamin manufacturers, and beverage companies. The fund's portfolio is usually packed with household names such as Philip Morris, PepsiCo, Kellogg, and Chiquita Brands. Management uses a value-based approach to investing and emphasizes companies whose price-earnings multiples lag the market. The fund's returns have lagged behind the overall market until recently. Long-term investors should be well rewarded with this fund.

**Annualized
Returns**
1-Year 9.7%
3-Year 16.1%
5-Year 13.8%

Portfolio Manager: William Mankivsky has managed the fund since April 1993. Previously, he managed Select Energy Service. He joined Fidelity in 1991, after receiving an M.B.A. from the University of Chicago.

Suitability: This fund is an ideal investment for all growth-oriented investors who possess a long-term view. Avoid the urge to trade this fund.

Portfolio Implications: The fund should be combined with other growth and aggressive growth funds. Because of the fund's industry concentration, allocations should be limited to no more than 20 percent of portfolio assets.

Risk: This fund has a low beta for a growth portfolio (0.75). However, it contains a modest degree of non-market-related volatility. The fund's portfolio declined a very modest 5 percent during the 1990 bear market. On balance, it is a low- to modest-risk portfolio.

Costs: There is an initial 3-percent front-end load; no sales charge (except a $7.50 exchange fee) when exchanging with other Select portfolios. The fund has a modest expense ratio (1.43 percent) but a high portfolio turnover ratio (124 percent).

Distributions: Income and capital gains distributions are paid in December.

How to Buy and Sell: The minimum initial investment is $2,500; subsequent investments $250; IRA $500. Unlimited telephone exchanges with other Select portfolios are permitted with a $7.50 exchange fee and 0.75-percent fee for shares held less than thirty days. Shares are also available through Schwab and Fidelity Brokerage (no transaction fees).

FIDELITY SELECT HEALTH CARE

Fidelity Distributors
82 Devonshire Street
Mail Zone L7B
Boston, MA 02109
800-752-2347

Inception: 1981
Total Assets: $1.27 Billion
Ticker Symbol: FSPHX
Home Page: http://www.fidelity.com

Objective and Strategy: This fund seeks capital appreciation by investing in a relatively concentrated portfolio of common stocks of companies in the health care industry, including those that provide products or services such as drugs and pharmaceuticals, medical equipment, and supplies and medical facilities management. With the majority of its holdings in pharmaceutical stocks, this fund has experienced a notable rebound during the last couple of years due to the lessening threat of a federal government-controlled health care program. Although emphasis on health care cost containment has diminished industry profit margins, health care continues to be one of the world's great growth industries. Long-term investors in this fund should continue to be well rewarded.

Annualized Returns

1-Year 17.8%
3-Year 28.2%
5-Year 13.9%

Portfolio Manager: Karen Firestone has managed the fund since July 1992. She also manages Select Biotechnology. She joined Fidelity in 1983 and has previously managed Select Air Transportation and Leisure.

Suitability: The fund's shares are suitable for highly aggressive, growth-oriented investors only and are recommended for investors with a long-term view (five years or more). Avoid the urge to trade this fund.

Portfolio Implications: Because of its industry concentration, the fund should be combined with diversified growth and aggressive growth funds.

Risk: The fund has a modest beta (0.96). However, its portfolio contains significant non-market-related volatility. The fund managed to dodge the 1990 bear market, with share price declining by less than 1 percent.

Costs: There is an initial 3-percent front-end load; no sales charge (except a $7.50 exchange fee) when exchanging with other Select portfolios. The fund has a modest expense ratio (1.31 percent) and a low portfolio turnover ratio (54 percent).

Distributions: Income and capital gains distributions are paid in December.

How to Buy and Sell: The minimum initial investment is $2,500; subsequent investments $250; IRA $500. Unlimited telephone exchanges with other Select portfolios with a $7.50 exchange fee and 0.75-percent fee for shares held less than thirty days. Shares are also available through Schwab and Fidelity Brokerage (no transaction fees).

FIDELITY SELECT LEISURE

Fidelity Distributors
82 Devonshire Street
Mail Zone L7B
Boston, MA 02109
800-752-2347

Inception: 1984
Total Assets: $119 Million
Ticker Symbol: FDLSX
Home Page: http://www.fidelity.com

Objective and Strategy: This fund seeks capital appreciation by investing in a relatively diversified portfolio of common stocks of companies that engage in all aspects of the leisure and entertainment industry. Currently, the fund's largest holdings are in the areas of broadcasting, entertainment, lodging, and gaming. Although the exposure to the booming cable and communications industry may provide for handsome returns and at the same time prevent the fund from experiencing an extreme decline, the leisure industry is always vulnerable to an environment of low consumer confidence. Although its communications stocks are long-term growth vehicles, many of its other holdings are highly cyclical and are quite vulnerable to the business cycle.

Portfolio Manager: Katherine Collins has been managing the fund since February 1996. Previously, she managed Select Construction and Housing. She joined Fidelity as an equity analyst in 1990.

Suitability: This fund is an ideal investment for all growth and aggressive growth investors who possess a long-term view (five years or more).

Annualized Returns

1-Year 10.5%
3-Year 11.7%
5-Year 18.4%

Portfolio Implications: Because of the fund's modest industry concentration, its shares should be combined with those of other growth and aggressive growth funds. The portfolio is dominated by large-cap companies. Consider combining this fund with a small-cap or value-seeking fund.

Risk: The fund has an average beta (1.01); however, its portfolio contains significant non-market-related volatility. The fund's share price plunged more than 24 percent during the 1990 bear market.

Costs: There is an initial 3-percent front-end load; no sales charge (except a $7.50 exchange fee) when exchanging with other Select portfolios. The fund has a modest expense ratio (1.64 percent) and a high portfolio turnover ratio (141 percent).

Distributions: Income and capital gains distributions are paid in December.

How to Buy and Sell: The minimum initial investment is $2,500; subsequent investments $250; IRA $500. Unlimited telephone exchanges with other Select portfolios are permitted with a $7.50 exchange fee and 0.75-percent fee for shares held less than thirty days. Shares are also available through Schwab and Fidelity Brokerage (no transaction fees).

FIDELITY SELECT MEDICAL DELIVERY

Fidelity Distributors
82 Devonshire Street
Mail Zone L7B
Boston, MA 02109
800-752-2347

Inception: 1986
Total Assets: $246 Million
Ticker Symbol: FSHCX
Home Page: http://www.fidelity.com

Objective and Strategy: As one would expect, this sector fund primarily invests in stocks of firms in the medical delivery field. The explosion in new forms of health care delivery creates many new business and investment alternatives. This specialized fund can target not only for-profit hospitals, nursing homes, and HMOs, but also acute-care psychiatric and specialized hospitals. Although this fund experienced weakness with the rest of the health care industry during the early 1990s, it has since rebounded significantly as health care providers have made great efforts to cut and control costs. Shareholders should continue to benefit from rapid growth in the demand for medical services.

Portfolio Manager: Steve Binder has managed the fund since December 1994. He joined Fidelity in 1989 and previously managed Select Regional Banks, Defense and Aerospace, and Financial Services.

Suitability: This fund's shares are suitable for highly aggressive, growth-seeking investors only and are recommended for investors with a long-term view (five years or more). Avoid the urge to trade this fund.

**Annualized
Returns**
1-Year 18.3%
3-Year 24.9%
5-Year 12.8%

Portfolio Implications: Because of its industry concentration, this fund should be combined with other diversified growth and aggressive growth funds.

Risk: The fund has a very high beta (1.21). In addition, its portfolio contains significant non-market-related volatility. The fund's portfolio declined by a modest 10 percent during the 1990 bear market.

Costs: There is an initial 3-percent front-end load; no sales charge (except a $7.50 exchange fee) when exchanging with other Select portfolios. The fund has a higher-than-average expense ratio (1.65 percent) and a high portfolio turnover ratio (132 percent).

Distributions: Income and capital gains distributions are paid in December.

How to Buy and Sell: The minimum initial investment is $2,500; subsequent investments $250; IRA $500. Unlimited telephone exchanges with other Select portfolios are permitted with a $7.50 exchange fee and 0.75-percent fee for shares held less than thirty days. Shares are also available through Schwab and Fidelity Brokerage (no transaction fees).

FIDELITY SELECT SOFTWARE AND COMPUTERS

Fidelity Distributors
82 Devonshire Street
Mail Zone L7B
Boston, MA 02109
800–752–2347

Inception: 1985
Total Assets: $437 Million
Ticker Symbol: FSCSX
Home Page: http://www.fidelity.com

Objective and Strategy: Investing in both large and small computer-application companies, this fund has been able to keep results positive for every one of its ten years in existence. This is no small feat, considering how weakly the computer industry performed in 1989 and 1990. With an above-average beta, this fund, not surprisingly, performs exceptionally well in a rising stock market environment. For long-term-oriented investors willing to bet on continued expansion in the computer software industry and on the future of the technology industry in general, this is a suitable fund.

Portfolio Manager: John Hurley has led this fund since August 1994. He joined Fidelity as an analyst covering software companies in 1993, after receiving an M.B.A. from Stanford University.

Suitability: The fund's shares are suitable for highly aggressive, growth-oriented investors only. This fund is recommended for investors with a long-term investment horizon (five years or more).

Portfolio Implications: Because of the fund's industry concentration, its shares

should be combined with diversified growth and aggressive growth funds. The portfolio will duplicate those of funds with a technology bent.

Risk: The fund's portfolio has an extremely high beta (1.37). In addition, it contains significant non-market-related volatility. The fund's share price plunged nearly 28 percent during the 1990 bear market.

Costs: There is an initial 3-percent front-end load; no sales charge (except a $7.50 exchange fee) when exchanging with other Select portfolios. The fund has a modest expense ratio (1.48 percent) but a very high portfolio turnover ratio (183 percent).

Distributions: Income and capital gains distributions are paid in December.

How to Buy and Sell: The minimum initial investment is $2,500; subsequent investments $250; IRA $500. Unlimited telephone exchanges with other Select portfolios are permitted with a $7.50 exchange fee and 0.75-percent fee for shares held less than thirty days. Shares are also available through Schwab and Fidelity Brokerage (no transaction fees).

Annualized Returns
1-Year 12.8%
3-Year 18.7%
5-Year 26.0%

FIDELITY SELECT TECHNOLOGY

Fidelity Distributors
82 Devonshire Street
Mail Zone L7B
Boston, MA 02109
800-752-2347

Inception: 1981
Total Assets: $479 Million
Ticker Symbol: FSPTX
Home Page: http://www.fidelity.com

Objective and Strategy: This fund, one of the original Select portfolios, began operations in 1981. It seeks capital appreciation by investing in a relatively concentrated portfolio of common stocks of companies operating in the technology sector, including cellular communications equipment, computer services and software, electronics, electronic instruments, and medical equipment and supplies. Depressed conditions in the technology sector greatly impaired returns during the late 1980s. However, if one can stomach the volatility, this industry is capable of generating explosive returns. Investors have received an annualized compound return in excess of 25 percent during the last five years. While these returns will be hard to duplicate, the fund should continue to provide market-topping numbers over the long run.

Portfolio Manager: Adam Hetnarski has been managing the fund since March 1996. He joined Fidelity in 1991 and previously served as an equity analyst.

Suitability: The fund's shares are suitable for highly aggressive, growth-seeking investors only. The fund is recommended for investors with a longer-term view (five years or more).

Annualized Returns

1-Year -4.9%
3-Year 19.6%
5-Year 21.2%

Portfolio Implications: Because of the fund's industry concentration, its shares should be combined with those of diversified growth and aggressive growth funds. This fund's portfolio will duplicate others with a technology bent.

Risk: The fund has an extremely high beta (1.34). In addition, its portfolio contains significant non-market-related volatility. The fund's share price sunk more than 22 percent during the 1990 bear market.

Costs: There is an initial 3-percent front-end load; no sales charge (except a $7.50 exchange fee) when exchanging with other Select portfolios. The fund has a modest expense ratio (1.40 percent) but a higher-than-average portfolio turnover ratio (112 percent).

Distributions: Income and capital gains distributions are paid in December.

How to Buy and Sell: The minimum initial investment is $2,500; subsequent investments $250; IRA $500. Unlimited telephone exchanges with other Select portfolios are permitted with a $7.50 exchange fee and 0.75-percent fee for shares held less than thirty days. Shares are also available through Schwab and Fidelity Brokerage (no transaction fees).

FIDELITY SELECT TELECOMMUNICATIONS

Fidelity Distributors
82 Devonshire Street
Mail Zone L7B
Boston, MA 02109
800-752-2347

Inception: 1985
Total Assets: $481 Million
Ticker Symbol: FSTCX
Home Page: http://www.fidelity.com

Objective and Strategy: This fund seeks capital appreciation by investing in a relatively concentrated portfolio of common stocks in the telecommunications sector, including broadcasting, cellular communications equipment, computers and office equipment, electrical equipment, and telephone services. Although funds with concentrated portfolios are capable of producing above-average returns during short-run periods, they tend to be more volatile than the typical diversified equity fund. Worldwide demand for telecommunications equipment and services is expected to grow at double-digit annual rates well into the twenty-first century. The fund should continue to perform well over the long run given its concentration of investments in this high-growth industry.

Annualized Returns

1-Year 0.3%
3-Year 9.7%
5-Year 17.3%

Portfolio Manager: Nick Thakore has been managing the fund since July 1996. He received a B.A. from the University of Michigan and an M.B.A. from the University of Pennsylvania in 1993.

Suitability: This fund's shares are suitable for highly aggressive, growth-oriented investors only. The fund is recommended for investors who can maintain a long-term view (five years or more).

Portfolio Implications: Because of its industry concentration, this fund should be combined with diversified growth and aggressive growth funds. Because of the fund's large-cap orientation, consider combining its shares with those of a small-cap or micro-cap fund.

Risk: The fund has a modest beta (0.98). However, its portfolio contains significant non-market-related volatility. The fund's share price plunged 20 percent during the 1990 bear market.

Costs: There is an initial 3-percent front-end load; no sales charge (except a $7.50 exchange fee) when exchanging with other Select portfolios. The fund has a modest expense ratio (1.52 percent) and an average portfolio turnover ratio (89 percent).

Distributions: Income and capital gains distributions are paid in December.

How to Buy and Sell: The minimum initial investment is $2,500; subsequent investments $250; IRA $500. Unlimited telephone exchanges with other Select portfolios are permitted with a $7.50 exchange fee and 0.75-percent fee for shares held less than thirty days. Shares are also available through Schwab and Fidelity Brokerage (no transaction fees).

FIDELITY SELECT UTILITIES

Fidelity Distributors
82 Devonshire Street
Mail Zone L7B
Boston, MA 02109
800-752-2347

Inception: 1981
Total Assets: $212 Million
Ticker Symbol: FSUTX
Home Page: http://www.fidelity.com

Objective and Strategy: Unlike most utility funds that stress a combination of current yield and growth, Select Utilities primarily seeks capital appreciation when making its utility stock selections. Thus, it should not be a surprise to find more than half of the fund's investments concentrated in the telephone services industry. As a result of the fund's affinity for growth, its current yield tends to be lower and its portfolio turnover ratio higher than those of the typical utilities fund. Although this strategy is capable of producing handsome returns, investors should be cautious of rising interest rates, as utility stocks tend to be underperformers in such an environment (as was evidenced in 1994).

Portfolio Manager: John Muresianu has managed this fund since December 1992. He also manages Fidelity Utilities, and previously has managed Select Natural Gas. He joined the company in 1986.

Suitability: This fund is suitable for both growth and growth and income seeking investors. Although the fund is growth-oriented, conservative growth investors should consider investing in it.

Annualized Returns

1-Year 6.0%

3-Year 4.5%

5-Year 10.2%

Portfolio Implications: Consider this a large-cap growth fund. Thus, it works best when combined with small-cap and value-seeking funds. Because the fund tends to avoid high-yield utility stocks, there is little need to hedge interest rate risk.

Risk: The portfolio has a below-average beta (0.72). However, it also contains significant non-market-related volatility. The fund managed to sidestep the 1990 bear market.

Costs: There is an initial 3-percent front-end load; no sales charge (except a $7.50 exchange fee) when exchanging with other Select portfolios. The fund has a low expense ratio (1.39 percent) and a below-average portfolio turnover ratio (65 percent).

Distributions: Income and capital gains distributions are paid in December.

How to Buy and Sell: The minimum initial investment is $2,500; subsequent investments $250; IRA $500. Unlimited telephone exchanges with other Select portfolios are permitted with a $7.50 exchange fee and 0.75-percent fee for shares held less than thirty days. Shares are also available through Schwab and Fidelity Brokerage (no transaction fees).

FRANKLIN GLOBAL HEALTH CARE

Franklin Advisors
777 Mariners Island Boulevard
San Mateo, CA 94404
800-632-2301

Inception: 1992
Total Assets: $136 Million
Ticker Symbol: FKGHX
Home Page: None

Objective and Strategy: This fund invests across a broad range of sectors within the health care industry, including HMOs, medical technology and supplies, pharmaceuticals, software and information systems, hospitals, and biotechnology. One of the unique features of this relatively young fund is that it invests globally. The fund will invest at least 70 percent of its assets in the stocks of companies domiciled in at least three different countries. Everyone in the world will use some form of health care over their lifetime, and the health care industry in industrialized nations is consuming an ever-growing percentage of GDP, ranging from 7 percent in Japan to 14 percent in the United States. In addition, the increase in the U.S. population above the age of 65 will continue to expand at a double-digit rate until the year 2030. Thus, the health care industry is virtually assured of maintaining a double-digit annual revenue growth rate well into the foreseeable future.

**Annualized
Returns**

1-Year 36.7%
3-Year 32.9%
5-Year NA

Portfolio Manager: Rupert H. Johnson, Jr. and Kurt von Emster have managed this fund since its inception in April 1992, with Evan McCulloch since April 1995. Mr. Johnson joined Franklin in 1965.

Suitability: The fund is suitable for highly aggressive, growth-seeking investors only. A long-term orientation (five years or more) is recommended.

Portfolio Implications: Because the fund's portfolio is industry concentrated, investment in it should be combined with diversified growth and aggressive growth funds. The fund offers some international exposure. Limit allocations to no more than 20 percent of portfolio assets.

Risk: The fund has an extremely high beta (1.36). In addition, the portfolio includes significant non-market-related volatility. This relatively new fund has yet to experience a severe bear stock market.

Costs: The fund is sold by brokers and financial planners with 4.50-percent front-end load. It also levies a 0.19-percent annual 12b-1 fee. It has a modest expense ratio (1.37 percent) and a relatively high portfolio turnover ratio (94 percent).

Distributions: Income distributions are paid in June and December, and capital gains are distributed in December.

How to Buy and Sell: The minimum initial investment is $100; subsequent investments $25; no minimum IRA requirement. Purchase shares through broker/dealer firms. Shares are also available at Fidelity Brokerage with no transaction fees. Telephone switches are permitted with other Franklin funds.

INVESCO STRATEGIC FINANCIAL SERVICES

Invesco Funds Group
P.O. Box 173706
Denver, CO 80217-3706
800-525-8085

Inception: 1986
Total Assets: $244 Million
Ticker Symbol: FSFSX
Home Page: http://
www.invesco.com

Objective and Strategy: Invesco Strategic Financial Services invests primarily in equity securities of companies engaged in such financial services as banking, leasing, brokerage, and insurance. Management trades rapidly in an effort to weed out stocks with deteriorating fundamentals and/or earnings momentum. This strategy has proven particularly beneficial. The fund's positions in regional and service-oriented firms provided for good resistance to decline in 1990, when the average financial stock declined by approximately 40 percent. Its rebound since then, fueled by falling interest rates, has been nothing short of phenomenal.

Portfolio Manager: R. Dalton Sim, chairman/president of Invesco Trust Company, has been managing the fund since May 1996. He replaced Douglas Pratt, who resigned to join another money management firm.

Suitability: The fund is suitable for both growth and growth and income seeking investors who possess a long-term view. Conservative investors should limit portfolio allocations to no more than 15 percent of portfolio assets.

Annualized Returns

1-Year 21.7%
3-Year 14.2%
5-Year 19.2%

Portfolio Implications: Because of its industry concentration, this fund should be combined with diversified growth and growth and income funds. A small gold fund allocation can be used to offset some interest rate risk.

Risk: The fund has a modest beta (0.89). In addition, its portfolio contains significant non-market-related volatility, including a high degree of sensitivity to interest rate changes. The fund's share price tumbled 22 percent during the 1990 bear market.

Costs: Fund shares are sold with a no-load format. The fund has a modest expense ratio (1.31 percent) and management fee (0.75 percent) but a relatively high portfolio turnover ratio (171 percent).

Distributions: Income and capital gains distributions are paid in late October.

How to Buy and Sell: The minimum initial investment requirement is $1,000; subsequent investments $50; IRA $250. Telephone switches with other Invesco funds are permitted. Shares are also available from Fidelity Brokerage and Schwab (no transaction fees).

INVESCO STRATEGIC HEALTH SCIENCES

Invesco Funds Group
P.O. Box 173706
Denver, CO 80217-3706
800-525-8085

Inception: 1984
Total Assets: $1.12 Billion
Ticker Symbol: FHLSX
Home Page: http://www.invesco.com

Objective and Strategy: As this fund's name implies, its assets are largely invested in the stocks of firms engaged in some facet of the health care field. Like the health care industry itself, the fund's investments span a wide variety of firms, ranging from pharmaceutical companies to exotic biotechnology concerns. Overall, this fund has produced spectacular returns. Although the threat of a government-sponsored health care plan sent most health care stocks reeling during 1992 and 1993, industry growth continued at double-digit annual rates. Although margins have been trimmed by implementation of health care cost containment efforts, the industry is capable of growing at a 12 to 14 percent annual rate well into the twenty-first century.

Annualized Returns
1-Year 25.4%
3-Year 25.0%
5-Year 11.3%

Portfolio Manager: John Schroer has managed the fund since 1996. He also serves as portfolio manager of Global Health Sciences and comanager of Emerging Growth. He earned a B.S. and an M.B.A. from the University of Wisconsin. Carol Werther was appointed comanager in May 1996.

Suitability: The fund is suitable for highly aggressive, growth-oriented investors only.

It is recommended for investors with a long-term view (five years or more). Avoid the urge to trade this fund.

Portfolio Implications: Because of its industry concentration, the fund should be combined with diversified growth and aggressive growth funds.

Risk: The fund has a higher-than-average beta (1.15). In addition, its portfolio contains significant non-market-related volatility. The fund's share price declined by 12 percent during the 1990 bear market.

Costs: Fund shares are sold with a no-load format. The fund has a low expense ratio (1.15 percent) but a higher-than-average portfolio turnover ratio (107 percent). It is one of the least expensive health care sector funds.

Distributions: Income and capital gains distributions are paid in late October.

How to Buy and Sell: The minimum initial investment is $1,000; subsequent investments $50; IRA $250. Telephone exchanges with other Invesco funds are permitted. Shares are also available through Fidelity Brokerage and Charles Schwab (no transaction fees).

INVESCO STRATEGIC LEISURE

Invesco Funds Group
P.O. Box 173706
Denver, CO 80217–3706
800–525–8085

Inception: 1984
Total Assets: $286 Million
Ticker Symbol: FLOSS
Home Page: http://www.invesco.com

Objective and Strategy: This fund normally invests 80 percent of its assets in companies in so-called leisure-time industries. While classified as a sector fund, it maintains a diverse portfolio that may include stocks of companies that supply travel services and lodging, operate amusement parks, produce tobacco and food products, manufacture toys and games, operate restaurants, and print and distribute newspapers. Given that most of these companies directly serve consumers, their stocks are highly sensitive to the business cycle and tend to suffer when the economy dips into a recession.

Portfolio Manager: Mark Greenberg has managed the fund since 1996, when he joined Invesco. He was formerly a global media analyst with Scudder, Stevens and Clark. He received a B.S.B.A. degree from Marquette University.

Suitability: This fund is an ideal investment for all growth and aggressive growth investors who have a long-term view (five years or more).

Annualized Returns
1-Year 9.3%
3-Year 7.4%
5-Year 17.9%

Portfolio Implications: Because of its modest industry concentration, the fund's shares should be combined with those of other growth and aggressive growth funds. The portfolio tends to be dominated by large-cap companies. Consider combining this fund with a small- or micro-cap fund.

Risk: The fund has a below-average beta (0.76). However, it contains significant non-market-related volatility, which can be severe during bear markets (as witnessed by the 27-percent share price decline it suffered during the 1990 bear market).

Costs: Fund shares are sold with a no-load format. The fund has an average expense ratio (1.29 percent) but a higher-than-average portfolio turnover ratio (119 percent).

Distributions: Income and capital gains distributions are paid in late October.

How to Buy and Sell: The minimum initial investment requirement is $1,000; subsequent investments $50; IRA $250. Telephone exchanges with other Invesco funds are permitted. Shares are also available through Fidelity Brokerage and Charles Schwab (no transaction fees).

INVESCO STRATEGIC TECHNOLOGY

Invesco Funds Group
P.O. Box 173706
Denver, CO 80217–3706
800-525-8085

Inception: 1984
Total Assets: $720 Million
Ticker Symbol: FTCHX
Home Page: http://www.invesco.com

Objective and Strategy: As its name suggests, this fund invests in the equity securities of companies principally engaged in the field of technology, including computers, communications, video, electronics, oceanography, office and factory automation, and robotics. The fund's portfolio has traditionally reflected a broad diversification across a number of areas. Favored segments in recent years include software, computer peripherals, and electronics stocks. With exceptionally strong five-year returns and a no-load format, this fund should appeal to long-term-oriented investors who can ignore short-term volatility in the pursuit of double-digit returns.

Portfolio Manager: Daniel Leonard has been co-portfolio manager since 1996 and portfolio manager from 1985. He joined Invesco in 1975. Gerard Hallaren, Jr., has been co-portfolio manager since 1996. He joined Invesco in 1994.

Suitability: This fund's shares are suitable for highly aggressive, growth-oriented investors only. The fund is recommended for investors with a longer-term view (five years or more).

Annualized Returns

1-Year	24.6%
3-Year	22.5%
5-Year	23.9%

Portfolio Implications: Because of the fund's industry concentration, its shares should be combined with those of diversified growth and aggressive growth funds. This fund should not be combined with any other fund with more than 25 percent of assets invested in technology stocks.

Risk: The fund has a higher-than-average beta (1.11). In addition, its portfolio contains significant non-market-related volatility. The fund's share price sunk a hefty 28 percent during the 1990 bear market.

Costs: Fund shares are sold with a no-load format. The fund has a low expense ratio (1.12) but a high portfolio turnover ratio (191 percent).

Distributions: Income and capital gains distributions are paid in late October or early November.

How to Buy and Sell: The minimum initial investment requirement is $1,000; subsequent investments $50; IRA $250. Telephone exchanges with other Invesco funds are permitted. Shares are also available through Fidelity Brokerage and Charles Schwab (no transaction fees).

INVESCO STRATEGIC UTILITIES PORTFOLIO

Invesco Funds Group
P.O. Box 173706
Denver, CO 80217-3706
800-525-8085

Inception: 1986
Total Assets: $148 Million
Ticker Symbol: FSTUX
Home Page: http://
www.invesco.com

Objective and Strategy: This fund is one of the few no-load funds that specializes in the utilities sector. Because utilities stocks possess lower-than-average price volatility due to the stability of their earnings and higher-than-average yields, this fund has a defensive quality. However, the fund's share price is slightly more volatile and its current yield is slightly below those of the typical utility portfolio because it has held a significant investment in telephone utilities stocks as well as in telecommunications equipment stocks in recent years. As with utilities stocks themselves, this fund's performance is highly sensitive to interest rate changes. The fund can be expected to perform best during a period of declining interest rates.

Portfolio Manager: Jeffrey Morris has managed this fund since 1995. He also has managed Strategic Environmental Services since 1995. He joined Invesco in 1991. He earned his B.S. degree from Colorado State University.

Suitability: This fund is suitable for both conservative growth and growth and income investors. It provides its best returns during a stable or declining interest rate environment.

Annualized Returns

1-Year 13.6%
3-Year 5.9%
5-Year 12.1%

Portfolio Implications: This fund is best combined with equity-income or diversified growth funds. It also makes an excellent addition to a bond fund portfolio. It can be combined with a small investment in a gold fund to offset some interest rate risk.

Risk: The fund has a very low beta (0.58). However, its portfolio contains significant non-market-related risk. Its share price is highly sensitive to interest rate changes. The fund's share price declined by less than 7 percent during the 1990 bear market.

Costs: The fund is sold with a no-load format. It has a low expense ratio (1.18 percent) but a high portfolio turnover ratio (185 percent).

Distributions: Income and capital gains distributions are paid in late October and early November.

How to Buy and Sell: The minimum initial investment is $1,000; subsequent investments $50; IRA $250. Telephone exchanges with other Invesco funds (minimum $250) are permitted. Shares are also available through Fidelity Brokerage and Charles Schwab (no transaction fees).

T. ROWE PRICE SCIENCE AND TECHNOLOGY

T. Rowe Price Investment Services
100 East Pratt Street
Baltimore, MD 21202
800-225-5132

Inception: 1987
Total Assets: $2.9 Billion
Ticker Symbol: PRSCX
Home Page: http://
www.troweprice.com

Objective and Strategy: This fund seeks aggressive growth of capital through investments in common stocks of companies that are expected to benefit from the development, advancement, and utilization of science and technology. Although the fund may invest in stocks of all sizes, it has substantial exposure to various small capitalization companies that are experiencing very rapid growth in earnings. The fund's affinity for emerging growth companies gives it enormous potential, as demonstrated during the past five years, but also makes it very vulnerable to sharp price corrections when market sentiment turns against secondary stocks and technology. Bold investors will like this fund's enormous potential.

Portfolio Manager: Charles Morris, chairman of the fund's investment committee, has managed this fund since 1991. He joined T. Rowe Price in 1987 and has been managing investments since 1991.

Suitability: This fund is suitable for aggressive, growth-oriented investors. It does not represent a balanced investment plan, and it is recommended for long-term-oriented investors only.

Portfolio Implications: Because of the fund's industry concentration, its shares should be combined with those of diversified growth and aggressive growth funds. The portfolio will duplicate other funds with a technology bent.

Risk: Although the fund possesses a modest beta (1.13), its concentration in a high-growth industry and its investment in stocks with very high price-earnings ratios add to its overall volatility, which at times can be quite high. During the 1990 bear market, the fund's share price tumbled nearly 30 percent.

Costs: Shares are sold with a 100-percent no-load format. The fund's expense ratio (1.01 percent) is well below that of the typical equity fund. However, it also possesses a high portfolio turnover ratio (130 percent), which can negatively impact net returns.

Distributions: Income and capital gains distributions are paid in late December.

How to Buy and Sell: The minimum initial investment is $2,500; subsequent investments $100; IRA $1,000. Telephone exchanges with other T. Rowe Price funds are permitted. However, the sponsor frowns on frequent switching. Shares are also available at Fidelity Brokerage, Charles Schwab, and Jack White.

Annualized Returns
1-Year 15.9%
3-Year 28.2%
5-Year 28.1%

PUTNAM HEALTH SCIENCES A

One Post Office Square
Boston, MA 02109
800-225-1581

Inception: 1982
Total Assets: $1.2 Billion
Ticker Symbol: PHSTX
Home Page: http://
www.putnaminv.com

Objective and Strategy: This fund seeks capital appreciation by investing at least 80 percent of its total assets in the health sciences industries. This includes companies engaged in the development, production, or distribution of products or services related to the treatment of diseases, disorders, or other medical conditions. Examples of such industries include pharmaceuticals; hospitals and rehabilitation centers; home health care; research and development, such as biotechnology; and medical equipment or supplies. The fund tends to invest in stocks of large, blue-chip companies rather than smaller firms. The fund may, from time to time, invest up to 20 percent of its assets in foreign securities.

Portfolio Manager: Joanne Soja has been managing the fund since 1993. Prior to joining Putnam in 1993, she was a portfolio manager at Chancellor Management.

Suitability: The fund is suitable for highly aggressive, growth-oriented investors only. It is recommended for investors with a long-term view (five years or more). Avoid the urge to trade this fund.

Annualized Returns

1-Year	23.2%
3-Year	26.5%
5-Year	13.7%

Portfolio Implications: Because of its industry concentration, this fund does not represent a balanced investment program. It should be combined with diversified growth and aggressive growth funds.

Risk: The fund possesses a modest beta (1.09) and weathered the 1990 bear market quite well, declining in value by less than 5 percent. However, the fund's portfolio contains significant non-market-related volatility.

Costs: A 5.75-percent front-end load and an ongoing 0.25-percent 12b-1 fee make this one of the more costly sector funds around. Because of the initial sales fee, investors should plan to stick around for a long time. However, the fund's expense ratio (1.12 percent) is low, as is portfolio turnover (20 percent).

Distributions: Income and capital gains distributions are paid in mid- to late December.

How to Buy and Sell: The fund is sold with three classes of shares (A, B, and M), which bear sales charges in different forms. The minimum initial investment is $500; subsequent investments $50; IRA $500. Telephone exchanges with other Putnam funds are permitted. Shares are also available through Fidelity Brokerage.

SELIGMAN COMMUNICATIONS AND INFORMATION A

100 Park Avenue
New York, NY 10017
800-221-2783

Inception: 1983
Total Assets: $2.14 Billion
Ticker Symbol: SLMCX
Home Page: None

Objective and Strategy: This fund seeks capital appreciation by investing primarily in securities of companies in the communications, information, and related industries. Companies engaged in the production of methods for using electronic technology to communicate information have made up a large portion of the fund's portfolio in recent years. Although the fund does not focus on company size when making its selections, the rapidly changing technologies and the expansion of the communications, information, and related industries have provided a favorable environment for small growth companies. With a large portion of its assets invested in small, rapidly growing companies, this fund has one of the best long-term track records in the mutual fund industry.

Portfolio Manager: Paul H. Wick has been managing the fund since 1995. He also comanaged Seligman Henderson Global Technology Fund. He joined Seligman in 1987 and became managing director in 1995.

Suitability: The fund is suitable for highly aggressive, growth-oriented investors only. Because of its hefty front-end sales fee, the fund is suitable for long-term investors only.

Annualized Returns

1-Year -13.9%
3-Year 26.0%
5-Year 28.8%

Portfolio Implications: As an industry-sector fund, this fund should be used as a small component of a diversified equity portfolio. Limit allocations to no more than 10 percent of portfolio assets.

Risk: The fund has a higher-than-average beta (1.18), but it is a bit lower than those of most technology-sector funds. The fund's portfolio contains significant non-market-related risk. The share price plunged more than 34 percent during the 1990 bear market.

Costs: Class A shares are sold with a 4.75-percent front-end load and an ongoing 0.25-percent 12b-1 fee. The fund has an above-average expense ratio (1.76 percent) but a modest portfolio turnover (65 percent). On balance, this is a relatively high-cost fund.

Distributions: Income and capital gains distributions are paid in late December.

How to Buy and Sell: Fund shares are sold in three classes (A, B, and D). The minimum initial investment is $2,500; subsequent investments $100; IRA $1,000. Telephone exchanges with other Seligman funds (with same class designation) are permitted. Shares are also available through Charles Schwab and Fidelity Brokerage.

STRONG AMERICAN UTILITIES

P.O. Box 2936
Milwaukee, WI 53201
800-368-1030

Inception: 1993
Total Assets: $125 Million
Ticker Symbol: SAMUX
Home Page: http://
www.strong-funds.com

Objective and Strategy: This fund seeks a combination of income and capital appreciation by investing in public utility companies headquartered in the United States, including water, gas, electric energy, and telecommunications, excluding public broadcasting companies. One of the unique features of this fund is that, at times, management will invest up to 25 percent of its assets in the stocks of energy companies. As with all utility funds, this fund's share price is highly sensitive to changes in interest rates. Its return, in recent years, has been hindered by heightened inflation fears, which caused interest rates to rise. However, a relatively large investment in telephone and energy stocks boosted returns. As a result, this fund, relative to its peers, has been one of the better performers. Continued growth in the telecommunications industry and a more benign interest rate environment should bode well for this growth and income sector fund.

**Annualized
Returns**

1-Year 10.0%

3-Year 7.9%

5-Year NA

Portfolio Manager: William Reaves has managed the fund since its inception and is employed by its subadviser (W. H. Reaves and Company). He has worked as a utilities analyst since 1946.

Suitability: The fund is ideally suited for conservative investors who desire a combination of current income and capital appreciation. The fund provides a needed inflation offset for income-seeking investors.

Portfolio Implications: The fund's investment in energy stocks gives it a growth bent that would fit well with most diversified growth or aggressive growth funds. There will be some duplication with energy-sector funds. This fund can be used to dampen volatility of an aggressive growth portfolio.

Risk: Strong American Utilities has a relatively high beta (0.86) for a utilities-sector fund. Because of the fund's utility stock investments, its share price is influenced by changing interest rates. This relatively new fund has yet to experience a significant bear stock market.

Costs: The fund is sold with a no-load format. It has a modest expense ratio (1.24 percent) and a low portfolio turnover ratio (56 percent). This is one of the lower-cost sector funds around.

Distributions: Income distributions are paid quarterly (March, June, September, and December). Capital gains are paid in late December.

How to Buy and Sell: The minimum initial investment is $1,000; subsequent investments $50; IRA $250. Telephone exchanges with other Strong funds are permitted. Shares are available with no transaction fees from Charles Schwab, Fidelity Brokerage, and Jack White and Company.

VANGUARD SPECIALIZED ENERGY

Vanguard Group
Vanguard Financial Center
P.O. Box 2600
Valley Forge, PA 19482
800-635-1511

Inception: 1984
Total Assets: $610 Million
Ticker Symbol: VGENX
Home Page: http://
www.vanguard.com

Objective and Strategy: This fund seeks growth of capital by investing in the securities of companies whose activities are related directly to the field of energy. These companies may engage in the production, transmission, marketing and control, or measurement of energy or energy fuels. As with all concentrated portfolios, the fund can experience wide fluctuations in its net asset value, which are not directly related to the market. In addition, earnings and dividends of companies in the energy industry are greatly affected by changes in the prices and supplies of oil and other fuels, which can fluctuate significantly over a short period of time.

Portfolio Manager: Ernst H. von Metzsch, senior vice president of Wellington Management, has managed the fund since its inception in 1984.

Suitability: Although fluctuating energy prices and a sector orientation can enhance volatility, this fund is suitable for a wide spectrum of investors, including those who pursue growth and those who desire a combination of growth and income. Investors should limit allocations to less than 15 percent of portfolio assets.

Portfolio Implications: Heavily packed with oil companies, this fund performs well in an inflation environment. It can be used as a substitute for a gold fund as an inflation hedge. Because of industry concentration, the fund is not a balanced investment program.

Risk: This fund contains a high degree of non-market and industry risk. Its beta of 1.16 may not adequately represent total portfolio risk. The fund is highly sensitive to the prices of oil and natural gas.

Annualized Returns
1-Year 28.9%
3-Year 9.8%
5-Year 12.4%

Costs: Like all Vanguard funds, this fund is highly cost-efficient. Its expense ratio is 0.51 percent, and it has a low (21 percent) portfolio turnover. It is sold in a no-load format. A 1-percent redemption fee is levied on shares held less than one year.

Distributions: Both income and capital gains distributions are made in late December. The low portfolio turnover reduces the possibility of large capital gains distribution.

How to Buy and Sell: The minimum initial investment is $3,000; subsequent investments $100; IRA $1,000. Shares are available through Jack White discount broker with a modest fee. Telephone switches with other Vanguard funds are permitted, but the fund family frowns on frequent switching.

VANGUARD SPECIALIZED HEALTH CARE

Vanguard Group
Vanguard Financial Center
P.O. Box 2600
Valley Forge, PA 19482
800-635-1511

Inception: 1984
Total Assets: $2.2 Billion
Ticker Symbol: VGHCX
Home Page: http://
www.vanguard.com

Objective and Strategy: This fund seeks capital appreciation by investing in securities of companies in the health care industry. Companies include pharmaceutical firms; those that design, manufacture, or distribute medical supplies, equipment, and support services; and those that operate hospitals and health care facilities. At times, the portfolio contains stocks of companies engaged in medical diagnostic, biochemical, and biotechnological research and development. Packed with large-cap stocks, this is the tamest fund investing in health care companies. Investors have recently benefitted from this fund's conservative nature, as it experienced nowhere near the decline of most health care funds in the early 1990s. Like all Vanguard offerings, it is a low-cost fund that passes along most of the returns it earns to its shareholders.

Annualized Returns
1-Year 28.0%
3-Year 26.5%
5-Year 17.9%

Portfolio Manager: Edward P. Owens, an investment professional with Wellington Management since 1974, has served as manager of this fund since its inception.

Suitability: The fund is suitable for long-term, growth-oriented investors. As a sector fund, it does not represent a complete investment program and should be avoided by investors who cannot tolerate a substantial degree of short-term volatility.

Portfolio Implications: Because of the fund's industry concentration, investors should limit allocations to no more than 10 percent of portfolio assets. Health care can be considered a defensive industry and provides some protection during a severe bear market.

Risk: With a beta of 0.97, this is the least volatile health care sector fund. However, the fund is sensitive to changes in health care cost reimbursement and other variables that impact the industry.

Costs: An expense ratio of 0.46 percent and a very low portfolio turnover ratio (13 percent) make this a highly efficient fund. It is sold in a no-load format. However, a 1-percent redemption fee is levied for shares held less than one year.

Distributions: The fund distributes both income and capital gains in late December. The modest turnover ratio can be expected to limit capital gains distributions.

How to Buy and Sell: The minimum initial investment is $3,000; subsequent investments $100; IRA $1,000. Shares can be purchased at Charles Schwab. Telephone switches with other Vanguard funds are permitted; however, the sponsor frowns on frequent switching.

VANGUARD SPECIALIZED UTILITIES

Vanguard Group
Vanguard Financial Center
P.O. Box 2600
Valley Forge, PA 19482
800-635-1511

Inception: 1992
Total Assets: $695 Million
Ticker Symbol: VGSUX
Home Page: http://
www.vanguard.com

Objective and Strategy: A relatively new addition to the Vanguard Specialized portfolios, this fund invests in equity and debt securities of companies engaged in the generation and distribution of electricity, gas, telecommunications, or water. With a bias toward fundamental value, management seeks to provide shareholders with income as well as some capital appreciation. Although utility stocks tend to decrease in value as interest rates rise, this fund's investments in telecommunications stocks has provided an additional amount of protection in a rising interest rate environment. With a no-load format and an extremely low expense ratio, this is an ideal investment for risk-conscious investors who prefer some current income and participation in the telecommunications revolution.

Annualized Returns
1-Year 7.5%
3-Year 5.4%
5-Year NA%

Portfolio Manager: In 1995, Mark J. Beckwith, a vice president of Wellington Management, replaced John Ryan, who had managed the fund since its inception in 1992. Beckwith is assisted by Paul Kaplan, who manages the portfolio's fixed-income investments.

Suitability: The fund is ideally suited for conservative investors who desire a combination of current income and capital appre-

ciation. The fund is an excellent substitute for a bond fund.

Portfolio Implications: Because the fund is highly interest rate sensitive, it is not a suitable companion to most bond funds. A modest allocation to a gold fund will offset some of the interest rate risk possessed by this fund.

Risk: Although this fund has a modest beta (0.77), its share price is highly sensitive to changes in interest rates, and investors can expect to lose money when interest rates are ballooning.

Costs: This is the lowest-cost utilities-sector fund you can find, with an expense ratio of 0.44 percent and a 35-percent portfolio turnover ratio. It is sold in a no-load format.

Distributions: Both income and capital gains distributions are paid in late December. Because of low portfolio turnover, capital gains distributions tend to be modest.

How to Buy and Sell: The minimum initial investment is $3,000; subsequent investments $100; IRA $1,000. Shares can be purchased through Schwab and Fidelity (no transaction fees). Telephone switches with other Vanguard funds are permitted, but the fund family frowns on frequent switching.

INDEX